UNDERSTANDING THE TIMES

A Summit Ministries Curriculum

Jordyn Wagner

Understanding the Times Curriculum
4TH EDITION, 2006

AUTHORS

David Noebel, Kevin Bywater, Jeff Myers, Connie Willems, Jeff Baldwin, Jr.,
Micah Wierenga, Todd Cothran, Jason Graham,
Mike Sligh, and Paul Ryle

EDITORS

Michael Bauman
Sharon Berry
James Bowers
Joel Brown
Jay Butler
Angela Bywater
Renee Cothran
John Dunham
Tom Eckblad
Chuck Edwards
Suzanne Florentine
Trudy Friesema
Ken Gasper
Holly Gooden
Sandi Gooden

Nancy Hay
Charissa Imken
Bill Jack
Abraham Lee
Amanda Lewis
Kara Linden
George Martin
Joel Putnam
Blake Roeber
David Rogers
Sarah Schultz
Jae Stellema
Sarah Tozlian
Sonnie Wierenga

Summit is an educational Christian ministry whose very existence is a response to our current post-Christian culture. Today, countless Christian youth have fallen victim to the popular ideas of our modern world. Most have adopted these ideas into their own worldview, while still others go on to renounce their Christian faith altogether.

Summit views its role in God's kingdom as a catalyst to counteract this alarming trend. However, our ultimate goal supersedes simply training. As Christians are challenged to stand strong in their faith and defend truth, they will also be equipped to have a positive influence on the society in which they live.

Sixth printing (2011), Printed by Mennonite Press (Newton, KS)

SPECIAL CONTRIBUTORS

Kerby Anderson is National Director of Probe Ministries International. He holds degrees from Oregon State University, Yale University, and Georgetown University. He is the author of several books, including *Genetic Engineering*; *Origin Science*; *Living Ethically in the 90s*; *Signs of Warning, Signs of Hope*; and *Moral Dilemmas*. He also served as general editor for *Marriage, Family and Sexuality*. Kerby is a nationally syndicated columnist whose editorials have appeared in the *Dallas Morning News*, the *Miami Herald*, the *San Jose Mercury*, and the *Houston Post*. He is the host of "Probe," and serves as host of "Point of View" (USA Radio Network).

Dr. Michael Bauman is Professor of Theology and Culture, and Director of Christian Studies at Hillsdale College, Hillsdale, Michigan. He also is a former president of the Evangelical Philosophical Society, and was once a member of the editorial department of *Newsweek* magazine. Dr. Bauman has published numerous books, articles and political editorials; his books include *God and Man in the Twentieth Century*, *Man and Creation*, and *Are You Politically Correct?* He is a contributing editor for *Ultra Cycling* magazine and co-editor of *The Schwarz Report*. His latest books are *90 Days in the Christian Classics* and *Christianity A to Z*.

Dr. Francis J. Beckwith is Associate Professor of Church-State Studies and Associate Director of the J. M. Dawson Institute for Church-State Studies at Baylor University. Among his books are *Do the Right Thing: Readings in Applied Ethics & Social Philosophy*, *Relativism: Feet Firmly Planted in Mid-Air*, and *Politically Correct Death: Answering the Arguments for Abortion Rights*. He and his wife Frankie currently reside in Woodway, TX.

Dr. E. Calvin Beisner is Associate Professor of Historical Theology and Social Ethics at Knox Seminary. He holds degrees from the University of Southern California, International College, and University of St. Andrews (Scotland). Prior to coming to Knox, Cal taught at Covenant College and has for many years been an author and lecturer on issues of Christian faith and practice. He is a CAPO (Center for the Advancement of Paleo-Orthodoxy) Fellow and has been a contributing editor for such publications as *World Magazine*, *Christian Research Journal*, and *Crosswinds*. He also has written a number of books including: *Where Garden Meets Wilderness*; *Man, Economy, and the Environment in Biblical Perspective*; and *Answers for Atheists, Agnostics, and Other Thoughtful Skeptics*.

Dr. John C. Bergstrom is the Richard B. Russell, Jr. Distinguished Professor of Public Policy at the University of Georgia, Athens, Georgia. He teaches and conducts research related to natural resource, environmental, and agricultural issues and policy. As a Christian professor, he is interested in the integration of biblical teaching on stewardship and our responsibilities as stewards and managers of God's creation. He lives in Watkinsville, Georgia with his wife and four children and is a member of Faith Presbyterian Church (PCA) in Watkinsville.

Dr. Craig Blomberg is currently a Distinguished Professor of New Testament at Denver Seminary. Craig completed his Ph.D. in New Testament, specializing in the parables and the writings of Luke through Acts, at Aberdeen University in Scotland. In addition to writing numerous articles in professional journals, multi-author works, and dictionaries or encyclopedias, he has authored or edited 15 books, including *The Historical Reliability of the Gospels*, *Interpreting the Parables*, *Matthew* for the New American Commentary series, *1 Corinthians* for the NIV Application Commentary series, *Jesus and the Gospels*, *Neither Poverty nor Riches*, *Making Sense of the New Testament*, *Preaching the Parables*, and *Contagious Holiness*.

Dr. Raymond G. Bohlin is President of Probe Ministries. He received his Ph.D. in molecular biology from the University of Texas at Dallas. Raymond is the co-author of the book *The Natural Limits to Biological Change*, served as general editor of *Creation, Evolution and Modern Science*, and has published numerous journal articles. Raymond was also named a 1997–98 and 2000 Research Fellow of the Discovery Institute's Center for the Renewal of Science and Culture.

Kevin Bywater is a researcher, author, and lecturer for Summit Ministries and a current Ph.D. candidate in New Testament at the University of Durham, England. He holds a bachelor's degree in philosophy and a master's degree in theology. As a former member of the Church of Jesus Christ of Latter-day Saints, Kevin is dedicated to helping Christians understand and effectively reach members of pseudo-Christian religions. He has published articles on cults, worldviews, and Islam, and has co-authored (with David A. Noebel and J. F. Baldwin) *Clergy in the Classroom: The Religion of Secular Humanism*. Kevin, his wife, Angela, and their five children currently live in both Colorado Springs, Colorado, and Oxford, England, where Kevin is the Resident-Scholar for the Summit Oxford Program.

J. Todd Cothran served as Director of Curriculum and Resource at Summit Ministries. He holds a B.A. in communications from the University of South Carolina as well as an M.A. in Christian Apologetics from Biola University. Todd, his wife Renee (whom he met here on summer staff in 1993), and their four children love and cherish their community of friends here at the Summit as well as the vibrant and committed body of believers at their local church where Todd serves as a shepherding elder, Bible study leader, and Sunday school teacher.

Gary DeMar is Founder and President of American Vision, a worldview and apologetics ministry in Atlanta, Georgia. He has published a number of articles and books including *The Reduction of Christianity*, *Surviving College Successfully*, *America's Christian History: The Untold Story*, and *War of the Worldviews*. Gary lives in Atlanta, Georgia with his wife Carol. They have two grown sons.

F. Carolyn Graglia served from 1954 through 1959 as Attorney, General Litigation Section, Civil Division, Department of Justice, Washington, D. C.; Law Clerk, Judge Warren E. Burger, Court of Appeals, District of Columbia Circuit; Special Counsel for Federal Housing Administration litigation, Department of Justice, Washington, D. C.; Attorney, Covington & Burling, Washington, D. C. She retired from legal practice in 1959 to become a homemaker and mother of three daughters. When the children were grown, she consulted for several years on constitutional law and antitrust litigation and then began to write and lecture on family issues. She has published articles in *The Harvard Journal of Law and Public Policy*, *The Texas Law Review*, *The Weekly Standard*, *The Wall Street Journal*, *The Women's Quarterly*, *Claremont Review of Books*, and *The Brigham Young University Law Review*. She is also author of the book *Domestic Tranquility: A Brief Against Feminism*. Mrs. Graglia has been married for over fifty years to Lino A. Graglia, Professor of Law, University of Texas Law School.

George Grant is Director of the King's Meadow Study Center, Teaching Pastor at Christ Community Church (PCA), coordinator of the Gileskirk Curriculum Project, and instructor at Franklin Classical School. He is the author of dozens of books in the areas of history, biography, politics, literature, and social criticism, and he has written hundreds of essays, articles, and columns. His work on behalf of the homeless, for international relief and development, for racial reconciliation, and for the sanctity of life has been profiled in such varied media outlets as *The Wall Street Journal*, *The Washington Post*, Focus on the Family, The 700 Club, The Coral Ridge Hour, Point of View, Crossfire, *World Magazine*, and *Christianity Today*. His books include *The Micah Mandate: Balancing the Christian Life*, *Shelf Life: How Books Have Changed the Destinies of Men and Nations*, and *Going Somewhere: A Novel*.

Joseph P. Gudel is a long-time contributing writer for the *Christian Research Journal*, an ordained pastor in the Lutheran Church—Missouri Synod and a Ph.D. candidate at Concordia Theological Seminary in Fort Wayne, IN.

Dr. Phillip E. Johnson is the Jefferson E. Peyser Professor of Law, Emeritus, at the University of California at Berkley, where he taught for thirty years. Known as a founding father of the Intelligent Design movement, he is the author of *Darwin on Trial*, *Reason in the Balance*, *Defeating Darwinism by Opening Minds*, and *Wedge of Truth*, among others. He is also a regular columnist for Touchstone and is active in scientific debate. Phillip has two children and currently lives with his wife, Kathie, in Berkeley, California.

Scott Klusendorf is Founder and President of Life Training Institute. He travels throughout the United States and Canada training pro-life advocates to graciously and incisively make a defense of the lives of the unborn. He also addresses students and other groups on key bioethical issues, training staff and students at pro-family organizations such as Focus on the Family, New Jersey Right to Life, Ohio Right to Life, and Southern California Right to Life, to name a few. He has participated in 23 debates on abortion at the collegiate and graduate level. As a guest lecturer in bioethics, Scott has taught pro-life apologetics at both the graduate and undergraduate level at Orange Coast College and Trinity International University Law School. Scott is a Magna Cum Laude graduate of UCLA.

Greg Koukl is Founder and President of Stand to Reason, a ministry dedicated to training Christians to think more clearly about their faith and to make an even-handed, incisive, yet gracious defense for Christianity and Christian values in the public square. An award-winning writer, Greg has published the book *Relativism: Feet Firmly Planted in Mid-Air* with Dr. Francis J. Beckwith, and is also the author of *Precious Unborn Human Persons*. Greg received his B.A. in Bible from Azusa Pacific University; his master's in Christian Apologetics from Simon Greenleaf University and is working on his master's in Philosophy of Religion and Ethics at Talbot School of Theology. He hosts his own radio talk show advocating clear-thinking Christianity and defending the Christian worldview.

Charles Moore grew up in California. At age seventeen, under the influence of Young Life, he decided to follow Christ. After college, he went on to seminary and graduate school, where he received degrees in Philosophy of Religion and Ethics. After ten years of teaching at Denver Seminary, he and his wife moved to New York to become members of the Bruderhof Community. Since then, he has been an assistant editor at Plough Publishing. Charles has written numerous articles for various publications and compiled and edited a variety of books, including *Provocations: The Spiritual Writings of Kierkegaard* and *Tolstoy: Essential Writings*.

Dr. J. P. Moreland is a Professor of philosophy at Talbot School of Theology, Biola University in La Mirada, California. Dr. Moreland has 4 earned degrees: a B.S. in chemistry from the University of Missouri, a Th.M. in theology from Dallas Theological Seminary, an M.A. in philosophy from the University of California-Riverside, and a Ph.D. in philosophy from the University of Southern California. He has been involved in planting churches, debating on over 200 college campuses around the country, and serving with Campus Crusade for Christ for over 10 years, as well as authoring and co-authoring numerous books, including *Scaling the Secular City*, *Does God Exist?*, *Immortality: The Other Side of Death*, and *Love Your God With All Your Mind*. He has also published in over 40 articles and journals which include *Philosophy and Phenomenological Research*, *American Philosophical Quarterly*, *Australian Journal of Philosophy*, *Metaphilosophy*, and *Faith and Philosophy*. He, his wife Hope, and daughters Allison and Ashley live in Yorba Linda, California.

Dr. Jeff Myers is Associate Professor of Communication Arts at Bryan College, Dayton, Tennessee. He's also President of the Myers Institute for Communication and Leadership. He speaks to more than 50,000 people each year in corporations, schools, homeschool conferences, parent groups and youth-serving organizations. Over the last decade, Dr. Myers has worked with Summit Ministries to develop cutting-edge leadership experiences in Colorado, Tennessee, North Carolina, and Alberta, Canada. He is the author of six books and three video coaching systems including *Understanding the Times*, the curriculum that introduced worldview training to America's Christian schools, and *Secrets of Great Communicators*. Dr. Myers earned a Doctor of Philosophy degree from the University of Denver. He and his wife Danielle have four children—Graham, Emma, Cate, and Stuart—and live in Tennessee.

Nancy Pearcey is the Francis A. Schaeffer scholar at the World Journalism Institute, where her book *Total Truth* serves as the basis for a worldview curriculum. After earning an M.A. from Covenant Theological Seminary, she pursued further graduate work in philosophy at the Institute for Christian Studies in Toronto. Currently she serves as a Visiting Scholar at the Torrey Honors Institute at Biola University, and a Senior Fellow at the Discovery Institute. Pearcey has authored or contributed to several works, including the ECPA Gold Medallion winner *How Now Shall We Live?* and *The Soul of Science*.

Dr. Walt Russell is Professor of New Testament at Talbot School of Theology. Walt is the author of numerous articles and books, including *Playing With Fire: How the Bible Ignites Change in Your Soul*. Walt lives in Southern California with his wife of over 30 years and their two children Elizabeth and Jonathan. He's "bonkers" about saltwater fishing, jazz, and classical music, and rabidly follows the Kansas City Chiefs and Royals with J. P. Moreland, his best friend for over 30 years.

Dr. Leland Ryken is the Clyde S. Kilby Professor of English at Wheaton College, where he has taught for over 40 years. He has published over 25 books on such varied topics as literature and the arts from a Christian perspective, the Bible as literature, work and leisure, the Puritans, and Bible translation.

John Stonestreet is Executive Director of Summit Ministries. Mr. Stonestreet holds a M.A. in Christian Thought from Trinity Evangelical Divinity School and is on the Biblical Studies faculty at Bryan College. A popular speaker at camps, conventions, and conferences, he works annually with thousands of parents, teachers, and students on developing a biblical worldview, understanding comparative worldviews, defending the Christian faith, applying a biblical worldview to education, and engaging important cultural issues. He is a Fellow of the Wilberforce Fellows, a division of Breakpoint, and is the co-author with W. Gary Phillips and William E. Brown of *Making Sense of Your World: A Biblical Worldview*, 2nd. ed., as well as numerous web and journal articles. John joined the Summit team in 1999, and has served numerous roles including directing the eastern Summit programs in Tennessee and Virginia. He, his wife Sarah, and three daughters live in Colorado Springs, Colorado.

Table of Contents

WORLDVIEW TRAINING

STUDENT MANUAL

UNDERSTANDING THE TIMES

Preparation

A Summit Ministries Curriculum

THE AIM OF THIS CURRICULUM

Many people think that those in the military, high government offices or important financial positions control the world. In this they are mistaken; our world revolves around *ideas*. Militaries exude power and authority, yet they are prisoners to the ideologies of their representative nations. Politicians and those in positions of governmental authority may think they rule the world, but they are held captive by the ideas they have embraced about government. Executives in large corporations may think they have the world by the tail, but they too are indebted to their ideas/beliefs about business practices/values and economic trends. Ideas lie behind every historical event and social policy. Ideas are the guiding force behind every twist and turn in public opinion; they determine what we accept or reject in the arts, media, business, medicine, education, government, church, family, etc.

We will never fully understand our world unless we understand the ideas that form its structure. Issues like stem-cell research, abortion, the homosexual rights movement, and political correctness will bewilder us if we divorce these issues from the ideas on which they are based. The reasons behind the cruelty of Ted Bundy, Joseph Stalin, or Adolf Hitler will elude us unless we understand their ideas. Without a thorough understanding of ideas, we will watch with feelings of helplessness and uncertainty as our world constantly tries to persuade us of the validity of its beliefs and practices.

Understanding the Times is about ideas. This curriculum will help you understand that everyone has a "worldview," a way of interpreting everything that happens in the world. The Bible has an explanation for the universe, but so does Islam, Secular Humanism, Marxism, Postmodernism, and the New Age movement. Each of these worldviews is founded upon ideas. A worldview will dictate (consciously or unconsciously) how we should interpret and respond to the world around us. If we can understand the prominent worldviews in our world, we will better understand the underlying framework of many issues that Christians face. We will learn how to anticipate the response of a Muslim, Secular Humanist, Marxist, Postmodernist, or New Ager. Where once you saw thousands of confusing issues, you will see a big picture. Moreover, as you journey through the complex yet enlightening information this curriculum contains, you will learn to see ideas from a biblical Christian perspective.

The goal of this curriculum is to help open your eyes to the war of ideas competing for your heart and mind. You will begin to realize that the worldly problems we call "issues" are symptoms, not the disease. The disease is found in Romans when Paul declares, "all have sinned and fall short of the glory of God" (3:23). Because all human beings are sinners (the *disease*), we will naturally produce and indulge in sin (the *symptoms*)—"For the wages of sin is death" (6:23a). We must start addressing the disease if we want to be effective in dealing with the symptoms.

Another way to look at this is to say that *ideas have consequences*. Since our world is utterly opposed to God, it produces bad ideas which, in turn, lead to bad consequences. Yet there is hope in the midst of this sinful world. Those who understand the ideas that rule the world will have the opportunity to influence the world of ideas. First Chronicles 12:32 tells the story of one small tribe in Israel that was chosen to lead because it "understood the times, and knew what Israel ought to do." It is our hope that you too will understand the times and thus know what God would have you do.

THE NEED FOR THIS CURRICULUM

Our goals for this curriculum are twofold. The first goal is defensive: we want to help protect Christian youth from being deceived by anti-Christian worldviews. The second goal is offensive: we want to train up Christian leaders who can actively champion the truth of Christianity in a culture of relativism, paganism, hedonism, and confusion.

> Nothing short of a great Civil War of Values rages today throughout North America. Two sides with vastly differing and incompatible world-views are locked in a bitter conflict that permeates every level of society… the struggle now is for the hearts and minds of the people. It is a war over ideas. And someday soon, I believe, a winner will emerge and the loser will fade from memory. For now, the outcome is very much in doubt.[1]

What James Dobson and Gary Bauer describe is the current struggle among worldviews as Christians, Muslims, Secular Humanists, Marxists, New Agers, and Postmodernists vie for the hearts and minds of

[1] James C. Dobson and Gary L. Bauer, *Children at Risk* (Dallas: Word, 1990), 19–20.

individuals. Many Christian students, parents, and teachers falsely assume that Christian youth are immune to false ideas simply because they have been raised in a Christian environment. However, even students raised in Christian homes, who attend church regularly, and are enrolled in Christian schools are vulnerable to non-Christian ways of thinking. Christian youth in large numbers are rejecting certain biblical truths or even turning away from Christianity altogether. Without proper worldview training, the trends outlined below will likely continue:

CHRISTIANS RENOUNCING THEIR FAITH IN COLLEGE: According to findings published in a UCLA dissertation, Dr. Gary Railsback notes that up to 59% of Christians renounce their faith before graduating from college (this is up from 51% in 1989). Shockingly, there is little statistical difference between Christian students enrolled at secular and Christian institutions.[2]

CHRISTIANS THINKING MORE LIKE HUMANISTS: Each year, thousands of Christian school students take the Nehemiah Institute worldview assessment test. Students are presented with a series of relevant questions, and then asked to pick the multiple-choice answer that best expresses their beliefs. Based on their answers, students are scored along a spectrum from "Biblical Christian" (100–70) to "Moderate Christian" (69–30) to "Secular Humanist" (29–0) to "Marxist" (anything below a '0' score). From 1988 until 2000, it was found that students enrolled in Christian schools moved from an average in the low 50s (meaning they scored at the lower end of "Moderate Christian") to an average of about 20 in the year 2000 (meaning they responded to key social, political, and religious issues like a Secular Humanist).[3]

REJECTION OF MORAL ABSOLUTES AMONG CHRISTIAN TEENS AND ADULTS: The well known Christian statistician George Barna reports that among teenagers, a mere 9% of Christian teens believe in moral absolutes versus 4% of non-Christian teens.[4]

While these trends are alarming, we must remember that God's truth is more powerful than the false ideas capturing the minds of our culture. For years, the Christian community has drawn a line between the *sacred* and the *secular*. Christians have been encouraged to focus only on "sacred" activities and avoid involvement with "secular" activities such as politics, culture, science, or philosophy. In reality, no such distinction exists. *Understanding the Times* is a call to understand the spiritual nature of the struggle between good and evil, and the way in which it impacts every area of life and culture—the distorted sexual mores, the rewriting of history to exclude God, and the attempt to impose a humanistic utopian vision on the world. This curriculum operates on the premise that *this* generation must be prepared to undertake a *pro-active* Christianity—one that seeks to *redeem* culture and all of God's creation, rather than *reject* it.

This curriculum does not teach that Christians are victims of some global conspiracy. It holds firmly, however, to the biblical description of evil as persuasive and in direct rebellion against God's will.

Years ago, Francis Schaeffer astutely noted that Christians were beginning to view the world in "bits and pieces instead of totals." In the twentieth century, Christians rather abruptly lost sight of their responsibilities in society, and gradually lost the ability to discern good from evil. Christianity entered a downward spiral in which we quickly lost the capacity to stand for righteousness and justice. Before long, complicated "issues" seemed so overwhelming that most Christians numbly retreated from their societal responsibilities into the comfort zone of *self*. Generally speaking, Christianity ceased to reflect God's love and character to the unbelieving world. Today, many Christians are more concerned with their personal faith, personal growth, and personal church than with the world at large that they are called to love and serve.

However, the current generation of Christians has started to notice the previous generation's shirking of cultural responsibilities, though they are perhaps unsure of what needs to change, how to take action, or even where they should begin. Assuming responsibility used be the mark of adulthood, but this timeless "rite of passage" between childhood and adulthood has become blurry. In its absence, young people often feel compelled to prove their adulthood by engaging in premarital sex, declaring independence, and so on.

---

[2] This study was done in 1989 by Gary Lyle Railsback, "An Exploratory Study of the Religiosity and Related Outcomes Among College Students," University of California at Los Angeles, 1994. The greatest losses were at Catholic universities, reporting 59% of Christian freshmen renounced their faith by their senior year. Protestant universities showed a 31% loss.

[3] In addition, Christian students in public schools scored considerably lower, with an average of 8.2 in 2004. Source: http://www. nehemiahinstitute.com/index.php

[4] Source: http://www.barna.org/cgi-bin/PagePressRelease.asp?PressReleaseID=106&Reference=C

Understanding the Times provides a constructive "rite of passage." Through it, we want to pass the torch to you, the next generation, by explaining the mistakes of the past and endowing you with the responsibility for shaping the future of the world.

USING THIS MANUAL
Before beginning this curriculum, it will be helpful to understand its structure and layout.

ICONS: The following icons are used throughout this manual in order to indicate the primary purpose and medium of the activity by which they appear.

Reading Assignment	Video Outline	Discussion Questions	Writing Assignment	Class Activity

UNITS: There are 10 units to this curriculum plus an Introduction and Conclusion section. The following elements are found within each unit:

1. **Table of contents:** At the beginning of each unit is a table of contents or section outline that lists the components and their corresponding page numbers. All textbook readings will be <u>underlined</u>, essays *italicized*, and videos "quoted."

2. **180-day and 90-day Syllabus:** Also at the beginning of each unit is both a two- and one-semester syllabus outlining your daily classroom and homework assignments.

3. **Video outlines:** Each unit has corresponding video presentations and outlines. Videos may be divided into multiple parts, and average between 20 to 40 minutes in length. Each presentation has a set of video outlines with fill-in-the-blank notes.

4. **Video discussion questions:** Each video (with the exception of the intro videos for each unit) has an accompanying set of discussion questions. These questions should be completed individually after watching each presentation, and then reviewed the following day with the entire class.

5. **Textbook reading assignments:** Each unit has a corresponding textbook reading assignment. These assignments are found within the book titled *Understanding the Times*.

6. **Textbook discussion questions:** Each textbook reading assignment has an accompanying set of discussion questions. These questions should be completed individually after reading, and then reviewed the following day with the entire class.

7. **Essay reading assignments:** Each unit has corresponding essay reading assignments.

8. **Essay discussion questions:** Each essay reading assignment has an accompanying set of discussion questions. These questions should be completed individually after reading, and then reviewed the following day with the entire class.

9. **Dear Doug essay assignment (180-day syllabus only):** Each unit (except Unit Five and Conclusion) has a corresponding essay assignment. These essays will be 1–2 page written responses to problems addressed in letters from Doug, a friend who has just begun college.

10. **Unit Test:** At the end of each unit (except Unit Five) is a corresponding unit test. The questions for these tests may be matching, multiple choice, true/false, fill-in-the-blank, or short answer. Each test is based on the video, textbook, and essay discussion questions as well as the Fact Sheets.

11. **Worldview Paper:** At the end of Unit Five there will be a 4–6 page paper defining and comparing the Christian, Islamic, Secular Humanist, Marxist, New Age, and Postmodernist worldviews.

12. **Comprehensive Exam:** At the end of the Conclusion Unit, there will be a comprehensive multiple choice exam covering all the materials from the course. Questions for the comprehensive exam are found in the video, textbook, and essay discussion questions as well as the Fact Sheets.

FACT SHEETS: A number of fact sheets are provided with the manual. They are categorized according to various worldview subjects, and provide helpful resources for college research and writing assignments.

TRANSLATION: For this curriculum, we have chosen to use the New King James Version of the Bible unless otherwise noted.

GRADING: There are 2000 points possible for this course (1500 for the one-semester):

180-Day

Assignments	Number	Points	Total Points	Points Earned
Dear Doug Letters	10	50	500	
Unit Tests	10	100	1000	
Worldview Paper	1	200	200	
Final Exam	1	300	300	

90-Day

Assignments	Number	Points	Total Points	Points Earned
Unit Tests	10	100	1000	
Worldview Paper	1	200	200	
Final Exam	1	300	300	

COLLEGE CREDIT: Bryan College (a nationally accredited university in Dayton, Tennessee) has teamed up with Summit Ministries to offer college credit to students taking the Understanding the Times course. For those following the 180-day syllabus, three credit hours are offered; for those following the 90-day syllabus, two credit hours are offered. You can earn college credit now!

Requirements:
1. Submit application and tuition to **Summit Ministries** by May 1st (halfway through the year)
2. Complete the *Understanding the Times* syllabus requirements (180- or 90-day) with at least a C:
    a. Read the revised 2nd edition textbook and all assigned supplemental essays
    b. Write the 4–6 page research paper
    c. Write 10 responsive Essays (3 credit hours only)
    d. Take 10 unit Tests and the Final Exam
3. Submit copies of your Unit Tests and Final Exam to **Summit Ministries** by June 1st

For more information, please visit the High School Curriculum page at www.summit.org. If you are interested in pursuing this option, ask your teacher for an application.

ADDITIONAL SUMMIT RESOURCES

SUMMIT HOMEPAGE: The online hub for Summit's conferences, curriculum, and resources. www.summit.org

SUMMIT TRUTH & CONSEQUENCES: A free monthly e-news article that reviews current issues from a worldview perspective. To sign up, visit the RESOURCES page at www.summit.org.

SUMMIT JOURNAL: A free monthly review of the news and cultural events, edited by Dr. David Noebel. To sign up, visit the RESOURCES page at www.summit.org.

SUMMIT WEBSTORE: For the most up-to-date selection of worldview-oriented books, videos, and CDs covering such topics as apologetics, Darwinism, Relativism, Pluralism, Skepticism, and many others, click on the STORE tab at www.summit.org.

SUMMIT JAT (JUST A THOUGHT): A Summit Ministries community discussion project aimed at thinking through issues of faith and worldview. To join in, visit the RESOURCES page at www.summit.org.

SUMMIT CONFERENCES: To learn more about our intensive two-week educational conferences that analyze the major worldviews of our day and contrast them with the Christian Worldview, please visit the CONFERENCES page at www.summit.org.

ADDITIONAL RESOURCES

Included below is a list of organizations and publications that can provide you with valuable information. To explore some of the topics you will be studying, we've provided you with places to begin your own research. Please note that this list is not intended to be comprehensive and that the inclusion of an organization on this list does not constitute an implicit endorsement of that organization by Summit Ministries.

PUBLICATIONS:
Note: Many organizations give free subscriptions to students.

Areopagus Journal | **Apologetics Resource Center** | www.arcapologetics.org | 205.408.0136 |

Biblical Worldview | **American Vision** | www.americanvision.org | 770.222.7266 |

Christian Research Journal | **Christian Research Institute** | www.equip.org | 888.700.0274 |

Citizen Magazine | **Focus on the Family** | www.fotf.org | 800.232.6459 |

First Things | **Institute of Religion and Public Life** | www.firstthings.com | 712.627.1985 |

Freeman Journal | **Foundation for Economic Education** | www.fee.org | 800.960.4333 |

Human Events | www.humanevents.org | 800.787.7557 |

Imprimis | **Hillsdale College** | www.hillsdale.edu | 517.437.7341 |

Intercollegiate Review | **Intercollegiate Studies Institute** | www.isi.org | 800.526.7022 |

Journal of the Evangelical Theological Society | **Evangelical Theological Society** | www.etsjets.org |

Philosophia Christi | **Evangelical Philosophical Society** | www.epsociety.org |

Southern Baptist Journal of Theology | **Southern Baptist Theological Seminary** | www.sbts.edu |

Summit Journal | **Summit Ministries** | www.summit.org | 719.685.9103 |

World Magazine | www.worldmag.com | 800.951.6397 |

ONLINE RESOURCES:
Access Research Network | www.arn.org | 719.633.1772 |

American Vision | www.americanvision.org | 770.222.7266 |

Christian Answers | www.christiananswers.net |

Christian Apologetics & Research Ministry | www.carm.org |

Christian Research Institute | www.equip.org | 888.700.0274 |

Discovery Institute | www.discovery.org | 206.292.0401 |

Leadership University | www.leaderu.com | 972.516.0516 |

Probe Ministries | www.probe.org | 972.480.0240 |

Stand to Reason | www.str.org | 719.685.9103 |800.273.2766

Summit Ministries | www.summit.org | 719.685.9103 |

Veritas Forum | www.veritas.org | 617.491.2055 |

THINK TANKS:
Cato Institute | www.cato.org | 202.842.0200 |

Concerned Women for America | www.cwfa.org | 202.488.7000 |

Eagle Forum | www.eagleforum.org | 618.462.5415 |

Family Policy Network | www.familypolicy.net | 202.657.5384 |

Family Research Council | www.frc.org | 800.225.4008 |

Federalist Society | www.fed-soc.org | 202.822.8138 |

Foundation for Thought and Ethics | www.fteonline.com |

Heritage Foundation | www.heritage.org | 202.546.4400 |

CAMPUS MINISTRIES:

Campus Crusade for Christ | www.campuscrusadeforchrist.com | 407.826.2000 |

Intercollegiate Studies Institute | www.isi.org | 800.526.7022 |

Probe Ministries | www.probe.org | 972.480.0240 |

Ravi Zacharias International Ministries | www.rzim.org | 770.449.6766 |

Reformed University Fellowship | www.ruf.org |

STUDENT MANUAL

UNDERSTANDING THE TIMES

Introduction

Topics:
Apologetics
Hermeneutics
Leadership
Worldviews

A Summit Ministries Curriculum

SECTION OUTLINE

180-DAY SYLLABUS

DAY	IN CLASS	HOMEWORK	
1	READ Student Manual 'Preparation'	READ UTT Textbook 'Introduction 0.1'	
2	WATCH "Introduction to Worldviews" video		
3	REVIEW "Introduction to Worldviews" video questions	READ UTT Textbook 'Introduction 0.2'	
4	REVIEW UTT Textbook 'Introduction 0.2' questions	READ UTT Textbook 'Introduction 0.3'	
5	REVIEW UTT Textbook 'Introduction 0.3' questions		
6	READ *Playing with Fire* essay	ASSIGN Dear Doug Letter	
7	REVIEW *Playing with Fire* essay questions		
8	WATCH "Loving God with Your Mind" video P1		
9	WATCH "Loving God with Your Mind" video P2		
10	REVIEW "Loving God with Your Mind" video questions		
11	WATCH "Ambassadors for Christ" video		
12	REVIEW "Ambassadors for Christ" video questions		
13	READ *Total Truth* essay		
14	REVIEW *Total Truth* essay questions	Dear Doug Letter assignment DUE	
15	TAKE Introduction Test		

90-DAY SYLLABUS

DAY	IN CLASS	HOMEWORK	
1	READ Student Manual 'Preparation'	READ UTT Textbook 'Introduction 0.1'	
2	WATCH "Introduction to Worldviews" video	READ UTT Textbook 'Introduction 0.2-0.3'	
3	REVIEW "Introduction to Worldviews" video questions		
4	REVIEW UTT Textbook 'Introduction 0.2-0.3' questions		
5	TAKE Introduction Test		

"INTRODUCTION TO WORLDVIEWS"
WITH KEVIN BYWATER

I. We Are in a ___battle.___

    A. Two kinds of people: ___captors___ and ___captives___

    B. **Colossians 2:8:** to not be taken ___captive___

    C. **2 Corinthians 10:3–5:** to take every thought ___captive___

    D. **2 Timothy 2:22–26:** to set the ___captive___ free

II. What is a Worldview?

"A world view is a way one views the whole world. And since people have vastly different views of the world, depending on the perspective from which they view the world, it is clear that one's world view makes a world of difference. A world view is a way of viewing or interpreting all of reality. It is an interpretive framework through which or by which one makes sense out of the data of life and the world." — Norman L. Geisler and William D. Watkins, *Worlds Apart*, 11.

"A worldview is the perspective through which you understand and approach life and the world."

Mr. Sowers favorite annalogy for a worldview: filter.

III. Illustrating Worldviews

    A. ___Glasses___

    B. ___Water filter___

    C. Optical illusions

IV. Questions Every Worldview Must Answer

    A. What is ___God___ ?

    B. What is ___mankind___ ?

V. The Worldview Triangle

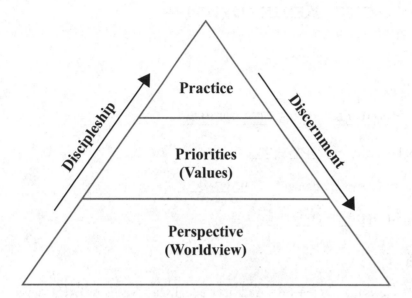

One key worldview principle: ___ideas___ have consequences

VI. Developing Your Own Worldview

A. Don't ___read___ your Bibles… ___study___ them!

B. Read other worldview materials.

C. Put yourself in challenging situations.

D. Stretch your intellectual boundaries.

E. Engage in ___cultural___ analysis.

F. Watch your time closely.

VII. The Goals of Developing a Christian Worldview

A. Be a faithful disciple of Christ.

B. Know ___what___ we believe ___why___ we believe.

C. Learn to think consistently.

D. Learn to engage our culture without compromise.

E. Be faithful ___ambassadors___ of Christ.

"INTRODUCTION TO WORLDVIEWS"
VIDEO QUESTIONS

Answer the questions below on a separate sheet of paper and be prepared to review your answers in class. Reflection Questions will not be found in the text. These are merely designed to help you start thinking about issues from a worldview perspective.

1. **What are three key verses used in the discussion of worldviews?**

2. **What is a worldview? What are some illustrations?**

3. **What questions must every worldview answer? Why are these questions relevant?**

4. **What is the purpose of the worldview triangle? Why is it important to develop a Christian worldview?**

5. **Reflection Question: What does the dictum "ideas have consequences" mean?**

UNDERSTANDING THE TIMES
INTRODUCTION QUESTIONS

Answer the questions below on a separate sheet of paper and be prepared to review your answers in class. Answers to the Reflection Questions will not be found in the text, but are designed to help you start thinking about issues from a worldview perspective.

INTRODUCTION 0.2

1. What is a worldview and what are some of the fundamental questions a worldview answers?

2. How do Norman Geisler and William Watkins define a worldview? What are two illustrations that demonstrate how a worldview works?

3. How is the term "worldview" defined in Understanding the Times?

4. **Reflection Question:** Does a person's belief in the existence of God affect his or her life? If yes, give an example of how that belief may affect his or her ideas about life.

5. **Reflection Question:** Francis Schaeffer said, "The basic problem of the Christians in this country in the last eighty years or so, in regard to society and in regard to government, is that they have seen things in bits and pieces instead of totals." What does Schaeffer mean by "bits and pieces?"

INTRODUCTION 0.3

6. Which verses from Genesis fit with the worldview disciplines listed in the *Understanding the Times* textbook?

7. In what way does the person of Jesus Christ underline the significance of each discipline?

8. According to 2 Corinthians 10:4–5, once we understand the world, what are we to do?

9. What evidence supports the claim that Secular Humanism is "religious" in nature?

10. What legal and constitutional problem should result from classifying Secular Humanism as a religion? Can humanist teaching be considered *neutral*? Why or why not?

PLAYING WITH FIRE
BY WALT RUSSELL

THE HAZARDS OF READING ON A BATTLEFIELD

As she worked her way toward the front of the room, I could tell the young woman was really angry with me. Her eyes were blazing and her jaw was set. This was surprising because the setting was fairly benign: speaking to a large evangelical church's singles group on "How to Interpret the Bible." At the beginning of my two times with them, however, I was already offending the troops! I braced myself.

Twenty-four year-old "Janet" (not her real name) was angry at my emphasis on seeking to discover authors' intentions when we read their texts. She was an evangelical Christian and a second grade teacher in a public school. She prided herself in helping her 20 students learn to love literature. She would read them a story as they gathered around her, and then ask each child, "What does the story mean to you?"

She prodded them to come up with their own unique meanings. With such strong encouragement, the class of 20 would eventually have 20 different meanings for the one story. Janet sensed that I was opposed to such "love of literature." Pouring a little emotional gasoline on the fire, I said, "Janet, you're certainly doing your part to insure that these 7 year-olds will never recover from a radically relativistic view of meaning!" Now I had her full attention.

Actually, Janet's and my little story about where a text's meaning resides is really part of a larger, more tangled story that's over a hundred years old. It started with some American literary critics early in the 20th century who shifted the focus from the author to the text. This literary perspective, later called "New Criticism," banished the author and focused instead on a "close reading" or "explication" of the text. When created, a text supposedly becomes an independent creation, like a newborn set free on its own. The autonomous text's meaning is discovered by studying the way it naturally goes together as a whole. New Criticism triumphed in the United States from about 1930 to 1960. As the text moved into the spotlight, authors were shuffled to the periphery.

But to understand Janet's and my little discussion we need to know the story from 1960 to the present. This is because the movement away from authors did not stop at the text. Rather, it continued its movement all the way to us as readers. In the last 40 years, reading and interpreting has been redefined from *seeking the intentions of authors* through reading their texts to *continually recreating the text through the presuppositions of readers*. Since the 1960s the emphasis has shifted to the astonishing assumption that readers not only create the meaning, but also in some sense *create the text itself* through the contouring of their presuppositions! With this view none of us can really share the same text!

The classical view of meaning is that a text is *a window* into an author's intentions. For example, we peer through the window of the biblical text to interpret what the Divine and human authors intend to say. By contrast, the postmodern sense is that a text is *a mirror* by which readers generate meaning. Janet was holding up a mirror to her second graders and encouraging them to generate their own meanings in light of their own images. The irony is that this does not teach a "love of literature," but rather fosters a self-centered fascination with one's own thoughts! If this is how Christians interpret the meaning of the Bible, then we are trapped within our own mirrors—our own set of presuppositions. We are not hearing God's voice, only our own. We are trapped inside our own heads.

The first problem with this view of meaning is that any positive presentation of it is self-refuting. In order to communicate "readers create meaning," relativistic authors have to scab off of the real world and the way meaning actually works to communicate their relativistic ideas. In other words, they expect us to interpret accurately their authorial intention that readers can't get to authorial intention! Or approach it from another perspective: If you're a student, ask your professor who expounds this view of meaning to reread your paper on which she gave you a D until she creates a meaning for it worthy of an A. Say that it's unfair that she graded *you* harshly for *her* poor reader-generated meaning! No one can live in a world where readers generate meaning because it doesn't exist.

Another problem with the present relativism in meaning in the West is the very fact that it is *in the West*. The 30 percent of the world that lives in the West has reaped the bitter fruit of a 500-year march toward extreme individualism. Those of us born right after World War II have reached the lunatic fringe in living out a radical and narcissistic self-absorption. It has destroyed our marriages, families, churches, national cohesion, and meaningful sense of community.

The good news is that our children have sensed the futility of this radical perspective and are saying, "We can't take it anymore! We don't want to deny the group dimension of ourselves anymore. We want to have meaningful connections with one another. We want to have stable community and long-lasting relationships."

Good move. Now simply stop denying the universal dimension of language too! Recognize that words, ideas, and genres are public, sharable things that we use in order to communicate with one another. While an individual intersects with them, the components of language are essentially group oriented things. They make individual communication possible. While we complicate the interpretive process with our individual presuppositions, they are not an insurmountable barrier. We simply recognize the "fuzzing" that our presuppositions can cause and seek to use good interpretive methods to transcend any clouding they may bring.

The Church in the West has been deeply impacted by this misunderstanding of meaning. We need go no further than the main question we ask when interpreting the Bible: "What does this verse mean to you?" The trickle-down of a century of bad interpretive theories has led to our widespread relativistic interpretation of the Bible. We have been profoundly wounded in the midst of the spiritual warfare that has surrounded the issue of meaning. Our anti-intellectualism has actually increased the casualty list.

Another culprit is our naiveté about the setting in which we read. We read right in the middle of a remarkable spiritual battlefield. While the casualties are initially subtler, they are ultimately more obvious. The spiritual warfare is blazing around us. It has effectively neutralized the greatest wealth of Bible study resources available in the history of the Church. Not by preventing their publication, but by undercutting their usefulness with a relativistic view of meaning! Why do I need a Bible dictionary to help determine Paul's meaning in Philippians 1:6 if the ultimate trump card is what it means to me? How brilliantly diabolical and strategic such a view of meaning is. It effectively cuts us off from God's voice and imprisons us within our own voice. It is Satan's ancient question, "Indeed, has God said?…" in postmodern dress.

Perhaps it is no overstatement to imagine that when you pick up your Bible and start reading it, you are instantly transported to the field of spiritual battle. Perhaps that funny odor is not burning pizza but flaming arrows; perhaps you need to avoid being a casualty! Probably not a bad idea also to be fighting for the right army! These are just some of the hazards of reading on a battlefield.

'INDIANS SLAY TIGERS' AND BRAKING FOR GENRES

"INDIANS SLAY TIGERS!"—the newspaper headline virtually screams out at you. The thought of something being slain is repulsive. You're gripped by a mental image of southern India's Bengal tiger. You imagine its beautiful face, its stripes and piercing eyes. Then your image is shattered by the sudden blast of a high-powered rifle. You see the exquisite creature writhe in pain, fall gracelessly in its tracks and die. Having read no further than the headline, you feel sick, as if you've witnessed something tragic.

But *should* you feel this way? The slaughter of an endangered species—especially one as magnificent as the Bengal tiger—is horrifying, no doubt. But suppose you failed to notice that the headline "INDIANS SLAY TIGERS!" appeared in the *sports page* of the morning paper. Clearly enough, it now refers to different Indians, different Tigers, and a different manner of slaying than you originally thought. And is it really that tragic that the Cleveland Indians badly beat the Detroit Tigers in a major league baseball game last night? Not unless you're a long-suffering Detroit Tigers' baseball fan. But how do you now know that the headline is about baseball and not tiger-slaying in India? You look at the words "INDIANS SLAY TIGERS" and you know exactly what each word means. When you combine these words, how can they not mean exactly what you first thought they did—that *Indians slay tigers*? Answer: because their meanings are communicated (as the meanings of *all* words are) through *genres*!

Whether we recognize that we are doing so or not, we interpret all things in life, from casual conversations to scholarly articles, in terms of their perceived genres or types of communication. When we develop an ability to discern cues within a text that indicate what kind of literature we're working with and what to expect (or not to expect) from it, we have achieved what some call "literary competence." We develop literary competence by growing up in a culture and learning its various genres—its various styles of communication. If we have literary competence, after reading "INDIANS SLAY TIGERS!" in the sports page, we would never picture tigers in India because we would instantly know that correct interpretation within *this* genre requires assuming that "TIGERS" and "INDIANS" refer to *teams* rather than people from India and large striped cats. Our interpretation of any section in the newspaper begins instantaneously when we recognize the genre and adjust our expectations accordingly. The beauty of genres is that they are public, sharable forms of communication that immediately enable the understanding of meaning. Genres are one of God's enduring gifts of common grace that help us communicate to one another with accurate understanding.

The *words* of the Bible are God-breathed, by the Holy Spirit, into the human-crafted *genres* exhibited in the Bible. We find every God-breathed word of Scripture within a genre. Because genres set limits on our possible interpretations of words, if God had *not* placed the words of Scripture within genres, we wouldn't understand one word of the Bible. So God has spoken to us "in many portions and many ways" (Hebrews 1:1) through particular biblical genres such as historical narrative, law, poetry, wisdom literature, apocalyptic literature, prophecy, gospels, letters, parables, and on and on. If our literary competence with the Bible approaches the literary competence we have with the morning newspaper, we should be able to jump into any part of the Scriptures and interpret its words accurately. But sadly, much of our Bible-reading parallels our weeping for Bengal tigers after reading a headline in the sports section of the newspaper!

In front of a large adult fellowship in an evangelical church, I recently spoke on the topic of being genre-sensitive in reading the Bible. To illustrate, I turned to Proverbs 22:6, "Train up a child in the way he should go, even when he is old he will not depart from it." I asked, "Can we claim this as a promise for parents?" Not wanting to appear a fool, no one ventured an answer. Most assumed that we could claim it as a promise and had, in fact, done so many times! To provoke them a bit further, I shared a proverb from American history—*early to bed, early to rise, makes a man healthy, wealthy, and wise.* "Anyone want to claim that as a promise?" I asked, rhetorically. "No. Why not?…Because it's a proverb," I said, answering my own question. "Then why do you think that you can change a *biblical* proverb into a promise?" I anticipated the answer that eventually emerged from the fog: "Because this proverb about child-raising is *in the Bible*!" I deadpanned, "So what?" Their response: "God can supernaturally do whatever He wants in the Bible."

True, God *can* do whatever He wants, in the Bible and elsewhere. If He *wants*, God can tell us how to make lasagna through the gospel of John, tell us that Christ died for our sins through a cookbook and, of course, promise the salvation of our kids through Proverbs 22:6. But how is this relevant? If their answer is correct and *we* can change *God's* proverbs into promises, then we really have no idea what God is saying in Proverbs, do we? If Proverbs 22:6 isn't a proverb (or *is* a proverb, but doesn't need to be *interpreted* as a proverb), then we don't know *what* it is or *how* to interpret it. Having no limit for its possible interpretation, it can morph into whatever *we* want it to be. It really has no genre except what we choose to give it, based on our present needs. One person can make it a promise, another can make it a riddle, and the cynical, burnt out parent can make it an ironic joke. Without genre, it is vague and meaningless, and we really don't know what God intended to say. What it does provide, however, is an occasion for us to craft God's words into whatever words we want to hear!

Hopefully, those of you familiar with such methods of interpretation get the idea of how foolish and dangerous much of our Bible reading has become. It is another example of the tragic shift in interpretive focus from seeking authors' intentions to unpacking readers' presuppositions. When we ignore genres in the interpretive process, we are ignoring one of the most important aids to understanding. Why? Because genres are one of those *community things* that authors and readers must share if they want to communicate clearly and efficiently with one another. When I ignore the chosen genre of a biblical passage, I effectively *individualize and privatize* the interpretive process and jerk the Bible out of everybody else's hands. Whether I'm teaching the passage or reading it, I have taken it out of the public arena where we can share and discuss its meaning.

The personal cost of ignoring biblical genres may also be great. I can still picture a distinguished, older gentleman I conversed with two decades ago. We were studying Proverbs that Saturday and I had just claimed that proverbs are not promises but instances of wisdom literature that emphasize wise choices. I used the example of Proverbs 22:6 and the earnest but erroneous claiming of that proverb by parents as a promise in child-rearing. The dear fellow literally stood up from his chair, red-faced and flustered. He and his wife had two boys who appeared to trust Christ as children but wandered from the faith as teenagers and had not returned as adults. As faithful parents, he and his wife had gotten on their knees and prayed for their wayward sons several times each week, claiming the "promise" of their return in Proverbs 22:6 for over 20 years! In the midst of their parental pain over the eternal well-being of their sons, they took comfort in the "promise" of Proverbs 22:6. Imagine the disillusionment in God and His "promises" that would inevitably accompany their years of false hope if their sons never returned to the Lord. What's worse, the pain and disillusionment were due to some well-intentioned but genre-ignoring saint who made a proverb into a promise—somewhere in the process of interpreting Proverbs 22:6, God's words became his words and God's intended meaning was distorted.

Such, however, does not have to be the case if we will brake for the genres of the Bible. As the diversity of biblical literature testifies, God seems to.

OVERCOMING VERSE-BITE CHRISTIAN CULTURE

"Never Read a Bible Verse!" That's the title of a little booklet my friend and Christian radio personality, Gregory Koukl, has written to help people read the Bible well. What great advice. "That's right, never read a Bible verse. Instead, always read a paragraph—at least." But the current is flowing the other way in our popular sound-bite culture. Not to be left out (or left behind!), the Church has its own version of sound-bite culture: *verse-bite culture*. In verse-bite culture we take a sentence or sentence-fragment from a biblical paragraph, memorize it out of context, write it on a little card, put it on a billboard, a plaque, a rock, etc. Somehow we think that just because this little chunk of Scripture has a verse number in front of it, it was meant to be a freestanding unit of thought. Nothing could be further from the truth.

Apart from the fact that chapter and verse divisions weren't added to the New Testament text until 1560—long after the New Testament's inspired authorship—there is a more important reason for never reading just a Bible verse, and instead reading at least the paragraph that contains it.

By nature, meaning comes from the top down, from a text's larger units to its smaller ones. The paragraph is there because of the *whole text's* thesis. The sentence (or "verse") is there because of the *paragraph's* thesis. The word is there because of the *sentence's* thesis. You get the idea. The contours of the larger units of a text determine the meaning of its smaller units. This is also the way our minds work—from the big idea down to its smaller parts. The same is true of the Bible. A biblical sentence (verse) is simply a part of a paragraph and develops some aspect of the *paragraph's* big idea. Therefore, the *minimal* unit of thought to read is the paragraph. A wise Bible reader will learn to think in terms of paragraphs and will regularly ask, "What's the big idea of this paragraph?"

Let's test this approach to reading the Bible by looking at a well-known verse of Scripture, 1 Thessalonians 5:22—"Abstain from all appearance of evil." I confess that whenever I encounter this verse, I picture old, withered saints shaking their bony fingers in younger believers' faces and exhorting them about some questionable behavior. In this recurring scenario, the godly, mature Christians find it necessary to exhort the younger saints not because they have done something that *actually is* evil, but simply because they behaved in a manner that could have the *appearance* of being evil.

This understanding of the teaching of 1 Thessalonians 5:22 can be traced back to the King James Version of 1611. The KJV chose the word "appearance" for the Greek word *eidos*, which means *visible form, outward appearance, kind or sort*. Since this translation emerged, well-intentioned Christians have focused only on the "outward appearance" aspect and concluded that we are not only to avoid evil, but we are also to avoid anything that could *outwardly appear* to be evil. Hence, the genesis of the widely used ethical dictum, "Avoid every appearance of evil." However, there are multiple problems with this interpretation.

One is that it doesn't fit into the big idea of the paragraph containing it. In fact, this understanding is totally secondary to the paragraph's big idea. Let me briefly explain.

1 Thessalonians is the Apostle Paul's letter to a group of new Christians being persecuted by their fellow citizens in northern Greece. It's an adversarial context for the church, so Paul spends much of his time defending his church-planting team's integrity and actions in chapters 1–3. In chapters 4–5 ("the moral

exhortation" section), he addresses five successive threats to the life of this church body. 1 Thessalonians 5:12–22 addresses the fifth and final significant issue facing this new band of Christians.

Verses 12–22 deal broadly with the concerns that arise when the church gathers for her weekly assembly. Paul gives instructions about fostering healthy church body life in this context by rightly esteeming leaders (verses 12–13), dealing sensitively with the saints' varying needs (verses 14–15), establishing a joyful assembly (verses 16–18), and not squelching the ministry of the Holy Spirit in prophetic utterances in the assembly (verses 19–22). Note that verse 22 helps develop the exhortation about prophecy in the church. While the paragraph covers a broad range of issues, these issues coherently develop the big idea of "what our body life should look like when the church gathers."

By briefly working our way down from the broader context of the whole letter to the paragraph (5:12–22), we're now ready to look at the immediate context for verse 22. Notice the logical flow of the argument about prophetic utterances in verses 19–22:

"¹⁹ **Do not quench the Spirit;**"—*This is the general exhortation of the argument.*

"²⁰ **do not despise prophetic utterances.**"—*A specific NEGATIVE aspect of the exhortation.*

"²¹ **BUT examine everything carefully;**"—*A contrasting POSITIVE aspect of the exhortation.*

"**hold fast to that which is good;**"—*What we should do with GOOD prophecies after examining them.*

"²² **abstain from every form of evil.**"—*Or "abstain from every evil form of utterance."—This is what we should do with EVIL prophetic utterances.*

Note that the topic is *very specific*. It is about the specific topic of prophetic utterances when the church officially gathers. As is generally the case with Scripture, God and the human authors are very specific in their discussions. They seldom sprinkle broad moral sayings like "avoid every appearance of evil" in free-standing fashion. Rather, they usually speak in a closely argued style developing a big idea, especially in the New Testament letters. Such is the case with 1 Thessalonians 5:22. Paul is exhorting the young Christians at Thessalonica to stay away from every evil prophetic utterance. However, by removing verse 22 from its very specific paragraph development, we abstract the language from its anchor and create a much more general, vague concept—*a verse-bite*. (Yes, in a nice tone, I've just said that *we distort God's words and thoughts!*) This seems to be an enormous price to pay for not taking a few extra seconds to read the unit of thought—at least the paragraph—containing the verse in question. The Bible's big ideas are expressed in the big ideas of its paragraphs and we should attend to them.

Moreover, if 1 Thessalonians 5:22 is a broad, moral dictum, did Jesus avoid every appearance of evil? I think not! One of His constant criticisms at the hands of religious people was that He spent time with "defiling people" like tax gatherers, swindlers, irreligious people ("sinners"), and probably even prostitutes. Though He was perfect, sinless—though He never did anything that was *actually* evil—by the standards of the religious, Jesus seemed regularly to have the *appearance* of evil. But perhaps this is the accusation we must bear along with Jesus rather than inappropriately withdrawing from the sin-scarred people in our lives. Perhaps this is also part of our rebuke at the hands of those who don't read 1 Thessalonians 5:22 in context. Perhaps this is part of the bitter fruit of a verse-bite Christian culture.

GRAVE LESSONS ABOUT APPLICATION

I was staring into the open grave of my son Christopher. It was an unspeakably painful moment. The nightmare all parents dread had become my life. Had I been physically able to muster more tears, I would have been weeping uncontrollably. As I watched four men struggle to lower a steel lid over the grave vault holding Christopher's miniature white casket, I realized I would see his little smiling face no more, and run my fingers through his beautiful blond hair never again. We would never snuggle together or touch one another again. Our time together was *over*. As I stood there, looking into what felt like an abyss, I realized that I was in the most despairing, skeptical, and faithless state I had ever been in. I felt like cursing God for the rest of my life. I was on the edge of the dark, bottomless pit of hell.

The excruciating pain of my son's death was a defining moment for me, profoundly shaping my view of God's Word. Previous to that moment, while God's Word had been central to my life, I thought its primary purpose was to give me guidance and doctrinal stability. While I knew His Word was about real human experiences (like suffering and death), it had seemed flat, two-dimensional, like a blueprint or a map. To me, it had been little more than a divinely inspired collection of *information*. I had experienced no great loss or defeat in life up to that point, and I even thought that 1 Thessalonians 4:13–18 (which deals with the death of loved ones) was about nothing more than the timing of Christ's return. Sure, a few Christians in Thessalonica died, but that was simply an occasion for Paul to teach about the end-times.

Over the years, I had logged quite a bit of time studying 1 Thessalonians 4:13–18, trying to understand it. I sought to comprehend the Apostle Paul's teaching about the relationship between death and Christ's coming for His church. I struggled to know the *facts* about Jesus' raising the dead at the rapture of the church, and once I knew these facts, I even meditated upon them. In other words, I laid a *basis of knowledge* about this part of God's Word. And part of my knowledge was the correct application of the passage: "Therefore encourage one another with these words" (verse 18).

In a culture that is rapidly moving into emotivism, the above paragraph is terribly out of step. How dare I use words like "study," "understand," "comprehend," "facts" and "knowledge" when talking about death?

I used these strong, cognitive words intentionally, because one of the purposes of the Word of God is to give us *knowledge*; we are instructed to *learn* about the things Scripture recounts. While this isn't the ultimate end of God's Word, it is certainly the essential beginning. The Bible has a very real cognitive dimension; *knowledge* of certain things is absolutely necessary for meaningful living on planet earth. Quite simply, we must know what biblical passages mean before we can apply their meaning to our lives.

As I pondered the fact that my son's little body was being covered by a steel lid and several feet of dirt, I wondered how God could possibly resurrect his body through such obstacles. It was at this curious, yet horrifying moment that God graciously reminded me of my study of 1 Thessalonians 4:13–18. I began to ponder with new tear-clouded eyes Paul's graveside theology for the grieving Thessalonians:

> [13]But we do not want you to be uninformed, brothers, about those who are asleep, that you may not grieve as others do who have no hope. [14]For since we believe that Jesus died and rose again, even so, through Jesus, God will bring with him those who have fallen asleep. [15]For this we declare to you by a word from the Lord, that we who are alive, who are left until the coming of the Lord, will not precede those who have fallen asleep. [16]For the Lord himself will descend from heaven with a cry of command, with the voice of an archangel, and with the sound of the trumpet of God. And the dead in Christ will rise first. [17]Then we who are alive, who are left, will be caught up together with them in the clouds to meet the Lord in the air, and so we will always be with the Lord. [18]Therefore encourage one another with these words. (ESV)

While these verses contained rich truths about the end times, this passage suddenly seemed far more oriented toward families and friends grieving the death of loved ones. It was theology wrapped in real, gritty, painful, emotion-filled experience. It was shaped to address not an abstract and mechanical interest in the end-times, but the tear-stained eyes of believers who had lost their friends and family members, even their children. It was addressed, at that moment, *to me*. It was God's Word to me, pulling me back from the abyss of despair and unbelief. It was God's Word to me, giving me emotional comfort and a hope that could overcome unspeakable tragedy. It was God's Word to me in my grief, so that I could grieve my heart out, yet "not grieve as others do who have no hope." In that graveside realization, I learned to apply God's Word in a very different way. Perhaps I began to apply it in the way God intended, with both my mind and heart, with *both* my intellect and my emotions. At that moment I learned how desperately I needed to apply God's Word to my life.

Although it has been almost 22 years since my graveside pondering of 1 Thessalonians 4:13–18, I continue to unpack the significance of this experience. It was pivotal in helping me wed the *informing* dimension of the Bible with its *transforming* one. My scales had been tipped toward the information/knowledge end and needed to be balanced with the corresponding transformational intention of the Scriptures. It is always a both/and. While my generation has emphasized the Bible's informing dimension, younger generations are hungering for its transforming dimension. Perhaps my generation's imbalanced emphasis on knowledge has fueled your generation's imbalanced emphasis on experience. Neither is complete by itself. We must know the Bible's *information* before we can experience the Bible's *transformation.* I could never have been comforted by the remarkable truths of Christ's uniting of loved ones at the "catching-up" of the church without first *knowing* those truths. More bluntly, I could never have experienced this timely application of God's Word in the midst of the darkest moment of my life if I hadn't first mastered the information about it. It was a grave lesson, but a life-changing one, about application.

---

*This essay originally appeared as a four-part series on the *Boundless* website:

Walter Russell, "The Hazards of Reading on a Battlefield," [article online] http://www.boundless.org/features/a0000825.html
Walter Russell, "Indians Slay Tigers," [article online] http://www.boundless.org/features/a0000842.html
Walter Russell, "Overcoming Verse-Bite Culture," [article online] http://www.boundless.org/features/a0000853.html
Walter Russell, "Grave Lessons about Application," [article online] http://www.boundless.org/features/a0000864.html

**Reproduction rights granted by *Boundless* and Walt Russell.

PLAYING WITH FIRE
ESSAY QUESTIONS

Answer the questions below on a separate sheet of paper and be prepared to review your answers in class.

1. Based on the context of 1 Corinthians 8:1, what does Paul mean when he states "knowledge puffs up, but love builds up?"

Using the principles that you have learned from this essay, answer the following questions regarding Matthew 18:19–20.

2. How are these verses typically understood?

3. To which paragraph do verses 19–20 belong?

4. What theme is presented in the verses 21–35?

5. What phrase is repeated in verses 15 and 21?

6. The first reference to "two or three witnesses" occurs in Deuteronomy 19:15. How is this phrase understood in the context of verses 15-21?

7. In what three places in the New Testament do we find the phrase "two or three witnesses?"

8. Because of the way this phrase is typically understood in the rest of the Bible, how should we understand it in the context of Matthew 18?

9. How do verses 19–20 contribute to our understanding of the rest of the paragraph?

10. How then should this passage be applied today?

"Loving God with Your Mind"
with J. P. Moreland

PART ONE

I. Being a Teenager Today

A. There were no "___teenagers___" until after World War II.

"Teenagers today have their own values and their own heroes—and many times those heroes and values are communicated through television commercials and through pop culture like music and movies. And they really end up being contrary—not all the time, but sometimes—to the cause of Jesus Christ."

B. Teenagers often don't have good adult role models.

II. How Did We Get Here?

A. The church

"Up until about the time of the Civil War… Christians worked really hard at thinking and learning how to understand what they believed and why."

"Around the middle to the late 1800s Christians became anti-intellectual. They began to emphasize feelings and private devotions. They began to devalue and lose their interest in knowing how to study and think and read the Bible, and to learn to really be learned about one's faith. The Church became kind of illiterate about its own faith."

  1. The awakenings in the middle 1800s

"The problem was that the evangelistic preaching that took place in these awakenings tended to be very, very anti-intellectual and tended to address people's emotions and feelings only."

  2. Secular attacks

"Right when the church had a whole bunch of new converts that didn't know very much about the Christian faith, a tremendous assault was launched against Christianity in the centers of higher learning."

"The Christian community was not prepared to address those assaults by argument against argument, and instead, they withdrew and retreated from culture."

B. Philosophy and science

    1. Immanuel Kant and David Hume (late 1700s)

    "Their ideas were, largely, that we can only know things if we can sense them with our five senses. And if you can see it, touch it, taste it, smell it, or hear it, you can know it's real. If you can't, you can't know it, even though you might believe in it."

    "The great truths of God, the soul, immortality, and right and wrong were banished from the realm of knowledge. That means that they are only matters of private faith and blind belief."

    2. Charles Darwin's *On The Origin of Species* (1859)

    3. The Scopes Trial (1926)

        i. Christians were unprepared in their thinking and were made to look ignorant.

        ii. Winning the trial, but losing the battle

        "We lost the battle in that trial because we communicated to the people watching the trial that the only reason we won was that we were still popular. We did not win because our arguments were better than our opponents' arguments."

III. Anti-intellectualism in the Church

A. The separation of _____faith_____ and reason

"In order to cope with a culture that was beginning to turn secular, the church began to separate faith and reason… Many people said that faith is one thing and reason is another thing… that evidence is a bad thing."

"The Bible teaches that faith is trusting what we have evidence to believe is true."

"If faith and reason aren't relevant to one another, then youth directors and pastors who preach and teach will try to address people's feelings, and will not argue their case before their people. The result is that we don't learn anything over a long period of time."

B. The separation of the _____sacred_____ and the secular

"Centuries ago, when a person fell in love with Jesus Christ, he or she thought that to be a disciple meant that 'everything in my life should be dedicated to Christ.' That meant that if I am a lawyer or a businessman or an educator, I should think as a Christian in what I do for a living. I had better learn about what Christ thinks about that subject matter."

"Today, there is a separation of the sacred and the secular. What I mean is that 95% of the church's teaching is directed to private, personal morality and holiness, and to my personal feelings of warmth and tenderness toward Jesus Christ… But we almost never hear of a Sunday school class that studies business or environmentalism or economic theory from a Christian point of view."

IV. The Gospel and Our Culture

"Because Christians have stopped emphasizing what we believe and why, we have changed how we present the gospel to non-Christians… We used to emphasize that the gospel is really true and makes sense, and you should believe it because it is true and makes sense."

"When you present Christ to people today, if people don't want to accept it, they don't reject it because they think it is false. Today, people don't view the gospel as relevant to their lives… They respond that way because we present the gospel as something to meet their personal needs rather than that it is simply true and real and makes sense."

V. What about World Missions?

"Missions have been hurt because we have spent all of our money in evangelism (which is important), but we haven't spent enough money in training thoughtful leadership for the churches in these cultures we have evangelized."

"There is sometimes a confusion in thinking that the Great Commission is fulfilled simply in evangelism, yet we lose sight of full-fledged discipleship [i.e. learning]."

VI. The Lack of Courage

"We have courage to speak about things we know something about… Now if a person doesn't really understand a whole lot about their own Christian faith… and they don't know how to defend their faith, they are not going to be really courageous about speaking out on behalf of their faith and when they do speak out they will come across as defensive and uninformed."

"We have not valued an informed commitment to Jesus Christ. We have not produced enough Christians who really have thought through the issues carefully and have a real intelligent view of the subject."

"What we need is for Christians to not only care about these issues, but to have more courage to speak about them… to be calm and confident because they have paid the price to study these issues and to know why they believe what they believe."

VII. The Empty Self

A. ___The empty self___ : a person who thinks about himself or herself, and not about his or her role in the community

B. ___The empty self___ : a person who believes everything exists to make him or her happy

My wife, my husband, my parents, my parents' car, my coach, my youth pastor, and even Jesus Christ himself exists to make me happy. If they don't make me happy, then I will turn to something else.

C. ___The empty self___: a person that is very preoccupied with his or her body and/or appearance and with pleasure

D. _The empty self_: a person who is a consumer of entertainment and incapable of creating

"Teenagers fight being individualistic, being self-centered, being infantile, and being passive. And if they don't overcome that, they're never going to grow up and become functional, healthy adults—and they will never be disciples of Jesus Christ who will change the world and fulfill the Great Commission."

PART TWO

VIII. Overcoming the Empty Self

A. Denying ourselves for Jesus' sake

1. Learn to _____serve_____ other people

2. It takes _practice_

B. Learn to understand why we believe what we believe

"It is only if we really know what and why we believe what we believe that we will have a standpoint to step back from our culture and be able to separate what is good and bad, and not get sucked into our culture. If they can do that, then people can resist the messages in their culture that encourage the empty self, and have the strength to resist those messages."

C. Knowledge is not bad

"Childlike faith is a heart that is ready to trust. But when Jesus is talking about a childlike faith, he is not talking about a faith that doesn't mature and become informed and learned."

1. It is the abuse of knowledge that is bad, not knowledge itself.

2. The solution to knowledge "puffing up" is not ignorance, but humility.

IX. The Biblical View of the Mind

A. The God of the Bible is pictured as a rational, intelligent, thoughtful God.

B. In certain Eastern religions you have to abandon your mind.

The God of the Bible does not say 'empty your mind and get rid of it'… He tells us, through the apostle Paul, that we are changed and transformed by having our minds renewed. — Romans 12:2

C. If you want to learn how to share your faith, read the book of Acts.

"When the apostles went to unbelievers, they reasoned and argued and gave evidence for the Christian religion. They learned and read non-Christian literature [see Acts 17]."

D. A specific command regarding our minds

You shall love the Lord your God with all your heart, with all your soul, with all your mind, and with all your strength. And you shall love your neighbor as yourself. — Matthew 22:37–39

"Our love for others grows deeper as we gain a greater knowledge and understanding of them... It's important, if we are going to have a real and full love for God, that we learn to think the way he thinks."

X. Developing a Christian Mind

A. Ask questions

1. Don't act as if you understand something that you do not.

2. Don't be obnoxious in asking your questions.

3. Unbelief is sin, but doubt and questions are not sin.

B. _____Study_____ the Bible

"The Bible for many people has become a rabbit's foot; we rub it for a short period of time in the morning and then hope that it will give us good luck throughout our day."

"Stop asking the question, 'What does this passage mean to you?' Start asking, 'What does this passage mean?' And 'Why do you think it means that?'"

"Get into the habit of reading entire books of the Bible in one sitting... Learn how to study a book rather than just read it."

C. Take your studies seriously.

D. Learn to think logically.

XI. As You Prepare for College

"Be prepared for the fact that there are going to be professors that are dead set on undermining your faith in Jesus Christ... Now when that happens you need to relax. You need to realize that you are eighteen and nineteen years old and if you can't answer your professors questions that it doesn't mean that there aren't Christians who can."

A. Ask questions, but be respectful.

B. Ask your professor if he or she has read contrary Christian opinions.

C. Find Christian resources relevant to your major area of study.

XII. Stretching Your Intellectual Boundaries

A. Band together in small study groups (apart from church).

1. Pick a hot-button issue, not a self-help book.

2. Act on your study (e.g. letters to the editor).

B. We need to change Sunday school in our churches.

XIII. Concluding Remarks

"Many of the important world-changing movements in history were started by teenagers and young people… and that is because they're still fresh enough and idealistic enough to believe the world can be changed."

"If you're going to change the world, you had better be informed about the issues before you change it… and have an informed commitment to changing the world, and not just a youthful zeal that is without knowledge."

"LOVING GOD WITH YOUR MIND"
VIDEO QUESTIONS

Answer the questions below on a separate sheet of paper and be prepared to review your answers in class.

1. What is it like being a teenager today?

2. What is the intellectual state of the church today? How did we get here?

3. How is the gospel often presented in our culture today? How have world missions been affected by the dumbing down of Christianity?

4. What are some characteristics of the empty self? How do we overcome the empty self?

5. What is the biblical view of the mind? How does one develop a Christian mind?

"AMBASSADORS FOR CHRIST"
WITH GREG KOUKL

I. An Ambassador

Therefore, we are ambassadors for Christ, as though God were speaking through us; we beg of you on behalf of Christ, be reconciled to God. — 2 Corinthians 5:20

A. As believers, we are already ambassadors.

B. People draw conclusions about the Sovereign based on _you (me)_

"People are drawing conclusions about your God and about your gospel and about your Savior and about your Bible and about your way of life based on you."

"As a Christian, you may be the only 'living Bible' that some people ever read."

C. We can be good ambassadors or bad ambassadors.

II. _Knowledge_ : An accurately informed mind

A. We are to be offensive and defensive.

Do not be taken captive by philosophy and empty deception, according to the tradition of men, and not according to Christ. — Colossians 2:8 (paraphrased)

We have weapons that are divinely powerful for the destruction of fortresses. We are tearing down speculations and every lofty thing raised up against the knowledge of God, and we are taking every thought captive to the obedience of Christ. — 2 Corinthians 10:3–5 (paraphrased)

1. Truth is our spiritual weapon.

2. We are in a battle for minds.

3. Jesus and Paul addressed ideas with _truth_ .

4. We are not to be taken captive; we are to defend the truth against false philosophies.

B. We need knowledge of the _answers_ .

1. The answers come from the Bible, but…

"Evangelicals have developed a dangerous habit: reading a passage looking for private messages from the Spirit instead of learning what the Spirit is teaching through the inspired writers."

2. We practice relativism (a false philosophy of our time).

"There is no Biblical justification for receiving private messages from text originally intended by God to teach something else. This is not Christianity… this is superstition. Bible verses do not change meaning. A text can never mean what it never meant."

3. Never read a Bible verse; always read a paragraph or more.

4. You can only get the answers by reading the Bible in _context_.

C. We need knowledge of the _questions_.

1. Questions are in the context of culture.

contextualize - take the message and fit it to the culture.

2. Two mistakes Christians often make:

i. Ridicule

ii. Throwing Bible verses

3. We need to know definitions.

4. We need to know the reasons for people's beliefs.

III. _Wisdom_: **An artful method**

A. Tactics: Maneuvering in conversation—ask questions

B. Clarity

1. Present the truth in a compelling way, i.e. get rid of Christian lingo. *(bad news 1st, then good news)*

2. Adapt your message to the specific person or circumstances.

IV. _Character_: **An attractive manner**

A. Two extremes

1. We are so nice we would never offend _anybody_.

2. We don't care what anybody thinks, so we offend _everybody_.

B. We are not to be bullies

1. Gentle and reverent (1 Peter 3:15)

2. Patient and not quarrelsome (2 Timothy 2:24–25)

C. Be ordinary

    1. Get rid of tired, worn-out words and phrases that have ceased to communicate something specific.

    2. Be a genuine, healthy, balanced, winsome, attractive, ~~likeable~~ human being.

D. Learn to say, "I could be wrong." *not true*

E. Learn to say, "That is a good point."

"Christianity is offensive enough. Don't add any more offense to it. But we dare not remove the offense inherent to the Gospel."

"AMBASSADORS FOR CHRIST"
VIDEO QUESTIONS

Answer the questions below on a separate sheet of paper and be prepared to review your answers in class.

1. What does it mean to be an ambassador for Christ?

2. What does it mean to reconcile and be reconciled? What can we learn from 2 Corinthians 5:20? What are three key elements for being an effective ambassador for Christ?

3. What does it mean to have knowledge while being an ambassador for Christ? Is the purpose offensive or defensive? How do we get knowledge of the answers?

4. What does it mean to have *wisdom* while being an ambassador for Christ?

5. What does it mean to have *character* while being an ambassador for Christ?

TOTAL TRUTH
BY NANCY PEARCEY

INTRODUCTION

"Your earlier book says Christians are called to redeem entire cultures, not just individuals," a schoolteacher commented, joining me for lunch at a conference where I had just spoken. Then he added thoughtfully, "I'd never heard that before."

The teacher was talking about *How Now Shall We Live?*[1] and at his words I looked up from my plate in surprise. Was he really saying he'd never even heard the idea of being a redemptive force in every area of culture? He shook his head: "No, I've always thought of salvation strictly in terms of individual souls."

That conversation helped confirm my decision to write a follow-up book dealing with the worldview themes in *How Now Shall We Live?* Just a few years ago, when I began my work on that earlier volume, using the term *worldview* was not on anyone's list of good conversation openers. To tell people that you were writing a book on *worldview* was to risk glazed stares and a quick change in subject. But today as I travel around the country, I sense an eagerness among evangelicals to move beyond a purely privatized faith, applying biblical principles to areas like work, business, and politics. Flip open any number of Christian publications and you're likely to find half a dozen advertisements for *worldview* conferences, *worldview* institutes, and *worldview* programs. Clearly the term itself has strong marketing cachet these days, which signals a deep hunger among Christians for an overarching framework to bring unity to their lives.

This book addresses that hunger and offers new direction for advancing the worldview movement. It will help you identify the secular/sacred divide that keeps your faith locked into the private sphere of "religious truth." It will walk you through practical, workable steps for crafting a Christian worldview in your own life and work. And it will teach you how to apply a worldview grid to cut through the bewildering maze of ideas and ideologies we encounter in a postmodern world. The purpose of worldview studies is nothing less than to liberate Christianity from its cultural captivity, unleashing its power to transform the world.

"The gospel is like a caged lion," said the great Baptist preacher Charles Spurgeon. "It does not need to be defended, it just needs to be let out of its cage." Today the cage is our accommodation to the secular/sacred split that reduces Christianity to a matter of private personal belief. To unlock the cage, we need to become utterly convinced that, as Francis Schaeffer said, Christianity is not merely religious truth, it is total truth—truth about the whole of reality.

POLITICS IN NOT ENOUGH

The reason a worldview message is so compelling today is that we are still emerging from the fundamentalist era of the early twentieth century. Up until that time, evangelicals had enjoyed a position of cultural dominance in America. But after the Scopes trial and the rise of theological modernism, religious conservatives turned in on themselves: They circled the wagons, developed a fortress mentality, and championed "separatism" as a positive strategy. Then, in the 1940s and 50s, a movement began that aimed at breaking out of the fortress. Calling themselves *neo-evangelicals*, this group argued that we are called not to escape the surrounding culture but to engage it. They sought to construct a redemptive vision that would embrace not only individuals but also social structures and institutions.

Yet many evangelicals lacked the conceptual tools needed for the task, which has seriously limited their success. For example, in recent decades many Christians have responded to the moral and social decline in American society by embracing political activism. Believers are running for office in growing numbers; churches are organizing voter registration; public policy groups are proliferating; scores of Christian publications and radio programs offer commentary on public affairs. This heightened activism has yielded good results in many areas of public life, yet the impact remains far less than most had hoped.

---

[1] *How Now Shall We Live?* was coauthored by Charles Colson (Wheaton, IL: Tyndale, 1991) and is hereafter cited as *How Now?* I would also like to recognize the contribution of Harold Fickett, an outstanding writer and storyteller, who wrote the chapter in *How Now?* consisting of extended stories. In offering the current book in part as an advance on themes developed in *How Now?* I'd like to clarify that all citations of that earlier volume refer solely to chapters that I authored.

Why? Because evangelicals often put all their eggs in one basket: They leaped into political activism as the quickest, surest way to make a difference in the public arena—failing to realize that politics tends to reflect culture, not the other way around.

Nothing illustrates evangelicals' infatuation with politics more clearly than a story related by a Christian lawyer. Considering whether to take a job in the nation's capital, he consulted with the leader of a Washington-area ministry, who told him, "You can either stay where you are and keep practicing law, or you can come to Washington and *change the culture*." The implication was that the only way to effect cultural change was through national politics. Today, battle-weary political warriors have grown more realistic about the limits of that strategy. We have learned that "politics is downstream from culture, not the other way around," says Bill Wichterman, policy advisor to Senate Majority Leader Bill Frist. "Real change has to start with the culture. All we can do on Capitol Hill is try to find ways government can nurture healthy cultural trends."[2]

On a similar note, a member of Congress once told me, "I got involved in politics after the 1973 abortion decision because I thought that was the fastest route to moral reform. Well, we've won some legislative victories, but *we've lost the culture*." The most effective work, he had come to realize, is done by ordinary Christians fulfilling God's calling to reform culture within their local spheres of influence—their families, churches, schools, neighborhoods, workplaces, professional organizations, and civic institutions. In order to effect lasting change, the congressman concluded, "we need to develop a Christian worldview."

LOSING OUR CHILDREN

Not only have we "lost the culture," but we continue losing even our own children. It's a familiar but tragic story that devout young people, raised in Christian homes, head off to college and abandon their faith. Why is this pattern so common? Largely because young believers have not been taught how to develop a biblical worldview. Instead, Christianity has been restricted to a specialized area of religious belief and personal devotion.

I recently read a striking example. At a Christian high school, a theology teacher strode to the front of the classroom, where he drew a heart on one side of the blackboard and a brain on the other. The two are as divided as the two sides of the blackboard, he told the class: The heart is what we use for religion, while the brain is what we use for science. An apocryphal story? A caricature of Christian anti-intellectualism? No, the story was told by a young woman who was in the class that day. Worse, out of some two hundred students, she was the only one who objected. The rest apparently found nothing unusual about restricting religion to the domain of the "heart."[3]

As Christian parents, pastors, teachers, and youth group leaders, we constantly see young people pulled down by the undertow of powerful cultural trends. If all we give them is a "heart" religion, it will not be strong enough to counter the lure of attractive but dangerous ideas. Young believers also need a "brain" religion—training in worldview and apologetics—to equip them to analyze and critique the competing worldviews they will encounter when they leave home. If forewarned and forearmed, young people at least have a fighting chance when they find themselves a minority of one among their classmates or work colleagues. Training young people to develop a Christian mind is no longer an option; it is part of their necessary survival equipment.

HEART VERSUS BRAIN

The first step in forming a Christian worldview is to overcome this sharp divide between "heart" and "brain." We have to reject the division of life into a sacred realm, limited to things like worship and personal morality, over against a secular realm that includes science, politics, economics, and the rest of the public arena. This dichotomy in our own minds is the greatest barrier to liberating the power of the gospel across the whole of culture today.

---

[2] Bill Wichterman, in discussion with the author. Wichterman develops his thesis in greater detail in "The Culture: Upstream from Politics," *Building a Healthy Culture: Strategies for an American Renaissance*, Don Eberly, ed. (Grand Rapids, MI: Eerdmans, 2001), 76–101. "While cultural conservatives bemoan judicial activism that reinterprets the plain meaning of the written Constitution, they forget that the courts are only finishing on parchment a job already begun in the hearts of the American people… Politics is largely an expression of culture."

[3] Cited in Mary Passantino, "The Little Engine That Can," a review of Phillip Johnson's *The Right Questions*, *Christian Research Journal* (April 2003).

Moreover, it is reinforced by a much broader division rending the entire fabric of modern society—what sociologists call the public/private split. "Modernization brings about a novel dichotomization of social life," writes Peter Berger. "The dichotomy is between the huge and immensely powerful institutions of the public sphere [by this he means the state, academia, large corporations]…and the private sphere"—the realm of family, church, and personal relationships.

The large public institutions claim to be "scientific" and "value-free," which means that values are relegated to the private sphere of personal choice. As Berger explains: "The individual is left to his own devices in a wide range of activities that are crucial to the formation of a meaningful identity, from expressing his religious preference to settling on a sexual life style."[4] We might diagram the dichotomy like this:

Modern societies are sharply divided:

PRIVATE SPHERE
Personal Preferences

PUBLIC SPHERE
Scientific Knowledge

In short, the private sphere is awash in moral relativism. Notice Berger's telling phrase "religious preference." Religion is not considered an objective truth to which we *submit*, but only a matter of personal taste which we *choose*. Because of this, the dichotomy is sometimes called the fact/value split.

Values have been reduced to arbitrary, existential decisions:

VALUES
Individual Choice

FACTS
Binding on Everyone

As Schaeffer explains, the concept of truth itself has been divided—a process he illustrates with the imagery of a two-story building: In the lower story are science and reason, which are considered public truth, binding on everyone. Over against it is an upper story of noncognitive experience, which is the locus of personal meaning. This is the realm of private truth, where we hear people say, "That may be true for you but it's not true for me."[5]

The two-realm theory of truth:

UPPER STORY
Nonrational, Noncognitive

LOWER STORY
Rational, Verifiable

When Schaeffer was writing, the term *postmodernism* had not yet been coined, but clearly that is what he was talking about. Today we might say that in the lower story is modernism, which still claims to have universal, objective truth—while in the upper story is postmodernism.

---

[4] Peter Berger, *Facing Up to Modernity: Excursions in Society, Politics, and Religion* (New York: Basic, 1977), 133.
[5] Francis Schaeffer deals with the divided concept of truth in *Escape from Reason* and *The God Who Is There*, which can be found in *The Complete Works of Francis Schaeffer* (Wheaton, IL: Crossway, 1982).

Today's two-story truth:

POSTMODERNISM
Subjective, Relative to Particular Groups

MODERNISM
Objective, Universally Valid

The reason it's so important for us to learn how to recognize this division is that it is the single most potent weapon for delegitimizing the biblical perspective in the public square today. Here's how it works: Most secularists are too politically savvy to attack religion directly or to debunk it as false. So what do they do? They consign religion to the value sphere—which takes it out of the realm of true and false altogether. Secularists can then assure us that of course they "respect" religion, while at the same time denying that it has any relevance to the public realm.

As Phillip Johnson puts it, the fact/value split "allows the metaphysical naturalists to mollify the potentially troublesome religious people by assuring them that science does not rule out 'religious *belief*' (so long as it does not pretend to be *knowledge*)."[6] In other words, so long as everyone understands that it is merely a matter of private feelings. The two-story grid functions as a gatekeeper that defines what is to be taken seriously as genuine knowledge, and what can be dismissed as mere wish-fulfillment.

JUST A POWER GRAB?

This same division also explains why Christians have such difficulty communicating in the public arena. It's crucial for us to realize that nonbelievers are constantly filtering what we say through a mental fact/value grid. For example, when we state a position on an issue like abortion or bioethics or homosexuality, *we* intend to assert an objective moral truth important to the health of society—but *they* think we're merely expressing our subjective bias. When we say there's scientific evidence for design in the universe, *we* intend to stake out a testable truth claim—but *they* say, "Uh oh, the Religious Right is making a political power grab." The fact/value grid instantly dissolves away the objective content of anything we say, and we will not be successful in introducing the *content* of our belief into the public discussion unless we first find ways to get past this gatekeeper.

That's why Lesslie Newbigin warned that the divided concept of truth is the primary factor in "the cultural captivity of the gospel." It traps Christianity in the upper story of privatized values, and prevents it from having any effect on public culture.[7] Having worked as a missionary in India for forty years, Newbigin was able to discern what is distinctive about Western thought more clearly than most of us, who have been immersed in it all our lives. On his return to the West, Newbigin was struck by the way Christian truth has been marginalized. He saw that any position labeled *religion* is placed in the upper story of values, where it is no longer regarded as objective knowledge. To give just one recent example, in the debate over embryonic stem cell research, actor Christopher Reeve told a student group at Yale University, "When matters of public policy are debated, *no religions should have a seat at the table*."[8]

To recover a place at the table of public debate, then, Christians must find a way to overcome the dichotomy between public and private, fact and value, secular and sacred. We need to liberate the gospel from its cultural captivity, restoring it to the status of public truth. "The barred cage that forms the prison for the gospel in contemporary western culture is [the church's] accommodation…to the fact-value dichotomy," says Michael Goheen, a professor of worldview studies.[9] Only by recovering a holistic view of total truth can we set the gospel free to become a redemptive force across all of life.

---

[6] Phillip E. Johnson, *The Wedge of Truth: Splitting the Foundations of Naturalism* (Downers Grove, IL: InterVarsity, 2000), 148, emphasis added. See also my review "A New Foundation for Positive Cultural Change: Science and God in the Public Square," *Human Events* (September 15, 2000), at www.arn.org.

[7] Lesslie Newbigin, *A Word in Season: Perspectives on Christian World Missions* (Grand Rapids, MI: Eerdmans, 1994); see especially the chapter titled "The Cultural Captivity of Western Christianity as a Challenge to a Missionary Church."

[8] "Reeve: Keep Religious Groups Out of Public Policy," The Associated Press (April 3, 2003), emphasis added.

[9] Michael Goheen, *"As the Father Has Sent Me, I Am Sending You"* (Zoetermeer: Uitgeverij Boekencentrum, 2000), 377.

MENTAL MAPS

To say that Christianity is the truth about total reality means that it is a full-orbed worldview. The term means literally a *view* of the *world*, a biblically informed perspective on all reality. A worldview is like a mental map that tells us how to navigate the world effectively. It is the imprint of God's objective truth on our inner life.

We might say that each of us carries a model of the universe inside our heads that tells us what the world is like and how we should live in it. A classic book on worldviews is titled *The Universe Next Door*, suggesting that we all have a mental or conceptual universe in which we "live"—a network of principles that answer the fundamental questions of life: Who are we? Where did we come from? What is the purpose of life? The author of the book, James Sire, invites readers to examine a variety of worldviews in order to understand the mental universe held by other people—those living "next door."

A worldview is not the same thing as a formal philosophy; otherwise, it would be only for professional philosophers. Even ordinary people have a set of convictions about how reality functions and how they should live. Because we are made in God's image, we all seek to make sense of life. Some convictions are conscious, while others are unconscious, but together they form a more or less consistent picture of reality. Human beings "are incapable of holding purely arbitrary opinions or making entirely unprincipled decisions," writes Al Wolters in a book on worldview. Because we are by nature rational and responsible beings, we sense that "we need some creed to live by, some map by which to chart our course."[10]

The notion that we need such a "map" in the first place grows out of the biblical view of human nature. The Marxist may claim that human behavior is ultimately shaped by economic circumstances; the Freudian attributes everything to repressed sexual instincts; and the behavioral psychologist regards humans as stimulus-response mechanisms. But the Bible teaches that the overriding factor in the choices we make is our ultimate belief or religious commitment. Our lives are shaped by the "god" we worship—whether the God of the Bible or some substitute deity.

The term *worldview* is a translation of the German word *Weltanschauung*, which means a way of looking at the world (*Welt* = world; *schauen* = to look). German Romanticism developed the idea that cultures are complex wholes, where a certain outlook on life, or spirit of the age, is expressed across the board—in art, literature, and social institutions as well as in formal philosophy. The best way to understand the products of any culture, then, is to grasp the underlying worldview being expressed. But, of course, cultures change over the course of history, and thus the original use of the term *worldview* conveyed relativism.

The word was later introduced into Christian circles through Dutch neo-Calvinist thinkers such as Abraham Kuyper and Herman Dooyeweerd. They argued that Christians cannot counter the spirit of the age in which they live unless they develop an equally comprehensive biblical worldview—an outlook on life that gives rise to distinctively Christian forms of culture—with the important qualification that it is not merely the relativistic belief of a particular culture but is based on the very Word of God, true for all times and places.[11]

NOT JUST ACADEMIC

As the concept of *worldview* becomes common currency, it can all too easily be misunderstood. Some treat it as merely another academic subject to master—a mental exercise or "how to" strategy. Others handle worldview as if it were a weapon in the culture war, a tool for more effective activism. Still others, alas, treat it as little more than a new buzzword or marketing gimmick to dazzle the public and attract donors.

---

[10] Albert M. Wolters, *Creation Regained: Biblical Basics for a Reformational Worldview* (Grand Rapids, MI: Eerdmans, 1985), 4.

[11] For a brief history of the term *worldview* from a Christian perspective, see Albert M. Wolters, "On the Idea of Worldview and Its Relation to Philosophy," in *Stained Glass*, Paul Marshall, Sander Griffioen, and Richard J. Mouw, eds. (Lanham, MD: University Press of America, 1989), 65–80. For a more detailed account, see David K. Naugle, *Worldview: The History of a Concept* (Grand Rapids, MI: Eerdmans, 2002). For a brief history from a non-Christian perspective, see the first two sections of Eugene F. Miller, "Positivism, Historicism, and Political Inquiry," *American Political Science Review* 66, no. 3 (September 1972): 796–817. Miller writes: "All human expressions point beyond themselves to the characteristic worldview (*Weltanschauung*) of the epoch or culture to which they belong. This underlying impulse or spirit makes the culture a whole and determines the shape of all thought and evaluation within it. We grasp the documentary meaning of human objectifications by seeing them as unconscious expressions of worldview. Even theoretical philosophy is but a channel through which the spirit of the age finds expression."

Genuine worldview thinking is far more than a mental strategy or a new spin on current events. At the core, it is a deepening of our spiritual character and the character of our lives. It begins with the submission of our minds to the Lord of the universe—a willingness to be taught by Him. The driving force in worldview studies should be a commitment to "love the Lord your God with all your heart, soul, strength, and mind" (see Luke 10:27).

That's why the crucial condition for intellectual growth is *spiritual* growth, asking God for the grace to "take every thought captive to obey Christ" (2 Corinthians 10:5). God is not just the Savior of souls, He is also the Lord of creation. One way we acknowledge His Lordship is by interpreting every aspect of creation in the light of His truth. God's Word becomes a set of glasses offering a new perspective on all our thoughts and actions.

As with every aspect of sanctification, the renewal of the mind may be painful and difficult. It requires hard work and discipline, inspired by a sacrificial love for Christ and a burning desire to build up His Body, the Church. In order to have the mind of Christ, we must be willing to be crucified with Christ, following wherever He might lead—whatever the cost. "Through many tribulations we must enter the kingdom of God" (Acts 14:22). As we undergo refining in the fires of suffering, our desires are purified and we find ourselves wanting nothing more than to bend every fiber of our being, including our mental powers, to fulfill the Lord's Prayer: "Thy Kingdom come." We yearn to lay all our talents and gifts at His feet in order to advance His purposes in the world. Developing a Christian worldview means submitting our entire self to God, in an act of devotion and service to Him.

---

*This essay originally appeared as a chapter in Nancy Pearcey, *Total Truth: Liberating Christianity from Its Cultural Captivity* (Wheaton, IL: Crossway, 2004), 17–25.

**Reproduction rights granted by Crossway Books.

TOTAL TRUTH
ESSAY QUESTIONS

Answer the questions below on a separate sheet of paper and be prepared to review your answers in class.

1. What is meant by the assertion that "politics tend to reflect culture, not the other way around?"

2. How has the concept of truth been divided in modern society?

3. According to our modern society, what are some examples of public and private truths?

4. Why is using the word "values" to describe religious claims a useful strategy for those who endorse the fact/value split?

5. How might the fact/value split affect the way modern culture understands the nature of marriage and the abortion debate?

DEAR DOUG
WRITING ASSIGNMENT

Hey there!

Well, I'm finally settled into my dorm room. You wouldn't think that it would take so long to move into a room the size of a closet, but when you're sharing that space with a roommate you have to be creative.

My roommate's name is Nathan and we hit it off pretty early. I can't say we have a lot in common, but we both like to talk and debate. After the first day of class we talked until four in the morning! At one point he noticed my Bible and asked if I was a Christian. When I said that I was, he asked me *why*. I've never really thought about it that deeply until that moment. Well, it isn't that I've never shared my faith with anyone before—it was just that he was asking me to supply deeper reasons. I told him that I believe in the God of the Bible, and that I had asked Jesus into my heart when I was young. I said that I believe God has a plan for my life and that the purpose of my life is to glorify him. Nathan got very confused. He said he didn't understand what I meant by "asking Jesus into my heart" and "God having a plan for my life" and that "the purpose of my life is to glorify God." When I really thought about it, I wasn't sure myself what all those phrases mean. I was just repeating what I'd heard in church.

Nathan is a really nice and intelligent guy. I'd like to be able to discuss my faith with him, but the questions he asks make me wonder if I've thought through my faith for myself. Nathan told me he holds to a non-Christian worldview, that he's "searching for truth." He's open to talking about Christianity, but says he has a hard time understanding my "Christianese." The problem is that I don't know how else to communicate with him. I've never thought about what some of the words and phrases we use at church really mean. How can I talk about my beliefs with non-Christians without using those terms?

Also, I didn't want to look ignorant, so I didn't tell Nathan that I'm not sure what he meant by "worldview." What is a worldview? He's interested in learning about my beliefs, but what does it mean to have a Christian worldview?

Well, it's already past midnight, so I'd better get some sleep. I have a class at eight tomorrow morning and can't skip breakfast if I want to have my brain awake that early!

Oh, one last thing… do you know why you are a Christian? I *know* that I am, but after my conversations with Nathan, I'm not sure I know *why* I am. Just curious.

Tell everyone hi,
Doug

INTRODUCTION

WORLDVIEW   TRAINING

STUDENT
MANUAL

UNDERSTANDING THE TIMES

Unit One

Topics:
Cults
Proof of God
Religious Pluralism
Theology

A Summit Ministries Curriculum

Section Outline

180-Day Syllabus

Day	IN CLASS	HOMEWORK	
1	Watch "Theology" video		
2	Read UTT Textbook 'Theology 1.1'	Read UTT Textbook 'Theology 1.2'	
3	Review UTT Textbook 'Theology 1.1-1.2' questions	Read UTT Textbook 'Theology 1.3'	
4	Read UTT Textbook 'Theology 1.4'		
5	Review UTT Textbook 'Theology 1.3-1.4' questions	Read UTT Textbook 'Theology 1.5'	
6	Read UTT Textbook 'Theology 1.6'		
7	Review UTT Textbook 'Theology 1.5-1.6' questions	Assign Dear Doug Letter	
8	Read *Are All Religions One?* essay		
9	Review *Are All Religions One?* essay questions		
10	Watch "Existence and Nature of God" video		
11	Review "Existence and Nature of God" video questions		
12	Watch "Marks of the Cults" video P1		
13	Watch "Marks of the Cults" video P2		
14	Review "Marks of the Cults" video questions	Dear Doug Letter assignment Due	
15	Take Unit One Test		

90-Day Syllabus

Day	IN CLASS	HOMEWORK	
1	Watch "Theology" video	Read UTT Textbook 'Theology 1.1-1.2'	
2	Review UTT Textbook 'Theology 1.1-1.2' questions	Read UTT Textbook 'Theology 1.3-1.4'	
3	Review UTT Textbook 'Theology 1.3-1.4' questions	Read UTT Textbook 'Theology 1.5-1.6'	
4	Review UTT Textbook 'Theology 1.5-1.6' questions		
5	Watch "Marks of the Cults" video P1		
6	Watch "Marks of the Cults" video P2		
7	Review "Marks of the Cults" video questions		
8	Take Unit One Test		

UNDERSTANDING THE TIMES
THEOLOGY QUESTIONS

Answer the questions below on a separate sheet of paper and be prepared to review your answers in class. Reflection Questions will not be found in the text. These are merely designed to help you start thinking about issues from a worldview perspective.

THEOLOGY 1.1

1. What are the two "foundations" upon which Christian theism rests?

2. What is the difference between general and special revelation? What does it mean that general revelation is "a necessary but insufficient" means of revelation? What is God's most direct form of special revelation?

3. What is a linchpin? How is special revelation "the linchpin of Christianity?" How does general revelation function as a "prod?"

4. When C. S. Lewis says, "Unless I believe in God, I can't believe in thought," what does he mean?

5. What are some of the characteristics of the personal God? From which biblical references do we learn about these characteristics?

THEOLOGY 1.2

6. What are the key beliefs of Islam? According to Islam, who is Muhammad? What roles do Jesus, Moses, and other biblical figures play in Islam?

7. What are the key practices (or pillars) of Islam?

8. What are the Qur'an and the Hadith?

9. What do Muslims believe regarding the doctrine of the Trinity? Why do they hold this view?

10. Muslims claim that Islam fulfills Christianity. What are the main problems with this view?

THEOLOGY 1.3

11. What term best describes Secular Humanist theology? How do Humanists view the supernatural? Myths

12. According to Corliss Lamont, from where did the idea of God or gods come?
From the cosmos.

13. What is the premise of the humanistic children's book *What About God?*
That God is a mythical character, and not real.

14. Why did life-long atheist Antony Flew abandon atheism and accept theism?
Science and reason drew him.

15. Reflection Question: According to Paul Kurtz, since there is no God, man must save himself. What does Kurtz mean by "save" himself?
That we are responsible for ourselves.

THEOLOGY 1.4

16. **What term best describes Marxist-Leninist theology?**

    Atheism

17. **How did Karl Marx view humanity and its role in history?**

18. **What well-known quote by Karl Marx best summarizes his sentiment toward religion?**

19. **Fyodor Dostoevsky said the problem with Communism is not economic, but what?**

    The problem of atheism.

20. **Reflection Question: Why did Marx and Lenin both desire to wipe "even the flirting of the idea of God" out of existence?**

THEOLOGY 1.5

21. **Why is the life of Christ important to Cosmic Humanists?**

    They say He is their role model of realizing their godhood.

22. **According to Cosmic Humanism, who is God?**

    Everyone, and every

23. **According to Cosmic Humanism, what happens when a person dies?**

    They are reincarnated.

24. **What is the theological view of Cosmic Humanism?**

    Pantheism - everything is god.

25. **Reflection Question: How have you seen pantheism portrayed in popular culture?**

    Star Wars

THEOLOGY 1.6

26. **What is the theological view of classical Postmodernism?**

    Religious Pluralism

27. **Why are Postmodernists such as Jacques Derrida and Michel Foucault unwilling to clearly state their theological beliefs?**

28. **What is deconstruction? How might this theory be applied to texts such as the Bible?**

29. **How has Postmodernism influenced the notion of religious pluralism?**

30. **Reflection Question: What do you think Friedrich Nietzsche is saying in his poem *The Madman*?**

ARE ALL RELIGIONS ONE?
BY DOUGLAS GROOTHUIS

We live in a culture of increasing religious diversity. Just walk around and look at bulletin boards on any university campus, and you will find advertisements for Hindu yoga, Buddhist meditation, Islamic societies, Christian fellowships, and a mind-numbing collection of assorted spiritual teachings and practices. A survey of the phone book yields the same result. There we find not only Christian churches and Jewish synagogues, but Buddhist and Hindu temples, as well as Muslim mosques. This fact is not altered by any amount of talk about America being, or having been, a "Christian nation."

Despite this increasing diversity, adherents of thee different religions routinely declare that their beliefs are both objectively true and essential for spiritual liberation. The dizzying plethora of religious options has led many to argue that religious claims to an exclusive and saving truth are persistent evidence of an unenlightened and outmoded dogmatism. Religions, therefore, must succumb to a saner and more humble estimation of themselves, in order to avert religious controversy and strife.

THE ELEPHANT AND THE BLIND MEN

According to many, a popular parable about an elephant and several blind men illustrates a vital truth about the relationship among the world's religions. The story promises that religious intolerance and even violence can be overcome through mutual understanding and humility. Can a mythical elephant and some blind men deliver the elixir for our religious struggles and confusions?

As the story goes, several blind men were feeling an elephant. (Just how the elephant became placid enough to endure this inspection is never explained.) The man who felt the tusk said the beast was smooth and hard. The one feeling the tail described the elephant as thin and wiry. The man who touched the ear believed the animal to be a soft and flexible creature. The man rubbing his hand over the hide said the elephant was hard and rough like clay. Each man had but a limited exposure and understanding of the entity he was assessing. Because of his ignorance of the whole truth, each man assumed the entire elephant matched his very limited description. Of course, the elephant is made of all the things the blind men described. The tusk is smooth, the ear is soft, the hide is rough, and the tail is wiry.

The moral of the story is that each religion has only partial knowledge, but each mistakenly thinks it has captured the essence of religious truth. From an enlightened vantage point, one sees that all religions are part of the one divine reality (the same elephant). Therefore, the squabbles, struggles and even wars that are fought over religious disagreements are pointless. All religions capture some important religious truths, and they should honor each other accordingly. Those who invoke this parable advise their audience to remember this story the next time they are tempted to make exclusive claims about their part of the religious elephant.

WHAT IS RELIGION?

We will return to our elephant and his friends in due time. First we need to consider the nature and function of religion in order to evaluate the claim that all religions are, in some significant sense, one.

Defining religion is notoriously difficult. We know that Buddhism, Islam, Christianity, Judaism and Hinduism are religions. What essential attribute do they share that makes them religions and not something else?

Some have argued that a sense of ultimate commitment is the defining feature of all religions. In that case, one could label Marxism a religion, although it is atheistic and advocates no methods for spiritual enlightenment, apart from understanding Marxist philosophy and fomenting revolution.

On the other hand, we know that Buddhism is a religion, yet Theravada Buddhists are either agnostic or atheistic. Theism, therefore, is not an essential aspect of religion. Furthermore, many who believe in God but adhere to no religious tradition would be called irreligious.

A loose but workable understanding of religion is that religions claim to explain the nature of the sacred and how humans can come to terms with it. All the major world religions make truth-claims about ultimate reality, the human condition, and how humans can find spiritual liberation.

A "truth-claim" is an assertion that claims to accurately represent or correspond with reality. This is the doctrinal dimension of religion, which is indispensable to its identity.[1] Religions founders, whether Buddha or Jesus or Muhammad, purport to have received knowledge of objective truth—truth that all need to know. The various truth-claims of religions have a strong experiential focus. A philosopher may speculate about the Absolute, but she will not gather a religious sect to follow her conjectures even to the death. Religions, on the other hand, pronounce truths that are viewed as momentous and life-changing.

For instance, after Siddhartha Gautama found enlightenment and became the Buddha ("enlightened one"), he preached the way to enlightenment (nirvana)—a teaching that could not be found in the Hindu systems of his time. The Buddha claimed that if one wanted release from the wheel of birth and rebirth (reincarnation), one must follow his teaching on the eightfold path to freedom from craving and suffering.

In another context, Jesus of Nazareth proclaimed that he himself was "the way the truth and the life," and that peace with God the Father could come only through him (John 14:6). These claims were not offered as idle speculations or religious opinions, but as transformational truths. Neither Buddha nor Christ were religious relativists who went around mumbling, "This is true for me, but it may not be true for you." They were far more sober than that.

Religions are embedded in cultures and serve a number of social and psychological functions. They serve to unite a community, to give hope, or to challenge or sanction secular powers. As William James pointed out in *The Varieties of Religious Experience*, despite the vast differences between religions "there is a certain uniform deliverance in which religions all appear to meet. This common element has two parts: (1) an uneasiness; and (2) its solution. (1) The uneasiness, reduced to its simplest terms, is a sense that there is something wrong about us as we naturally stand. (2) The solution is a sense that we are saved from the wrongness by making proper connection with the higher powers."[2]

However, the nature of the problem and the manner of the solution proposed have been defined in widely differing ways. Religions may be similar in form and function, but they claim contradictory things about ultimate reality, the human condition, and spiritual liberation. G. K. Chesterton made this point in his classic work Orthodoxy when he countered the idea that "the religions of the earth differ in rites and forms, but they are the same in what they teach." This idea, he maintained,

> is false; it is the opposite of the fact. The religions of the earth do not greatly differ in rites and forms; they do greatly differ in what they teach... The truth is that the difficulty of all the creeds of the earth is not as alleged in this cheap maxim: that they agree in meaning, but disagree in machinery. It is exactly the opposite. They agree in machinery; almost every great religion on earth works with the same external methods, with priests, scriptures, altars, sworn brotherhoods, special feasts. They agree in the mode of teaching; what they differ about is the thing to be taught... Creeds that exist to destroy each other both have scriptures, just as armies that exist to destroy each other both have guns.[3]

Chesterton emphasizes that the use of certain cultural forms does not imply any agreement on the actual religious teachings propounded through those forms. For instance, both socialists and capitalists have strongly held worldviews that they express in magazines and books. However, the common use of literature to promote beliefs does nothing to harmonize conflicting beliefs. When Chesterton says that creeds exist to destroy each other, he is not arguing that religions should take up arms against each other.

He means that every religion issues truth-claims about essential elements of its worldview that cannot be squared with the essential truth-claims of other religions. For instance, Hindus, Christians, and Muslims all pray; yet they differ in their idea of the God to whom they pray.

One straightforward way to test the idea that all religions are one is to compare the essential teachings of three major religious traditions. If all the major world religions were ultimately expressions of the same reality, we would expect them to agree on matters of *ultimate reality, the human condition, and spiritual liberation*. At the very least we would expect to find some strategy by which to unify their apparently

---

[1] On truth-claims and religion, see Mortimer Adler, *Truth in Religion: The Plurality of Religions and the Unity of Truth* (New York: Macmillan, 1990) and Harold Netland, *Dissonant Voices: Religious Pluralism and the Quest for Truth* (Grand Rapids, MI: Eerdmans, 1991).

[2] William James, *The Varieties of Religious Experience: The Works of William James*, ed. Frederick Burkhardt (Cambridge: Harvard University Press, 1985), 400.

[3] G. K. Chesterton, *Orthodoxy* (Garden City, NY: Doubleday, 1959), 128–29.

contradictory teachings, as with the elephant story.

A chief temptation in the study of comparative religion is to alter religious teachings in order to squeeze them into a common system. In a recent popular book, *Living Buddha, Living Christ*, the Buddhist monk Thich Nhat Hanh describes the Christian ceremony of Communion as a way in which Christians reflect on their interconnections with the earth, as represented by the wine and the bread. He says:

> If we allow ourselves to touch the bread deeply, we become reborn, because our bread is life itself. Eating it deeply, we touch the sun, the clouds, the earth, and everything in the cosmos. We touch life, and we touch the Kingdom of God.[4]

Hanh straps Christian Communion onto the Procrustean bed of Buddhism so as to describe it in a manner that denies the Christ-centered practice of remembering Jesus' broken body (the bread) and shed blood (the wine) which were offered through his death on the cross. This maneuver does nothing to bring greater understanding to religious discussion, because it does not honor the intrinsic meaning of the religion being described. The kingdom of God, biblically understood, is not a matter of oneness with the cosmos, but of God's personal reign and redeeming presence.

To test the idea that all religions are one, we will compare the teachings of Christianity, Islam, and non-dualistic Hinduism in these three basic areas; ultimate reality, the nature of humanity, and spiritual liberation. We will be careful to describe each system of belief in a way that is faithful to the different traditions—and leave the Procrustean bed to Procrustes and his erring followers.

ULTIMATE REALITY: TRINITY, ALLAH, OR BRAHMAN?

What Christianity Says:

Both the Old and the New Testaments reveal God to be the unique and supreme Creator of the universe. "In the beginning God created the heavens and the earth" (Genesis 1:1). God is the eternal Creator; he cannot be identified with the cosmos because he is transcendent, separate from creation in his essential being. Paul preached that God is a self-existent being upon whom the universe depends (Acts 17:25). God announced himself to Moses in the burning bush as "I AM WHO I AM" (Exodus 3:14). God is a self-reflective, personal being–a center of consciousness in relation to his creation. The prophet Isaiah repeatedly describes God's unmatched power and excellence in personal and sovereign terms: "Turn to me and be saved, all you ends of the earth; for I am God, and there is no other" (Isaiah 45:22). When Jesus taught his disciples to pray, he said they should address God as their "Father" (Matthew 6:9). The personal language the Bible uses to describe God refers to God's very character; it is not a poetic accommodation used to describe a being beyond personality, as in some forms of Hinduism.

Beyond being merely monotheistic, Christianity is Trinitarian, which distinguishes it from other forms of theism. There is one God (Deuteronomy 6:4), who eternally exists in three equal persons: the Father (Ephesians 1:3), the Son (John 1:1) and the Holy Spirit (Acts 5:1–5). The doctrine of the Trinity does not imply that one equals three, which would be a logical contradiction. Instead it teaches that there is one divine essence or substance that exists in three persons. So God is one in one sense and three in a different sense. This doctrine is not explicit in the Old Testament, but it is intimated and certainly not precluded.[5] The New Testament writings teach that Jesus is God Incarnate, the promised Messiah of the Old Testament. Jesus said, "I and the Father are one," which his audience identified as a claim to deity (John 10:30). The apostle Paul affirmed that Jesus suspended some of his divine prerogatives by becoming a human servant for the purpose of redeeming his erring creatures (2 Corinthians 8:9; Philippians 2:6–11).

What Islam Says:

Islam claims to be a fulfillment of Christianity, yet it denies many essential Christian teachings. The Qur'an,

---

[4] Thich Nhat Hanh, *Living Buddha, Living Christ* (New York: G.P. Putnam's Sons, 1995), 31. Hanh often redefines Christianity in Buddhist terms.

[5] On this see Millard Erickson, *God in Three Persons: A Contemporary Interpretation of the Trinity* (Grand Rapids, MI: Baker, 1995), 159–74.

Islam's holy book, teaches that God (Allah) is an absolute unity that allows for no distinctions of persons. Islam insists that Allah is the Creator and sovereign Lord of the universe and is the ultimate Judge of all people. In his passionate condemnation of idolatry, Muhammad, the prophet of Allah, rejected the idea that Jesus, a human being, could in any sense be God. Jesus was hailed as a great prophet of Allah and even as the Messiah, but not God Incarnate. Islam rejects the worship of Jesus as *shirk* (the sinful worship of the creature instead of the creator). The Qur'an affirms that

> Allah is One, the Eternal God.
> He begat none, nor was He begotten.
> None is equal to Him (Surah 112:1–4).

In claiming that "He begat none," these verses deny the biblical claim that Jesus is the "only begotten Son" (John 3:16 KJV). It is very likely that Muhammad never understood the orthodox view of the Trinity and instead rejected several heretical views common during his time, including Adoptionism, the teaching that Jesus became God after first existing as a human.[6] Nevertheless, Islam continues to reject the idea that the divine unity can include three coeternal and equal persons.

Islam and Christianity are both monotheistic: there is but one God, and he cannot be identified with his creation. God alone is worthy of worship and honor. They agree on this doctrine. However, Islam contradicts the New Testament witness that God is most fully revealed in Jesus Christ and that Jewish monotheism anticipated the fuller revelation of God as triune. When Muslims worship God without Christ, Christians remember the apostle John's statement "No one who denies the Son has the Father" (I John 2:23). When Christians worship God in three persons and Christ as the incarnation of God, Muslims pronounce them guilty of shirk and cite a passage in the Qur'an where Jesus is said to deny his deity (Surah 5:115–118). This is a titanic divide between the two faiths.

What Nondualistic Hinduism Says:

Outside the monotheistic traditions lies the worldview of nondualistic (or Advaita Vedanta) Hinduism. Hinduism is a religion of great variety, with six major schools and plenty of theological disagreements. I have chosen one school as representative of pantheistic monism, a worldview that has recently influenced the West largely through Transcendental Meditation and the New Age movement.[7] In its classic form as taught by Sankara (A.D. 788–820), nondualistic Hinduism claims that reality is ultimately one (monism). All apparent distinctions, dualities and diversities are not real but illusory (*maya*) and due to ignorance (*avidya*) of the ultimate reality. This great oneness or nonduality is Brahman, the supreme deity of Hindu scripture. Brahman is the totality of reality (pantheism); there is nothing but Brahman.

Monism cannot become a partner with monotheism. Nondualism denies the duality of the Creator-creature distinction that is affirmed by both Islam and Christianity. While Islam and Christianity teach that the creation must not be worshiped, nondualistic Hinduism teaches that there is nothing but the divine. The dualistic idea of separating Creator from creation must be dropped. The self itself is divine in essence. In one famous Hindu scripture, the Chandogya Upanishad, a son asks his father about the nature of God. He is told, "That art thou."[8] The self is identical with God.

Furthermore, the God of nondualistic Hinduism is not a personal being but an impersonal principle or essence which is beyond personality. Although nondualists may accommodate popular sentiments by allowing worship of a personal God (*saguna Brahman*), this is deemed a lower and inadequate understanding from which one should graduate to a higher knowledge of God as impersonal (*nirguna Brahman*).[9] Brahman is not a personal agent who enters into relationship with his creatures. There are no agents, no creatures, no relationships. All is one.[10]

---

[6] See Geoffrey Parrinder, *Jesus in the Qur'an* (New York: Oxford Press, 1977), 137.

7 On the relationship between pantheistic monism and New Age perspectives, see Douglas Groothuis, *Unmasking the New Age* (Downers Grove, IL: InterVarsity, 1986) and *Confronting the New Age* (Downers Grove, IL: InterVarsity, 1988).

8 Swami Prabhavananda and Frederick Manchester, *The Upanishads: Breath of the Eternal* (New York: Mentor, 1957), 70.

9 For an insightful discussion and critique of this distinction, see Stuart Hackett, *Oriental Philosophy: A Westerner's Guide to Eastern Thought* (Madison: University of Wisconsin Press, 1979), 145–67.

10 For a good general treatment of pantheistic monism see James Sire, *The Universe Next Door*, 2nd ed. (Downers Grove, IL: InterVarsity, 1988), 135–55.

The notion that the teachings of all religions are essentially the same has not fared well so far in our analysis of differing views of ultimate reality. As we look at the different views of human nature and spiritual liberation, we will discover more fundamental disagreements.

THE HUMAN CONDITION: SINFUL, DEFECTIVE, OR DIVINE?

What Christianity Says:

To borrow a phrase form Blaise Pascal, Christianity sees humans as deposed royalty.[11] Man and woman were made in the image and likeness of God for the purpose of having fellowship with God and each other, and in order to cultivate and develop God's good creation (Genesis 1–2). Scripture roots humanity not in an impersonal deity but in the creative activity of God. We share a God given dignity as persons created by a personal God. However, humans disobeyed the wise will of God and fell into disobedience and sin (Genesis 3). Ever since, all people have suffered both by nature and by choice from the effects of this Fall from grace (Romans 3). We were divinely created, but we bear the marks of rebellion. According to Paul, "All have sinned and fall short of the glory of God" (Romans 3:23). The Bible views sin as a force that has corrupted every aspect of human nature and affects all areas of life. It is primarily a moral offense against a morally perfect God, and it severs the divine-human relationship (Psalm 51:4).

What Islam Says:

Islam also teaches that humans are creations of God but have lost their original innocence before God (Surah 20:116–22). Yet, as Harold Netland notes:

> Although Islam does acknowledge Adam's sin and expulsion from the Garden, it does not have anything corresponding to the Christian doctrine of original sin and the total depravity of human nature. There is, of course, a sense of sin in Islam, but it seems to signify more a weakness, defect, or flaw in human character rather than the radical corruption of human nature.[12]

Men and women are not enslaved to sin, according to Islam. With resolution of will, they are able to obey Allah and resist human and demonic temptations. This teaching opposes the Christian understanding of sin as entrenched and pervasive. As Bishop Stephen Neill put it, "At the heart of the Muslim-Christian disagreement, we shall find a deep difference in the understanding of the nature of sin."[13]

What Nondualistic Hinduism Says:

According to nondualistic Hinduism, human beings are inherently one with Brahman. The individual self (sometimes referred to as Atman) is not a creature of Brahman or distinct from Brahman in being. The sense of separation comes only from ignorance of one's ultimate identity. Since God is impersonal and all-encompassing, there is not notion of sin as a moral offense against a holy God. There is a breach in the divine-human relationship through immortality. The core problem is a lack of awareness of one's true essence as divine. As Sankara taught, "The difference between the individual self and the highest Lord is owing to wrong knowledge only, not to any reality."[14]

SPIRITUAL LIBERATION: FAITH, WORKS, OR ENLIGHTENMENT?

Lastly, we come to the vital matter of spiritual liberation. As William James observed, all religions offer purported solutions to the human condition. Just what is wrong? How can it be corrected? Again we find three entirely different sets of answers.

---

[11] Blaise Pascal, *Pensees* 116/398 (New York: Penguin, 1966), 59.

[12] Netland, *Dissonant Voices*, 89.

[13] Stephen Neill, *Crises of Belief: The Christian Dialogue with Faith and No Faith* (London: Hodder & Stoughton, 1984), 88.

[14] Quoted from *A Sourcebook in Indian Philosophy*, ed. Sarvepalli Radhkrishnan and Charles A. Moore (Princeton, NJ: Princeton University Press, 1957), 515.

What Christianity Says:

Christians hail Jesus as the Lord and Savior of humanity. Contrary to Islam, Christians esteem Jesus and God Incarnate, who lived a perfect life, died a sacrificial death on the cross so that people could be reconciled to a holy God, and rose from the dead to vindicate his mission (Romans 1:4). Jesus proclaimed that "God so loved the world that he sent his one and only Son, that whosoever believes him shall not perish but have eternal life" (John 3:16). Paul taught that there is one mediator between God and humanity, Christ Jesus, who gave himself as a ransom for all people (I Timothy 2:5–6). In Christianity, spiritual liberation bestows on the believer the complete forgiveness of sins and a righteous standing before God. This is received by faith alone in Christ alone through God's grace alone (Ephesians 2:8). The sincere believer can be assured that he or she has received eternal life because "the Spirit himself testifies with our spirit that we are God's children" (Romans 8:16).

What Islam Says:

In Islam there is no mediator between Allah and his creatures. Muhammad is a bearer of information about Allah, but not a savior.[15] He may be emulated as an example, but he is never looked to for salvation. One must stand or fall on one's merit, according to one's obedience to the commands of Allah: "no soul shall bear another's burden and... each man shall be judged by his own labours" (Surah 53:38). The Qur'an breathes the last judgment in its every chapter (*surah*). Judgment hangs heavily in the air: "On that day no soul shall suffer the least injustice. You shall be rewarded according to your deeds" (Surah 36:45; compare 82:19). Deeds will determine paradise or hell. Salvation comes through works, not by faith alone. Yet no Muslim is assured of his or her eternal fate at the judgment.[16]

What Nondualistic Hinduism Says:

Spiritual liberation (*moksha*) for nondualistic Hindus is attained through the proper yoga (spiritual practice). Sankara taught that *jnana* yoga (the yoga of knowledge) was the means to realize the self's identity as Brahman. Sankara said that "the man who has once comprehended Brahman to be the Self does not belong to this transmigratory [reincarnational] world as he did before. He, on the other hand, who still belongs to this transmigratory world as before has not comprehended Brahman to be the Self."[17] One who experiences *moksha* is released from the wheel of reincarnation and rests in the divine identity. Faith in an external being (a personal God) is excluded because there is no external being. All is one. Good works done to earn salvation are also eliminated, since salvation is not given by another being. Everyone is Brahman (whether one knows it or not). The knowledge of one's divine essence is what brings salvation.

ASSESSING THE DIFFERENCES

Let us return to the proverb of the elephant and the blind men. What can this story do to harmonize the conflicting accounts of spiritual reality? We should first realize that the elephant story puts the world's religions in the position of blind men! No world religion would accept this assessment, because they each claim to reveal ultimate and universal truths, not partial insights needing elaboration from other religions. The religious interpreter who employs the elephant story is claiming to look down on all the religions from an elevated vantage point that none of them have attained. In essence, the interpreter is creating a new supra-religion that denies the particular claims of the actual religions he or she is assessing.[18] But can the supposedly elevated view really reconcile the divergent claims we have discovered?

Although an elephant can be rough in one spot and smooth in another, it cannot be smooth all over and rough all over simultaneously. When Islam claims that God is absolutely unitary with no allowance for three persons or the Incarnation, it excludes the Christian doctrine of the Trinity. It cannot be harmonized with this doctrine by saying that part of God is absolutely unitary and part is a Trinity. God cannot possess contradictory attributes (nor can anything else). Neither can we align the nondualistic views of impersonal

---

[15] See Josef van Ess, "The Image of God and Islamic Mysticism, the Image of Man and Society," in *Christianity and the World's Religions*, ed. Hans Kung, Heinrich von Stietencron and Heinze Bechert (Garden City, NY: Doubleday, 1986), 71.

[16] See Netland, *Dissonant Voices*, 90–91.

[17] Quoted in Radhkrishnan and Moore, ed., *Sourcebook*, 513.

[18] On this see Lesslie Newbigin, *The Gospel in a Pluralist Society* (Grand Rapids, MI: Eerdmans, 1989), 9–10.

Brahman with the thoroughly personal notions of deity found in Islam and Christianity. God's nature cannot be both personal and impersonal because personality cancels out impersonality and vice versa. One either has personality or does not. An elephant may be partially smooth and partially rough at the same time. Neither can God be both personal and impersonal.

The same difficulties are encountered with the different religious teachings on human nature and spiritual liberation, concepts closely tied to the varying doctrines of ultimate reality. Humans cannot be both one with Brahman and distinct from their Creator. Sankara's assessment of our ignorance of our divinity is at odds with monotheism.

Neither can the disagreement between Islam and Christianity be solved through recourse to the elephant story. If we are morally incapacitated by sin (Christianity), we are not merely wounded by sin (Islam) and vice versa. It follows that if we can be saved by works (Islam), it is false to say we are saved by faith alone through the grace of God totally apart from works (Christianity). Differing descriptions of ultimate reality lead to differing descriptions of the human problem and to differing prescriptions for its solution. It seems that the elephant and its benighted observers have let us down.

Nevertheless, several modern thinkers–of whom John Hick is the most prominent—have tried to harmonize the world's religions.[19] Hick's theory of religions pluralism is too involved to be adequately criticized here.[20] However, we can inspect some important elements of his approach in order to highlight its problems.

JOHN HICK'S RELIGIOUS PLURALISM

Hick believes that all the major religions produce saintly people; therefore, salvation cannot be restricted to one religion. His strategy for reconciling conflicting truth-claims involves creating an all-encompassing category called the Real, which signifies the ultimate reality that is the source of the diverse manifestations of the major world religions. Hick knows that religions disagree on the nature of ultimate reality, humanity and spiritual liberation. Rather than siding with one religion against the others, he claims that all express "the Real" in different but equal ways.

However, this removes from the Real any meaningful intellectual content. We cannot say it is personal, because this would oppose pantheism; neither can we say it is impersonal, because this would oppose theism. We cannot even say it is divine, since Theravada Buddhism does not equate nirvana with a deity. The upshot is that Hick's idea of the Real becomes itself unreal. How can something be neither personal nor impersonal? Furthermore, why would the Real manifest itself in one religion by offering salvation only through Christ and in another religion by offering it through a mystical intuition of Brahman? The Real would be perjuring itself.

Hick tries to handle these disagreements by claiming that whenever a religion makes exclusive claims about reality (as they all do in one way or another), the religion overextends itself. The enlightened vantage point sees all religions as partial expressions of the Real–even if the religions themselves allow no such category. Again, Hicks creates a suprareligious (and ultimately irreligious) category in order to harmonize religions. In so doing, he hauls out the old Procrustean bed, this time fitted with more modern sheets.

Another problem haunts Hick's efforts. In his system, the Real is really unknowable or ineffable. He claims that it is beyond the reach of concepts. Hick is forced into this position if he is to defend the equality of mutually contradictory religious claims. This appeal to the unknowable really solves nothing and triggers an avalanche of problems. If all Hick can say of the Real is that it exists and is the source of the world's religions, he can say nothing specific about its actual nature. Hick admits that we cannot refer to the Real as having knowledge or as being powerful, good or loving. The blind men knew more about the elephant than Hick says religions know about the Real! If the Real is unknowable, it cannot adequately explain the nature of the world's religions. If our concepts about the Real never capture its essential nature, why should we trust the concept that the Real is the source of religious manifestations, especially when these traditions explicitly contradict each other on fundamental doctrines? The real becomes mute—and meaningless.

---

[19] The most developed statement of Hick's position is *An Interpretation of Religion* (New Haven, CT: Yale University Press, 1988).

[20] For more thorough critiques, see Netland, *Dissonant Voices*, especially chaps. 5–7, and Ronald Nash, *Is Jesus the Only Savior?* (Grand Rapids, MI: Zondervan, 1995), chapters. 1–6.

ACCOUNTING FOR JESUS CHRIST

The ideas of Hick and other religious pluralists finally collapse when they meet the person of Jesus Christ. They cannot accept him as he is presented in the New Testament and still claim that all religions are one.

Although many religions claim that God intervenes in or influences the world, Christianity is unique in claiming that God became a human being in history, once and for all, for the purpose of our redemption. Hinduism teaches that the impersonal Brahman sometimes takes a personal form as an avatar to help enlighten the ignorant. Avatars are often historically shadowy figures and have little in common with Christ.[21] Although the Buddha and Christ are often compared, the historical Buddha made no claims of divinity or even of being an oracle of God. Rather, he taught of way of liberation based on meditation and right action, irrespective of any deity.[22] And Islam insists that although Muhammad is Allah's prophet, Allah himself cannot be embodied.

The historical narratives of the New Testament all affirm that Jesus of Nazareth was a man–but more than a man. We find Jesus announcing that he came to seek and to save what was lost and "to give his life as a ransom for many" (Matthew 20:28). He claimed the divine "authority on earth to forgive sins" (Mark 2:10). When debating religious leaders of his day he said, "Before Abraham was, I am" (John 8:58), a clear assertion of being identified with the divine "I AM WHO I AM" of the Old Testament (Exodus 3:14).

Jesus backed up these claims with impeccable and unrepeatable credentials. He healed the sick, raised the dead, taught with unparalleled authority, associated with the lowly, and fulfilled a score of Old Testament prophecies concerning the promised Messiah, the suffering servant who was to be wounded for our transgressions but vindicated by God (Isaiah 53). The apostle Paul proclaimed that this vindication burst forth in Jesus' resurrection from the dead (Romans 1:4), a verifiable fact of history (I Corinthians 15:1–9).[23]

Are all religions one? Given their contradictory claims and the nature of truth, they cannot all be one with the truth. They offer vastly different views of spiritual reality and salvation. Yet in Christ, we are offered spiritual reality in the flesh, a reality that welcomes all to partake of his grace. As Jesus said:

> Come to me, all you who are weary, and burdened, and I will give you rest. Take my yoke upon you and learn from me, for I am gentle and humble in heart, and you will find rest for your souls. For my yoke is easy and my burden is light (Matthew 11:28–29).

Jesus himself welcomes into his family needy people from every race and religious background. All who know Christ as Lord are brothers and sisters in God's adopted family. By turning away from our sinful patterns of life and by turning toward Jesus as Savior, we also embrace a rich variety of God's multicolored and multiethnic people worldwide. The spiritual unity found in Jesus Christ (Galatians 3:26–28) is a tonic to the ethnocentrism and racism that plague the planet.

The apostle Paul taught that Jesus' death on the cross reconciles us to God and allows us to be reconciled to each other in order to create a new humanity (Ephesians 2:15). All religions are not one, but all people can find oneness at the foot of Christ's cross.

---

*This essay originally appeared as a booklet produced by InterVarsity Press

  Douglas Groothuis, *Are All Religions One?* (Downers Grove, IL: InterVarsity, 1999).

**Reproduction rights granted by InterVarsity Press.

---

[21] On the avatar doctrine in relation to the Incarnation, see Geoffrey Parrinder, *Avatar and Incarnation* (New York: Barnes and Noble, 1970).

[22] For an insightful comparison between Buddha and Jesus, see Russell Aldwinkle, *More Than a Man: A Study in Christology* (Grand Rapids, MI: Eerdmans, 1976), 211–46.

[23] See William Lane Craig, "Did Jesus Rise from the Dead?" in *Jesus Under Fire: Modern Scholarship Reinvents the Historical Jesus*, ed. Michael J. Wilkins and J. P. Moreland (Grand Rapids, MI.: Zondervan, 1995), 141–76.

ARE ALL RELIGIONS ONE?
ESSAY QUESTIONS

Answer the questions below on a separate sheet of paper and be prepared to review your answers in class.

1. **What is the moral of the elephant illustration?**

2. **How is religion defined?**
They explain the nature of the sacred and how humans can come to terms with it.

3. **Why weren't Buddha, Christ, or Muhammad religious relativists?**
They pronounced truths that are viewed as momentous and life-changing

4. **According to Christianity, why can God not be identified with the cosmos?**
Because He created them and he is transcendent, separate from creation

5. **How is non-dualism incompatible with both Christianity and Islam?**
Non-dualism says that the creator + creation are one and not separate.

6. **What happens when a religious pluralist tries to harmonize contrary religious beliefs?**
He has to change one or both of them.

7. **How do Christianity, Islam, and non-dualistic Hinduism view the human condition?**
Sin is death, sin is a weakness you can overcome, and lack of awareness of

8. **How does one find spiritual liberation according to Christianity? Islam? Non-Dualistic Hinduism?**
ones true essence as divine.

9. **In the elephant illustration, who are the blind men and who is the interpreter? Why wouldn't world religions accept the elephant illustration?**

10. **What is a truth-claim? Why does religious pluralism ultimately fail when applied to religions that are making truth-claims?**

"Existence and Nature of God"
with Frank Beckwith

"Your faith does not rest on the latest argument by the best philosopher that came out yesterday… your faith rests on what you know to be true by your commitment to Christ. The arguments and reasons are part of the puzzle; they give you reinforcement as to why you believe."

I. Attributes of God

"One of the great paradoxes of believing that everyone is part of God is that most people don't realize it… if you were God, wouldn't you know it? Being omniscient and not knowing it is a really big problem."

A. Creator and sustainer (of all *else* that exists)

　　1. "Who made God?" misses the point

　　2. Acts 17:25; Colossians 1:16; Romans 11:36

B. ___Omnipotent___: All-powerful

　　1. Nonsense question: "Can God make a rock so big that he cannot lift it?"

　　　　"Omnipotence does not mean that God can do anything that you can string together in words. Stringing together things in words may not be anything that is actually even possible… For example, God cannot make a married bachelor… but that doesn't count against God. If it is not a thing that is conceptually possible, then God cannot do it."

　　2. Things that God cannot do:

　　　　i. Make square circles or married bachelors (nonsensical things)

　　　　ii. Sin, lie, cease to exist (goes against his perfection)

　　　　　　"Neither do we lessen God's power when we say that he cannot die or be deceived. This is the kind of inability, which, if removed, would make God less powerful than he is. It is precisely because he is omnipotent that some things are impossible." — Saint Augustine

C. ___Omniscient___: All-knowing

　　1. Knows past, present, and future

　　2. Psalm 139:17–18; Isaiah 46:10, 41:21–24

D. _____Disembodied_____: Spirit

  1. Everywhere: Aware of everything and sustains everything

  2. Nowhere: Transcends time and space

  3. John 4:24

E. ___Necessary___: Cannot not exist

F. ___Rational Agent___: A person or being (not an "it" or a force)

II. The Existence of God

  A. God's existence is not dependent upon us.

    1. Our belief in him does not make God real.

    2. He exists independently of our minds.

  B. We cannot observe God in his fullness.

III. Arguments for the Existence of God

"To present an argument to those who do not believe… is not saying that in order for you to believe you must have an argument. There are numerous people on this planet who are perfectly rational for believing in God who are not philosophers."

  A. ___Transcendental___ Argument

    1. Atheistic/naturalistic worldview

      i. Only physical things exist—no soul, mind, or morality

      ii. Human beings are the result of blind chance and evolution.

    2. Theistic Christian worldview

      i. Physical and non-physical things exist—morality, minds, souls, numbers

      ii. While physical things change, non-physical things do not—e.g. logic.

    3. If your mind is the result of blind chance, how can you trust your own mind?

      "If you knew that a computer had software downloaded at random, would you buy that computer? No… because you know it wouldn't give you true information. Your mind according to the naturalistic worldview is not only physical, but the result of chance and survival of the fittest… it may be that we've survived as the result of us not knowing the truth about the world. Maybe our minds lie to us and that helps us survive. How do you know that you know anything? In an atheistic worldview, you have no assurance of even knowledge itself."

    4. Evil only makes sense if there is an objective good

B. __Kalan Cosmological__ Argument

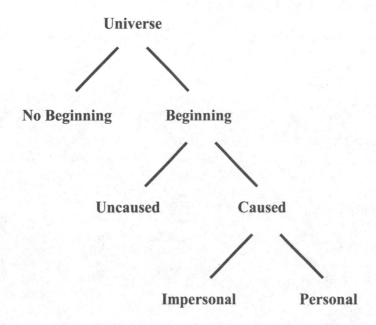

1. No beginning vs. beginning

   i. Big Bang Theory: Something came from nothing

   ii. Second Law of Thermodynamics: Universe is moving toward heat death

   iii. Actual infinite: unlimited set

      1) Logically impossible

      2) If the past were infinite, we couldn't be here today.

2. Uncaused vs. caused

   i. If the universe were uncaused, then it would have always existed.

   ii. An actual infinite is logically impossible.

3. Impersonal vs. personal

IV. Conceptually Possible vs. Logically Impossible

A. Miracles are both conceptually and logically possible.

1. Virgin birth

2. Prior to the 1900s, flying in an airplane

B. Nonsense is neither conceptually nor logically possible.

"EXISTENCE AND NATURE OF GOD"
VIDEO QUESTIONS

Answer the questions below on a separate sheet of paper and be prepared to review your answers in class.

1. **Who made God?**

2. **How is God omnipotent? Are there things God cannot do? How is God omniscient? How is God omnipresent?**

3. **What is the Transcendental Argument for the existence of God?**

4. **What is the Kalam Cosmological Argument for the existence of God?**

5. **What is the difference between conceptually possible concepts and logically impossible concepts?**

"Marks of the Cults"
with Kevin Bywater

PART ONE

"Idolatry is idolatry, whether it is metal or mental."

"We human beings are perpetual idol factories and if we will not worship the true God who made us, then we will make gods to worship." — John Calvin

I. What is a Cult?

A. ___Psychologists___ definition: mind-control, brain-washing

B. ___sociologists___ definition: a sub-group that deviates from the norm

C. ___Dictionary___ definition: from *cultus* (Latin); a group of people having common beliefs and practices; a religion

D. A cult *is* a religion.

E. Pseudo-Christian religion

"A pseudo-Christian religion is a group of people gathered around an individual (or a group of individuals or an organization), who, while claiming to be the true Christian Church and teach true Christianity, actually distorts and denies the foundational and distinctive doctrines of the Christian faith."

But I am afraid that just as Eve was deceived by the serpent's cunning, your minds may somehow be led astray from your sincere and pure devotion to Christ. For if someone comes to you and preaches a Jesus other than the Jesus we preached, or if you receive a different gospel from the one you accepted, or a different Spirit from the one you received, you put up with it easily enough. — 2 Corinthians 11:3–4

1. They use our vocabulary, but not our dictionary.

For such people are false apostles, deceitful workers, masquerading as apostles of Christ. And no wonder, for Satan himself masquerades as an angel of light. It is not surprising, then, if his servants masquerade as apostles of Christ. Their end will be what their actions deserve. — 2 Corinthians 11:13–15

But even if we or an angel from heaven should preach a gospel other than the one we preached to you, let him be eternally condemned. As we have said before, so now I say again: If anybody is preaching to you a gospel other than what you accepted, let him be eternally condemned. — Galatians 1:6–9

2. How can we discern true teachers from false teachers?

    i. We must study what is true.

    and

    ii. We must study what is false.

> You, dear children, are from God and have overcome them, because the one who is in you is greater than the one who is in the world. They are from the world and therefore speak from the viewpoint of the world, and the world listens to them. We [apostles] are from God, and whoever knows God listens to us; but whoever is not from God does not listen to us. This is how we recognize the Spirit of truth and the spirit of falsehood. — 1 John 4:1–6

3. We need to know the Word of God.

II. Cults Add to the Word of God (John 17:17; 2 Timothy 3:15–17; 2 Peter 1:3)

They may deny…

A. The reliability of the Bible

> "The Bible is the word of God, written by men. It is basic in Mormon teaching. But the Latter-day Saints recognize that errors have crept into this sacred work because of the manner in which the book has come to us. Moreover, they regard it as not being complete as a guide… Supplementing the Bible, the Latter-day Saints have three other books: the *Book of Mormon*, the *Doctrine and Covenants*, and the *Pearl of Great Price*. These with the Bible constitute the standard works of the church." — *What of the Mormons?*, 9, 11.

    1. Missing Books

        i. Which books are missing?

        ii. How do you know these books were supposed to be Scripture?

        iii. Do we really need these books?

        iv. Do you have those books? (Isaiah 40:8)

    2. Did Jesus and the Apostles criticize the Old Testament?

B. The clarity of the Bible (2 Peter 3:15–16, Psalm 119:105)

> "Is [the Bible] too puzzling and complex to be understood? Can the average person understand it? What help is needed for one to grasp the meaning of the Scriptures?… It is obvious that we need help if we are to understand the Bible… [T]he fact is that we cannot understand the Bible on our own. We need help… Jehovah, through his organization, however, has allowed his loyal servants to understand its meaning today… You too can gain this understanding with the assistance of those who are experienced in 'handling the word of the truth aright'…

All who want to understand the Bible should appreciate that the 'greatly diversified wisdom of God' can become known only through Jehovah's channel of communication, the faithful and discreet slave [i.e. The Watchtower Bible and Tract Society]." — *The Watchtower* (1 October 1994), 4, 6, 8.

C. The sufficiency of the Bible (2 Timothy 3:15–17, Proverbs 30:5–6)

III. Cults Subtract from the Trinity

They may teach…

A. ___Unitarianism___ : The Father is God, the Son is merely a creature, and the Holy Spirit is an impersonal force (Hebrews 1–2)

"Jesus Christ further deserves honor because He is Jehovah's chief angel, or archangel." Footnote 9: "Why do we conclude that Jesus is the archangel Michael…?" — *The Watchtower* (1 February 1991), 17.

In [the] beginning the Word was, and the Word was with God, and the Word was a god. — John 1:1 *The New World Translation of the Holy Scriptures*

1. Don't argue from John 1:1, 8:58, 20:28

2. Use Isaiah 45:22–23 = Philippians 2:9–11   Heb.

B. ___Modalism___ : Only one person in the godhead who appears as three persons: the Father in the Old Testament, the Son in the New Testament, and the Holy Spirit today (Matthew 3:16–17, Matthew 26)

C. ___Tritheism___ : Three separate gods (Isaiah 40–46)

"Many men say there is one God; the Father, the Son and the Holy Ghost are only one God. I say that is a strange God anyhow—three in one, and one in three! It is a curious organization… All are to be crammed into one God, according to sectarianism. It would make the biggest God in all the world. He would be a wonderfully big God—he would be a giant or a monster." — *Teachings of the Prophet Joseph Smith*, 372.

"I have always declared God to be a distinct personage, Jesus Christ a separate and distinct personage from God the Father, and that the Holy Ghost was a distinct personage and a Spirit; and these three constitute three distinct personages and three Gods." — *Teachings of the Prophet Joseph Smith*, 370.

"…for I am going to tell you how God came to be God. We have imagined and supposed that God was God from all eternity. I will refute that idea, and take away the veil, so you may see… he was once a man like us; yea, that God himself, the Father of us all, dwelt on an earth, the same as Jesus Christ himself did; and I will show it from the Bible… Here, then, is eternal life—to know the only wise and true God, and you have got to learn to be Gods yourselves, and to be kings and priests to God, the same as all Gods have done before you." — *Teachings of the Prophet Joseph Smith*, 345–46.

IV. Cults Multiply the Terms of Salvation (Ephesians 2:8–10, Titus 2:11–14; 3:4–8)

They may have…

A. A high view of human nature (Ephesians 2:1ff, Romans 5:12ff)

"The Church of Jesus Christ of Latter-day Saints discounts the notion of Original Sin and its ascribed negative impact on humanity… [W]e believe that we are not born sinners… In other words, we're born good; we learn to sin as we grow older." — M. Russell Ballard, *Our Search for Happiness*, 87.

"Indeed, we honor and respect Adam and Eve for their wisdom and foresight. Their lives in the Garden of Eden were blissful and pleasant; choosing to leave that behind so they and the entire human family could experience both the triumphs and travails of mortality must not have been easy. But we believe they did choose mortality, and in so doing made it possible for all of us to participate in the Heavenly Father's great, eternal plan." — M. Russell Ballard, *Our Search for Happiness*, 87.

"The decision of Adam and Eve to eat the forbidden fruit was not a sin, as it is sometimes considered by other Christian churches. It was a transgression—an act that was formally prohibited but not inherently wrong." — *Preparing for Exaltation*, Lesson 3

B. A low view of the atonement of Christ (Colossians 2:13, Galatians 2:21)

C. An unbiblical view of heaven

    1. Too restrictive

      or

    2. Too inclusive

D. No assurance of salvation

V. Cults Divide Their Followers' Loyalties

They may…

A. Divide families

    1. Separatistic

    2. Exclusivistic

B. Be authoritarian

    1. Demanding

    2. Controlling

C. Become the mediator (1 Timothy 2:5)

VI. Witnessing Essentials

A. Be prayerful

B. Be prepared

    1. Know what you believe.

    2. Know what others believe.

    3. Ask what others believe.

C. Be patient

D. Be persistent

"MARKS OF THE CULTS"
VIDEO QUESTIONS

Answer the questions below on a separate sheet of paper and be prepared to review your answers in class.

1. What are the different ways of defining a cult? Ultimately, what is a cult? What is a pseudo-Christian religion? How do we discern false teaching?

2. In what ways do cults add to the Word of God?

3. In what ways do cults subtract from the Trinity?

4. In what ways do cults multiply the terms of salvation?

5. In what ways do cults divide their followers' loyalties?

DEAR DOUG
WRITING ASSIGNMENT

Hey!

Okay, first off… our football team is number one! Game days are crazy around here. Just wait until you're a freshman. I made it through orientation and figured out my schedule. My major classes for this semester are psychology, biology, ethics, as well as philosophy—which hits right after lunch, so I'm always falling asleep!

I think I'm getting the hang of college life. Now if only I had someone to do my laundry, everything would be perfect. My roommate Nathan and I are getting along great. We have even started hanging out regularly with a few other people from the dorm—Muhammad, Sarah, Paige, and Mark. Last night we went to a coffee shop off University Ave. to listen to this guitarist Sarah likes. I think it was the first time he'd ever played in front of a live audience!

Anyway, afterwards we all started talking about theology and religion. It was a very interesting conversation. You should have heard the questions they all were asking each other.

Nathan had a question for me—if God created all of nature, wouldn't that make everything divine? I wasn't sure what he meant, so I couldn't really respond to him. And Muhammad wanted to know more about the Trinity, but I didn't really know much about that either. I hope you can help me understand this: how can God be three and one at the same time?

Sarah believes there isn't a God at all, that we just invented the idea of him and an afterlife to make ourselves feel better, and Mark completely agreed. He said that we would never find peace until we could evolve past our need for God. He sees the idea of religion as a human invention, with God as a father figure to help us all feel safer. I guess anything's possible. Do you think God is a human invention? At the end, Paige said that since we can't know for sure which religion is true, we should just be tolerant of everyone's beliefs.

I wasn't really sure how to respond to them. I mostly just listened to what everyone else had to say. They had some good questions and I hadn't actually thought much about all this. Everyone expected me to represent the Christian side of the conversation. What is the Christian view of God?

Well, I should go. I have a date tonight… that's right, a real date! I'll tell you about it some other time. Thanks for all your help. I want you to know that I really appreciate your friendship.

I'll keep in touch,
Doug

WORLDVIEW TRAINING

STUDENT MANUAL

UNDERSTANDING THE TIMES

Unit Two

Topics:
Critical Thinking
Philosophy
Postmodernism
Theodicy

A Summit Ministries Curriculum

Section Outline

180-Day Syllabus

Day	IN CLASS	HOMEWORK	
1	WATCH "Philosophy" video		
2	READ UTT Textbook 'Philosophy 2.1'	READ UTT Textbook 'Philosophy 2.2'	
3	REVIEW UTT Textbook "Philosophy 2.1-2.2" questions	READ UTT Textbook 'Philosophy 2.3'	
4	READ UTT Textbook 'Philosophy 2.4'		
5	REVIEW UTT Textbook 'Philosophy 2.3-2.4' questions	READ UTT Textbook 'Philosophy 2.5-2.6'	
6	REVIEW UTT Textbook 'Philosophy 2.5-2.6' questions	ASSIGN Dear Doug Letter	
7	WATCH "Understanding Postmodernism" video P1		
8	WATCH "Understanding Postmodernism" video P2		
9	REVIEW "Understanding Postmodernism" video questions		
10	WATCH "Evil and Suffering" video P1		
11	WATCH "Evil and Suffering" video P2		
12	REVIEW "Evil and Suffering" video questions	READ *Critical Thinking* essay P1	
13	REVIEW *Critical Thinking* essay questions P1	READ *Critical Thinking* essay P2	
14	REVIEW *Critical Thinking* essay questions P2	Dear Doug Letter assignment DUE	
15	TAKE Unit Two Test		

90-Day Syllabus

Day	IN CLASS	HOMEWORK	
1	WATCH "Philosophy" video	READ UTT Textbook 'Philosophy 2.1-2.2'	
2	REVIEW UTT Textbook "Philosophy 2.1-2.2" questions	READ UTT Textbook 'Philosophy 2.3-2.4'	
3	REVIEW UTT Textbook "Philosophy 2.3-2.4" questions	READ UTT Textbook 'Philosophy 2.5-2.6'	
4	REVIEW UTT Textbook "Philosophy 2.5-2.6" questions		
	WATCH "Understanding Postmodernism" video P1		
	WATCH "Understanding Postmodernism" video P2	READ *Critical Thinking* essay P1	
	REVIEW *Critical Thinking* essay questions P1		
5	TAKE Unit Two Test		

UNDERSTANDING THE TIMES
PHILOSOPHY QUESTIONS

Answer the questions below on a separate sheet of paper and be prepared to review your answers in class.

PHILOSOPHY 2.1

1. How do some Christians use Colossians 2:8 to support their belief that faith does not need to be defended on philosophical grounds? What is wrong with this interpretation?

2. What led former atheist C.E.M. Joad to embrace the Christian view of the universe?

3. What does "faith precedes reason" mean? How does Edward T. Ramsdell explain this idea?

4. What is Christianity's basis for special revelation?

5. What is the Christian view of the relationship between the natural and the supernatural? How does this view differ from that of the naturalist?

PHILOSOPHY 2.2

6. Which system of philosophy influenced Islamic philosophers? What kind of problem does this create for the Islamic view of God?

7. Which argument did Muslims develop for the existence of God?

8. Are Muslims naturalists or supernaturalists? Why? Do Muslims believe in life after death?

9. Do Muslims believe in miracles? Does the fact that Muhammad did not perform any miracles cause a problem for Muslims?

10. How do Muslims interpret Deuteronomy 18:15–18 and John 14:16? How do Christians usually interpret these verses?

PHILOSOPHY 2.3

11. What is the essence of naturalism?

12. How did Roy Wood Sellars regard the Christian worldview? In his opinion, what has rendered Christianity obsolete?

13. What is the cosmology of the Secular Humanist?

14. For the naturalist, what is the ultimate means of perception?

15. How does the naturalist's *monistic* view of the mind and body differ from the Christian's *dualistic* view? What are two troubling implications of a naturalistic answer to the "mind-body" question?

16. How does Lenin describe matter?

17. What is the Marxist view of truth and knowledge (epistemology)?

18. What is the Marxist dialectic and how does it work?

19. What is the Marxist metaphysical belief?

20. How does Marxism address the mind-body question? What is the problem with their explanation?

PHILOSOPHY 2.5

21. Are Cosmic Humanists in agreement with the tenets of naturalism?

22. What is the Cosmic Humanist view of philosophy?

23. How do Cosmic Humanists understand truth? Where does the Cosmic Humanist look to find truth?

24. Why do different Cosmic Humanist thinkers express different interpretations of reality?

25. According to Cosmic Humanism, what is the only substance that actually exists?

PHILOSOPHY 2.6

26. Why is the statement "God so loved the world" nonsensical to a Postmodernist?

27. What is literary deconstruction? What does this theory mean for the Bible?

28. What is the "correspondence theory" of truth? Why do Postmodernists reject this theory?

29. What is the primary idea behind "word play?"

30. What four points does Kevin J. Vanhoozer use to summarize Postmodern philosophy?

"UNDERSTANDING POSTMODERNISM"
WITH JOHN STONESTREET

PART ONE

I. Understanding Postmodernism

A. Both a ___philosophy___ and a ___cultural mood___ that describes "our times"

B. We are all, in a sense, postmodern

II. Historical Perspective

A. Pre-modern Period: < to 1600

    1. Strong belief in the ___supernatural___

    2. Authority of oral and written traditions to give the "Big Story"

    3. Truth is objective, corresponds to reality, and may be known via:

        i. Revelation

        ii. Faculties (reason and senses)

        iii. Experience

B. Modern Period: 1600 to 1960

    1. ___Skepticism___ of the supernatural

    2. Authority of observation, human reason, and science to give the "Big Story"

        i. Belief in progress

    3. Truth is objective, corresponds to reality, and may be known via:

        i. Revelation

        ii. Faculties (reason and senses)

        iii. Experience

C. Postmodern Period: 1960 to ?

    1. Skeptical of all claims to knowledge

    2. Rejects all authorities claiming to give a "Big Story"

        i. Disbelief in progress

3. Truth and reality are only ___subjective___ constructs attained via:

    i. Revelation

    ii. Faculties (reason and senses)

    iii. Experience

PART TWO

III. Key Thinkers

  A. Friedrich Nietzsche (1844–1900)

    1. *Beyond Good and Evil* (1891)   *"The godfather"*

    2. "God is dead"

    3. "Truth is an illusion"

  B. Jacques Derrida (1930–2004)

"When words lose meaning people lose their lives."
—Confucius

    1. *Of Grammatology* (1976)

    2. Deconstruction: no real meaning to any text

  C. Michel Foucault (1926–1984)

    1. *Madness and Civilization* (1960)

    2. Critique of the discourses of power (language is used to oppress others)

  D. Richard Rorty (1931– ?)

    1. *Philosophy and the Mirror of Nature* (1979)

    2. Anti-foundationalism

    3. Anti-essentialism

    4. Truth is a social construct

IV. Postmodernism: The Philosophy

  A. Rejection of "___Essentialism___"

Things don't exist until we name them. Things can be whatever we want them to be.

    1. Things do not have real qualities independent of our knowing them.

    "In the naming, the things named are called into their thinging; thinging they unfold world, and thus are abiding ones." — Martin Heidegger

    2. There are only interpretations in different ways by different people

3. What is "normal" (i.e. knowledge) is really determined by power.

4. What one believes to be true is only the product of his/her cultural situation.

5. Truth is nothing more than interpretation.

> "Truth is… a mobile army of metaphors, metonymies, anthropomorphisms, a sum, in short, of human relationships which, rhetorically and poetically intensified, ornamented and transformed, come to be thought of, after long usage by a people, as fixed, binding, and canonical. Truths are illusions, worn-out metaphors now impotent to stir the senses, coins which have lost their faces and are considered metal rather than currency." — Friedrich Nietzsche

B. Rejection of _Universal Explanations_ (Big Stories)

1. There are no legitimate metanarratives.

2. Any universal theory rejects and suppresses something or someone.

3. All metanarratives are tools of oppression.

C. Role of the "interpretive" community

"If you claim to know history you are oppressing some one else."

1. Meaning can only be derived from one's cultural context ("history is bunk").

2. Words create (not reflect) reality and have no normative meanings.

3. Meaning is created by one's interpretive community.

D. Rejection of _Traditional Logic_

1. Everything is interpretation.

2. All interpretations are valid.

3. Coherence and consistency are illusions.

V. Where You Will Find It

A. **Literature**: Deconstructionism

B. **Philosophy**: Relativism, pragmatism

not reflecting, but creating reality.

C. **Art**: Dada, surrealism, pop-nihilism

They offer a different kind of salvation.

D. **History**: Revisionist (anti-metanarrative)

E. **Sociology**: Multiculturalism

Don't base your worldview on your feelings but on the truth.
Judge your feelings by truth or judge truth by your feelings.

VI. The Contradictions

A. Proposing that "there is no truth," which is a truth statement *(if they say yes, are you sure? and if they say no then how can you know then?)*

B. Asking that we agree with the postmodern interpretation that there is nothing but interpretation

C. Announcing authoritatively that authoritative announcements are invalid

D. Offering the metanarrative that there are no metanarratives *giving a story to everyone that there can be no stories to everyone.*

E. Claiming it is immoral to oppress people with morality

VII. The Culture

A. Truth is not objective, but based on personal feelings.

B. There are no universal values that apply everywhere to everyone.

C. Basis for moral action is not universal rights and morals, but relationship with the other person.

D. We are the product of our culture; nothing more.

E. No one has the right to tell others that they are wrong in their interpretation.

VIII. Postmodernism and Christianity

A. Christianity IS a __metanarrative__. *(Postmodernism denies metanarrative.)*

B. Christianity IS __historical__. *Postmodernism says you can't know history. (history is just an interpretation)*

C. Christianity DOES propose moral norms, authority, and objective truth.

D. What becomes of Scripture and interpretation of Scripture?

E. There are points of agreement:

1. __Modernism__ is flawed. *(Reason can't solve all of our problems. you need revelation, too)*

2. Community is vitally important. *(strong relationships)*

3. Without God, knowledge is impossible. *God is the only answer to the Big story*

"I came to realize that the search of the philosophers for a grand scheme that would encompass everything was illusory. Only a theism that combined a God with equal measures of truth, love, and justice could do the trick. But since I could not imagine myself being religious, and had indeed become more raucously secular, I did not consider that an option for me." — Richard Rorty, *Trotsky and the Wild Orchids*

Base their belief on their feelings not the truth.

"UNDERSTANDING POSTMODERNISM"
VIDEO QUESTIONS

Answer the questions below on a separate sheet of paper and be prepared to review your answers in class.

1. **How can we historically divide the pre-modern, modern, and postmodern periods? How did each period view truth?**

2. **What four elements define the philosophy of Postmodernism?**

3. **In what five ways is Postmodernism a contradiction?**

4. **On what areas do Christianity and Postmodernism disagree?**

5. **What do Christianity and Postmodernism have in common?**

"EVIL AND SUFFERING"
WITH JOHN STONESTREET

I. Defining Evil

A. ___Moral evil___ : Evil that is the result of human choices (Sept. 11, murder, etc.)

B. ___Natural evil___ : Evil where there is no human will involved (natural disasters, etc.)

C. ___Maximum evil___ : Gratuitous evil, innocent suffering (kids killed)

II. Approaching the Problem of Evil

A. Logical side (Focus—the existence of evil)

  1. How could an omniscient, omni-benevolent, omnipotent God allow evil?

  2. Logical syllogism

> Proposition 1: If God were all-*good*, he *would* destroy evil
>
> Proposition 2: If God were all-*powerful*, he *could* destroy evil
>
> Proposition 3: Evil has not been destroyed
>
> Conclusion: There is no all-good, all-powerful God

B. Personal side (Focus—the existence of pain and suffering)

  1. Why did God allow that evil to happen to me?

  2. We struggle with this side most.

C. Other worldviews and the problem of evil

  1. **Naturalism**

    i. Physical world is all there is.

    ii. There is no real evil, only bad luck.

    iii. Evil has no meaning.

  2. **Transcendentalism** [Non-naturalism]

    i. Physical world is an illusion.

ii. Evil is an illusion.

iii. Evil is the result of karmic debt (and is deserved).

3. **Theism**

i. God allowed evil in the world for his own purposes.

ii. Islamic position

"The gist is that good and evil are foreordained. What is foreordained comes necessarily to be after a prior act of divine volition. No one can rebel against God's judgment; no one can appeal His decree and command. Rather, everything small and large is written and comes to be in a known and expected measure." — Al-Ghazali, *Theodicy in Islamic Thought*

III. Bad Solutions

A. _Fideism_ : the problem should be ignored   Romans 8:28   Isaiah 55:8   *really a condemnation, not an encouragment*

Redefines man's ability to know God

B. _Illusionism_ : evil does not exist

Redefines evil *or* the world

C. _Finitism_ : God cannot control all evil

Redefines God's power

Proposition 2: If God were all-*powerful,* he *could* destroy evil

D. _Transmoralism_ : God is beyond moral categories

Redefines God's goodness

Proposition 1: If God were all-*good,* he *would* destroy evil

PART TWO

IV. Biblical Resolution

A. A view of the past

1. God's creation was very good (Genesis 1).

2. Free will is an essential component of true humanity (Genesis 2).

3. We are not good (Genesis 3).

B. A view of the future

"These are they who have come out of the great tribulation; they have washed their robes and made them white in the blood of the lamb. Therefore, they are before the throne of God and serve Him… He who sits on the throne will spread His tent over them. Never again will they hunger, never again will they thirst. For the Lamb at the center of the throne will be their Shepherd; He will lead them to springs of living water. And God will wipe away every tear from their eyes." — Revelation 7:14–17

Proposition 1: If God were all-*good*, he *would* destroy evil

Proposition 2: If God were all-*powerful*, he *could* destroy evil

Proposition 3: Evil has not **YET** been destroyed

Conclusion: Evil will one day be destroyed by an all-good, all-powerful God

---

(factor of time)

1. All evil will be destroyed one day.

2. The end will be better than the beginning.

   i. Revelation 4 and 5 — 24 other thrones (elders) — most authority 3 worship God
   4 beasts w/ eyes — see all of creation at all times
   God the redeemer takes the focus off of God the creator then.

   ii. A world redeemed is better than a world that never fell.

   iii. God doesn't just forgive sins, he redeems.

C. A view of the present

   1. What is the answer for personal suffering?

   "But He was pierced for our transgressions, He was crushed for our iniquities; the punishment that brought us peace was upon Him, and by His wounds we are healed." — Isaiah 53:5

   "Surely He took up our infirmities and carried our sorrows." — Isaiah 53:4

   "It is the woman who has been raped that understands what rape is, not the rapist. It is the person who has been slandered who understands what slander is, not the slanderer. It is the one who died for our sins who understands what evil is, not the skeptics." — Ravi Zacharias

   2. Our God suffers with us

   "For we do not have a high priest who is unable to sympathize with our weaknesses, but we have one who has been tempted in every way, just as we are—yet without sin." — Hebrews 4:15

"EVIL AND SUFFERING"
VIDEO QUESTIONS

Answer the questions below on a separate sheet of paper and be prepared to review your answers in class.

1. What are three types of evil? What are some examples? Which is the hardest type to deal with and why?

2. What are two different sides to the problem of evil and suffering? Which side do we struggle with the most?

3. How do differing worldviews view the existence of evil?

4. What are some bad solutions to the problem of evil? Why are these solutions problematic?

5. What is the biblical resolution to the problem of evil and suffering?

CRITICAL THINKING

BY THE SUMMIT STAFF

INTRODUCTION

In the following essay, we will briefly discuss the nature of an argument, the law of non-contradiction, and a selection of informal fallacies. We will also present a helpful cache of tough questions, which can be used when engaging various worldviews. Finally, we will look at how to discern the assumptions behind the information presented in the media. This survey is designed to provide you with an introduction to the art of critical thinking.

LOGIC

Why are so many people in today's society swayed by mere emotionalism, or trapped by the most recent propaganda disseminated across our airwaves, television, or in the classroom? While there are several factors involved in answering this question, one primary reason is that people do not think critically.

What is an argument? Most people think an argument occurs when people get together, raise their voices, and call each other names. Properly speaking, this is not an argument, but an altercation. An argument, understood in a philosophical or logical context, is where we draw conclusions from various premises. There are several words that we use to indicate when we are presenting a premise and when we are presenting a conclusion. When indicating a premise, we use such words as *because, for, for this reason, as, if, based on the fact that*, etc. When demonstrating a conclusion, we typically use *therefore, thus, consequently, hence, it follows that*, etc. It's good to keep these indicators in mind so that you can detect an argument.

It is common for arguments to be confused with assertions. Assertions are the expressions of opinions without supporting premises. For example, it is common to hear someone assert that there are contradictions in the Bible, but just *saying* so doesn't *make* it so. When you hear assertions like this, the proper response is to ask questions, such as, "Can you give me some examples?"[1]

The Law of Non-Contradiction: This law is the foundation for all logical thinking. It may be defined as follows: a statement (a proposition) cannot be true and not true at the same time and in the same respect. For example: It cannot be both raining and not raining at the same time and in the same respect.

Humans did not invent the laws of logic any more than they invented the laws of nature—such as the law of gravity. In fact, throughout the Bible, the law of non-contradiction is implied. Without this law, nothing could be interpreted as true or false. Right thinking imitates God's thinking; and because God does not contradict himself (his Word cannot be broken—John 10:35; he cannot lie—Hebrews 6:18), Christians should seek to avoid contradiction. Without the law of non-contradiction we would never be able to detect a lie.[2]

In fact, if someone wants to deny the law of non-contradiction, that person immediately runs back into it, because he or she would have to presuppose that it's true in order to prove that it's false. Imagine the following conversation:

> "Hey, I don't think the law of non-contradiction is really that important. In fact, I believe we don't need to follow it at all."
> "Really? So you think we need to follow the law of non-contradiction. You really believe it's that important?"
> "Didn't you hear me? I said just the opposite of what you said I said."
> "If the law of non-contradiction really isn't important, then we are both correct."

---

[1] Of course, there are "hard passages" in the Bible (cf. 1 Peter 3:15ff. to see that even Peter could acknowledge that). If you have questions about such difficult passages, we recommend Gleason Archer, *New International Encyclopedia of Bible Difficulties*.
[2] A lie is a contradiction of the truth. It is a denial of reality.

When expressing a denial or affirmation of any claim, proposition, belief, or idea, one must presuppose the law of non-contradiction. It is fundamental to any kind of distinctions: right and wrong, good and bad, true and false.[3]

LOGICAL FALLACIES

A fallacy is simply a faulty argument. In the process of reasoning, there are two types of fallacies that occur: formal and informal. Formal fallacies deal with the actual *form* of the argument. When an argument is structured incorrectly it is fallacious. Even when an argument is *formally* correct, it may still be *informally* fallacious. The conclusion may not actually follow from the premises due to a faulty gathering of information, circular reasoning, or some other mistake. Informal fallacies are the more common of the two types of fallacies, and will be covered in this paper.

Below we provide a list of some common informal fallacies, a brief explanation of each, and an illustration or two. We have not provided an exhaustive catalogue because there seem to be an endless number of ways that people can make mistakes in their thinking, and we do not have the space to explain them all.

Fallacies of Ambiguity: Communication can be difficult. Difficulties arise from differing cultures, age groups, races, prejudices, and especially from differing worldviews. One of the most important ground rules for clear communication is clear definitions. We may be unnecessarily frustrated if others misunderstand what we say because they either don't know what a word means, or we simply have not supplied clear definitions for the words we use.

Equivocation

The fallacy of equivocation occurs when we use different definitions for the same word, or when a word is taken in a different way than intended (a different definition). Many words have different meanings depending on their context. Consider the following examples:

> "All men are created equal? If that were so, then there wouldn't be so many rich people."
> "If all men are created equal, then why am I so short?"

The difficulty that arises in these examples is that the statement "all men are created equal" means that all men should be equally valued as human beings. It was never intended to mean that we are all clones of one another, or that we would have equal incomes.

There is a special type of equivocation that can occur with relative terms like *tall* or *short*. These types of words must be understood in relation to something else. To claim that something or someone is tall assumes a relation to other people or things. The vagueness of these types of terms can only be clarified by context.

It should be noted that much of our humor rests in equivocations. In a humorous context, we call it a "play on words." Also, sometimes an equivocation can be intentional and witty, such as when Ben Franklin declared, "We must all hang together, or, most assuredly, we shall all hang separately." The word *hang* is intended to be understood quite differently in each usage.

When Christians are witnessing to people who are involved in pseudo-Christian religions (i.e. cults), they need to be very careful to define their words so as not to be misunderstood. For example, while Mormons and Jehovah's Witnesses both use the name of Jesus Christ, they have completely different meanings. The Jehovah's Witness believes that Jesus was the first *created* being and was, in fact, the Archangel Michael before he became the man Jesus. The Mormons, on the other hand, believe that Jesus is literally our older brother from a pre-existence. Jesus is believed to be the firstborn of the Father and one of many gods. Given these differences, we need to make sure that we dig deeper into the meanings of what people say and not stay at a superficial level of communication.[4]

---

[3] Of course, there are some people who still insist that such dichotomous thinking is incorrect. If it is not correct, however, then that means there is such a state as being correct. That then poses a dichotomy. They can't escape the nature of reality.

[4] The Apostle Paul warned the early Church about those who teach a different Jesus and a different gospel (see 2 Corinthians 11:2–4, 13–15; Galatians 1:6–9; 1 John 4:1–6). For a good survey and theological refutation of various pseudo-Christian religions, see Richard Abanes, *Defending the Faith* (Minneapolis: Bethany, 1997)

Fallacies of Relevance: This section will deal with fallacies that occur when something irrelevant to the question of truth is added to an argument in the attempt to persuade.

Appeal to Pity

This fallacy occurs when one tries to persuade by invoking the listener to feel sorry for the individual or group for whom one is arguing. Many times, pity is an appropriate reaction, but it is not always a valid means of persuasion.

For example, sometimes abortion advocates will argue that if you make poor women carry their babies to term, they may not be cared for properly, or that if you outlaw abortion, then women will have to return to the "back alley butchers" to get abortions. While these arguments may be emotionally persuasive, they are not relevant to the issue at hand. One is never justified in killing a child just because life becomes harder for the mother.

Ad Hominem

Ad hominem means "argument to the person." This fallacy is committed when, instead of dealing with what a person is arguing, someone attacks his or her character. This is fallacious because a person's character typically has no bearing on the truth or falsehood of his or her claims. Here are some examples:

"You are wrong because you are an intolerant, closed-minded, right-wing fundamentalist."
"You can't trust anything he says. He is a liberal pagan atheist and has no basis for morality."

Appeal to Ignorance

This fallacy can occur in two ways. 1) To argue that something is true because it hasn't been proven to be false; or 2) to argue that something is false because it hasn't been proven to be true. Just because there is no proof against your position does not prove your position true. Likewise, just because a position has not been proven does not mean that it is false. Here are a couple examples:

"You cannot prove God does not exist, therefore God exists."
"You cannot prove God does exist, therefore God does not exist."

Red Herring

A herring is a fish that can be used to distract and confuse bloodhounds on the scent of game. Similarly, this fallacy is the introduction of an irrelevant side issue into an argument which ultimately distracts and confuses the case being presented. Often positive (or even negative) reasons offered for a conclusion have nothing to do with conclusion. Here are a couple of examples:

"Of course she's a good doctor. She drives a great car and is really funny."
"You believe abortion is murder, yet you are in support of capital punishment?"

Fallacies of Presumption: Fallacies of presumption are those fallacies where someone holds to an unjustified conclusion. This is usually caused by overlooking, denying, evading, or distorting the facts.

Hasty Generalization

When you wish to make an argument for a certain position, you need to gather information for support. In doing this, you must be very careful to gather sufficient evidence to support your conclusion. The fallacy of hasty generalization is committed when a person gathers too little information to support the conclusion being argued.

Just because one or two taxi drivers are rude and obnoxious does not mean that you can generalize that all (or even most) taxi drivers behave this way. All that can legitimately be drawn from such a sampling is that the particular taxi drivers you have encountered were rude and obnoxious. In the same way, just because a person may encounter a couple of Christian TV evangelists who have questionable character does not mean one can conclude that all Christians have questionable character.

These examples get at the heart of the most common way this fallacy is manifest: prejudices. Our prejudices are typically built on a very small sampling, and then are generalized and applied to an entire group (or sub-group) of people or things.

Sweeping Generalization

The fallacy of sweeping generalization is committed when one takes a general rule and applies it absolutely to all instances, not recognizing that there are exceptions. The generalization might be a very fair one, but the application in particular, uncommon, or unique instances may not be valid.

For example, exercise is generally a good thing. Yet what if you have a heart condition? One could say, "Aerobics is the best way to exercise, and Jenny really needs exercise for her heart condition." The problem is that while aerobics might be "the best way to exercise," it would obviously not be the right way for Jenny. Instead of it helping her, it might kill her. Here are a couple more examples:

"I haven't met a single moral atheist. Therefore, no atheists are moral."
"All Christians hate homosexuals. At least, all the ones I know do."

Begging the Question

This fallacy occurs when one simply assumes what he or she is trying to prove. This situation can be demonstrated in the following conversation between two thieves who just stole three bars of gold:

Thief A: "So how are we going to divide the gold?"
Thief B: "I should get two bars and you can have one."
Thief A: "Why should you get two bars?'
Thief B: "Because I am the leader."
Thief A: "How did you get to be the leader?"
Thief B: "Because I have two bars."

Faulty Dilemma

This fallacy occurs when a person states that there are only a certain number of options, and you must choose between them, when in fact there are more options available. In John 9:2–3 the disciples posed a faulty dilemma when, concerning a man who had been blind from birth, they asked, "Rabbi, who sinned, this man or his parents, that he was born blind?" This is an either/or type of question. Instead of answering the question with one of the suggested responses, Jesus denies both and supplies a third. Jesus said, "Neither this man nor his parents sinned, but this happened so that the work of God might be displayed in his life."

Complex Question

One common attempt by unbelievers to stump believers is to ask the age-old question: "Can God create a rock so big that he can't lift it?" If you answer yes, then God's omnipotence (all-powerfulness) is denied due to the fact that he can't lift the rock. If you answer no, however, then God's omnipotence is denied because he can't create such a rock. Neither of these answers is satisfying to a Bible-believing Christian. How does one reason out of this dilemma?

This example can be classified as the fallacy of a complex question, or loaded question. What if I asked you, "Have you stopped beating your wife yet?" If you answer yes, that implies that you have been beating her. If you answer no, then you are still beating her. The problem lies in the question; it is one of those that is simply not fair to ask. You would have to respond that you have never beaten your wife, and that the question presupposes that you have. You can't answer with a simple yes or a no.

Now back to God and the big rock. You cannot answer this question with a simple yes or no. What you have to do is show that the question is not fair. (It might be good to provide the question about beating one's wife as an illustration of this.) You see, by definition, since God is omnipotent (and that is what the Bible teaches), he could create the largest rock possible. Also, because God is omnipotent, he could lift the largest possible rock. The problem with the question is that it is faulty; the question was loaded. You cannot set the creative expression of an omnipotent being against the abilities of an omnipotent being. That would be just as illogical as asking whether or not God could create a square circle or if God could count higher than infinity. It is not within the realm of reality to speak of such illusions, and they do not in any way illustrate any limitation in God's power and abilities.

False Analogy

An analogy is said to be fallacious or false if it compares two objects that are actually relevantly dissimilar or if the points of comparison are used to draw a conclusion that simply does not follow.[5] Consider the following example:

> "You Christians claim to have miracles to support your religion, but so do other religious traditions, such as Mormonism. Thus there is no reason to believe that Christianity is true."

The two objects being compared are Christians and Mormons. Their status as religions and their claim that miracles occur and support their validity are the points of commonalities. However, the conclusion that Christianity is false because another religion claims miracles does not follow. For example, it is possible that miracles occur within both religions traditions. It is also possible that either Christianity or Mormonism have lied or believed falsely regarding the miracles claimed by their religion.

False Cause

This fallacy is committed when a person believes that just because one thing followed another there must be a causal connection. In many ancient cultures, people believed that the gods caused all sickness. These cultures would therefore attempt to placate the wrath of their gods by means of various sacrifices. At times, the sickness would go away after the sacrifices. Because of this, their beliefs were reinforced. They believed that the gods had been placated, and the sickness was removed because of the sacrifice. Mere chronological sequence does not prove causation.

Straw Man

The straw man fallacy occurs when a person misrepresents another's view so as to easily discredit it. This can happen intentionally or unintentionally. The image this fallacy conjures up is that of a person building a straw man simply to knock it over. One might say, "You say that the New Testament teaches that we are not under law, and that we are saved by grace through faith alone. Therefore, what you teach is that we can sin all we want after we are saved." This is a straw man according to Paul in Romans 6:15ff. The person making such an argument simplified the New Testament's stance on the law, sin, and salvation in order to easily defeat a teaching they either didn't understand or with which they didn't agree.

Appeal to Majority

We see this fallacy when we appeal to a group of people to prove that something is true or false, right or wrong. Many times Americans fall into this trap. For example, some people think that certain sexual practices are justified because over 50% of the American public believes that they are permissible. We cannot determine right and wrong by majority vote. In the past, many people believed that the earth was flat. But just because they believed this, does it mean that the earth was indeed flat? Does majority vote make things true or right today? Just because a great number of Americans think that abortion is acceptable, does that make it so? In the end, we cannot determine right/wrong or true/false by majority vote. Such a thing can be decided only by legitimate reasons and evidence.

Appeal to Tradition

This fallacy occurs when one appeals either to what is old, or to what is new in the attempt to establish the truth. Someone may appeal to what is traditional. "We have always done it this way, it must be right." However, there may be a better way. More often today, we hear an appeal to the modern. "We moderns don't believe in the existence of God. That was for ages past when people believed in mythology." Merely because something is old or new does not make it right or true.

---

[5] This is not to say that the objects being compared do not share points of commonality; rather, the objects being compared are not supported by the analogy.

ASKING QUESTIONS[6]

Francis Scott Key, the man who penned the words of the *Star-Spangled Banner*, was also a great Christian apologist. He once wrote, "I do not believe there are any new objections to be raised to the truth of Christianity. Men may argue ingeniously against our faith, but what can they say in defense of their own?"

Mr. Key understood a profound, yet little known principle of defending the Christian faith: the best defense is a good offense. Both sides of an issue should be able to defend their position. We need to practice making our opponents[7] stand up for what they believe, and the best way to make them defend their position is by asking strategic questions.

The strategy of asking questions is a powerful one, but it must be done with the correct demeanor. We must always question the ideas presented, although we should be careful not to challenge the authority of the professor.

In addition, we must keep in mind that if we ask questions of others, they will likely ask questions of us. That means that while we want to challenge other people to defend their beliefs, they will challenge us as well. We need to know why we believe what we believe.

By asking questions we engage in worldview apologetics. We are able to go beyond someone's appearance or behavior in order to reveal and engage their worldview.

How you ask questions—the attitude revealed in your style of inquiry—will reveal whether you want to persuade someone of the truth or just win arguments. We hope that you will desire the former so that you can graciously demonstrate Christian living to unbelievers.

Asking questions is an excellent strategy for three reasons. First, it is low risk. If your opponent becomes angry or defensive at your questions, then you can simply stop asking questions, or change the subject.

Second, asking questions helps you to understand your opponent's train of thought—where they began their thinking, how their thinking progressed, and the exact conclusion for which they are trying to argue. In other words, asking questions helps you to understand them. And understanding is a primary step in seeking to persuade people of the truth.

Third, asking questions can help someone to have a better understanding of where they stand on an issue. In other words, instead of giving them an explanation, you can cause them to think through their position more clearly.

What sort of questions should we be asking? Start with questions that strike at the heart of your opponents' worldview. Such questions force them to back up and defend their assumptions. Along this line, we suggest a series of *tough questions*.

Question 1: What do you mean by that? Always begin by asking your opponents to define their terms. If they say something like, "There is no such thing as a traditional family left in the United States today," then ask, "What do you mean by traditional family?" If they say "God cannot exist because there is too much evil," then ask, "What do you mean by evil?"[8]

Question 2: How did you come to that conclusion? This question is especially helpful in coming to understand how people think. You can find out where their thoughts began, how they progressed, and how they arrived at their conclusion. Along the way, you can ask further questions about any of their points of reasoning.

Question 3: How do you know that to be true? Here we are seeking an understanding of why they believe what they believe. Ask them to supply some good support for what they are claiming to be true.

---

[6] Special thanks to Bill Jack and Jeff Myers for help on earlier editions of this material. Both Bill and Jeff are great examples of how to live inquisitively.

[7] By opponent, we mean the person of whom you are asking questions. It does not mean your enemy.

[8] To combat this particular argument, you can ask by which standard do they judge between good and evil. Keep in mind that atheists have no final universal standards by which to judge between good and evil. The existence of evil is actually a good argument for the existence of God. In the end, if God does not exist, then there is no such thing as evil either.

Question 4: Why do you believe that you are right? We should be ready to ask, "Why do you believe as you do?" This question forces one's opponent to admit when they are simply assuming their beliefs and when they have actually reasoned through their beliefs. It also helps to reveal any evidence they might offer for their arguments. Christians should, in turn, always be ready to give rudimentary reasons for their beliefs on any given subject.

Question 5: Where do you get your information? Students should be trained to ask, "Where do you get the information to prove that what you are saying is true?" This question can help distinguish between mere hearsay and documented data.

Question 6: What happens if you are wrong? Nobody likes to think about the consequences if what they believe is wrong. Yet there have been some outstanding examples of people who were willing to do just that. One such person was Blaise Pascal, a brilliant mathematician, known for his famous wager. It goes something like this: "If I become a Christian and live my life in the service of mankind, and then die only to find out that Christianity is not true, I will have lost nothing. But if I do not become a Christian and live my life selfishly, and then die only to discover that Christianity is true, I will have lost everything." Pascal's wager is a direct way of asking, "What do I have to lose if I am wrong?"[9]

Question 7: Can you give me two sources that disagree with you and explain why they disagree?[10] College professors often hold to one position very strongly against all others. In class, they may assert, either implicitly or explicitly, that what they believe to be true is the objective truth. Therefore, they may give little or no merit to any disagreements, or they may even ridicule their opponents. The astute Christian student will ask such professors to explain clearly the opposing viewpoints, along with good documentation, and then explain why they disagree. In this way, you can see if your professors have weighed different sides of the issues and made informed decisions. The professor has two options: give the merits of the opposing side (thus demonstrating to the class that his is not the only way to think about the issue), or admit that he has not studied the opposing viewpoints and has thus made an uninformed decision without weighing all the available information.

Question 8: Why is this significant? Many professors will fail, unless challenged by students, to provide the connection between their worldview and the point they are making. For example, if they claim "people are basically good, not sinful, by nature," you might ask why this point is significant. This might prompt them to explain that this justifies another view, maybe a socialistic view of the world, or elimination of the need for a savior.

Question 9: How do I know you are telling me the truth?[11] If the opponent has any hidden agenda, it will surface at this point. We should not trust someone simply because he has a Ph.D. after his name. People are fallible, and we all make mistakes. Remember, the Bereans were *nobler* because they checked the Apostle Paul against the Old Testament (Acts 17:11). A poor professor will respond simply by listing his or her qualifications. A good professor will say "Don't take my word for it. Go check it out for yourself."

Question 10: Can you give me an alternative explanation for this phenomenon? This is a good way to move a discussion back onto logical ground. Many individuals will emotionally assert things like, "His budget cuts are responsible for all of the economic ills in this nation." This is an absurd generalization, something that will become evident when asking this question.

---

[9] Be careful with this question because it can always be thrown back at you.

[10] Another way of asking this question is, "Can you give us some sources who disagree with your opinion, explain their positions, and tell us what is wrong with their views?"

[11] Another way of asking this question is, "Why should I believe you?" But you really need to be careful here. It is difficult to ask this question in a way that doesn't seem snobbish.

ANALYZING MEDIA REPORTS

People need to recognize that most of their information about the world comes to them through the media. Yet, the media isn't some massive channel that simply dumps unbiased facts into our laps. As we have seen, everyone has a worldview: the *actors* in a news story, the *experts* who comment on it, the *reporters* of the story, even the *editors/executives* who decide which story to cover. Each of their worldviews has an impact on the information that eventually reaches you.

At times, the influence of a particular worldview may be subtle. However, it wouldn't take very long to discover that many of them don't just have a job; they have a mission. Their mission is to make a difference in the world through what they do. In fact, for many people, this is not an unusual goal. Students needs to be aware that we all approach information and life with a bias. It is simply unavoidable.

In the vast majority of cases, the editors and reporters are making an effort to be balanced. Yet what does *balanced* mean? It means reporting both sides of the issue with no indication that either side of the story has more merit. Is that true? As Christians, we believe that some things are right and other things are wrong.

As one learns to analyze media reports, he or she should apply the rules on logical thinking that are presented in this section. They should also keep the following factors in mind:

1. What is reported? It is easy to think that by reading your daily newspaper and watching the evening news you have received a thorough representation of anything relevant in your community. Students should realize that each media outlet has a limited amount of space and ability to deal with everything that is important. Think of a media outlet as a spotlight on a dark night. The spotlight will illuminate things that you would never see otherwise, but there is no way it can shine on everything at once.

Recognize also that each individual news form has restrictions and limitations. In order to make a story acceptable for television, it must have pictures. This may seem inconsequential until you realize that there are some things—like the arrival of a new bear at the local zoo—which are reported because they make great pictures and can be reported in two minutes. Yet perhaps the same day the bear arrived, the city council made a change in the zoning laws that will affect your school. City council meetings make horrible pictures, and zoning laws don't fit well into concise sound bites. Which story is truly important?

What makes an event newsworthy? Most events that are truly life-changing are not considered newsworthy: marriages, deaths, and births. Rarely do these events appear on the front page. Conversely, many events that make the front page are life changing for only a few people, or intriguing for the moment.

2. Which sides are presented? Is a response from each side presented? Does the news story even indicate that someone might think differently? For instance, in an article in the *Chicago Tribune* entitled "Life Gets Earlier Date of Origin,"[12] an Australian scientist is reported as having found that life evolved much earlier than was previously thought—going from chemical soup to living cells in just 500 million years, rather than 1 1/2 billion years. The article is well written, and acknowledges disagreement within the scientific community. However, it does not acknowledge that anyone might disagree with evolution altogether.

There are many reasons for this type of omission. Sometimes it is deliberate. At other times, a reporter may not be aware that another viewpoint exists or know a credible contact to represent a position. Also, there may not be time to consider another opinion due to deadlines.

Another reason for omitting a position on an issue is based on worldviews. How we think will affect what we believe to be credible, or even possible. For example, we know that the world is round, but some people still believe it to be flat. If you were going to write an article examining a change in a major ocean current and its effect on weather, would you contact the Flat Earth Society for comment?

In the same way, a reporter who firmly believes that the material world is all that exists may do a human-interest piece on a *miraculous* recovery from cancer. Although they might mention the chance that there might be a supernatural element involved, a *natural* cause of recovery will be sought and favored.

The reporter knows that there is no way God could have healed the patient, so this possibility is as absurd as the idea of a flat earth.

---

[12] "Life Gets Earlier Date of Origin," *Chicago Tribune* (May 2, 1993).

3. What is the tone of the report? Does the tone of the writing or speaking carry meaning in itself? Does the tone match the issue being reported? Consider the following example from an article concerning the ethical discussions raised by the movie *Indecent Proposal* (where a billionaire offers another man 1 million dollars for one night with his wife). The reporter spoke with a woman who is shocked by the number of women who would agree to take the money and sleep with the man. The reporter is writing in the first person.

> "I was really shocked," she said. "I think these people are telling the truth. Kidding is one thing, but this was a serious discussion. I love my husband. This would never even be cause for five minutes of deliberation. I would never do it. I can't believe they would."
>
> She talks as if this is going to go on record as the final rip in modern morality.
>
> "And what do you think?" she wanted to know.
>
> The woman is 53 years old, the grandmother of three. And by her own admission, she is 35 pounds overweight. I told her I could see how this would be a great moral challenge. But I thought she had the strength to get through it.
>
> "I think you can go back to worrying about Somalia, the economy, and whether Donald will marry Marla," I said. "I just don't think this is going to come up."
>
> "That's not the point," she said.
>
> "Yes, it is," I replied.[13]

4. What underlying assumptions does the news story hold? Students should become skilled in seeking *underlying assumptions* held in the report of a story. The *Twin Cities Star Tribune* ran an article entitled, "If every kid cared, the world would change,"[14] describing the impact of a few sixth graders concerned about the environment. The piece is inspiring, but the assumption is that it is permissible to do whatever is necessary to make your point (the children disobeyed school officials in holding a protest, and were suspended from school). This disobedience was presented in a positive light.

5. Who are the sources and how are they characterized? Does an article on environmentalism only quote extremist groups, or do they use more moderate sources? If the article quotes Christians, which groups or spokespersons are quoted? Are these the best sources? Why were these sources used? Consider also how the sources are characterized or described. Are they seen in a positive or negative light? The following quote is from an Associated Press article reporting on several Italian towns that banned bikinis on city streets.

> ROME (AP)—Limits on topless bathing or skimpy suits on city streets are not new. But this time the prudery illuminates attitudes about a political force that has arrived like an awkward adolescent shouldering his way onto the school bus.
>
> The prudish officials belong to the Northern League, a regionally based anti-corruption party backed by small businessmen and the middle class, with upright morals to match.
>
> The bans reflect the culture clash between the League and its rivals from traditional parties, particularly on the left, which regard the League as part of a conservative backlash.[15]

6. How are words used to describe people or organizations?
- To describe the incident: Was someone *taken* to jail or *thrown* into jail?
- To describe the people involved: A *local church* or a *fundamentalist religious group*?[16]
- To describe a position: Is someone *pro-life* or *anti-abortion*?
- To convey emotion: One article described citations by the Thomas Jefferson Center for the Protection of Free Expression. The organization cited the Federal Communications Commission

---

[13] "Premise of 'Indecent Proposal' Disturbing," Marilyn Schwartz, *Dallas Morning News*, in *Gazette Telegraph*, Colorado Springs, CO (April 26, 1993).

[14] "If every kid cared, the world would change," *Twin Cities Star Tribune*, Minneapolis (April 22, 1993).

[15] "Bikini ban in 2 Italian cities underlines new cultural clash," *Standard Examiner*, Ogden, UT (July 20, 1993).

[16] Be aware of the use of the word "fundamentalist." It is being applied indiscriminately to any religious group, whether a local church is protesting the location of an adult bookstore or David Koresh's Branch Davidian cult near Waco, Texas.

for censorship for "trying to gag controversial radio personality Howard Stern."[17] *Censorship* and *gag* are emotional words, and convey meaning.

- To give positive or negative connotations: "Focus on the Family, the Christian media conglomerate, should be up-front about its 'extreme and un-American' political agenda, a national civil liberties watchdog group said Wednesday."[18] Think of the words with generally positive connotations: *civil liberties* and *watchdog*. Negative connotations come from the words *agenda* and *conglomerate*.

- To simply describe a thing: A fascinating example of this comes from an article titled "Doctors try to save brain-dead mom's fetus." The baby is referred to as a fetus throughout the article, except when a hospital spokesman is quoted as saying, "The odds are very slim, but the baby's heart is beating."[19] Also consider Colorado's Amendment Two, which would prevent laws giving gays protected civil rights status such as those that protect minority groups. Contrast that description with "the amendment would ban laws that prevent discrimination against homosexuals,"[20] as it was described by the Associated Press.

- Even punctuation can be used to convey meaning. In the following examples, a prayer rally is presented as something a bit odd, if not downright unsavory.
  1. "Abortion clinics brace for Operation Rescue."
  2. "Saturday 'prayer rally' set for Robbinsdale."
  3. "Operation Rescue officials confirmed Wednesday that their national director, the Rev. Keith Tucci, will be in the Twin Cities this weekend and will lead a "prayer rally" in front of a Robbinsdale abortion clinic on Saturday."[21]

7. How are actions described? What are the outcomes or results of the event being reported? Are these accurate? Consider an article entitled, "Teaching multicultural history instills pride, sense of place, educators find."[22] The results of implementing a multicultural curriculum are presented as overwhelmingly positive. However, the writer does not examine the results of this curriculum on the students' standardized test scores. The program has raised self-esteem, but is that the only crucial criteria for evaluation?

8. What statistics are used? Statistics can prove just about anything—and they can be misleading. A prime example is the *accepted* statistic that homosexuals comprise 10% of the population.[23] Recent studies indicate that 2–3% is more appropriate,[24] yet the 10% figure continues to be used.

9. What is left out of the news story? This can include background sources, supporting materials or studies, and opposing viewpoints. Sometimes this omission is deliberate. However, in many cases it is simply irresponsible reporting. For example, consider the following news brief that was sent on the United Press International newswire:

(TRENTON, NJ)— Some 15 million people could be getting parched if there is more global warming without an increase in rainfall. The U.S. Geological Survey says the Delaware River Basin which feeds Pennsylvania, New Jersey, and New York could be facing a serious drought if the overall temperature rises by just four degrees. That would cause stream flow to drop 27 percent and allow saltwater to back up in the Delaware into freshwater aquifers.[25]

---

[17] "Official's ban of fairy tale earns 'citation' for censorship," *The Clarion-Ledger*, Jacksonville, MS (April 14, 1993).

[18] "Watchdog says Focus hides aims," D'Arcy Fallon, *Gazette Telegraph*, Colorado Springs, CO (April 29, 1993).

[19] "Doctors try to save brain-dead mom's fetus," *The Commercial Appeal*, Memphis, TN (April 24, 1993).

[20] "Amendment 2 Boycott," Associated Press newswire (May 7, 1993).

[21] "Abortion clinics brace for Operation Rescue," Tim Nelson, *Pioneer Press*, St. Paul, MN (April 22, 1993).

[22] "Teaching multicultural history instills pride, sense of place, educators find," Sandy Kleffman, *San Francisco Chronicle*, in *Gazette Telegraph*, Colorado Springs, CO (April 19, 1993).

[23] Alfred C. Kinsey, *Sexual Behavior in the Human Male* (Philadelphia: Saunders, 1948).

[24] June M. Reinisch, *The Kinsey Institute New Report on Sex* (New York: St. Martin's Press, 1990), 147. See also Abraham Maslow and James M. Sakoda, "Volunteer Error in the Kinsey Study," *Journal of Abnormal and Social Psychology* 47 (April 1952), 259–62.

[25] *First-Pennsylvania News in Brief*, UPI Newswire (May 18, 1993).

That is the entire story! Almost every possible detail was left out—why the U.S. Geological Survey said what it did, any supporting statistics or studies, or support for the controversial idea of global warming in general. This example also begins with the faulty assumption that global warming is already occurring, and points out the inherent difficulties in reporting news. This news clip was intended for a radio broadcast which leaves very little time for in-depth information. Also notice the conditional words, like *could* and *if*.

10. Where is the reader or listener led into faulty reasoning? Consider the following example from United Press International:

> (MALDEN, MA)—The state Board of Education Tuesday approved a policy that encourages local school officials to implement programs to protect gay students from harassment and educate faculty members about gay issues.
>
> The policy, believed to be [the] first of its kind in the nation, was approved as part of an overall strategy intended to curb an increasing level of violence in schools, which in recent months has included the fatal shootings of a student and a librarian.
>
> The board, however, stopped short of recommending a gay studies curriculum to be offered in the public schools.[26]

Unless the reader is thinking critically, he or she might assume that the shootings cited in paragraph two were gay related—not so. The reader is led to assume that with increasing violence, gays will need protection.

TAKING ACTION

One of the difficulties with analyzing media reports is that the more you think critically, the more critical you become. It will become much harder to simply *absorb* the news. There are some positive actions you and your class can take to promote a more balanced approach to the news in your area. One key action is to make sure your local media outlets have access to credible sources. Gary Bauer, of the Family Research Council, is quoted often in secular media simply because he is one of the few people they know to contact for the "conservative Christian" viewpoint.

One of the best ways to do this is to distribute a media guide to all your local news sources. Find spokespeople on a variety of topics: women's issues, the family, religion, education (private schools, Christian education, home school), abortion, etc. Make sure your spokespeople are reasonable and articulate—choose carefully. Be sure to include teens from your school who are willing to be interviewed. List the topics and spokespersons—including addresses, day and evening phone numbers, and a short biography will lend credibility.

Send the media guide with a cover letter to all newspapers, and radio and television stations in your area. They may or may not use it, but it will be kept on file. A reporter always appreciates a source who can be reached when a deadline is looming, and is willing to speak up in a manner that is easily quotable.

Also, begin to think of good stories for your local media. Some of the community service projects your class is doing could make a great "warm fuzzy" story. Let them know.

If your local newspaper or television station doesn't have a "teen council" composed of students from area high schools—find a couple of interested students who would be willing to make the suggestion and serve on the council. Council members could serve as a sounding board on community issues affecting youth, be reporters, and take turns writing a weekly or daily "teen editorial."

---

[26] "Mass. Board of Education approves policy on gay students," UPI newswire (May 18, 1993).

CRITICAL THINKING
ESSAY QUESTIONS

Answer the questions below on a separate sheet of paper and be prepared to review your answers in class. The following are a list of statements/arguments that are fallacious in some way. Your teacher will guide you through this exercise.

PART ONE

1. The end of a thing is its perfection; death is the end of life; therefore, death is the perfection of life. *Equivocation*

2. Marijuana can't be all that bad. Everyone knows about barroom brawls, but marijuana makes people peaceful. *Red Herring*

3. Women are so sentimental. My mother and sisters always cry at the movies; my father and I never do. *Hasty generalization*

4. The Senator is incorruptibly honest; no one has ever uncovered a scandal involving him. *Appeal to ignorance*

5. The so-called theories of Einstein are merely the ravings of a mind polluted with liberal, democratic nonsense, which is utterly unacceptable to German men of science. *Ad Hominen*

6. Exercise keeps everyone healthy. Therefore, if Tim would just run more, it might help his heart condition. *Sweeping Generalization*

7. Those who favor gun control also favor disarming the police and disbanding the National Guard. *Straw man*

8. "Death should be held of no account, for it brings but two alternatives: either it utterly annihilates the person and his soul, or it transports the spirit or soul to some place where it will live forever. What then should a good man fear if death would bring only nothingness or eternal life." — Cicero *Faulty dilemma*

9. I'm on probation, sir. If I don't get a good grade in this course, I won't be able to stay in school. Please, could you let me have at least a C? *Appeal to pity*

10. I join 2 presidents, 27 senators, and 83 representatives in describing this woman as a liar. *Appeal to majority*

11. Of course the Bible is true. It says that it is true. *Begging the question → goes in a circle*

12. It's the old time religion and it's good enough for me. *Appeal to tradition*

13. In defense of suicide, David Hume said, "It would be no crime in me to divert the Nile or Danube from its course, were I able to effect such purposes. Where is then the crime of turning a few ounces of blood from their natural channel?" *False analogy*

14. Why do you want to throw your money away like that? *Complex question*

15. I think his daughter's marriage must have worried him dreadfully, because his hair began to turn white after the wedding. *False cause*

16. I fail to see why hunting should be considered cruel when it gives me tremendous pleasure.

Red herring

17. You are either a conservative or a liberal.

Faulty dilemma

18. Pro-lifers believe that a fetus should be protected because it is a "potential" human. Today I will prove that a "potential" human is not a human and therefore should not be protected.

Straw man - we say it's d baby, they are mischaracting our argument

19. There must be intelligent life in outer space, because no one has been able to prove that there isn't.

Appeal to ignorance

20. All Christians hate homosexuals—at least all the ones I know do.

Hasty generalization

21. You're wrong because you are an intolerant, closed-minded, right-wing fundamentalist.

Ad Hominem

22. The Golden Rule is basic to every system of ethics ever devised. Everyone accepts it in some form or other. It is, therefore, an undeniably sound moral principle.

Appeal to majority

23. The sign stated, "Fine for parking here." Since it said "fine," I parked here.

Equivocation

24. These rules were written 100 years ago and we have always followed them. Therefore, there is no need to change them.

Appeal to tradition

25. Of course I am right. I am always right.

Begging the question

26. Everyone has a right to own property. Just because Jon has been declared insane doesn't mean that you can take his weapon away.

Sweeping generalization

27. If we outlaw abortion, countless women will die during back alley abortions.

Appeal to pity

28. Are you still a heavy drinker?

Complex question

29. Employees are like nails. Just as nails must be hit in the head in order to make them work, so must employees.

False analogy

30. Immediately after walking under a ladder, my leg fell off. I haven't hobbled under a ladder since.

False cause

PART TWO

Read the following fictitious news story and answer the corresponding questions.

P.A.G.A.N. Invades Christian Town

Long time anti-Christian activist organization removes pro-God public display from government arena.

SHELBYVILLE — In a little–known, mid-sized, midwestern town, there was great outrage over the events of this past weekend. With little more than a court order, the lawsuit-happy organization known as P.A.G.A.N. (People Against God And Normalcy) arrived at the steps of Shelbyville's City Hall late Friday afternoon with a crane. Local judge Rod Snider, a staunch liberal, had signed an order that morning giving P.A.G.A.N. the authority to steal the town's symbol of religious freedom and moral guidance—a 50-foot statue of the Virgin Mary. I watched in disbelief as the statue honoring Christianity as the town's established religion was removed from the city steps and strapped to a rundown flatbed truck. Judge

Snider sat idly by as a number of citizens protested the forced removal of the town's glorious icon. P.A.G.A.N. and its motley crew, seemingly unmoved by the demonstrations, pressed on with their desecration.

The statue has been taken to a nearby state-owned warehouse and veiled in retired green army blankets where it will be held hostage while the judge's decision is being appealed to a higher court.

The statue was generously donated to the town around six months ago after being commissioned by the respected religious leader Reverend Timothy Love. He noted that the statue was a token of the church's appreciation "to the good folks of Shelbyville."

The honorable reverend's wife, Helen Love, insists that P.A.G.A.N. is in her town largely because of the complaints of one irreligious man, Joe Sylack. Mr. Sylack, a local bar owner, rarely attends church and has apparently never appreciated the community's sacred stone image. Mrs. Love asserts that this is simply an example of a few atheists trying to make everyone else respect their religious beliefs. But Mrs. Love wants to know, "What about the town's religious beliefs?"

I interviewed one of Love's knowledgeable parishioners, Ned Landers, about the situation. He insists, "This is just another example of how our town is going to hell in a hand basket." Mr. Landers blames the situation on rock music, daytime television, and foreigners. After witnessing this contemptible event, I believe the majority of Shelbyville's citizens would agree with Mr. Lander's assessment. It seems clear that P.A.G.A.N. and Judge Snider have no respect for property, the will of the people, or God Himself.

Kent Beckman
The Shelbyville County Times

1. **What incident is being reported?**

2. **Which sides are presented?**

3. **What is the tone of the report?**

4. **On what underlying assumption is the news story based?**

5. **Who are the article's sources and how are they characterized?**

6. **What words are used to describe people or organizations?**

7. **How are the parties' actions described throughout the article?**

8. **What statistics are used?**

9. **What is left out of the news story?**

10. **What logical fallacies are used to lead the reader or listener into faulty reasoning?**

DEAR DOUG
WRITING ASSIGNMENT

Hey, it's me again!

I love college! There's always something going on—games, intramurals, parties, concerts, late nights with friends—it's awesome! In fact, college life would be perfect if all those annoying classes didn't get in the way. With all the stuff to do here on campus, I can barely make time for class. Don't worry, though. So far my grades have been pretty good... well, all except for Philosophy 101. Half the time I don't have a clue what the prof is saying. She might as well be speaking Chinese!

That class is the worst. I keep waiting for her to just give us the answers, but she only asks a lot of questions. Sometimes it seems like we just focus on what a lot of dead guys thought about reality, knowledge, morality, whatever. I have an essay due next week about my own take on the stuff we've been learning, but I've got no idea where to start. Science tells us that evolution is a fact, so I guess reality is composed of things I can see and touch. Do you think reality, truth, and knowledge can be explained by naturalism? But then some people (like the guy down the hall) believe that nothing is natural at all—that the world is only a spiritual illusion. I'm just really confused. I believe that there is a God who created everything. So does that mean reality, truth, etc. can be explained by non-naturalism? It doesn't seem like both views can be right.

And if that's not enough, I'm supposed to be able to explain the differences between Karl Marx's philosophy and plain old atheistic materialism. What's the difference between naturalism and Marx's "dialectical materialism" anyway?

I've got so many questions and no one here seems able to answer them. Here's an important one we're not even dealing with in class. All this philosophy stuff is explained by other worldviews, like Marxism. But what does the Christian worldview say about philosophy? Is it even covered in the Bible? I'm sorry to keep bugging you with all these questions, but I really want to know.

Enough thinking for now. I'm dying to tell you about my date a couple of weeks ago. It was great! We caught an Indie flick and then headed over to the coffee shop to talk. Her name is Amber and she's lots of fun and very smart. When I made some comment about faith, she said she was an agnostic and changed the subject. It didn't bother me too much—I mean, we have such a good time together. Besides, it isn't serious... yet.

Hope to hear from ya soon,
Doug

STUDENT
MANUAL

UNDERSTANDING THE TIMES

Unit Three

Topics:
Bioethics
Biotechnology
Ethics
Moral Relativism

A Summit Ministries Curriculum

SECTION OUTLINE

180-Day Syllabus

Day	IN CLASS	HOMEWORK	
1	Watch "Ethics" video		
2	Read UTT Textbook 'Ethics 3.1'	Read UTT Textbook 'Ethics 3.2'	
3	Review UTT Textbook 'Ethics 3.1–3.2' questions	Read UTT Textbook 'Ethics 3.3'	
4	Read UTT Textbook 'Ethics 3.4'		
5	Review UTT Textbook 'Ethics 3.3–3.4' questions	Read UTT Textbook 'Ethics 3.5–3.6'	
6	Review UTT Textbook 'Ethics 3.5–3.6' questions	Read *Living as if People Mattered* essay	
7	Review *Living as if People Mattered* essay questions	Assign Dear Doug Letter	
8	Watch "Responding to Relativism" video P1		
9	Watch "Responding to Relativism" video P2		
10	Watch "Responding to Relativism" video P3		
11	Review "Responding to Relativism" video questions		
12	Watch "Biotechnology" video P1		
13	Watch "Biotechnology" video P2		
14	Review "Biotechnology" video questions	Dear Doug Letter assignment Due	
15	Take Unit Three Test		

90-Day Syllabus

Day	IN CLASS	HOMEWORK	
1	Watch "Ethics" video	Read UTT Textbook 'Ethics 3.1–3.2'	
2	Review UTT Textbook 'Ethics 3.1–3.2' questions	Read UTT Textbook 'Ethics 3.3–3.4'	
3	Review UTT Textbook 'Ethics 3.3–3.4' questions	Read UTT Textbook 'Ethics 3.5–3.6'	
4	Review UTT Textbook 'Ethics 3.5–3.6' questions		
5	Watch "Biotechnology" video P1		
6	Watch "Biotechnology" video P2		
7	Review "Biotechnology" video questions		
8	Take Unit Three Test		

UNDERSTANDING THE TIMES
ETHICS QUESTIONS

Answer the questions below on a separate sheet of paper and be prepared to review your answers in class. Reflection Questions will not be found in the text. These are merely designed to help you start thinking about issues from a worldview perspective.

ETHICS 3.1

1. Why are Christian ethics and theology inseparable? What did Francis Schaeffer mean when he said that not all things are the same to God?

2. What did Schaeffer conclude about a society without moral absolutes? Do we see this in society?

3. On what authority do Christians base their belief in moral absolutes? How specific is this authority?

4. Ethically speaking, what are Christians called to do?

5. What did Dietrich Bonhoeffer mean by the question, "Where are the responsible people?"

ETHICS 3.2

6. Why do Muslims view Muhammad as morally exemplary even though the Hadith does not paint a flattering portrait of his life?

7. How do Christianity and Islam differ in relation to their beliefs about ethical absolutes?

8. In what two ways is the term *jihad* used?

9. What motivates Muslims to behave ethically?

10. Which motivation is the strongest?

ETHICS 3.3

11. What is the ultimate ethical question for a Secular Humanist? What questions did Morris B. Storer outline in his book *Humanist Ethics*?

12. Why are there such diverse views and conflicts regarding humanistic ethics?

13. Who proposed the "no-truth thesis" and what does it state?

14. How do most humanists attempt to dodge the "no-truth thesis?" How does Corliss Lamont address this issue?

15. What did Arthur E. Gravatt, Joseph Fletcher, Herbert W. Schneider, and Paul Kurtz have to say about ethics?

ETHICS 3.4

16. How did Karl Marx and Friedrich Engels view the issue of morality?

17. What is the Marxist-Leninist morality of the future? How will it be determined?

18. What is the Marxist-Leninist view of "old morality?"

19. What is the Marxist code of ethics according to the book *Scientific Communism*?

20. What means have Marxists historically believed would bring about a society without class distinctions? What have been the results of such an ethical system?

ETHICS 3.5

21. What is the foundation for Cosmic Humanism's ethical system?

22. According to Cosmic Humanist ethics, can anyone judge another's actions?

23. How is the word "tolerance" used by Cosmic Humanists?

24. How is the line between good and evil blurred in Cosmic Humanist ethics?

25. In what system of justice do Cosmic Humanists believe?

ETHICS 3.6

26. What is the foundation of Postmodern ethics?

27. According to Postmodernists, how does a community create its own ethical standards?

28. Why are Postmodernists hesitant to use the term relativism?

29. According to Richard Rorty, how do ethics develop within a Postmodern community? Do all Postmodernists agree with his assessment?

30. Reflection Question: What are the possible consequences when a community is allowed to sever ethics from an absolute standard and negotiate its own ethical system?

LIVING AS IF PEOPLE MATTERED
BY GEORGE GRANT

> One of the strangest disparities of history lies between the sense of abundance felt by older and simpler societies and the sense of scarcity felt by the ostensibly richer societies of today.
> —Richard Weaver

I remember only too well the first time I met Francis Schaeffer. In 1979 I was puttering around in one of my favorite used bookstores—on Locust Street, just a couple of blocks from the beautiful and magnificent Christ Church Cathedral in downtown St. Louis. The cathedral is a vivid reminder of the remarkable flowering of creativity and beauty that the Gospel has always provoked through the ages.

Just out of sight of the great Easter pinnacle is a little row of quirky stores and businesses. There are a couple of musty antique dealers, a disreputable-looking chili restaurant, a jaunty coffee shop, a boutique specializing in platform shoes from the seventies, and, of course, the bookstore—stocking a rather eccentric jumble of old magazines, cheap paperbacks, and fine first editions arranged in no apparent order.

I had just discovered a good hardback copy of Scott's *Ivanhoe* and a wonderful turn-of-the-century pocket edition of Ruskin's *Seven Lamps of Architecture*—both for less than the cost of new paperback copies—when I rounded a corner and bumped into Dr. Schaeffer. Literally.

I had been reading his books since the late sixties and looked to him as my spiritual and intellectual mentor. Not only did he express his orthodox Reformed faith in a clear and thoughtful fashion, his appreciation for the great heritage of Christendom's art, music, and ideas and his commitment to practical justice and true spirituality made him a beacon light of hope to me. In 1948, he had gone to live in the Swiss Alps just below Villars. There, in a little mountain chalet, he established a unique missionary outreach to all who might find their way to his door.

Over the years, thousands of students, skeptics, and searchers found their way to that door. He named the ministry L'Abri—a French word meaning shelter—an apt description for the function it served to the rootless generation of the Cold War era. It had always seemed to me that L'Abri was precisely the kind of witness that the church at the end of the twentieth century desperately needed.

I'd like to say that as I stood face-to-face with my hero, I was able to articulate my appreciation for all that he had done for my faith and my walk with Christ. I'd like to say that I was able to express my gratitude and then perhaps strike up a stimulating conversation about, say, epistemological self-consciousness. I'd like to say that as providence afforded me the opportunity I was able to think of all the questions I'd always wanted answered.

Unfortunately, that was not the case. Instead, the first thought that sprang into my mind was: "Oh my, he's short!" My second thought was: "What a haircut!" My third thought was: "And what's the deal with the knickers?"

In shock, I realized that I couldn't think of a single intelligent thing to say. I had fallen epistemologically unconscious.

Evidently, Dr. Schaeffer could read the awkward consternation in my eyes. He chuckled, introduced himself to me, and struck up a conversation. Amidst my embarrassed befuddlement he was cheerfully gracious and kind. He commended me on my selections and then showed me a couple other books he thought I might like—a fine paperback copy of Van Til's *The Calvinistic Concept Of Culture* and a rare edition of Schaeffer's *The Principle of Protestantism*.

Here was one of the brightest minds of our generation giving his time and attention to a gawky young Christian who couldn't even string together a coherent sentence. I later discovered that this was typical of him. Though he was often passionate, stubborn, and irascible, his life was suffused with a clear sense of calling—a calling to serve others. He demonstrated that calling on a daily basis—not just through heroic feats of sacrifice but through the quiet virtue of ordinary kindness. He believed that the Reformation doctrine of the priesthood of all believers was best portrayed in the beauty of caring human relationships. And so he listened. He cared. He gave. He put into motion Christ's tender mercies through the simplest acts of humble service.

I came away from that first brief encounter with Dr. Schaeffer with an entirely new understanding of biblical mercy. With a servant's heart, he treated me as if I mattered. He treated me the way we are all to treat one another.

SERVICE

Service is a much ballyhooed concept these days. The literature of business success and personal management tosses it about rather profligately. We are told, for instance, that our industrial economy has been almost completely transformed into a service economy by the advent of the information age. The service factor is the new by-word for success in the crowded global marketplace. Good service guarantees customer loyalty, management efficiency, and employee morale. It provides a competitive edge for companies in an increasingly cut-throat business environment. It is the means toward empowerment, flexibility, and innovation at a time when those qualities are essential for business survival. It prepares ordinary men and women to out-sell, out-manage, out-motivate, and out-negotiate their competition. It enables them to "swim with the sharks without being eaten alive."[1]

According to Jack Eckerd and Chuck Colson, service on the job and in the workplace can mean many things: "Valuing workers. Managing from the trenches. Communicating. Inspiring excellence. Training. Using profits to motivate."[2]

Virtually all the corporate prognosticators, strategic forecasters, motivational pundits, and management consultants agree—from Tom Peters, John Naisbitt, and Stephen Covey to Richard Foster, Michael Gerber, and Zig Ziglar. They all say that service is an indispensable key to success in business or success in life.

According to these analysts, service in business is essentially a complex combination of common courtesy, customer satisfaction, and the "spirit of enterprise." It is simply realizing that the customer is always right and then going the extra mile. It is a principle-centered approach to human relationships and community responsibilities. It is putting first things first.[3]

This new emphasis on service is not just confined to the corporate world. It has also suddenly reappeared as a stock-in-trade public virtue in the discourse of politics. Candidates now offer themselves for public service rather than to merely run for office. They invoke cheery images of community service, military service and civic service as evidence of their suitability to govern the affairs of state. Once in office they initiate vast federal programs for national service. They charge the lumbering government bureaucracy with the task of domestic service. And they offer special recognition for citizens who have performed exemplary volunteer service.

Again, service is defined rather broadly in a series of happy platitudes as an expansive sense of public-spiritedness, good neighborliness, community-mindedness, or big-hearted cooperativeness. All of these things are certainly admirable. They are fine and good as far as they go. But they are not at all what the Bible has in mind when it speaks of service—as Francis Schaeffer would no doubt have readily attested.

Biblical service isn't a tactic designed to boost profit margins, protect market shares, keep customers happy, or improve employee relations. It isn't a strategy designed to inculcate patriotism, strengthen community relations, or attract more investments. It is not a technique to pad resumes, garner votes, or patronize constituents. It isn't a style of leadership, a personality bent, or a habit of highly effective people.

Instead, biblical service is a priestly function of mercy. The Hebrew word often used for service in the Old Testament is *sharath*. It literally means "to minister" or "to treat with affection." Similarly, in the New Testament the Greek word *diakoneo* is often used. It literally means "to care for" or to "offer relief."

In both cases, the priestly connotations and the merciful intentions of service are quite evident. In both cases, the emphasis is on the interpersonal dimension rather than the institutional dimension, on mercy rather than management, on true righteousness rather than mere rightness. Biblical service is far more concerned about taking care of souls than about taking care of business.

[1] *Houston Chronicle*, 18 May 1986; *Forbes*, 14 September 1992; *Forbes*, 9 September 1993; *Wall Street Journal*, 16 April 1992; Harvey Mackay, *Swim with the Sharks* (New York: William Morrow, 1988), 1.

[2] Chuck Colson and Jack Eckerd, *Why America Doesn't Work* (Dallas: Word, 1991), 168.

[3] George Gilder, *The Spirit of Enterprise* (New York: Simon & Schuster, 1984); Michael Gerber, *Power Point* (New York: HarperCollins, 1991); Tom Peters, *Thriving on Chaos* (New York: Knopf, 1987); Stephen Covey, Roger Merrill, and Rebecca Merrill, *First Things First* (New York: Simon & Schuster, 1994).

This distinction between the ministry of service and the business of service is like the difference between faith in God and faith in faith.[4]

DOING UNTO OTHERS

God is merciful and just. He works righteousness and justice for all. Morning by morning, He dispenses His justice without fail and without partiality. All his ways are just, so that injustice is an abomination to Him. Thus, He is adamant about ensuring the cause of the abused, the meek, and the weak. Time after time, Scripture stresses this important attribute of God:

The Lord abides forever; He has established His throne for judgment, and He will judge the world in righteousness; He will execute judgment for the peoples with equity. The Lord also will be a stronghold for the oppressed, a stronghold in times of trouble. (Psalm 9:7–9 NASB)

"Because of the oppression of the weak and the groaning of the needy, I will now arise," says the Lord. I will protect them from those who malign them." (Psalm 12:5)

A father to the fatherless, a defender of widows, is God in his holy dwelling. God sets the lonely in families, he leads forth the prisoners with singing; but the rebellious live in a sun-scorched land. (Psalm 68:5–6)

God cares for the needy. And His people are to do likewise. If God has comforted us, then we are to comfort others. If God has forgiven us, then we are to forgive others. If God has loved us, then we are to love others. If He has taught us, then we are to teach others. If He has borne witness to us, then we are to bear witness to others. If He has laid down His life for us, then we are to lay down our lives for one another.[5]

Whenever God commanded the priestly nation of Israel to imitate Him in ensuring justice for the wandering homeless, the alien, and the sojourner, He reminded them that they were once despised, rejected, and homeless themselves. It was only by the grace and mercy of God that they had been redeemed from that low estate. Thus they were to exercise compassion to the brokenhearted and the dispossessed. They were to serve.

Priestly privilege brings priestly responsibility. If Israel refused to take up that responsibility, then God would revoke their privilege. If they refused to exercise reciprocal mercy, then God would rise up in His anger to visit the land with His wrath and displeasure, expelling them into the howling wilderness once again. On the other hand, if they fulfilled their calling to live lives of merciful service, then they would ever be blessed.[6]

The principle still holds true. Those of us who have received the compassion of the Lord on High are to demonstrate tenderness in kind to all those around us. This is precisely the lesson Jesus was driving at in the parable of the unmerciful slave (Matthew 18:23–35).

The moral of the parable is clear. The needy around us are living symbols of our own former helplessness and privation. We are therefore to be living symbols of God's justice, mercy, and compassion. We are to do as He has done. God has set the pattern by His gracious working in our lives. We are to follow that pattern by serving others in the power of the indwelling Spirit.

In other words, the Gospel calls us to live daily as if people really matter. It calls us to live lives of selfless concern. We are to pay attention to the needs of others. In both word and deed, in both thought and action we are to weave ordinary kindness into the very fabric of our lives.

But this kind of ingrained mercy goes far beyond mere politeness. We are to demonstrate concern for the poor. We are to show pity toward the weak. We are to rescue the afflicted from violence. We are to familiarize ourselves with the case of the helpless, give of our wealth, and share of our sustenance. We are to put on "compassion, kindness, humility, gentleness and patience" (Colossians 3:12). We are to take up

---

[4] Faith in God is personal and objective. Faith in faith is impersonal and subjective. Faith in God transcends self-interest and self-fulfillment. Faith in faith descends into self-reliance and self-assurance. Faith in God is a belief in someone who has revealed himself to man "at many times and in various ways" (Hebrews 1:1). Faith in faith is simply "a belief" in something or any thing (James 2:19).

[5] To see these principles demonstrated in Scripture, read 2 Corinthians 1:4; Ephesians 4:32; 1 John 4:11; Matthew 28:20; John 15:26–27; 1 John 3:16.

[6] See Isaiah 1:11-17; Exodus 22:24; Psalm 41:1–2.

"the case of the stranger" (Job 29:16). We are to love our neighbors as ourselves (Mark 12:31) and "rescue those being led away to death" (Proverbs 24:11–12).

According to the Scriptures, this kind of comprehensive servanthood emphasis is, in fact, a primary indication of the authenticity of our faith: "Religion that God our Father accepts as pure and faultless is this: to look after orphans and widows in their distress and to keep oneself from being polluted by the world" (James 1:27).

We are called to do "righteousness and justice" (Genesis 18:19 NASB). We are to be ministers of God's peace, instruments of His love, and ambassadors of His kingdom. We are to care for the helpless, feed the hungry, clothe the naked, shelter the homeless, visit the prisoner, and protect the innocent. We are to live lives of merciful service.

GOOD DEEDS

In writing to Titus, the young pastor of Crete's pioneer church, the apostle Paul pressed home this fundamental truth with a clear sense of persistence and urgency. The task before Titus was not an easy one. Cretan culture was terribly worldly. It was marked by deceit, ungodliness, sloth, and gluttony (Titus 1:12). Thus, Paul's instructions were precise. Titus was to preach the glories of grace, but he was also to make good deeds evident. Priestly mercy and selfless servanthood were to be central priorities in his new work:

> For the grace of God has appeared, bringing salvation to all men, instructing us to deny ungodliness and worldly desires and to live sensibly, righteously and godly in the present age, looking for the blessed hope and the appearing of the glory of our great God and Savior, Christ Jesus; who gave Himself for us, that He might redeem us from every lawless deed and purify for Himself a people for His own possession, zealous for good deeds. (Titus 2:11–14 NASB)

Paul tells Titus he should build his entire fledgling ministry around works of mercy: He was to be an example of good deeds (Titus 2:7). He was to teach the people to watch for chances to do good (3:1). They were all to "learn to devote themselves to doing what is good, in order that they might provide for daily necessities and not live unproductive lives" (3:14). Some within the church professed to know God, "but by their actions they deny him. They are detestable, disobedient and unfit for doing anything good" (1:16). Titus was to "rebuke them sharply, so that they will be sound in the faith" (1:13).

As a pastor, Titus had innumerable tasks that he was responsible to fulfill. He had administrative duties, doctrinal duties, discipling duties, preaching duties, counseling duties, and arbitrating duties. But intertwined with them all, fundamental to them all, were his servanthood duties.

TO THE UTTERMOST

Paul called himself a servant (Galatians 1:10). Similarly, James, Peter, Epaphroditus, Timothy, Abraham, Moses, David, and Daniel were all called servants.[7] In fact, even before they were called "Christians," all of the first century believers were called "servants" (1 Corinthians 7:22).

Whenever and wherever the Gospel has gone out, the faithful have emphasized the priority of good works, especially works of compassion toward the needy. Every great revival in the history of the church, from Paul's missionary journeys to the Reformation, from the Alexandrian outreach of Athanasius to the Great Awakening in America, has been accompanied by an explosion of priestly service. Hospitals were established. Orphanages were founded. Rescue missions were started. Almshouses were built. Soup kitchens were begun. Charitable societies were incorporated. The hungry were fed, the naked clothed, and the unwanted rescued. Word was wed to deeds.[8]

This fact has always proven to be the bane of the church's enemies. Unbelievers can argue theology. They can dispute philosophy. They can subvert history. And they can undermine character. But they are helpless in the face of extraordinary feats of selfless compassion.[9]

---

[7] James 1:1; 2 Peter 1:1; Colossians 4:12; 2 Timothy 2:24; Psalm 105:42; Nehemiah 9:14; Psalm 89:3; Romans 6:20.
[8] George Grant, *Bringing in the Sheaves: Transforming Poverty into Productivity* (Brentwood, TN: Wolgemuth & Hyatt, 1985).
[9] George Grant, *Third Time Around* (Brentwood, TN: Wolgemuth & Hyatt, 1990).

Thus, Martin Luther said: "Where there are no good works, there is no faith. If works and love do not blossom forth, it is not genuine faith, the Gospel has not yet gained a foothold, and Christ is not yet rightly known."[10]

Likewise, the Westminster Confession asserted:

> Good works, done in obedience to God's commandments, are the fruits and evidences of a true and lively faith: and by them believers manifest their thankfulness, strengthen their assurance, edify their brethren, adorn the profession of the Gospel, stop the mouths of the adversaries, and glorify God whose workmanship they are.[11]

All too often in our own day though, we have tended to decline those priestly responsibilities—yielding the work of service to government bureaucrats or professional philanthropists. Grave societal dilemmas that have always busied the church before—like defending the sanctity of life, caring for the aged, and protecting the helpless—have been mentally and practically separated from our other "spiritual" responsibilities. They have been relegated to the status of "issues," even declared "political" and put on the other side of the fence from us in "the separation of church and state."

From a biblical perspective, though, these things are not "issues"; they cannot be separated from our tasks as believer-priests. They are our tasks as believer-priests. They are central to our purpose and calling in the world.

Many Christians have observed—only partly in jest—that if God doesn't judge America soon, He's probably going to have to apologize to Sodom and Gomorrah. That may well be true—but not for the reason that we think. God did not judge Sodom and Gomorrah because of their rampant greed, perversity, and corruption. He judged them because, those who were charged with serving didn't (Ezekiel 16:49–50). If God's wrath ever does utterly consume America, it will be for precisely the same reason. When biblical service is replaced by its worldly counterfeits, the effects go far beyond rising taxes, bloated bureaucracies, welfare graft, urban blight, and sundered families. When we fail to do the priestly work of mercy and compassion, judgment becomes inevitable. Sava of Trnova, writing at the end of the seventh century, said:

> The chief spiritual works in the world are sevenfold: to admonish sinners, to instruct the ignorant, to counsel the doubtful, to comfort the sorrowful, to suffer wrongs patiently, to forgive injuries, and to pray for all men at all times. Thus, we are to feed the hungry, give drink to the thirsty, to clothe the naked, to ransom the captives, to shelter the homeless, to visit the sick, and to rescue the perishing, for only in these corporal acts of service may this world of carnality be guarded from the full consequences of judgment.[12]

The Bible tells us that if we will obey the command to be generous to the poor, we ourselves will taste joy. If we will serve the needy, God will preserve us. If we will offer priestly mercy to the afflicted, we ourselves will be spared. We will prosper, our desires will be satisfied, and we will even be raised up from beds of sorrow and suffering.[13] God will ordain peace for us, authenticate our faith, and bless our witness to the world.[14] But only if we will serve.

Charles Haddon Spurgeon, the great Victorian pastor, not only was a masterful pulpiteer, administrator, writer, and evangelist, he was a determined champion of the deprived and the rejected. He gave more than half of his incredibly busy schedule to one or another of the sixty organizations or institutions he founded for their care and comfort. Explaining his furious activity on behalf of the poor and needy, Spurgeon said:

> God's intent in endowing any person with more substance than he needs is that he may have the pleasurable office, or rather the delightful privilege, of relieving want and woe. Alas, how many there are who consider that store which God has put into their hands on purpose for the poor and needy, to be only so much provision for their excessive luxury, a luxury which pampers them but yields them neither benefit nor pleasure.[15]

---

[10] John Dillenberger, ed., *Martin Luther* (New York: Doubleday, 1961), 18.
[11] *Confession*, XVIII:2.
[12] *Terra Ecalivat*, VI: 82.
[13] Proverbs 14:21; Psalm 41:1-2; Proverbs 28:27; Proverbs 11:24; Proverbs 11:25; Psalm 41:3.
[14] Isaiah 26:12; James 2:14-26; Isaiah 58:6–12.
[15] George H. Neville, *Good Works* (Edinburgh: McGavock, 1956), 202.

Wherever committed Christians have gone, throughout Europe, into the darkest depths of Africa, to the outer reaches of China, along the edges of the American frontier, and beyond to the Australian outback, selfless care for the needy has been in evidence. In fact, most of the church's greatest heroes are those who willingly gave the best of their lives to the less fortunate. Service was their hallmark. Mercy was their emblem.

A LIFE OF SERVICE

According to the majority of eighteenth- and nineteenth-century historians, the most remarkable event during America's founding era did not take place on a battlefield. It did not occur during the course of the constitutional debates. It was not recorded during the great diplomatic negotiations with France, Spain, or Holland. It did not take place at sea, or in the assemblies of the states, or in the counsels of war.

In a humble demonstration of servanthood, the field commander of the continental armies surrendered his commission to the congressional authorities at Annapolis.

At the time, he was the idol of the country and his soldiers. The army was unpaid, and the veteran troops, well-armed and fresh from their victory at Yorktown, were eager to have him take control of the disordered country. Some wanted to crown him king. Others thought to make him a dictator—rather like Cromwell had been a century earlier in England.

With the loyal support of the army and the enthusiasm of the populace, it would have been easy enough for him to have made himself the ruler of the new nation. But instead, General George Washington resigned his officer's commission. He appeared before President Thomas Mifflin and his cabinet and submitted himself to their governance.

Though he had often wrangled in disagreement with his superiors over matters of military strategy, pay schedules, supply shipments, troop deployment, and the overlap of civil and martial responsibilities, there was never any question of his ultimate loyalty or allegiance. In the end, he always submitted himself to the authority God had placed over him.

And that was no mean feat.

Washington had faithfully served under eleven different American presidents at a time of severest crisis. The first two held office prior to the signing of the Declaration of Independence—Peyton Randolph of Virginia and Henry Middleton of South Carolina. The next six held office between the time of the Declaration and the ratification of the first constitution—John Hancock of Massachusetts, Henry Laurens of South Carolina, John Jay of New York, Samuel Huntington of Connecticut, Samuel Johnson of North Carolina, and Thomas McKean of Delaware. The last three held office under the Articles of Confederation—John Hanson of Maryland, Elias Budinot of New Jersey, and finally, Thomas Mifflin of Pennsylvania. Another four presidents would hold office during Washington's short interlude away from public life prior to the ratification of the current constitution—Richard Henry Lee of Virginia, Nathaniel Gorham of Massachusetts, Arthur St. Clair of Pennsylvania, and Cyrus Griffin of Virginia. During all those trying days, under each of those varied men, General Washington gave himself wholeheartedly to the loyal task of selfless service.

He obeyed orders. He rendered due respect. He yielded to the authority of lawful office and jurisdiction. He met the needs of the hour. He set aside personal ambition, preference, security, and at times, personal opinion in order to serve.

"His true greatness was evidenced," said the pundit Henry Adams, "in the fact that he never sought greatness, but rather service."[16] The dean of American historians, Francis Parkman, concurred that it was this "remarkable spirit of the servant" that ultimately "elevated him even higher in his countrymen's estimations than he already was."[17]

George Washington lived a life of service. He practiced what we today call servant-leadership. He would settle for nothing less. He would strive for nothing more. And he left the disposition of the matter of his life and fortune in the hands of God.

Though we generally think of mercy more in terms of charity or philanthropy, Washington's balanced and selfless perspective actually comes closer to the biblical ideal. Kindness, helpfulness, compassion, and

---

[16] B. L. Cartwright, *Washington* (Boston: Little, Brown, & Co., 1924), 166.
[17] Ibid.

care are the natural outgrowths of a servant's heart. Where personal ambition and a lust for self-fulfillment are subdued, true mercy is sure to follow.

GOOD SERVICE

The prophet Micah condemned the people of his day for their heartless defrauding and victimizing of the needy (Micah 2:1–2). He asserted that the imminent judgment of their land was due to their tolerance of sin, their blatant selfishness, and their refusal to undertake their servanthood responsibilities (3:2–4).

Instead, they were concerned only with their own comforts and pleasures (2:8–11). They were intent on their own personal peace and affluence, often at the cost of oppression and exploitation (3:5–11). They had thus violated the covenant (5:10–15).

Where there is no mercy there is no hope.

Thus, the Micah Mandate was not only a call to the people to repent and to return to the path of righteousness, it was a proclamation of reconciliation and healing. It was a promise of better things to come. The prophet asserted that the remnant would be regathered (Micah 4:6). The shame of affliction would be lifted (4:7). And the lost fortunes of the land would be restored (4:8).

Where there is mercy there is hope.

Therefore let us too be "zealous for good deeds" (Titus 2:14 NASB).

ZEALOUS FOR GOOD DEEDS

> "He has showed you, O man, what is good. And what does the Lord require of you? To act justly and to love mercy and to walk humbly with your God" (Micah 6:8).

Through the ages, the great heroes of the faith were notable as much for their charity and kindness as they were for their doctrinal fidelity. They were invariably men and women of mercy who lived lives of selfless service. Examples abound:

Not only did *John Wycliffe* (1329–84) revive interest in the Scriptures during a particularly dismal and degenerate era with his translation of the New Testament into English, he also unleashed a grassroots movement of lay preachers and relief workers that brought hope to the poor for the first time since the peasants' land had been taken more than two generations before. Those common Lollards—as they were most often called—carried Wycliffe's determined message of grace and mercy to the entire kingdom, laying the foundations for the Reformation in England more than a century and a half later.

John Calvin (1509–64) established Geneva as the epicenter of the Reformation with his profound theological insight and his rich devotional piety. His careful and systematic codification of the biblical foundations for Reform was like a magnet for the best and brightest throughout Christendom. The city quickly became an island of intellectual integrity and economic prosperity. In addition, though, it became renowned for its charitable compassion. It was a kind of safe haven for all of Europe's poor and persecuted, dispossessed and distressed. There they found that Calvin had not only instructed the people in such things as the providence of God, but he had also taught them the importance of mercy in balancing the Christian life.

Dwight L. Moody (1837–99) was America's foremost evangelist throughout the difficult days that immediately followed the cataclysm of the War Between the States and disruption of Reconstruction. Literally thousands came to know Christ because the former shoe salesman faithfully proclaimed the Gospel wherever and whenever he had opportunity—pioneering the methods of both modern crusade evangelism and Sunday-school outreach. But in addition to preaching to the masses, he cared for the masses. He was responsible for the establishment of some one hundred and fifty schools, street missions, soup kitchens, clinics, colportage societies, and other charitable organizations. He believed it was essential that Christians proclaim the Gospel in both word and deed. As a result, his impact on the nation is still felt through many of those institutions that continue their vital work—nearly a century after his death.

Dozens of others could be cited throughout the wide span of history: Polycarp (d. 155), Ambrose (d. 397), Angelica of Brescia (d. 1540), Edmund Arrowsmith (d. 1628) David Brainerd (d. 1747), George Mueller (d. 1898), and Florence Nightingale (d. 1910). Each made the priestly message of their lips manifest

Unit Three

by the servanthood message of their hands. Thus, each became an emblem of mercy in this often merciless world.

DO A GOOD TURN DAILY

"He has showed you, O man, what is good. And what does the Lord require of you? To act justly and to love mercy and to walk humbly with your God" (Micah 6:8).

An entire catalog of Scripture exhorts us to act mercifully to those around us.[18] Do a brief concordance study—looking up the verses that deal with mercy, kindness, and compassion—to get a good overview of the subject. Try to make a list—from memory, if possible—of all the saints and heroes of the past whose stories of mercy, service, and compassion you have heard in sermons, Sunday school, missions conferences, Bible studies, or devotions. What does your list tell you about the importance and impact of mercy ministry on the overall history of the church? There are needs all around us. It doesn't matter what section of the country we live in. It doesn't matter what kind of neighborhood we call home. Single mothers silently struggle to make ends meet. Elderly couples try to get by on fixed incomes. Young families are stymied by debt, underemployment, illiteracy, physical handicaps, or prejudice. There are undernourished and poorly clothed children, third- and fourth-generation welfare dependents. There are hurting, lonely, desperate people. They may be right next door, down the street, around the block, across the tracks, or on the other side of town. But they are there. Stop. Look. Listen. See if you can't develop new eyes to see those needs where they are. Now, get busy. You may not have abundant resources or even much time to spare, but none of us is too strapped to care about—and then do something about—the needs of others.

Exodus 22:25	Proverbs 29:7	Romans 12:8–20
Leviticus 19:10	Proverbs 31:8–9	2 Corinthians 1:3–4
Leviticus 23:22	Isaiah 1:10–17	2 Corinthians 8:1–24
Leviticus 25:35–37	Isaiah 10:1–2	2 Corinthians 9:7
Numbers 18:24	Isaiah 32:6–8	Galatians 5:6
Deuteronomy 14:29	Isaiah 58:1–12	Galatians 6:2
Deuteronomy 15:1–2	Amos 5:1–27	Galatians 6:9–10
Deuteronomy 24:19–21	Matthew 5:16	Ephesians 2:8–10
Ruth 2:1-23	Matthew 7:12	Ephesians 5:2
Ruth 4:1-12	Matthew 10:8	2 Thessalonians 3:6–10
Psalm 41:1-3	Matthew 25:31–46	1 Timothy 5:8
Proverbs 11:25	Mark 12:44	1 Timothy 6:18–19
Proverbs 14:21	Luke 3:11	Titus 2:11–14
Proverbs 14:31	Luke 6:38	Titus 3:1
Proverbs 17:5	Luke 9:48	Titus 3:8
Proverbs 21:13	Luke 10:30–37	Titus 3:14
Proverbs 22:9	Luke 11:41	Hebrews 13:16
Proverbs 28:27	Luke 12:33–34	James 2:14–26
	Acts 20:35	1 John 3:17

*The essay originally appeared as a chapter in the book *The Micah Mandate*
   George Grant, *The Micah Mandate* (Chicago: Moody Press, 1995), 111–128.
**Reproduction rights granted by Moody Press.

---

[18] The following list is by no means comprehensive, but it may provide you with a good starting place for personal study.

LIVING AS IF PEOPLE MATTERED
ESSAY QUESTIONS

Answer the questions below on a separate sheet of paper and be prepared to review your answers in class. Reflection Questions will not be found in the text. These are merely designed to help you start thinking about issues from a worldview perspective.

1. **What is the worldly function of service?**

2. **What is the biblical function of service?**

3. **How are we to imitate God in his mercy and justness?**

4. **What happened to the nation of Israel when they refused their responsibility to imitate God in mercy and justness? Does this principle hold true today?**

5. **What responsibilities did Paul give to Titus in relation to the Cretan church?**

6. **How important have service and good works been to Christianity in the past?**

7. **What has become of Christian good works in our own day?**

8. **Why were the actions of General Washington so momentous?**

9. **Why did the prophet Micah condemn the Israelites of his day and foretell their imminent judgment?**

10. **Reflection Question: How might this generation be able to serve those that are needy?**

"RESPONDING TO RELATIVISM"

WITH FRANK BECKWITH AND GREG KOUKL

I. What Is Moral Relativism?

"Moral relativism is the belief that ethics (morality) are simply reducible to either the culture or the individual—that is, there are no absolute or universal moral standards that apply to every person in every place and in every time." — Frank Beckwith

"Moral relativism is a kind of subjectivism… There are no moral rules that are outside the subject, that are objective features of the world, that we discover; rather, concepts of right and wrong are what individuals make up and invent for themselves. It's a personal choice when it comes to morality." — Greg Koukl

II. What Are Some Motivations for Moral Relativism?

A. Sometimes they want to ___get along___ with other people.

1. *Problem #1:* They can't seem to get along with the moral objectivists. They have to say that the objectivists are wrong.

2. *Problem #2:* This assumes that it is a morally objective norm that we ought to get along with other people. But if relativism is true, there are no morally objective norms.

3. *Problem #3:* This motive presupposes objective moral norms, such as tolerance. But there are no moral norms if relativism is true.

4. *Problem #4:* Relativism robs meaning from such concepts as justice, fairness, and moral discourse. Even the word "tolerance" becomes meaningless.

B. Sometimes they want to engage in a certain immoral ___behavior___.

III. Subjectivism and Objectivism

A. What does it mean for something to be "subjective?"

"It basically says that when it comes to moral questions—those questions of right and wrong, whether people are moral or immoral, ethical or unethical—the final standard is determined by what individual subjects decide. And so in moral relativism, it is not the case that moral rules are out there somewhere, that they are features of the universe, that they are objective realities in the world—kind of like math principles that we might discover—but rather they are personal preference items. They are the kinds of things that we choose because they resonate with our own self-interests or our own tastes. So, there is a sense in which when morals are viewed as relative, they are viewed more like tastes in ice cream than something like medicines. Medicines you choose to cure an objective illness. And if you choose the wrong medicine, you'll suffer from the illness and maybe die. But when it comes to ice cream, you don't choose ice cream to solve an external problem, you choose ice cream to satisfy a personal taste. And so in the area of moral relativism, morals then turn out to be relative to the subject, and subjects choose their own moral system, their own values system, based on what appeals to them." — Greg Koukl

B. What does it mean for something to be "objective?"

"An objective claim is one that is true apart from my own mind. For example, that Ronald Reagan was president of the United States between 1981 and 1989 is true whether I believe it or not. It is objectively true. Now, objective doesn't mean publicly proved, it just means that it's something true apart from me. So let's say I know where a hidden treasure is. That may be something that nobody knows except me—and it has not been publicly proved, but it is something that is objectively true. Because if I were to die, that buried treasure would still be there, although nobody would actually know that it exists... So, subjective truths refer to our feelings, our perceptions, those things that we can only know in a first person context. Objective truths are truths that are true apart from whether I believe them or not, or whether I exist or not." — Frank Beckwith

IV. Preference Claims and Moral Claims

A. **Preference Claim**: what somebody __likes__ or __dislikes__

   1. A claim about what someone prefers

   2. Example—"I like vanilla ice cream."

B. **Moral Claim**: what somebody __should__ or __shouldn't__ do

   1. A claim about what ought to be

   2. Example—"It is wrong to torture people."

   3. A person may *prefer* something that is *morally wrong*.

Problem: sometimes we like the bad things and we want to do them, but we still know they are wrong so we don't do them. We might actually prefer something that is wrong.

"Part of the moral life is actually elevating your preferences so they can reach the standard of doing the right thing. To tell somebody, "Look, morality is simply what you prefer," is to advocate the morality of the sociopath. That is what the sociopath does; he does whatever he wants because he likes it. It's a dangerous thing to tell people." — Frank Beckwith

V. Three Main Types of Relativism

A. "__society does__" **Relativism** (Cultural Relativism)

   1. Different cultures have different moral values.

   2. Nobody has the right to say that one morality is better than the other.

   3. *Response*: Just because people disagree does not mean that no one is correct.

      i. Example—We used to think the earth was flat.

      ii. Example—We used to practice slavery.

B. "__Society Says__" **Relativism** (Conventionalism)

   1. We ought to do what society says we should do.

2. Each culture is its own source of morality.

3. *Response*:

    i. There could be nothing like an immoral society.

    ii. Morality is reduced to ___law___ and ___power___.

    iii. Moral reformers (e.g. Martin Luther King) are immoral because they defy the law.

C. "___I Say___" **Relativism** (Individual Ethical Relativism)

1. The individual is the deciding factor.

2. *Response*: If moral relativism were true, then…

    i. there would be no immoral individuals

    ii. there would be no heroes

    iii. there is no such thing as evil

    iv. there is no such thing as wrong-doing

    v. there is no such thing as justice or fairness

    vi. there is no moral obligation of tolerance

    vii. there is no sensibility to moral discourse

    viii. there is no way to morally improve

VI. Postmodernism

A. **Modernism**: morality is relative

B. **Postmodernism**: truth is relative

C. Epistemological Relativism

1. **Epistemology**: the study of how we know what we know—the study of knowledge

2. **Epistemological Relativism**: the idea that there is no objective knowledge of the world *[handwritten: Bigger claim than moral relativism]*

    i. Example—Political correctness

    ii. *Response*:

        1) You allow them to rationalize their own prejudices and bigotries.

2) It's a _Self-refuting_ claim.

    a) It is a claim that does not fulfill it own standards of truthfulness ("I have a brother who is an only child").

    b) To claim that epistemological relativism is universally true is to make a truth claim.

PART TWO

VII. Responses to Common Slogans

A. "Who are you to say?" or "Who are you to judge?"

"They have missed the point entirely. I don't expect people to believe my point of view just because I say it. I'm not speaking on my own authority. I'm trying to reason with them about moral rules." — Greg Koukl

"I think the claim or the proposition comes back on the person, because when they do that, *they're judging you.* So one way you can respond to it is, "Well, who are you to ask the question, 'Who are you to judge?' " And you're telling them, "Look, you are in the same position you are claiming I'm in. You're judging me!" — Frank Beckwith

"Look, I'm perfectly qualified to judge. I am a rational adult who is aware of certain moral principles. I think I'm perfectly qualified to judge. Who else do you want to judge things, dogs and cats? I mean, if human beings can't be the ones to make moral judgments, then who is left? I mean, in many ways, she's abdicating her responsibility. People who raise this question are abdicating their responsibility as human persons… 'I prefer to make no judgments whatsoever.' But of course, as we know, that turns out to be just another judgment." — Frank Beckwith

B. "You should be open-minded"

    1. The assumption is that if you come to a _Conclusion_, you are not open-minded.

    2. If there is such a thing as the _truth_, then why be open-minded at all?

VIII. Moral Relativism in Our Society

A. _Values Clarification_: a theory of moral education that essentially tells kids to understand and appreciate their own *personal* values, and that there are really no objective moral values, that we each are sort of stuck with our own perspectives

"When you give my children the most difficult moral problems people can face in life, and then you tell them that there are no rules to guide them, that there is no morality to give insight to the circumstances, but instead, that it is up to them, that's not neutral. That is a moral point of view called moral relativism." — Greg Koukl

B. Multiculturalism

    1. _____Weak_____ **Multiculturalism**: reading and learning about diverse cultures around the world, and looking at the accomplishments of those cultures, and finding something that is good and true and beautiful in those cultures *"Truth is something we can learn from other cultures"*

    2. _____Strong_____ **Multiculturalism**: is the belief that all cultures are equal. No single culture has accomplished more than any other.

        i. What do we do with Nazi culture?

        ii. What do we do with cultures that engage in genocide and bizarre immoral practices?

C. Political Correctness

    1. _____Speech codes_____: rules of speech on college campuses that forbid students from making disparaging remarks about another student's religion, ethnicity, or gender

    2. *Response*:

        i. As Christians we can embrace a code that forbids harassing people.

        ii. Speech codes have been used on some universities to shut up legitimate discussion.

            1) Example—writing an editorial about homosexuality, even if respectful

            2) Harassing and/or coercing individuals to *accept* a morally liberal view

IX. Evolution, Science, and Morality

A. You don't need God for morals; morals are the kinds of things that have just simply evolved

B. *Response*: Morality can't be reduced to mere _____behavior_____.

"All evolution can do is describe why we behaved in certain ways in the past. What it can't do is tell us why we ought to be good in the future; it can't prescribe behavior, it can just describe behavior. And morality is not about description… it's about prescription. Morality is about what you and I ought to do in the future. And no evolutionary explanation can speak to that issue." —Greg Koukl

"The way we know about moral beliefs is that we discover them, and we discover them by reflecting on human nature, we discover them in Scripture. And sometimes they just are things that strike us as true. Think about when children play. Children many times are not taught when they are young about morality and ethics in any systematic way. And yet, when they play they'll say things like 'That's not fair!' They understand what fairness is. It's part of the way they're created." — Frank Beckwith

X. Same-Sex Marriage

A. Is it a question of liberty?

"It's really not a question about liberty, because when we talk about what freedom is, we have to ask the question 'What is the nature of freedom?' Is freedom simply license to do whatever I want, or does it mean the opportunity to do the right thing or to do the good? And I think there are two different views of freedom in our society." — Frank Beckwith

B. What is the nature of human sexuality?

"If human beings are the sorts of beings that are made with a purpose, and if gender has a purpose to it—that is, that men and women are the foundation of society. And that is to say when they are married they create the first government, so to speak… If, in fact, there is a unitive significance to marriage, then there really can be, in principle, no such thing as same sex marriage… because sex really means a union between a man and a woman." — Frank Beckwith

C. Understanding the battle of worldviews

"One worldview says, 'All sexual unions are equal as long as everybody consents'… The [Christian] view says that not all sexual unions are equal, that in fact, some are better than other, because in the case of heterosexual monogamy, it has unitive significance and serves as a foundation for society. Without that, we cannot expect to have a society in which children are nurtured and brought up in ways that would result in the benefit and good of society." — Frank Beckwith

D. Both views limit people

"The first view says that if you believe that men and women should be the exclusive members of a marriage, then you are narrow, intolerant, and bigoted, and you ought not to have your views figured in any way in the public square or reflected in any way in the law… The other view says the opposite about the same sex marriage proponent." — Frank Beckwith

E. Contrasting understanding of the nature of sexuality

"The same sex proponents are sexual Nihilists, or sexual egalitarians. They don't believe sex has an intrinsic purpose, it is simply there as an instrumental good for people to achieve pleasure… The other side says pleasure is an aspect of sexuality, but it is not the only aspect of it. It ultimately has intrinsic value because it has unitive significance as the foundation of society." —Frank Beckwith

F. *Response*: Use counter-intuitive examples

   1. What about incest?

   2. Could I marry my pet?

G. Shouldn't the state remain neutral?

1. On abortion?

"But now the state permits abortion. Isn't the state then saying that fetuses are not human persons; that they don't belong to the membership of the human community? Because, if they did belong as full-fledged members of the human community, then we ought to protect them. And the state ought to be in the process of doing so… [so] the state isn't neutral. The state is saying fetuses are *not* a part of our moral community, and for that reason we are not going to protect them from being harmed." — Frank Beckwith

2. On same-sex marriage?

"Once the state says all sexual unions are equal, it is not neutral. It is making a claim about the nature of human sexuality. And so by permitting same-sex marriage, or let's say polygamous same-sex marriage, or incestuous marriage, or some other bizarre union, they are in fact then treating all those unions as all equal in the eyes of the state. That *is* a position." —Frank Beckwith

---

PART THREE

XI. Tactics for Responding to Relativism

A. People can say they believe in relativism, but nobody can _____live_____ as a relativist.

B. *Tactic #1:* Self-refutation

1. "You shouldn't push your morality on others"

2. *Response:* _____Why not_____?

"What this question does is push the burden of proof on the other person. The other person is going to have a very, very hard time answering the question why one person should not push their morality on another without at the same time imposing one of his own moral rules upon you." — Greg Koukl

Ok so now we had admitted we are both pushing ours on eachother, why don't we talk about them and see which one is better.

C. *Tactic #2:* Pressing hot buttons

"If people claim that there is no morality, then their own pet moral peeves can't really apply. They're going to have to surrender them; but people don't want to do that. And so one way to show that this person's point of view isn't really going to work is to press that button." — Greg Koukl

1. True moral intuitions are shown by _____reactions_____ rather than by actions.

2. Look for words like *should, ought, shouldn't*, and the like

"If morals are relative, there are no *shoulds* and *oughts* of any kind; and every time a person utters a sentence that begins with *should* or *ought*, they are doing something incoherent according to their own professed view of morality." — Greg Koukl

D. *Tactic #3:* Forcing the tolerance issue

   1. "We should be tolerant"

   2. *Response*:

      i. If relativism is true, there is no moral rule that you ought to be tolerant.

      ii. Only moral objectivists can say that there is a moral rule like "you should be tolerant."

   3. Tolerance implies disagreement

      "Traditionally tolerance has implied condemnation. That is, if I tolerate you, *I am in fact saying you are wrong*, but I am willing to be civil with you and to get along with you."
      —Frank Beckwith

      "Today it has been translated to mean something like, 'Well, to judge somebody is to be intolerant,' which is odd, because I don't *tolerate* what I agree with. I agree with it! I only tolerate that which I disagree with." — Frank Beckwith

   4. Tolerance is not affirmation or approval.

      i. Christians may tolerate other religions, but we don't affirm them.

      ii. Much of what goes by the name of tolerance today is really coerced affirmation.

XII. God and Morality

   A. The argument from evil

      1. The most compelling argument against the existence of God?

      2. Actually, it is one of the best arguments in favor of the existence of God.

         i. What is the definition of "evil?"

         ii. Evil means that things aren't as they should be—they have departed from good.

         iii. That would mean that there is a standard for goodness.

            "I wouldn't have known what crooked was unless I knew what straight was." — C. S. Lewis

            "In order for somebody to complain about evil, there must be some transcendent standard of good that it departs from. That can only be the case if God exists." — Frank Beckwith

B. Can we have moral laws without God?

    1. Atheism teaches that only material things exist, but moral laws are not material.

    2. A law is something that is a _____ between two persons.

        i. If laws are random mistakes, why obey them?

            "Or let's say I was playing a game of Scrabble and the letters randomly read, 'Go to Baltimore.' Would that mean that I should go? 'I better get on a plane and go to Baltimore?' I wouldn't take it seriously because I know that there is no mind behind the random collection of letters." — Frank Beckwith

        ii. Moral law, in order to have justification and force, has to have a mind behind it

XIII. Three Options Regarding Moral Laws

    A. *Option #1:* Morals are ____imaginary____.

    B. *Option #2:* They happened by ____acident____.

    C. *Option #3:* They are designed and are purposed.

    D. *Response*:

        1. *Option #1:* Believing morals are imaginary is moral relativism.

        2. *Option #2:* If morals happened by chance, "Why ought we to obey them?"

        3. *Option #3:* Moral rules do have a sense of 'oughtness' to them.

            i. Commands always have a commandee and a commander

            ii. Laws have a law-giver

            "This explains our feelings of guilt, our expectation of punishment; and further than that, it becomes pretty clear to people that if that's the case, when they violate a moral rule, which we do frequently, that we are not just breaking a rule, but we are offending the rule-maker. We have accountability." — Greg Koukl

"RESPONDING TO RELATIVISM"
VIDEO QUESTIONS

Answer the questions below on a separate sheet of paper and be prepared to review your answers in class.

1. What is moral relativism? What are some motivations for moral relativism? What are some problems with the motivations?

2. What is objectivism? What is subjectivism? How do these ideas relate to moral relativism?

3. What are moral claims? What are preference claims? How does this distinction relate to the subject of moral relativism?

4. What are the three types of moral relativism? What are some of their problems?

5. What is Epistemological Relativism? What are some problems with this position?

6. What are some common relativistic slogans? What are some problems with these slogans and possible responses?

7. How has moral relativism advanced in our society? What are some problems and responses?

8. Why can the state not take a neutral position on issues like same-sex marriage or abortion?

9. What are some tactics for responding to moral relativism?

10. How can evil be a proof of God's existence?

"Biotechnology"

with John Stonestreet

PART ONE

I. Understanding Our Times

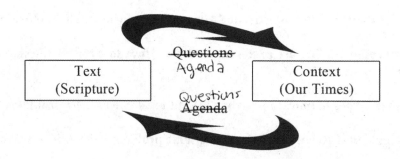

Text (Scripture) ← Questions ~~Agenda~~ / ~~Questions~~ Agenda → Context (Our Times)

"There is nothing in Scripture about these things [Islam, stem cell research, xenotransplantation], but Scripture is full of stuff about these things. And we have to take the questions that emerge from our times, and that should drive us back to the text so that we can understand how we ought to live for 'such a time as this.'"

"If Christianity should happen to be true—that is to say, if God is the real God of the universe—then defending it may mean talking about anything and everything. Things can be irrelevant to the proposition that Christianity is false, but nothing can be irrelevant to the proposition that Christianity is true." — G. K. Chesterton

"Cloning and the biotech agenda are even worse news for human dignity than abortion. Not only are we taking upon ourselves the godlike prerogative of ending human life as we choose, but we also are attempting to appropriate the prerogative of making human life as we choose." — Charles Colson

II. What the Biotech Age Promises: (taken from Mitchell, *Bioethics in the New Millennium*)

A. Creation of life in a lab

B. Predetermination of the sex and genetic makeup of children

C. Pharmacogenomics

D. Programming of human genes

E. Identifying disease genes and genetically derived cures for cancer, AIDS, etc.

F. Repair of damaged spinal cords and brain cells

G. Cloning of mammals, including humans

H. Control of aging and obesity

I. Animals growing replacement organs for humans

---

110 **Unit Three**

J. Transgenic vegetables that will inoculate the world's poor against disease

K. Trees that can grow in a few years instead of decades

L. Plants that can produce substitutes for raw materials in plastic

M. Stronger materials, fibers, and adhesives

N. Wearable computers

O. Bionics

P. Bioelectric noses, ears, tongues, etc.

Q. Biosynthetic skin, blood, bones, muscles, etc.

III. What is Biotechnology?

A. ___Bio___ : Natural and living

B. ___Technology___ : Application of technique in an attempt to control, enhance, or manipulate

C. **Biotechnology**: Industrial use of living organisms or the application of technique to living organisms

IV. Different Areas of Biotechnology

A. Stem Cell Research

    1. **Stem Cells**: Cells in your body that have not been diversified and have not stopped reproducing

    2. Embryonic stem cells

        i. Kills the embryo when extracted

        ii. No scientific achievement

    3. Non-embryonic (or adult) stem cells

        i. Does not kill a human being

        ii. Has produced much scientific advancement

B. Genetics

    1. Human genome project

    2. Reproductive technology

C. ___Xenotransplantation___ : Use of animal tissues, organs, or cells transplanted to or used for contact with human subjects

D. ___Transgenics___ : Insertion of DNA of one species into the genetic code of another

E. Robotics

F. _Nanotechnology_: Engineering and manufacturing at the molecular level

   1. Medicine

   2. National defense

G. _Artifical Intelligence_ : An artificial mechanism that can mimic human thinking

H. _Cybernetics_ : Integration of man and machine

I. _Medical technology_ : Antibiotics, medicines, organ transplants, alternative medicines, etc.

J. _Life issues_ : Birth control, abortion, euthanasia, assisted suicide, etc.

PART TWO

V. Bioethics : Right conduct in the area of biotechnology

"Bioethics is at least thirty years behind biotechnology."

VI. The Challenges of Biotechnology

A. Biotechnology is carried out in the context of a false worldview.

"The most dangerous ideas in a society are not the ones that we argue, but the ones that we assume." — C. S. Lewis

"A worldview is not just a view of the world; a worldview gives you a view of yourself. And if you have a wrong view of yourself, then there are negative consequences from that."

B. We don't know what human is.

"The idols of the nations are silver and gold, made by the hands of men. They have mouths but cannot speak, eyes but they cannot see; they have ears but cannot hear, nor is there breath in their mouths. Those who make them will be like them, and so will all who trust in them." — Psalm 135:15–18

   1. We become what we worship.

      i. We worship stuff (e.g. music, celebrities, power, money, self, sex).

      ii. People have become stuff.

   2. People are seen only as machines.

"The huge modern heresy is to alter the human soul to fit modern social conditions, instead of altering modern social conditions to fit the human soul." — G. K. Chesterton

   3. Only humans were created to bear God's image.

C. The Re-evaluation of humanity

    1. We judge the value of stuff by what it can do and what it looks like.

    2. We judge human beings by what they can do and what they look like.

    3. What makes humans valuable?

        i. Biblical Christianity: Human = _Imago Dei_

           1) Humans are specially created in the image of God.

           2) God has endowed all humans with significant value.

           3) All humans have purpose and value.

               a) Value not based on what we can do

               b) Value not based on what we look like

               c) Value based on the fact that God has given us his image

       ii. Naturalism: Human = _Body_

           1) Humans have no intrinsic value.

           2) Some humans have qualities that others do not.

           3) We decide which humans have value.

> "If we compared the characteristics of different individuals, irrespective of species… we would have to go much further down the evolutionary scale before we reached a point at which non-human animals had capacities as limited as the most severely retarded humans… Pigs, cows, and chickens have a greater capacity to relate to others, better ability to communicate, and far more curiosity, than most severely retarded humans." — Peter Singer, Princeton University bio-ethicist

D. The commodification of humanity

> "Intelligent, Athletic Egg Donor Needed for Loving Family. You must be at least 5'10" / Have a 1400+ SAT score / Possess no major family medical issues." Fee Offered: $50,000 — Ad from the _Harvard Crimson_

E. Are we really in control?

    1. 276 embryos failed [deformed fetuses] to produce Dolly

    2. Dolly ultimately euthanized

    3. Unused embryos are destroyed in human in-vitro fertilization

    4. Embryo ownership

5. Mix-ups during in-vitro fertilization

"Unless human choices control technology, technology will control human choices." — Andrew Kimbrell, *The Human Body Shop*

F. Not all knowledge is ___good___ (Genesis 11)

"According to God, nothing is impossible for collective humanity."

VII. How to Live in a Biotech Age

A. Commit to the value of all *imago Dei*.

"It is a serious thing… to remember that the dullest and most uninteresting person you talk to may one day be a creature which, if you saw it now, you would be tempted to worship, or else a horror and a corruption such as you now meet, if at all, only in a nightmare. All day long we are, in some degree, helping each other to one or other of these destinations… There are no ordinary people. You have never talked to a mere mortal. Nations, cultures, arts, civilizations—these are mortal, and their life is to ours as the life of gnat. But it is immortals whom we joke with, work with, marry, snub, and exploit—immortal horrors or everlasting splendors." — C. S. Lewis

B. Send Christians to the "mission field" of biotechnology.

"What we want is not more little books about Christianity, but more little books by Christians on other subjects—with their Christianity latent. You can see this most easily if you look at it the other way around… it is not the books written in direct defense of Materialism that make modern man a Materialist; it is the materialistic assumptions in all the other books. In the same way, it is not books on Christianity that will really trouble him. But he would be troubled if, whenever he wanted a cheap popular introduction to some science, the best work on the market was always by a Christian." — C. S. Lewis

C. Be part of the educated public.

1. Learn terminology and follow new developments.

2. Offer hope (1 Peter 3:15).

"BIOTECHNOLOGY"
VIDEO QUESTIONS

Answer the questions below on a separate sheet of paper and be prepared to review your answers in class.

1. What is biotechnology? What does Scripture say about biotechnology?

2. What are stem cells? Why is research being done on stem cells?

3. What are the differences between embryonic and non-embryonic stem cells? Which type of stem cells has produced scientific achievement?

4. What are some different areas of biotechnology? What are some promises that these areas hold? What are some concerns?

5. What is bioethics? What are some of the ethical challenges of biotechnology? What makes human beings valuable?

Unit Three

DEAR DOUG
WRITING ASSIGNMENT

Hey there!

Well, I can't believe that we are almost halfway through the semester. Midterms are starting to loom and everybody's getting a little panicked. I'm barely holding my grades, so I've had to give up on some of the partying—but not football, never football.

I think we should start a club, the way our group keeps meeting spontaneously at the coffee shop! Paige even showed up today—guess her sorority didn't have any meetings today. As she and Sarah walked in the door, they were talking about the fact that there is no universal standard of right and wrong. Humans create their own ethics, Sarah said, and since these standards change from situation to situation—even from person to person—we need to be tolerant of everyone's beliefs and decisions. Paige said that it was wrong for people to force their beliefs on others. Do you believe there is a universal standard of right and wrong?

Nathan's argument was similar to what the girls stated, but he said that if we break our own ethical rules, we'd have to pay for it in our next life. He said that if our "good" deeds don't outweigh the "bad," we could come back as a toad or something. But does his idea of "karma" make sense?

Mark got all fired up about the differences between the wealthy and the poor. He defined wrong as anything the wealthy do to oppress the poor and right as anything that relieves the suffering of the underprivileged. But that would sanction everything from revolution to murder, as long as it was done for the "right" reasons. What are your thoughts?

Muhammad said there is a standard of right and wrong set by God and that if we break it we'll have consequences in this life and the next to deal with. He seemed to think that by doing enough good things we can outweigh the bad things we do and find Allah's favor. But is simply adding up good deeds a big enough standard to live by? I've always assumed that the Bible taught there was an external set of rules we had to live by, but I could be wrong. What does Christianity really teach about ethics?

Well, I gotta run. There's a big game tonight and not even cramming for tomorrow's quiz could make me miss it. Besides, I'm picking Amber up and we're going out for ice cream afterwards. You know how girls are… they want you to be on time, even if they aren't!

Keep in touch,
Doug

WORLDVIEW TRAINING

STUDENT MANUAL

UNDERSTANDING THE TIMES

Unit Four

Topics:
Biology
Naturalism
Icons of Evolution
Intelligent Design

A Summit Ministries Curriculum

Section Outline

180-Day Syllabus

DAY	IN CLASS	HOMEWORK	
1	WATCH "Biology" video		
2	READ UTT Textbook 'Biology 4.1'	READ UTT Textbook 'Biology 4.2'	
3	REVIEW UTT Textbook 'Biology 4.1–4.2' questions	READ UTT Textbook 'Biology 4.3'	
4	READ UTT Textbook 'Biology 4.4'		
5	REVIEW UTT Textbook 'Biology 4.3–4.4' questions	READ UTT Textbook 'Biology 4.5'	
6	READ UTT Textbook 'Biology 4.6'		
7	REVIEW UTT Textbook 'Biology 4.5–4.6' questions	ASSIGN Dear Doug Letter	
8	WATCH "Icons of Evolution" video P1		
9	WATCH "Icons of Evolution" video P2		
10	REVIEW "Icons of Evolution" video questions		
11	WATCH "Mysteries of Life's Origins" video P1		
12	WATCH "Mysteries of Life's Origins" video P1		
13	REVIEW "Mysteries of Life's Origins" video questions	READ *What is Darwinism?* essay	
14	REVIEW *What is Darwinism?* essay questions	Dear Doug Letter assignment DUE	
15	TAKE Unit Four Test		

90-Day Syllabus

DAY	IN CLASS	HOMEWORK	
1	WATCH "Biology" video	READ UTT Textbook 'Biology 4.1–4.2'	
2	REVIEW UTT Textbook 'Biology 4.1–4.2' questions	READ UTT Textbook 'Biology 4.3–4.4'	
3	REVIEW UTT Textbook 'Biology 4.3–4.4' questions	READ UTT Textbook 'Biology 4.5–4.6'	
4	REVIEW UTT Textbook 'Biology 4.5–4.6' questions		
5	WATCH "Icons of Evolution" video P1		
6	WATCH "Icons of Evolution" video P2		
7	REVIEW "Icons of Evolution" video questions		
8	TAKE Unit Four Test		

UNDERSTANDING THE TIMES
BIOLOGY QUESTIONS

Answer the questions below on a separate sheet of paper and be prepared to review your answers in class.

BIOLOGY 4.1

1. What are some problems with the theory of theistic evolution?

2. What aspects of the Christian worldview were foundational to the development of science?

3. Define the following topics: teleology, DNA, spontaneous generation, Second Law of Thermodynamics, and gene pool. How do they relate to the debate over origins?

4. According to Walter Brown, what should we see in the fossil record if evolution is true?

5. What problems does the theory of punctuated equilibrium avoid? What problems must it face?

BIOLOGY 4.2

6. What is the Islamic view of creation?

7. According to Islam, how many days did creation take?

8. According to Islam, did creation happen in literal days or longer periods of time?

9. Do Muslims believe that the universe displays design?

10. Does Islam incorporate a belief in evolution?

BIOLOGY 4.3

11. What do the *Humanist Manifestos I* and *II* state about humanity's origins?

12. Why must "modern" science rule out creation? Does this reasoning pose a problem for evolution as well? Why or why not?

13. What is spontaneous generation? Why is this theory important to evolutionists?

14. Define the following topics: natural selection and struggle for existence (or survival). How do they relate to the debate over origins?

15. Upon what six planks does Secular Humanist biology rest?

16. Why was Charles Darwin's work so important to Karl Marx? What connection does Friedrich Engels make between Darwin and Marx?

17. Where did Engels place his faith and was there any way to persuade Engels against spontaneous generation?

18. Why do Marxists ultimately deem Darwinism as inconsistent with their worldview?

19. What form of evolution does Marxism embrace?

20. What stunning indictment does Stephen J. Gould make against the fossil record? How does this relate to his theory of punctuated evolution?

21. What is the main evolutionary concern for Cosmic Humanists? What is this approach called? Cosmic Humanists believe that mankind is moving upward toward an age of higher consciousness.

22. How do Cosmic Humanists view science? In what ways do they believe it has been harmful? Do they believe science supports their ideas about reality?

23. How does the evolutionary view of Cosmic Humanism differ from the evolutionary theory purported by Marxist-Leninists and Secular Humanists?

24. How is John White's version of the Second Coming different from the one described in the New Testament?

25. What is the *Gaia Hypothesis*? How does this hypothesis undermine the Darwinian ideal of survival of the fittest?

26. What are three prominent theories of evolution? Why are many Postmodernists unwilling to endorse any particular theory of origins?

27. What is Paul Feyerbend's opinion of how science works?

28. How does Thomas Kuhn describe the nature of scientific investigation?

29. What do evolutionary Postmodernists believe about man's role in the process of evolution?

30. Although Christians acknowledge that scientists have biases and presuppositions, what reasons are given for believing that true knowledge about reality is possible?

"ICONS OF EVOLUTION"
VIDEO OUTLINE

I. Haeckel's Drawings

    A. Artistic drawings of vertebrate embryos

        1. Fraudulent drawings

        2. Omits the earliest stages of development

        3. Highlights stages and classes that look the most similar

        4. Omits the classes that don't look similar

    B. _Icons_ : distortions of pro-evolution evidence found in textbooks

II. Galapagos Finches — _not an example of macroevolution_

    A. Finch beaks change in size and shape

        1. The changes are temporary.

        2. They oscillate back and forth.

    B. _micro-evolution_ : small changes within the species of a gene pool

    C. _macro-evolution_ : the origin of fundamentally new organisms and plants

III. Four-Winged Fruit Flies

    A. Anomaly: Fruit fly with two sets of wings

        1. No muscles attached to wings

        2. Hopeless cripple

        3. Can only survive in the laboratory

        4. Would be "selected out" by natural selection

        5. Other fruit flies will not mate with them.

    B. _Neo-darwinism_ : randomly occurring mutations provide the raw material needed for evolution

IV. Antibiotic Resistance

A. Bacteria strains resistant to antibiotics

    1. When the parent is re-introduced, the resistant bacteria disappear.

    2. The resistant bacteria is crippled.

B. _fitness cost_ : how well mutant bacteria survive when the antibiotic is removed

---

PART TWO

V. Homology

A. _Homology_ : similarity in structure between different organisms

    1. The similarity shows that all living things have common ancestry.

    2. Complex life descended from simple life.

B. Darwin thought that similar animals shared similar genes.

C. Homologous structures can be produced by different genes.

    1. The body of the fruit fly

    2. The body of the wasp

D. Homologous structures can follow different patterns of development

    1. Shark gut—develops in upper cells of embryonic cavity

    2. Lamprey gut—develops in lower cells of embryonic cavity

    3. Frog gut—develops in upper and lower cells of embryonic cavity

VI. Cambrian Explosion

A. Biology textbooks

    1. Depict the progress of life from simple to complex

    2. Over hundreds of millions of years

B. _Cambrian explosion_ : the sudden geological appearance of most major groups of animals

    1. Animals appeared with major differences.

    2. No fossil evidence that they came from a common ancestor

C. Chengjiang's fossils

    1. Complex life at the bottom

    2. Sudden appearance

    3. Pre-Cambrian fossils not ancestors

D. _Hox genes_ - genes turned on after development

"ICONS OF EVOLUTION"
VIDEO QUESTIONS

Answer the questions below on a separate sheet of paper and be prepared to review your answers in class.

1. How do Haeckel's drawings seem to support Darwin's theory?

2. What was the problem with Haeckel's drawings?

3. Why is the change in a finch's average beak size a good example of natural selection?

4. What evidence do the Galapagos finches supply for macro-evolution?

5. What is neo-Darwinism?

6. What evidence does the four-winged fruit fly supply for neo-Darwinism?

7. How can antibiotic resistance be demonstrated in the laboratory? What is the fitness cost?

8. What evidence do antibiotic resistant bacteria provide for neo-Darwinism?

9. What is homology? Does the Darwinian theory of homology fit the available evidence?

10. What is the Cambrian explosion? How does it challenge evolution's "bottom-up" progression of life?

"MYSTERIES OF LIFE'S ORIGINS"
VIDEO OUTLINE

PART ONE

I. Fundamental Questions

    A. What brought life into existence?

        1. Chance and necessity?

        2. Purpose, plan, and design?

    B. Darwin saw life as the product of undirected natural forces.

        1. Time, chance, and natural selection

        2. Example: finch beaks

II. Doubts about Darwinism

    A. _Flagellum_ : miniature molecular machines

    B. _Irreducible complexity_: if any part is removed, the system loses function

        1. Mouse trap (5 essential parts)

        2. Bacteria flagellum (40 essential parts)

    C. Intelligent Design

III. _Co-option_ : natural selection's ability to borrow components from one machine to build another

    A. Borrowing from nothing

    B. Assembly sequence

    C. Irreducibly complex borrowed components

IV. How Did Life Begin?

    A. How do you get new living forms and structures from life that already exists?

    B. How did life originate in the first place?

V. Proteins: 30,000 distinct types made from a sequence of 20 different amino acids

    A. **Biochemical predestination**: life was inevitable due to attractions between amino acids

        1. Where did the genetic assembly instructions come from?

        2. How can proteins assemble without instructions from DNA?

VI. First Cell

    A. Chance alone

    B. Natural selection could not have existed before the first living cell.

VII. Cell Factory

    A. _____: storehouse for instructions to build every protein in an organism

    B. _____: process where DNA is unwound to expose instructions for RNA

    C. _____: carries the genetic information out of the cell

    D. _____: process where information is translated and protein is built

    E. _____: translates and builds specific amino acids from information

    F. Strain folded into protein

    G. Protein moved to where it is needed

VIII. The Design Inference

    A. Improbable object/event

    B. Recognizable pattern

    C. _Information_____: small probability and specification

        1. **SETI**: searching for information

        2. **DNA**: world of information

"MYSTERIES OF LIFE'S ORIGINS"
VIDEO QUESTIONS

Answer the questions below on a separate sheet of paper and be prepared to review your answers in class.

1. **What is irreducible complexity? What are some examples?**

2. **What is co-option? What are some problems with the idea?**

3. **How does Darwinism theorize that life first began? What are some problems with the idea?**

4. **What is the process of protein production within the cell?**

5. **What is design inference? What are some examples?**

WHAT IS DARWINISM?

BY PHILLIP E. JOHNSON

SUMMARY

The debate between creationism and Darwinism is often depicted as a dispute between naive biblical literalists, who ignore the overwhelming evidence for evolution, and scientifically enlightened intellectuals. But this is a caricature that serves the purpose of helping to perpetuate a worldview hostile to Christian faith: atheistic naturalism. The debate hinges on five key terms: creationism, evolution, science, religion, and truth. Instead of trying to Christianize evolution we ought instead to challenge the assumption that atheistic naturalism is true.

The popular television game show Jeopardy reverses the usual order of things. Instead of being asked a question to which they must supply the answer, contestants are given the answer and asked to provide the appropriate question. This format suggests an insight that is applicable to law, to science, and indeed to just about everything. More important than knowing all the answers is knowing what question is being asked.

That insight is the starting point for my inquiry into Darwinian evolution and its relationship to creation, because Darwinism is the answer to two very different kinds of questions. First, Darwinian theory tells us how a certain amount of diversity in life forms can develop once we have various types of complex living organisms already in existence. If a small population of birds happens to migrate to an isolated island, for example, a combination of inbreeding, mutation, and natural selection may cause this isolated population to develop different characteristics from those possessed by the ancestral population on the mainland. When the theory is understood in this limited sense, Darwinian evolution is uncontroversial and has no important philosophical or theological implications.

Evolutionary biologists are not content merely to explain how variation occurs within limits. They aspire to answer a much broader question—how complex organisms like birds, flowers, and human beings came to exist at all. The Darwinian answer to this second question is that the creative force that produced complex plants and animals is essentially the same as the mechanism producing variations in flowers, insects, and domestic animals before our very eyes. In the words of Ernst Mayr, the dean of living Darwinists, "Transspecific evolution [i.e., macroevolution] is nothing but an extrapolation and magnification of the events that take place within populations and species."

Neo-Darwinian evolution in this broad sense is a philosophical doctrine so lacking in empirical support that Mayr's successor at Harvard, Stephen Jay Gould, in a reckless moment once pronounced it "effectively dead. "Yet neo-Darwinism is far from dead. On the contrary, it is continually proclaimed in textbooks and the media as unchallengeable fact. How does it happen that so many scientists and intellectuals, who pride themselves on their empiricism and open-mindedness, continue to accept an unempirical theory as scientific fact?

DEFINING THE ISSUES

The answer to that question lies in the definition of five key terms—creationism, evolution, science, religion, and truth. Once we understand how these words are used in evolutionary discourse, the continued ascendancy of neo-Darwinism will be no mystery, and we need no longer be deceived by claims that the theory is supported by "overwhelming evidence." As we shall see, there are powerful vested interests in this area that thrive in the midst of ambiguity and confusion. Those who insist on defining terms precisely and using them consistently may find themselves regarded with suspicion and hostility, and even accused of being enemies of science.

Creationism

The first word is creationism, which means simply a belief in creation. In Darwinist usage, which dominates not only popular and professional scientific literature but also the media, a creationist is a person who takes the creation account in the Book of Genesis as true in the most literal sense. The earth was created in a single week of six 24-hour days no more than 10,000 years ago; the major features of the geological record were produced by Noah's flood; and there have been no major innovations in the forms of life since the beginning. It is a major theme of Darwinist propaganda that the only persons who have any doubts about Darwinism are young-earth creationists of this sort, who are always portrayed as rejecting the clear and convincing evidence of science to preserve a religious prejudice. The implication is that citizens of modern society are faced with a choice that is really no choice at all. Either they reject science altogether and retreat to a premodern worldview, or they believe everything the Darwinists tell them.

In a broader sense, however, a creationist is simply a person who believes in the existence of a creator who brought about the world and its living inhabitants for a purpose. Whether the process of creation took a single week or billions of years is relatively unimportant from a philosophical or theological standpoint. Creation by gradual processes over geological ages may create problems for biblical interpretation, but it creates none for the basic principle of theistic religion. Creation in this broad sense, according to a 1991 Gallup poll, is the creed of 87 percent of Americans. Is creation in this sense consistent with evolution?

Evolution

The answer is no, when evolution is understood in the Darwinian sense. To Darwinists evolution means naturalistic evolution, an insistence that science must assume that the cosmos is a closed system of material causes and effects, which can never be influenced by anything outside of material nature, such as God. In the beginning, an explosion of matter created the cosmos, and undirected, naturalistic evolution produced everything that followed. Thus, no intelligent purpose guided evolution. If intelligence exists today, that is only because it has itself evolved through purposeless material processes.

At bottom the theory must be based on chance, because that is what is left when we have ruled out everything involving intelligence or purpose. But theories invoking only chance are not credible. One thing everyone acknowledges is that living organisms are enormously complex—far more so than, say, a computer or an airplane. That such complex entities came into existence simply by chance is clearly less credible than that they were designed and constructed by a creator. To back up their claim that this appearance of intelligent design is an illusion, Darwinists therefore need to provide a building force that is mindless and purposeless. Natural selection is by far the most plausible candidate.

If we assume that random genetic mutations provided the new genetic information needed, say, to give a small mammal a start towards wings, and if we assume that each tiny step in the process of wing building gave the animal an increased chance of survival, then natural selection ensured that the favored creatures would thrive and reproduce. It logically follows that wings can and will appear as if by the plan of a designer. Of course, if wings or other improvements do not appear, the theory explains their absence just as well. The needed mutations didn't arrive, or "developmental constraints" closed off certain possibilities, or natural selection favored something else. There is no requirement that any of this speculation be confirmed by either experimental or fossil evidence. To Darwinists just being able to imagine the process is sufficient to confirm that something like that must have happened.

Biologist Richard Dawkins calls the process of creation by mutation and selection "the blind watchmaker," by which he means that a purposeless, materialistic designing force substitutes for the "watchmaker" deity of natural theology. The creative power of the blind watchmaker is supported only by very slight evidence, such as the famous example of a moth population in which the percentage of dark moths increased during a period when the birds were better able to see light moths against the smoke-darkened background trees. This may be taken to show that natural selection can change organisms, but not that it can create organisms that were not already in existence.

Even such slight evidence is more than sufficient, however, because evidence is not really necessary to prove something that is practically self-evident. The existence of a potent blind watchmaker follows deductively from the philosophical premise that nature had to do its own creating. There can be argument about the details, but if God was not in the picture something very much like Darwinism simply has to be true, regardless of the evidence.

Science

That brings me to my third term, science. We have already seen that Darwinists assume as a first principle that the history of the cosmos and its life forms is fully explicable on naturalistic principles. This reflects a philosophical doctrine called scientific naturalism, a necessary consequence of the inherent limitations of science. What scientific naturalism does, however, is transform the limitations of science into limitations on reality, in the interest of maximizing the explanatory power of science and its practitioners. It is, of course, entirely possible to study organisms scientifically on the premise that they were all created by God, just as scientists study airplanes and even works of art without denying that these objects are intelligently designed. The problem with allowing God a role in the history of life is not that science would cease, but rather that scientists would have to acknowledge the existence of something important that is outside the boundaries of natural science. For scientists who want to be able to explain everything, this is an intolerable possibility.

The second feature of scientific naturalism that is important for our purpose is its set of rules governing the criticism and replacement of a paradigm. A paradigm is a general theory, like the Darwinian theory of evolution, which has achieved general acceptance in the scientific community. The paradigm unifies the various specialties that make up the research community, and guides research in all of them. Thus, zoologists, botanists, geneticists, molecular biologists, and paleontologists all see their research as aimed at filling out the details of the Darwinian paradigm.

If molecular biologists see a pattern of apparently neutral mutations, which have no apparent effect on an organism's fitness, they must find a way to reconcile their findings with the paradigm's requirement that natural selection guides evolution. This they can do by postulating a sufficient quantity of invisible adaptive mutations, supposedly accumulated by natural selection. Similarly, if paleontologists see new fossil species appearing suddenly in the fossil record, and remaining basically unchanged thereafter, they must perform whatever contortions are necessary to force this recalcitrant evidence into a model of incremental change through the accumulation of micromutations.

Supporting the paradigm may even require what in other contexts would be called deception. As Niles Eldredge candidly admitted, "We paleontologists have said that the history of life supports [the story of gradual adaptive change], all the while knowing it does not."[1] Eldredge explained that this pattern of misrepresentation occurred because of "the certainty so characteristic of evolutionary ranks since the late 1940s, the utter assurance not only that natural selection operates in nature, but that we know precisely how it works." This certainty produced a degree of dogmatism that Eldredge says resulted in the relegation of paleontologists to the "lunatic fringe" who reported that "they saw something out of kilter between contemporary evolutionary theory, on the one hand, and patterns of change in the fossil record on the other."[2] Under the circumstances, prudent paleontologists understandably swallowed their doubts and supported the ruling ideology. To abandon the paradigm would be to abandon the scientific community; to ignore the paradigm and just gather the facts would be to earn the demeaning label of "stamp collector" (i.e., one who does not theorize).

As many philosophers of science have observed, the research community does not abandon a paradigm in the absence of a suitable replacement. This means that negative criticism of Darwinism, however devastating it may appear to be, is essentially irrelevant to the professional researchers. A critic may point out, for example, that the evidence that natural selection has any creative power is somewhere between weak and nonexistent. That is perfectly true, but to Darwinists the more important point is this: If natural selection did not do the creating, what did? "God" is obviously unacceptable, because such a being is unknown to science. "We don't know" is equally unacceptable, because to admit ignorance would be to leave science adrift without a guiding principle. To put the problem in the most practical terms: it is impossible to write or evaluate a grant proposal without a generally accepted theoretical framework.

The paradigm rule explains why Gould's acknowledgment that neo-Darwinism is "effectively dead" had no significant effect on the Darwinist faithful, or even on Gould himself. Gould made that statement in a paper predicting the emergence of a new general theory of evolution, one based on the macromutational speculations of the Berkeley geneticist Richard Goldschmidt.[3] When the new theory did not arrive as anticipated, the alternatives were either to stick with Ernst Mayr's version of neo-Darwinism or to concede that biologists do not know of a naturalistic mechanism that can produce biological complexity. That was no choice at all. Gould had to beat a hasty retreat back to classical Darwinism to avoid giving aid and

---

[1] Niles Eldredge, *Time Frames* (Portsmouth, NH: Heinemann, 1986), 144.
[2] Ibid., 93.
[3] Stephen Jay Gould, "Is a New and General Theory of Evolution Emerging?" *Paleobiology 6* (1980): 119–30, reprinted in Maynard Smith, ed., *Evolution Now: A Century after Darwin* (New York: W. H. Freeman, 1982).

comfort to the enemies of scientific naturalism, including those disgusting creationists. Having to defend a dead theory tooth and nail can hardly be a satisfying activity, and it is no wonder that Gould lashes out with fury at people such as myself who call attention to his predicament.[4] I do not mean to ridicule Gould, because I have a genuinely high regard for the man as one of the few Darwinists who has recognized the major problems with the theory and reported them honestly. His tragedy is that he cannot admit the clear implications of his own thought without effectively resigning from science.

The continuing survival of Darwinist orthodoxy illustrates Thomas Kuhn's famous point that the accumulation of anomalies never in itself falsifies a paradigm, since "to reject one paradigm without substituting another is to reject science itself."[5] This practice may be appropriate as a way of carrying on the professional enterprise called science, but it can be grossly misleading when it is imposed on persons who are asking questions other than the ones scientific naturalists want to ask. Suppose, for example, that I want to know whether God really had something to do with creating living organisms. A typical Darwinian response is that there is no reason to invoke supernatural action because Darwinian selection was capable of performing the job. To evaluate that response, I need to know whether natural selection really has the fantastic creative power attributed to it. It is not a sufficient answer to say that scientists have nothing better to offer. The fact that scientists don't like to say "we don't know" tells me nothing about what they really do know.

I am not suggesting that scientists have to change their rules about retaining and discarding paradigms. All I want them to do is to be candid about the disconfirming evidence and admit, if it is the case, that they are hanging on to Darwinism only because they prefer a shaky theory to having no theory at all. What they insist on doing, however, is to present Darwinian evolution to the public as a fact that every rational person is expected to accept. If there are reasonable grounds to doubt the theory, such dogmatism is ridiculous, whether or not the doubters have a better theory to propose.

To believers in creation, Darwinists seem thoroughly intolerant and dogmatic when they insist that their own philosophy must have a monopoly in the schools and the media. Darwinists do not see themselves that way, of course. On the contrary, they often feel aggrieved when creationists (in either the broad or narrow sense) ask to have their own arguments heard and considered. To insist that schoolchildren be taught that Darwinian evolution is a fact is, in their minds, merely to protect the integrity of science education; to present the other side of the case would be to allow fanatics to force their opinions on others. Even college professors have been forbidden to express their doubts about Darwinian evolution in the classroom, and it seems widely believed that the Constitution not only permits but actually requires such restrictions on academic freedom.[6]

Religion

To explain this bizarre situation, we must define our fourth term: religion. Suppose that a skeptic argues that evidence for biological creation by natural selection is obviously lacking, and that in the circumstances we ought to give serious consideration to the possibility that the development of life required some input from a preexisting, purposeful creator. To scientific naturalists, this suggestion is "creationist" and therefore unacceptable in principle, because it invokes an entity unknown to science. What is worse, it suggests the possibility that this creator may have communicated in some way with humans, perhaps with real prophets—persons with a genuine knowledge of God. Such persons could be dangerous rivals for the scientists as cultural authorities.

Naturalistic philosophy has worked out a strategy to prevent this problem from arising: it labels naturalism as science and theism as religion. The former is then classified as knowledge, and the latter as mere belief. The distinction is of critical importance, because only knowledge can be objectively valid for everyone; belief is valid only for the believer, and should never be passed off as knowledge. The student who thinks that 2 and 2 make 5, or that water is not made up of hydrogen and oxygen, or that the theory of evolution is not true, is not expressing a minority viewpoint. He or she is ignorant, and the job of education

---

[4] See Stephen Jay Gould, "Impeaching a Self-Appointed Judge," *Scientific American* (July 1992), 118–22. *Scientific American* refused to publish my response, but the response did appear in the March 1993 issue of *Perspectives on Science and Christian Faith: The Journal of the American Scientific Affiliation*.
[5] Thomas S. Kuhn, *The Structure of Scientific Revolutions* (Chicago: University of Chicago Press, 1970), 79.
[6] This issue is discussed in my article "What (If Anything) Hath God Wrought?" at www.arn.org.

is to cure that ignorance and to replace it with knowledge. Thus, students in the public schools must be taught at an early age that "evolution is a fact," and as time goes by they will gradually learn that evolution means naturalism.

The proposition that God was in any way involved in our creation is effectively outlawed, since naturalistic evolution is by definition in the category of scientific knowledge and what contradicts knowledge is implicitly false, or imaginary. That is why it is possible for scientific naturalists in good faith to claim on the one hand that their science says nothing about God, and on the other to claim that they have said everything that can be said about God. In naturalistic philosophy both propositions are at bottom the same. All that needs to be said about God is that there is nothing to be said of God, because on that subject we can have no knowledge.

Truth

Our fifth term is truth. Truth as such is not a particularly important concept in naturalistic philosophy. The reason for this is that "truth" suggests an unchanging absolute, whereas scientific knowledge is a dynamic concept. Like life, knowledge evolves and grows into superior forms. What was knowledge in the past is not knowledge today, and the knowledge of the future will surely be far superior to what we have now. Only naturalism itself, and the unique validity of science as the path to knowledge, are absolute. There can be no criterion for truth outside of scientific knowledge, no mind of God to which we have access.

This way of understanding things persists even when scientific naturalists employ religious-sounding language. For example, the physicist Stephen Hawking ended his famous book A Brief History of Time with the prediction that humanity might one day "know the mind of God." This phrasing gives some friends of mine the mistaken impression that he has some attraction to theism. In context, Hawking was not referring to a supernatural eternal agent, but to the possibility that scientific knowledge will eventually become complete and all-encompassing because it will have explained the movements of material particles in all circumstances.

The monopoly of science in the realm of knowledge explains why evolutionary biologists do not find it meaningful to address the question whether Darwinism is true. They will gladly concede that the theory is incomplete and that further research is needed. At any given point in time, however, the reigning theory of naturalistic evolution represents the state of scientific knowledge about how we came into existence. Scientific knowledge is by naturalistic definition the closest approximation of absolute truth available to us. To ask whether this knowledge is true is to miss the point, and to betray a misunderstanding of "how science works."

CHRISTIANS AND DARWINISM

So far I have described the metaphysical categories by which scientific naturalists have excluded the topic of God from rational discussion, and thus ensured that Darwinism's fully naturalistic creation story is effectively true by definition. There is no need to explain why atheists find this system of thought control congenial. What is more difficult to understand—at least at first—is the strong support Darwinism continues to receive in the Christian academic world. Attempts to investigate the credibility of Darwinist evolution are regarded with little enthusiasm by many leading Christian professors of science and philosophy, even at institutions that are generally regarded as theologically conservative. Given that Darwinism is inherently naturalistic and therefore antagonistic to the idea that God had anything to do with the history of life, and that it plays the central role in ensuring agnostic domination of the intellectual culture, one might have supposed that Christian intellectuals (along with religious Jews) would be eager to find its weak spots.

Instead, the prevailing view among Christian professors has been that Darwinism—or "evolution," as they tend to call it—is unbeatable, and that it can be interpreted to be consistent with Christian belief. In fact Darwinism is unbeatable as long as one accepts the thought categories of scientific naturalism that I have been describing. The problem is that those same thought categories make Christian theism, or any other theism, absolutely untenable. If science has exclusive authority to tell us how life was created, and if science is committed to naturalism, and if science never discards a paradigm until it is presented with an acceptable naturalistic alternative, then Darwinism's position is impregnable within science. Yet the same reasoning that makes Darwinism inevitable also bans God from taking any action within the history of the Cosmos, which makes theism illusory. Theistic naturalism is self-contradictory.

Some hope to avoid the contradiction by asserting that naturalism rules only within the realm of science, and that there is a separate realm called "religion" in which theism can flourish. The problem with this, as we have already seen, is that in a naturalistic culture scientific conclusions are considered to be knowledge, or even fact. What is outside of fact is fantasy, or at best subjective belief. Theists who accommodate scientific naturalism therefore may never affirm that their God is real in the same sense that evolution is real. This rule is essential to the entire naturalistic mindset that produced Darwinism in the first place.

If God exists he could certainly work through scientifically explainable processes if that is what he wanted to do, but he could also create by some means totally outside the ken of our science. Once we put him into the picture, there is no good reason to attribute the creation of biological complexity to random mutation and natural selection. Direct evidence that these mechanisms have substantial creative power is not to be found in nature, the laboratory, or the fossil record. An essential step in the reasoning that establishes that Darwinian selection created the wonders of biology, therefore, is that nothing else was available. Theism says that something else was available.

Perhaps the contradiction is hard to see when it is stated at an abstract level, so I will give a more concrete example. Persons who advocate the compromise position called "theistic evolution" are in my experience always vague about what they mean by "evolution." They have good reason to be vague. As we have seen, Darwinian evolution is by definition unguided and purposeless, and such evolution cannot in any meaningful sense be theistic. For evolution to be genuinely theistic it must be guided by God, whether this means God programmed the process in advance or stepped in from time to time to push it in the right direction. To Darwinists evolution guided by God is a soft form of creationism—that is to say, it is not evolution at all. To repeat, this understanding goes to the very heart of Darwinist thinking. Allow a preexisting supernatural intelligence to guide evolution, and this omnipotent being can do a whole lot more than that.

Of course, theists can think of evolution as God-guided whether naturalistic Darwinists like it or not. One problem with having a private definition for theists, however, is that the scientific naturalists have the power to decide what the term "evolution" means in public discourse, including the science classes in the public schools. If theistic evolutionists broadcast the message that evolution as they understand it is harmless to theistic religion, they are misleading their constituents unless they add a clear warning that the version of evolution advocated by the entire body of mainstream science is something else altogether. That warning is never clearly delivered, because the main point of theistic evolution is to preserve peace with the mainstream scientific community. Theistic evolutionists therefore unwittingly serve the purposes of the scientific naturalists by helping persuade the religious community to lower its guard against the incursion of naturalism.

We are now in a position to answer the question, What is Darwinism? Darwinism is a theory of empirical science only at the level of microevolution, where it provides a framework for explaining phenomena such as the diversity that arises when small populations become reproductively isolated from the main body of the species. As a general theory of biological creation Darwinism is not empirical at all. Rather, it is a necessary implication of a philosophical doctrine called scientific naturalism, which is based on the nonscientific assumption that God was always absent from the realm of nature. Evolution in the Darwinian sense is inherently antithetical to theism, although evolution in some entirely different and nonnaturalistic sense could conceivably (if not demonstrably) have been God's chosen method of creation.

To return to the game of Jeopardy with which we started, let us say that Darwinism is the answer. What, then, is the question? The question is: "How must creation have occurred if we assume that God had nothing to do with it?" Theistic evolutionists err in trying to Christianize the answer to a question that comes straight out of the agenda of scientific naturalism. What we need to do instead is challenge the assumption that the only questions worth asking are the ones that assume that naturalism is true.

*This essay originally appeared in the *Christian Research Journal*:
    Phillip Johnson, "What is Darwinism?," *Christian Research Journal* Vol. 19, No. 4, (1997), 20–26.
**Reproduction rights granted by the *Christian Research Journal*.

Unit Four

WHAT IS DARWINISM?
ESSAY QUESTIONS

Answer the questions below on a separate sheet of paper and be prepared to review your answers in class.

1. What are the two tenets of Darwinian evolution?

2. What defines a creationist?

3. What is Darwinian evolution?

4. How does naturalism affect science?

5. Why is the paradigm of naturalism revered so highly among Darwinists?

6. Why is Darwinism generally a dogmatic belief?

7. What distinction do Darwinists make between religion and science?

8. What is the Darwinian view of truth?

9. Why are Christianity and Darwinism incompatible?

10. What is Darwinism?

Hello again!

Last week before Thanksgiving break! I can hardly remember what life feels like without classes to worry about—nothing to do next week but sleep in and eat!

Speaking of classes, biology is driving me crazy. I have to read the textbook in order to pass the class, but it is so full of evolution that I hate to open it. The prof has been going on and on about how the facts of evolution have been scientifically proven and how college is supposed to be where our childish beliefs are replaced with the truth. Of course, everyone knew he was talking about me. I made the mistake last week of casually mentioning creation, and he hasn't missed a chance yet to bash it.

I have to tell you though… some of this stuff is starting to make sense. After all, evolution has a scientific basis, while creation is just a religious belief. I'm not sure how we can say that the Bible should take precedence over all the scientific evidence supporting evolution.

We were all talking about this the other day at lunch. Sarah said that scientists have pretty well proven that life evolved through a slow gradual process of natural selection, with random mutations making each generation better than the last one. Our biology professor did share some pretty good pieces of proof— finches, peppered moths, bacteria mutation, etc. But I'm just not sure if those examples explain evolution on a grand scale. Do you think Darwin's theory of evolution explains how life began?

Mark has been arguing with the professor, though. He thinks the original concept of evolution is too slow and that instead life evolved in big leaps separated by long static pauses. He says this explains why there is a lack of transitional life forms. But does this explain how we got here any better than regular Darwinism? Nathan agreed with Mark, but said he was being too "naturalistic"—that the physical side isn't as important as our steps toward becoming more enlightened and even divine. For a Christian, that kinda makes sense. At least Nathan believes we have a spiritual side. Do you think life is only a search for enlightenment?

Afterwards, Muhammad walked back to the dorm with me and told me that he didn't think we evolved. He asked me what I thought, but I wasn't sure how to answer him. I'd like to believe the Bible, but in this area, it just doesn't seem to be adequate, especially with all the verifiable evidence the biology prof uses. What does Christianity really have to say about how life began?

Thanks for being my resource on all these questions—I don't feel quite so awkward asking you. Anyway, gotta run. There's a paper I have to turn in before I leave, and maybe I can squeeze in lunch with Amber. I'd love to have you meet her sometime!

Talk to you later,
Doug

Creationism isn't just religious b/c it can explain all the design that evolution can't. Not based on religious premesis, its based on the evidence, and the evidence points to intelligence.

Unit Four

UNDERSTANDING THE TIMES

Unit Five

Topics:

Homosexuality

Psychology

A Summit Ministries Curriculum

SECTION OUTLINE

180-DAY SYLLABUS

DAY	IN CLASS	HOMEWORK	
1	WATCH "Psychology" video		
2	READ <u>UTT</u> Textbook 'Psychology 5.1'	READ <u>UTT</u> Textbook 'Psychology 5.2'	
3	REVIEW <u>UTT</u> Textbook 'Psychology 5.1–5.2' questions	READ <u>UTT</u> Textbook 'Psychology 5.3'	
4	READ <u>UTT</u> Textbook 'Psychology 5.4'		
5	REVIEW <u>UTT</u> Textbook 'Psychology 5.3–5.4' questions	READ <u>UTT</u> Textbook 'Psychology 5.5'	
6	READ <u>UTT</u> Textbook 'Psychology 5.6'		
7	REVIEW <u>UTT</u> Textbook 'Psychology 5.5–5.6' questions		
8	READ *Homosexuality, Fact or Fiction?* essay		
9	REVIEW *Homosexuality, Fact or Fiction?* essay questions		
10	READ *That Which is Unnatural* essay		
11	REVIEW *That Which is Unnatural* essay questions		
12	WRITE Worldview Paper		
13	WRITE Worldview Paper		
14	WRITE Worldview Paper		
15	Worldview Paper DUE		

90-DAY SYLLABUS

DAY	IN CLASS	HOMEWORK	
1	WATCH "Psychology" video	READ <u>UTT</u> Textbook 'Psychology 5.1–5.2'	
2	REVIEW <u>UTT</u> Textbook 'Psychology 5.1–5.2' questions	READ <u>UTT</u> Textbook 'Psychology 5.3–5.4'	
3	REVIEW <u>UTT</u> Textbook 'Psychology 5.3–5.4' questions	READ <u>UTT</u> Textbook 'Psychology 5.5–5.6'	
4	REVIEW <u>UTT</u> Textbook 'Psychology 5.5–5.6' questions	READ *Homosexuality, Fact or Fiction?* essay	
5	REVIEW *Homosexuality, Fact or Fiction?* essay questions		
6	WRITE Worldview Paper		
7	WRITE Worldview Paper		
8	Worldview Paper DUE		

UNDERSTANDING THE TIMES
PSYCHOLOGY QUESTIONS

Answer the questions below on a separate sheet of paper and be prepared to review your answers in class.

PSYCHOLOGY 5.1

1. Why does William Kirk Kilpatrick refer to Christianity and psychology as competing faiths?

2. Why should Christians bring God's truth to the discipline of psychology?

3. What is the Christian view of ontology (the study of being)? What is "unity of identity?"

4. According to Christianity, what is the key to healing non-organic mental illnesses?

5. How do Secular Humanists and Christians differ in their views of suffering?

PSYCHOLOGY 5.2

6. What do Muslims believe about being created in the "image of God?" What is their view of human nature?

7. What is the Islamic view of the Fall?

8. What is the Islamic view of Christ's work on the cross? How does one attain salvation in Islam?

9. What is the Islamic view of the Final Judgment and forgiveness?

10. What are the ramifications of denying Jesus' death on the cross?

PSYCHOLOGY 5.3

11. What is behaviorism? Why is Secular Humanism's rejection of behaviorist psychology inconsistent with its worldview?

12. Why do so few Secular Humanists accept behaviorism?

13. What do Secular Humanists believe about the innate nature of mankind?

14. Why do Secular Humanist psychologists justify self-centeredness as a worthwhile goal? How does this contrast with the Christian view?

15. What is the Secular Humanist psychologist's source of ethics? How does this line of thinking tend toward elitism?

PSYCHOLOGY 5.4

16. What aspects of behaviorism do Marxists accept? What aspects of behaviorism do they reject?

17. How do Marxists avoid accepting the determinism dictated by behaviorism?

18. According to Marxists, what is the major problem with society? Why?

19. How does the Marxist view of the dialectic affect their psychology?

20. How do Marxists define freedom?

PSYCHOLOGY 5.5

21. What role does psychology play in Cosmic Humanism?

22. According to Cosmic Humanism, how do individuals achieve a healthy well-being?

23. According to Cosmic Humanism, why do people suffer health problems?

24. According to Cosmic Humanism, where do criminal tendencies originate?

25. What methods do "fourth force" psychology employ to induce states of higher consciousness in willing individuals?

PSYCHOLOGY 5.6

26. How has the concept of soul become obsolete in the Postmodern era?

27. How do Gilles Deleuze and Felix Guattari view the soul?

28. What is the definition of "self" according to Jacques Lacan and Michel Foucault?

29. What is the theory of "multiple selves" according to Mitchell Stephens and Kenneth Gergen?

30. What are some inherent problems with the notion of a socially constructed self?

HOMOSEXUALITY, FACT OR FICTION?
BY JOSEPH P. GUDEL

"People should live and let live!" "To each his own, let them live as they wish." "Let the gays have their freedom." "Whatever makes you happy, live with it."[1]

Comments like these are commonly heard when the topic of homosexuality comes up for discussion. The debate over homosexuality and homosexual rights has steadily grown over the past two decades and will only continue to do so.

In the course of this debate, however, numerous inaccuracies, half-truths, fallacies, and overt propaganda have been disseminated to the public as uncontested truth. It is the purpose of this article to examine these claims and separate fact from fiction. Before anyone can give intelligent and compassionate answers, the questions must be clarified and brought into focus. I believe that when this is done the impartial reader will be able to agree with the analogy made by Dr. James D. Mallory, a psychiatrist and the director of the Atlanta Counseling Center: "A physician would be guilty of malpractice if he didn't warn a diabetic of his condition because he didn't want to hurt his feelings. Simply letting the person continue eating excessive carbohydrates without proper treatment condemns him to a worsening physical condition. The most loving act one can do is point out that an abnormality exists, and offer help. This needs to be done—but not in a spirit of condemnation—with homosexuality."[2]

HOMOPHOBIA?

Homophobia is defined in *The Kinsey Institute New Report on Sex* as the "fear, dislike, or hatred of homosexuals."[3] The Greek word *phobia* denotes an "irrational fear." The word *homo* literally means "same," but the word is frequently used as a shortened form of *homosexual*—one who is sexually attracted to his or her own sex. Thus, strictly speaking, homophobia denotes an irrational fear or hatred of homosexuals. However, the gay rights movement (and, by-and-large, the media) places this label on anyone who opposes any of the movement's goals and objectives; specifically, anyone opposing the full acceptance of the homosexual lifestyle as healthy and "normal."

While indeed there are many people who hate or irrationally fear homosexuals, to say that anyone who opposes the homosexual lifestyle or disagrees with the gay rights political agenda is a homophobe is simply not true. This tactic is clearly intended to divert attention from the argument and onto the person. As we will see below, there are many who oppose homosexuality on psychological, sociological, medical, and moral grounds.

TEN PERCENT OF THE POPULATION?

Perhaps the most fascinating statistic cited (constantly and confidently) in research of homosexuality is that ten percent of the United States population is homosexual. The implication is that this is probably just as true in most other societies as well. I say this is fascinating because virtually nobody knows (or at least cites) where this statistic comes from.

The Family Research Institute asks, "How many homosexuals are there? *USA Today* said '25 million gay men and lesbians' [i.e., about 10% of the US population]. The *Washington Times* said '10 percent of American men are homosexual and 5 percent of women are lesbian.' The American Psychological Association assures us that homosexuality is 'an orientation found consistently in about ten percent of the male population and approximately five percent of the female population.'"[4]

Just this week, as I was preparing to put this article together, I watched "Teen Connection," a public broadcast program.[5] Its topic was "Sexual Orientation," with a panel consisting of a homosexual teenage

---

[1] Quotes from members of the studio audience on *The Geraldo Show*, "Can Gays and Lesbians Go Straight?" (June 11, 1991).
[2] James D. Mallory, "Homosexuality: Part III—A Psychiatrist's View," *Christian Life* (October 1977).
[3] June M. Reinisch, dir., *The Kinsey Institute New Report on Sex* (New York: St. Martin's Press, 1990), 147.
[4] *Family Research Report* (Family Research Institute, Washington DC), 1.
[5] *Teen Connection*, "Sexual Orientation," Wisconsin Public Television (May 19, 1992).

boy, the boy's mother, a young lady who is a lesbian, and an adult homosexual counselor. Within the course of an hour the ten percent figure was cited three times, being adduced as evidence of just how many people out there need our encouragement and understanding. They had a panel of phones for those who had questions or needed counseling themselves. I called in and asked them where the ten percent figure came from. The lady I spoke with did not know, and neither did another phone counselor she asked.

The truth is that this ten percent statistic comes from a report published more than 40 years ago—the famous 1948 study led by Alfred Kinsey.[6] The only problem with this report is that its findings were terribly flawed by the methodology used to collect the supposedly representative sample of the U.S. population.[7]

Why were his findings flawed? For several reasons, first and foremost being that approximately 25 percent of the 5,300 individuals Kinsey studied were prison inmates, "who by the nature of their confinement, couldn't have heterosexual intercourse." In addition, 44 percent of these inmates had had homosexual experiences while in prison.[8] This was hardly a representative sample of the American population.

But there were other major flaws in the group selected for the research. Kinsey admitted that "several hundred male prostitutes" were used in his sample. This alone would make a major difference in his findings.[9]

In addition there was clearly a "volunteer bias." In attempting to select a representative group to work with, one does not merely run an ad and accept anyone who responds. Research has shown that those responding to a study as intimate as the one Kinsey was doing would *not* be representative of the general population. In fact, the widely renowned psychologist Abraham Maslow pointed this out to Kinsey before his findings were published, but he refused to listen.[10]

To make matters worse, the people who refer back to this old and flawed study do not quote it accurately. Kinsey did not say that 10 percent of the entire U.S. population was homosexual. Rather, he affirmed that ten percent of white American males were "more or less" exclusively homosexual for at least three years of their lives between the ages of 16 and 65. The statistic for females was five percent. The actual percentage of those thought to be *exclusively* homosexual for their entire lives was only four percent of men and two or three percent of women, all based on his allegedly representative sample of the population.[11]

What are the real figures as far as we can tell today? One recent study of men conducted between 1984 and 1987 by David Forman, the senior staff scientist at the Radcliffe Infirmary (Oxford, England), found that only 1.7 percent of the sample study had ever had homosexual intercourse.[12] An even more recent study, conducted at the University of Chicago in 1989 and reported at the 1990 meeting of the American Association for the Advancement of Science, resulted in a figure "less than 1% exclusively homosexual."[13]

Are these results significant? Well, they are significant in at least setting the record straight as to the actual scope or parameters of the debate. There is quite a difference between one or two percent of the population being homosexual as opposed to ten percent of the population. Obviously, the higher the percentage cited as being homosexual, the more influence those in the gay rights movement can wield.

IS HOMOSEXUALITY AN ILLNESS? IS IT "NORMAL"?

An even more important question, though, is if homosexuality constitutes pathological behavior. Is it an illness? Gay rights groups continually assert that homosexuals are as "normal" as heterosexuals, that homosexuality is not an illness or psychological disorder. For example, Peri Jude Radecic, a member of the National Gay and Lesbian Task Force (NGLTF), asserted on the ABC news show *Nightline*, "Homosexuality is not an illness, it is not something that needs to be cured. We are normal, healthy people."[14]

[6] Alfred C. Kinsey, et al., *Sexual Behavior in the Human Male* (Philadelphia: Saunders, 1948).
[7] See Abraham Maslow and James M. Sakoda, "Volunteer Error in the Kinsey Study," *Journal of Abnormal and Social Psychology 47* (April 1952), 259–62.
[8] "The Ten Percent Solution, Part II," *Peninsula* 3:2 (October/November 1991), 7. Also see Judith A. Reisman and Edward W. Eichol, *Kinsey, Sex and Fraud* (Lafayette, LA: Huntington House, 1990), 23.
[9] Kinsey, 216.
[10] Maslow and Sakoda, 259–62.
[11] Reinisch, 140.
[12] Reisman and Eichol, 194.
[13] Ibid., 195.
[14] *Nightline*, ABC News (August 30, 1991).

Moreover, these groups universally contend that all competent psychiatrists and psychologists are in agreement on this. As proof of this, the American Psychiatric Association's (APA) 1973 declassification homosexuality as a mental disorder is always cited.

Before examining the contention that all competent psychiatrists and psychologists agree that homosexuality is normal and healthy, we need to look at the APA's 1973 decision for a moment. For 23 years homosexuality had been listed as a mental disorder by the APA. Why was it decided, at that particular point in time, that it was not pathological?

I do not have the space to go into a detailed analysis of the history leading up to the APA's decision.[15] Nonetheless, it is a misconception to think that this came about only after dispassionate and scholarly discussion, and only after listening equally to all sides of the issue. Also, it is important to note that the APA's vote was anything but unanimous.

In the three years leading up to the 1973 APA meeting, the previous national meetings had been repeatedly disrupted by gay activists. At the 1970 meeting in San Francisco certain sessions were broken up with shouts and jeers, prohibiting any rational discussion or debate.

At the APA's 1971 meeting in Washington, threats and intimidation accomplished what discussion could not. Ronald Bayer, in a work sympathetic toward homosexuality and the gay rights movement, recounts: "Using forged credentials, gay activists gained access to the exhibit area and, coming across a display marketing aversive conditioning [i.e., punishing an organism whenever it makes a particular response] techniques for the treatment of homosexuals, demanded its removal. Threats were made against the exhibitor, who was told that unless his booth was dismantled, it would be torn down. After frantic behind-the-scenes consultations, and in an effort to avoid violence, the convention leadership agreed to have the booth removed."[16]

These tactics continued in the same manner at the APA's 1972 national meeting. It was against this backdrop that the association's trustees finally made its controversial 1973 decision. When a referendum on this was sent out to all 25,000 APA members, only a quarter of them returned their ballots. The final tally was 58 percent favoring the removal of homosexuality from their list of disorders.

Four years later, Dr. Charles Socarides—who was at the meetings and was an expert in the area of homosexuality, having treated homosexuals for more than twenty years—described the political atmosphere leading up to the 1973 vote. He writes that during this time, "militant homosexual groups continued to attack any psychiatrist or psychoanalyst who dared to present his findings as to the psychopathology [i.e., the study mental disorders from all aspects] of homosexuality before national or local meetings of psychiatrists or in public realms."[17] Elsewhere Socarides stated that the decision of the APA trustees was "the medical hoax of the century."[18]

Was this the end of the debate? Did the vast majority of "competent" psychiatrists agree with the APA's decision? In 1977 ten thousand members of the APA were polled at random, asking them their opinion on this. In an article entitled "Sick Again?" *Time* magazine summarized the results of the poll: "Of those answering, 69% said they believed 'homosexuality is usually a pathological adaptation, as opposed to a normal variation,' 18% disagreed, and 13% were uncertain. Similarly, sizable majorities said that homosexuals are generally less happy than heterosexuals (73%) and less capable of mature, loving relationships (60%). A total of 70% said that homosexuals' problems have more to do with their own inner conflicts than with stigmatization by society at large."[19]

But what about today? Has this issue been resolved in current medical opinion and research? Concerning this, Dr. Stanton L. Jones, professor of psychology at Wheaton College, states that there is a "mixed scorecard" among professionals on this. He writes: "I would not regard homosexuality to be a

---

[15] For those interested in the history leading up to the APA's 1973 removal of homosexuality from their *Diagnostic and Statistical Manual of Psychiatric Disorders*, see Ronald Bayer, *Homosexuality and American Psychiatry: The Politics of Diagnosis* (New York: Basic, 1981), 101–54; and William Dannemeyer, *Shadow in the Land* (San Francisco: Ignatius, 1989), 24–39.

[16] Bayer, 105–6.

[17] Charles W. Socarides, *Beyond Sexual Freedom* (New York: Quadrangle Books, 1977), 87. Prior to the 1973 vote, Dr. Socarides led the APA's task force studying homosexuality, which issued a report unanimously declaring homosexuality to be a disorder of psychosexual development. This report, considered to be too politically inflammatory, was shelved, only later being published as a "study group" report in 1974.

[18] Charles W. Socarides in Robert Kronemeyer, *Overcoming Homosexuality* (New York: Macmillan, 1980), 5.

[19] "Sick Again? Psychiatrists Vote on Gays," *Time* (February 20, 1978), 102.

psychopathology in the same sense as schizophrenia or phobic disorders. But neither can it be viewed as a normal 'lifestyle variation' on a par with being introverted versus extroverted."[20]

One may debate whether or not homosexuality is a pathological disorder, but it is clear that the APA's 1973 decision cannot be cited as medical consensus that homosexuality is a "normal" condition. Later in this article I will examine in some detail the assertion that homosexuality is a healthy lifestyle.

BORN GAY?

Perhaps the most dangerous myth disseminated today by the pro-homosexuality movement is that modern science has proven that homosexuality is innate and immutable. That is, homosexuals are *born* gay, much like being born left handed or with blue eyes. The inference, of course, is that if they are born that way, then homosexuality cannot be considered immoral or unnatural; the homosexual is just following his or her genes. However as Congressman William Dennemeyer put it, "if homosexuality is a perversion of what is natural, then homosexuals must look at their own conduct in an entirely different light and explain it in less satisfying terms."[21]

It is well beyond the scope of this article to summarize all the findings concerning the genesis of homosexuality. However, the scientific evidences for its origins are usually classified in terms of either biological causes (i.e., genetic/hormonal) or environmental factors (e.g., psychological causes, volitional, and so forth).

1. Biological Causes

The most recent research suggesting that homosexuality may be caused by biological factors came out in 1991 with the publication of some preliminary findings of Dr. Simon LeVay, a neuroscientist at the Salk Institute for Biological Studies in San Diego. His research consisted of studying the brains of 41 cadavers, including 19 homosexual males. He found that "a tiny area believed to control sexual activity [the hypothalamus] was less than half the size in the gay men than in the heterosexuals."[22]

This study was seized upon by many as "irrefutable evidence" that homosexuals are born gay, something the homosexual community has been proclaiming for many years. However, "instead of resolving the debate," a *Newsweek* article suggests, "the studies may well have intensified it. Some scientists profess not to be surprised at all by LeVay's finding of brain differences. 'Of course it [sexual orientation] is in the brain,' says Johns Hopkins University psychologist John Money, sometimes called the dean of American sexologists. 'The real question is, when did it get there? Was it prenatal, neonatal, during childhood, puberty? That we do not know.'"[23]

Other problems with his findings include: (1) all 19 of the homosexual men had died of AIDS, something that many researchers believe could very well account for or contribute to the differences; (2) there was no way to know the sexual history of the "heterosexual" men; (3) there is no way to determine if the smaller hypothalamuses were the *cause* or the *result* of homosexuality; and (4) Dr. LeVay, a homosexual himself, admitted that his study was not entirely a dispassionate scientific endeavor.[24]

2. Environmental Factors

There are probably just as many, if not more, psychiatrists and psychologists who believe that homosexuality arises from various environmental factors. The majority of these say that homosexuality's root causes are psychological, not biological. But these are not cited nearly as often by the media as the others—perhaps a pro-homosexual bias by the media? And they are virtually never even acknowledged by the homosexual community, because most homosexuals want to believe that they were born that way and had no choice (conscious or subliminal) in the matter.

In any case, some of the most noteworthy and respected researchers and therapists in the world deny that homosexuality is determined by biological factors. For example, therapists helping homosexuals who are

---

[20] Stanton L. Jones, "Homosexuality According to Science," in J. Isamu Yamamoto, ed., *The Crisis of Homosexuality* (Wheaton, IL: Victor, 1990), 107.

[21] Dannemeyer, 40–41.

[22] Charlene Crabb, "Are Some Men Born to Be Homosexual?," *U. S. News & World Report* (September 9, 1991).

[23] David Gelman, et al., "Born or Bred?" *Newsweek* (February 24, 1992).

[24] Simon LeVay on *The Phil Donahue Show*, "Genetically Gay: Born Gay or Become Gay?"(January 3, 1992).

unhappy with their condition can cite one case history after another showing that negative early childhood experiences are the one common factor found in almost all their patients. The vital factor here is that these people were raised in a very unloving home environment, never knowing love or acceptance from their father. According to these studies, the child's reaction to this rejection and lack of nurturing is formulated at a very early age, usually before five years old. The follow reference illustrates these findings.

William H. Masters (co-director of the Masters and Johnson Institute), Virginia E. Brown, and Robert C. Kolodny stated categorically in their 1982 work *Human Sexuality*: "The genetic theory of homosexuality has been generally discarded today."[25]

Robert Kronemeyer, in his work *Overcoming Homosexuality*, writes, "With rare exceptions, homosexuality is neither inherited nor the result of some glandular disturbance or the scrambling of genes or chromosomes. Homosexuals are made, not born 'that way.' I firmly believe that homosexuality is a learned response to early painful experiences and that it can be unlearned. For those homosexuals who are unhappy with their life and find effective therapy, it is 'curable.'"[26]

John DeCecco, professor of psychology at San Francisco State University and the editor of the 25-volume *Journal of Homosexuality*, expressed the same view in a 1989 *USA Today* article. "'The idea that people are born into one type of sexual behavior is entirely foolish,' says John DeCecco. Homosexuality, he says, is 'a behavior, not a condition,' and something that some people can and do change, just like they sometimes change other tastes and personality traits."[27]

One thing is clear: it is hardly an established scientific fact accepted by the entire medical field that homosexuality is solely or even primarily caused by biological factors. This brings us to the question just raised above: Can those who are homosexual change?

IS CHANGE IMPOSSIBLE?

The question of whether or not one should want to change his or her sexual preference will be addressed shortly. But before looking at the desirability of changing, we need to ascertain whether change is even possible. I say that this is important to investigate because a host of individuals concerned with homosexual issues deny that this is a possibility.

Those in the gay rights movement, as well as numerous researchers, psychotherapists, and so forth, decry any attempt to change the homosexual's sexual orientation or preference. Rick Notch, a homosexual man who at one time claimed to have become an ex-gay, stated on *The Geraldo Show*: "The only choice we have is to learn to accept ourselves and to find a way to live a responsible, moral life."[28] Dr. Richard Isay, a psychiatrist who heads the APA's committee on gay issues, likewise asserted: "The core orientation in a gay man cannot be changed."[29]

But even a perfunctory examination of the available testimonies and case studies shows that this simply is not true. First of all, do all of the other psychiatrists and psychologists agree with the assertion that change is not possible? By no means! In fact, most believe that change is possible. William H. Masters and Virginia E. Johnson, hardly homophobes, write in their work *Homosexuality in Perspective*: "Providing therapeutic support for the homosexually oriented man or woman who wishes to convert or revert to heterosexuality has been an integral part of the practice of psychotherapy for decades."[30]

Likewise, in the *Kinsey Institute New Report on Sex* (1990) we find the statement that "sexual orientation, whether heterosexual or homosexual, *is not readily changed* by any type of intervention" (emphasis added).[31]

---

[25] William H. Masters, Virginia E. Brown, and Robert Kolodny, *Human Sexuality* (Boston: Little, Brown, 1982), 319.

[26] Kronemeyer, 7.

[27] Kim Painter, "A Biological Theory for Sexual Preference," *USA Today* (January 1, 1989). Also see Alan P. Bell, et al., *Sexual Preference* (Bloomington, IN: Indiana University Press, 1981), 221. While not believing that biology determines sexual preference, neither do they believe that the parents somehow caused it. Instead, they believe there is a causal relationship in children having early "gender identity" problems and their becoming homosexual.

[28] Rick Notch, *The Geraldo Show* (June 11, 1991).

[29] Richard Isay, quoted on *20/20*, ABC News (April 24, 1992).

[30] William H. Masters and Virginia E. Johnson, *Homosexuality in Perspective* (Boston: Little, Brown, 1979), 333. Also, after a ten-year study of homosexuality they found that those desiring "conversion" to heterosexuality had only a 21 percent failure rate (p. 396). However, after making certain adjustments the conversion failure rate could be as high as 45 percent.

[31] Reinisch, 143.

Thus, while it is not easy, changing one's sexual orientation is nonetheless possible—which could not be the case if homosexuality was innate and immutable.

This was confirmed on a recent segment of ABC's *20/20*, which had a story dealing with Dr. Joseph Nicolosi. Nicolosi is a psychologist and psychotherapist who has been helping homosexual men convert to heterosexuality for a number of years now.[32]

I already referred above to the work of Dr. Robert Kronemeyer. If the interested reader pursues this work, he or she will find eight case histories cited—true accounts of people who sought relief from their lives of homosexual bondage (their own description of their lifestyles) and were converted to heterosexuality.[33]

Another area where we see the fruit of changed lives is in the numerous Christian ministries reaching out to homosexuals desiring help. Space limitations will not allow me to go into great detail. Those interested can find the references in the endnotes.

Are there really changed lives? There is Darlene Bogle, a woman who "struggled with lesbianism" for 17 years.[34] She was raised in an environment where she was sexually abused by different men and boys, the first at the age of three. Her parents divorced when she was only five. Her new stepfather frequently abused her, both verbally and physically. In her own words she was raised in "a home that lacked nurturing, that was void of positive role models and void of love."[35] Today, through the grace and mercy of God, she has been completely free for 15 years from her former lifestyle and is currently a counselor at Paraklete Ministries in Hayward, California.

There is Frank Worthen, a practicing homosexual for 25 years. In 1973 he turned back to Jesus Christ, who delivered him from that lifestyle. Since then he has remained free, without once falling back into his old secular behavior. Today he and his wife Anita are missionaries in the Philippines with Exodus International.[36]

There is Andrew Comiskey, a former homosexual who is now the director of Desert Stream Ministries.[37]

There is Joanne Highley, a lesbian from the ages of 13 to 23, who has now been freed from that lifestyle for the past 35 years. She has been married to the same man during those 35 years, is a mother and grandmother, and with her husband is co-director of L.I.F.E. Ministries in New York City.[38]

Are there really changed lives, people who were exclusively homosexual and became heterosexual? *Yes*. Have there not been those who have fallen back into their old lifestyles? Again, the answer is yes, which is to be expected. Just like in Alcoholics Anonymous, the road is rarely easy and involves a tremendous commitment by the individual seeking recovery and healing. Sometimes individuals stumble and never get back up again. Sometimes they stumble, get back up, and continue on in the process of recovery. And occasionally, individuals are healed instantly and never turn back again. But the fact remains that there are many former homosexuals, ex-gays, who have been transformed by the power of Jesus Christ.

A HEALTHY LIFESTYLE?

As noted above, those in the gay rights movement constantly assert that they are both normal and healthy individuals. We have already discussed the "normality" of homosexuality. The question of whether or not it is a healthy lifestyle can be addressed in two areas: promiscuity and actual sexual practices.

1. Promiscuity

If one agrees with the assertion that being promiscuous is not healthy, from either an emotional or physical standpoint, then homosexuality as typically practiced must be termed extremely unhealthy. *Homosexualties*, an official publication of The Institute for Sex Research founded by Alfred Kinsey, Alan Bell, and Martin Weinberg, reported that only ten percent of male homosexuals could be termed as "relatively monogamous"

---

[32] *20/20*, ABC News (April 24, 1992).
[33] Kronemeyer, 141–67.
[34] Darlene Bogle, "Healing from Lesbianism," in Yamamoto, 15.
[35] Ibid., 17.
[36] Bob Davies, "The Exodus Story: The Growth of Ex-gay Ministry," in Yamamoto, 47–59. Also see Kent Philpott, *The Gay Theology* (Plainfield, NJ: Logos International, 1977), 20–37.
[37] Andrew Comiskey, *Pursuing Sexual Wholeness: How Jesus Heals the Homosexual* (Lake Mary, FL: Creation House, 1989).
[38] Joanne Highley, L.I.F.E. Ministries, P.O. Box 353, New York, NY 10185.

or "relatively less promiscuous." Additional findings showed that 60 percent of male homosexuals had more than 250 lifetime sexual partners, and 28 percent of male homosexuals had more than 1,000 lifetime sexual partners. Another startling fact is that 79 percent admitted that more than half of their sexual partners were strangers.[39]

Just a few years after the publication of this report, Dr. William Foege, the director of the Centers for Disease Control, stated: "The average AIDS victim has had 60 different sexual partners in the past twelve months."[40] In contrast with this, "the average heterosexual male has—throughout his life—from five to nine sex partners."[41]

What about lesbian relationships? Are homosexual women less promiscuous than homosexual men? While less research has been done on lesbians, the data shows that they are much more monogamous than homosexual men. However, their relationships are still not very secure. Yvonne Zipter, a lesbian writing in Chicago's gay journal *Windy City Times*, in an article entitled "The Disposable Lesbian Relationship," notes that the "lasting lesbian relationship" is a "mythic entity."[42]

2. Sexual Practices

A second item that cannot be avoided in a discussion of the health aspects of homosexuality is the actual sexual practices of homosexuals. Are these healthy? Once again, the vast preponderance of medical evidence is resoundingly negative.

Many different medical sources document the physical aberrancy of homosexual sexual practices. The following information comes from an article entitled "Medical Perspective of the Homosexual Issue." It was written by Dr. Bernard J. Klamecki, a proctologist (rectal specialist) for more than 30 years.

Dr. Klamecki states in this article that when he began his medical practice in 1960, only one percent of his patients were homosexuals. By 1988 this number had grown to 25 percent of his patients, the majority being referred by a local gay free clinic. The following material comes from one who is known and respected by the homosexual community, a medical professional who has care and compassion for all his patients and who donates a good deal of his time to their service.

Unit Five

[39] Alan P. Bell and Martin S. Weinberg, *Homosexualities* (New York: Simon & Schuster, 1978), 308.
[40] Walter Isaacson, "Hunting for the Hidden Killers," *Time* (July 4, 1983), 51.
[41] Kronemeyer, 32.
[42] Yvonne Zipter, "The Disposable Lesbian Relationship," Chicago, *Windy City Times* (December 25, 1986).
[43] Bernard J. Klamecki, "Medical Perspective of the Homosexual Issue," in Yamamoto, 116–17.

Dr. Klamecki then continues, discussing the various bacterial diseases and viral diseases he regularly encounters with his homosexual patients—the most prominent being AIDS (the current figure is that 70 percent of Americans with AIDS are male homosexuals or bisexuals). In addition, he asserts that up to 86 percent of homosexual males use various drugs to enhance and increase their sexual stimulation.[44]

Is the homosexual lifestyle a healthy one? The information presented above just scratches the surface showing the pathological nature of these sexual practices. Much more could be shared (e.g., the homosexual is three times more suicidal than the heterosexual; a recent study shows the life expectancy of homosexual men and women *without AIDS* being about 33 years shorter than that of the heterosexual; and so forth),[45] but space will not permit it. I believe that any unbiased reader would have to admit that homosexuality is neither a healthy lifestyle nor a natural one.

THE CHRISTIAN'S TASK

Before closing I need to clarify that while I believe that homosexuality is anatomically aberrant, psychologically deviant, and morally bankrupt, it is also just as true that we are all sinners. The Bible states that we have *all* turned our backs on God and gone our own way. As Martin Luther once put it, we each "sin often and daily."

Except for the grace and mercy of God, each one of us would be left in our own little world of sin, alone and helpless. The good news, though, is that God has reached out to us, coming down to become one with us in our humanity, dying and rising again—that we may be free from the bondage of sin.

For anyone struggling with the bondage of homosexuality, or the bondage of any other sin, there is freedom available at the cross of Calvary. Our task as Christians is to lovingly reach out to all people with the gospel of Jesus Christ.

---

*This essay originally appeared in the Christian Research Journal:
   Joseph Gudel, "Homosexuality: Fact or Fiction," *Christian Research Journal* 15:1 (1992), 21–33.
**Reproduction rights granted by the Christian Research Journal.

---

[44] Ibid., 123, 119.
[45] Paul Cameron, William L. Playfair, and Stephen Wellum, "The Homosexual Lifespan," *Family Research Institute* (February 14, 1992).

HOMOSEXUALITY, FACT OR FICTION?
ESSAY QUESTIONS

Answer the questions below on a separate sheet of paper and be prepared to review your answers in class.

1. How is homophobia defined in *The Kinsey Institute New Report on Sex*? According to this definition, are Christians homophobes? Why or why not?

2. It is often cited that 10 percent of the population in the United States is homosexual; from where does this statistic come?

3. Is the 10 percent figure accurate? Why or why not?

4. What other studies have been done regarding the percentage of homosexuals in our society? What were their findings?

5. Does the APA's 1973 decision to remove homosexuality from its list of disorders substantiate the claim that homosexuality is normal? Why or why not?

6. What is the best evidence for homosexuality being biological? What are the main problems with this evidence?

7. Is there any evidence that would indicate an environmental cause for homosexuality?

8. Is it possible for homosexuals to revert or convert to heterosexuality? Cite at least one example.

9. For what two reasons is homosexuality not a healthy lifestyle?

10. What is the Christian task in relation to homosexuals?

Unit Five

THAT WHICH IS UNNATURAL
BY JOSEPH P. GUDEL

THE GAY RIGHTS MOVEMENT'S POLITICAL AGENDA

In Part One of this series I went into some detail showing that even from a secular perspective the unbiased reader is forced to admit that homosexuality is neither a healthy nor a natural lifestyle. However, over the past 20 years or so there has been a growing gay rights movement within America. This movement has been militantly demanding not just the homosexuals' right to do whatever they wish to do behind closed doors, but, more importantly, that society fully accept their lifestyle as both healthy and normal, even demanding special rights and legislation as an "oppressed minority."

Concerning the demands of the gay rights movement, gay spokesperson Jeff Levi in a 1987 speech to the National Press Club in Washington stated: "We are no longer seeking just a right to privacy and a protection from wrong. We also have a right—as heterosexual Americans already have—to see government and society affirm our lives."[1]

As far back as 1975, in an article entitled "Gays on the March," *Time* magazine quotes gay activist Barbara Gittings, "What the homosexual wants, and here he is neither willing to compromise nor morally required to compromise—is acceptance of homosexuality as a way of life fully on a par with heterosexuality."[2] In response to this, *Time* wisely reflected: "It is one thing to remove legal discrimination against homosexuals. It is another to mandate approval… It is this goal of full acceptance, *which no known society past or present has granted to homosexuals*, that makes many Americans apprehensive" (emphasis added).[3]

In view of their stated goals, it is extremely significant that today there is legislation pending in the United States Congress which proposes to do just what the gay rights movement has demanded: fully legitimize homosexuality as an acceptable and sanctioned alternative lifestyle. The Senate version, sponsored by Senator Edward Kennedy, is bill S. B. 574. The House version, sponsored by Representative Barney Frank (an openly avowed homosexual), is measure H. R. 1430. [*Editor's Note: Neither of these bills passed.*]

For most Americans it is shocking simply to have a bill like this being considered in the halls of Congress.[4] What is even more amazing is that already it has approximately 140 congressional sponsors, as well as the full support of President Bill Clinton.[5]

If passed, this bill would make it illegal for any organization, including Christian businesses and churches, to refuse employment to practicing homosexuals. It would legalize same-sex "marriages," something not now recognized in any U.S. jurisdiction. [*Editor's Note: As of 2009, Massachusetts, Connecticut, Iowa, Vermont, and New Hampshire have legalized same-sex marriage, while the issue is actively being debated in California and Maine. In addition, New York, California, and Washington D.C. recognize same-sex marriages, although they are not currently performed in those states.*] Homosexual "couples" would have the right to adopt children. And every school system would have to include homosexuality as a positive alternative lifestyle in any sex education course offered.

Concerning the radical gay rights agenda now being advanced, Dr. John F. Harvey—a nationally known professor of moral theology at De Sales School of Theology and someone actively involved in counseling homosexual persons for over thirty years—writes: Homosexual activists… are not requesting merely the right to live their lifestyle in private, to be left alone; to use their own words, they want to convince all elements of society—even children—that "gay is as acceptable as straight"… I think that gay-rights legislation would harm children at an impressionable, malleable, and gullible age. There is plenty of evidence for the position that homosexual propaganda can sway young people into homosexual activity and, perhaps, permanent orientation in that direction.[6]

---

[1] Jeff Levi, in William Dannemeyer, *Shadow in the Land* (San Francisco: Ignatius, 1989), 86.

[2] "Gays on the March," *Time* (September 8, 1975), 43.

[3] Ibid.

[4] In a 1991 Gallup Poll, 61% of Americans believed that "tolerance of the gay lifestyle has been bad for society." *Nightline* (September 8, 1992).

[5] Gregory Bray, "Where Are Dems on Family Values?" Augusta, GA, *The Augusta Chronicle*, reprinted in the *Oshkosh Northwestern* (August 22, 1992).

[6] John F. Harvey, *The Homosexual Person* (San Francisco: Ignatius, 1987), 114–15.

As evidence that influencing children at a very early age is part of the gay rights agenda one need look no further than New York City's public school curriculum. Included in the curriculum materials are four pro-homosexual books aimed at very young children. One, *Heather Has Two Mommies*, is a children's book about a lesbian couple having a child through artificial insemination. Another book, *Daddy's Roommate*, describes a boy with divorced parents who visits his father and his father's new male roommate (obviously his lover). In a third book, *Gloria Goes to Gay Pride*, part of the text reads: "Some women love women, some men love men, some women and men love each other. That's why we march in the parade, so everyone can have a choice."[7]

The rationale for these books is found on page 145 of the city's "Children of the Rainbow" first-grade curriculum which states that teachers must "be aware of varied family structures, including . . . gay or lesbian parents," and "children must be taught to acknowledge the positive aspects of each type of household."[8]

In an article describing this, John Leo writes in *U.S. News and World Report,* "A line is being crossed here; in fact, a brand new ethic is descending upon the city's public school system. The traditional civic virtue of tolerance (if gays want to live together, it's their own business) has been replaced with a new ethic requiring approval and endorsement (if gays want to live together, we must 'acknowledge the positive aspects' of their way of life)."[9]

It is clear that the gay community wants much more than simply the right to privacy. But what about their civil rights? Are new laws really essential to protect those in the gay community? In answer to this Roger J. Magnuson, a nationally renowned trial lawyer, states: "Homosexuals have all of the same rights heterosexuals do. They are protected by the Bill of Rights, by federal and state statutes, and by common-law decisions. They have the same status before the law as do other citizens... The issue is not whether rights have been infringed. The issue is whether new rights, not previously recognized, should be created."[10]

There is no question about the homosexual's right to practice whatever deviations he or she wants to in the privacy of his or her own home. There are many questions, however, about their attempt to codify their behavior as acceptable and good, to force their lifestyle on the rest of society, and to influence those too young to understand the moral implications of this issue.

It is simply an emotional ploy to attempt to portray this issue as involving civil rights for an oppressed minority. No one would ever say it is a sin to be black or Hispanic, just as no one would say it is a sin to be female or to be physically handicapped. But God's Word does say it is a sin to engage in homosexual behavior, as we shall see below.

HOMOSEXUALITY AND THE CHURCH

Very few churches today come right out and affirm homosexuality as official church teaching. There are a few, though, which do. Foremost among these is the Metropolitan Community Church, founded by Troy Perry in 1968, largely for practicing homosexuals.

The only mainline denomination that has actually called for affirming and fully accepting homosexuals is the United Church of Christ (UCC). As far back as 1975 they voted to end any "discrimination" based on sexual preference and left it to individual UCC congregations to decide for themselves what they believed on this matter. In 1983 the UCC General Synod passed a resolution stating that "a person's sexual orientation is not a moral issue."[11] Finally, in 1991 the UCC General Synod approved the call for its congregations to "boldly affirm, celebrate, and embrace the gifts for ministry of lesbians, gays, and bisexual persons."[12]

Many other denominations are close to this view. Some, such as the Episcopal Church, have openly practicing homosexual clergy, with the full knowledge of their church's governing bodies. Others, such as the United Methodist Church (UMC), have officially rejected homosexual practice as incompatible with the Christian faith. However, at least 44 UMC congregations "have formally opened their doors to homosexuals" and called on their bishops to bless "same-sex union ceremonies."[13] Similarly, the Evangelical

---

[7] *Nightline.*
[8] John Leo, "Heather Has a Message," *U.S. News & World Report* (August 17 1992).
[9] Ibid.
[10] Roger J. Magnuson, *Are Gay Rights Right?* updated edition (Portland: Multnomah, 1990), 78.
[11] "UCC Admits Gay Church," *The Christian Century* (May 30, 1990).
[12] "Bar Homosexual Clergy, Conservative Disciples Say," *Religious News Service,* in *The Christian News* (Sept. 30, 1991).
[13] "UMC and Gay Unions," *The Christian Century* (June 27 1990).

Lutheran Church in America's 1991 study guide on sexuality affirms that "no absolutistic judgments can be drawn" concerning homosexuality.[14] However, the guide then goes on to promote "committed" homosexual relationships.[15] A new gay magazine which describes itself as a "journal for gay and lesbian Christians" has a 10-page listing of "Christian" churches and organizations that "welcome gays and lesbians into full membership and participation."[16]

Very few Christian denominations today have remained faithful to the Bible's clear affirmation that homosexuality is a sin. Among these would be the Roman Catholic Church, the Southern Baptist Convention, the Lutheran Church-Missouri Synod, the Wisconsin Evangelical Lutheran Synod, and the Greek Orthodox Church.

THE BIBLE AND HOMOSEXUALITY

The Authority of the Scripture

It is extremely revealing to note that almost every pro-gay group within the church shares one thing in common: *they reject the Bible as being fully the Word of God*. Of the above mentioned denominations which have accepted homosexuality or are sympathetic to it, none of them believe that we have God's inerrant Word in the Old and New Testaments. Likewise, the many pro-homosexual books that have come out almost all reject—or even ridicule—the church's historic stance on the inspiration and authority of Scripture.

Three different lines of attack on Scripture are found in the various pro-homosexual literature. The first is simply to ignore the biblical writers on the grounds that they were men who oftentimes made mistakes, and thus to reject what Scripture says as being morally authoritative. Thus John Barton states that "the Bible is not a code at all; it is a big baggy compendium of a book, full of variety and inconsistency, sometimes mistaken on matters of fact and theology alike."[17] And elsewhere, in John Boswell's widely cited work, we find, "In considering the supposed influence of certain biblical passages... one must first relinquish the concept of a single book containing a uniform corpus of writings accepted as morally authoritative."[18]

A second attack relates to the first—that is, the biblical writers were ignorant about homosexuality. They did not know all that we do today, it is argued, and so we must judge and interpret the Bible with our modern understanding of biology, psychology, sociology, and so forth. "With the quantum leaps that have been achieved in biology, psychology, and sociology, minds in the twentieth and twenty-first centuries must subject traditional religious arguments about nature to more thorough and critical analyses."[19]

It is not within the purview of this article to give a detailed defense of the inspiration and reliability of the Bible.[20] However, the simple response to these attacks is that both Judaism and Christianity have always held to the full authority of Scripture, as did Jesus Himself. In speaking of the Old Testament, for example, our Lord succinctly declared, "Scripture cannot be broken" (John 10:35). Parts of Scripture cannot be accepted while other parts are rejected. And in speaking of the guidance His apostles would receive, including guidance on their future writings (i.e., the New Testament), Jesus told them: "But the Helper, the Holy Spirit, whom the Father will send in My name, He will teach you all things, and bring to your remembrance all things that I said to you" (John 14:26; cf. 2 Tim. 3:16).

It is ludicrous to believe that the Creator of the universe, in guiding the biblical authors, was ignorant concerning the things we now know about homosexuality through modern biology, psychology, sociology, and so forth. To deny scriptural statements about homosexuality on these grounds is to completely deny God's superintendence in the authorship of Scripture.

---

[14] Evangelical Lutheran Church in America, *Human Sexuality and the Christian Faith* (Minneapolis: ELCA, 1991), 44.

[15] Ibid., 41–46.

[16] *Christus Omnibus*, premier issue, front cover and 18.

[17] John Barton, "The Place of the Bible in Moral Debate," *Theology* 88 (May 1985), 206.

[18] John Boswell, *Christianity, Social Tolerance, and Homosexuality* (Chicago: University of Chicago Press, 1980), 92.

[19] Jeannine Gramick, "What Is Natural?" in Robert Nugent and Jeannine Gramick, eds., *Building Bridges* (Mystic, CT: Twenty-Third Publications, 1992), 46. Also see Letha Scanzoni and Virginia Ramey Mollenkott, *Is the Homosexual My Neighbor?* (New York: Harper & Row, 1978), 71.

[20] See Norman L. Geisler and William E. Nix, *A General Introduction to the Bible* (Chicago: Moody, 1968).

A third type of attack is to state that it really does not matter what heterosexuals think the Bible says about homosexuality, because homosexuals must interpret Scripture in view of their own experiences. Hence, in the book *Building Bridges* we find the statement that "the Scriptures contain some insights that can be made known to the Christian community only through the testimony of lesbian and gay people." Thus homosexuals must "interpret the Scriptures in the light of their own experiences."[21]

The problem with this is that a person could justify *any* type of behavior by saying that Scriptures pertaining to a particular behavior can only be understood by those who engage in such behavior (e.g., incest, adultery, fornication, and even bestiality). Those who believe this should remember the words of our Lord, "Therefore take heed that the light which is in you is not darkness" (Luke 11:35).

Human Sexuality

Genesis 1–2

For those who believe that statements of the Bible are normative for our daily lives, the most important question to consider regarding homosexuality is: What was God's *purpose* in creating human sexuality? The answer to this question is more important than any other area of discussion.

From the very beginning of His revelation to humankind, God has revealed His order of creation, especially as it relates to sexuality. In Genesis 1 we are told that one purpose in creating the two sexes was *procreative*—through the sexual union of male and female we could reproduce the race: "Male and female He created them. Then God blessed them, and God said to them, Be fruitful and multiply; fill the earth and subdue it" (Gen. 1:27b–28).

More detail is provided in Genesis 2, however, where we are told that in addition to *procreation*, there is a *unitive* function of sexuality that has to do with fulfilling our need for companionship: "And the Lord God said, 'It is not good that man should be alone; I will make him a helper comparable to him'" (Gen. 2:18). Then, after God created Eve and presented her to Adam, Adam rejoiced in his God-given companion. The chapter concludes: "Therefore a man shall leave his father and mother and be joined to his wife, and they shall become one flesh" (Gen. 2:24–25).

In this second chapter several items emerge. First, man has need for companionship: "It is not good that man should be alone" (Gen. 2:18); second, God makes provision to meet this need: the creation of woman (2:19–23). Concerning this, Samuel Dresner, Visiting Professor at Jewish Theological Seminary, states: "Woman is formed and becomes his partner. In her, man finds completion."[22] And third, God ordains the institution of marriage. We are told that the man would (1) "leave his father and mother," (2) "cleave to his wife," and (3) "they shall become one flesh." Thus we find that heterosexuality is proclaimed to be God's natural order of creation.

In the New Testament, whenever the subject of sexuality comes up, the heterosexual norm of marriage is always upheld. For example, Jesus, in answer to a question, quoted Genesis 1 and 2: "Have you not read, that He who made them at the beginning 'made them male and female,' and said, 'For this reason a man shall leave his father and mother and be joined to his wife, and the two shall become one flesh'? So then, they are no longer two but one flesh. Therefore what God has joined together, let not man separate" (Matt. 19:4–6).

In addition, the apostle Paul reaffirms the norm of heterosexuality in several of his letters, also quoting the Genesis passages (e.g., Eph. 5:25–33; cf. 1 Cor. 7:2–3, 10–16; 1 Tim. 3:2, 12). And while some protest that we cannot take Genesis 1 and 2 as modern scientific treatises,[23] these chapters nonetheless teach us spiritual truths concerning God's intended order for His creation.

It is *only* in the heterosexual union of marriage that we find the fulfillment of God's intended order, both procreative *and* unitive. However, pro-homosexual writers argue that while homosexual activity in and of itself cannot be procreative it can still fulfill the unitive role of Genesis 2. In response to this Harvey writes:

21 Jeanine Gramick, "Lesbian/Gay Theology and Spirituality," *Building Bridges*, 190–91.

22 Samuel H. Dresner, "Homosexuality and the Order of Creation," *Judaism* 40: 3 (Summer 1991), 309; also see Richard F. Lovelace, *Homosexuality and the Church* (Old Tappan, NJ: Fleming H. Revell, 1978), 102 ff.

23 Ralph Blair, *Homosexualities* (New York: Ralph Blair, 1991), 13.

One does not need a Ph.D. to realize that homosexuality is anatomically aberrant; that is, there is a created biological order intended in our sexuality. As an editorialist at Harvard's Peninsula journal writes, "How can (homosexual) people be happy when they're persistently deceiving themselves, believing that it is just as natural for sperm to swim into feces as it is to swim into eggs?"[25] "The true religious goal of human sexuality can be seen, not as *satisfaction*, but as *completeness*."[26]

This fulfillment is unattainable in homosexuality. Now that we have considered God's positive purpose in creating human sexuality, we are ready to look at biblical texts which explicitly address homosexuality. Space precludes a detailed response to pro-homosexual interpretations of these passages. The interested reader can check the resources listed in the endnotes for further reading.

Leviticus 18 and 20

"You shall not lie with a male as with a woman. It is an abomination" (Lev. 18:22).

"If a man lies with a male as he lies with a woman, both of them have committed an abomination. They shall surely be put to death" (Lev. 20:13).

Although these prohibitions explicitly condemn homosexuality as an abomination before God, we are told that they are not relevant today. Why? First, the pro-homosexual interpretation is that since these condemnations are contained in the "Holiness Code" of Israel, they were only applicable to ancient Israelites, to keep them separate from the pagan practices of their neighboring tribes.[27]

Second, parts of this code are not kept today. Letha Scanzoni and Virginia Ramey Mollenkott assert that "consistency and fairness would seem to dictate that if the Israelite Holiness Code is to be invoked against twentieth-century homosexuals, it should likewise be invoked against such common practices as eating rare steak, wearing mixed fabrics, and having marital intercourse during the menstrual period."[28]

Much effort need not be expended answering these objections. First, God did not condemn certain behavior for the Israelites only because Israel was to be kept separate from Canaanite practice. Otherwise, if the Canaanites did not practice child sacrifice and bestiality, would these then have been all right for the Israelites? Of course not! Having sexual relations with an animal and killing one's child are inherently wrong and evil, even when they are not related to pagan worship; they are abominations before God. And yet, these specific prohibitions also are listed in this passage, both immediately before and after the condemnation of homosexuality (Lev. 18:21–23).

Other prohibitions listed in Leviticus include incest and adultery (Lev. 18:6ff; 20:10). Were these too only condemned because of the Canaanites? To argue in this fashion is dishonest and denies that there are eternal moral absolutes.

What of the fact that other parts of the Holiness Code in Leviticus are not kept today? Again, the answer is simple. The Holiness Code contained different types of commands. Some were related to dietary regulations or to ceremonial cleanliness, and these have been done away with in the New Testament (Col. 2:16–17; Rom. 14:1–3). Others, though, were moral codes, and as such are timeless. Thus incest, child sacrifice, homosexuality, bestiality, adultery, and the like, are still abominations before God.

---

[24] Harvey, 101.

[25] R. Wasinger, "If You're Gonna Call Me Names," *Peninsula* 3:2 (October/November 1991), 25.

[26] R. T. Barnhouse, *Homosexuality: A Symbolic Confusion* (New York: Seabury Press, 1977), in Natalie Shainess, "Homosexuality — Today," *Judaism* 32: 4 (Fall 1983), 414.

[27] Boswell, 100–106.

[28] Scanzoni and Mollenkott, 60–61.

Romans 1:18–27

"For this reason God gave them over to degrading passions; for their women exchanged the natural function for that which is unnatural, and in the same way also the men abandoned the natural function of the woman and burned in their desire toward one another, men with men committing indecent acts and receiving in their own persons the due penalty of their error" (Rom. 1:26–27).

If there were no other passage than this which condemns homosexuality, those engaged in this lifestyle would still be, in Paul's own words, "without excuse" (Rom. 1:20). Paul's intent in Romans 1–3 is to show that all have sinned, Jew and Gentile alike, and turned from God. It is not an accident that the apostle begins his argument with a reference to the Creator and His creation (1:16–20). His Jewish/Christian audience would immediately have connected this with Genesis 1–2, which, as we have seen, tells us not only about God's created order, but also about the complementary design of male and female within that order.

In his catalogue of sins (Rom. 1:18–32) Paul lists homosexuality and lesbianism first after idolatry not because they are the most serious sins, but because they are warning signs that a violation of reason and nature has occurred. Men have inverted God's order by worshipping the creature rather than the Creator, and as a signal of this error, like the blinking red light on the dashboard of a car which is functioning improperly, God has given them up to "dishonorable desires" in the inversion of their sexual roles.[29]

Two main arguments are raised against the historic understanding of this passage. The first is that Paul was not referring to true homosexuality here because he stated that they exchanged "the natural function for that which is unnatural." It is argued that for those with a true homosexual orientation, that is their "natural" sexual expression. Hence he could only mean heterosexuals who were leaving their heterosexual relations for what was against their natures.[30]

This argument involves an amazing anachronism. That is, those saying this are attempting to place a very recent twentieth century understanding of homosexuality back into the first century mindset of Paul. People in the first century did not think in terms of "sexual orientation." It is inconceivable for Paul to have even attempted to make a psychological differentiation such as this. Concerning this, Richard Hays writes: "The idea that some individuals have an inherent disposition towards same-sex erotic attraction and are therefore constitutionally 'gay' is a modern idea of which there is no trace either in the NT or in any other Jewish or Christian writings in the ancient world."[31]

The second attempt to refute Paul's clear condemnation of homosexuality argues that his words "unnatural" or "against nature" do not refer to a certain created order, but rather use "nature" in the sense of "current convention" or "current custom."[32] While "nature" is sometimes used in this fashion (e.g., 1 Cor. 11:14), the context of Paul's argument in Romans 1 clearly is that of creation and the natural order established by the Creator Himself (Rom. 1:20, 25). Thus Paul is asserting that homosexuality is a gross violation of God's natural design for His creation. In addition, it should be noted that the phrase "against nature" was used in connection with homosexual intercourse by both Philo and Josephus, contemporaries of Paul.[33]

1 Corinthians:9 and 1 Timothy 1:10

"Do you not know that the wicked will not inherit the kingdom of God? Do not be deceived: Neither the sexually immoral nor idolaters nor adulterers nor male prostitutes nor homosexual offenders… " (1 Cor. 6:9, NIV).

In both 1 Corinthians 6:9 and 1 Timothy 1:10 the apostle Paul states that those guilty of sexual immorality will not inherit the kingdom of God. At the time Paul wrote his letters there was no word in classical, biblical, or patristic Greek which corresponded with our English term "homosexual." Instead, homosexual behavior *was described* (e.g., Rom. 1:26–27). The words Paul uses here—*malakoi* ("male

---

[29] Lovelace, 92.

[30] Boswell, 109ff.

[31] Richard B. Hays, "Relations Natural and Unnatural: A Response to John Boswell's Exegesis of Romans l," *The Journal of Religious Ethics* 14:1 (Spring 1986), 200; also see David F. Wright, "Homosexuality: The Relevance of the Bible," *Evangelical Quarterly* 61:4 (1989), 291–300.

[32] Boswell, 110ff.

[33] Philo, *Spec. Leg.* 3.39; Josephus, *Against Apion*, 2.273.

prostitute") and *arsenokoitai* ("homosexual offenders")—have been translated in different ways. Because of this those condoning homosexuality have tried to lessen the impact of these verses, saying that all Paul was condemning was either homosexual prostitution or pederasty (i.e., men having sexual relations with boys).[34]

Virtually every Greek lexicon, however, including all of the standard English ones, has understood these words (especially *arsenokoitai*) to be referring to homosexuality.[35] Arndt and Gingrich's lexicon says *malakoi* refers to persons who are "soft, effeminate, especially of catamites, men and boys who allow themselves to be misused homosexually."[36] Likewise, *arsenokoites* means "a male homosexual, pederast, sodomite."[37]

We also find these terms in classical Greek literature (e.g., Lucian and Aristotle) "sometimes applied to obviously gay persons."[38] As well, if Paul were only condemning certain types of homosexuality he would certainly have specified this. Instead, he used a term directly based on the Greek Septuagint translation of the prohibitions against homosexuality in Leviticus:

> *meta arsenos ou koimethese koiten*
> *gynaikos* (Lev. 18:22)
> *koimethe meta arsenos koiten*
> *gynaikos* (Lev. 20:13)[39]

Paul, a rabbi thoroughly trained in the Torah, was certainly mindful of these Levitical condemnations and the Septuagint translation of them when he chose his wording in 1 Corinthians and 1 Timothy.

Law and Gospel

Is homosexuality natural and healthy, as the gay rights movement wants us to believe? The answer from Scripture is no, and as Christians we must not be involved in homosexuality nor be among those who, as Paul warns, "approve of those" who are engaged in it (Rom. 1:32). The Roman Catholic church is correct in stating that homosexuality is "an intrinsic moral evil."[40]

At the same time, though, we must reach out to all people with the love of Jesus Christ and His gospel, which alone has the power to change lives. And we must speak out against hatred and violence directed toward any group, remembering that we are all sinners, worthy only of God's judgment. We all have sin in our lives, and we are all tempted in different ways (whether it be toward homosexuality, adultery, incest, greed, violence, pridefulness, or whatever else).

Paul used the Law to show us, his readers, our sin and the fearful judgment awaiting us. But then, to those who truly desired to follow after God, he announced the good news of the Gospel: "For the wages of sin is death, but the gift of God is eternal life, through Jesus Christ our Lord" (Rom. 6:23).

For all who accept this gift, including homosexuals, there is reconciliation to God, regeneration as His children, and "grace to help in time of need" (Heb. 4:16).

---

*This essay originally appeared in the *Christian Research Journal*:
   Joseph Gudel, "That Which is Unnatural: Homosexuality in Society, the Church, and Scripture," *Christian Research Journal* 15:3 (1993), pp. 9–15.
**Reproduction rights granted by the *Christian Research Journal*.

---

[34] Boswell, 106–7.

[35] Ibid., 341–42.

[36] Walter Bauer, *A Greek-English Lexicon of the New Testament and Other Early Christian Literature*, ed. William F. Arndt, trans. F. Wilbur Gingrich (Chicago: University of Chicago Press, 1957), 489.

[37] Ibid., 109.

[38] P. Michael Ukleja, "Homosexuality in the New Testament," *Bibliotheca Sacra* 140: 560 (October-December 1983), 351.

[39] Wright, 297ff.

[40] Joseph Ratzinger, *On the Pastoral Care of Homosexual Persons* (Boston: Daughters of St. Paul, 1986), 2.

THAT WHICH IS UNNATURAL
ESSAY QUESTIONS

Answer the questions below on a separate sheet of paper and be prepared to review your answers in class.

1. Of what are homosexual activists trying to convince society?

2. What types of legislation are homosexual activists trying to pass?

3. How is the homosexual agenda being promoted in public schools?

4. Are new laws needed to protect homosexuals?

5. Point out three lines of attack being used by a number of Christian denominations to circumvent God's Word regarding homosexuality. What are some of the problems with these lines of attack?

6. What was God's purpose in creating human sexuality?

7. Are the prohibitions against homosexuality in Leviticus still relevant today?

8. What two arguments are raised against the historic understanding of Romans 1:18–27? How might the historic reading be defended?

9. How should we translate the Greek words *malakoi* and *arsenokoitai*? Why?

10. How should the Church respond to homosexuality and homosexuals?

Unit Five

WORLDVIEW PAPER
WRITING ASSIGNMENT

REQUIREMENTS

Write a paper comparing the most fundamental elements of the six worldviews presented in this course. These elements include theology, philosophy, ethics, and biology. You should also explain how each of these elements logically interacts with the others (e.g. since Secular Humanists are atheists, they explain the origin of life by methods that exclude God—some form of evolution).

This paper should be 4–6 pages in length, double-spaced, Times New Roman 12 point font with 1 inch margins. You must use at least 3 sources (one source can be your textbook), and all citations must be documented with footnotes. The suggested outline for your paper is below:

1. **INTRODUCTION** (25 points possible)
   - Define the term "worldview"
      1. In your own words
      2. Cite an expert
      3. Use an analogy (e.g. triangle, pyramid, bundle of sticks, tree, etc.)
      4. Do not merely list the disciplines
   - Practically explain how a person's worldview influences the way he or she lives (e.g. Christians pray because their worldview includes a belief in a personal God)

2. **CHRISTIAN WORLDVIEW** (25 points possible)
   - Overview
   - Theology, philosophy, ethics, and biology

3. **ISLAMIC WORLDVIEW** (25 points possible)
   - Overview
   - Theology, philosophy, ethics, and biology

4. **SECULAR HUMANIST WORLDVIEW** (25 points possible)
   - Overview
   - Theology, philosophy, ethics, and biology

5. **MARXIST-LENINIST WORLDVIEW** (25 points possible)
   - Overview
   - Theology, philosophy, ethics, and biology

6. **COSMIC HUMANIST WORLDVIEW** (25 points possible)
   - Overview
   - Theology, philosophy, ethics, and biology

7. **POSTMODERN WORLDVIEW** (25 points possible)
   - Overview
   - Theology, philosophy, ethics, and biology

8. **CONCLUSION** (25 points possible)
   - Compare, contrast, and critique the above worldviews

WORLDVIEW   TRAINING

STUDENT MANUAL

UNDERSTANDING THE TIMES

Unit Six

Topics:
Community
Marriage and Family
Radical Feminism
Sociology

A Summit Ministries Curriculum

180-Day Syllabus

DAY	IN CLASS	HOMEWORK	
1	Watch "Sociology" video		
2	Read UTT Textbook 'Sociology 6.1'	Read UTT Textbook 'Sociology 6.2'	
3	Review UTT Textbook 'Sociology 6.1–6.2' questions	Read UTT Textbook 'Sociology 6.3'	
4	Read UTT Textbook 'Sociology 6.4'		
5	Review UTT Textbook 'Sociology 6.3–6.4' questions	Read UTT Textbook 'Sociology 6.5'	
6	Read UTT Textbook 'Sociology 6.6'	Assign Dear Doug Letter	
7	Review UTT Textbook 'Sociology 6.5–6.6' questions	Read *Doing Life Together* essay	
8	Review *Doing Life Together* essay questions		
9	Watch "Love, Sex, and Marriage" video P1		
10	Watch "Love, Sex, and Marriage" video P2		
11	Review "Love, Sex, and Marriage" video questions		
12	Read *Domestic Tranquility* essay P1		
13	Read *Domestic Tranquility* essay P2		
14	Review *Domestic Tranquility* essay questions	Dear Doug Letter assignment Due	
15	Take Unit Six Test		

90-Day Syllabus

DAY	IN CLASS	HOMEWORK	
1	Watch "Sociology" video	Read UTT Textbook 'Sociology 6.1–6.2'	
2	Review UTT Textbook 'Sociology 6.1–6.2' questions	Read UTT Textbook 'Sociology 6.3–6.4'	
3	Review UTT Textbook 'Sociology 6.3–6.4' questions	Read UTT Textbook 'Sociology 6.5–6.6'	
4	Review UTT Textbook 'Sociology 6.5–6.6' questions		
5	Watch "Love, Sex, and Marriage" video P1		
6	Watch "Love, Sex, and Marriage" video P2		
7	Review "Love, Sex, and Marriage" video questions		
8	Take Unit Six Test		

Unit Six

UNDERSTANDING THE TIMES
SOCIOLOGY QUESTIONS

Answer the questions below on a separate sheet of paper and be prepared to review your answers in class. Reflection Questions will not be found in the text. These are merely designed to help you start thinking about issues from a worldview perspective.

SOCIOLOGY 6.1

1. According to the Bible, what are the three basic institutions of society? Why do sociologists differ when describing the origin of these institutions and their relationship to the individual?

2. According to Christianity, what is the source of humanity's problems?

3. What scriptural references support the institutions of family, church, and state?

4. Reflection Question: What impact did the Fall have on human relationships? How does this relate to the area of sociology?

5. Reflection Question: What does it mean to be created in the image of God and how was this image marred?

SOCIOLOGY 6.2

6. How do some Islamic writings characterize women?

7. What is the Islamic view of polygamy? Is polygamy the norm?

8. How was Muhammad's disregard for the restriction on polygamy resolved?

9. What does the Bible have to say about polygamy?

10. How do Muslims view the institution of the state? What two forms of government do Muslims promote?

SOCIOLOGY 6.3

11. How is sociology different from psychology? What problem do both secular psychologists and sociologists face?

12. What are some adjectives used by Secular Humanists to describe traditional marriage?

13. What must Secular Humanists use to reshape people's thinking socially and economically?

14. How does the new social order propose to handle childrearing?

15. Reflection Question: How might state-sponsored childrearing change society?

Unit Six

SOCIOLOGY 6.4

16. How does Marxism's reliance on evolution as a basis for its social theory influence its perception of the mechanisms of society?

17. According to Karl Marx, what determines a person's consciousness?

18. How do Marxists view religion in relation to the evolution of society?

19. Once the proletariat has ushered in a socialistic system, what role does the Marxist sociologist envision education taking?

20. How will children be cared for according to Marxist sociology?

SOCIOLOGY 6.5

21. What is the ultimate goal of Cosmic Humanist psychology and sociology?
to achieve higher consciousness

22. What is the Cosmic Humanist view of traditional marriage and family?
outdated + unenlightened institutions

23. What does Shakti Gawain say about divorce in the New Age society?

24. What does Kevin Ryerson say about sexuality in the New Age society?

25. How do Cosmic Humanists view education?

SOCIOLOGY 6.6

26. According to Michel Foucault, why is the social order important?

27. What do Postmodernists believe about the family, sexuality, traditional values, and the church? How is the Postmodernist view of sociology best defined?

28. According to Walter Truett Anderson, what role does education play within society? How do Postmodernists plan to equalize the playing field?

29. How are Postmodernists seeking to restructure society?

30. Why is Dada art a good representation of the Postmodern mood? What words best describe Postmodern art and music?

Objects on this page are no smaller than they appear.

If you can read this, you are too close to your workbook.

Doing Life Together

by Charles Moore

Fellowship is life, and lack of fellowship is death;
fellowship is heaven, and lack of fellowship is hell;
and the deeds that ye do upon the earth
it is for fellowship's sake that ye do them.
William Morris

If I've read the New Testament right, as followers of Christ, we are members of Christ's body (1 Cor. 12:14–21), and hence, by definition, we belong to each other. We cannot intentionally follow Christ solo. Interdependence, not independence, is God's pattern. In other words, there is no such thing as a lone ranger Christian. When we fail to connect with each other we are failing to connect with Jesus.

But what does it mean to *connect* with one another? Sadly, superficiality is a disease of our time. Shallow friendships and fragile relationships mark not only our society but also the church. Even our language betrays such superficiality. Consider how we use the word "fellowship" in Christian gatherings. In Acts 2:42 we read that the early Christians "devoted themselves to the fellowship." They did not occasionally have fellowship (verb). They *were* the fellowship (noun); marked by a shared life together. They were devoted *to each other*, and so they were being woven together in mutual care. It involved a common, daily, material life of unity and sharing. The early church experienced daily life *together* in Christ, and this was how they were constituted as a fellowship.

Biblically speaking, therefore, fellowship is far more than spilling coffee on one another on Sunday morning. It extends far beyond "getting together" and experiencing a rush of relational warm fuzzies during hyped-up religious happenings. Sadly, very few of us experience our life together as did the early Christians. They did not consider what they had as their own. Theirs was a common, daily, material life of unity and sharing. We, however, assemble and associate and meet at regular intervals, but our lives and pocket books are still very much our own. Our *lives* really don't intersect. We share commonly very little.

Re-Membering the Body

From what I have read and heard, right after the collapse of the Twin Towers, one might inadvertently come across a human body part, like a finger or a toe. The thought of dismemberment both shocks and repulses us. It not only is incongruous, but a severed body part is not quite human; removed from the body it is horrendously out of place.

Now if we would but step back and actually see how fractured and dismembered our country has become, how severed and alienated, and how conflicted and fearful we are of each other, if we could but see how frightfully alone we have become, we might become more repulsed and begin to see what it is that ails us both individually and socially. We might also discover anew the plan and purpose of God revealed in Christ's prayer for unity: "That they may be one, Father, as you and I are one… " (John 17:21ff).

Herein lies the gift and witness of Christ's body: the church on earth. God's people can, by their manner of life together, be the very thing the world cannot achieve on its own steam. But it is important to grasp that following Jesus is nothing if it is not a way, a life, a living, and a living together. It's all about *togetherness*. Consider, for example, the reciprocal pronoun "one another" (*allelon*) in the New Testament. This one word alone highlights the significance of doing life together:

- Outdo one another in showing honor (Rom. 12:10)
- Live in harmony with one another (Rom. 12:16)
- Admonish one another (Rom. 15:14)
- Greet one another with a holy kiss (Rom. 16:16)
- Wait for one another (1 Cor. 11:33)
- Have the same care for one another (1 Cor. 12:25)
- Be servants of one another (Gal. 5:13)
- Bear one another's burdens (Gal. 6:2)
- Comfort one another (1 Thess. 5:11)
- Build one another up (1 Thess. 5:11)
- Be at peace with one another (1 Thess. 5:13)
- Do good to one another (1 Thess. 5:15)
- Put up with one another in love (Eph. 4:2)
- Be kind and compassionate to one another (Eph. 4:32)
- Submit to one another (Eph. 5:21)

Unit Six

- Forgive one another (Col. 3:13)
- Confess your sins to one another (James 5:16)
- Pray for one another (James 5:16)
- Love one another from the heart (1 Pet. 1:22)
- Be hospitable to one another (1 Pet. 4:9)
- Meet one another with humility (1 Pet. 5:5)

Now when we reflect on the above list, one thing is clear: Virtually none of the above exhortations make sense without a serious level of *commitment* to one another. How are we to bear another person's burden unless the burden is known and unless we are willing to actually carry it? How are we to "put up with each other" unless we relate closely enough to get on each other's nerves? How are we to forgive one another unless we are in each other's lives enough to hurt and let down one another? How can we learn to submit to one another unless we struggle with differences? In other words, if we are to connect (or reconnect) our lives with one another, it will demand much more of us than we normally give. To be the church, and not just go to church, demands a great deal more than many of us are willing to give.

Few of us are ready to build up a common, committed life with others on a daily level, especially if it costs us a pay raise or causes us to forgo our personal preferences. If we are honest, we take our primary social cues from the broader culture. We consider our lives as "ours," independent of or above the church in some way. But experiencing genuine Christian community will never happen if you are hanging on to your own life or if your schedule only allows for a couple of "religious" meetings a week. New lifestyle habits will have to form. Sacrifices of convenience and of giving up private spaces and personal preferences will have to be made. It will involve making concerted choices so that others can more naturally and easily be in, and not just around, your life. Doing life together demands commitment. But it involves more than this. Without engaging in some very concrete practices, life together, instead of being a joy, may be hell.

LIFE TOGETHER

Commitment is the basis, but community in Christ is the aim. What might this look like in more concrete terms? What are the marks that signify authentic Christian fellowship beyond going to church on Sundays? What does a shared life really look like in which the Spirit bears its fruit?

Time

Perhaps the first fruit of commitment is *time*. Those who love one another spend time with each other. When I was in college and seminary I purposely took fewer credits than I could handle, just so I could make more time for others. As the years have gone by, finding time for others has become more difficult. A stark example of this occurred when I was living in an intentional Christian community in downtown Denver. A group of us, mostly in our thirties, lived in four duplexes right next to each other. We wanted to go on a back-packing trip together, but wouldn't you know, there was not one available weekend in the summer where we could all be together. Though we managed to share "space" together, our time was another matter.

Time is important because without being available to each other, fulfilling the biblical "one anothers" is virtually impossible. Take the construction metaphor of "building one another up." Building is a process that requires effort and persistence. Leaving a project undone will do damage to the materials. And if it is not done *together* who knows what will result? Or take the command to "do good to one another." It takes time to discern what is good for another person. I remember very well when I accidentally put a young college student into an emotional tailspin. I gave her a very strong challenge that completely backfired. I didn't realize she had been severely abused as a child and constantly struggled with suicidal feelings. If I had taken the time to know her better, I would have handled things very differently.

Time is crucial if we are really to "serve one another." Interestingly, the New Testament concept of service means performing lowly, thankless deeds—as a slave would do. This is what Jesus modeled when he washed his disciples' feet. The slave serves the master as *he* has need. Our gifts are less important than our readiness to serve. This hit home to me while I was in seminary. Jake, a fellow seminarian, and his wife Sharon were struggling to keep their home sane. They had two small boys, and Sharon had several medical needs. Their house, especially their kitchen, was a disaster. I was busy myself, but not at 10:30 PM. That was downtime before bed. I felt a nudge inside me that I should offer to do their dishes at that time. Did I want to? No. But a slave of Christ doesn't have the luxury of choosing which service to perform and when. They accepted my offer, and for two years this is what I did. Jake has been a life-long friend ever since.

Space

As important as time is, so is sharing space. This may or may not mean living with one another under the same roof. But it will mean finding practical ways of becoming more proximate with each other. The notion of a commuter marriage is an oxymoron. So is a commuter church. Unless we are physically present in each other's lives, unless our personal spaces are made available to one another, sharing life will only be skin deep.

Throughout history believers have found various ways of sanctifying space together. The earliest Christians formed neighborhoods within cities. The Celtic church created entire villages, sharing everything in common. Then there were various monastic orders, and during the Reformation radical reformers, like the Anabaptists, formed outright communities, some consisting of as many as 2,000 people. Today there are churches that revolve around cluster groups and there are groups like Jesus People USA in Chicago, or Community of Sojourners in San Francisco, or the Community of Jesus on Cape Cod, who have forged their own unique ways of drawing together in close proximity. Whatever its size, shape, or form, a living fellowship will seek very physical ways to share life together.

Of course, community demands more than sharing time and space. A fellowship of Christians is not the same things as a *Christian* fellowship. Doing life together must be done *in Christ*—in other words, in a way where Christ's authority holds sway. For this to happen, we must learn to listen to the Word—both in the Bible and as the Spirit speaks through others—and obey it *together*. Personal study of the Scriptures is vital, but God's Word has always been primarily addressed to his people—as a people! Interestingly, almost all the New Testament Epistles are written to churches! And when we think about the various "one another" commands, they can be fulfilled only if they are accomplished with others. Being under the Word is not just a matter of listening to a sermon together, but seeking with each other, by way of dialogue and prayer, what it means to obey Christ together. In my own church community, for instance, we regularly read the Scriptures together and then ask: "What must *we* do?" Recently, we felt convicted by how much unnecessary "stuff" we all had. So on a Saturday we all went through our houses, and with feedback from each other, got rid of piles of things that we really didn't need. We brought everything to one place to be either hauled away or sold. We did this all together in order to show God that we were serious about doing his Word. And by doing it together, we dealt a deathblow to the spirit of Mammon that wreaks so much havoc in our world. This was obviously not easy to do, but discipleship certainly isn't easy, and it definitely involves discipline (1 Cor. 9:24–27).

[handwritten annotation: - But we cant forget about needing to go out and be the salt of the earth.]

Resources

Another mark of life together is being open-handed with the excess that we have. "*Koinonia*" is not solely translated as "fellowship." In fact, its predominate use denotes the sharing of resources. The Macedonian and Achaian churches, for example, set up a common fund (*koinonian*) for the impoverished church in Jerusalem. Since the Gentiles shared (*ekoinonesan*) in the Jew's spiritual blessing, they in turn served their material need (Rom. 15:26,27; also 12:13). Out of their extreme poverty, they urgently pleaded with the apostles for the privilege of taking part (*koinonian*) in this service to the saints (2 Cor. 8:4). Such generosity marked a liberality of fellowship (*aploteti tes koinonias*—2 Cor. 9:13). It demonstrated the effectual working of God's grace (2 Cor. 8:1). On this basis and for this reason, Paul commands those of material means to generously extend their fellowship (*einai koinonikous*) by sharing with those in need (1 Tim. 6:17–19).[1]

For Paul, the right hand of fellowship (*koinonias*) authenticated his apostolic mission: he was committed to taking the gospel to the Gentiles and to obtaining funds for the needy in Jerusalem (Gal. 2:9,10). This sacrifice of sharing (*koinonias*), according to Paul, is what pleases God (Heb. 13:16).[2] Similarly, those receiving instruction in the gospel were to share (*koinoneito*) the good things of this life with their instructor (Gal. 6:6). For this reason Paul praises the Philippian church as ones who partook (*sugkoinonous*) in God's grace, who shared (koinonia) in the work of the gospel, and who were partners (*sugkononesantes*) in his

---

[1] It was only because of who the early church was *as a fellowship* that Paul could literally *command* the wealthier members to give generously. To hold back was a denial of their common life.

[2] The contribution for the needy Jewish Christians in Jerusalem, taken up by the Gentile Christians in the Hellenistic world was "a theological expression of the validity of his [Paul's] work among Gentiles, a sure sign that they had been completely accepted into God's work among the Jews." J. R. McRay, "Fellowship," *Evangelical Dictionary of Theology,* Walter E. Elwell, ed. (Grand Rapids, MI: Baker, 1984), 414.

troubles, for only they shared (*ekoinonesen eis logon*—lit. "opened an account") in giving to him and his companions the aid they needed (Phil. 1:5,7;4:14–16). This was indeed a "fragrant offering, an acceptable sacrifice, pleasing to God" (4:18).

The fellowship of the early church, therefore, was marked by how it shared material life together. It was this very practical expression of love that so impressed pagan society. Their love for one another was not in words, but in deeds—demanding real, physical sacrifices. It was assumed that those who belonged to Christ would have their material needs met (Acts 4:34; 2 Cor. 8:13–15). What a contrast to how we practice church today, where money matters are almost entirely private and personal.

This "none of your business" attitude can work both ways: for those who give and those who receive. Many years ago Cheryl, a good friend of mine who was a part of our local fellowship, lost her job. When she came to tell my wife and me about it, she was literally shaking, in tears, gripped with fear. After sharing with us, it dawned on me: Cheryl feels alone because, in terms of money, she was. It would be up to her to fend for herself. *She* lost her job, and *she* would have to find another. We as a fellowship hadn't lost a source of income; she had, and it was her welfare, not ours, that was on the line. She was no more willing to ask the church for help, than the church was willing to supply it. We were far from being a New Testament community.

I am currently a member of a community movement that consists of several intentional communities throughout the world. One thing we've vowed together is that amongst ourselves we will never charge each other money. Our services to each other are free. Why? Because we don't want money issues to divide or distract us. Nor do we want to be caught up in the snares of the world, which can so easily choke the inner life. Jesus said that we cannot serve both God and Mammon, and that if we seek first the kingdom of God and his justice, all our needs will be provided for (Matt. 6:33). We know which god the world worships; the church, by contrast, must do everything it can to show that it worships a very different God. What better way is there than to be free of the love of money?[3]

What so many Christians seem to miss is how it is possible to shape everyday life itself—including one's work—on the basis of faith. *In Christ*, all things can be made new, including those areas that tend to have a momentum all their own, as they especially do when it comes to career or business. If God's people would join together and redeem the workplace itself, both in terms of what is done and how, then a corporate work—a "Kingdom work"—of transformation can be achieved. A different social-spiritual material reality would emerge, one woven together by the diverse strands of everyday life where Jesus is proclaimed Lord, not just in word, but in deed.

Money and business matters are one thing, our homes are another. We mustn't forget how significant the injunction to "show hospitality to one another" is. It's a resource we often fail to use. It demands a different kind of personal investment—one that is often more telling. Showing hospitality is more than entertaining one another at our convenience. It means providing for each other's needs by offering what is most intimately "yours." Writing a check is easy compared to providing a night's lodging for someone who needs it. Eating at a restaurant with friends may be "fun," but what about taking the time and effort to prepare an equally nice meal? Giving hospitality communicates that you are giving your life, not just your possessions.

Accountability

Now all of this—be it our time, our space, our resources—demands a great deal of trust. Invariably, life together means not only building each other up, but letting each other down. For the struggle against sin, both within ourselves and how we are with each other, is an ongoing one. Life together requires that we be our brother's and sister's keeper.

At the very minimum, holding each other accountable demands that we speak the truth in love. Jesus instructed us clearly on this matter: if a brother is in sin, go to him. If he doesn't listen, get help. If he still

---

[3] One very practical way to show this is to find common ways to work together. Rondout House, in New York, consists of a group of Christians who run a cleaning and maintenance business together. Norwood Community, outside of Cincinnati, operates a café. Danthonia Community, in Australia, makes and sells custom signs together. Rose Creek Community in Tennessee runs a restaurant and a business in solar tinting, construction, and home improvement. Shepherdfield's Community, in Missouri, earns part of its living through organic homemade goods. And in my own community, Catskill Bruderhof, we manufacture specialized handicap equipment.

doesn't listen, then bring the matter to the whole church (Matt. 18:15–20). His point? Don't let sin destroy your brother or sister, nor let it mar my Body.

We have a "rule" in our community. It is paramount for experiencing real joy together. It goes as follows:

> There is no law but that of love (1 John 4:7–8). Love means having joy in others. Then what does being annoyed with them mean? It is thus out of the question to speak about another person in a spirit of irritation or vexation (Eph. 4:29–32). There must never be talk, either in open remarks or by insinuation, against another, against their individual characteristics—under no circumstances behind the person's back. Talking in one's own family is no exception.

> Without this rule of silence there can be no loyalty, no community. Direct address is the only way possible; it is the spontaneous service of love we owe anyone whose weaknesses cause a negative reaction in us (Eph. 4:2–3). An open word spoken directly to the other person deepens friendship and is not resented.

A truthful word spoken in love can be extremely powerful. A few years ago I met two fellow members of my community in a rather heated argument—right in the middle of work. Keith, one of our shop foremen, had made a bad machining mistake and had gotten overly defensive (and excited) about it. A few minutes later a couple of co-workers came over to try and sort things out. Then, all of a sudden, they all walked out of the factory. Later I learned that the whole scene was a result of something deeper, unrelated to work. Keith and his wife had been struggling in their marriage and it was starting to take its toll on Keith's general attitude on the floor. Fortunately, with the help of different ones in the community, they were able to find each other's hearts again.

To cite another example, some members of our community once spent a fair amount of money on hotel accommodations while on a mission trip. My wife and I got upset. Why hadn't that money, which we helped to earn, been put to better use? But in the course of our confrontation, and after several others had spoken honestly to us, we realized that our so-called concern was a cover up for cold-heartedness and self-righteousness. We weren't really interested in understanding their situation or their needs. We were more concerned with principles than with warm-blooded, everyday people. I'm glad we were called up short.

Having open, free and honest relationships demands work. And speaking the truth in love doesn't always work out. When Jim fell in love with Karen, who was married to Sean in our community in Denver, it was a burden to bear. But when they began to spend time together alone, and when Karen began to have feelings toward Jim, then something needed to be done. Neither, however, wanted Sean or others to know what was happening. And neither was willing to humble themselves to get help or to ask forgiveness. Sadly, two years later Karen and Sean divorced.

Karen and Jim were not solely to blame. If our community had been more committed to them, and had brought them up short and battled for their relationship openly, then the alluring power of sin might have been nipped in the bud. Recently, when some friends of mine inadvertently discovered a six-pack of beer in Greg's room, they right away talked to him about it. When it happened again, our whole fellowship confronted Greg. In so doing, we came to realize that it wasn't just drinking Greg struggled with, but a whole host of other things: vanity, sexual impurity, and loneliness. Fortunately, Greg wanted things to be different, and so he unburdened his conscience and heart with one of our pastors. He's been a new person ever since!

Forging life together in Christ with others is never easy. We fail each other—and God—all the time. This is why speaking truth in love must always be accompanied by forgiving one another. The Christian fellowship, the community, the church, or whatever one may call life together in Christ is ultimately the place of forgiveness. It is here that the cross comes alive. As Jean Vanier of the L'Arche Community, writes: "In spite of all the trust we may have in each other, there are always words that wound, self-promoting attitudes, situations where susceptibilities clash. That is why living together implies a certain cross, a constant effort, and an acceptance which is daily and mutual forgiveness."[4]

There's a reason why Jesus told his disciples to forgive seventy times seven times. Forgiveness is perhaps the most essential quality necessary for an ongoing and vibrant life with others. Without it our worship is not only false (Matt. 5:23–26), but we violate the very Body of Christ (1 Cor. 11:17ff). We

---

[4] Jean Vanier, *Community and Growth* (New York: Paulist Press, 1979), 10.

actually make a mockery of the cross. For in the cross, Jesus came to mend what is broken, and reconcile estranged relationships (Eph. 2:11ff). Harboring judgment, grudges, mistrust, and fear of each other denies the mystery of why Jesus came.

There are many other attributes one could list that mark being Christians together. But to reiterate, because disciples of Jesus follow a different road map than that of the world, the way in which we live and relate to each other will be markedly different. The path we are on is meant to be traveled together, for our destination is towards a kingdom the first fruits of which can already be felt and seen. Coming together in Christ, if it is real, can show the world that Jesus is Lord both in heaven and on earth.

BECOMING AN APOLOGETIC

It is a misnomer to think that a highly committed fellowship is an "exclusive" or a "reclusive" one. In fact, there is no greater witness to the reality of God's coming kingdom than a biblically formed life together. A fully functioning fellowship of love demonstrates the truth of the gospel far better than apologetic arguments over abstract ideas. As Stanley Hauerwas argues, "What is crucial is not that Christians know the truth, but that they be the truth." The strongest argument for Christianity's truthfulness consists of the lives it produces. Jesus was quite clear about this when he said, "All people will know that you are my disciples if you love one another" (John 13:35). What the world needs most is not words, but living testaments who embody the power of his love. Only our unity will convince the world of Christ's reality (John 17:22–23). For Jesus, the medium and the message are one.

As scientific theories are judged by the fruitfulness of the activities they generate, so is the Christian story. Christian truth is ultimately to be judged by the richness of moral character and the authenticity of relationship it generates. How else can the power of the gospel be *known* (1 Cor. 4:20)?

Therefore, it is how we are together, not just how smart or intellectually astute we are, that vindicates Christ. This is what characterized the witness of the early Christians and permeated the writing of all the early apologists. Athenagoras, for example, wrote:

> Among us you will find uneducated persons, and artisans, and old women, who, though in words are unable to prove the benefit of our doctrine, by their deeds exhibit the benefit arising from their persuasion of its truth. They do not rehearse speeches, but exhibit good works. When struck, they do not strike again; when robbed, they do not go to law. They give to those that ask of them, and love their neighbors as themselves.[5]

Athenagoras' words are not exaggerated. For example, the type of care the early Christians had for one another, revolutionary in comparison with pagan society, extended to all its members: to widows, orphans, the elderly and sick, those incapable of working and the unemployed, prisoners and exiles, Christians on a journey and all other members of the church who had fallen into special need. Care was also taken that the poor received a decent burial. Those no longer able to work received the support of the community.

Such care extended beyond the community's own ranks to include those abandoned and rejected by the unbelieving. For this reason, Christian compassion often received high praise, even from enemies of the faith. The Roman Emperor Julian writes:

> Why don't we notice that it is their [the Christians'] benevolence to strangers, their care for the graves of the dead and the pretended holiness of their lives that have done the most to increase atheism [i.e. Christianity]?... When these impious Galileans support not only their own poor but ours as well, everyone sees that our people lack aid from us.[6]

This failure, combined with the church's deeds, is what convinced the ancient world of Christianity's truth. The church's life together was its logic. Hence, Origen did not hesitate to say, "The evidences of Jesus' divinity are the Churches of people who have been helped."[7] It was not the rationality of its beliefs per se, but the lives the early church produced that persuaded the world. It was the church's ethical transformation that silenced her critics and their desperate accusations. This is how it always is. Christ's truth is both

---

[5] A. Roberts and J. Donaldson, eds., *The Ante-Nicene Fathers*, vol. II (Grand Rapids: Eerdmans), 134.
[6] W. C. Wright, *The Works of the Emperor Julian*, vol. 3 (LCL, 1923), 69,71.
[7] Henry Chadwick, *Origen: Contra Celsum* (Cambridge: Cambridge University Press, 1953), 150.

validated and vindicated when it is being lived out. A moral revolution, set in motion, not argument set in propositions, is what convinces.

Consider again the early church and the extraordinary role healing miracles played. For example, the apologist Origen takes for granted the healing power of Christ as he regularly saw with his own eyes those who were miraculously cured. And Cyprian, in his letter to Demetrianus, describes how the Spirit whips demons and drives them away from the believing. He thus challenges Demetrianus: "Come yourself and see how true it is what we say. You will see how we are entreated by those (i.e. the demons) whom you entreat and feared by those whom you fear and worship." In this vein, the church fathers repeatedly pointed out that the most profound miracles did not consist in people being healed of their infirmities but in their ability— against all human striving and expectation—to break with their pagan past and to embark on a new life.

In other words, the early Christians did not just believe in the power of Christ's resurrection, they lived in and by this power. C. S. Lewis writes, concerning the New Testament's resurrection narratives, that they "are not a picture of survival after death; they record how a totally new mode of being has arisen in the Universe. Something new had appeared in the Universe: as new as the first coming of organic life." A new mode of being has arisen, the first fruits of which were given to the Church to partake. For this reason, Clarence Jordan declares: "The crowning evidence that Jesus was alive was not a vacant grave, but a spirit-filled fellowship. Not a rolled-away stone, but a carried-away church." Such people were the direct evidence of the kingdom—the God movement.

While there is a place for demonstrating Christianity's truthfulness and historicity on certain documentary and experiential "facts," believers ultimately need to become the evidence—a living epistle—necessary to support its claims. Are the Scriptures reliable? How can this ever be answered unless there exists a people who consistently live by them and bear good fruit? Are miracles possible? Jesus' reply to John the Baptist was: "Look and see!" Do we live in such a way that the only satisfactory explanation for its existence is the power of God in its midst? Was Christ raised from the dead? Did he actually die for the world's sin? Well, are there or are there not communities of faith marked by the new life of the Spirit who reconciles all things?

CONCLUSION

In his book *Life Together*, Dietrich Bonhoeffer writes: "It is grace, nothing but grace, that we are allowed to live in community with Christian brothers and sisters." This but echoes the words of the Psalmist who wrote: "How good and pleasant it is when brothers live together in unity!" (Psalm 133:1). This gift of life together opens up the way to God and to our brother and sister.

This gift of community is not simply Christians who are really nice to their friends and the people they go to church with. In the end, Christian community is not even living together and sharing cars, money, and bagels. Genuine community is more like a movement where groups of people have been set free by Christ to pursue radically different agendas with their life and lifestyles.

The Apostle Paul reminds us that love is the greatest gift. This is precisely why Jesus gave up his body on the Cross and gave it back again in the Church. Doing life together in a way where we really need each other brings Christ and his kingdom very close to this earth. For Jesus once dwelt among us as a humble servant; and he continues to dwell among us in this same way. As Paul writes in Philippians, Jesus takes up residence in brothers and sisters, his corporate body, who, "being like-minded, having the same love, being one in spirit and purpose," consider others better than themselves and look to the interests of others above their own. It is they who "shine like stars in the universe" and hold out the word of life.

---

*This essay was commissioned by Summit Ministries for this curriculum.
** Reproduction rights granted by Charles Moore.

DOING LIFE TOGETHER
ESSAY QUESTIONS

Answer the questions below on a separate sheet of paper and be prepared to review your answers in class. Reflection Questions will not be found in the text. These are merely designed to help you start thinking about issues from a worldview perspective.

1. What is interdependence and why is it important? What makes us so independent?

2. What is fellowship? How does biblical fellowship differ from common Christian experience today?

3. How can we apply the "one another" statements in the Bible to a fellowship?

4. How is *time* important to a life together as the fellowship? What are some examples from your own experience? What are some improvements you can make?

5. How is *space* important to a life together as the fellowship? What are some examples from your own experience? What are some improvements you can make? Why do we find it difficult to share our space with others?

6. How are *resources* important to a life together as the fellowship? What are some examples from your own experience? What are some improvements you can make?

7. How is accountability important to a life together as the fellowship? What are some examples from your own experience? What are some improvements you can make?

8. What role does church discipline play in accountability? How have you seen this work in your own fellowship? How should we look at failure?

9. What does it mean to be an apologist? How did the early church practice this?

10. Reflection Question: How can your fellowship be a more authentic apologetic in our culture today?

"LOVE, SEX, AND MARRIAGE"
WITH JEFF MYERS

PART ONE

I. The Story of the Family (Genesis 1:26–31)

II. God's Plan for Creation (Genesis 2:15–25)

    A. Bear God's image

    B. Name the animals—take responsibility

    C. Be fruitful and multiply   *force into submission*

    D. Fill the earth and subdue (*kabash*) it—turn entire earth into a garden

III. Man's Rebellion (Genesis 3:1-15)

    A. Irresponsibility

    B. Paranoia

    C. Blame

IV. Satan's Plan

    A. The _____curse_____ ensured Satan's doom.

    B. Offspring (*zera*)

        1. One person who epitomizes the group

        2. Whole line of descendents as a group

    C. "The God of peace will soon crush Satan under your feet" (Romans 16:20).

V. Satan's Attack

"It can be demonstrated from history that no society has ever survived after its family life deteriorated." — Paul Popenoe

    A. Kill ____*babies*____

    B. Make people fear or despise ____*marrige*____

    C. Destroy existing marriages

    D. Promote ____*promiscuity*____

Unit Six

E. "Alternatives" to marriage

women view living together as a step to marriage and men do not. — they see it as having sexual relations w/o strings

F. Homosexuality

G. Pornography

H. Trivialize __sex__

I. Practice for __divorce__

J. Create a wedge between parents and kids

K. Get people to deceive themselves
- make people think they are the exception to the rule.

PART TWO

VI. Responding to Satan's Attacks

A. Understand this is a __worldview__ battle

1. Secular Humanist View *- family is what you want it to be.*

"All societies have long recognized that the family commitment is not merely biological, but rests on a complex foundation of contract, custom, and emotional commitment. Families have taken many forms—some, we have outgrown. The core of the modern family is two or more individuals who see themselves as a family, and who accept long-term responsibility for one another's health, security, independence, and happiness." — Council for Secular Humanism

2. Marxist-Leninist View
- family should be abolished

"With the transfer of the means of production into common ownership, the single family ceases to be the economic unit of society. Private housekeeping is transformed into a social industry. The care and education of the children becomes a public affair; society looks after all children alike, whether they are legitimate or not." — Frederick Engels

3. Cosmic Humanist View
- we have evolved beyond needing family

"Relationships and families as we've known them seem to be falling apart at a rapid rate. Many people are panicky about this; some try to re-establish the old traditions and value systems in order to cling to a feeling of order and stability in their lives. It's useless to try to go backward, however, because our consciousness has already evolved beyond the level where we were willing to make the sacrifices necessary to live that way." — Shakti Gawain

4. Christian View

"The act of uniting a man and woman for life… marriage was instituted by God himself for the purpose of preventing the promiscuous intercourse of the sexes, for domestic felicity, and for securing the maintenance and education of children." — Webster's 1828 dictionary

marriage {

i. _Covenant_ with community and God

ii. As the means through which to fulfill the creation mandate (Genesis 1–2)

iii. As a picture of _Christ_ and the church (Ephesians 5:31–33)

B. Live out our God-given design – don't try to be other people, be who God made you to be. clear differences between men + women

C. Commit to _purity_ of body and mind

lack purity = I will act to fulfill myself

"Self-governing people require a robust culture founded on marriage and family, which nurtures the qualities that permit self-rule: deferred gratification, self-sacrifice, respect for kinship and law, and property rights. These qualities are founded upon sexual restraint, which permits people to pursue long-term interests, such as procreating and raising the next generation, and securing benefits for one's children." — Robert Knight

purity: means not putting yourself at the center

D. Model the love of Christ

–understand than be understood

E. Love kids

F. Be _reconciled_ to one another

"People's hearts are seldom changed if they are not changed when young. Seldom indeed are men converted when they are old. Habits have long roots. Sin once allowed to nestle in your bosom will not be turned out at your bidding. Custom becomes second nature, and its chains are threefold cords not easily broken." — J. C. Ryle

start living for God in the way He wants you to now!

"LOVE, SEX, AND MARRIAGE"
WITH JEFF MYERS

Answer the questions below on a separate sheet of paper and be prepared to review your answers in class.

1. What can we learn about the family in Genesis 1–3?

2. What is Satan's plan to ensure his survival? How has this plan been implemented?

3. What are the Secular Humanist, Marxist-Leninist, and Cosmic Humanist views of marriage and the family?

4. What is the Christian view of marriage and the family?

5. How can we as Christians thwart Satan's attacks on marriage and the family?

DOMESTIC TRANQUILITY

BY E. CAROLYN GRAGLIA

PART ONE

Since the late 1960s, feminists have very successfully waged war against the traditional family, in which husbands are the principal breadwinners and wives are primarily homemakers. This war's immediate purpose has been to undermine the homemaker's position within both her family and society in order to drive her into the work force. Its long-term goal is to create a society in which women behave as much like men as possible, devoting as much time and energy to the pursuit of a career as men do, so that women will eventually hold equal political and economic power with men. This book examines feminism's successful onslaught against the traditional family, considers the possible ramifications of that success, and defends a woman's choice to be a homemaker. Feminists have used a variety of methods to achieve their goal. They have promoted a sexual revolution that encouraged women to mimic male sexual promiscuity. They have supported the enactment of no-fault divorce laws that have undermined housewives' social and economic security. And they obtained the application of affirmative action requirements to women as a class, gaining educational and job preferences for women and undermining the ability of men who are victimized by this discrimination to function as family breadwinners.

A crucial weapon in feminism's arsenal has been the status degradation of the housewife's role. From the journalistic attacks of Betty Friedan and Gloria Steinem to Jessie Bernard's sociological writings, all branches of feminism are united in the conviction that a woman can find identity and fulfillment only in a career. The housewife, feminists agree, was properly characterized by Simone de Beauvoir and Betty Friedan as a "parasite," a being something less than human, living her life without using her adult capabilities or intelligence, and lacking any real purpose in devoting herself to children, husband, and home.

Operating on the twin assumptions that equality means sameness (that is, men and women cannot be equals unless they do the same things) and that most differences between the sexes are culturally imposed, contemporary feminism has undertaken its own cultural impositions. Revealing their totalitarian belief that they know best how others should live and their totalitarian willingness to force others to conform to their dogma, feminists have sought to modify our social institutions in order to create an androgynous society in which male and female roles are as identical as possible. The results of the feminist juggernaut now engulf us. By almost all indicia of well-being, the institution of the American family has become significantly less healthy than it was thirty years ago.

Certainly, feminism is not alone responsible for our families' sufferings. As Charles Murray details in *Losing Ground*,[1] President Lyndon Johnson's Great Society programs, for example, have often hurt families, particularly black families, and these programs were supported by a large constituency beyond the women's movement. What distinguishes the women's movement, however, is the fact that, despite the pro-family motives it sometimes ascribes to itself, it has actively sought the traditional family's destruction. In its avowed aims and the programs it promotes, the movement has adopted Kate Millett's goal, set forth in her Sexual Politics, in which she endorses Friedrich Engels's conclusion that "the family, as that term is presently understood, must go;" "a kind fate," she remarks, in "view of the institution's history.[2] This goal has never changed: feminists view traditional nuclear families as inconsistent with feminism's commitment to women's independence and sexual freedom.[3]

Emerging as a revitalized movement in the 1960s, feminism reflected women's social discontent, which had arisen in response to the decline of the male breadwinner ethic and to the perception—heralded in Philip Wylie's 1940s castigation of the evil "mom"[4]—that Western society does not value highly the roles of wife and mother. Women's dissatisfactions, nevertheless, have often been aggravated rather than alleviated by

[1] Charles Murray, *Losing Ground* (New York: Basic, 1984).

[2] Kate Millett, *Sexual Politics* (Garden City, NY: Doubleday, 1969), 127.

[3] This is a theme, for example, of Ellen Willis's *No More Nice Girls: Countercultural Essays* (Wesleyan University/University Press of New England, 1993).

[4] Philip Wylie, *Generation of Vipers* (New York: Holt, Rinehart, & Winston, 1942), 52–53.

the feminist reaction. To mitigate their discontent, feminists argued, women should pattern their lives after men's, engaging in casual sexual intercourse on the same terms as sexually predatory males and making the same career commitments as men. In pursuit of these objectives, feminists have fought unceasingly for the ready availability of legal abortion and consistently derogated both motherhood and the worth of full-time homemakers. Feminism's sexual teachings have been less consistent, ranging from its early and enthusiastic embrace of the sexual revolution to a significant backlash against female sexual promiscuity, which has led some feminists to urge women to abandon heterosexual sexual intercourse altogether.

Contemporary feminism has been remarkably successful in bringing about the institutionalization in our society of the two beliefs underlying its offensive: denial of the social worth of traditional homemakers and rejection of traditional sexual morality. The consequences have been pernicious and enduring. General societal assent to these beliefs has profoundly distorted men's perceptions of their relationships with and obligations to women, women's perceptions of their own needs, and the way in which women make decisions about their lives.

TRADITIONAL HOMEMAKING DEVALUED

The first prong of contemporary feminism's offensive has been to convince society that a woman's full-time commitment to cultivating her marriage and rearing her children is an unworthy endeavor. Women, assert feminists, should treat marriage and children as relatively independent appendages to their life of full-time involvement in the workplace. To live what feminists assure her is the only life worthy of respect, a woman must devote the vast bulk of her time and energy to market production, at the expense of marriage and children. Children, she is told, are better cared for by surrogates, and marriage, as these feminists perceive it, neither deserves nor requires much attention; indeed, the very idea of a woman's "cultivating" her marriage seems ludicrous. Thus spurred on by the women's movement, many women have sought to become male clones.

But some feminists have appeared to modify the feminist message; voices—supposedly of moderation—have argued that women really are different from men. In this they are surely right: there are fundamental differences between the average man and woman, and it is appropriate to take account of these differences when making decisions both in our individual lives and with respect to social issues. Yet the new feminist voices have not conceded that acknowledged differences between the sexes are grounds for reexamining women's flight from home into workplace. Instead, these new voices have argued only that these differences require modification of the terms under which women undertake to reconstruct their lives in accordance with the blueprint designed by so-called early radicals. The edifice erected by radical feminism is to remain intact, subject only to some redecorating. The foundation of this edifice is still the destruction of the traditional family. Feminism has acquiesced in women's desire to bear children (an activity some of the early radicals discouraged). But it continues steadfast in its assumption that, after some period of maternity leave, daily care of those children is properly the domain of institutions and paid employees. The yearnings manifested in women's palpable desire for children should largely be sated, the new voices tell us, by the act of serving as a birth canal and then spending so-called quality time with the child before and after a full day's work.

Any mother, in this view, may happily consign to surrogates most of the remaining aspects of her role, assured that doing so will impose no hardship or loss on either mother or child. To those women whose natures make them less suited to striving in the workplace than concentrating on husband, children, and home, this feminist diktat denies the happiness and contentment they could have found within the domestic arena. In the world formed by contemporary feminism, these women will have status and respect only if they force themselves to take up roles in the workplace they suspect are not most deserving of their attention. Relegated to the periphery of their lives are the home and personal relationships with husband and children that they sense merit their central concern.

Inherent in the feminist argument is an extraordinary contradiction. Feminists deny, on the one hand, that the dimension of female sexuality which engenders women's yearning for children can also make it appropriate and satisfying for a woman to devote herself to domestic endeavors and provide her children's full-time care. On the other hand, they plead the fact of sexual difference to justify campaigns to modify workplaces in order to correct the effects of male influence and alleged biases. Only after such modifications, claim feminists, can women's nurturing attributes and other female qualities be adequately expressed in and truly influence the workplace. Manifestations of these female qualities, feminists argue, should and can occur in the workplace once it has been modified to blunt the substantial impact of male aggression and competitiveness and take account of women's special requirements.

Having launched its movement claiming the right of women—right allegedly denied them previously—to enter the workplace on an *equal* basis with men, feminism then escalated its demands by arguing that female differences require numerous changes in the workplace. Women, in this view, are insufficiently feminine to find satisfaction in rearing their own children but too feminine to compete on an equal basis with men. Thus, having taken women out of their homes and settled them in the workplace, feminists have sought to reconstruct workplaces to create "feminist playpens" that are conducive to female qualities of sensitivity, caring, and empathy. Through this exercise in self-contradiction, contemporary feminism has endeavored to remove the woman from her home and role of providing daily care to her children—the quintessential place and activity for most effectively expressing her feminine, nurturing attributes.

The qualities that are the most likely to make women good mothers are thus redeployed away from their children and into workplaces that must be restructured to accommodate them. The irony is twofold. Children—the ones who could benefit most from the attentions of those mothers who do possess these womanly qualities—are deprived of those attentions and left only with the hope of finding adequate replacement for their loss. Moreover, the occupations in which these qualities are now to find expression either do not require them for optimal job performance (often they are not conducive to professional success) or were long ago recognized as women's occupations—as in the field of nursing, for example—in which nurturing abilities do enhance job performance.

TRADITIONAL SEXUAL MORALITY TRADUCED

The second prong of contemporary feminism's offensive has been to encourage women to ape male sexual patterns and engage in promiscuous sexual intercourse as freely as men. Initially, feminists were among the most dedicated supporters of the sexual revolution, viewing female participation in casual sexual activity as an unmistakable declaration of female equality with males. The women in our society who acted upon the teachings of feminist sexual revolutionaries have suffered greatly. They are victims of the highest abortion rate in the Western world. More than one in five Americans is now infected with a viral sexually transmitted disease which at best can be controlled but not cured and is often chronic. Sexually transmitted diseases, both viral and bacterial, disproportionately affect women because, showing fewer symptoms, they often go untreated for a longer time. These diseases also lead to pelvic infections that cause infertility in 100,000 to 150,000 women each year.[5]

The sexual revolution feminists have promoted rests on an assumption that an act of sexual intercourse involves nothing but a pleasurable physical sensation, possessing no symbolic meaning and no moral dimension. This is an understanding of sexuality that bears more than a slight resemblance to sex as depicted in pornography: physical sexual acts without emotional involvement. In addition to the physical harm caused by increased sexual promiscuity, the denial that sexual intercourse has symbolic importance within a framework of moral accountability corrupts the nature of the sex act. Such denial necessarily makes sexual intercourse a trivial event, compromising the act's ability to fulfill its most important function after procreation. This function is to bridge the gap between males and females who often seem separated by so many differences, both biological and emotional, that they feel scarcely capable of understanding or communicating with each other.

Because of the urgency of sexual desire, especially in the male, it is through sexual contact that men and women can most easily come together. Defining the nature of sexual intercourse in terms informed by its procreative potentialities makes the act a spiritually meaningful event of overwhelming importance. A sexual encounter so defined is imbued with the significance conferred by its connection with a promise of immortality through procreation, whether that connection is a present possibility, a remembrance of children already borne, or simply an acknowledgment of the reality and truth of the promise. Such a sex act can serve as the physical meeting ground on which, by accepting and affirming each other through their bodies' physical unity, men and women can begin to construct an enduring emotional unity. The sexual

---

[5] *New York Times* (April 1, 1993). This study by the Alan Guttmacher Institute estimates that if "current trends continue, one-half of all women who were 15 in 1970 will have had [pelvic inflammatory disease] by the year 2000."

encounter cannot perform its function when it is viewed as a trivial event of moral indifference with no purpose or meaning other than producing a physical sensation through the friction of bodily parts.

The feminist sexual perspective deprives the sex act of the spiritual meaningfulness that can make it the binding force upon which man and woman can construct a lasting marital relationship. The morally indifferent sexuality championed by the sexual revolution substitutes the sex without emotions that characterizes pornography for the sex of a committed, loving relationship that satisfies women's longing for romance and connection. But this is not the only damage to relationships between men and women that follows from feminism's determination to promote an androgynous society by convincing men and women that they are virtually fungible. Sexual equivalency, feminists believe, requires that women not only engage in casual sexual intercourse as freely as men, but also that women mimic male behavior by becoming equally assertive in initiating sexual encounters and in their activity throughout the encounter. With this sexual prescription, feminists mock the essence of conjugal sexuality that is at the foundation of traditional marriage.

MARRIAGE AS A WOMAN'S CAREER DISCREDITED

Even academic feminists who are considered "moderates" endorse doctrines most inimical to the homemaker. Thus, Professor Elizabeth Fox-Genovese, regarded as a moderate in Women's Studies, tells us that marriage can no longer be a viable career for women. But if marriage cannot be a woman's career, then, despite feminist avowals of favoring choice in this matter, homemaking cannot be a woman's goal, and surrogate child-rearing must be her child's destiny. Contrary to feminist claims, society's barriers are not strung tightly to inhibit women's career choices. Because of feminism's very successful efforts, society encourages women to pursue careers, while stigmatizing and preventing their devotion to childrearing and domesticity.

It was precisely upon the conclusion that marriage cannot be a viable career for women that *Time* magazine rested its Fall 1990 special issue on "Women: The Road Ahead," a survey of contemporary women's lives. While noting that the "cozy, limited roles of the past are still clearly remembered, sometimes fondly," during the past thirty years "all that was orthodox has become negotiable." One thing negotiated away has been the economic security of the homemaker, and *Time* advised young women that "the job of full-time homemaker may be the riskiest profession to choose" because the advent of no-fault and equitable-distribution divorce laws" reflect, in the words of one judge, the fact that " society no longer believes that a husband should support his wife."[6]

No-fault divorce laws did not, however, result from an edict of the gods or some force of nature, but from sustained political efforts, particularly by the feminist movement. As a cornerstone of their drive to make women exchange home for workplace, and thereby secure their independence from men, the availability of no-fault divorce (like the availability of abortion) was sacrosanct to the movement. *Time* shed crocodile tears for displaced homemakers, for it made clear that women must canter down the road ahead with the spur of no-fault divorce urging them into the workplace. Of all *Time*'s recommendations for ameliorating women's lot, divorce reform—the most crying need in our country today—was not among them. Whatever hardships may be endured by women who would resist a divorce, *Time*'s allegiance, like that of most feminists, is clearly to the divorce-seekers who, it was pleased to note, will not be hindered in their pursuit of self-realization by the barriers to divorce that their own mothers had faced.[7]

These barriers to divorce which had impeded their own parents, however, had usually benefited these young women by helping to preserve their parents' marriage. A five-year study of children in divorcing families disclosed that "the overwhelming majority preferred the unhappy marriage to the divorce," and many of them "despite the unhappiness of their parents, were in fact relatively happy and considered their situation neither better nor worse than that of other families around them."[8] A follow-up study after ten years demonstrated that children experienced the trauma of their parents' divorce as more serious and long-lasting than any researchers had anticipated.[9] *Time* so readily acquiesced in the disadvantaging of homemakers and

---

[6] *Time* (Fall 1990).

[7] Ibid., 12.

[8] Judith S. Wallerstein and Joan Berlin Kelly, *Surviving the Breakup: How Children and Parents Cope with Divorce* (New York: Basic, 1980), 4–5, 10–11.

[9] Judith S. Wallerstein and Sandra Blakeslee, *Second Chances: Men, Women & Children a Decade After Divorce* (New York:

Unit Six

the disruption of children's lives because the feminist ideological parameters within which it operates have excluded marriage as a *proper* career choice. Removing the obstacles to making it a *viable* choice would, therefore, be an undesirable subversion of feminist goals.

That *Time* would have women trot forward on life's journey constrained by the blinders of feminist ideology is evident from its failure to question any feminist notion, no matter how silly, or to explore solutions incompatible with the ideology's script. One of the silliest notions *Time* left unexamined was that young women want "good careers, good marriages and two or three kids, and they don't want the children to be raised by strangers." The supposed realism of this expectation lay in the new woman's attitude that I don't want to work 70 hours a week, but I want to be vice president, and you have to change." But even if thirty hours were cut from that seventy-hour workweek, the new 'woman would still be working the normal full-time week, her children would still be raised by surrogates, and the norm would continue to be the feminist version of child-rearing that *Time* itself described unflatteringly as "less a preoccupation than an improvisation."[10]

The illusion that a woman can achieve career success without sacrificing the daily personal care of her children—and except among the very wealthy, most of her leisure as well—went unquestioned by *Time*. It did note, however, the dissatisfaction expressed by Eastern European and Russian women who had experienced as a matter of government policy the same liberation from home and children that our feminists have undertaken to bestow upon Western women. In what *Time* described as "a curious reversal of Western feminism's emphasis on careers for women," the new female leaders of Eastern Europe would like "to reverse the communist diktat that all women have to work." Women have "dreamed," said the Polish Minister of Culture and Arts, "of reaching the point where we have the choice to stay home" that communism had taken away."[11] But blinded by its feminist bias, *Time* could only find it "curious" that women would choose to stay at home; apparently beyond the pale of respectability was any argument that it would serve Western women's interest to retain the choice that contemporary feminism—filling in the West the role of communism in the East—has sought to deny them.

Nor was its feminist bias shaken by the attitudes of Japanese women, most of whom, *Time* noted, reject "equality" with men, choosing to cease work after the birth of a first child and later resuming a part-time career or pursuing hobbies or community work. The picture painted was that of the 1950s American suburban housewife reviled by Betty Friedan, except that the American has enjoyed a higher standard of living (particularly a much larger home) than has the Japanese. In Japan, *Time* observed, being "a housewife is nothing to be ashamed of." Dishonoring the housewife's role was a goal, it might have added, that Japanese feminists can, in time, accomplish if they emulate their American counterparts.

Japanese wives have broad responsibilities, commented Time, because most husbands leave their salaries and children entirely in wives' hands; freed from drudgery by modern appliances, housewives can "Pursue their interests in a carefree manner, while men have to worry about supporting their wives and children.[12] Typically, a Japanese wife controls household finances, giving her husband a cash allowance, the size of which, apparently, dissatisfies one-half of the men. Acknowledging that Japanese wives take the leadership in most homes, one husband observed that "things go best when the husband is swimming in the palm of his wife's hand." A home is well-managed, said one wife, "if you make your men feel that they're in control when they are in front of others, while in reality you're in control."[13] It seems like a good arrangement to me.

Ticknor & Fields, 1989). In *The Divorce Culture* (New York: Knopf, 1996), Barbara Dafoe Whitehead presents a heartrending picture of the blighting of children's lives and the permanent damage they suffer because of their parents' divorce. Rather than calling for a reform of no-fault that would reinstitute strict legal controls over divorce, she would rely on exhorting parents to behave more responsibly towards their children and each other.

[10] *Time* (Fall 1990).

[11] Ibid., 32. Christina Hoff Sommers has described the incredulity of American feminists when Russian women writers, alleging that socialism "had denied women their femininity," encouraged women "to pay more attention to their traditional role as 'keepers of the hearth,'" and proclaimed that they "have nothing to do with feminism." *Who Stole Feminism? How Women Have Betrayed Women* (New York: Simon & Schuster, 1994), 39–40.

[12] *Time* (Fall 1990).

[13] Nicholas D. Kristof, "Japan Is a Woman's World Once the Front Door Is Shut," *New York Times* (June 19, 1996). The contrast between Japanese women's public powerlessness and private authority is analyzed by Takie Sugiyama Lebra in *Japanese Women: Constraint and Fulfillment* (Honolulu: University of Hawaii Press, 1984).

Instead of inquiring whether a similar carefree existence might appeal to some American women, *Time* looked forward to the day when marriage would no longer be a career for Japanese women, as their men took over household and child-rearing chores, enabling wives to join husbands in the workplace. It was noted, however, that a major impediment to this goal, which would have to be corrected, was the fact that Japanese daycare centers usually run for only eight hours a day. Thus, *Time* made clear that its overriding concern was simply promoting the presence of women in the work force. This presence is seen as a good *per se*, without any *pro forma* talk about the economic necessity of a second income and without any question raised as to whether it is in children's interest to spend any amount of time—much less in excess of eight hours a day—in communal care.

IRONIES WITHIN FEMINISM

Feminist success in reshaping social attitudes has been facilitated by our media's eagerness to adopt and propagate the feminist perspective and by feminism's ability to piggyback on the black civil rights movement by portraying women as victims. In acquiring "minority" status, women (who are the sexual majority) secured preferential entitlement to educational and employment opportunities afforded to blacks and other minorities. Feminists have also promoted their goals through a large body of law developed under the rubric of "women's rights," much of it laid down by the United States Supreme Court in decisions invalidating distinctions on the basis of sex.

Contemporary feminism's remarkable ability to enlist social institutions in its war on the traditional family has entailed two ironies, the first relating to the women spearheading the attack and the second to feminist reliance on the black civil rights movement to obtain preferential treatment for women. As detailed in *The Sisterhood*,[14] the most influential leaders of the women's movement that was revived in the 1960s were Betty Friedan, Kate Millett, Germaine Greer, and Gloria Steinem. Including the international movement, Simone de Beauvoir was a fifth. Of these five women, only Betty Friedan had both married and borne children. But she was unhappy with her marriage and life in the suburban home, which she compared to a "comfortable concentration camp" in which the housewife performs "endless, monotonous, unrewarding" work that "does not require adult capabilities" and causes "a slow death of mind and spirit." She felt "like a freak, absolutely alone" and afraid to face her "real feelings about the husband and children you were presumably living for."[15]

Denying that contemporary women could "live through their bodies" and derive satisfaction from child-bearing as the "pinnacle of human achievement" that it was on Margaret Mead's South Sea Islands, Friedan recommended the path of women who remained in the workplace by "juggling their pregnancies" and relying on nurses and housekeepers. Characterizing her marriage as one based not "on love but on dependent hate," Friedan concluded that she could no longer continue "leading other women out of the wilderness while holding on to a marriage that destroyed my self-respect."[16] And so the self-proclaimed Moses from the New York suburbs obtained her divorce.

While Betty Friedan had tasted a life devoted to marriage and motherhood and pronounced it foul, the remaining four women were unacquainted with the experience. Kate Millett and Simone de Beauvoir, both bisexuals, agreed that women were prevented from becoming free human beings by the myths revering maternity and the expectations that women should personally care for their children. Gloria Steinem declared that she deliberately chose childlessness because "I either gave birth to someone else" or "I gave birth to myself."[17] Germaine Greer, who was the best known of the feminist sexual revolutionaries and wrote the very popular *The Female Eunuch*, was childless and argued that marriage was outmoded. Greer indicated a certain distaste for the female body, opining with respect to menstruation that women "would rather do without it."[18] Later, as a revisionist and to the regret of other feminists, she attacked sexual permissiveness and lauded motherhood and fertility. Her preference for abstinence, anal intercourse, and *coitus interruptus* over other contraceptive methods, however, suggested a lingering distaste for the womb as well as for

---

[14] Marcia Cohen, *The Sisterhood* (New York: Simon & Schuster, 1987).
[15] Betty Friedan, *The Feminine Mystique* (New York: Dell, 1984), 307–08, 381.
[16] Ibid., 140–41, 376, 381, 394.
[17] *Time* (May 2, 1988), 88. Steinem's name was on a list published of prominent women who had had an illegal abortion. Katherine Dalton, "Hard Cases," *The American Enterprise* (May/June 1995), 71.
[18] Germaine Greer, *The Female Eunuch* (New York: McGraw Hill, 1970), 43.

phallic potency.[19]

Although she never married or shared living quarters with him, Simone de Beauvoir maintained a lifelong liaison with Jean-Paul Sartre. Their relationship was based on sexual freedom for both, and as one commentator has described it, "her role was not unlike that of a eunuch in charge of a harem," inspecting the women who wished to have affairs with Sartre and "disposing of past sexual partners of his who became troublesome in their continued affection for him.[20] Simone de Beauvoir's life was a blueprint for the woman "liberated" through radical feminism: a bisexual[21] who was neither wife nor birth mother, but an aborted woman, a fact she disclosed in an advertisement by women who had obtained illegal abortions.[22]

Reflecting the female's hypergamous impulse, de Beauvoir allied herself with a man she considered her intellectual superior. Upon meeting Sartre as a university student, she recognized that he "had a deeper and wider knowledge of everything," "a true superiority over me." She recalled "the calm and yet almost frenzied passion with which he was preparing for the books he was going to write." In comparison, her "frantic determination seemed weak and timid" and her "feverish obsessions," "lukewarm." Their early discussions, she said, were "the first time in my life that I had felt intellectually inferior to anyone else;" "Day after day, and all day long I set myself up against Sartre, and in our discussions I was simply not in his class;" "he soon demolished" my theories and in "the end I had to admit I was beaten."[23] De Beauvoir's evident excitement at being bested by this superior man is familiar to women (it was not entirely with regret that I realized my future husband might beat me in an argument). This excitement can serve women well. But while losing to a superior man may enhance a woman's sexual as well as intellectual satisfaction, whatever intellectual pleasure a heterosexual man may derive from being bested by a superior woman, he is unlikely to find the experience sexually affirmative.

Eschewing marriage and childbirth, de Beauvoir undertook to live a life of the intellect on the basis of presumed equality with a man she believed to be superior and who achieved greater fame. When compared to "great men," she said, the woman of achievement seems mediocre,"[24] a view echoing Beatrice Webb's assertion that women lacked "that fullness of intellectual life which distinguishes the really able man."[25] According to Paul Johnson, Sartre's superiority was more apparent than real: de Beauvoir was "in a strictly academic sense, abler." She almost beat Sartre for first in the philosophy degree, the examiners thinking her "the better philosopher." Johnson thinks her "in many respects a finer" writer, her novel, *Les Mandarins*, being "far better than any of Sartre's."[26]

It has been the norm for women to ally themselves with men who achieve greater market success than they. David M. Buss has established the biological basis for our attraction to the powerful, superior men best able to protect and care for us while we bear children.[27] Her affinity for a superior man well serves a woman who enjoys the many rewards afforded by marriage and child-bearing. But it must surely bring discontent to the woman who confines her life to seeking achievement in the workplace as the equal of that superior man. Not only was de Beauvoir unmarried and childless, but "there are few worse cases," says Johnson, "of a man exploiting a woman." She "became Sartre's slave from almost their first meeting and remained such for all her adult life until he died;" yet, although she was his "mistress, surrogate wife, cook and manager, female bodyguard and nurse," she never held "legal or financial status in his life." Their sexual relationship, moreover, ended in the mid-1940s as she became a "sexually-retired, pseudowife," while he pursued innumerable affairs with ever younger mistresses, one of whom, in his ultimate humiliation of de Beauvoir, he legally adopted so that she was his sole heir and literary executor.[28]

[19] Germaine Greer, *Sex and Destiny: The Politics of Human Fertility* (New York: Harper & Row, 1984), 124–43, 149–53, 353–55, 363–64.

[20] *Insight* (June 8, 1987), 62–3.

[21] De Beauvoir's adopted daughter, Sylvie Le Bon, published de Beauvoir's letters to Sartre which discussed her sexual trysts with young female students. Simone de Beauvoir, *Letters to Sartre*, edited and translated by Quintin Hoare (New York: Little, Brown, 1992). After charges were brought by the parents of one of her female students, de Beauvoir was barred from the university and lost her license to teach anywhere in France. Paul Johnson, *Intellectuals* (New York: Harper, 1988), 238–39.

[22] *Time* (April 28, 1986), 77.

[23] Simone de Beauvoir, *Memoirs of a Dutiful Daughter* (New York: Harper, 1974), 340–44.

[24] Simone de Beauvoir, *The Second Sex* (New York: Knopf, 1978), 711.

[25] Norman and Jeanne MacKenzie, eds., *The Diary of Beatrice Webb: Two* (Cambridge, MA: Belknap, 1983), 52.

[26] Johnson, *Intellectuals*, 235.

[27] David M. Buss, *The Evolution of Desire: Strategies of Human Mating* (New York: Basic, 1994), 19–48.

28 Johnson, *Intellectuals*, 235, 239, 251. Ronald Hayman, a biographer of Sartre, has noted that in a fifty-year friendship, the

In *The Coming of Age*, de Beauvoir attested to the bitterness of life's fruits, describing old age as "life's parody" and "a degradation or even a denial of what has been." "What," she repined, "is the point of having worked so hard if one finds that all is labour lost" and "if one no longer sets the least value upon what has been accomplished?" Those old people who do not "give up the struggle" but stubbornly persevere, continued her lament, "often become caricatures of themselves."[29] Only with great difficulty, one must think, can it be otherwise for those who forgo the bearing of children that can fill our lives with the richest meaning, enabling us to greet old age with equanimity and the expectation that we too will "come proud, open-eyed and laughing to the tomb."[30] To trade the rewards of child-bearing for an aborted fetus and production of intellectual constructs—however great their merit—seems, to some of us, an unsatisfactory exchange.

Upon this exchange—in theory, if not fact—were grounded the lives of all, save one, who spearheaded the contemporary feminist movement. Their qualifications to speak for women as a class are rarely questioned, however, nor are they viewed simply as representing the interests of lesbians and other women who forgo marriage and reproduction. The one exception, Betty Friedan, had concluded that a life devoted largely to marital and maternal responsibilities could never be satisfying. It was these jaundiced abdicants from traditional femininity who led the assault on the traditional wife and mother, the kind of woman only one had ever been, and none would choose to be. Their aim was to make this woman's domestic role untenable; their method was to revile, disdain, and calumniate her. Which leads us to the second irony of their offensive.

Feminism's ability to piggyback upon the black civil rights movement has greatly facilitated women's acquisition of educational, job, and other market preferences. Yet, the principal weapon feminists have employed to devalue the housewife's status has been an attack based on stereotypical analysis, arrant bigotry, and undisguised contempt, all the antithesis of respect for the worth and integrity of each individual that was the wellspring of our civil rights movement. To see this clearly, one need only substitute the word "African-American," "Jew," or "Hispanic" for the word "housewife" in the statements of Betty Friedan and her sisters in the movement. These feminists (who surely thought themselves good people and committed to liberal values) would recoil from characterizing any other group in society in the degrading terms they have routinely applied to the housewife.

PART TWO

FEMINISM'S FALSIFICATION OF REALITY

Contemporary feminism is the creation of women who rejected the traditional family and traditional femininity, who were career-oriented, and who either rejected motherhood altogether, or believed it should play a very subordinate role in a woman's life. The ideology they developed is based on misrepresentation of the facts—feminism's falsification of reality. Feminist success has depended on convincing both men and women that a woman's devotion to home and children is a sacrifice, a virtually worthless pursuit which affords no opportunity to use the energies and intelligence of even an average woman.

A crucial step towards inculcating this attitude has been to foster the belief that mothers previously stayed at home to rear their children only because they had no alternative. The allegation that women have been discriminatorily denied jobs has been, of course, the predicate for giving women job preferences within the legal framework of affirmative action remedies. But this allegation also has been essential to the task of convincing younger generations of women that, if older generations had been permitted to do so, they themselves would have pursued careers rather than staying at home to rear their children.

The major complaint of working mothers is usually not workplace discrimination in the ordinary sense, but their exhaustion, lack of leisure time, and the discrepancy between their own image of what being a good mother entails and the reality of their lives. One feminist response has been to demand alteration of workplace requirements to accommodate child-rearing responsibilities. In addition to these palliative

---

sexual relationship lasted only about sixteen. Ronald Hayman, "Having Wonderful Sex, Wish You Were Here," *The New York Times Book Review* (July 19, 1992).

[29] Simone de Beauvoir, *The Coming of Age* (New York: Putnam, 1972), 539, 540.

[30] William Butler Yeats, *Vacillation* (1932).

measures, feminists have also undertaken to alter the traditional image of a good mother. They began by creating the myth that the decision of women of an earlier generation to decline participation in the workplace did not arise from their own vision of motherhood; rather, they stayed at home with their children only because they had been denied any opportunity to enter or succeed in the workplace. To feminists, who were certain they themselves would never willingly stay at home to rear children, this myth was believable and accorded with the view of sociologist Jessie Bernard that a woman who said she enjoyed being a homemaker had to be somewhat mentally disturbed.

Feminist myth-making meant that women of my generation who had willingly exchanged market production for child-rearing found ourselves represented as victims in analyses designed to document the denial of career opportunities to women. Workplace discrimination in fact played no part in the decisions many of us made to cease working outside the home. We were impelled to stay with our children by the strong emotional pull they exercised on us and because we thought our presence in the home was the single best guarantee of their well-being. A life caring for them at home, we often discovered, was good for us as well. We were confident, moreover, that society respected us and believed us to be engaged in a valuable activity—not acting as sacrificial victims—when we functioned as full-time homemakers.

It is this confidence that contemporary feminism has destroyed by successfully propagating the idea that homemakers' activities are largely valueless, convincing younger generations of men and women that society disdains a woman's domestic role. Yet feminism has been less successful in expunging women's own image of a good mother and relieving working mothers of their ambivalence and feelings of guilt about leaving their children. While workplace modifications can help accommodate working mothers, they offer, at best, mild palliatives for those mothers who do yearn to be with their children and for those children who never find an adequate replacement for lost maternal care.

Workplace modifications can usually only compensate slightly for what is often a mother's nearly insupportable burden of dual responsibility. Instituting these changes serves a very important function, nevertheless, by helping assuage mothers' guilt. The message conveyed through these changes is that society is willing to impose the cost upon taxpayers and consumers because it believes a mother should work outside the home and that her presence at home would be of little value to either mother or child. Reinforcing this message is the fact that costs of workplace modifications benefiting working mothers will be disproportionately borne by one-income families which must pay for, while not sharing in, these benefits.

Like all special interest groups, feminists seek subsidies for themselves. Their economic interests and professional advancement have been greatly enhanced by claims of past societal discrimination against women, including the claim of being forced to assume a sacrificial role as homemaker.

My own experience differs sharply from the tales feminists tell. I was a practicing lawyer in the 1950s. From the time in junior high school when I decided to become a lawyer until I ceased working in order to raise a family, I always received unstinting encouragement and support. It was scarcely possible that someone from the working class, living on the edge of poverty with a divorced mother, could have succeeded otherwise. My entire college and law school educations were funded by scholarships and my employment. Teachers and counselors in high school and college energetically assisted in my efforts to secure these scholarships and other aid, without ever questioning the suitability of my aspirations for a woman. Not once in all the sessions where we discussed my educational options and planned how I would pay for them was this issue ever raised.

Contrary to the received opinion that society consistently discouraged women's market activity, I found social acquaintances were extremely supportive, while employers and many colleagues generously encouraged my pursuit of a career. At the same time, those of my female friends in the 1950s who were traditional housewives little resembled the stereotype, so effectively popularized by Betty Friedan, of intellectually shallow, bored, underachieving child-wives. Nor do I believe the stereotype accurately applied to me when I, too, became a homemaker.

Attending law school and practicing law during a period when feminists would have us believe women were systematically discriminated against, I was treated as well as, and I sometimes thought even better than, the men with whom I was competing. But feminists tell a very different story. Justice Ruth Bader Ginsburg, for example, upon her nomination to the United States Supreme Court, reiterated the feminist mythology. Paying homage to her mother, Justice Ginsburg expressed the hope that she herself would be all her mother "would have been had she lived in an age when women could aspire and achieve." Reflected in these words are the feminist assumptions that women can "achieve" only through market production and that failure to achieve within the workplace cannot have been a willing choice. Cannot Justice Ginsburg conceive that her mother may not have wanted to sacrifice the time at home with her child that would have been required to gain what that child has achieved?

The nominee also attested to the discrimination she faced when, having graduated from Columbia University Law School (on the Law Review and tied for first in her class), "not a law firm in the entire city of New York bid for my employment as a lawyer." It was reported—surely inaccurately—that she had to take a job as a legal secretary.[31] The phrasing of her remarkable statement raises the question whether, resume in hand, she had actually sought a job with every law firm in New York City or simply waited to receive "bids."

When I graduated from the same law school several years before justice Ginsburg (also on the Law Review, but not first in my class) and began my job search, I received an offer from a major Wall Street law firm. As I recall, most of the fourteen women in my class sought and obtained legal positions,[32] although only two of us were on the Law Review and none was first in the class. It is true that the other woman on the Law Review (who was Jewish) did not share my good fortune of receiving an offer from any of the major Wall Street law firms, which did discriminate at that time against Jews and other ethnics. My future husband, for example, who graduated with me—also on the Law Review and with a virtually identical record but without the advantage of being a "Pennington"—was among the many men who could claim they were so discriminated against. Many Jewish graduates during that period, including women, took jobs with what were known as the midtown Jewish law firms, and it seems hardly possible that this avenue was foreclosed to a woman who had graduated first in her class. If her complaint is that she received no offers from major Wall Street firms, my own experience and that of my classmates would indicate the controlling variable was not her sex. It is, of course, more beneficial to plead sex, rather than ethnic, discrimination. Reparation for the latter still leaves her in competition with all the men who share her ethnicity.

Similarly, Barbara Aronstein Black, at the time Dean of Columbia Law School, discussed what it was like for her and other women to go to law school when they did not think they could get jobs or have a career: "We all knew that once we attempted to move into practice (but of course I never did), we would meet active discrimination. That was perfectly clear, and we were pretty angry about it."[33] But we did *not* all know this; it was *not* perfectly clear. The then-Barbara Aronstein graduated from Columbia Law School the year after I did. I never was part of such discussions and never doubted that I could obtain a good legal job and pursue a career for as long as I wanted. Like most of my classmates, male and female, I set out with my resume and obtained a job. Those women, who, like Barbara Aronstein Black, were Jewish or members of other ethnic groups, did know—just as similarly situated men knew—that for them the job search would be harder and that they were unlikely to receive offers from major Wall Street law firms. The distinction then usually made—but certainly not always—was between white, Anglo-Saxon Protestants and ethnics, not between men and women.[34] Now that it has become fashionable to plead one's victimization at every opportunity, what I find most interesting is that my classmates who were disadvantaged because of their ethnicity rarely did seem angry, but only determined to overcome whatever obstacles they faced.

Feminist Susan Brownmiller entered Cornell University as a freshman the year after I had finished my undergraduate work there and gone on to law school. In a letter to the *Cornell Alumni News* of April 1973,

---

[31] *New York Times* (June 15, 1993). Although this lead article on her nomination stated that her first job was as a "legal secretary," a letter from the Columbia Law Women's Association detailing her alleged victimization by sex bias states that when "she could not find a job in a law firm commensurate with her credentials," she served "as law clerk to Judge Edmund L. Palmieri of the United States District Court, Southern District of New York." This is confirmed in *Columbia, The Magazine of Columbia University* (Summer 1980) and it was so reported in *The Wall Street Journal* (June 15, 1993).

[32] The same is true for women graduates of Harvard Law School. Because she transferred to Columbia in her final year at Harvard Law School, Justice Ginsburg is a member of the Harvard Law class of 1959. On the occasion of that class's 25th reunion, an examination of the careers of its female members disclosed that "most of the women in the class ended up following career paths similar to the men—law firm partners, judges, academics, public-interest lawyers and in-house corporate lawyers. In the late 1970s and 1980s, many found themselves established as the senior women in their field—and enjoying the benefits." Jill Abramson, "Class of Distinction," *The Wall Street Journal* (July 20, 1993).

[33] "Barbara Aronstein Black: A Conversation," *The Observer* (Columbia Law School Alumni Association, August 1986), 4.

[34] Ethnicity would sometimes be overlooked in the presence of other factors—for example, the ability to bring business to the firm.

Myth: that staying home to raise kids + be a homemaker is a huge sacrifice. And that a woman who chooses to do it must either be crazy or a saint.

Brownmiller wrote that when she entered Cornell in 1952, "I had secret hopes of going to Law School. Two years later I abandoned that goal as a rather unseemly ambition for a woman." She does not say who made her believe this ambition was unseemly—perhaps it was her family. I doubt it was any of the faculty or administrators with whom I dealt at Cornell. After my first year, I was given a job that enabled me to earn my room and board without working so many hours that I would be unable to maintain the grades required for my full-tuition scholarship; this job was given only to students whose ambition was thought serious and seemly. The Registrar at Cornell Law School took my aspirations very seriously. My only doubt about those aspirations was that it might be foolish for one as poor as I to continue her education. The Registrar always encouraged me to pursue my ambitions, and he helped me to choose the law schools where I should apply and then to decide between Harvard, Yale, Columbia, and Cornell. That these law schools accepted me and offered me scholarships and other aid belies the claim that being a lawyer was considered unseemly for a woman.

My own career pursuits elicited a vastly more tolerant reaction four decades ago than is now evoked by a decision to devote oneself to being a full-time mother and housewife, a choice that, in recent years, has usually been depicted as a waste of time and talent. What were once considered valuable and respected activities—raising children, attending to a husband's needs, and managing a household—the present society created by contemporary feminism views as benighted and beyond rational justification. No woman with a brain in her head, feminists have largely convinced society, could possibly be happy devoting herself to what they portray as worthless, even degrading, activities. No woman, as Justice Ginsburg implied, would *willingly* live a life of such limited achievement.

Feminists have inaccurately depicted women's past lives both in home and workplace and falsely claimed that the intensive devotion of a woman at home cannot significantly benefit her marriage and children. But feminists are accurate when they deny that women should be expected to become mothers. The denial seems superfluous, however, since it has rarely been asserted that motherhood must be every woman's destiny. Monasteries and nunneries, for example, have been among the social institutions recognizing that reproduction is not expected of everyone. Clearly, some women are not suited to motherhood and some mothers prefer delegating child-rearing to others in order to pursue a career or other interests. The insidiousness of the women's movement is that, while claiming—and being perceived by society—to speak for all women, it has represented only these two groups.

THE AWAKENED BRUNNHILDE

The woman who wishes to rear her children within a traditional marriage, to whom contemporary feminism has been an implacable enemy, I call the "awakened Brunnhilde." Best-known from Richard Wagner's *The Ring often Nibelung*, Brunnhilde is a warrior maiden who was transformed by her love for the hero Siegfried. The Brunnhilde I seek to defend is a woman who finds that the satisfactions of full-time commitment to being a wife and mother outweigh the rewards of pursuing a career. This realization is part of what I call her awakened femininity.

But Brunnhilde's choice, according to societal consensus, is a sacrifice. It is viewed as a sacrifice because society has acquiesced in feminism's depiction of the homemaker's role as worthless, boring, unrewarding, unfulfilling, and incapable of using a woman's talents. Even those who support this choice as being in children's best interest will speak of it as a sacrifice. For women like me, however, the sacrifice lies in precisly the opposite choice. It would have been a virtually unendurable sacrifice for me to have left my children with anyone (including my husband who, while possessing many virtues, was ill suited to a mother's role) in order to remain in the workplace.

I have been happy in every period of my adult life: attending college and law school, practicing law, staying at home to raise a family, and creating a new life once my family responsibilities had largely ended. Yet those many years I spent as a mother at home from the birth of my first child until the last left for college were the best, the ones I would be least willing to have forgone. Feminists recount endless tales of women's oppression throughout the ages, but one of the greatest injustices to women is feminists' own success in convincing society to treat as a sacrifice what for some women can be the most rewarding occupation of their lives.

By undermining the status and security of awakened Brunnhilde, contemporary feminism has inflicted undeserved injury upon many good women. And society itself has been weakened by its curtailing of women's domestic role, which contributes substantially possibly more than any other single activity—to societal health and stability. All indicia of familial well-being demonstrate that our society was a significantly better place for families in the decade before the feminist revival—when the primary concerns of most mothers were their husbands, their children, and their home. Those of us who concluded that our marriages and families would thrive better if we devoted ourselves to home and children rather than to market production find our belief validated by studies showing that "when women can support themselves, there is a lesser degree of bonding between husband and wife and more relaxed sexual mores" and that "the higher the relative degree of power attributed by respondents to the male partner, the lower the rate of marital dissolution."[35] These findings are consistent with the long-known fact that the women "with high incomes and/or graduate degrees have the highest divorce rate—a rate far higher than successful men."[36]

Our belief is also confirmed by several findings of a recently concluded long-term study of married couples: (1) husbands "who do more household tasks are less satisfied with the way the tasks are distributed," and this division of tasks "is associated with declines in their love for their wives;" (2) the "more fathers in dual-earner marriages are involved with child care, the more negativity in the marriage," and those fathers "who report more negative interaction tend to be less satisfied with the division of child care tasks and also tend to be less in love with their wives;" and (3) the extent to which husbands who are the sole bread-winners are involved in child care is unrelated to the amount of negativity toward their wives, and "the more single-earner fathers are in love with their wives, the more (rather than less) involved they are in child care and leisure activities alone with their children.[37]

That mothers provide daily care for their children is in the interest of those men who would resist the feminist effort to refashion them into mother-substitutes, a role for which men are usually not well-suited. It is in the interest of those children who would have both a father and a mother, each filling different roles, and who would be spared the daycare and surrogate mothering that can be a source of misery and are likely to be inferior to care at home from a competent and contented mother. And it is in the interest of those women who could find a motherhood that is unencumbered by marketplace commitments to be an incomparable joy.

Admittedly, life at home with their children cannot be a joy—either incomparable or ordinary—for women who regard that life as a sacrifice. It is not my purpose to convince these women otherwise. Such persuasion, my own experience has taught me, is more likely to spring from their own physical and emotional experience than from discussion. It is the experiences in her marital relationship, together with the experiences of pregnancy and childbirth—forces more subtle than intellectual reasoning—that will usually awaken a woman's response to her children and then mold the dimensions of that response.

I use the term "awakened femininity" to describe Brunnhilde's response to her sexual experiences and to her children. The purpose of the feminist endeavor was to discourage a response like Brunnhilde's and encourage what I call women's "spiritual virginity." This is the term I use to describe a response that permits a woman to resist the emotional pull exerted by her child so that she can continue her life as a market producer after childbirth. At the same time as feminists promoted the sexual revolution that mocked women's premarital sexual virginity and marital chastity, they vilified and disadvantaged those women who refused to adopt a feminist "spiritual virginity," but chose, instead, to become homemakers and child-rearers.

Clearly, some women do experience full-time child-rearing as a joy, not a sacrifice, even when their initial decision to stay at home is prompted by the altruistic motive that this will be best for their children. That these women should find life at home to be enjoyable and rewarding is, I contend, at least reasonable. It is, therefore, scarcely debatable that society should support, not undermine, their lives at home. In the interests of such women, their families, and society, we should begin to restore the level playing field that the women's movement has destroyed.

[35] Kingsley R. Browne, "Sex and Temperament in Modern Society: A Darwinian View of the Glass Ceiling and the Gender Gap," *Arizona Law Review* 37 (1995), 995, n.112, 1089, n.810.

[36] George Gilder, *Sexual Suicide* (New York: Quadrangle, 1973), 67.

[37] Ted L. Huston, "Path to Parenthood," *Discovery: Research and Scholarship at The University of Texas At Austin* 14 (1996), 59, 63.

Feminists actually think they're doing a good thing. Failure to realize that there is another way of looking at things. They think that since they think this way, all women do.

We must recognize that proposals with an initial appeal can often have detrimental effects on traditional families and must therefore be resisted by those who want to support such families. The proposed equal rights amendment, for example, would have forbidden denial of "equality of rights under the law... on account of sex." It was intended to make sex distinctions identical to distinctions on the basis of race so that men and women—like blacks and whites—would have to be treated alike for all purposes. The amendment was intended, like many of the judicial decisions reached under the Fourteenth Amendment's equal protection clause, to promote the feminist goal of an androgynous society. It would forbid, among other things, the existence of publicly run schools, classes, or athletic activities for one sex only and require drafting of women for military service, including combat. Feminists sought the amendment to signify that our nation endorsed the aim of the National Organization for Women to disfavor the traditional family with a breadwinner husband and homemaker wife. Like no-fault divorce laws, the amendment was designed to force women to abandon their traditional roles and refashion themselves after the feminist role models who promoted it.

Similarly, government-funded child care programs must inevitably harm traditional families. The greatest financial need in our society exists in households with children. It is not this financial need, however, which leads the women's movement to endorse government-funded child care, but its firm belief that a woman's proper place is in the work force, rather than in the home caring for her children. Financial hardships of families with children could be alleviated by increasing the federal income tax exemption for dependents or providing family allowances (through tax credits or some other method) that would benefit *all* families with children, including those in which the mother stays at home. Such reforms would lighten the financial burden of one-wage-earner families and permit some women to leave the work force.

But any outcome that enables women to exchange market activities for life at home is disfavored by the women's movement. It consistently argues, instead, for government-funded institutional child care that would require expenditures rivaling social security and Medicare. The lure of subsidized child care, together with the resulting tax burden imposed on all families, would serve feminist goals by encouraging women to continue working and enticing women into the work force who prefer caring for their children at home. Through the legislation they seek, feminists demonstrate their preference for a government policy that disfavors families where the mother remains at home with her children by taxing these families in order to pay for child care, as well as other benefits, for families in which the mother works outside the home. Acting upon their belief that women should do market work rather than care for their children, feminists advocate discriminatory methods designed to deprive women of a real choice and push them into living in accordance with the feminist ideology.

In *1984*, George Orwell describes an old man in a pub who, having survived revolution and purges, is one of the "last links that now exist with the vanished world of capitalism." When told by the barman that there are no pints of beer, the old man responds that "a pint's the 'alf of a quart, and there's four quarts to the gallon," to which the barman replies that he'd never heard of them: "liter and half liter—that's all we serve."[38] All that is now served by the reigning cultural elite are views like feminist Karen DeCrow's: "No man should allow himself to support his wife—no matter how much she favors the idea, no matter how many centuries this domestic pattern has existed, no matter how logical the economics of the arrangement may appear, no matter how good it makes him feel... It will diminish and destroy affection and respect... Love can flourish between adults only when everyone pays his or her own way."[39] *crazy*

Contained within DeCrow's brief statement is the entire feminist ideology. Andrea Dworkin had earlier stated it even more briefly, asserting that "to have what men have one must be what men are."[40] This ideology dictates that marriage should not be an institution in which a man and a woman assume different, complementary roles, but a relationship like that of roommates, each fully and independently committed to market production—something resembling a homosexual relationship, yet between heterosexuals. DeCrow assumes that only a paycheck can fulfill a woman's half of the marital bargain. To Brunnhilde, however, the arrangement DeCrow proposes, in which the woman (who for all purposes could just as well be another man) must pay her own way, has two fatal flaws: first, the arrangement requires child-rearing by surrogates;

---

[38] George Orwell, *1984* (New York: Harcourt, Brace, 1949), 86–87.
[39] Letters to the Editor, *The New York Times Magazine* (May 31, 1992).
[40] Andrea Dworkin, *Intercourse* (New York: Free Press, 1987), p. 100.

second, it discards the different, complementary roles that she believes are most likely to produce a stable marriage, enlivened by satisfying sexuality. DeCrow's market-oriented roommates, who are little more than clones of each other, are the least likely to satisfy what Roger Scruton identified—Brunnhilde believes accurately—as the foundation of heterosexual sexual excitement: "the energy released when man and woman come together is proportional to the distance which divides them when they are apart."[41]

That this feminist ideology is now substantially institutionalized in our society is evidenced by the wide acceptance of Justice Ginsburg's assumption that what can properly be considered achievement occurs only within the marketplace. A woman who seeks an alternative achievement within the domestic arena is dismissively described by Ginsburg—in words reflecting the same ideological assumptions as those of DeCrow and Dworkin—as being "reduced to dependency on a man."[42] It is beyond the ken of these feminists to perceive the homemaker—in the way I have always viewed myself—not as being "reduced," but as happily being spared the market work which would have required an unbearably constricted maternal role.

Feminism's ideological victory has been a significant factor in producing the conditions cited by public school administrators when recommending full-day public school education for very young children because government institutions must take responsibility for children at ever younger ages. One administrator, for example, stated at a public hearing that children are no longer being reared by their families since the family "as we once knew it, has been destroyed." The family, he said, "is gone" and so "we are going to have to do something else." "You can forget the family part."[43] But not all those mothers whose employment has contributed to creating this situation celebrate it as the social advance it is to feminists. Some of these mothers, instead, acknowledge a strong yearning to be at home with their children and guilt because of the choices they have made.[44]

If this maternal yearning is ever to influence behavior, it must be powerful enough to overcome the feminist triumph that has entrenched within our society views of elite opinion-makers like those expressed by justice Ginsburg and Karen DeCrow. The traditional family that the women's movement targeted as its enemy is, like the pints and quarts of *1984*, on its way to extinction. While not yet dead and gone, as the school administrator claimed, it will be unless those who believe in the value of this family structure attempt to reverse feminism's victory. Such an attempt will not succeed until society begins again to respect and support—rather than disfavor, patronize, and demean—the woman who undertakes a traditional role and the man who makes it possible for her to do so.

---

*The essay originally appeared as a chapter in the book *Domestic Tranquility: A Brief Against Feminism*:
   E. Carolyn Graglia, *Domestic Tranquility: A Brief Against Feminism* (Dallas: Spence Publishing, 1998), 1–30.
**Reproduction Rights granted by E. Carolyn Graglia and Spence Publishing.

---

[41] Roger Scruton, *Sexual Desire: A Moral Philosophy of the Erotic* (New York: Free Press, 1986), 273.
[42] *New York Times* (June 27, 1993).
[43] Transcript of Proceedings, United States Commission on Civil Rights, Forum on Early Childhood Education, Dallas, TX (May 20, 1989), 90, 103.
[44] These are the typical reactions of the working mothers and women considering motherhood who were surveyed by anthropologist Katherine S. Newman in her study of a New York suburban community. *Declining Fortunes: The Withering of the American Dream* (New York: Basic, 1993). In *Feminism Is Not the Story of My Life* (New York: Doubleday, 1996), 194, Elizabeth Fox-Genovese describes how "the pull between family and work can drive working mothers to distraction" and "the feelings of guilt may become almost too much to bear."

DOMESTIC TRANQUILITY
ESSAY QUESTIONS

Answer the questions below on a separate sheet of paper and be prepared to review your answers in class.

1. What are the similarities and differences between radical feminists and moderate feminists?

2. What are two consequences of the mass migration of women into the workforce?

3. What are the consequences of the feminist-supported sexual revolution?

4. What have been the consequences of no-fault divorce laws?

5. What is the irony of feminism's alignment with the black civil rights movement?

6. What myth has helped lead to feminism's success?

7. Why does the feminist movement support government-funded child care?

8. Why do feminists refuse to support incentives that would benefit a single-income family?

9. What type of marital relationship is most likely produced by feminism's dictum that "a woman must pay her own way?"

10. What problems can arise from this type of marital relationship?

DEAR DOUG
WRITING ASSIGNMENT

Hello again!

A new semester has begun! I'm determined not to slack off this year—let's just say my grades pointed out exactly how many parties I went to. My new class sheet says I'm signed up for economics, law and politics, history, and sociology this spring.

That last class is going to be interesting, just from looking at the textbook. We've already had a coffee discussion about it and everyone brought up lots of issues. I walked in late and they were talking about the church's effect on society. Mark was saying that religion is a hindrance to progress—it dumbs people down so they can't influence change in society. Sarah agreed because she thinks women aren't allowed enough power in the church. I've never thought of Christians as being outdated.

Mark was also saying that the government should take a much larger role in raising kids so that they aren't brainwashed by their parents into believing in religion. Sarah thought that was a great idea because it would free women from the constraints of the home. Without children tying them down, they would be able to exercise the same power and sexual freedoms as men. I'm not sure I agree with them, though. What do you think about the government taking on the full responsibility of educating children?

Nathan and Paige pretty much agreed, adding that the church is sexist and homophobic—it doesn't care about anything but rules and regulations and being perfect. Paige said religion in general limits what women can do and Nathan told a story about a gay friend of his who got kicked out of church because of his lifestyle. I guess I've never seen church from that angle… at least I didn't see it that way in our youth group. How would you respond to that accusation?

In addition to all this, I had a fight with Amber. I took her out last night and during dinner we started talking about what we wanted to do after college. Her plan had a lot to do with career and nothing at all about marriage. When I asked her about it, she said that would be like throwing away everything women have gained over the past several decades.

I must've had a strange look on my face, because she stopped eating and jumped into this tirade about how there really isn't any difference between the sexes—men have just been forcing their will on women and women have let them get away with it. Then she headed into abortion and how women everywhere deserve the right to decide what happens to their own bodies, not religious fanatics or the government. By the time she ran out of steam, I didn't have a clue what to say. How's a Christian supposed to handle this issue, anyway? Seems to me any side I take I'm going to be wrong, just because I'm a guy.

Sorry to dump all this on you just after we both got back in the school routine, but I really need some advice. Does the Bible have anything to say about social issues like feminism and the role of the church in society?

Later,
Doug

WORLDVIEW TRAINING

STUDENT
MANUAL

UNDERSTANDING THE TIMES

Unit Seven

Topics:
Arts
Entertainment
Law

A Summit Ministries Curriculum

180-DAY SYLLABUS

DAY	IN CLASS	HOMEWORK	
1	WATCH "Law" video		
2	READ UTT Textbook 'Law 7.1'	READ UTT Textbook 'Law 7.2'	
3	REVIEW UTT Textbook 'Law 7.1–7.2' questions	READ UTT Textbook 'Law 7.3'	
4	READ UTT Textbook 'Law 7.4'		
5	REVIEW UTT Textbook 'Law 7.3–7.4' questions	READ UTT Textbook 'Law 7.5'	
6	READ UTT Textbook 'Law 7.6'		
7	REVIEW UTT Textbook 'Law 7.5–7.6' questions	ASSIGN Dear Doug Letter	
8	WATCH "Entertainment" video P1		
9	WATCH "Entertainment" video P2		
10	REVIEW "Entertainment" video questions		
11	READ *The Creative Arts* essay P1		
12	REVIEW *The Creative Arts* essay questions P1		
13	READ *The Creative Arts* essay P2		
14	REVIEW *The Creative Arts* essay questions P2	Dear Doug Letter assignment DUE	
15	TAKE Unit Seven Test		

90-DAY SYLLABUS

DAY	IN CLASS	HOMEWORK	
1	WATCH "Law" video	READ UTT Textbook 'Law 7.1–7.2'	
2	REVIEW UTT Textbook 'Law 7.1–7.2' questions	READ UTT Textbook 'Law 7.3–7.4'	
3	REVIEW UTT Textbook 'Law 7.3–7.4' questions	READ UTT Textbook 'Law 7.5–7.6'	
4	REVIEW UTT Textbook 'Law 7.5–7.6' questions		
5	WATCH "Entertainment" video P1		
6	WATCH "Entertainment" video P2		
7	REVIEW "Entertainment" video questions		
8	TAKE Unit Seven Test		

Unit Seven

UNDERSTANDING THE TIMES
LAW QUESTIONS

Answer the questions below on a separate sheet of paper and be prepared to review your answers in class.

LAW 7.1

1. Why do law systems that reject God as Lawgiver ultimately fail?

2. Why does public trust in law disappear if the fundamental principles of law are undermined? How could this affect other areas of life?

3. Why do Christians believe that law exists? Why do Christians believe it is possible to develop a just system of law?

4. In what two ways has God revealed his law to mankind?

5. What are the five basic precepts of Christian law?

LAW 7.2

6. What is Shari'ah law? What are its main tributaries? What is *fiqh*?

7. Which legal schools do the Sunnis promote? Which legal schools do the Shi'ites promote? Why do the legal traditions of the Shi'ites give them an edge over their Sunni counterparts in contemporary culture?

8. What are the five categories of behavior within Shari'ah law?

9. How does the Islamic view of humanity and law differ from the view held by Christianity? What form of government does the Islamic view usually produce? How does India's system of government differ from most Islamic governments?

10. Can the Muslim community find a basis for individual freedom within its religion? What examples are given as restrictions of these freedoms?

LAW 7.3

11. What is the basic assumption upon which Secular Humanist law is founded?

12. What are some key foundational principles of Secular Humanist law?

13. What is natural law?

14. How do the theistic and Secular Humanistic views of natural law differ?

15. What view of law must consistent Humanists accept? What danger is inherent in such a view?

Unit Seven

16. According to Marxism, where do rights and laws originate?

17. What is bourgeoisie law? What two problems do Marxists have with bourgeoisie law? How do Marxists propose that society overcome the corrupt rule of bourgeoisie law?

18. How is Marxist legal theory similar to Secular Humanist law? How does Marxist legal theory differ from that of the Secular Humanist?

19. What is the ultimate source for determining justice in a Marxist society?

20. What is the ultimate fate of law in the future communist utopia?

LAW 7.5

21. According to Cosmic Humanists, where does all authority reside and why?

22. According to Cosmic Humanism, what is sacrificed when we choose to honor a set of rules other than our own inner truth?

23. What must societies abandon to become more conducive to a Cosmic Humanist view of law?

24. Under the Cosmic Humanist legal perspective, what makes an action right or wrong?

25. What problems do Cosmic Humanists have with a Christian view of law?

LAW 7.6

26. Why are Postmodernists opposed to Western law? What do they desire to see in its place?

27. What is the Critical Legal Studies movement?

28. In what ways have the ideas of Michel Foucault and Jacques Derrida influenced CLS?

29. How is Susan Estrich's view of law different from the traditional view?

30. What techniques do Postmodernists prefer over objective reasoning and why?

"ENTERTAINMENT"

WITH JOHN STONESTREET

I. Christianity and Culture

A. _Offended_ by culture

  1. Tend to withdraw

  2. We are neither in the world nor of the world

  3. Scopes Monkey Trial

> "We really took the approach, by and large as the church, that we couldn't handle the tough questions and that we were going to get made fun of, so we withdrew from the culture… Today Christians are much better known for what they are against than what they are for."

B. _Distracted_ by culture

> "For the first time in recorded history there is no significant difference between the way Christians and non-Christians live their lives and make decisions." — George Barna

1. We become just like our culture

    i. We forget about morality

    or

    ii. We take everything the world is doing and put "Christian" on it

2. We are in the world and of the world

C. _Distressed_ by culture

> While Paul was waiting for them in Athens, he was greatly distressed to see that the city was full of idols. So he reasoned in the synagogues… as well as in the marketplace day by day… 'Men of Athens, I see that in every way you are very religious. For as I walked around and looked carefully at your objects of worship… ' — Acts 17

  1. We need to know both the word of God and the world of God

  2. We are to be *in* the world but not *of* the world

Unit Seven

II. Exegeting Entertainment

A. It is an overwhelming and culture-shaping force in our world

"It is not any 'ism' but entertainment that is arguably the most pervasive, powerful, and ineluctable force of our time—a force so overwhelming that it has finally metastasized into life." — Neal Gabler

"I feel like I have a duty. I, as an architect, have a need to impose my worldview on the culture." — Courtney Love

"We don't shoot for fourteen year-olds, we own them." — President of MTV

"If a man were permitted to write the ballads of a nation, he need not care who writes its laws." — Andrew Fletcher

"First art will imitate life, then life will imitate art, then life will find its very meaning from the arts." — Unknown

B. How entertainment shapes culture:

1. It ___embodies___ worldview ideas

"The most dangerous ideas in a society are not the ones being argued, but the ones that are assumed." — C. S. Lewis

2. It ___changes___ how we know and think:

   i. The rapid pace discourages reflection and evaluation

   ii. Images and ideas given and juxtaposed out of context fragment and trivialize life

   iii. Celebrity-ism, escapism, and addiction

   "We risk being the first people in history to have been able to make their illusions so vivid, so persuasive, so 'realistic' that they can live in them." — Daniel Boorstin

---

PART TWO

III. Approaching Entertainment

A. Wrong "Christian" approaches

1. Avoid it and it will go away

2. Just listen/watch "___Christian___" music and movies

   i. What is a Christian song or movie?

   ii. Entertainment changes how we know and think

   "Entertainment makes us silly." — Neil Postman

"If entertainment makes us silly, then Christian entertainment makes us silly Christians… Instead of having a meaningful time with the Lord, we listen to a CD."

"A good song, a good movie, and a good book take you deeper into life. A bad song, a bad movie, and a bad book distract you from life."

3. The Rating System (G, PG13, R, etc.)

4. Cusswords + Sex = Acceptability

5. **Wrong Question:** "Where do I draw the ___line___?"

"Life is not a line; life is a direction… We are either running toward life or running toward death."

B. **The right approach:** "How should I live as a Christian in an entertainment-based culture?"

1. *With the right goal*: cultural impact

2. *With the right mind*: engaged, not "___amused___"

i. Recognize and utilize where possible the culture's search for meaning

ii. Live above the triviality

iii. Do not condone sin, but warn of it

3. *With the right framework*: Scripture (Philippians 4)

hope looks the dispare in the world right in the eye and deals w/ it. Positivity just ignores the problems + dispare in life.

i. Form	➡	Quality (Is it well done?)	➡	Excellent
ii. Content	➡	Message (What is it saying?)	➡	True
iii. Function	➡	Effect (What is its purpose?)	➡	Noble

4. *With the right tool*: discernment

5. Use available resources for selectivity

"ENTERTAINMENT"
VIDEO QUESTIONS

Answer the questions below on a separate sheet of paper and be prepared to review your answers in class.

1. **What are two bad approaches Christians have taken with regards to culture? What is wrong with these approaches?**

2. **How should Christians approach culture? How did Christ and Paul approach culture?**

3. **In what two ways does entertainment shape culture?**

4. **What are some faulty ways Christians can approach entertainment? What is wrong with these approaches?**

5. **What is a good approach Christians can take with entertainment?**

Objects on this page are no smaller than they appear.

If you can read this, you are too close to your workbook.

THE CREATIVE ARTS
BY LELAND RYKEN

PART ONE

This is the final essay in a series that defines a Christian worldview and applies that framework to leading areas of intellectual life. We must not allow the final position of this essay to mislead us into thinking that the creative arts are the extraneous "dessert" in a person's worldview, an intellectual delicacy that cannot hope to compare in importance to such staples as philosophy and the physical and social sciences.

Creativity and imagination permeate all human activity. It is important to note at the outset, therefore, that the qualities that I attribute to the creative arts are present in other intellectual pursuits as well. My focus will be on the arts; I leave it to each reader to decide how widely my statements apply to the humanities in general and the social and natural sciences.

THE PLACE OF THE ARTS IN A WORLDVIEW

The creative arts play a crucial role in shaping the worldview of every person and culture. They are an implied declaration that a worldview consists of more than abstract ideas or theoretical concepts. A world picture is a map of reality made up of images, symbols, myths and stories as well as theoretical concepts. Contemporary psychology has given us such terms as *preconceptual sensing* and *nonverbal cognition* and *the right side of the brain* to identify what I will call images.

The arts are rooted in the image-making and image-perceiving nature of people. People do not live by ideas alone. They also express their affirmations and denials through the paint on a canvas, the tension and release of sound, and poems and stories. A noted theologian has said that "we are far more image-making and image-using creatures than we usually think ourselves to be and… are guided and formed by images in our minds… Man… is a being who grasps and shapes reality… with the aid of great images, metaphors, and analogies."[1]

Who can doubt it? People organize their lives and make their decisions partly in terms of such images as heroes and villains, cross and altar, national emblem and patriotic legend, love song and hymn, landscape painting and portrait. These images have an ideational aspect to them but also communicate meanings that do not become focused into the form of theoretical propositions.[2]

By their very nature, therefore, the arts serve the salutary function of reminding people, including Christians, that to regard their worldview as being solely the domain of theoretical thought is to invite unawareness about themselves. People may not accede to the accumulation of possessions, but if their minds are filled with images of big houses and fancy clothes, their actual behavior will run in the direction of materialism. People may theoretically believe in the ideals of chastity and faithful wedded love, but if their minds are filled with images of exposed bodies and songs of seduction, their sexual behavior will have a large admixture of lust and sexual license in it.

Unless we recognize the powerful role of images in a worldview, our worldview and the behavior it produces will continue to be the muddled things they often are. We also need to recognize that the quality of our life and character is heavily affected by the quality of the images that we habitually take into our minds and imaginations.

The contribution that the arts make to a person's worldview is rooted in the fact that they all employ a "language" of images. The visual artist, for example, uses physical materials such as paint and stone to produce images that we can see and touch. Music employs physical instruments to produce sounds that we hear with our ears and feel in our muscles. Poets use words to evoke imagined sensations, objects and emotions. And storytellers describe such tangible realities as people performing actions in physical settings.

[1] H. Richard Niebuhr, *The Responsible Self* (New York: Harper & Row, 1963), 151–52, 161.
[2] Michael Polanyi's way of saying this is that "we can know more than we can tell" (*The Tacit Dimension* [Garden City, NY: Doubleday, 1966], 4).

The Imagination

The human faculty or capacity that enables the arts to image forth reality in this way is the imagination. Imagination is what the arts share. By "imagination" I mean simply the image-making and image-perceiving capacity that we all have; I do not have in mind any particular theory of artistic creativity or mental association. Modern aesthetic theory is based on the imagination as the key to everything, and it has stressed two aspects of the imagination.

Imagination implies, first of all, the notion of "image," that is, sensory concreteness or experiential immediacy. The arts are a *presentational* form. Instead of talking about human experience, they present the experience. The arts show rather than tell. They incarnate their meanings in concrete images of human experience or the external world. Instead of primarily asking our intellects to grasp an idea, the arts ask us to undergo an experience, which may or may not eventuate in a proposition or concept. The fiction writer Flannery O'Connor has said regarding her particular art form that "the whole story is the meaning, because it is an experience, not an abstraction."[3] We can view the arts as analogous to a picture accompanying the instructions for assembling an appliance or piece of furniture: if we have a good picture, we may not even need the written instructions.

The second thing that imagination implies is a fictional or imaginary element. Fictional literature is the most obvious illustration of the "made up" quality of art, but in fact all art is an imaginary reconstruction of actual reality. Looking at a painted landscape is never the same as standing in an actual landscape. Music gives us combinations of sounds that we never encounter in real life. Only in poems do people speak in rhyme and regular meter.

The arts are never a mere copy of life. They are always a distillation of some aspect of reality. All artists use techniques of highlighting, omission, selectivity, exaggeration, arrangement and juxtaposition to heighten our perception of some aspect of life. Music, for example, artificially produces arrangements of sounds that awaken feelings of serenity or exultation or reverence. A painting can give us a heightened sense of something as common as flowers and household utensils, as in the still-life paintings of the Dutch realists. Literary tragedy distills the essence of human suffering and silhouettes it with clarity.

The arts, in short, are based on a grand paradox. They are imaginary constructions that "distort" reality in order to increase our awareness of it. In the words of Pablo Picasso, "Art is a lie that makes us realize truth."[4] Or as Samuel Johnson put it, works of fiction "are not mistaken for realities, but... bring realities to mind."[5] The truth that the arts are particularly adept at capturing is enduring, elemental human experience. Whereas the newspaper and history book tell us what *happened*, the arts tell us what *happens*—the reality that never goes out of date because it is universal in human experience.

Imagination and the Bible

If we now ask how the artistic imagination fares in a Christian worldview, it is at once apparent that Christianity affirms the artistic enterprise. The Bible itself endorses both the image-making and imaginary impulses of the arts. There are four main lines of evidence to support this claim.

The first is that God is portrayed in the Bible as a creator of images. A dominant theme throughout the Old Testament is God's creation of the natural world of created objects. These visible images, in turn, are said to communicate truth about God himself (Psalm 19:1–4; Romans 1:19–20). The New Testament counterpart is the Incarnation of Jesus, who is declared to be God in tangible human form.

We should note secondly the literary nature of the Bible. The one thing that the Bible is not is what we so often picture it as being—a theological outline with proof texts attached. The bulk of the Bible consists of stories, poems, visions and letters, all of them literary forms. When asked to define neighbor, Jesus told a fictional story (Luke 10:25–37). When he wished to teach a lesson in servanthood, he washed his disciples' feet (John 13:1–20). Jesus taught religious truth by making up stories about sheep and pearls and seed and fish. Oliver Cromwell rightly said that Jesus "Spoke things." Jesus trusted the ability of literary images to convey religious truth when he told his disciples to "remember Lot's wife" (Luke 17:32). The Bible repeatedly affirms the image-making tendency of the arts.

---

[3] Flannery O'Connor, *Mystery and Manners*, eds. Sally and Robert Fitzgerald (New York: Farrar, Straus & Giroux, 1961), 73.
[4] Pablo Picasso, *The Arts*, May 1923.
[5] Quoted in Charles Kaplan, ed., *Criticism: The Major Statements* (New York: St. Martin's Press, 1975), 264.

Third, the Christian sacraments of communion and baptism have also been important in attempts to arrive at a Christian aesthetic (philosophy of the arts). The Christian sacraments affirm the sign-making impulse of the arts. The sacraments, after all, use the physical elements of water, bread, and wine to express and impart spiritual realities. While the Christian sacraments do not lend sanction to every manifestation of the creative imagination in a fallen world, they do nonetheless confirm the principle that images and symbols can express truth to the glory of God and the edification of people.

A fourth biblical validation of the arts is the descriptions of worship that we find especially in the Old Testament. Worship in the Bible is surrounded by a wealth of music and visual and verbal art.[6] As the Old Testament worshipers approached the Temple in Jerusalem, they saw two gigantic freestanding bronze pillars over twenty-five feet high (1 Kings 7:15–22). These monoliths had no architectural function other than to be beautiful and suggest by their aesthetic properties something of the grandeur, stability and power of God. The pillars were specimens of one prominent type of art in the Temple, namely, abstract or nonrepresentational art.

Representational and symbolic art were also present in Old Testament worship. The ten stands of bronze at the Temple were engraved with lions, oxen and palm trees (1 Kings 7:27–37). Sculptures of winged cherubim were prominent in both the tabernacle (Exodus 25:18–20; 26:31) and the Temple (1 Kings 7:29). Symbolic art also abounded, with such tangible objects as a golden table for the sacred bread, a golden altar, lampstands of pure gold and basins serving as visual symbols of such spiritual realities as communion with God, sacrifice, revelation, and cleansing.

There can be no doubt that the tabernacle and Temple were the Old Testament believer's most intense encounter with artistic beauty. If we doubt this, we need only read the chapters of the Bible that describe the visual properties of these places (Exodus 25–31; 35–39; 1 Kings 5–7; 2 Chronicles 2–4). The descriptions testify to an overwhelming value accorded to beauty. Some of the artistic embellishment in these places of worship awakened the worshipers' awareness of the other great source of beauty in their life—nature, as seen, for example, in the carved flowers about which we read repeatedly (1 Kings 7).

The beauty associated with the tabernacle and Temple included the purely imaginary as well as the realistic. The pomegranates on Aaron's robe were colored blue, purple and scarlet. In nature there are no blue pomegranates. One of the most attractive artifacts at the Temple was a molten sea forty-five feet in circumference, filled with water and resting on twelve statuesque oxen (1 Kings 7:23–26). Where in the real world can one find a sea held up on the backs of oxen? Francis Schaeffer rightly comments that "Christian artists do not need to be threatened by fantasy and imagination… The Christian is the one whose imagination should fly beyond the stars."[7]

Music was as prominent at the Temple as were the visual arts. David appointed four thousand musicians to conduct the music of the Temple (1 Chronicles 23:5). The Psalms, moreover, are a Temple hymnbook. If we catalog the musical instruments mentioned in the Psalms, they show the same wide use of available art forms that the visual arts in the Temple do.

It is no wonder that Christianity has been the most artistic religion in the world. Much of its doctrine has been enshrined in music, visual symbol, poem and story. The authoritative book of this revealed religion is itself a largely literary work in which story, character, and image are the customary ways of embodying truth. For more than fifteen centuries of Western history, Christianity provided the main influence and content for the creative arts. That it lost its dominance is one of the tragedies of both Western civilization and Christendom. That the arts will someday regain their lost place among Christians is a thing to be hoped.

PERSPECTIVE IN THE ARTS

The main thesis of the entire book—that a person's worldview affects all human pursuits—emphatically applies to the creation and study of the arts. The arts by their very nature are value-laden. They embody and express human values. Even the aspects of human experience that painters and composers and writers choose for artistic portrayal are an implied comment about what is important and worthy of attention.

---

[6] The best discussions are by Gene Edward Veith, Jr., *The Gift of Art* (Downers Grove, IL: InterVarsity, 1983) and Francis A. Schaeffer, *Art and the Bible* (Downers Grove, IL: InterVarsity, 1974).
[7] Schaeffer, *Art and the Bible*, 61.

And once they have selected their subject, artists express an attitude toward the subject. The arts are *affective*: they are constructed so as to encourage an audience to share the artist's way of experiencing or perceiving reality. Works of art by their nature awaken attitudes or feelings of sympathy, aversion, approval, and disapproval toward the whole range of human experience.

While the importance of perspective in works of art is probably a truism, it is too often overlooked that the *study* of art, music and literature is just as influenced by perspective. Critics and teachers of the arts have a bias, too. They even reveal a bias in the works they choose to discuss or include in a course syllabus. And once they have chosen their works, they reveal a perspective in the aspect of a work that they single out for comment and in the attitudes they express toward the topics they have chosen for scrutiny. What critics and teachers of the arts *omit* from discussion can tell us as much about their bias as what they include. It would be a drastic mistake, therefore, to think that what a literature or art teacher says about works of art is any more "objective" than what a teacher of philosophy or biology says.

If art is inherently value-laden, so is the assimilation of art. As readers, viewers and listeners, we assimilate works of art within the framework of our personal experiences and worldview. Experiencing and interpreting works of art are subjective activities. The final meaning of a painting or symphony or story is a fusion of what the work itself puts before a person and the content that a person is able to bring to the words on a page or the sound from an instrument or the colors and objects on a canvas.

If experiencing art is this subjective, we are free as consumers of art to be ourselves when we read and listen and look. We do not need to repress our values or apologize for having a worldview when we read a novel or visit an art gallery or attend a concert. We do, however, need to be self-aware about our responses. We should acknowledge the presuppositions that lead us to see certain elements in a work of art, and we need to extend the same charitable privilege to people who do not share those presuppositions and therefore respond differently.

Current aesthetic theory stresses the idea of "interpretive communities"—groups of people who view the creative arts from a common core of interests and assumptions and values. Christians are one such interpretive community. They are not inherently better artists or critics than other people are. But they have their own "agenda" of interests springing from their coherent worldview. They also share beliefs and attitudes that they bring to their artistic and critical pursuits. The purpose of this essay is to delineate the Christian principles that have a special relevance to the arts.

As an organizing framework, we should note that artists perform three interrelated activities: (1) they create aesthetic objects and artistic form (2) they present human experience for our contemplation; and (3) they offer an interpretation of the experiences they present. Perspective affects all three activities, which I will discuss individually.

ARTISTIC CREATIVITY IN CHRISTIAN PERSPECTIVE

Human creativity is active in all human pursuits, but it has always, and rightly, been especially regarded as an attribute of the arts. For one thing, the arts are the province of the imagination, and the imagination is never limited solely to observable reality. Oscar Wilde once commented that art "has flowers that no forests know of, birds that no woodland possesses… She can work miracles at her will, and when she calls monsters from the deep they come. She can bid the almond-tree blossom in winter, and send the snow upon the ripe cornfield."[8] Artists are the orators of the imagination. A work of art is a new creation that cannot be fully explained by any previously existing model.

In addition to the creative element of the arts, the related qualities of form, beauty, technique and craftsmanship are an essential ingredient of art. The elements of artistic form that all of the arts share are theme or centrality, pattern or design, organic unity (also called unity in variety or theme and variation), repetition or recurrence, rhythm, balance, contrast or tension, symmetry, harmony or "fittingness," unified progression and coherence. No single work of art needs to possess all of these, and some are more appropriately applied to one of the arts than the others. Nor should we limit these elements of artistic form to classical or Platonic aesthetic standards. Modern art also possesses its version of these formal qualities, even when artists claim that they are not using them.

---

[8] Oscar, Wilde, "The Decay of Lying," as reprinted in *The Modern Tradition: Backgrounds of Modern Literature*, eds. Richard Ellmann and Charles Feidelson, Jr. (New York: Oxford University Press, 1965), 20.

The elements of artistic form are what the arts share. They differ in the medium by which they incarnate them. Music presents these elements of form through the medium of sound, literature through words, and painting through color, line and texture.

Artistic beauty or proficiency consists of the skillful composition and manipulation of the elements of aesthetic form. Such proficiency in the control of artistic technique is an important part of the value that we attach to the arts; sometimes the creation of beauty is virtually the whole point of a work of art. This is especially true of much abstract or nonrepresentational art. Abstract art such as the symmetrical designs of a Persian carpet, an ornamental wrought-iron railing, or music without words have as their main purpose to present an artistic pattern for the pleasure of the beholder or listener.

And even in representational art, where part of the attention is focused on some aspect of human experience or external reality, the technical excellence remains an important part of the total effect. "Our primal aesthetical experience," writes one aesthetic theorist, is "a response of enchantment to 'beauty' (in a very wide sense of the term)."[9]

To gauge the importance of creativity and form in the artistic enterprise, we need only note the statements and practices of artists. They attribute creativity to a process of inspiration, however conceived. The revisions and refinements that they continue to lavish on their unfinished works are almost always directed toward a better crafted artistic form and rarely toward the ideational content of the work.

The poet Dylan Thomas wrote over 200 manuscript versions of his poem "Fern Hill." Beethoven sketched and resketched his compositions. Leonardo da Vinci drew a thousand hands. The Christian poet Gerard Manley Hopkins theorized that the purely artistic dimension of poetry exists "for its own sake and interest even over and above its interest of meaning."[10] And even when artistic excellence is not the main purpose of art, as when art is used in religious worship, for example, the formal beauty of a work enhances its effectiveness.

When we ask how the high value that the arts place on creativity and artistic form fits into a Christian worldview, it is apparent at once that the two are in total accord. In contrast to much of the prevailing cultural climate of our time, biblical Christianity asserts that human creativity and artistry are not only desirable but indispensable.

The Doctrine of Creation

The starting point for thinking Christianly about creativity and beauty is the doctrine of creation, especially as described in the first chapter of the Bible. We learn in these verses that God himself is a creator who pronounced his handiwork "very good" (Genesis 1:31). Equally important is the precise kind of nature of world that God created. It is a world that is beautiful as well as functional.

From a purely utilitarian point of view, God need not have created a world filled with symmetrical shapes and beautiful colors and pleasing sounds and varied textures. What we find in the visible creation is evidence not only of a functional mind but also an artistic imagination.

What kind of environment did God intend people to inhabit? Genesis 2:9 tells us: When God created Paradise, he "made to grow every tree that is pleasant to the sight and good for food." The conditions for human welfare are double—aesthetic and functional. Along with nature, the human arts have been the largest source of beauty in people's lives.

Not only did God create a universe filled with beautiful forms, he also created people in his own image (Genesis 1:26–27). Exactly what does this mean? Theology has rightly stressed human rationality, morality and holiness as the things that people share with God. But in its narrative context in Genesis 1, where we first hear about God's image in people, something else is even more obvious, namely, the idea of creativity.

---

[9] Auriel Kolna, "Contrasting the Ethical with the Aesthetical," *British Journal of Aesthetics* 12 (1972):340. Although the word *beauty* has fallen out of vogue in scholarly circles, partly because it is inappropriate to modern art whose subject is ugliness, I am unwilling to relinquish the term for the simple reason that I have found again and again that it is the term with which ordinary people resonate. Whatever synonym we might choose, we obviously need some term by which to term *beauty* can continue to serve this function has been argued by Guy Sircello, *A New Theory of Beauty* (Princeton, NJ: Princeton University Press, 1975).
[10] Gerard Manley Hopkins, "Poetry and Verse," as quoted in *Gerard Manley Hopkins: The Major Poems*, ed. Walford Davies (London: J. M. Dent and Sons, 1979), 38.

The classic study of what the image of God in people means to aesthetic theory is Dorothy L. Sayers' book *The Mind of the Maker*, where we read this regarding the Genesis statement about God's image in people:

> Had the author of Genesis anything particular in his mind when he wrote? It is observable that in the passage leading up to the statement about man, he has given no detailed information about God. Looking at man, he sees in him something essentially divine, but when we turn back to see what he says about the original upon which the "image" of God was modeled, we find only the single assertion, "God created." The characteristic common to God and man is apparently that: the desire and the ability to make things."[11]

The image of the creative God in people is the theological reason why people create. The doctrines of creation and the image of God in people affirm human creativity as something good in principle. Abraham Kuyper once wrote,

> As image-bearer of God, man possesses the possibility both to create something beautiful, and to delight in it… The world of poetic ideas, can have no source other than God; and it is our privilege as bearers of His image, to have a perception of this beautiful world, artistically to reproduce, and humanly to enjoy it.[12]

Can a Christian in good conscience do something as non-utilitarian as spending an afternoon at an art gallery or an evening at a concert? Can a student justify the time spent taking a course in fiction writing or painting or music composition? In a Christian scheme of things, the answer is clear: to be artistically creative, and to enter into the creativity of others, is to exercise the image of God within oneself.

The Doctrine of Stewardship

The Christian doctrine of stewardship leads to the same conclusion. A steward is a person put in charge of the resources of his or her master. Christian stewardship means serving God with the talents with which he has endowed us (see especially the parable of the talents in Matthew 25:14–30). A duty of cultivation attaches to every ability and capacity that we possess.

What, then, are the talents with which God has endowed the creative artist? The classic answer is given in Exodus 31:3–5 in the description of the building of the tabernacle. We read that the Lord filled Bezalel "with the Spirit of God, with ability and intelligence, with knowledge and all craftsmanship, to devise artistic designs, to work in gold, silver, and bronze, in cutting stones for setting, and in carving wood, for work in every craft." These are the gifts of the artist. To cultivate them is to exercise stewardship. It is worthy of note, too, that "God called Bezalel" to exercise his creative ability (Exodus 31:2). The creation and study and dissemination of art is a calling. The "creation mandate" that God gave to Adam and Eve when he told them to exercise dominion over the creation (Genesis 1:26–30) is by extension also a cultural mandate to rule human culture in the name of God.

It is evident from what I have said that thinking Christianly about the arts involves rejection of the utilitarian mindset that scorns aesthetic form and beauty. The non-utilitarian aspect of the arts is not a mark against them. God did not create a purely utilitarian world. He filled his creation with much that is simply beautiful and delightful. When he created the perfect human environment, it included every tree that is pleasant to the sight (Genesis 2:9). The garments of Aaron were embellished "for glory and for beauty" (Exodus 28:2). We should note that well: beauty is worthy in itself, just as truth and goodness are.

The embellishments of the Temple served no architectural weight bearing function. They simply beautified the place. As H. R. Rookmaaker writes in his monograph *Art Needs No Justification*, "God gave humanity the skill to make things beautiful, to make music, to write poems, to make sculpture, to decorate things… Art has its own meaning. A work of art can stand in the art gallery and be cherished for its own sake. We listen to a piece of music simply to enjoy it."[13] Art nearly always has a gratuitous, more-than-functional quality to it. By its very nature it involves a willingness to go beyond the purely utilitarian.

---

[11] Dorothy L. Sayers, *The Mind of the Maker* (Cleveland, OH: World Publishing, 1956), 34.
[12] Abraham Kuyper, *Calvinism* (Grand Rapids, MI: Eerdmans, 1967), 10.
[13] H. R. Rookmaaker, *Art Needs No Justification* (Downers Grove, IL: InterVarsity, 1978), 38–39.

While it is an overstatement to attribute automatic moral effects to the arts, one of the virtues that the arts tend to foster is an inherent rejection of the materialism and acquisitiveness that are always threatening to overwhelm the human race. Because the enjoyment of artistic beauty is essentially non-utilitarian, it draws a boundary around human acquisitiveness and clears a ground in which people can recover and celebrate distinctively human values. Any worldview that finds a place for artistic delight has a built-in curb against the purely acquisitive mindset that sees value only in practical activities that serve a utilitarian function.

Creativity and the Fall

We must, of course, not overstate the case for artistic creativity. Human creativity did not escape the effects of the Fall. Artistic creativity, too, is subject to moral and intellectual criticism. A painting or song or novel has no claim to our reverence or admiration simply because it is the product of human creativity. We must differentiate between noble and ignoble manifestations of the creative impulse.

One criterion is the purpose or *telos* that governs an artist's effort. Art composed to feed an artist's greed for fame or wealth has a less noble purpose than art designed to serve one's fellow humans or to glorify God. Art that caters to the coarse taste for pornography is less worthy than creativity that aims to dignify and refine human taste.

Another criterion for judging the worthiness of human creativity is the effect of art on its audience. We rightly admire art, music and literature whose effect is to make people more sensitive, moral or humanly refined. And we should judge negatively art whose effect is to encourage people to behave selfishly, immorally or coarsely.

Yet another standard by which we can judge artistic creativity is aesthetic excellence. Poorly executed paintings or musical compositions or stories might be the products of someone's creativity, but they do not for that reason merit our admiration. Technical excellence, on the other hand, is one of the very aims of artistic creativity. In fact, the lack of artistic excellence detracts from the impact of the Christian content.

Artistic creativity is a great gift, but it is not inherently sacred or good. For at least a century now, non-Christian enthusiasts for the arts have tended to find in art a substitute for the Christian religion. Nietzsche virtually deified free creativity. The romantic poets regarded the imagination as the religious faculty by which we have contact with the supernatural. Such people elevate the imagination to a religious role that the Bible reserves for a person's "heart" or "soul."

Artistic creativity can never hold such an esteemed place in a Christian worldview. There is wisdom and beauty but not salvation in a sonnet. Art can satisfy some of the same longings that religion does. It speaks to the human capacity for illumination, mystery, order, and beauty. But a Christian finds the ultimate satisfaction of these longings in God, not in art. It is this conviction that lies behind this statement of C. S. Lewis:

> The Christian will take literature a little less seriously than the cultured Pagan… The unbeliever is always apt to make a kind of religion of his aesthetic experiences… But the Christian knows from the outset that the salvation of a single soul is more important than the production and preservation of all the epics and tragedies in the world.[14]

The Christian religion encourages a balanced view toward artistic creativity. To a technological world that values only what is utilitarian, Christianity declares that whatever is beautiful, whether it is a tree or a sonata, has worth in itself because a creative God has conferred the capacity for artistry on his human creatures. To enthusiasts for the arts who make an idol of the imagination and its products, Christianity asserts that God the Creator is always separate from his creation, whether nature or culture.

[14] C. S. Lewis, *Christian Reflections* (Grand Rapids, MI: Eerdmans, 1967), 10.

THE PORTRAYAL OF HUMAN EXPERIENCE IN THE ARTS

The arts take human experience as their subject. They are above all the expression of human response to reality. When a painter paints a landscape, he or she is suggesting something of the human response to nature. Music is particularly adept at expressing the inner weather of the human emotions or condition. Literature is even more comprehensive in its ability to present the contours of human experience in the world. The novelist Joseph Conrad wrote, "My task... is, by the power of the written word to make you hear, to make you feel—it is, before all, to make you see."[15] So rooted are the arts in reality that the oldest and most influential of all aesthetic theories has regarded the arts as an imitation of reality.

Creative artists are sensitive observers of reality. "The writer should never be ashamed of staring," writes novelist Flannery O'Connor.[16] The American painter Andrew Wyeth once told an interviewer, "I love to study the many things that grow below the corn stalks and bring them back into the studio to study the color. If one could only catch that true color of nature—the very thought of it drives me mad."[17] The creative artist's vocation is to stare at the created and human worlds and to lure the rest of us into a similar act of contemplation.

The arts stay close to the way things are in the world. The knowledge that they convey is an experiential knowledge of the physical and human worlds. Whether or not this is a knowledge worth having depends on one's values and worldview. Plato viewed such knowledge as rather frivolous, a knowledge hardly worth having.

A Christian viewpoint disagrees with this denigration of physical and human reality. It does so partly on the basis of the doctrine of creation. Things are real because God made them. And because he made them, they are worthy of study and celebration and love. Not only did God make things. He created people in such a way that they perceive them as much through their physical senses as their minds. The color and smell of a rose are not irrelevant or illusory.

The Christian doctrine of Incarnation points in the same direction. When Jesus took on human form in order to redeem people, he demonstrated that earthly, human experience is of immense worth. Christianity is not escapist. It does not substitute a heavenly world for the earthly one. It brings a spiritual reality into the earthly order.

Simply at the level of subject matter, then, the Christian doctrines of creation and Incarnation have far-reaching implications for the arts. Visual artists are assured that their preoccupation with the scenes and people and colors that they paint or mold are worthy of such attention. Musicians need not doubt the significance of the human feelings and attitudes embodied in their sounds. Poets and storytellers and dramatists can be convinced that their portrayal of the whole range of human experience in the natural and social worlds is a worthwhile endeavor. Christian artists can take all of life as their subject, just as the writers of the Bible did.

VALUES AND REALITY: THE ARTIST'S PERSPECTIVE

We might think that the mere subject matter of an artistic work is philosophically neutral and that perspective enters only when artists add their interpretive slant to the subject of portrayal. But the worldview of creative artists emerges even from the subjects they select for portrayal. The details that an artist includes in the limited confines of a single work carry a burden of meaning larger than themselves and are understood to be representative of a bigger sense of life. Artistic subject matter implies a statement about both values and reality.

In the realm of *values*, artists imply what they regard as worthy of human attention whenever they put brush to canvas or pen to paper. Why did the French painter Courbet shock the artistic norms of his day by painting common stonebreakers and a peasant burial? Because his very choice of such subject matter implied that true worth resides in people of humble social standing instead of people with aristocratic status.

---

[15] From the preface of Joseph Conrad, *The Nigger of the Narcissus* (New York: Collier Books, 1962), 19.

[16] O'Connor, *Mystery and Manners*, 84.

[17] Quoted by Virginia Stem Owens in *The Christian Imagination*, ed. Leland Ryken (Grand Rapids, MI: Baker, 1981), 380.

Bach wrote church music on sacred themes because he valued supremely the worship of God. Wordsworth's nature poems, simply at the level of subject matter, express his attitude toward what is important in human experience.

What an artist chooses to portray is a comment about *reality* as well as values. Artists create out of the habitual furniture of their minds. What they exclude is as important as what they include. Writers whose poems or stories never portray God, spiritual reality or Christian values exhibit, simply at the level of subject matter, a secular worldview. We can tell by looking at the table of contents of the works of Mendelssohn and Handel that their view of reality was Christian. Flannery O'Connor theorized that "it is form the kind of world the writer creates, from the kind of character and detail he invests it with, that a reader can find the intellectual meaning of a book."[18]

We might think that abstract or nonrepresentational art and music are free from perspective, but they, too, are an implied comment about reality. A symphony in which organization dominates the composition conveys a different sense of life from a symphony in which disorganization dominates. A vastly different worldview emerges from the intricate harmony of a Persian tapestry and most modern abstract art. When a graduate student who works in abstract sculpture recently had his work critiqued by his department, he was asked why his nonrepresentational sculptures possessed an order and gracefulness and clean lines so atypical of prevailing contemporary trends. His answer was that his sculpture expressed his Christian view of the world as ultimately orderly.

Artistic content is inherently laden with perspective. Christians have a picture of reality and a value system stemming form their Christian worldview. As they assimilate works of art, therefore, they should self-consciously assess the adequacy of artistic pictures of the world in terms of a Christian framework.

The central tenets in that worldview are the existence of God and an unseen spiritual world, the worth of physical reality, the value of the individual person and social institutions, the fact of human evil and fallenness, the availability of God's redemptive grace, and a view of human history as being under God's purposeful providence and headed toward a goal.

As Christians look at the subject matter of artistic works through the lens of their convictions, some of the objects they see come into focus. Other objects remain out of focus. In either case, art has served its useful purpose; it has furnished the recipient with an occasion to exercise intellectual discrimination on questions of values and reality. Some value systems and views of reality are wrong, but Christians have an obligation to understand the world in which they minister.

THE INTERPRETATION OF REALITY IN WORKS OF ART

Artists do more than present human experience; they also *interpret* it from a specific perspective. Works of art make implied assertions about reality. This is simply one of the conventions with which people approach the artistic enterprise, whether as creators or recipients. The primary convention of the arts is what aesthetic theorist Jonathan Culler calls "the rule of significance," meaning that we should look on works of art "as expressing a significant attitude to some problem concerning man and/or his relation to the universe."[19] Artists intend meanings, and audiences can scarcely avoid looking for them.

Art's Implied Assertions

Works of art make implied assertions, just as history and science and philosophy do. For convenience, we can say that the arts make implied claims about the three great issues of life:

1. Reality: what really exists, and what is its nature?
2. Morality: what constitutes right and wrong behavior?
3. Values: what really matters, and what matters most and least?

For purposes of illustration, I turn first to a pair of nineteenth-century English painters, Constable and Turner. They both chose nature as their paintings convince us not simply that physical nature is an important

---

[18] O'Connor, *Mystery and Manners*, 75.
[19] Jonathan Culler, *Structuralist Poetics: Structuralism, Linguistics, and the Study of Literature* (Ithaca, NY: Cornell University Press, 1975), 115.

part of reality but also that it is something of great worth in human experience.

But along with these similarities we notice obvious differences in how Constable and Turner interpreted nature. What do we see as we look at Constable's famous paintings of Salisbury Cathedral? We see the beauty and harmony of nature. We see nature in a religious light and as the friend of people. The human and natural worlds are unified. Constable himself said that he painted nature as benevolent because he sensed God's presence in nature.

Turner offers quite a different interpretation of nature. His colors are more intense, his brush strokes much broader and more passionate. There is an element of terror in many of his nature scenes. One of his paintings shows a gigantic avalanche ready to overwhelm a matchbox cabin under it furious weight. In such a painting nature is not nurturing, as in paintings by Constable and the Dutch realists, but hostile. The one is not necessarily more Christian than the other, though we should not minimize how artists select details that suggest their overall view of human possibilities in the universe.

For a literary illustration, consider the following sonnet, entitled "God's Grandeur," by Gerard Manley Hopkins:

> The world is charged with the grandeur of God.
> It will flame out, like shining from shook foil.
> It gathers to a greatness, like the ooze of oil
> Crushed. Why do men then now not reck his rod?
> Generations have trod, have trod, have trod;
> And all is seared with trade; bleared, smeared with toil;
> And wears man's smudge and shares man's smell: the soil
> Is bare now, nor can foot feel, being shod.
>
> And for all this, nature is never spent;
> There lives the dearest freshness deep down things;
> And though the last lights of the black West went
> Oh, morning, at the brown brink eastward, springs—
> Because the Holy Ghost over the bent
> World brooks with warm breast and with ah! bring wings.

The subject of the poem is the permanent freshness of nature. The perspective from which we view that reality is the grandeur of God. What really exists? According to this poem, the physical world of sun and trees and the spiritual world that includes the Triune God are equally real. What constitutes moral and immoral behavior? To live morally is to live in reverence before God's creation. To desecrate nature in pursuit of selfish acquisitiveness is immoral. What values are most worthy of human pursuit? God's nature.

The Audience's Responsibility

If works of art are this laden with meaning, what are the implications for those who constitute the audience of the arts? Today it is commonplace to appropriate works of art in terms of our own values, morality and view of reality. A Christian worldview asserts specific ideas in all three areas. To assimilate the arts in a Christian way means to interact with their implied assertions within a framework of Christian doctrine, as derived from the Bible.

Because the three big subject areas of the arts are God, people and nature, it is especially crucial for Christians to have a grasp of Christian truth about these topics whenever they encounter works of art. In a Christian view, God is the ultimate reality and object of devotion. God is the one who has created everything that exists in the universe. Several important corollaries follow. One is that God is transcendent over reality and never to be equated with the creation. Another is that since God is the ultimate source and end of reality, everything else derives its identity from God. Thus people are the creatures of God, moral goodness consists of doing God's will, history is the outworking of God's purposes, human institutions such as state and family are ordained by God, and so forth.

Christianity postulates a threefold view of people: good and worthy in principle because God made them in his image, evil or fallen by virtue of their sinful actions, and capable of restoration by God's grace.

Judged by such a standard, any view of people is inadequate if it sees them as *only* evil or *only* good. In a Christian scheme, people are evil by their inclinations but good as they participate in God's grace. In either case, human choice is both possible and necessary. A lot of art is *truthful* without telling the whole *truth*. It accurately portrays part of the truth about human nature, but still falls short of a Christian perspective because it fails to do justice to the comprehensive balance in a Christian view of people.

The Christian view of nature runs parallel to the view of people. Nature was created by God and it is under his providential control. This means on the one hand that nature itself is not divine and on the other that it is worthy of love and reverence. A lot of artistic portrayals of nature err in either overvaluing or undervaluing it. Medieval painting and music were so preoccupied with heaven and angels and Madonnas and grace that they suffer from an unbiblical denigration of nature. The reverse has been true of the arts during the last two centuries.

At the heart of the Christian worldview is a balance or tension between good and evil, hope and despair, optimism and pessimism. Is a work of art unchristian in its viewpoint if it portrays only a sense of despair or discord? Isn't the Fall a keystone of Christian doctrine? If so, why should Christians not endorse the protest music and literature and painting that are so dominant in the twentieth century?

The best framework that I have seen for grappling with this issue is Francis Schaeffer's commonsensical suggestion that Christianity consists of two themes.[20] One is the pessimistic fact of sin, despair and lostness in human experience. The other theme is the hope, meaningfulness and redemptive potential in life. A Christian worldview embraces both halves of this tension. The sense of life that emerges from artistic works is less than Christian if it omits either side of the tension. The garbage can behind the house and the rose bush in front of the house are equally real.

To summarize, artists inevitably offer a perspective on such basic human issues as what really exists, how people should act and what values are worthy of human devotion. The obligation of Christian artists is to convey a Christian viewpoint in their stories and paintings and musical compositions. The task of all Christians is to discern and evaluate the perspectives that artists offer for their approval whenever they read of look or listen.

TRUTH IN ART

We are now in a position to consider the question that inevitably arises when art is considered in terms of a worldview. Do the arts tell the truth? There is no single answer to the question because there are various types or levels of truth in art. There is a range of ways in which a work of art can be true or false. I will discuss them under the headings of human values, representational truth, and ideational or perspectival truth.

Human Values

To begin, the arts as a whole tell us the truth about what is foundational in human experience. Simply at the level of content, the arts keep calling us back to bedrock humanity. The arts are probably the most accurate index to human preoccupations, values, fears and longings that we possess. If we wish to know what people want and do not want, we can go to their stories and poems and songs and paintings.

This is why we often feel that we have learned more from art than from life. In real life the essential patterns and values are usually obscured by the sheer complexity and pressures of living. The arts, however, awaken our awareness of the central realities of human experience—realities such as nature and God and family and love and pain. A work of art is a distillation of experience in which the irrelevancies are stripped away. The knowledge that the arts give us is rarely new information but rather a bringing to consciousness of what we already know but to which we become oblivious in daily living.

The arts are therefore a great organizing force in human life. When people say that the arts help them to understand or make sense of life, they usually mean the ability of the arts to cut through the clutter and put them in touch with what is enduring in human experience. This, then, is one level of truth in the arts: truthfulness to the fears, longings, and values of the human race. The arts possess such truth regardless of the philosophical perspective of an artist. Such knowledge about human experience is a type of truth that Christians need; it is one of their bonds with the human race.

---

[20] See Schaeffer, *Art and the Bible*, 56–59.

Representational Truth

A second level of truth in the arts is representational truth, by which I mean truthfulness to the way things are in the world. Artists are sensitive observers of reality. They present human experience in their chosen artistic medium. Whenever a writer or composer or visual artist accurately captures the contours of human experience or external reality, we can say that the resulting work of art is true to reality.

A work of art can be true at this level even though the perspective from which the subject is viewed might be wrong. As with the previous level of truth (art as a truthful repository of what is most essential in human experience), we can make very large claims for the truth of art in its faithfulness to reality. We have all looked at paintings or read stories and poems that struck us as false to reality, to the way things are, but the overwhelming majority of art is true to reality.

Of course the arts are not "photographically" real. They use artistic techniques of highlighting, selectivity, omission, juxtaposition, and distortion in their portrayal of reality. There is a certain indirection to art. Thus the "truthfulness" of a painted portrait of a person is not measured in terms of photographic realism but in terms of whether it captures the reality of grief or serenity or the beauty of the human face. Coleridge's *Rime of the Ancient Mariner* contains such fantastic elements as ghosts and surrealistic landscapes and an albatross with supernatural powers. But these elements of fantasy accurately suggest such realities as sin, guilt, alienation, and renewal. The imaginative details in a work of art are a lens or window through which we look at life.

Perspectival Truth

The third level at which the truthfulness of a work of art needs to be tested is the level of perspective or implied assertion. I noted earlier that artists inevitably offer an interpretation of the human experiences that they portray. Not all art forms are equally laden with perspective. Literature, because it consists of words, is the most consistently perspectival. Music, being the most nonrepresentational, is least likely to bear ideational perspective. The visual arts fall somewhere between the two.

The perspectives or themes embodied in artistic works range from a general sense of life at one end of the spectrum to very specific assertions at the other. At the general end, artistic perspective consists of such attitudes as order or lack of it, hope or despair, the presence or absence of a supernatural reality, meaning or futility. As works of art become more explicitly laden with perspective, they embody specific ideas about God, people, society and nature, or about what constitutes good and bad behavior, or about what values are worthy and unworthy of human devotion.

As people assimilate a work of art, they do so in terms of their own worldview. They measure the perspective in works of art by their own convictions. The more committed they are to a standard of truth that they regard as authoritative, the more consciously they will assess art in terms of their own worldview.

Two-Stage Criticism

Christians surely fall into the category of people committed to a standard of truth. The methodology for integrating one's encounter with works of art and one's Christian faith has been succinctly summarized in T. S. Eliot's theory that the criticism of artistic works

> should be completed by criticism from a definite ethical and theological standpoint… It is… necessary for [Christians] to scrutinize… works of imagination with explicit ethical and theological standards… What I believe to be incumbent upon all Christians is the duty of maintaining consciously certain standards and criteria of criticism over and above those applied by the rest of the world; and that by these criteria and standards everything… must be tested.[21]

Notice that Eliot envisions a two-stage process of criticism. First we must receive the work on its own terms and allow it to say what it really says. Then we must exercise our prerogative of agreeing or disagreeing with the artist's interpretation of reality and experience.

What are the "explicit ethical and theological standards" by which Eliot thinks Christians should assess the truth content of art? They are based ultimately on the Bible, the only final authority for belief

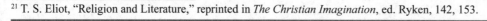

[21] T. S. Eliot, "Religion and Literature," reprinted in *The Christian Imagination*, ed. Ryken, 142, 153.

in what is, after all, a *revealed* religion. The insights of Christian creeds based on the Bible and Christian thinkers who are gifted to codify and state the implications of biblical doctrine become important elements in a person's understanding of a Christian worldview. In the application of Christian doctrine to specific artistic assertions about life, biblical revelation obviously needs to be supplemented by human reason in any Christian critique of art.

Judging the truthfulness of the implied assertions of art is a form of intellectually testing the spirits to see if they are from God. The criteria by which the ideational or perspectival truth of art is judged are the same intellectual standards as applied to the other disciplines. The arts, for all their beauty and delightfulness and imaginative power, do not allow us to take a holiday from the mind. The task of completing artistic criticism with a Christian assessment of an artist's perspective or worldview needs to be informed by insights from philosophy, theology, ethics and psychology. It can never rest solely on aesthetic considerations.

Common Grace

The truthfulness of a work of art does not depend on an artist's Christian orthodoxy. The doctrine of common grace asserts that God endows all people, believers and unbelievers alike, with a capacity for goodness, truth, creativity and so forth. All truth is God's truth. It is not suspect if it happens to be expressed by non-Christian artists.

The Bible itself affirms that unbelieving artists can express truth. In the New Testament, Paul several times quotes with approval from pagan Greek poets.[22] When Solomon needed visual artists who could express the beauty of holiness, he hired the best available artists, who happened to be pagans.[23] As John Calvin wrote regarding the application of the doctrine of common grace to the arts, "All truth is from God; and consequently, if wicked men have said anything that is true and just, we ought not to reject it; for it has come from God."[24]

Does art tell the truth? There is no single answer to the perennial question. A lot of misleading eulogistic overstatements and denigrating understatements have been made about the truthfulness of art by people who ignore the range of ways in which art can be true and false.

Virtually all art tells us the truth about the foundational preoccupations, values, fears and longings of the human race. Most art is true as a representation of some aspect of human experience or external reality. At the level of intellectual perspective or interpretation of reality, most of the world's art, music and literature has not measured up to a Christian standard of truth.

Of course it is possible to state the theme of a work of art so broadly that virtually no one, including Christians, would disagree with the statement. But when pressed more specifically at the level of implied philosophical assertion, most art through the centuries has deviated from Christian doctrine, despite the predominantly Christian tenor of European culture during the Middle Ages and Renaissance.

Not all art is Christian in viewpoint, but it is always of interest to Christians because it clarifies the human situation to which the Christian faith speaks. Encountering the moral and philosophic viewpoints of artistic works is an avenue to understanding the people with whom we live and the culture that is our daily environment. Measuring those viewpoints by a Christian norm serves as an invaluable catalyst to a Christian's thinking about human issues.

WHY CHRISTIANS NEED THE ARTS

The arts serve many functions in human culture. They are functions that Christians should welcome and that they avoid to their own harm.

One of the functions of art can be summed up under such related words as refreshment, recreation, entertainment, and the enjoyment of artistic form or beauty. The arts are a celebration of life. The goal of our excursions into the realm of imaginative art is to send us back to real life with a renewed zest for it. The arts awaken us to the hidden beauty of the world and are themselves an extension of that beauty. The arts

---

[22] The passages include Acts 17:28; 1 Corinthians 15:33; and Titus 1:12. For commentary on the importance of this data for aesthetic theory, see my book *Triumphs of the Imagination: Literature in Christian Perspective* (Downers Grove, IL: InterVarsity, 1979), 161–63.

[23] See Veith, *The Gift of Art*, pp. 57–58, for the details.

[24] John Calvin, *Commentaries on the Epistles to Timothy, Titus, and Philemon*, trans. William Pringle (Grand Rapids, MI: Eerdmans, 1948), 300–301.

affirm the humanness of humans. Even when the subject of art is human evil, suffering, and ugliness, the artistic skill with which the subject is rendered is a tribute to human achievement.

The arts are useful as well as delightful. They are a great ordering force in human culture. As the arts present human experience for our contemplation, they intensify our involvement with life, heighten our awareness, expand our range of experiences, and enlarge our human sympathies and compassion. The arts sharpen and reward the senses and do justice to the emotional and imagining side of human nature. They give shape to our own experiences, thereby satisfying the human urge for adequate expression of insights and feelings.

Because the arts are interpretive in nature, they speak to our intellect. They offer a diagnosis, definition and explanation for the human condition. With their implied assertions about life, the arts force us to think, ponder alternative views of life, to commit ourselves to our own convictions of truth. They provide the materials for us to exercise and expand our own angle of vision.

These are the gifts of art. They are even more important to Christians than to non-Christians because to the human reasons for art a Christian can add an even more ultimate rationale—the glory of God. This, indeed, is the appointed consummation of the arts. The person who can revere the ultimate source and end of human creativity has an added reason to cherish the ability of the arts to intensify human awareness and compassion, to enhance human enjoyment and understanding.

---

*This essay originally appeared in the book *The Making of a Christian Mind*:
   Leland Ryken, "The Creative Arts," *The Making of a Christian Mind*, ed. Arthur Holmes (Downers Grove, IL: InterVarsity, 1985), pp. 105–131.
**Reproduction rights granted by Leland Ryken.

THE CREATIVE ARTS
ESSAY QUESTIONS

Answer the questions below on a separate sheet of paper and be prepared to review your answers in class.

PART ONE

1. What role do the arts play in affecting worldviews?

2. How does imagination relate to art?

3. In what ways does the Bible endorse both the image-making and imaginary impulses of the arts?

4. What role does one's worldview play in interpreting and experiencing art?

5. Besides creativity, what essential elements do the arts share in common?

6. Besides rationality, morality, and holiness, what other aspect do human beings share in common with God?

7. What do the arts have to do with the doctrine of stewardship?

8. How can the arts foster a rejection of materialism and acquisitiveness?

9. How do we judge between noble and ignoble human creativity?

10. Is artistic creativity inherently sacred or good?

PART TWO

11. What role do *values* and *reality* play in the arts?

12. What are the three big subject areas of the arts and what is the Christian view of these subjects?

13. What three types of truth are discussed in relation to the arts? How is each unique?

14. How should a Christian judge the truthfulness of art?

15. Why do Christians need the arts?

Unit Seven

DEAR DOUG
WRITING ASSIGNMENT

Hey there!

Just when you think spring might be around the corner, February changes your mind! Last week I was ready to break out the sunscreen, but now I'm back to wearing a sock cap and long underwear. Next time, remind me to pick a college someplace warm… like Hawaii.

At least brisk weather makes a steaming cup of coffee more inviting—and where there's coffee, there's discussion! This week we were talking about some issues our law professor brought up in class. He had stated that mankind is the author of all laws, and Sarah agreed with him. She said that she didn't believe that laws came from a higher power, but were created by society. I've always assumed that most laws had their foundation in God and the Bible. Who do you think makes the laws?

Nathan thought her basic idea was correct, but he changed it a bit. He said that we don't write laws because of society, but for ourselves—that the laws you should keep are the ones you believe in. This didn't really make sense to me, though. I mean, that would let someone who didn't think stop signs applied to him put everyone else on the road in danger. Are there laws that apply to everyone in every situation?

Nathan's comment got Paige started. She said that the people in power write laws, pretend they are objective, and then use them to enforce their will on society. It's like the religious right passing laws against gay marriage, she said. I had never thought about it that way before. Are laws only based on the beliefs of the people in power?

After listening to everyone else, Muhammad spoke up. He was adamant that law comes from Allah and that only laws based on principles found in the Qur'an and Islamic tradition can be trusted. How are laws from biblical principles different than laws taken from the Qur'an?

I guess everyone agreed that laws have to have a credible source in order to be trustworthy. We just differed on the source itself—Muhammad said the Qur'an, Sarah and Nathan said humanity or society, and Paige said whoever's in power. But none of these sources seem big enough. What is the Christian position on law?

All right, enough serious thinking for now… my brain is starting to hurt. I wonder—can a brain cramp become permanent, like those faces my mother said would stick if I kept making them?!

Talk to you later!
Doug

UNDERSTANDING THE TIMES

Unit Eight

Topics:
Abortion
Euthanasia
Politics

A Summit Ministries Curriculum

SECTION OUTLINE

180-DAY SYLLABUS

DAY	IN CLASS	HOMEWORK	
1	WATCH "Politics" video		
2	READ UTT Textbook 'Politics 8.1'	READ UTT Textbook 'Politics 8.2'	
3	REVIEW UTT Textbook 'Politics 8.1–8.2' questions	READ UTT Textbook 'Politics 8.3'	
4	READ UTT Textbook 'Politics 8.4'		
5	REVIEW UTT Textbook 'Politics 8.3–8.4' questions	READ UTT Textbook 'Politics 8.5'	
6	READ UTT Textbook 'Politics 8.6'		
7	REVIEW UTT Textbook 'Politics 8.5–8.6' questions	ASSIGN Dear Doug Letter	
8	WATCH "The Case Against Abortion" video P1		
9	WATCH "The Case Against Abortion" video P2		
10	WATCH "The Case Against Abortion" video P3		
11	REVIEW "The Case Against Abortion" video questions		
12	READ *The Shifting Focus in the Abortion Debate* essay		
13	REVIEW *The Shifting Focus...* essay questions	READ *The Battle for Life* essay	
14	REVIEW *The Battle for Life* essay questions	Dear Doug Letter assignment DUE	
15	TAKE Unit Eight Test		

90-DAY SYLLABUS

DAY	IN CLASS	HOMEWORK	
1	WATCH "Politics" video	READ UTT Textbook 'Politics 8.1–8.2'	
2	REVIEW UTT Textbook 'Politics 8.1–8.2' questions	READ UTT Textbook 'Politics 8.3–8.4'	
3	REVIEW UTT Textbook 'Politics 8.3–8.4' questions	READ UTT Textbook 'Politics 8.5–8.6'	
4	REVIEW UTT Textbook 'Politics 8.5–8.6' questions		
5	READ *The Shifting Focus in the Abortion Debate* essay		
6	REVIEW *The Shifting Focus...* essay questions	READ *The Battle for Life* essay	
7	REVIEW *The Battle for Life* essay questions		
8	TAKE Unit Eight Test		

UNDERSTANDING THE TIMES
POLITICS QUESTIONS

Answer the questions below on a separate sheet of paper and be prepared to review your answers in class. Reflection Questions will not be found in the text. These are merely designed to help you start thinking about issues from a worldview perspective.

POLITICS 8.1

1. What two aspects of human nature did America's founding fathers understand?

2. Why does mankind need a civil government?

3. How can mankind be protected from government abuses?

4. **Reflection Question:** What are some current government activities that go beyond the limited sphere suggested by the text?

5. **Reflection Question:** What explanations can be made for why Christians are hesitant to be involved in politics? What logically follows if Christians retreat from political involvement?

POLITICS 8.2

6. What are two ways in which the term *jihad* can be used?

7. How did the attitudes of Jesus and Muhammad differ toward those who opposed them?

8. What reason do some Muslims offer in defense of bloodshed in the name of Allah? Does this argument seem plausible in light of history?

9. What are four points that support the belief that violent forms of *jihad* are intended to be in force until Islam is a global reality?

10. For what reason were the Crusades fought? How should Christians handle this issue?

POLITICS 8.3

11. How does the Secular Humanist conception of democracy differ from the more common attitude?

12. Why do Secular Humanists favor globalism?

13. Why do most Secular Humanists call for universal disarmament and expanded power for the United Nations?

14. Why does Humanistic globalism call for the international compromise of ideologies?

15. How can Secular Humanism justify defending its ideology while viewing other ideologies as opposed to democracy?

Unit Eight

16. How do Marxists view the notion of democracy?

17. For the Marxist, what is the ideal state?

18. According to Marxism, what is the first step in the transition from capitalism to communism?

19. Why is a proletariat dictatorship crucial for obtaining communism? What is the role of the communist party in this dictatorship?

20. According to Marxism, how did the state come into being? What is the ultimate fate of the state under communism? What is the ultimate political aim of Marxism?

21. What is the political goal of Cosmic Humanism?

22. Why do Cosmic Humanists believe that a New World Order is guaranteed?

23. What type of government system will humanity have in the New World Order?

24. What is the fate of centralized government, according to Cosmic Humanism?

25. Reflection Question: Does the New World Order sound like anarchy? Will this system of government ever work?

26. What is the Postmodernist position toward politics?

27. What is identity politics?

28. What is an example of identity politics in action? Does identity politics strive to establish truthful theories?

29. How do Postmodernists manipulate language to achieve their political goals?

30. According to Postmodernists, what is social justice? How is social justice to be achieved?

"THE CASE AGAINST ABORTION"
WITH SCOTT KLUSENDORF

PART ONE

I. Task #1: Restore Meaning to the Word "Abortion"

A. Our current culture

   1. _____Visual_____ **culture:** We live in a culture that thinks and learns visually.

      i. We predominantly learn through images.

      ii. We no longer learn through books and linear thought.

   2. _____Postmodern_____ **culture:** Postmodernism, simply stated, says that there is no objective truth.

      i. Debate is no longer over what happens to the fetus, if the fetus feels pain, or if abortion is moral.

      ii. Debate is now about the circumstances of individual women and the right to privacy.

      iii. Truth has been reduced to personal experience.

      [handwritten margin notes: · size · level of development · environment · degree of dependency]

      iv. Christians have not been a movement of thinkers.

   3. _____Avoidance_____ **culture:** We live in a culture that wants difficult life problems to "just go away."

      "Our generation is the first generation of people [that] having demanded the right to kill its children through abortion is now demanding the right to kill its parents through doctor-assisted suicide." — Greg Cunningham

B. The challenge we face

      "How do we communicate truth on abortion to a culture that thinks and learns visually, that wants difficult life problems to 'just go away,' and thinks that truth on abortion is elusive and is nothing more than a personal story or subjective experience?… The answer is we have to show the culture abortion; it is not enough to talk about it… We don't use images in place of good arguments; rather we use them to support our arguments."

   1. Tell people what they are about to see; don't trick them.

   2. Tell them there is no narration, only instrumental music.

   3. Stress the fact that our Lord is eager to forgive the sin of abortion.

[side margin: Unit Eight]

II. Task #2: Simplify the Abortion Debate

A. What is the unborn?

1. The debate is not over choice and who gets to decide.

2. When someone kills a toddler, everyone agrees that a human was killed.

3. Are fetuses human beings like toddlers?

4. You cannot answer the question "Can I kill this?" until we ask the question, "What is it?"

B. Tactic: _Trot out the toddler_

"Every time someone gives you an objection to the pro-life view or offers you a justification as to why abortion ought to be allowed, ask yourself if this works as a good argument for killing a toddler."

Note: This tactic is not designed to show that the fetus is a human. It is designed to show that this is the question and that everything else is irrelevant, for example:

1. Unwanted children

2. Psychological pain/rape

3. Back-alley abortions

"If the unborn aren't human, then no justification for elective abortion is necessary. If they are human, then no justification for elective abortion is adequate." — Gregory Koukl

C. Showing that the unborn are human

1. Scientific evidence

   i. _law of biogenesis_: Living things reproduce after their own kind.

      "How is it possible for human parents to produce an offspring that is not human but later becomes human?"

   ii. Some individuals claim that the unborn are biologically human, but not persons.

      "What is the difference between being a human and being a person?"

2. Philosophic evidence

   i. _size_: Large people are not more human than small people.

   ii. _level of development_: A four-year-old is not less human than a fourteen-year-old.

iii. _____environment_____ : A newborn in an incubator is not less human than a child outside the womb.

iv. _____degree of dependency_____ : People on insulin are less viable but no less human.

"[For] any physical change to your body that does not kill you, you remain yourself through that change, because you have a human nature that was present from the moment you were conceived that allows us to say that we are the same person now that was conceived 19 or 20 years ago. The only difference is function—your abilities have changed but your essential nature is the same."

III. Task #3: Responding to Five Common Objections

A. Pro-abortion rhetoric assumes the unborn are not human.

1. _____begging the question_____ : When people assume what they are trying to prove

"The statement 'a woman has a right to an abortion' assumes there is no child in her womb that also has a right to live."

"The statement 'a woman has a right to control her own body' assumes there is only one body involved in the act of abortion."

2. They are asserting rather than arguing

i. _____assertion_____ : A claim without evidence

ii. _____argument_____ : A claim supported with evidence and/or reasons

3. Tactic: _____raising the roof_____

"In order for an argument to be valid it must have walls supporting it. You want to force them to provide walls [justification] for their house [assertion]."

4. Tactic: _____ghost busters_____

"Sometimes there is an invisible wall in an argument. For example, some assert that 'the Bible is silent on abortion; therefore it is fine.' Now the Bible doesn't expressly condemn cutting up your neighbor and feeding him to sharks, or drive-by shootings, or lynching homosexuals, but does that mean we are morally correct if we do those things?"

Ask, "Are you saying that whatever the Bible doesn't expressly condemn, it permits?"

B. Pro-abortion rhetoric often attacks the character of pro-lifers rather than refuting the argument.

1. _____Ad—Hominnen_____ : Attacking the person rather than the argument

i. You're a man.

"Arguments don't have genders, people do."

ii. How many unwanted babies have you adopted?

2. Tactic: ___Clumbo___

"How does my alleged unwillingness to adopt a child justify an abortionist killing one? The issue is, 'What is the unborn?' "

PART THREE

C. Pro-abortion rhetoric confuses moral claims with preference claims.

1. ___moral / truth___ **claim:** Does not address what we like, but what we believe is true or right.

2. ___preference___ **claim:** Has nothing to do with what is true or right, but with what we personally like.

"Here is the problem: we are saying to the culture that abortion is wrong and they are hearing we like chocolate ice cream rather than vanilla. They are taking our truth claim and changing it into a preference claim."

"When we are talking about what is right and wrong, we are not talking about what we like. In fact, there are a lot of things I would like to do, but I do not do because it would be morally wrong. And morality is about not doing some things we would *like* to do. That is why the bumper sticker 'don't like abortion; don't have one' is so off the mark. Imagine me saying 'don't like owning slaves, that's fine don't own one.' "

3. Why relativism fails

i. It cannot live up to its own standard.

"When someone says 'You shouldn't force your view on me,' they are forcing their view on you… "When someone says 'You shouldn't force your view on me,' your reply is, 'Why not?' Any answer they give you will be an example of them forcing their view on you."

ii. You can't say anything is right or wrong, including intolerance.

D. Pro-abortion rhetoric confuses functioning as a person with being one.

1. Rights are not based on current capacity but inherent capacity.

"If our rights are based on functional ability, we are all on a gigantic bell curve. We start off with very little rights of personhood; as we age and mature and reach our physical and intellectual peaks we have maximum rights of personhood and then as we grow old and decline we lose personhood… It also results in savage inequality… Keep in mind there is a difference between functioning as a person and being a person."

2. The issue of personal identity

"Ask, 'Were you ever an unborn child?' If the answer is yes, they have conceded a fundamental point of the pro-life view, that is, that human identity is a continuum from conception to death. If they answer that they were never an unborn child, ask them, 'What were you?'"

E. Pro-abortion rhetoric disguises its true position.

    1. The case of rape

        "Would you be willing to fight with me to end the practice of abortion for every instance except rape?"

        "Rape is a tragic thing but should the child be executed for the crime of its father? Or is it fair to demand that the child be killed so that its mother can feel better?… Would it be okay to kill a two-year old so its mother can feel better?"

    2. The real issue is not rape, incest, or anything else. It is, "What is the unborn?"

IV. Questions and Answers

A. How can we respond to those who say that they are personally against abortion but would not make it illegal?

"You personally oppose abortion because it takes the life of an innocent human baby, but you think it should be legal to kill babies?"

B. How can we respond to the claim that "Even if we outlaw abortion, people will still get them?"

"Laws against rape don't stop all rape, but we still have laws against it. Laws against car theft don't stop all cases of car theft but it does stop most of them. The law is a moral teacher."

C. How should we respond to pregnancies that endanger the life of the mother?

"It is better to save one person than lose both."

D. How can we respond to partial-birth abortion?

"First, these abortions are done for convenience. Second, if the mother's life is in danger why would the doctor use a three-day technique… If this is a life or death situation for the mother, you could do a c-section in a matter of minutes."

"THE CASE AGAINST ABORTION"
VIDEO QUESTIONS

Answer the questions below on a separate sheet of paper and be prepared to review your answers in class.

1. What three negative characteristics of our current culture complicate the abortion debate?

2. How do we restore meaning to the word "abortion" in our culture?

3. How do we simplify the abortion debate?

4. How do we convey both scientifically and philosophically that the unborn are human beings?

5. What are five common pro-abortion objections to the pro-life position and how might one best respond?

THE SHIFTING FOCUS
OF THE ABORTION DEBATE
BY FRANCIS J. BECKWITH[1]

Pro-lifers in the United States have always assumed that if they could demonstrate beyond a reasonable doubt that the fetus is a human person, then it would be only a matter of time before the courts and legislatures would declare nontherapeutic abortion—the willful destruction of a living fetus—unjustified homicide. Thus the pro-life view would be vindicated and nontherapeutic abortion would once again be illegal.

Even pro-abortion Supreme Court Justice Harry Blackmun, who wrote the majority opinion in *Roe v. Wade* (1973), agrees with this assumption: "If the suggestion of personhood [of the unborn] is established, the appellant's case, of course, collapses, for the fetus's right to life is then guaranteed specifically by the [Fourteenth Amendment]."[2] The scholarly and popular literature produced by evangelicals on the issue of abortion seems to make this assumption as well.[3]

In 1985, however, evangelical philosopher Robert Wennberg[4] defended a moderate pro-choice position employing an argument first presented in 1971 by MIT philosopher Judith Jarvis Thomson. Thomson argued that even if the fetus is a human person, abortion—at least in the early months of pregnancy—is *still* morally justified.[5] Unfortunately, nearly all the books published by evangelical opponents of abortion since the release of Wennberg's *Life in the Balance* (with the exception of recent works by John and Paul Feinberg,[6] Keith J. Pavlischek,[7] and myself[8]) have failed to address this important argument.[9]

This is so despite the fact that this argument—though nearly a quarter of a century old—is now being suggested by a number of legal scholars as a way to circumvent the problems of fetal personhood which they believe were mishandled in *Roe v. Wade.*

THOMSON'S ARGUMENT: THE FETUS'S PERSONHOOD DOES NOT MATTER

In her 1971 article, which by 1986 had become "the most widely reprinted essay in all of contemporary philosophy,"[10] Professor Thomson argued that even if the fetus is fully a human person with a right to life, this does not mean a woman must be forced to use her bodily organs to sustain its life. It is much the same, we are told, as the case in which one does not have a right to use another's kidney if one's kidney has failed. Consequently, a pregnant woman's removal of a fetus from her body, even though it will probably result in its death, is no more immoral than an ordinary person's refusal to donate his or her kidney to another in need of one, even though this refusal will probably result in the death of the prospective recipient. Thomson illustrates her position with the following story:

---

[1] This article under a different title was presented at the conference "The Christian Stake in Bioethics" (May 19–21, 1994), at Trinity Evangelical Divinity School, Deerfield, Illinois. Another version of this article (titled "From Personhood to Bodily Autonomy: The Shifting Legal Focus in the Abortion Debate") was published in *Bioethics and the Future of Medicine*, Nigel Cameron, David Schiedermayer, and John Kilner, eds. (Cumbria, UK: Pasternoster Press, 1995).

[2] Justice Harry Blackmun, "The 1973 Supreme Court Decisions on State Abortion Laws: Excerpts from Opinion in Roe v. Wade," in *The Problem of Abortion*, Joel Feinberg, ed. (Belmont, CA: Wadsworth, 1984), 195.

[3] See, for example, Harold O. J. Brown, *Death Before Birth* (Nashville: Thomas Nelson, 1977); Francis A. Schaeffer and C. Everett Koop, *Whatever Happened to the Human Race?* (Old Tappan, NJ: Revell, 1979); and John Warwick Montgomery, *Slaughter of the Innocents* (Westchester, IL: Crossway, 1981).

[4] Robert Wennberg, *Life in the Balance: Exploring the Abortion Controversy* (Grand Rapids: Eerdmans, 1985).

[5] Judith Jarvis Thomson, "A Defense of Abortion," in *The Problem of Abortion*, 173–87. All references to Thomson's article in this essay are from this book. This article was originally published in *Philosophy and Public Affairs* 1 (1971): 47–66.

[6] John S. Feinberg and Paul D. Feinberg, *Ethics in a Brave New World* (Wheaton, IL: Crossway, 1993), 66–69.

[7] Keith J. Pavlischek, "Abortion Logic and Paternal Responsibilities: One More Look at Judith Thomson's 'A Defense of Abortion,'" *Public Affairs Quarterly* 7 (October 1993): 341–61.

[8] Beckwith, *Politically Correct Death: Answering the Arguments for Abortion Rights* (Grand Rapids: Baker, 1993), chapter 7.

[9] See, for example, R. C. Sproul, *Abortion: A Rational Look at an Emotional Issue* (Colorado Springs, CO: NavPress, 1990); Randy Alcorn, *Pro Life Answers to Pro Choice Questions* (Portland: Multnomah, 1992); and F. LaGard Smith, *When Choice Becomes God* (Eugene, OR: Harvest, 1990).

[10] According to her editor, William Parent, in Judith Jarvis Thomson, *Rights, Restitution, and Risk* (Cambridge: Harvard University Press, 1986), vii.

You wake up in the morning and find yourself back to back in bed with an unconscious violinist. A famous unconscious violinist. He has been found to have a fatal kidney ailment, and the Society of Music Lovers has canvassed all the available medical records and found that you alone have the right blood type to help. They have therefore kidnapped you, and last night the violinist's circulatory system was plugged into yours, so that your kidneys can be used to extract poisons from his blood as well as your own. The director of the hospital now tells you, "Look we're sorry the Society of Music Lovers did this to you—we would never have permitted it if we had known. But still, they did it, and the violinist now is plugged into you. To unplug you would be to kill him. But never mind, it's only for nine months. By then he will have recovered from his ailment, and can safely be unplugged from you." Is it morally incumbent on you to accede to this situation? No doubt it would be very nice of you if you did, a great kindness. But do you *have* to accede to it? What if it were not nine months, but nine years? Or still longer? What if the director of the hospital says, "Tough luck, I agree, but you've now got to stay in bed, with the violinist plugged into you, for the rest of your life. Because remember this. All persons have a right to life, and violinists are persons. Granted you have a right to decide what happens in and to your body, but a person's right to life outweighs your right to decide what happens in and to your body. So you cannot ever be unplugged from him." I imagine that you would regard this as outrageous.[11]

Thomson's argument makes some very important observations that have gone virtually unnoticed. She is asking, "What happens if, for the sake of argument, we allow the premise [that the unborn are fully human or persons]? How, precisely, are we supposed to get from there to the conclusion that abortion is morally impermissible?"[12] That is to say, from the fact that a certain living organism is fully a human person, how does it logically follow that it is *never* permissible to kill that person?

Although a near unanimous number of ethicists maintain that it is *prima facie* wrong to kill an innocent human person, a vast majority agree that there may be some circumstances in which taking a human life or letting a human being die is justified, such as in the event of a just war, capital punishment, self-defense, or withdrawing medical treatment. Thomson's argument, however, includes abortion as one of these justified circumstances. She maintains that, since pregnancy constitutes an infringement by the fetus on the pregnant woman's personal bodily autonomy, the ordinary abortion—though it results in the death of an innocent human person—is not *prima facie* wrong.

One can immediately appreciate the appeal of this argument, especially in light of what is arguably the most quoted passage from *Roe*: "We need not resolve the difficult question of when life begins. When those trained in the respective disciplines of medicine, philosophy, and theology are unable to arrive at any consensus, the judiciary, at this point in the development of man's knowledge, is not in a position to speculate."[13] The Court, however, did not choose to employ Thomson's argument, though there is little doubt that it was brought to its attention. Consequently, the *Roe* Court assumed the major premise of the pro-life position: If the fetus is a person, then abortion in almost every case is unjustified homicide. This, according to a growing number of scholars, was a fatal mistake—a mistake that energized the right-to-life movement.

It appears that the first leading legal scholar to have recommended Thomson's argument to the judiciary was Michigan Law School professor, Donald Regan, in a law review article that appeared in 1979.[14] More recently, Professor Laurence Tribe of Harvard Law School, whose influence on the Court's liberal wing is well-known, suggested in a 1990 book on abortion that the Court should have seriously considered Thomson's argument. Tribe writes: "Perhaps the Supreme Court's opinion in Roe, by gratuitously insisting that the fetus *cannot* be deemed a 'person,' needlessly insulted and alienated those for whom the view that the fetus is a person represents a fundamental article of faith or a bedrock personal commitment... The Court could instead have said: Even if the fetus *is* a person, our Constitution forbids compelling a woman to carry it for nine months and become a mother."[15]

In his highly acclaimed book *The Culture of Disbelief* (1993), Stephen Carter of Yale Law School also recommended Thomson's argument:

---

[11] Thomson, "A Defense of Abortion," 174–75.
[12] Ibid., 174.
[13] Blackmun, 195.
[14] Donald Regan, "Rewriting Roe v. Wade," *Michigan Law Review* 77 (1979).
[15] Laurence Tribe, *Abortion: The Clash of Absolutes* (New York: W. W. Norton, 1990), 135.

As many theorists have recognized, the right to choose abortion, if indeed it survives, must be based on an approach that allows abortion *even if the fetus is human*—instead of an approach that denies that humanity under cover of the pretense that the definition is none of the state's business. The conclusion of fetal humanity by no means ends the argument; it simply forces the striking of a balance... My point is that the only fair way around a successful legislative effort to define the fetus as human—the only option that does not deride religiously based moral judgments as inferior to secular ones—is to argue for a right to abortion despite it. And an argument of that kind does not require an attack on the religious motivations of any abortion opponents.[16]

In addition to what has already been mentioned, a subtle philosophical shift seems to have occurred on the Supreme Court as well as society at large, which would indicate an openness to Thomson's argument. First, in a 1985 article Justice Ruth Bader Ginsburg, who was a Clinton appointee to the Supreme Court, chided the Court for appealing to the right to privacy rather than the equal protection clause in its grounding of abortion rights. She argued that since women are unique in their ability to be burdened by pregnancy—giving men a distinct advantage in social and political advancement—women should have the right to abortion based on the constitutional principle that all people, regardless of gender, deserve equal protection under the law. Thus, Ginsburg argued, by permitting women to undergo abortions on the basis of the equal protection clause, the Court would have made a clear stand for gender equity on firm constitutional grounds rather than basing its decision on the controversial and constitutionally vague right to privacy.[17]

Second, consider the recent physician-assisted suicide cases in Washington state and Michigan, in which a judge in the first case and a jury in the latter acquitted physicians who had killed consenting patients by appealing to an almost absolute principle of personal autonomy. The judge in Washington claimed she could find this principle in the 14th Amendment, the same place Justice Blackmun found the right to privacy in order to constitutionally ground *Roe*.

Third, in the 1992 case that upheld *Roe* as precedent, *Casey v. Planned Parenthood*, the Court asserted the following about the meaning of the 14th Amendment:

> Our law affords constitutional protection to personal decisions relating to marriage, procreation, family relationships, child rearing, and education... These matters, involving the most intimate and personal choices a person may make in a lifetime, choices central to personal dignity and autonomy, are central to the liberty protected by the Fourteenth Amendment. At the heart of liberty is the right to define one's own concept of existence, of meaning, of the universe, and of the mystery of human life. Beliefs about these matters could not define the attributes of personhood were they formed under compulsion by the State.[18]

Evidently the Supreme Court has chosen to abandon a rigorous defense of philosophical argument in the free marketplace of ideas only to replace it with a New Age mantra ("define your own reality") in the convenience store of slogans.

In any event, there is little doubt that a shift is occurring in the abortion debate. This shift should be addressed by those who oppose abortion as well as those who, regardless of their stand on abortion, see Thomson's argument as a threat to the moral force of parental obligations. Let us, therefore, take a critical look at Professor Thomson's argument.

WHY FETAL PERSONHOOD MATTERS

Although there are a number of problems with Thomson's argument, the following five are sufficient for the judiciary to reject it from consideration.

---

[16] Stephen L. Carter, *The Culture of Disbelief: How American Law and Politics Trivialize Religious Devotion* (New York: HarperCollins, 1993), 257–58.

[17] Ruth Bader Ginsburg, "Some Thoughts on Autonomy and Equality in Relation to *Roe v. Wade*," *University of North Carolina Law Review* (1985).

[18] Justice O'Connor, Justice Kennedy, and Justice Souter, "Planned Parenthood v. Casey (1992)," *The Abortion Controversy: A Reader*, Louis P. Pojman and Francis J. Beckwith, eds. (Boston: Jones & Bartlett, 1994), 54.

1. Thomson assumes that all moral obligations are voluntary.

By using the violinist story as a paradigm for all relationships, Thomson implies that moral obligations must be voluntarily accepted in order to have moral force. Thus she mistakenly infers that all true moral obligations to one's offspring are voluntary.

Consider the following story. Suppose a couple has a sexual encounter that is fully protected by several forms of birth control short of abortion (condom, the Pill, IUD, and so forth), but nevertheless results in conception. Instead of getting an abortion, the mother of the conceptus decides to bring it to term, although the father is unaware of this decision. After the birth of the child the mother pleads with the father for child support. Because he refuses, she seeks legal action and takes him to court. Although he took every precaution to avoid fatherhood—thus showing that he did not wish to accept such a status—according to nearly all child support laws in the United States he would still be obligated to pay support *precisely because* of his relationship to this child.[19]

As Michael Levin points out, "All child-support laws make the parental body an indirect resource for the child. If the father is a construction worker, the state will intervene unless some of his calories he extends lifting equipment go to providing food for his children."[20]

For this reason, Keith Pavlischek argues that "given the logic of" Thomson's argument, "the most reasonable course to follow would be to surrender the defense of paternal support laws for those children whose fathers would rather have had their children aborted." This "will lend some credence not only to the pro-life insistence on the corollary—that an intimate connection exists between the way we collectively relate to the unborn and the way we relate to our children after birth—but also to the claim made by pro-life feminists that the abortion mentality simply reaffirms the worst historical failings, neglect, and chauvinism of males."[21]

2. A case can be made that the unborn <u>does</u> have a prima facie right to her mother's body.

Assuming there is such a thing as a special obligation to one's children that does not have to be voluntarily accepted to have moral force, it is obvious that the unborn entity in ordinary circumstances (that is, with the exception of significant life-endangerment to the mother) *does* have a natural *prima facie* claim to her mother's body. There are several reasons to suppose that the unborn entity had such a natural claim.

First, unlike Thomson's violinist, who is artificially attached to another person in order to save his life and is therefore not naturally dependent on any particular human being, the unborn entity is a human being who is by her very nature dependent on her mother. This is how human beings *are* at this stage of their development.

Second, this period of a human being's natural development occurs in the womb. This is the journey we all must take and is a necessary condition for any human being's post-uterine existence. And this fact alone brings out the most glaring disanalogy between the violinist and the unborn: the womb is the unborn's *natural* environment, whereas being artificially hooked-up to a stranger is *not* the natural environment for the violinist. It would seem, then, that the unborn has a *prima facie* natural claim upon its mother's body.

Third, this same entity, when it becomes a newborn, has a natural claim upon her parents to care for her, regardless of whether her parents "wanted" her (see the above story of the irresponsible father). This is why we prosecute child abusers, people who throw their babies in trash cans, and parents who abandon their children.

Although it should not be ignored that pregnancy and childbirth entail certain emotional, physical, and financial sacrifices on the part of the pregnant woman, these sacrifices are also endemic *of parenthood in general* (which ordinarily lasts much longer than nine months). And these sacrifices do not justify the execution of troublesome infants and younger children whose existence entails a natural claim to certain financial and bodily goods that are under the ownership of their parents. If the unborn entity is fully human, as Thomson is willing to grant, why should the unborn's natural *prima facie* claim to her parents' goods differ *before* birth from what it will be *after* departing her mother's womb?

---

[19] See Carolyn Royce Kastner and Lawrence R. Young, eds., *In the Best Interest of the Child: A Guide to State Child Support and Paternity Laws*, (Child Support Enforcement Beneficial Laws Project, National Conference of State Legislatures, 1981).

[20] Michael Levin, review of *Life in the Balance* by Robert Wennberg, *Constitutional Commentary* 3 (Summer 1986): 511.

[21] Pavlischek, 343.

Of course, a court will not force a parent to donate a kidney to her dying offspring. But, as in the case of the unconscious violinist, this sort of dependence on another's body is highly unusual and is not part of the ordinary parental obligations associated with the *natural* process of human development.

Professor Stephen Schwarz points out that "the very thing that makes it plausible to say that the person in bed with the violinist has no duty to sustain him; namely, that he is a stranger unnaturally hooked up to him, is precisely what is absent in the case of the mother and her child." That is to say, the mother "does have an obligation to take care of her child, to sustain her, to protect her, and especially, to let her live in the only place where she can now be protected, nourished, and allowed to grow, namely the womb."[22]

It is evident that Thomson's violinist illustration undermines the *deep natural bond* between mother and child by making it seem no different than two strangers artificially hooked-up to each other so that one can "steal" the service of the other's kidneys. Rarely if ever has something so human, so natural, so beautiful, and so wonderfully demanding of our human creativity and love been reduced to such a brutal caricature.

This is not to say that the unborn has an *absolute* natural claim to her mother's body, but simply that she has a *prima facie* natural claim. One can easily imagine a situation in which this natural claim is outweighed by other important *prima facie* values, such as when pregnancy significantly endangers the mother's life.

3. Thomson ignores the fact that abortion is indeed killing, not merely withholding treatment.

Thomson makes an excellent point in her use of the violinist story; namely, there are times when withholding and/or withdrawing medical treatment is morally justified. For instance, one is not morally obligated to donate his kidney to Fred (one's next-door neighbor) simply because Fred needs a kidney in order to live. In other words, one is not obligated to risk his life so that Fred may live a few years longer. Fred should not expect that. If, however, one donates a kidney to Fred, one will have acted above and beyond the call of duty, since he will have performed a supererogatory moral act. But this case is not analogous to pregnancy and abortion.

Levin argues that there is an essential disanalogy between abortion and the unplugging of the violinist. In the case of the violinist (as well as one's relationship to Fred's welfare), "the person who withdraws [or withholds] his assistance is not completely responsible for the dependency on him of the person who is about to die, while the mother is completely responsible for the dependency of her fetus on her. When one is completely responsible for dependence, refusal to continue to aid is indeed killing."

For example, "if a woman brings a newborn home from the hospital, puts it in its crib and refuses to feed it until it has starved to death, it would be absurd to say that she simply refused to assist it and had done nothing for which she should be criminally liable."[23] Just as the withholding of food kills the child after birth, in the case of abortion it is the *abortion* that kills the child. In neither case is there any ailment from which the child suffers and for which highly invasive medical treatment (with the cooperation of another's bodily organs) is necessary in order to cure this ailment and save the child's life.

Or consider the case of a person who returns home after work to find a baby at his doorstep (as was the case in the film *Three Men and a Baby*, starring Tom Selleck, Ted Danson, and Steve Guttenberg). Suppose that no one else is able to care for the child, but this person only has to care for the child for nine months. (After that time a couple will adopt the child.) If we assume with Thomson that the fetus is as much a person as you or me, would "withholding treatment" (i.e., nourishment and protection) from this child and its subsequent death be justified on the basis that the homeowner was only "withholding treatment" from a child who could not benefit him, and for whom he did not ask? Is any person, born or unborn, obligated to sacrifice his life because his death would benefit another person?

Is it accurate to think of abortion as the withholding of support or treatment? Professors Schwarz and R. K. Tacelli make the important point that although "a woman who has an abortion is indeed 'withholding support' from her unborn child… abortion is far more than that. It is the active killing of a human person—by burning him, by crushing him, by dismembering him."[24] Euphemistically calling abortion the "withholding of support or treatment" makes about as much sense as calling suffocating someone with a pillow the withdrawing of oxygen.

---

[22] Stephen D. Schwarz, *The Moral Question of Abortion* (Chicago: Loyola University Press, 1990), 118.
[23] Michael Levin, *Feminism and Freedom* (New Brunswick: Transaction Books, 1987), 288–89.
[24] Stephen D. Schwarz and R. K. Tacelli, "Abortion and Some Philosophers," *Public Affairs Quarterly* 3 (April 1989), 85.

Unit Eight

4. Thomson's argument ignores family law.

Thomson's argument is inconsistent with the body of well-established family law, which presupposes parental responsibility of a child's welfare. And, of course, assuming as Thomson does that the unborn are fully human, this body of law would also apply to parents' responsibility for their unborn children.

According to legal scholars Dennis J. Horan and Burke J. Balche, "All 50 states, the District of Columbia, American Samoa, Guam, and the U.S. Virgin Islands have child abuse and neglect statutes which provide for the protection of a child who does not receive needed medical care." They further state that "a review of cases makes it clear that these statutes are properly applied to secure emergency medical treatment and sustenance (food or water, whether given orally or through intravenous or nasogastic tube) for children when parents, with or without the acquiescence of physicians, refuse to provide it."[25] Evidently, "pulling the plug" on a perfectly healthy fetus, assuming that it is a human person, would clearly violate these statutes.

In a case in New York, for example, the court ruled that the parents' actions constituted neglect when they failed to provide medical care to a child with leukemia: "The parent… may not deprive a child of lifesaving treatment, however well-intentioned. Even when the parents' decision to decline necessary treatment is based on constitutional grounds, such as religious beliefs, it must yield to the State's interests, as *parens patriae*, in protecting the health and welfare of the child."[26] The fact is that the "courts have uniformly held that a parent has the legal responsibility of furnishing his dependent child with adequate food and medical care."[27]

It is evident, then, that child-protection laws reflect our deepest moral intuitions about parental and community responsibility and the utter helplessness of infants and small children. These moral scruples are undoubtedly undermined by "brave new notions" of a socially contracted "voluntaristic" family (Thomson's view). Without such scruples the protection of children and the natural bonds and filial obligations that undergird family life (and, through it, society itself) will become a thing of the past. This seems too high a price to pay for "bodily autonomy."

5. Thomson's argument implies a "macho" view of bodily control that is inconsistent with true feminism.

Some pro-life feminists have pointed out that Thomson's argument and/or the reasoning behind it, which is supposed to be consistent with feminism, is actually quite anti-feminist.[28] In response to a similar argument from a woman's right to control her own body, one feminist publication asked the question, "What kind of control are we talking about? A control that allows for violence against another human being is a macho, oppressive kind of control. Women rightly object when others try to have that kind of control over them, and the movement for women's rights asserts the moral right of women to be free from the control of others." After all, "abortion involves violence against a small, weak and dependent child. It is macho control, the very kind the feminist movement most eloquently opposes in other contexts."[29]

Professor Celia Wolf-Devine makes the observation that "abortion has something… in common with the behavior ecofeminists and pacifist feminists take to be characteristically masculine; it shows a willingness to use violence in order to take control. The fetus is destroyed by being pulled apart by suction, cut in pieces, or poisoned."

Wolf-Devine goes on to point out that "in terms of social thought… it is the masculine models which are most frequently employed in thinking about abortion. If masculine thought is naturally … oriented toward power and control, then the interests of the fetus (who has no power) would naturally be suppressed in favor of the interests of the mother. But to the extent that feminist social thought is egalitarian, the question must be raised of why the mother's interests should prevail over the child's… Feminist thought about abortion

[25] Dennis J. Horan and Burke J. Balch, *Infant Doe and Baby Jane Doe: Medical Treatment of the Handicapped Newborn*, Studies in Law and Medicine Series (Chicago: Americans United for Life, 1985), 2.

[26] Quoted in ibid., 2–3, regarding Storar, 53 N.Y. 2d 363, 380–81, 420 N.E. 2d 64, 73, 438 N.Y.S. 2d 266, 275 (1981).

[27] Horan and Balch, 3–4.

[28] Although not dealing exclusively with Thomson's argument, Celia Wolf-Devine's article is quite helpful. "Abortion and the 'Feminine Voice,'" *Public Affairs Quarterly* 3 (July 1989). See also Sidney Callahan, "Abortion and the Sexual Agenda," *Commonweal* 113 (25 April 1986); and Janet Smith "Abortion as a Feminist Concern," Jeff Lane Hensley, ed., *The Zero People* (Ann Arbor: Servant, 1983).

[29] *Sound Advice for All Pro-life Activists and Candidates Who Wish to Include a Concern for Women's Rights in Their Prolife Advocacy: Feminists for Life Debate Handbook* (Kansas City, MO: Feminists for Life, no date), 15–16.

has… been deeply pervaded by the individualism which they so ardently criticize.[30]

Despite the recent suggestion in legal scholarship that fetal personhood ought not be the question that determines the morality of abortion, we have seen that if such a move is carried out by the courts the result would be morally and legally disastrous. For this reason, opponents of abortion ought to master the contents of this article and be prepared to engage this old philosophical, though new legal, challenge to human dignity.

---

*This essay originally appeared in the *Christian Research Journal*:
Francis Beckwith, "The Shifting Focus in the Abortion Debate: Does the Humanity of the Unborn Matter Anymore?," *Christian Research Journal* Vol. 17, No. 3 (1995), pp. 17–19, 32–34.
** Reproduction rights granted by the *Christian Research Journal*.

---

[30] Wolf-Devine, 86–87.

THE SHIFTING FOCUS
OF THE ABORTION DEBATE
ESSAY QUESTIONS

Answer the questions below on a separate sheet of paper and be prepared to review your answers in class.

1. **In relation to the personhood of the fetus, how has the abortion debate shifted?**

2. **Granting the personhood of the fetus, how does Thomson support the pro-choice position?**

3. **On what basis does Justice Ruth Bader Ginsburg base her belief in a right to abortion? What about *Casey v. Planned Parenthood*?**

4. **What are the first two objections made against Thomson's argument?**

5. **What other objections are made against Thomson's argument?**

THE BATTLE FOR LIFE
BY RAYMOND G. BOHLIN AND KERBY ANDERSON

THE HISTORY OF EUTHANASIA

The debate over euthanasia is not a modern phenomenon. The Greeks carried on a robust debate on the subject. The Pythagoreans opposed euthanasia, while the Stoics favored it in the case of incurable disease. Plato approved of it in cases of terminal illness.[1] But these influences lost out to Christian principles as well as the spread of acceptance of the Hippocratic Oath: "I will neither give a deadly drug to anybody if asked for it, nor will I make a suggestion to that effect."

In 1935 the Euthanasia Society of England was formed to promote the notion of a painless death for patients with incurable diseases. A few years later the Euthanasia Society of America was formed with essentially the same goals. In the last few years, debate about euthanasia has been advanced by two individuals: Derek Humphry and Dr. Jack Kevorkian.

Derek Humphry has used his prominence as head of the Hemlock Society to promote euthanasia in the United States. His book *Final Exit: The Practicalities of Self-Deliverance and Assisted Suicide for the Dying* became a bestseller and further influenced public opinion.

Another influential figure is Jack Kevorkian, who has been instrumental in helping people commit suicide. His book *Prescription Medicide: The Goodness of Planned Death* promotes his views of euthanasia and describes his patented suicide machine which he calls "the Mercitron." He first gained national attention by enabling Janet Adkins of Portland, Oregon, to kill herself in 1990. They met for dinner and then drove to a Volkswagen van where the machine waited. He placed an intravenous tube into her arm and dripped a saline solution until she pushed a button which delivered first a drug causing unconsciousness, and then a lethal drug that killed her. Since then he has helped dozens of other people do the same.

Over the years, public opinion has also been influenced by the tragic cases of a number of women described as being in a "persistent vegetative state." In the U.S. the first was Karen Ann Quinlan. Her parents, wanting to turn the respirator off, won approval in court. However, when it was turned off in 1976, Karen continued breathing and lived for another ten years. Another case was Nancy Cruzan, who was hurt in an automobile accident in 1983. Her parents went to court in 1987 to receive approval to remove her feeding tube. Various court cases ensued in Missouri, including her parents' appeal that was heard by the Supreme Court in 1990. Eventually they won the right to pull the feeding tube, and Nancy Cruzan died shortly thereafter. Most recently in 2005, Terri Schiavo's fate was sealed by the U.S. 11th circuit court of appeals, which granted Terri's husband the right to remove her feeding tube. The decision was unsuccessfully challenged by Terri's parents.

Seven years after the Cruzan case, the U.S. Supreme Court had occasion to rule again on the issue of euthanasia. On June 26, 1997 the Supreme Court rejected euthanasia by stating that state laws banning physician-assisted suicide were constitutional. Some feared that these cases (*Glucksburg v. Washington* and *Vacco v. Quill*) would become for euthanasia what *Roe v. Wade* became for abortion. Instead, the justices rejected the concept of finding a constitutional "right to die" and chose not to interrupt the political debate (as *Roe v. Wade* did), and instead urged that the debate on euthanasia continue, "as it should in a democratic society."

VOLUNTARY ACTIVE EUTHANASIA

It is helpful to distinguish between "mercy killing" (or active euthanasia) and what could be called "mercy dying" (or passive euthanasia). Taking a human life is not the same as allowing a terminal patient to die, that is, allowing nature to take its course. The former is immoral (and perhaps even criminal), while the latter is not.

However, drawing a sharp line between these two categories is not as easy as it used to be. Modern medical technology has significantly blurred the line between hastening death and allowing death. Certain analgesics, for example, ease pain, but they can also shorten a patient's life by affecting respiration. An

---

[1] Plato, *Republic* 3. 405.

Unit Eight

artificial heart will continue to beat even after the patient has died and therefore must be turned off by the doctor. So the distinction between actively promoting death and passively allowing nature to take its course is sometimes difficult to determine in practice. But this fundamental distinction between "mercy killing" and "mercy dying" is still an important philosophical distinction.

Another concern with active euthanasia is that it eliminates the possibility for recovery. While this should be obvious, somehow this problem is frequently ignored in the euthanasia debate. Terminating a human life eliminates all possibility of recovery, while passively ceasing extraordinary means may not. Miraculous recovery from a bleak prognosis sometimes occurs. A doctor who prescribes active euthanasia for a patient may unwittingly prevent a possible recovery he did not anticipate.

A further concern with this so-called voluntary active euthanasia is that these decisions might not always be freely made. The possibility for coercion is always present. Richard D. Lamm, former governor of Colorado, said that elderly, terminally ill patients have "a duty to die and get out of the way." Though those words were reported somewhat out of context, they nonetheless illustrate the pressure many elderly feel from hospital personnel.

The Dutch experience is also instructive. A survey of Dutch physicians was done in 1990 by the Remmelink Committee. They found that 1,030 patients were killed without their consent. Of these, 140 were fully mentally competent and 110 were only slightly mentally impaired. The report also found that another 14,175 patients (1,701 of whom were mentally competent) were denied medical treatment without their consent and died.[2]

A more recent survey of the Dutch experience is even less encouraging. Doctors in the United States and the Netherlands have found that though euthanasia was originally intended for exceptional cases, it has become an accepted way of dealing with serious or terminal illness. The original guidelines (that patients with a terminal illness make a voluntary, persistent request that their lives be ended) have been expanded to include chronic ailments and psychological distress. They also found that 60 percent of Dutch physicians do not report their cases of assisted suicide (even though reporting is required by law) and about 25 percent of the physicians admit to ending patients' lives without their consent.[3]

INVOLUNTARY ACTIVE EUTHANASIA

Involuntary active euthanasia requires a second party who makes decisions about whether active measures should be taken to end a life. Foundational to this discussion is an erosion of the doctrine of the sanctity of life. Ever since the Supreme Court ruled in *Roe v. Wade* that the life of unborn babies could be terminated for reasons of convenience, the slide down society's slippery slope has continued even though the Supreme Court has been reluctant to legalize euthanasia.

The progression was inevitable. Once society begins to devalue the life of an unborn child, it is but a small step to begin to do the same with a child who has been born. Abortion slides naturally into infanticide and eventually into euthanasia. In the past few years doctors have allowed a number of so-called "Baby Does" to die—either by failing to perform lifesaving operations or else by not feeding the infants.

The progression toward euthanasia is inevitable. Once society becomes conformed to a "quality of life" standard for infants, it will more willingly accept the same standard for the elderly. As former Surgeon General C. Everett Koop has said, "Nothing surprises me anymore. My great concern is that there will be 10,000 Grandma Does for every Baby Doe."[4]

Again the Dutch experience is instructive. In the Netherlands, physicians have performed involuntary euthanasia because they thought the family had suffered too much or were tired of taking care of patients. American surgeon Robin Bernhoft relates an incident in which a Dutch doctor euthanized a twenty-six-year-old ballerina with arthritis in her toes. Since she could no longer pursue her career as a dancer, she was depressed and requested to be put to death. The doctor complied with her request and merely noted that "one doesn't enjoy such things, but it was her choice."[5]

---

[2] R. Finigsen, "The Report of the Dutch Committee on Euthanasia," *Issues in Law and Medicine* (July 1991), 339–44.

[3] Herbert Hendlin, Chris Rutenfrans, and Zbigniew Zylicz, "Physician-Assisted Suicide and Euthanasia in the Netherlands: Lessons from the Dutch," *Journal of the American Medical Association* 277 (June 4, 1997): 1720–2.

[4] Interview with C. Everett Koop, "Focus on the Family" radio broadcast.

[5] Robin Bernhoft, quoted in *Euthanasia: False Light*, produced by IAETF, P.O. Box 760, Steubenville, OH 43952.

WHY PEOPLE SEEK EUTHANASIA

Why is such a large segment of our society enamored with the possibility of physician-assisted suicide? While there can be many roads that will lead to this conclusion, the primary one is fear. People today fear being at the mercy of technology, of being kept alive with no hope of recovery by machines. Few seem to realize that it is already legal for a terminally ill patient to refuse life-prolonging measures. We must realize that there is a difference between simply allowing nature to take its course when someone is clearly dying and taking direct measures to hasten someone's death. Former Surgeon General C. Everett Koop acknowledges,

> If someone is dying and there is no doubt about that, and you believe as I do that there is a difference between giving a person all the life to which he is entitled as opposed to prolonging the act of dying, then you might come to a time when you say this person can take certain amounts of fluid by mouth and we're not going to continue this intravenous solution because he is on the way out.[6]

Extraordinary measures are not required to keep a dying person alive at all costs. But some people fear exactly that. Removing this fear will take a lot of the wind out of the euthanasia sails.

Secondly, people fear the pain of the dying process. Intractable pain is a real fear, but few people today realize that most of the pain of terminally ill patients can be dealt with. Many doctors, particularly in the U.S., are not aware of all the measures at their disposal. There are new ways of administering morphine, for example, that can achieve effective pain management with lower doses and therefore a lower risk of respiratory complications.

Dr. Paul Cundiff, practicing oncologist and hospice care physician with 18 years of experience treating dying patients says,

> It is a disgrace that the majority of our health care providers lack the knowledge and the skills to treat pain and other symptoms of terminal disease properly. The absence of palliative care training for medical professionals results in sub-optimal care for almost all terminally ill patients and elicits the wish to hasten their own deaths in a few.[7]

But many would even be willing to live with the pain if they knew that they would not be left alone. The growth in the hospice movement will help alleviate this fear as well. The staff at a hospice is trained to deal not only with physical pain, but with psychological, social, and spiritual pain as well. If you have seen pictures of the many people Jack Kevorkian has assisted to commit suicide, you cannot help but notice that these are lonely, miserable people. Pain has had little to do with their desire to commit suicide.

As a nation we have in large part abandoned our elderly population. When God commanded Israel to honor their fathers and their mothers, this was understood to mean primarily in their older years. Extended families no longer live together even when the medical needs of parents are not severe or terribly limiting. No one wants to be a burden or to be burdened.

WHY LIFE IS WORTH LIVING

As we discuss the issue of euthanasia and physician-assisted suicide, it is critical that we not only understand what is going on in the world around us but that we also understand what the Bible clearly teaches about, life, death, pain, suffering, and the value of each human life.

First, the Bible teaches that we are made in the image of God and therefore, every human life is sacred (Genesis 1:26). In Psalm 139:13–16 we learn that each of us is fearfully and wonderfully made. God himself has knit us together in our mother's womb. We must be very important to him if he has taken such care to bring us into existence.

Second, the Bible is very clear that God is sovereign over life, death, and judgment. In Deuteronomy 32:39 The Lord says, "See now that I myself am He! There is no god besides me, I put to death and I bring to life, I have wounded and I will heal, and no one can deliver out of my hand." Psalm 139:16 says that it

---

[6] C. Everett Koop, "The Surgeon General on Euthanasia." *Presbyterian Journal* (Sept. 25, 1985):8.
[7] David Cundiff, quoted in review of *Euthanasia is NOT the Answer: A Hospice Physician's View* by Debbie Decker, *CURRENTS in Science, Technology, and Society*, 1(2):20.

is God who has ordained all of our days before there is even one of them. Paul says essentially the same thing in Ephesians 1:11.

Third, to assist someone in committing suicide is to commit murder and this breaks God's unequivocal commandment in Exodus 20:13.

Fourth, God's purposes are beyond our understanding. We often appeal to God as to why some tragedy has happened to us or someone we know. Yet listen to Job's reply to the Lord in Job 42:1–3:

> I know that you can do all things; no plan of yours can be thwarted. [You asked,] 'Who is this that obscures My counsel without knowledge?' Surely I spoke of things I did not understand, things too wonderful for me to know.

We forget that our minds are finite and his is infinite. We cannot always expect to understand all of what God is about. To think that we can step in and declare that someone's life is no longer worth living is simply not our decision to make. Only God knows when it is time. In Isaiah 55:8–9 the Lord declares, "For my thoughts are not your thoughts, neither are your ways my ways. As the heavens are higher than the earth, so are my ways higher than your ways and my thoughts higher than your thoughts."

Fifth, our bodies belong to God anyway. Paul reminds us in 1 Corinthians 6:15,19 that we are members of Christ's body and that we have been bought with a price. Therefore we should glorify God with our bodies. The only one to receive glory when someone requests doctor-assisted suicide is not God, not the doctor, not even the family but the patient for being willing to "nobly" face the realities of life and "unselfishly" end everyone else's misery. There is no glory for God in this decision.

Lastly, suffering draws us closer to God. In light of the euthanasia controversy, listen to Paul's words from 2 Corinthians 1:8:

> We were under great pressure, far beyond our ability to endure, so that we despaired even of life. Indeed, in our hearts we felt the sentence of death. But this happened that we might not rely on ourselves but on God, who raises the dead.

Not only does He raise the dead but there is nothing that can separate us from His love (Romans 8:38). For an inspiring and thoroughly biblical discussion of the euthanasia issue, read Joni Earickson Tada's book *When is it Right to Die?* (Zondervan, 1992). Her testimony and clear thinking is in stark contrast to the conventional wisdom of the world today. We must do the same.

WHAT WILL YOU DO? WHAT CAN YOU DO?

The Christian Medical and Dental Society has produced an excellent resource on physician-assisted suicide titled *The Battle for Life*.[8] As a part of the package they provide several cases to test your grasp of the principles involved and to help Christians be aware of the tough decisions that have to be made. I would like to share two of those with you and then discuss what you can do now to combat the "right to die" forces in this country.

Test Case 1:

Your 80 year-old grandmother has been fighting cancer for some time now and feels the emotional strain. She feels like she'll become a burden to the family. Her doctor notes that she seems to have lost her desire to live. Should she be able to have her doctor give her a prescription expressly designed to kill her? This is precisely what the courts have legalized and precisely what God's word says is wrong. It is wrong because it would be taking her life into our hands and violating God's sovereignty. Because physician-assisted suicide goes beyond letting someone die naturally to actually causing the death, it violates God's commandment, "You shall not murder." There is a clear distinction between allowing death to take its natural course in

---

[8] *The Battle for Life* is an educational resource kit produced by the Christian Medical and Dental Society. The kit includes an award winning video, *Euthanasia: False Light*, a leader's presentation guide with discussion questions, handouts for Christian and secular audiences, overhead transparencies, biblical principles summary, research synopsis, cassette tape of public service announcements, and bulletin inserts. The $30 kit is available from the Christian Medical and Dental Society, P.O. Box 5, Bristol, TN, 37621, Phone (615) 844-1000, FAX: (615) 844-1005. The kit can also be purchased through Probe Ministries.

someone who is clearly dying with no hope of a cure, and taking specific measures to end someone's life. There comes a time when the body is imminently dying. Bodily functions begin to shut down. At this point, people should be made as comfortable as possible, be supported and encouraged by their family and doctors, and allowed to die. This is death with dignity. Taking a lethal injection or breathing poisonous carbon monoxide takes life out of God's hands and into our own.

Test Case 2:

Your spouse has an incurable fatal disease, has lost control of bodily functions, and is unable to communicate. Special treatment and equipment can extend your spouse's life for a few weeks or even months but will involve much pain and exhaustion. Would it be morally right for you to not arrange for the treatment? Many would accept a decision not to arrange for treatment because that would not be killing but simply allowing death to take its natural course. Such decisions are not always clear-cut, however, and a physician and family members must take into account the pros and cons of intervention versus a faster natural death. Sometimes we rationalize that we need to keep the patient alive as long as possible because God may still work a miracle. But just how much time does God need to work a miracle? If God is going to intervene He will do so on His time and not ours.

Now that we have a better understanding of the issues, you may be wondering just what we can do about this threat among us. Three things:

Pray — Pray that God will turn the hearts of people back to Himself and back to protecting life. Pray for righteousness and justice in our legal system, that we enact laws that preserve life, punish the guilty and protect the innocent.

Speak Out — Present this information to other groups. Talk with your friends and family and discuss the reasons for protecting life. Contact your state and federal legislators and tell them to stand against physician-assisted suicide.

Reach Out — Visit the elderly, care for those who can't care for themselves, comfort the sick. Consider joining or starting a church ministry to the elderly, handicapped, or other individuals with special needs. As Christians we must lead the way with our hearts and actions and not just our words. If we devote our energies to providing quality and loving care and effective pain control, the euthanasia issue will die from a lack of interest.

---

*This essay originally appeared as two separate essays on the *LeaderU* website:
    Raymond G. Bohlin, "Euthanasia: The Battle for Life"
    Kerby Anderson, "Euthanasia"
**Reproduction rights granted by Raymond G. Bohlin and Kerby Anderson.

THE BATTLE FOR LIFE
ESSAY QUESTIONS

Answer the questions below on a separate sheet of paper and be prepared to review your answers in class.

1. What is active euthanasia? What is passive euthanasia?

2. What is voluntary euthanasia? What is involuntary euthanasia? What are some concerns connected with each?

3. What are some similarities between the society's general acceptance of euthanasia and the practice of abortion?

4. Why do individuals seek euthanasia?

5. How does the Bible teach that all life is valuable?

DEAR DOUG
WRITING ASSIGNMENT

It's me again!

I'm finally getting back into the swing of college life. It's been a little tough balancing everything so there's time left over for fun, but I think I've got it licked. Oh, yeah, the big news is I got a job—I'm working four evenings a week at a restaurant about a block from the dorm. Nice place, with good customers.

Nathan and I had everyone over last night to watch a movie. Can you picture the six of us crammed into a college dorm room? We were draped everywhere, but it was great! Paige brought the popcorn and Mark brought the movie, some new futuristic action-adventure.

When it was over, we started talking about what the world would look like in a couple of decades. Sarah thinks we'll have a unified global government… after all, the first steps have already been taken, when you consider the UN and Europe's adoption of the Euro. Everyone's always talking about "world peace" and this would be one way to get it, but I'm worried about how to keep it from becoming tyrannical. What do you think about a worldwide government?

Muhammad believes that a global government would only be possible under the control of Islamic leaders—a government unified by religious fervor. That didn't sit too well with me, since Christianity and Islam don't seem to mix. What are your thoughts on a global Islamic government?

Nathan supported having a single global power, but wanted to know what would happen to everyone's individual rights. Mark said we would only have those rights granted to us by the state, at which point Paige jumped on him. She wanted to know how they were going to protect women's rights. Nothing is certain in life, she said, and she wanted to make sure that she would keep total control over her own body.

That got the girls started on the topic of abortion and why the religious fanatics can't just leave women alone. Sarah said that it's her body and nobody should tell her what to do with it. A fetus is not really human until it's born, after all, and a mistake like getting pregnant shouldn't mess up her life and career. Paige added that legalized abortion is saving all those women who would die having back-alley abortions if the laws were overturned. By the time the conversation was over, both of them were pretty disgusted with the pro-life movement. How is a Christian supposed to deal with the issue of abortion anyway?

The whole issue of government and politics is pretty new to me. I mean, I've only been old enough to vote for a couple of years. Does Christianity have a position on politics?

Well, I've gotta get changed and head out to work.

Talk to you later!
Doug

STUDENT MANUAL

UNDERSTANDING THE TIMES

Unit Nine

Topics:
Economics
Radical Environmentalism
Stewardship
Welfare

A Summit Ministries Curriculum

180-DAY SYLLABUS

DAY	IN CLASS	HOMEWORK	
1	WATCH "Economics" video		
2	READ __UTT__ Textbook 'Economics 9.1'	READ __UTT__ Textbook 'Economics 9.2'	
3	REVIEW __UTT__ Textbook 'Economics 9.1–9.2' questions	READ __UTT__ Textbook 'Economics 9.3'	
4	READ __UTT__ Textbook 'Economics 9.4'		
5	REVIEW __UTT__ Textbook 'Economics 9.3–9.4' questions	READ __UTT__ Textbook 'Economics 9.5'	
6	READ __UTT__ Textbook 'Economics 9.6'		
7	REVIEW __UTT__ Textbook 'Economics 9.5–9.6' questions	READ *Heart, Soul, and Money* essay	
8	REVIEW *Heart, Soul, and Money* essay questions	ASSIGN Dear Doug Letter	
9	WATCH "Radical Environmentalism" video		
10	REVIEW "Radical Environmentalism" video questions		
11	READ *Principles of a Christian...* essay		
12	REVIEW *Principles of a Christian...* essay questions		
13	WATCH "The Dangerous Samaritan" video		
14	REVIEW "The Dangerous Samaritan" video questions	Dear Doug Letter assignment DUE	
15	TAKE Unit Nine Test		

90-DAY SYLLABUS

DAY	IN CLASS	HOMEWORK	
1	WATCH "Economics" video	READ __UTT__ Textbook 'Economics 9.1–9.2'	
2	REVIEW __UTT__ Textbook 'Economics 9.1–9.2' questions	READ __UTT__ Textbook 'Economics 9.3–9.4'	
3	REVIEW __UTT__ Textbook 'Economics 9.3–9.4' questions	READ __UTT__ Textbook 'Economics 9.5–9.6'	
4	REVIEW __UTT__ Textbook 'Economics 9.5–9.6' questions	READ *Principles of a Christian...* essay	
5	REVIEW *Principles of a Christian...* essay questions		
6	WATCH "The Dangerous Samaritan" video		
7	REVIEW "The Dangerous Samaritan" video questions		
8	TAKE Unit Nine Test		

Unit Nine

UNDERSTANDING THE TIMES
ECONOMICS QUESTIONS

Answer the questions below on a separate sheet of paper and be prepared to review your answers in class.

ECONOMICS 9.1

1. What is the distinction between socialism and the free market system?

2. What biblical support is offered for private property? What happens when private ownership is denied?

3. What is the principle of comparative advantage? How does competition stifle mankind's sinful tendencies?

4. What are two mistaken assumptions often made about the wealthy?

5. What is the relationship between freedom and the economic system a country employs?

ECONOMICS 9.2

6. What similarities exist between the Islamic and Christian approaches to economics?

7. What are the four foundational principles of Islamic economics as described by Syed Hawab Haider Naqvi?

8. What economic system do Muslims favor?

9. What do the terms *zakat* and *jizrah* mean?

10. How does Islam treat inheritance? What is the Islamic view of charging interest?

ECONOMICS 9.3

11. Why do a number of current leading Secular Humanists favor capitalism?

12. Why did most of Secular Humanism's earliest proponents favor socialism?

13. On what form of economics does almost every Humanist agree?

14. Why do many Secular Humanists believe in interventionism?

15. How do Secular Humanists propose that we achieve a more "equal" society?

Unit Nine

16. According to Karl Marx, what two flaws within capitalism cause it to be exploitative?

17. According to Marxism, what will be the fate of capitalism?

18. What is the difference between socialism and communism?

19. Why must a transitional phase necessarily exist between capitalism and communism?

20. What do Marxists believe the benefits of communism will be?

21. Why are Cosmic Humanists vague when defining their ideal economic system?

22. How do Cosmic Humanists encourage individuals to decide on a vocation?

23. According to Cosmic Humanism, what is the best way to achieve a higher income?

24. According to Cosmic Humanists, what does God desire for us?

25. According to New Agers, why can the enlightened trust the world to bring them material possession?

26. What is the "decentered self" and why is it important to Postmodern economics?

27. Why do Postmodernists denounce capitalism? How do Postmodernists propose that we fix the problems inherent in capitalism?

28. What is interventionism?

29. Since all economic theories have problems, what do Postmodernists claim should be done?

30. Why are Postmodernists hesitant to offer a positive economic theory?

HEART, SOUL, AND MONEY
BY CRAIG BLOMBERG[1]

INTRODUCTION

More than a billion people out of earth's six billion inhabitants live in desperate poverty. Natural disasters, war, corrupt governments, lack of education, disease, unfair trade laws, and false religions all play their part in creating this situation. Conservatively, at least 200 million (one-fifth) of these poor are Bible-believing, born-again Christians.

In North America, trends over the last thirty years demonstrate an increasing disparity between rich and poor, irrespective of which political party has been in power at any given time. More and more, the growing gap between rich and poor follows racial lines: whites and Asians growing richer; blacks and Hispanics growing poorer.

Meanwhile middle- and upper-class Americans, including Christians, have markedly changed their spending patterns. We now eat out on average for nearly 30% of all our meals, compared to only 10% a mere twenty years ago. The amount of money spent on such nonessentials as sports and recreation, lawn care, video and computer games, home entertainment centers, pets and dieting has skyrocketed. At the same time Christians' per capita giving to charitable causes of all kinds has steadily declined in the last forty years from just under 4% of their total annual income to barely above 2%.

We are in the midst of the largest transfer of wealth in human history from the World War II generation to their children, the baby boomers. The possibilities of funding Christian ministry to address people's spiritual and physical needs at home and abroad are at an all-time high. But all the trends suggest that overall those inheriting this wealth are spending the vast majority of it on themselves, either to get out of all-time, global record levels of debt or to continue to fuel their self-centered interests.

Christian trend-watchers have made two staggering calculations. On the one hand, if every American Christian simply tithed, the additional amount of money that would be raised above and beyond current giving levels would be enough to eradicate world poverty in our lifetime. Of course, the sinful behavior of fallen humanity would prevent this from ever fully happening, but we could certainly make substantially greater progress than we currently are making. Second, the average age of major donors in both church and para-church organizations is now, for the first time ever, well over sixty-five. Current Christian work is being funded largely by retired people, who lived a more frugal lifestyle a generation ago. Thus, unless patterns of Christian giving change dramatically, a majority of currently existing ministries will close their doors for lack of finances within one generation.

Astonishingly, while all this is happening, some Christian leaders are promoting a "health-wealth" gospel that pretends that it is God's desire for the already affluent Western Christian to become even richer. In striking contrast, every once in a while someone else seems to argue that well-to-do Christians should trade places with the poor. Both of these extremes prove unbiblical and probably discourage some of the rest of us from taking any action at all.

I have written on this subject, therefore, because I have discovered that many Christians today are not willfully choosing to be disobedient to the Scriptures in the area of financial stewardship. They merely are unaware of the Bible's teaching on the topic and often unaware of the plight of the world and the kinds of trends I have just described. Many gladly increase their giving after a careful study of the Bible and current realities.

HISTORICAL BACKGROUND TO NEW TESTAMENT PASSAGES

In order to accurately understand the biblical instruction on any subject, but especially this one, we need to understand the context in which the message was communicated. First and foremost, unlike our relatively large middle class of America today, in Jesus' time about 80% of the Jews were poor, hoping each year's

---

[1] This essay was adapted from a study guide of the same name by Craig Blomberg published by College Press (www. collegepress.com) in 2000. For an expanded study of this topic or to find the sources for Dr. Blomberg's facts stated in this essay, please consult his book *Neither Poverty nor Riches: A Biblical Theology of Possessions* (InterVarsity, 1999).

crops would get them through that year. For these believers the Lord's prayer "give us this day our daily bread," was a present reality and an understandable request.

By the first century, a tiny handful of Jewish and Roman landlords owned vast tracts of land in Palestine. Small landowners found it harder and harder to get by. Eventually many of them sold their property and went to work as hired hands of the rich, tilling the same land they once owned. When they were unable to pay their taxes, they took out loans and amassed debts on which they often had to default. In the most acute cases, some were thrown into debtors' prisons. Some even died there.

While the Jewish synagogues and temple regularly took up collections to benefit their poor, the Greco-Roman world, pertinent to the background of the traveling apostles, had no equivalent institutions. The Roman empire in general lacked any kind of welfare system. Greco-Roman ways of thinking often viewed poverty as the fault and just punishment of the poor. So it was very common for people to become disabled or diseased, homeless and helpless, with few if any people in the empire who cared.

Both the Jewish and Greco-Roman cultures reflected widespread frustration with the economic disparities between rich and poor that increased in severity throughout the first century. Little wonder, then, that many Jews looked for a military Messiah who would help them overthrow Rome and reestablish an independent state of Israel in which they could revert to the more just laws and practices of their Scriptures. Many of them became disenchanted with Jesus, who claimed to be the Messiah but had little interest in political revolution. Little wonder, too, that many Greeks and Romans warmed to the apostles' message of equality in Christ across the wide, humanly created socioeconomic divides of their world.

However, we should recognize that at least some of Jesus' twelve disciples were more middle-class than poor. Matthew's tax collecting business probably vaulted him into this class, though through ill-gotten gain if he resembled others of his day. James and John, the sons of Zebedee, may have come from one of the handful of more prosperous fishing businesses, because Mark 1:20 speaks of their family having "hired men." Even households with meager resources often had one servant, rescuing him or her from total poverty, but more than one "employee" in a household suggested some measure of prosperity.

Just as we ought not think of all twelve of the disciples and Jesus as uniformly poor, neither may we imagine them as having permanently divested themselves of all their property. True, Peter can declare, "We have left everything to follow you!" (Mark 10:28). But he will later lead a group of the disciples back to their fishing boats after the resurrection (John 21:3), demonstrating that they had not sold their property but merely left it for a time. Likewise when Jesus says, "The Son of Man has nowhere to lay his head" (Matt. 8:20), this does not mean that he is homeless. Mary still lived in Nazareth (Joseph may have died by this time), and Jesus himself seems to have had a house in Capernaum (Mark 2:1). Instead, Jesus is stressing his voluntarily chosen path of itinerant ministry.

Further insight into how Jesus and the twelve supported themselves comes from Luke 8:1–3, in which we read of several wealthy women who supported the little traveling troupe out of their personal means. A pair of apparently secret followers of Jesus who were also extremely rich were Joseph of Arimathea and Nicodemus (Matt. 27:57; John 19:38–40—the amount of spices used to anoint Jesus' body came close to that used in the burial of kings). Thus when we read in 2 Corinthians 8:9 that "you know of the grace of our Lord Jesus Christ, that though he was rich, yet for our sakes he became poor, so that you through his poverty might become rich," we are not to understand literal poverty and riches to be in view. Christ in his incarnation gave up the incomprehensible privilege of sitting at the Father's right hand to be humiliated as a human and ultimately executed. That is how he became "poor." Similarly, we become rich in spiritual blessings, not necessarily earthly ones, as we become disciples of Christ.

Major Themes

Any attempt to summarize the dominant emphases in any large swathe of biblical material inevitably oversimplifies. So, too, our comments here do not adequately encompass the wealth of detail discussed in the books from which this essay derives. Nonetheless, these broad strokes should help provide a framework through which to think about stewardship in general and your personal stewardship in particular. In the body of this paper, we will consider the five most important conclusions to emerge from a survey of the Bible's teaching on material possessions.

1. Material possessions are a good gift from God meant for his people to enjoy.

The Scriptures begin and end with one of the most important principles about possessions in the Bible. Like all of the rest of the material world, God created them as something good to be enjoyed by all humanity (Genesis 1:4, 10, 12, 18, 21, 25, 31). Unique among his creation, humans were fashioned in God's image and called to be stewards of everything else God had created (vv. 26–28). Even after the Fall, that calling does not give us permission to be cruel to animals or to destroy the environment, but it does grant us authority over "animal, vegetable, and mineral" to mold and reshape creation in ways that make our lives more productive and rewarding.

Throughout the Old Testament, Job, Abraham, David, Solomon and a variety of other figures demonstrate that riches and godliness can coexist, at least for a time. The very fact that God promised Israel the land of Canaan, with its abundant natural resources, demonstrates his commitment to providing the blessings of the material world as a pre-eminent, good gift for his people (Numbers 14:8). The proverbial literature offers riches as a reward for wholesome work. The New Testament likewise recognizes an increasing number of well-to-do Christians throughout the early history of Christianity who host churches in their homes, make business trips and fund itinerant ministries. The community of disciples shares its material resources with one another, not so that all will be equally impoverished, but so that there will be 'no needy persons among them' (Acts 4:34). This is part of the principle behind those with extra giving to those who lack. That those of us who have more than others should work to help those who have less to have at least a little more to enjoy. Even in the harshest of scenarios, the very luxuries that can lead to the demonic (Revelation 17–18) will be available for all of God's redeemed people in a very material age to come (Revelation 21–22).

Thus Paul concludes 1 Timothy by commanding "those who are rich in this present world not to be arrogant nor to put their hope in wealth, which is so uncertain, but to put their hope in God" (6:17). But he balances this with the reminder that God "richly provides us with everything for our enjoyment." Paul is no ascetic, the material world still includes good gifts for God's people, and Christ does not call a majority of his followers to permanently divest themselves of all of their property. Verse 18 explains how we can enjoy a measure of prosperity with a good conscience—when we simultaneously are "rich in good deeds," "generous and willing to share."

2. Material possessions are simultaneously one of the primary means of turning human hearts away from God.

It is not impossible to be both rich and Christian, but consistently throughout biblical and church history, lower percentages of believers are found among the richer than among the poorer segments of society.

Adam and Eve coveted the attractive but forbidden fruit of the garden, and everything was corrupted or cursed quickly thereafter. Possession of, or desire for, too many material goods leads to rejection of God, interpersonal hostility and exploitation or neglect of the poor. Thus most of the property laws of the Torah set limits on the amounts to be accumulated. The celebration of the Jubilee year (Leviticus 25:8–55) alone would have allowed for a family to start afresh once a lifetime (once every 50 years), no matter how irresponsibly they had handled their finances or how far into debt they had fallen. However, it is uncertain whether this special sabbatical year was ever observed. Therefore the loss of ancestral properties to wealthy aristocrats who bought up vast tracts of land forever altered the economic landscape and widened the gap between rich and poor.

The enormous wealth of the monarchy, even though enjoyed by some like David who remained faithful to God, fuelled social injustice and prophetic critique. Ezekiel 22:29, Micah 2:2, and Amos 5:11–12 are three of numerous passages that stress how the rich in Israel were trying to get richer at the expense of the poor. Instead of honoring the Torah's commitment that inheritance remain within families so that all can own at least modest amounts of property, numerous illegal and unethical maneuvers were being concocted to concentrate wealth in the hands of fewer and fewer.

Not all poor people follow God and not all rich people deny him, but increasingly the Israelites experience what many other cultures have recognized throughout history: levels of religious commitment are consistently higher among the less well-to-do, who recognize they must depend on God for their wellbeing, than among the affluent, who think their buying power can meet all of their human needs.

UNDERSTANDING THE TIMES

For Jesus, mammon was God's rival. In addition to his statement in Matthew 6:24, Jesus taught this to his followers in a number of parables. In the parable of the Sower, one of the kinds of soils that proves unfruitful is that which is crowded by thorns and thistles. Jesus explains that the seed sown here corresponds to those who "hear the word; but the worries of this life, the deceitfulness of wealth, and the desires for other things come in and choke the word" (Mark 4:18–19). In the parable of the Rich Fool (Luke 12:13–21), an inheritance dispute leads Jesus to warn about covetousness (vv. 13–15). Then he illustrates by telling the story of a farmer who had an unexpected bumper crop and had to build extra barns to store it all (vv. 16–20). Six times in the text, the man speaks about himself with the first-person pronoun "I." Never does he suggest that any of this surplus ought to help the needy who, as we have seen in the introduction, would have constituted about 80% of the peasants and villagers surrounding him. Suddenly, his life comes to an end and he can't take his riches with him. Jesus concluded, "This is how it will be with those who store up things for themselves but are not rich toward God" (v. 21).

This same idea leads Paul to proclaim, "The love of money is the root of all kinds of evil" (1 Timothy 6:10). Paul does not say that "money is the root of all evil" but speaks of "the love of money." The love of money is one important root, but not the only one, of all kinds of evil. Still, we must not lose the force of Paul's warning. Even translated correctly, as in the NIV, the verse still reminds us of all the ways wealth or its pursuit distracts us from godly priorities in our lives. In 1 Timothy 3:3 and 8, under the criteria for church leaders, Paul includes the prohibitions against being lovers of money and pursuing dishonest gain. The terms used are both synonyms for being greedy. Thus we should not be surprised when in Titus 1:11 false teachers are described as seeking dishonest gain, while in 2 Timothy 3:2,4 the terrible people that will arise in the last days are said to be lovers of money and lovers of pleasure.

James (4:13–17) rebukes well-to-do believers for planning an entire year or more of their lives without taking God's will into account. These businesspeople may well be part of the small middle class of the ancient Roman empire rather than truly wealthy, but either way the point is that the early Christians were not uniformly poor. But the "practical atheism" of the behavior of these traders closely parallels the long-term planning of middle-class people, including Christians, in our world today. The book of James contains an implicit criticism of the behavior of wealthy (at least not poor) Christians that reminds us that affluent Christians have particular obstacles they must overcome. They are tempted to think that their material possessions can replace God, that they deserve better treatment than poorer people do, and that life can be secured against all crises.

Both 2 Peter and Jude describe false teachers whose influence Christians should avoid. Among their evil character traits appears "greed" (2 Peter 2:3,14). Second Peter 2:14–15 describes them literally as "well trained in covetousness!" Jude 11 speaks of those who "rushed for profit into Balaam's error," a reference to Numbers 25 and 31:16 in which the pagan prophet who had earlier refused to curse Israel (Numbers 22–24) later seduced her into idolatry. In each of these contexts, it is interesting to see how sins of out-of-control spending are combined with references to sexual immorality. Both involve one's inability to delay gratification of one's wants and desires. Fulfilling one's immediate urges is all that counts for such people. It has been said that in our culture, too, one of the best barometers of Christian obedience is how a person uses his or her "wallet and zipper."

3. A necessary sign of a life in the process of being redeemed is transformation in the area of stewardship.

This will look different for every Christian, and it is dangerous to compare or contrast ourselves with anyone else, but over time some noticeable change in this arena will occur if a person is truly being indwelt by the Holy Spirit. Ultimately, one's entire life should be dedicated to God, but a particularly telling area for determining one's religious commitment involves one's finances. The wealthy but godly patriarchs and kings of the Old Testament are, without exception, said to have shared generously with the poor and needy. Even though none of the patriarchs—Abraham, Isaac, Jacob, and Joseph—ever experiences the complete fulfillment of this promise, each lives in the land for part of his life and amasses enormous wealth. Early on in the Bible, then, we learn that it is possible to be both rich and obedient to God (Genesis 20:14–16; 24:35; 26:13; 30:43; 47:27). At the same time, Genesis points out that the patriarchs are also generous in sharing their wealth with needier people around them (Genesis 13:1–18; 14:20,23; 32:13–16; 41:57).

Similar accounts are found in the historical books of the Old Testament. Those blessed by God with wealth during Israel's tenure within the Promised Land regularly and generously share that wealth with the poor. Boaz in the little book of Ruth and Nehemiah after the return from exile (especially Nehemiah 5) are two often neglected examples. One of the most frequent refrains of the Torah, Psalms, and Prophets is God's concern for the 'widow, fatherless, alien and poor', a concern which should lead his people ruthlessly to avoid every form of exploitation and to seek ways to meet the genuine needs of the marginalized and to address the causes of their misery. By way of contrast, one of the sins that makes someone like Ahab so wicked is his endless covetousness, so that he has Naboth, a small landowner near his palace, murdered just so he can add that property to his already vast holdings (1 Kings 21).

The book of Job reminds us that sometimes the wicked prosper and the righteous are impoverished (Job 21:7–21; 24:1–12). So Job keeps his possessions in proper perspective: "Naked I came from my mother's womb, and naked I shall depart. The Lord gave and the Lord has taken away; may the name of the Lord be praised" (1:21). Less well known is the fact that Job was always generous in sharing his possessions with the poor and often opposed injustice (29:12–17; 31:16–23). Thus he can declare, "If I have put my trust in gold or said to pure gold, 'You are my security,' if I have rejoiced over my great wealth, the fortune my hands had gained… so that my heart was secretly enticed… then these also would be sins to be judged, for I would have been unfaithful to God on high" (31:24–28).

In the New Testament, Jesus simply presupposes the practice of giving from one's surplus to help those who do not have daily essentials and some to enjoy. This comes through most clearly in the Sermon on the Mount: "So when you give to the needy… " (Matthew 6:2–3). Riches (or any amount of money) should not be our greatest goal. Instead, as Jesus teaches in the parables of the Hidden Treasure and the Pearl of Great Price, one must be prepared to give up whatever it takes, including material possessions, to enter the kingdom (Matthew 13:44–46). In the Good Samaritan, compassion for the helpless victim across ethnic and racial lines is illustrated by open-ended financial help (Luke 10:34–35).

Luke and Paul enjoin generous almsgiving. As part of Paul's farewell address to the Ephesian elders at Miletus, "I have not coveted anyone's silver or gold or clothing. You yourselves know that these hands of mine have supplied my own needs and the needs of my companions. In everything I did, I showed you that by this kind of hard work we must help the weak, remembering the words the Lord Jesus himself said: 'It is more blessed to give than to receive'" (Ephesians 20:33–35). Instead of endlessly amassing wealth for oneself, the ideal in most of the first-century empire (and in the modern West!), Paul quotes an otherwise unknown saying of Jesus that it is better to give some of one's wealth away.

First Corinthians 16:1–4 introduces a topic that will consume much of Paul's attention in his second letter to Corinth—a collection for the still impoverished Christians in and around Jerusalem. Here is the first reference in the New Testament, chronologically, to Christians gathering on the first day of the week (Sunday) rather than on the Jewish Sabbath (Saturday). And part of their weekly worship was to involve an offering. "Passing a collection plate" has formed a part of Christian worship services ever since.

Second Corinthians 8–9 forms the longest, sustained teaching passage in the New Testament on Christian stewardship. Here Paul returns to his instructions regarding the collection for Jerusalem, applying principles that give guidance for the church's giving in every era of her history. The Corinthians were initially eager to participate but have now lagged behind in fulfilling their pledges. The poorer Macedonian Christians have actually given more in a shorter period of time. So Paul encourages the Corinthians to complete what they started (8:1–11). En route he makes clear that this giving is the voluntary outgrowth of the larger Christian process of sanctification (vv. 4–5). It is a demonstration of the grace of God and of believers' spiritual giftedness (vv. 1,7). And it is the least we can do when we think of how much Jesus gave up in leaving his heavenly home and becoming incarnate and dying for our sakes (v. 9).

The epistle of James is best known for its hard-hitting teaching about faith and works. More ink has been spilled since the Protestant Reformation about James 2:18–26 than over all the rest of the letter put together. Martin Luther established the pattern by questioning whether James belonged in the canon of Scripture since it appeared to contradict Paul's teaching on salvation by grace through faith alone. Modern scholars of many theological persuasions have agreed that Paul does not contradict James: both recognize that true saving faith will produce tangible fruit (cf. Galatians 5:6).

But what is often lost sight of in this discussion is the context in which James's teaching about faith without works being dead emerges. In 2:14–17, James uses the illustration of help for the materially needy fellow Christian as the prime example of whether one performs the kinds of works that demonstrate the genuineness of one's faith. Interestingly, whereas the word "brother" in ancient Greek (and elsewhere in James) regularly functioned generically to include both men and women, here James explicitly adds the Greek word for "sister" (*adelphe*) in verse 15. As with the widows in 1:27, women in general were more likely to be impoverished and outcast in the biblical cultures, but James makes it clear that God does not approve.

The Greek also clarifies what remains ambiguous in English translations of verse 14. In the question, "Can such faith [professed belief in one God without any change of behavior, including helping the poor] save them?" the Greek uses an adverb (*me*) that implies a negative answer: "No, such 'faith' is not true saving faith." Put bluntly, if a person claims to be a Christian, is aware of the acute physical needs of desperately poor believers at home or abroad, is in any position to help, but never does a single thing except wish them well, that person's inaction disproves his or her profession of faith.

Two common misinterpretations of Scripture need to be dealt with before moving to the next point. First, there exists the mistaken idea of equating 'spiritual growth' with growth in material possessions. Not surprisingly, Christians who think that it is God's ideal for all believers to be rich regularly cite the arrangements God made with Israel during Old Testament times. What they fail to observe is that God made these arrangements with no other nation. Whereas the prophets can rebuke foreign nations for their injustice or mistreatment of the poor, demonstrating that the principles of the Mosaic Law apply at some level to all peoples, no other piece of geography is ever called a Promised Land. No other people are ever formed into a "theocracy," a country in which, even when there are human kings, God reigns and can overrule a king's command. Interestingly, the New Testament repeats all of the broad principles that we find in the Old Testament with respect to poverty and wealth with one notable exception. No Christian is ever promised material prosperity as the result of adequate obedience to Christ!

Another mistake is to read more into Acts 2:44 than the context permits. Acts 2:44 says, "All the believers were together and had everything in common." Verses 45–46 qualify the apparently absolute statement of the previous verse by explaining how people periodically sold property to meet various needs. Apparently not everyone sold everything as an entrance requirement for joining the church. It is interesting that the clause in verse 45, which could be translated "to each according to his need" combines with one in Acts 11:29— "from each according to his ability" to form the two halves of Karl Marx's famous Communist manifesto. Marx after all had thoroughly studied Christianity before rejecting it. It has been argued that Marx's ideal is indeed Christian and that what doomed it to failure were his means of implementing it: by coercion and legislation rather than voluntary cooperation and by divorcing it from its religious underpinnings. At any rate, if we cannot deduce a timeless, unalterable system for addressing issues of rich and poor from Acts 2, neither should we go to the opposite extreme and call the early Christian "communalism" an ill-advised, failed experiment. Luke as narrator makes it clear that he believes God has approved of and blessed these arrangements (Acts 2:47; 4:33; 5:13–14).

4. There are certain extremes of wealth and poverty that are in and of themselves intolerable.

These vary from person to person and culture to culture but involve, on the one hand, unused and unusable surplus and, on the other hand, the inability to meet even one's basic human needs of adequate food, clothing, shelter, and access to health care. It is one thing to generate income which is then channeled into kingdom purposes (Luke 16:9; 19:11–27); it is quite another to accumulate and hoard resources which are likely to be destroyed or disappear before being put to good use (Luke 16:19–31; James 5:1–6). In the latter case, such a surplus prevents others from having a better opportunity for a reasonably decent standard of living. Such hoarding or accumulation is sin, and if left unchecked proves damning (Luke 12:31–21; 16:19–31).

God created the material world completely good, but humanity in its sin regularly abuses that world so that all of creation is now in a corrupted state. Laws, therefore, must be enacted to keep human greed and violence in check. God does not believe in pure *laissez-faire economics*.[2] Sinful human beings, including

---

[2] *Laissez-faire economics* is defined as "an economic doctrine that opposes governmental regulation of or interference in commerce beyond the minimum necessary for a free-enterprise system to operate according to its own economic laws." Taken from *The American Heritage Dictionary of the English Language*, fourth ed. (New York: Houghton Mifflin, 2000).

Christians, will find ways to amass goods for themselves at the expense of the poor and needy of the world under any economic system. We must therefore recognize that all we have is on loan from God and that he calls us to be good stewards of all of it. Precisely because private property is a desirable good, we should work to see that everyone in the world has a fair shot at owning at least enough to live with some decency.

A closer look at James 5:1–6 may be helpful. James employs the literary figure of speech known as "apostrophe" to address rhetorically people who are probably not physically present to hear James's letter read as it circulated among his churches. Here he clearly is speaking about the rich non-Christian, and he is equally clearly warning them about the horrifying judgment that awaits them when Christ returns if they do not repent. What is frightening is to observe what is true in our world that was not the case in James's day—numerous, perhaps even a majority of American Christians living "on earth in luxury and self-indulgence" and fattening themselves "in a day of slaughter" (verse 5).

Lest we think this is referring only to the excessively wealthy, we must observe what made the rich landlords' behavior so heinous in this text: they were growing wealthier at the expense of the impoverished day-laborers (we might call them migrant workers in the U.S. or sweat-shop employees in the Two-Thirds World). In America alone, in the last thirty years, the number of poor and homeless has steadily grown, even as the number of upper middle-class and wealthy has skyrocketed. Abroad, even greater inequities abound. For example, in the mid-1990s Michael Jordan earned more money in promoting shoes for Nike™ than did Nike's entire 18,000 person Indonesian workforce that produced those shoes. But unless Western Christians become more informed and refuse to support companies that act like this, they remain unwitting coconspirators in the very crimes James condemned in his day!

In addition to rebuke, the New Testament contains appropriate instructions for wealthy Christians as they consider giving to kingdom work. Perhaps the most important section of 2 Corinthians 8–9 comes in 8:12–15. Here Paul seems to teach the principle that some have called "the graduated tithe." If ever there were a context in which one would expect a New Testament author to speak about tithing, if Christians were required to give exactly 10% of their income, this would be it. Instead Paul talks about giving "according to your means" (v. 11) and "according to what one has" (v. 12). To what do these expressions refer? Verses 13–15 hint at the answer. Paul is not calling on the more affluent to trade places with the less affluent but wants to create "equality" (vv. 13, 14).

The Greek word used here (*isotes*) could also be translated "that which is fair or equitable." Paul cites the illustration of the Israelites collecting manna in the wilderness. "Equality" for them did not mean that each person collected or consumed the same amount, but that no one had "too much" or "too little." Similarly, Paul does not imagine all Christians having the identical amount of material possessions. But he does recognize that many have unused surplus that qualifies as "too much," while others cannot even meet their basic needs and thus have "too little." To require the poorest of believers in our world today to give ten percent of their income would often just create added hardship for them. To permit affluent believers to give only ten percent would often let them off the hook well before their giving had become truly generous or sacrificial. Thus it seems reasonable to suggest that the implementation of Paul's principles here should call on Christians who earn more than others to give a higher percentage of their income to the Lord's work, including caring for the poor.

First Timothy 5 contains considerable teaching on stewardship that is often overlooked. While much attention is devoted in Christian churches to the "offices" of overseer and deacon dealt with in chapter 3, the similar "office" of widow in chapter 5 is almost never studied. Widows, as examples of the most dispossessed in Paul's world, who have no family members to care for them and who are too old to work, should be supported by the church (vv. 3–5). On the other hand, working-age relatives have the responsibility to provide for elderly or infirm family members. This is the context of verse 8, which thus says nothing about a man having to be the breadwinner for his nuclear family. (The word "anyone" in verse 8 is simply a generic pronoun referring to men and women alike.) That an adult who refuses to obey this command "has denied the faith and is worse than an unbeliever" does not mean they have lost their salvation, merely that they are acting less nobly than the pagan world around them which uniformly recognized this responsibility to care for needy relatives. Contemporary application can take many forms because of the changes in our society and the numerous methods available for providing for the elderly, but it does mean that children have a lifelong responsibility to their parents to see that they are properly taken care of.

A particularly clear example of the principle of moderation comes with God's provision of manna for the Israelites in the wilderness (Exodus 16:18), an episode cited by Paul as he encouraged the Corinthians to greater generosity in the giving (2 Corinthians 8:15). The principle of moderation lies behind the redistribution of property in sabbatical and Jubilee years and behind the prophetic critique of life under the monarchy and aristocracy of Israel. Its reduction of disparity between the 'haves' and 'have-nots' inspired early Christian communalism in Acts and ongoing collection for the poor throughout the New Testament. The principle of moderation explains Jesus' and Paul's concerns to live simply, particularly while engaged in ministry, so as to afford no unnecessary cause for bringing the gospel into disrepute. And it summarizes a large swathe of wisdom literature, particularly as epitomized in Proverbs 30:8: 'Give me neither poverty nor riches.'

Finally, in light of the biblical mandate to give to the poor and moderation, we must not neglect—nor overstate—the biblical example of occasional extravagance. The Song of Solomon primarily discusses the appropriate delights of sexual union within the context of a king's marriage to his beloved. But its picture of their lavish wedding (3:6–11) reminds us that once-in-a-lifetime ceremonies are often proper places for more extravagant expenditures. The question for many Americans, and especially Christians, today is whether the exception has become the norm.

5. Above all, the Bible's teaching about material possessions is inextricably intertwined with more "spiritual" matters.

No one is ever saved by stewardship; all the charitable giving in the world does not make one right with God if a person does not trust in Jesus as Savior and Lord. On the other hand, someone who never gives to the Lord's work or cares for the poor in any way demonstrates that nothing has ever happened in their lives that could qualify as "regeneration." Nor do we find any ungodly poor people exalted as models for emulation. The rich are not necessarily wicked, but frequently surplus goods have led people to imagine that their material resources can secure their futures so that they ignore God, from whom alone comes any true security. That was certainly a recurring trend in ancient Israel. Conversely, when the Jews found themselves in desperate circumstances, they more often than not turned back to God. It has not always been so in the history of humanity, but it frequently has been.

The good news of the kingdom that Jesus proclaimed is consistently "holistic." Jesus was concerned with both body and soul. All the charitable deeds in the world prove meaningless if a person is not a true follower of Christ; that individual will still be damned for all eternity. On the other hand, anyone who professes to be a disciple must demonstrate the reality of that profession by transformed living, including in the areas of personal spending and giving. Different people will experience that transformation in different ways and to different extents, but the person who never displays any concern for the Lord's work and for the poor and who never gives anything to help them by definition is not someone whom the power of the Spirit has touched. So it is wrong to claim, as some do, that Jesus does not envision any rich Christians. But it is correct to observe that the Gospels never depict a well-to-do person who is a genuine believer and yet who is not simultaneously generous in giving of his or her treasure.

In his summary of the sins of the "world"—the fallen nature of contemporary humanity—John lists "the cravings of sinful people, the lust of their eyes and the boasting of what they have and do" (1 John 2:16). The New Living Translation captures these thoughts even more powerfully: "the lust for physical pleasure, the lust for everything we see, and pride in our possessions"! To avoid these powerful forces within each of us, we must give from our surplus. First John 3:17–18 puts it quite bluntly: "If anyone of you has material possessions and sees a brother or sister in need but has no pity on them, how can the love of God be in you? Dear children, let us not love with words or tongue but with actions and in truth."

APPLICATIONS

The possibilities are enormous and the list of what Christians could do nearly endless. But it may help to list a few practical suggestions that most all readers of this essay could implement or implement further (now or in the future).

(1) Maintaining a budget helps people to see where their money is going. The more detailed records we keep, the more we can identify purchases that are not truly necessities so as to free up more money for

our giving. We must beware of our culture's daily attempts to seduce us through advertising into thinking that luxuries are necessities. Many Christians could easily spend less on housing, cars, recreation, home entertainment centers, phone and computer-related technologies, heating and cooling their environments, lawn care, and food (recall our comments in the Introduction on eating out) without sacrificing a generally comfortable lifestyle. Most would be surprised how many additional funds would be freed up for Christ and his kingdom.

(2) Avoiding debt wherever possible should be another priority. Most Americans could live most of their lives without ever owing debts on anything besides property and, at times, cars, or schooling. Credit cards should never be used if a person cannot pay the bills interest-free at the end of a month. Those who have already amassed crippling debts should take whatever action is necessary to implement a realistic plan to get out of debt as quickly as possible; Christian financial counselors can help.

(3) The graduated tithe offers an excellent opportunity for those whom God blesses with growing incomes (above the annual cost-of-living increases) to give higher percentages to the Lord's work. A young person or couple just beginning full-time employment can commit to giving 10%, and, without necessarily following any fixed tables, commit to increasing that percentage as their income grows. Others can start wherever they are and commit to similar increases. Churches should model similar practices. If a congregation is not yet giving 10% of its total income in a year to missions, it could begin with that commitment and then pledge to add 1% a year whenever their income increases.

(4) Christians must choose churches to belong to, in part, on the basis of how those churches spend their money. They should look for congregations that give generously to the poor and to outreach at both home and abroad. Because few churches are ever likely to give enough support to these areas to make enough difference in our world, believers should consider giving to individuals and organizations that more directly help the needy on top of their giving to their churches. Groups like World Vision, Food for the Hungry, Compassion International, and others are particularly successful and reputable organizations in this respect.

CONCLUSION

Countless other possibilities remain. But, in closing, it is worth stressing that attitudes are crucial in all this as well. Does reading an essay like this leave you resentful of the areas of your life into which it has "pried"? If so, it might be good to reflect on all the ways God has been enormously generous with you in your life, above all in providing salvation by grace which we could never have earned. Can we be any less generous in helping others, spiritually and materially? Do you feel a measure of guilt as a result of this study? Some may claim that they are being "manipulated by guilt." If that is the case, then it is important to realize that there is both true guilt and false guilt. If you are already being generous in giving from your surplus, you may need to focus on those portions of Scripture that stress how God gives us material possessions as good gifts for us to enjoy! Relax, put away your false guilt, and delight in God and his goodness. On the other hand, if you realize that there are numerous ways you could free up more money for the Lord and you just haven't been doing it, then guilt is a healthy and biblical motivation. Repent, change your ways, and then you can justifiably "feel good" about yourself!

---

*This essay originally appeared as a booklet produced by College Press Publishing Company.
   Craig L. Blomberg, *Heart, Soul, and Money: A Christian View of Possessions* (Joplin, MO: College Press, 2000).
**Reproduction rights granted by Craig L. Blomberg.

Unit Nine

HEART, SOUL, AND MONEY
ESSAY QUESTIONS

Answer the questions below on a separate sheet of paper and be prepared to review your answers in class. Reflection Questions will not be found in the text. These are merely designed to help you start thinking about issues from a worldview perspective.

1. What biblical evidence is there for the idea that Jesus and his disciples were not likely materially poor?

2. What are the first two biblical themes discussed by Dr. Blomberg? What are two biblical texts or ideas the author uses to support these themes?

3. What are the third and fourth biblical themes discussed by Dr. Blomberg? What are two biblical texts or ideas the author uses to support these themes?

4. In relation to the topic of stewardship, what should one look for when choosing a church?

5. **Reflection Question:** How do you keep the needs of poor brothers and sisters in mind when we live in a relatively affluent culture?

"RADICAL ENVIRONMENTALISM"
WITH CAL BEISNER

I. Environmentalism

A. <u>Radical environmentalism</u>: Biocentric (nature as central concern)

B. <u>Old line environmentalism</u>: Anthropocentric (man as central concern)

"Radical Environmentalism sees life—all biology (human, animal, plant) as a matter of concern—at an equal level. Whereas old line environmentalism saw our responsibility toward nature as a matter of our responsibility toward ourselves. We wanted to conserve resources and preserve beautiful places for… the benefit of future generations. Christian environmentalism should be neither. It should be theocentric."

C. <u>Christian environmentalism</u>: Theocentric (God as central concern)

"Christian environmentalism should be theocentric (God is at the center of our concern and our responsibility to the world around us stems from God)… then man, and then the rest of creation."

1. World created for God's enjoyment (Job)

2. World created for mankind (Psalm 115:16)

II. Types of Radical Environmentalism

A. Green political parties

1. Favor socialism as nature's only hope

2. Work through the political process using legislation, treaties, etc.

3. Tied to respectable organizations—*Environmental Defense Fund, Sierra Club*, etc.

B. Deep ecologists

1. Pantheists: All life is fundamentally one

2. Spiritual and religious (druidism, goddess worship, eastern religions)

3. Darwinian

4. Tied to radical organizations—*Green Peace, Earth First, Sea Shepherds*, etc.

5. <u>Biological egalitarianism</u>: All life is fundamentally equal

"Man is no more important than any other species and it may well take our species to set things straight." — Dave Foreman, *Earth First* founder

C. Animal rights movement

    1. Avoid all killing of animals (for any reason, even food)

    2. Darwinian

    3. No qualitative distinction between species

    4. Assume that animals must have rights if they are to be treated humanely

III. Radical Environmentalism vs. Christianity

A. Population

    1. Radical environmentalists

        i. People are naturally destructive—they consume resources and emit pollutants

        ii. Human population should be reduced

    2. Christianity

        i. People are created in God's image and creative

        ii. Population growth is a blessing

B. Animals

    1. Radical environmentalism

        i. Animals must not be harmed

        ii. Animals and human beings have equal rights to life

    2. Christianity

        i. Animals are for food

        ii. Human beings are created higher than animals

C. Nature

    1. Radical environmentalism

        i. Man is part of nature

        ii. Nature is good and perfect, man is the only destructive element

        iii. Human population must be reduced

2. Christianity

      i. Nature has been given to man to watch over and care for

      ii. Nature was good, but has been cursed

      iii. Man must restore the earth from the curse (part of the great commission)

IV. Summary of Radical Environmentalism

A. All life, including man, is one

B. Man is a part of nature, not above it

C. Man is an intruder on the earth, using up resources and polluting

D. Favor reducing human population

"RADICAL ENVIRONMENTALISM"
WITH CAL BEISNER

Answer the questions below on a separate sheet of paper and be prepared to review your answers in class.

1. **What is radical environmentalism? How are radical environmentalism, conventional environmentalism, and Christian environmentalism different?**

2. **What are three types of radical environmentalism?**

3. **How do radical environmentalism and Christianity differ about population?**

4. **How do radical environmentalism and Christianity differ about animals?**

5. **How do radical environmentalism and Christianity differ about nature?**

PRINCIPLES OF A
CHRISTIAN ENVIRONMENTAL ETHIC
BY JOHN C. BERGSTROM

"Where do you live?" is a question most people have been asked many times. When answering this question, our automatic response is most likely to think about the place where our homes made out of brick, wood, or stone are located. How would God answer the question of where each one of us lives? What physical home or homes has God given to all people?

The Bible teaches that when we put our faith and trust in Jesus Christ, he will lead us to an eternal heavenly home prepared by God. But, until we are called to live forever with God in our heavenly homes, we must live within the physical homes God has provided for us. These physical homes include the entire planet earth, the various natural environments found on the planet, our towns and cities, and the houses or apartments where we lay our heads down at night to sleep.

Thus, upon further reflection, the question of "Where do you live?" can be answered from a number of different perspectives and is perhaps a much more thought-provoking question than one may initially imagine. The perspective we are most interested in for this paper is the concept of the entire planet earth and different natural environments as places God has deliberately and carefully designed as homes for the people, plants, and animals he has created.

Because we all live on the same planet and are ultimately dependent on the natural fruits of the earth for life-support, everyone has a stake in how elements of nature and natural systems are used and managed. When a specific natural resource or environmental issue or problem arises, individuals and groups often disagree on the appropriate course of action to resolve the issue or problem. At the core of these disagreements are different values and beliefs related to nature itself, and the use and management of nature by people. Scholars in the humanities, social sciences, and physical and biological sciences have emphasized that environmental issues and problems are fundamentally interrelated with ethical issues and problems.[1] Consequently, we are hearing more voices saying that in order to solve environmental issues and problems, people need to develop and follow an appropriate "moral basis" for dealing with nature. This recognizes a basic tenant of human behavior taught in the Bible: true change starts from within a person's heart, mind, and spirit and works outwardly as reflected by attitudes and actions. In all areas of our lives, the substance of our inner faith determines the living out or practice of our faith.

The system of values and beliefs that influences how a persons thinks and acts is known as that person's ethical system or ethics. The purpose of this paper is to discuss three general principles of a Christian environmental ethic and applications of this ethic to natural resource and environmental stewardship. The three general principles of a Christian environmental ethic are: 1) God created and therefore values all of his works of creation (Principle of Creation Value); 2) God created and sustains all elements and systems in his creation within particular orders to meet certain ongoing purposes (Principle of Sustained Order and Purpose); and 3) Everything in the created world and universe is subject to corruption by sin and ultimate redemption through Jesus Christ (Principle of Universal Corruption and Redemption).

CHRISTIAN ENVIRONMENTAL ETHIC PRINCIPLES

The three general principles of a Christian environmental ethic are consistent with a careful study of God's Word found in the Holy Bible as illuminated by a number of historical and recent authors.[2] The meaning and biblical basis for these principles are discussed in more detail in this section.

---

[1] See for example Herman E. Daly, "The Steady-State Economy," *Valuing the Earth: Economics, Ecology, Ethics* (Cambridge, MA: MIT Press, 1993); Paul H. Santmire, *The Travail of Nature* (Philadelphia, PA: Fortress Press, 1985); Francis Schaeffer, *Pollution and the Death of Man: The Christian View of Ecology* (Wheaton, IL: Crossway, 1992); Ruth Goring Stewart, *Environmental Stewardship* (Downers Grove, IL: InterVarsity, 1990); Fred VanDyke, David C. Mahan, Joseph K. Sheldon, and Raymond H. Brand, *Redeeming Creation: The Biblical Basis for Environmental Stewardship* (Downers Grove, IL: InterVarsity, 1996); and Lynn White, Jr., "The Historical Roots of Our Ecological Crisis," *Science*, Volume 155, March 1967, 1203–1207.
[2] See for example Schaeffer, *Pollution and the Death of Man* and VanDyke, et. al., *Redeeming Creation*.

Principle of Creation Value

The Principle of Creation Value first recognizes that God created the heavens and earth and all things found therein (Genesis 1; Psalm 146:6; Acts 14:15). For example, Revelation 4:11 states: "You are worthy, our Lord and God, to receive glory and honor and power, for you created all things, and by your will they were created and have their being."[3] The Bible also teaches that although God allows people to utilize elements of nature, God retains ownership of all his creation (Psalm 89:11; Leviticus 25:23; Colossians 1:15–16). For example, Psalm 24:1 states; "The earth is the Lord's, and everything in it, the world, and all who live in it."

The Bible teaches that God loves and enjoys all that he has created. Psalm 145:16–17 reads: "You open your hand and satisfy the desires of every living thing. The Lord is righteous in all his ways and loving toward all he has made." Thus, an important implication of the Principle of Creation Value from an ethical standpoint is that God places value on elements of nature independent of human use and human-centered values (Genesis 1:25; Psalm 104:31; Psalm 148:9–13). This God-centered inherent value of nature is termed *theistic intrinsic value*.[4]

Plato's philosophy influenced the Gnostic view of the physical world that arose within the first century Christian church. Followers of Gnosticism taught that the spiritual world contains all that is good, and that everything in the physical or material world is bad.[5] Thus, under Gnosticism, nature would have a negative value and is something that should be disregarded in a person's life.

Christians in the modern church who say that "nature really doesn't matter because it's part of the physical world" are carrying on the heritage of Plato and the Gnostics. This position, which has a very low view of nature's value, is not supported by the Scriptures. As pointed out by Schaeffer,[6] the greatest testimony to the lasting value and importance of the physical world is that Jesus Christ's physical body was resurrected from the dead and exists today in the unseen spiritual world. In the new heaven and earth that God will someday create, Scripture teaches that in addition to Christians being given new, resurrected bodies, nature will also be renewed. As discussed in more detail later in the paper, both people and nature will therefore have existence and value in eternity.

The other extreme position on the value and importance of the physical world and nature that Christians should not fall into is one that improperly elevates the status of nature to being equal to or even above people. The "equality between people and nature" viewpoint in considered first. In modern times, certain secular environmental ethics or philosophies such as "deep ecology" teach that people and nature have equal status and value in the world.[7] Such viewpoints on the parity between people and nature can enter into the church as erroneous teaching.[8] Scripture teaches that although God values nature, he places a special higher value on people who he "crowned with glory and honor" as the climax of his creation (Genesis 1:26–30; Psalm 8:5–8). The "nature above people" viewpoint is considered next.

Romans 1:20–23 states: "For since the creation of the world God's invisible qualities—his eternal power and divine nature—have been clearly seen, being understood from what has been made, so that men are without excuse. For although they knew God, they neither glorified him as God nor gave thanks to him, but their thinking became futile and foolish hearts were darkened. Although they claimed to be wise, they became fools and exchanged the glory of the immortal God for images made to look like mortal man and birds and animals and reptiles." This passage refers to people who knew or at least knew of God but elevated nature to be objects or idols of worship. The worship of anything in nature violates the Second Commandment in which God states: "You shall not make for yourself an idol in the form of anything in heaven above or on the earth beneath or in the waters below. You shall not bow down to them or worship them" (Exodus 20:4–5).

---

[3] All Scripture references are taken from the New International Version (Grand Rapids, MI: Zondervan, 1985).

[4] Christopher B. Barrett and John C. Bergstrom, "The Economics of God's Creation," *Bulletin of the Association of Christian Economists*, Issue 31, Spring 1998, 4–23.

[5] Colin Brown, *Philosophy and the Christian Faith* (Downers Grove, IL: InterVarsity, 1968).

[6] Schaeffer, *Pollution and the Death of Man*.

[7] Donald VanDeVeer and Christine Pierce, *The Environmental Ethics and Policy Book* (Belmont, CA: Wadsworth Pub., 1998).

[8] See for example Kevin L. Burrell, "The Ethics of Environmentalism," *Faith and Practice*, Volume 2, Fall 1996, 16–24; and Tony Campolo, *How to Rescue Earth without Worshiping Nature* (Nashville: Thomas Nelson, 1992).

Principle of Sustained Order and Purpose

The Principle of Sustained Order and Purpose implies that God originally created all elements of nature to fit and function together in an orderly fashion within interrelated systems to meet certain ongoing purposes. God's direct involvement in natural systems did not end after the original creation period described in Genesis 1. The triune God continues to hold together or sustain the functioning of nature, accomplishing his intended order and purpose of all nonliving and living elements of nature and natural systems.

What are the various purposes of nature according to the Bible? One of the reasons God created and continues to sustain nature, as discussed above under the Principle of Creation Value, is for God himself to love and enjoy. Another purpose is to help meet people's needs such as food and shelter (Genesis 2:15; Genesis 9:3). A third major purpose of nature is to glorify and reveal God to people everywhere (Psalm 19:1–4; Romans 1:18–20). For example, Psalm 19:14 states: "The heavens declare the glory of God; the skies proclaim the work of his hands. Day after day they pour forth speech; night after night they display knowledge. There is no speech or language where their voice is not heard. Their voice goes out into all the earth, their words to the ends of the world."

To meet their intended purposes, God created and sustains all of creation within particular orders. The first large-scale Creation ordering of interest is the biblical hierarchy between God, people, and nature. Understanding and applying a Christian environmental ethic requires a proper interpretation of Biblical verses establishing and describing this basic hierarchy. A key verse is Genesis 1:28, which states: "So God created man in his own image, in the image of God he created him, male and female he created them. God blessed them and said to them, 'Be fruitful and increase in number; fill the earth and subdue it. Rule over the fish of the sea and the birds of the air and over every living creature that moves on the ground.'"

Genesis 1:28 establishes that in God's basic ordering of Creation, people have dominion over nature. However, this verse also clearly states that people are creations of God. As creations of God, people are under the authority or dominion of God. Thus, from the perspective of God's authority and control, people and nature are in the same class or order—all of Creation, including people, must submit to God's plans and ways. The basic biblical relationships and ordering between God, people, and nature are illustrated in Figure 1. A similar illustration is provided and discussed by Schaeffer.[9]

Figure 1. Principle of Sustained Order and Purpose
General Biblical Hierarchy

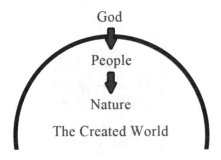

In Figure 1, it is first shown that there is a fundamental separation between God and his creation including people. God is above people and nature and both people and elements of nature such as plants and animals must interact and live together within the same created world governed by God's ways and plans. Thus, people share a common heritage and bond with plants, animals, and other elements of nature as fellow creations of God. People, like plants and animals, must also cope with living in a physical world and universe created and controlled by God.

The diagram also illustrates that within the physical world and universe, people are above nature. People are above nature by the grace and will of God only—not by our own power and ingenuity. God created people in his image to exercise Godly dominion over nature. Godly dominion over nature, as discussed in more detail later in the paper, means that people act as stewards or caretakers of nature who are ultimately responsible to God for their use and management of nature.

---

[9] Schaeffer, *Pollution and the Death of Man.*

In addition to the major large-scale relationships or orders between God, people, and nature illustrated in Figure 1, God created and sustains elements of nature within particular orders to meet deliberate purposes. The food chain system shown in Figure 2 illustrates how living and nonliving elements of nature in an ecosystem fit and function together to provide life-support for each other.

Figure 2. God's Order within Nature:
Simple Food Chain or System

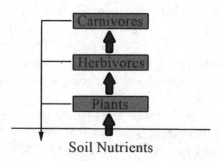

As illustrated in Figure 2, living plants take nutrients from the soil. Herbivores such as rabbits or deer eat plants for food. Carnivores such as mountain lions eat other animals for food. When plants and animals die, microorganisms in the environment decompose the plant and animal body material into basic chemicals that go back into the soil. These chemicals are then taken up by plants for nutrients completing the cycling of life-supporting chemicals through the environment.

People are also dependent on the food chain and chemical cycling systems illustrated in Figure 2. The linkages and interrelationships between people and elements of nature and natural systems are illustrated at a broader scale in Figure 3. Figure 3 illustrates the planet earth home God has provided for all of us, and the global interrelationships between people and nature.

Figure 3. Global Interelationships between
People and Nature on God's Earth

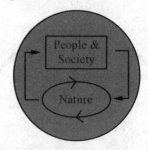

The scientific study of natural life-support systems falls under the realm of ecology. The word ecology is derived from the Greek root words *eco-* meaning "house" and *-logy* meaning "study." Ecology can therefore be literally interpreted to mean "house study" or the "study of the house." The "house" being referred to here is the planet earth and its natural systems. Before describing how the earth's natural systems provide life-support, consider the artificial life-support systems that people build into the various dwellings we call home at a small scale.

The actual physical dwellings in which we live were constructed by people with certain life-support systems in mind. These artificial life-support systems include: air circulation systems to regulate oxygen (O_2) and carbon dioxide (CO_2) levels so that indoor air is healthy to breathe; water systems to provide safe and secure drinking water supplies; heating and cooling systems to regulate indoor temperatures at healthy levels; and waste disposal systems that help to prevent illness by safely and regularly removing potential germ-producing human wastes and garbage.

The planet earth and different environments such as forests, deserts, oceans, lakes, and rivers were created by God with natural life-support systems in his mind and design. God built several major chemical cycles into our planet earth home. Each of these cycles helps to provide all that is needed to support life on earth. For example, the carbon and oxygen cycle helps to provide breathable air and regulate global temperatures at livable levels. The hydrologic cycle helps to provide water to drink and for a multitude of other purposes.

The different chemical cycles also contribute to the provision of mineral resources such as coal, oil, and natural gas that we use as fuel for transportation, electricity, and heating. These cycles also support renewable resources such as trees and fish and wildlife. We use trees for consumptive uses such as lumber and to support non-consumptive uses such as recreation and aesthetic enjoyment. We use fish and wildlife for consumptive uses such as harvesting ocean fish for food and hunting of wildlife on public and private lands. We also use fish and wildlife for non-consumptive recreational uses and aesthetic enjoyment such as wildlife observation and photography.[10]

When people use elements of nature for commercial production and consumption, and even recreational and aesthetic enjoyment, some level of waste by-products enter the environment. Smokestacks into the air and effluent discharge pipes into rivers are obvious evidence of these waste by-products. When people use a forest or park for recreation, waste by-products are emitted into the air from automobiles, RVs, ATVs and motorboats. Solid wastes in the form of litter are also often left behind. God has built waste assimilation and treatment capabilities into natural systems. For example, scientists have documented the natural ability of wetlands to filter chemicals out of water that are potentially harmful to human health. However, excessive use of a particular natural system such as a wetland area by people for waste by-product disposal may threaten the continued ability of that natural system to assimilate and treat wastes.

The God-given role of people as caretakers or managers of elements of nature and natural systems is illustrated through several linkages. People manage nature, for example, by cultivating the land to grow and harvest crops for food through agriculture and to grow and harvest trees for wood products through forestry. People manage lakes and rivers for producing electricity, providing drinking water and supporting many types of recreational activities such as boating and swimming. People may also be involved in managing entire ecosystems to provide fish and wildlife habitat and other broad environmental services such as protection of regional air and water quality or even regulation of global climate.

People also manage nature through waste and pollution management and policy. For example, people design and build waste treatment facilities to filter harmful materials out of human sewage waste water before the water is discharged into the environment. People also design and implement "best management practices" for reducing waste run-off from construction sites, farms, and forest and mining operations. Other people are trained and hired to develop and enforce policies and laws for regulating the discharge or emissions of waste by-products into the environment from a variety of sources including point sources (e.g., manufacturing plants) and non-point sources (e.g., automobiles).

This section discussing the Principle of Sustained Order and Purpose has emphasized that God created people and nature with order and purpose. In God's ordering, people are over nature, meaning that people may take from nature to meet their needs. However, God also expects people to give back to nature, as one of God's intended purposes for people is to act as responsible caretakers of nature.

Principle of Universal Corruption and Redemption

The Principle of Universal Corruption and Redemption has familiar implications with respect to the relationship between men and women created in God's image by God their Creator. The Scriptures are clear that all men and women have sinned and fall short of God's expectations for a righteous life. Thus, we are all in need of forgiveness and saving faith through a personal relationship with Jesus Christ (1 John 1:8–9). The Scriptures also teach that all of creation has been corrupted by sin (Romans 8:20–22). The effects of this universal corruption include not just separation of people from God, but also separation of people from themselves, each other, and nature.

The separation of people from nature as a result of sin entering the world at the time of the Fall of Mankind taught in the Bible (Genesis 3) is of particular interest to the topic of this paper. First, this separation

---

[10] Barrett and Bergstrom. "The Economics of God's Creation."

occurs at a physical level. Nature provides beneficial services to people, but since the Fall nature can also be the source of physical harm to people; the physical harm caused by tornadoes and hurricanes is a graphic example. The Fall also has resulted in a spiritual separation between people and nature. Prior to the Fall, God, people, and nature had close spiritual fellowship with each other. The introduction of sin into the world and its corrupting effects on all of God's created works broke apart this fellowship.

For people, forgiveness and saving faith through Jesus Christ assures personal redemption of the believer before God, and restoration of the believer's relationship and fellowship with God. Scripture teaches that God will also redeem nature and restore the relationship and fellowship between God, people, and nature in the eternal world. God's plan for redeeming nature is reflected in the creation covenant.[11] The creation covenant is God's promise to redeem, restore, and renew the physical world in the new heaven and earth that he will create when the earth we now call home no longer exists (2 Peter 3:13; Revelation 21:1).

In the New Testament, Romans 8:19–23 speaks to the creation covenant, saying: "For the creation waits in eager expectation for the sons of God to be revealed. For the creation was subjected to frustration, not by its own choice, but by the will of the one who subjected it, in hope that the creation itself will be liberated from its bondage to decay and brought into the glorious freedom of the children of God. We know that the whole creation has been groaning as in the pains of childbirth right up to the present time. Not only so, but we ourselves, who have the firstfruits of the Spirit, groan inwardly as we wait eagerly for our adoption as sons, the redemption of our bodies." This passage teaches that the physical universe including nature is not destined for eternal destruction when the world we now live in ends when Jesus Christ returns. Rather, when God gives Believers new bodies in the new heaven and earth, He will also provide a new beginning for nature and rest of the physical world.

In the new heaven and earth, nature will be restored to its pre-Fall magnificence and perfection. In this new Creation of God, both people and nature will be freed from the sufferings caused by the imperfections of the world we live in today, including death and decay. People and nature will also no longer battle against each other as so often is the case in our world today.

In the Old Testament, there is a precedent for divine covenants or promises that incorporate nature. Consider, for example, this passage from Genesis 9: "Then God said to Noah and to his sons with him: 'I now establish my covenant with you and with your descendants after you and with every living creature that was with you—the birds, the livestock and all the wild animals, all those that came out of the ark with you—every living creature on earth. I establish my covenant with you: Never again will all life be cut off by the waters of a flood; never again will there be a flood to destroy the earth'" (Genesis 9:8–11). The beautiful natural rainbow is God's sign and reminder of His covenant with Noah not to destroy life on earth again with a great flood. This covenant clearly includes plants and animals and every "living creature on earth."

The creation covenant referred to in Romans 8 can be thought of as an extension of God's covenant with Noah that includes a promise to protect and sustain both people and nature. God's concern for protecting and sustaining all living creatures was illustrated by Jesus Christ who, when speaking about sparrows, said that "not one of them will fall to the ground apart from the will of your Father" (Matthew 10:29). Providing for the continued and restored existence of nature in the new heaven and earth is consistent with what the Bible teaches about God's love and concern for all of his large and small works of Creation.

PRACTICING A CHRISTIAN ENVIRONMENTAL ETHIC THROUGH STEWARDSHIP

The three general principles of a Christian environmental ethic have practical implications for the role of people as caretakers or managers of nature. The Bible teaches that as caretakers or managers of nature, people are to practice good stewardship. The words "steward" and "stewardship" are used throughout the Old and New Testaments (Genesis 15:2, 44:1; 1 Chronicles 28:1; Matthew 20:8; 1 Corinthians 4:2; Luke 12:42, 16:1–2). The word used for steward in the Bible can also be interpreted as manager or servant.

When the word for steward (manager, servant) is used in the Bible, it refers to a person who is put in charge of taking care of something that does not belong to him or her. This meaning is consistent with the *Webster's Dictionary* definition of a steward as "one employed in a large household or estate to manage domestic concerns." As stewards of nature, people have been appointed by God to manage the "domestic environmental concerns" of our planet earth home.

---

[11] See again Schaeffer, *Pollution and the Death of Man* and VanDyke, et al, *Redeeming Creation*.

According to the Bible, general characteristics and responsibilities of a steward include being faithful, wise, and responsible. The steward should be concerned with meeting daily needs and is not to abuse or waste what he or she has been put in charge of managing. The steward is to maintain self-control (not overindulging), be a "problem-solver," and follow the household or estate owner's wishes and instructions with respect to management (Luke 12:42–46, 16:1–9).

How are stewards held accountable according to the Bible? Proper management actions are rewarded with "true riches" (spiritual riches). Improper actions are punished (something is taken away). Stewards in charge of more are held more accountable, especially if they do wrong when they know better.

Stewardship and the Principle of Creation Value

Under the Principle of Creation Value, all of God's creations are important and valuable to God. People hold a special particular value to God as living beings created in his image (Genesis 1:26–30). Part of God's provision for the well-being of people is the use of plants, animals, minerals and other elements of nature for meeting our material needs. These uses, for example, include farming the land to meet food and fiber needs and harvesting trees from forests to meet wood product needs.

When using elements of nature for human benefit, the Christian environmental steward keeps in mind that all of creation ultimately belongs to God and is valuable to God independent of human use. This knowledge, when put into practice, means that the Christian environmental steward respects and even loves elements of nature out of respect and love for their Creator, the Triune God—Father, Son and Holy Spirit.

Godly respect and love for elements of nature leads the Christian environmental steward to be a responsible caretaker of nature who does not abuse or misuse what has been entrusted into his or her care by God. The Christian steward or manager of a farm, forest, park or natural area, for example, would not deliberately kill plants and animals under his or care without good reason. Although the Christian environmental steward demonstrates Godly love and care for nature, he or she does not worship nature, only God who is its Creator.

Stewardship and the Principle of Sustained Order and Purpose

Genesis 1 establishes that although both people and nature are created works of God and under God's authority, God has given people dominion over nature. But, how are people to exercise this dominion? God created people in his own image—as his representatives on earth. Because we are under God's authority in all things, we are to do God's will when exercising our dominion over nature.

In Genesis 1:28, God tells people to subdue nature. The word "subdue" is translated from the Hebrew word *kabash*, which means to make to serve, by force if necessary. But "subdue" does not mean "abuse," just as the phrase "rule over" in the Bible does not mean "exercise tyranny over." Some specific instructions pertaining to managing nature are given in Genesis 2:15, which says, "The Lord God took the man and put him in the Garden of Eden to work it and take care of it." The phrase "to work it" means "to till it" or "to cultivate it," and the general meaning is to use productively. The phrase to "take care of it" means "to keep," "to guard," or "to exercise great care over." The intent of "keeping, guarding, caring over" is to sustain the function for which the element of nature or natural system being cared for was originally designed. Sustaining the original God-designed functions of nature is a very important objective from theological, ethical, and practical standpoints.

In summary, the "good steward" according to the Bible will manage nature in a wise, self-controlled, and non-wasteful manner, always taking care to sustain the original functions of elements of nature and natural systems. The "poor steward," in contrast, lacks self-control, is wasteful and irresponsible, and cannot be trusted to take proper care of what he or she has been put in charge of managing. The "poor steward" allows the original functions of elements of nature or natural systems to be degraded or ruined.

In the "natural economy" of God's creation, human use and management of natural environments can have positive or negative consequences. Negative consequences of poor use and management can be illustrated by thinking about the end results of not properly maintaining the life-support systems built into a house or apartment building. The most serious consequence of this poor management is that the health and well-being of the dwelling's occupants would likely suffer. In extreme cases, such as when improper use or management of heating equipment allows CO_2 in the indoor air to build up to unhealthy levels, death of the dwelling's occupants may result.

If we misuse and mismanage nature, the ability of nature to support provision of goods and commodities of consumptive or non-consumptive value to people may be significantly reduced. In extreme cases, essential life-support systems may be degraded to the point that plant, animal, and human health and life are seriously threatened.[12] However, if we use and manage nature properly as God expects us to, natural systems can continue to provide essential life-support services and various goods and commodities of consumptive or non-consumptive value to people.

Unfortunately, the poor management or stewardship model often describes how men and women of the world improperly exercise their dominion over nature. An example of poor stewardship from agriculture is farming a tract of land until the soil is totally "burned out" and incapable of further production. An example from forestry is over-harvesting a forest so that new trees can no longer be grown. Exceeding the capacity of air and water resources to absorb and disperse pollution so that air and water become unsafe to consume is an example of poor stewardship in the environmental pollution management area.

The Christian environmental steward understands that the elements of nature or natural systems that he or she may be involved in using or managing are ultimately controlled by God according to his ways and plans. Whether he or she is involved in the use and management of farmland, forestland, parks, natural areas, or air and water resources on a large scale, the Christian environmental steward realizes that human uses and management of nature that run counter to God's ways and plans are detrimental to nature and ultimately to people. There is also a realization that whenever we go our own way rather than following God, he is grieved by our actions.

To carry out his or her responsibilities, the Christian environmental steward attempts to learn as much as he or she can about the God-intended order and purpose of nature. This effort includes learning about individual elements of nature, and how these elements of nature function within natural systems created and sustained by God. The Christian environmental steward puts this knowledge into practice by doing his or her best to use and manage nature within the boundaries of God's ways and plans.

Stewardship and the Principle of Universal Corruption and Redemption
An important overarching implication of the Principle of Universal Corruption and Redemption for the practice of Christian environmental stewardship is that everyone who is involved in the study, use, and management of nature is corrupted by sin. Dealing with the effects of sin in our own lives and the lives of others represents a major challenge to Christians involved in the use and care of nature through education, administration or direct management in the field. To effectively meet this challenge, the Christian manager of nature applies Biblical values and guidance to manage both nature and people in a positive manner.

The Christian environmental steward also acknowledges that God will redeem both people and nature in the new heaven and earth. Knowing that God intends one day to redeem nature (rather than completely destroy it, as some in the church today may think) should motivate Christians to view and act differently towards nature. Christians should also be involved as much as possible in the process of redeeming nature here and now on earth as an expression of our own redemption and salvation and the "living out" of our faith (Philippians 2:12–13; James 2:14–25). In the case of a Christian forester or ecologist, for example, being involved in the restoration of a healthy forest ecosystem is consistent with and honors God's ultimate plan for redeeming nature. In contrast, being responsible for widespread and complete destruction of a particular forest ecosystem does not seem consistent with nor honors God's plan for redeeming nature.

PRINCIPLES AND PRACTICE OF A CHRISTIAN ENVIRONMENTAL ETHIC: CONCLUSIONS
We are faced in the world today with many natural resource and environmental issues and problems. There are issues and problems related to managing nature and the natural resources provided by nature to provide food for eating, paper for writing, lumber for construction, and areas for people to participate in outdoor recreation and experience aesthetic enjoyment of nature. There are issues and problems related to protecting nature from many sources of degradation or damage by people.[13] If nature is degraded or damaged by people (or even by itself), there are issues and problems related to how to go about repairing or mitigating the environmental damage.

---

[12] Calvin B. DeWitt, "Seven Degradations of Creation," *Perspectives* (February 1989), 4–8.
[13] Ibid.

Christians are in a unique position to offer thoughtful solutions to the natural resource and environmental problems and issues we face in the world today. As mentioned at the beginning of this paper, there is growing recognition on the part of people from a variety of professional and personal backgrounds that effective, long-term solutions to natural resource and environmental problems and issues requires an appropriate moral basis for action. God's word found in the Holy Bible provides this moral basis in the form of a Christian environmental ethic that results in responsible and caring stewardship of all of God's creation.

The foundation of a Christian environmental ethic are the Principle of Creation Value, the Principle of Sustained Order and Purpose, and the Principle of Universal Corruption and Redemption. To practice effective Christian environmental stewardship, we must work on increasing our knowledge of these principles from biblical, scientific and practical policy and management perspectives. But stale book knowledge of these principles is not enough to get the job done.

In Romans 12:2, the Apostle Paul says, "Do not conform any longer to the pattern of this world, but be transformed by the renewing of your mind. Then you will be able to test and approve what God's will is—his good, pleasing and perfect will." This passage implies that before we can effectively manage or take care of nature according to God's ways and plans, we must renew our minds. This renewal process first requires that we become new persons through a personal relationship with Jesus Christ as Savior and Lord. As it is said in the Scriptures, "if anyone is in Christ, he is a new creation; the old has gone, the new has come!" (2 Corinthians 5:17).

Once we have become a new creation or person in Christ, our minds and thinking can be and are renewed in many areas of our lives. In the area of environmental stewardship, a deep personal understanding of the way God loves and sustains all of His creation gives us a new and proper perspective of the temporal and eternal value and purposes of nature. This understanding, when taken to heart, transforms how we view and carry out our God-given role as caretakers of nature.

Christian caretakers of nature may be farmers, foresters, or fishermen who manage and harvest the land and waters of the earth in a productive and sustainable manner. They may be professional biologists, botanists, ecologists, or other environmental scientists who study nature and develop scientific solutions to problems and challenges related to managing specific parts of nature or entire natural systems. They may be toxicologists or other human health specialists who study the effects of environmental pollutants on people in order to develop waste management and pollution control strategies that protect and maintain our health and quality of life.

Christian caretakers of nature may be professional economists, sociologists, or political scientists who study economic and social systems in order to help solve problems and challenges related to people's use of natural resources and impacts on the environment. They may also be philosophers or theologians who help us to understand the proper biblical perspectives on the worth and purposes of people and nature. Professors at colleges and universities and teachers at secondary schools can also be Christian caretakers of nature through teaching, research, and public service activities that focus on providing needed information and equipping others to meet natural resource and environmental problems and challenges now and in the future in a Christian manner.

The above listing of possible professions of Christian caretakers of nature is meant to be illustrative, not exhaustive. The fact of the matter is that every Christian can and should be a Christian caretaker of nature no matter what his or her vocation or position in life happens to be. What characteristics distinguish the Christian caretaker of nature from others involved in the caring for and managing of nature? The proper model for the stewardship of nature from a biblical perspective is the Christian stewardship model (Genesis 2; Luke 12:16).

The Christian steward of nature first recognizes that nature, like everything else in heaven and earth, was created by God, belongs to God, and is valued by God for itself. The Christian steward helps to utilize nature as God intended in the service of both God and people. When making use of nature, the Christian steward recognizes that he or she has a responsibility to manage or take care of nature in a way that is not wasteful or destructive of the original functions of nature designed by God.

The Christian steward respects plants, animals, and other elements of nature in their created order out of respect for the Triune God—Father, Son and Holy Spirit—who created and continues to sustain the entire earth and universe. The Christian steward also respects and values nature because he or she knows that both people and nature will share in redemption and renewal in the new eternal heaven and earth. Respecting and valuing nature never makes nature the object of a Christian steward's worship. Rather, credit and honor and worship always go to the Creator of nature and not nature itself in the same way that credit and honor for a magnificent piece of art work do not go to the artwork itself, but to the artist who created it.

---

*This essay originally appeared on the *LeaderU* website:
    John C. Bergstrom, "Principles of an Christian Environmental Ethic."
**Reproduction rights granted by John C. Bergstrom.

PRINCIPLES OF A CHRISTIAN ENVIRONMENTAL ETHIC
BY JOHN C. BERGSTROM

Answer the questions below on a separate sheet of paper and be prepared to review your answers in class.

1. What is the Principle of Creation Value?

2. What are three non-biblical views of nature?

3. What is the Principle of Sustained Order and Purpose?

4. What is the hierarchy between God, people, and nature?

5. How do people manage nature?

6. What is the Principle of Universal Corruption and Redemption?

7. What does it mean to be a steward?

8. How can we practice stewardship in relation to the Principle of Creation Value?

9. How can we practice stewardship in relation to the Principle of Sustained Order and Purpose?

10. How can we practice stewardship in relation to the Principle of Universal Corruption and Redemption?

"The Dangerous Samaritan"
with Michael Bauman

"If you are a Christian, you have an interest in aiding the poor wisely. That is a harder job than you might think it is, because when it comes to aiding the poor, good intentions are not enough."

"If you want to do the right thing, you must learn to think with your head and not just your heart. Good public policy comes from clear thinking."

I. Minimum Wage Laws

"We forget that a wage is not just a selling price for a worker; it is a purchase price for an employer. So we pass laws that prevent the least desirable workers from selling their services at a price that prospective employers (and ultimately you the consumer) can afford to pay."

A. __Artificially__ high prices forces consumers to look elsewhere (e.g. $30k Fords)

"When you put an artificially high price on someone's service, you put them out of business. You make it impossible for them to get a job, because no one is going to want to pay that price for their service."

B. Ultimately harms rather than helps

1. Forces wage raises all the way up the corporate ladder

2. Forces an increase in the price of the company's product

3. The consumers may no longer want to buy the product

4. The company may be forced out of business

5. Minimum wage laws always lead to greater unemployment

C. Good examples are Ray Croc and Dave Thomas

1. Provide fast food for the poor

2. Provide job opportunities for the poor

3. Provide an opportunity for skills

"You can't make a career flipping hamburgers, but you can start a career by flipping hamburgers. Because you can get those important marketplace skills like punctuality, teamwork, appearance, deference, accuracy, dependability—you can get all those skills plus gain a reference and a little money to boot."

"12 percent (almost 1/8th) of the entire American workforce has worked for McDonalds or Wendy's at one time or another."

Unit Nine

II. Rent Control Laws

A. Create incentives for landowners to ___convert___ property (e.g. condos)

    1. Supply and demand

        i. Reduces the supply of cheap apartments

        ii. Aids the wealthy, injures the poor

    2. Can lead to homelessness

B. Quality of apartments can deteriorate

    1. Landowners cannot afford maintenance

    2. The condition of an apartment will always reflect its ___price___

C. Creates incentives for landowners to ___sell___ (e.g. parking lot)

III. Welfare Programs

A. Transferring of money

    1. The intention is to alleviate suffering

    2. The intention is to help the poor escape poverty

        "Since we started the welfare society programs in America in the late 1960s under Lyndon Johnson until today, we have transferred somewhere above 9 trillion dollars… and all the while poverty got worse because poverty is not a money problem… don't ever think that poverty is a money problem."

        "If you took the money earmarked for welfare in the national budget this year and gave it directly to all those people the government designates as poor, you could raise every man, woman, and child in America above the poverty line and have 54 billion dollars left over."

    3. ___Moral hazard___: When insurance against a disaster actually creates an incentive for the disaster to occur

        i. Fire insurance can cause fires (e.g. restaurant is worth more if set on fire)

        ii. Life insurance can cause death (e.g. beneficiaries better off if the insured is dead)

        iii. Medical insurance can causes illness (e.g. treatment for petty sicknesses)

        "Welfare is in some ways poverty insurance, and if your welfare insurance pays off too well, you are going to cause the very problem you are trying to alleviate."

B. Payment for illegitimacy

"One of the rules of government is this: whatever you tax you get less of; whatever you subsidize you get more of... We pay people to have illegitimate children... Inside the inner cities in urban American more than 80% of all black children were born without fathers to take care of them. Our welfare programs have actually made black men, in their families, unnecessary... Poverty circles around broken homes, especially homes led by single mothers... We are encouraging people to do the very things that make them poor and keep them poor."

    1. Worse in Sweden

    2. Incentive for mothers not to get married and to have children with different men

    3. Incentive for fathers to have sex outside marriage, government will pick up the tab

IV. False Charity

A. Success is not an entitlement; it is an achievement.

B. Bearing false witness against the wealthy.

    1. The rich haven't stolen from the poor.

    2. The rich didn't get wealthy by cheating.

C. Capitalism

    1. Does not begin with greed

    2. It begins with your neighbor

        i. Must offer your neighbor a product he wants at a price he can afford

        ii. The marketplace requires people to act decently.

D. Paul: "If you don't work, you don't eat."

E. Donate money to organizations that are part of the solution, not part of the problem

V. Improving Welfare Programs

A. Transfer welfare programs to contributors and away from government bureaucrats

B. Redefine poverty

    1. 40% own their own homes, 70% own their own cars, 60% own two or more televisions

    2. Poor used to mean a lack of food, shelter, and/or clothing

    3. Poverty programs ought not offer dollars

C. Re-educate politicians and poor

    1. Politicians should promote morality and responsibility

    2. Politicians should remember that welfare payments can be psychologically addictive

        "It is not a shame to be poor; it is a shame to be lazy and unproductive."

D. Provide tax credits for companies that hire and train welfare beneficiaries.

E. Welfare reform proposals should be local, timely, and situation specific.

F. Churches should provide food, shelter, and clothing.

    1. Provide example

    2. Know the people you are helping

    3. Know how they got where they are

    4. Be good stewards

    5. Make them change their lives

    6. Don't injure those you are trying to help

"THE DANGEROUS SAMARITAN"
VIDEO QUESTIONS

Answer the questions below on a separate sheet of paper and be prepared to review your answers in class.

1. What are three ways in which minimum wage laws can hurt the poor? How are Ray Croc and Dave Thomas counterexamples of this?

2. What are two ways in which rent control laws can hurt the poor?

3. How can welfare programs hurt the poor?

4. What are some false ideas people hold about capitalism and the wealthy?

5. What are six ways to improve welfare programs?

DEAR DOUG
WRITING ASSIGNMENT

Hello again!

Wow, I realized this morning that we only have a month and a half before the semester is over. It doesn't seem like the weeks could have sped by that fast, but they have. There's just a hint of spring in the air. Nothing big yet—like flowers blooming—but enough to get you thinking of summer! Speaking of which, spring break is coming up. I don't have any big plans—just a few days back at home.

Nathan's loved the milder temps we've had the past week. It seems to have brought out this tree-hugger streak in him that I can't quite relate to. He's been going on and on about protecting the environment and saving the whales and ending pollution. He says that since we are all one with nature, we're only harming ourselves by misusing the earth's resources. He's even gone vegan, though I can't see how not eating a hamburger is going to save the world. Does the Bible have anything to say about environmentalism?

Sarah's thing this week has been helping the poor. Both she and Mark think that government welfare programs are the only way to correct the imbalance between rich and poor. Mark, of course, blamed the gap on capitalism. He even said it is the state's moral responsibility to take care of the poor. I've always thought the church had a duty to help the less fortunate, but if it'll come out of my taxes anyway, maybe I don't need to contribute to the church relief fund. What do you think about welfare?

The longer Sarah and Mark talked the more they decided the government should take over in order to redistribute wealth evenly. Mark even suggested having the state own everything so the people could learn to share things equally. He said that owning land and property causes greed and greed leads to immorality. This sounds awfully close to communism. Do you think such a "socialistic" system can work?

I guess I haven't thought much about economics… been too busy worrying about my credit card bill. Does Christianity have anything to say about economics?

By the way, Amber and I are back together. She wouldn't talk to me for weeks after our fight, but I saw her at the library last week and invited her to a concert with a big group of us. She met me there and we went out for Chinese afterward. We talked and laughed like nothing had happened. I hope we can keep moving forward, because I really missed her.

Later,
Doug

Unit Nine

STUDENT
MANUAL

UNDERSTANDING THE TIMES

Unit Ten

Topics:

History

Historical Jesus

Historical Revisionism

Scriptural Reliability

A Summit Ministries Curriculum

Section Outline

180-Day Syllabus

DAY	IN CLASS	HOMEWORK	
1	WATCH "History" video		
2	READ UTT Textbook 'History 10.1'	READ UTT Textbook 'History 10.2'	
3	REVIEW UTT Textbook 'History 10.1–10.2' questions	READ UTT Textbook 'History 10.3'	
4	READ UTT Textbook 'History 10.4'		
5	REVIEW UTT Textbook 'History 10.3–10.4' questions	READ UTT Textbook 'History 10.5'	
6	READ UTT Textbook 'History 10.6'		
7	REVIEW UTT Textbook 'History 10.5–10.6' questions	READ *Censoring the Past* essay	
8	REVIEW *Censoring the Past* essay questions	ASSIGN Dear Doug Letter	
9	WATCH "The Reliability of Scripture" video P1		
10	WATCH "The Reliability of Scripture" video P2		
11	REVIEW "The Reliability of Scripture" video questions P1		
12	REVIEW "The Reliability of Scripture" video questions P2		
13	WATCH "The Historical Jesus" video		
14	REVIEW "The Historical Jesus" video questions	Dear Doug Letter assignment DUE	
15	TAKE Unit Ten Test		

90-Day Syllabus

DAY	IN CLASS	HOMEWORK	
1	WATCH "History" video	READ UTT Textbook 'History 10.1–10.2'	
2	REVIEW UTT Textbook 'History 10.1–10.2' questions	READ UTT Textbook 'History 10.3–10.4'	
3	REVIEW UTT Textbook 'History 10.3–10.4' questions	READ UTT Textbook 'History 10.5–10.6'	
4	REVIEW UTT Textbook 'History 10.5–10.6' questions	READ *Censoring the Past* essay	
5	REVIEW *Censoring the Past* essay questions		
6	WATCH "The Historical Jesus" video		
7	REVIEW "The Historical Jesus" video questions		
8	TAKE Unit Ten Test		

UNDERSTANDING THE TIMES
HISTORY QUESTIONS

Answer the questions below on a separate sheet of paper and be prepared to review your answers in class.

HISTORY 10.1

1. How important is historical validation to Christianity?

2. What are two common objections made against the Bible's reliability? How do Christians respond?

3. What external evidence exists to support the historicity of Jesus Christ?

4. Who witnessed Christ's resurrection? What effect did his resurrection have upon the disciples?

5. According to Christianity, what is the purpose of history?

HISTORY 10.2

6. What is the history of Muhammad's life?

7. How did the two dominant Islamic factions come into existence?

8. What is Sufism?

9. According to Muslims, what is the purpose of history and the vision for the future?

10. How will Muslims attain this vision for the future?

HISTORY 10.3

11. How does Secular Humanism's belief in evolution influence its optimism for the future?

12. How does Secular Humanism's belief in naturalism influence its optimism for the future?

13. In order to shape history, what must mankind do, according Secular Humanism?

14. According to Secular Humanists, which ideologies are worthy of shaping history? Why?

15. According to Secular Humanism, what is mankind's role in shaping the future?

Unit Ten

HISTORY 10.4

16. What term describes the Marxist view of history? What is this view?

17. According to Karl Marx, what is the real force behind history?

18. Why do Marxists believe that global communism is inevitable? How does the dialectic play a role?

19. What effect does the belief in historical determinism have on free will?

20. According to Marxists, what does the future look like? What is the fate of the dialectic?

HISTORY 10.5

21. What do Cosmic Humanists place their faith in for a better future?

22. How do Cosmic Humanists view the role of Christianity?

23. According to Cosmic Humanism, what is the goal of evolution?

24. Are all Cosmic Humanists satisfied with an evolutionary explanation? Why or why not?

25. According to David Spangler, what role does each individual have in history?

HISTORY 10.6

26. What is the Postmodern approach to history?

27. How did Michel Foucault approach history?

28. What is historical revisionism?

29. How does the Postmodern approach to history mimic the Marxist approach?

30. How does the Postmodern approach to history differ from the Marxist approach?

CENSORING THE PAST
BY GARY DeMAR

There is a lot of talk today about censorship. Recent art exhibits, funded by tax dollars and promoted by the National Endowment for the Arts, have come under severe attack. Many Americans rightly criticize these exhibits as inappropriate, certainly for viewing, but most assuredly for government support and funding. Museums, government-funded artists, Hollywood activists, homosexual groups, and the government-funded NEA (National Endowment for the Arts)[1] are crying "censorship" over such protests.

Another battle is raging over the selling of pornography in popularly trafficked bookstores. Rev. Donald Wildmon and his American Family Association have targeted Waldenbooks, a subsidiary of K-Mart, for selling pornography. Harry Hoffman, president of Waldenbooks, says that Wildmon and others like him "want to censor and stop the sales of constitutionally protected publications they deem objectionable."[2]

Protests against pornography and government-funded art are not acts of censorship. Censorship is a mandate by the civil government which prohibits the publication, sale, or distribution of material it deems to be politically harmful. As civil libertarian Nat Hentoff describes it, "Legally, censorship in violation of the First Amendment can only take place when an agent or agency of the state—a public school principal, a congressman, a President—suppresses speech."[3]

It is not censorship for a government to refuse to pay for objectionable material. In the case of pornographic "art," the protestors are only asking that their tax money not be used to fund the offensive material. Rev. Wildmon is not asking the government to prohibit Waldenbooks from selling *Playboy* and *Penthouse*; he is only calling on concerned citizens to stop doing business with K-Mart and its subsidiaries.[4] He wants the same freedoms that the pornographers are claiming belong only to them. Wildmon writes: "We don't want K-Mart, *Playboy*, and *Penthouse* drawing the line for the rest of us. The First Amendment belongs to all Americans, not just to pornographers."[5]

THE CENSOR BAND WAGON

Literature of all types has been scrutinized by numerous groups from different ends of the political and religious spectrum. Those on the political left have denounced classic works like Charles Dickens's *Oliver Twist* as being "anti-semitic." William Shakespeare's *King Lear* has been condemned as "sexist." *Tom Sawyer*, Mark Twain's coming-of-age classic, has suffered a double blow with denouncements of "racism" and "sexism." Beatrix Potter's *The Tale of Peter Rabbit* and *The Tale of Benjamin Bunny* have been criticized "because they are about 'middle-class rabbits.'"[6]

In 1988, librarians in Cobb County, Georgia, removed the Nancy Drew and Hardy Boys mysteries from the library shelves. The librarians cited lack of shelf space as the reason for the exclusion of the popular mystery series. Mary Louis Rheay, director of the Cobb County Library System, tells a different story, saying that "series books are poorly written and do not meet library standards for book selection."[7] In 1994 the library board in Wellesley, Massachusetts, voted 5 to 1 to keep *Playboy* on the shelves. The board said the magazine, like all its material, is protected by free speech provisions. "There is something in the library to offend everyone," librarian Anne Reynolds said. "We cannot be in the position of censoring everything. Those days are gone." Trustee Carol Gleason, who voted to remove the magazine, said, "If minors cannot buy the magazine in a store, why should they be able to obtain it in the library?"[8]

[1] Miriam Horn with Andy Plattner, "Should Congress censor art?," *U.S. News and World Report* (September 25, 1989); Bo Emerson, "Civil War over Censorship: Morality is the Issue on Battlefield of Culture," *Atlanta Journal/Constitution* (July 25, 1990); and "Four artists to NEA: Who are you to judge?," *The Atlanta Constitution* (March 19, 1991).

[2] Harry Hoffman, "Protect the Right to Buy and Sell Books," *USA Today* (April 25, 1990).

[3] Nat Hentoff, *Free Speech for Me—But Not for Thee* (New York: HarperCollins, 1992), 2.

[4] Those who promote liberal causes are not opposed to boycotts of companies and products they deem objectionable. See Cathy Lynn Grossman, "Boycotting is popular resort for activists," *USA Today* (October 11, 1994).

[5] Donald C. Wildmon, "Protect the Right to Boycott Pornography," *USA Today* (April 25, 1990).

[6] Joseph W. Grigg, "'Peter Rabbit' banned from London schools," *Atlanta Journal/Constitution* (April 7, 1988).

[7] Peggie R. Elgin, "Hardy Boys banned from Cobb libraries," *Marietta Daily Journal* (January 13, 1988).

[8] "Residents want 'Playboy' out of library," *Marietta Daily Journal* (October 18, 1994).

WHO DRAWS THE LINE?

An ad hoc public school committee supported the removal of books by Dr. James Dobson, a Christian psychologist, from the library of the Early Childhood Family Education Program of the Mankato, Minnesota, school system. They were removed because the staff "disagreed with Dobson's views on child discipline, which includes an endorsement of spanking, and because of the religious nature of his philosophy."[9]

Donated books are often refused by libraries because of religious content. *The Closing of the American Heart*, written by Dr. Ronald H. Nash, was donated to the Haggard Library in Plano, Texas, by a group of concerned citizens. Nash is a former professor of religion and philosophy at Western Kentucky University who presently teaches at Reformed Theological Seminary in Orlando, Florida. He has also served as an advisor to the United States Civil Rights Commission. Why was his book refused? Certainly not because of his academic and professional credentials. Book donations had to pass the library's evaluation criteria.[10] *The Closing of the American Heart* did not pass because of its Christian perspective.

Each year People for the American Way (PAW), a liberal political advocacy group, publishes a report on censorship and "book banning." Most of the books which are brought into question deal with occultic themes, promiscuous sexual content, and advocacy of homosexuality. Most of the protestors are parents who send their children to government-controlled (public) schools. PAW considers such parental concern over what children read "attacks on the freedom to learn."[11] What PAW does not tell its unsuspecting audience is that incidents of so-called censorship are negligible compared to the number of schools and libraries in existence. For example, the most challenged book, *Scary Stories to Tell in the Dark*, "was challenged only 7 times out of 84,000 public schools and never removed." In fact, Kristi Harrick, press secretary for the Family Research Council, reports that "none of the most challenged books were censored."[12]

Eric Buehrer, a former public-school teacher and president of Gateways to Better Education in Lake Forest, California, states that "PAW has confused the issues of material selection and censorship. What used to be called discernment is now called censorship."[13] Why is it called "censorship" when parents apply standards for book selection but called "meeting library standards" when a librarian evaluates a book?

Judgments are constantly made as to what children should read and what books should appear on library shelves. As we've seen, librarians appeal to "library standards" when selecting books. There is nothing wrong with having "standards."

Unfortunately, these "library standards" are neither applied consistently in libraries and schools nor always reported in the same way by the press.[14] It seems that when concerned Christian parents voice objections to the content of books, they are said to be censors. But when books with Christian themes are refused by libraries or when teachers are denied the right to read a Bible silently during a reading period,[15] we learn that the rejection is based upon the religious nature of the literature. Rarely are such actions by libraries and schools said to be "censorship" by even the strongest opponents of book banning.

WILL THE REAL CENSORS PLEASE STAND UP?

It is instructive how one segment of our society screams "censorship" every time its views are questioned, but when Christians claim "censorship" of the facts of history, they are ignored by the guardians of the First Amendment.

Liberal media coverage of world events is just one example of the anti-Christian bias of mainstream contemporary society. Consider journalistic coverage of events in Eastern Europe. Rev. Laszlo Tokes, the Hungarian pastor who sparked the Rumanian Revolution, stated that "Eastern Europe is not just in a political revolution but a religious renaissance." How many people read in their local newspapers or

[9] Willmar Thorkelson, "Book Ban Considered," *Washington Post* (September 1, 1990).

[10] Reported in "Texas Report," a supplement to the *Christian American* (July/August 1992).

[11] Andrew Mollison, "Group says efforts to ban schoolbooks focus on alleged satanic, occult content," *Atlanta Constitution* (August 29, 1991).

[12] "PAW Cries Censor-Wolf: Attempt to Keep Parents Out of Schools, Says FRC," *Family Research Council Press Release* (August 31, 1994).

[13] Quoted in "The Great 'Censorship' Hoax," *Citizen* (September 19, 1994).

[14] David Shaw, "Abortion Bias Seeps Into News" and Al Knight, "School races turn nasty," Denver Post (October 10, 1993). Knight writes: "The term *religious right*, in the hands of PAW and other groups, has become one of the most elastic political labels in memory. It is routinely stretched to include nearly anyone who might be motivated by conservative, religious, or moral concerns."

[15] John W. Whitehead, *The Rights of Religious Persons in Public Education* (Wheaton, IL: Crossway, 1994), 112–13.

saw on the evening news that Rev. Tokes believed he had been saved from execution through "divine intervention"? Explicitly Christian themes are regularly excluded from news articles: "References to 'Jesus,' the 'Christian spirit,' and Czechoslovakia's role as the 'spiritual crossroads of Europe' were omitted from excerpts of President Vaclav Havel's New Year's Day address. *The New York Times*, *The Washington Post*, and *Newsweek* were among the sinful censors."[16]

None of these examples should surprise the informed Christian. The present educational establishment, to cite just one group, has been obscuring the past so that our children have no way of comparing the facts of history with the distorted version promoted by biased secular historians.

CENSORSHIP AT WORK IN THE CLASSROOM

Public school textbooks are fertile ground for the seeds of willful historical deception. Paul C. Vitz, professor of psychology at New York University, spent months of careful analysis of sixty textbooks used in elementary schools across the country. The study was sponsored by the National Institute on Education. The texts were examined in terms of their references to religion, either directly or indirectly. "In grades 1 through 4 these books introduce the child to U.S. society—to family life, community activities, ordinary economic transactions, and some history. None of the books covering grades 1 through 4 contain one word referring to any religious activity in contemporary American life."[17] Dr. Vitz offers an example of how this translates into the real world of classroom instruction:

> Some particular examples of the bias against religion are significant. One social studies book has thirty pages on the Pilgrims, including the first Thanksgiving. But there is not one word (or image) that referred to religion as even a part of the Pilgrims' life. One mother whose son is in a class using this book wrote me to say that he came home and told her that "Thanksgiving was when the Pilgrims gave thanks to the Indians." The mother called the principal of this suburban New York City school to point out that Thanksgiving was when the Pilgrims thanked God. The principal responded by saying "that was her opinion"—the schools could only teach what was in the books![18]

In 1986 school children in Seattle, Washington, were given a large dose of revisionist history in the booklet *Teaching about Thanksgiving*. The children were told that "the Pilgrims were narrow-minded bigots who survived initially only with the Indians' help, but turned on them when their help wasn't needed anymore." The Pilgrims "had something up their sleeves other than friendship when they invited the Indians to a Thanksgiving feast, and it was the Indians who ended up bringing most of the food, anyway."[19] The booklet has obvious biases and is filled with historical inaccuracies. For example, supposedly Increase Mather preached a sermon in 1623 where he reportedly "gave special thanks to God for the plague of smallpox which had wiped out the majority of Wampanoag Indians, praising God for destroying 'chiefly young men and children, the very seeds of increase, thus clearing the forests for a better growth.'"[20] This sermon could not have been preached by Increase Mather, at least not in 1623, because he was not born until 1639.

The rewriting of history has even reached the pages of the Sunday comics. A story recently appeared about "Squanto and the First Thanksgiving." As all children know, Squanto was a great help to the Pilgrims. But was Squanto so much of a help that the first Thanksgiving was given in his honor? According to the author of the Squanto column, we learn that "the Pilgrims so appreciated Squanto's generosity that they had a great feast to show their thanks."[21] William Bradford, governor of Plymouth and the colony's first historian, continually makes reference to "the Lord Who never fails," "God's blessing," and "the Providence of God," in times of both plenty and want.[22] How uncharacteristic it would have been for the Plymouth settlers to ignore thanking God during a time of harvest. Edward Winslow, in his important chronicle of the history of

[16] Barbara Reynolds, "Religion is Greatest Story Ever Missed," *USA Today* (March 16, 1990).
[17] Paul C. Vitz, *Censorship: Evidence of Bias in Our Children's Textbooks* (Ann Arbor, MI: Servant Books, 1986), 1.
[18] Ibid., 3.
[19] Carey Quan Gelernter, "The Real Thanksgiving," *Seattle Post-Intelligencer* (November 23, 1986).
[20] Ibid.
[21] "Squanto and the First Thanksgiving," Rabbit Ears, *Atlanta Journal/Constitution* (November 27, 1994).
[22] William Bradford, *Bradford's History of the Plymouth Settlement: 1608–1650*, rendered into modern English by Harold Paget (Portland, OR: American Heritage Ministries, 1988).

Unit Ten

Plymouth, reports the following eyewitness account of the colony's thanksgiving celebration:

> Our harvest being gotten in, our governor sent four men out fowling, that so we might, after a special manner, rejoice together after we had gathered the fruit of our labors. They four in one day killed as much fowl as, with a little help beside, served the company almost a week. At which time, among other recreations, we exercised our arms, many of the Indians coming among us, and among the rest their greatest king, Massasoit, with some ninety men, whom for three days we entertained and feasted; and they went out and killed five deer, which they brought to the plantation, and bestowed on our governor, and upon the captain and others. And although it be not always so plentiful as it was at this time with us, yet by the goodness of God we are so far from want, that we often wish you partakers of our plenty.[23]

Squanto was an example of God's providential care of the Pilgrims. He taught them how to farm in the New World and led them on trading expeditions. There is no doubt that these early Christian settlers thanked the "Indians" in general and Squanto in particular for their generosity in supplying venison to supplement the Pilgrims' meager Thanksgiving rations. As the historical record shows, however, thanksgiving was ultimately made to God. "Governor Bradford, with one eye on divine Providence, proclaimed a day of thanksgiving to God, and with the other eye on the local political situation, extended an invitation to neighboring Indians to share in the harvest feast… This 'first Thanksgiving' was a feast called to suit the needs of the hour, which were to celebrate the harvest, thank the Lord for His goodness, and regale and impress the Indians."[24]

CENSORSHIP THROUGH CREATIVE EDITING

Dr. Vitz is not the only person to uncover the way public school texts minimize the role that Christianity played in the founding of our nation. Consider how a teacher's guide for the high school history text *Triumph of the American Nation*, published in 1986, omits material from the Mayflower Compact without informing the teacher that the document has been edited. In discussing the document students are left with an incomplete understanding of what motivated these early founders because they do not have all the facts. The Mayflower Compact is depicted solely as a political document with its more striking religious elements deleted. Here is the document as presented by the textbook company. The bold face portions are missing from the textbook version:

> In the name of God, Amen. We whose names are underwritten, **the loyal subjects of our dread sovereign lord, King James, by the grace of God, of Great Britain, France, and Ireland, King, Defender of the Faith, etc.,** having undertaken **for the glory of God and advancement of the Christian faith and honor of our king and country,** a voyage to plant the first colony in the northern parts of Virginia, do **by these presents** solemnly and in the presence of God, and one another, covenant and combine ourselves together into a civil body politic… [25]

These brave men and women had more on their minds than political freedom. Missionary zeal and the advancement of the Christian faith were their primary motivations as they risked life and property to carve out a new home in an uncertain wilderness.

The critics of America's early Christian origins have steadily removed such references from textbooks and have created a tense legal environment that frightens many teachers from even raising evidence contradicting the censored texts. Will a member of the ACLU threaten legal action against a teacher who decides to cite original source material to support a view that differs from the historical perspective of the textbook?

[23] Edward Winslow, "How the Pilgrim Fathers Lived," *CD Sourcebook of American History* (Mesa, AR: Candlelight Publishing, 1992), 2:116. Also see Mourt's *Relation: A Journal of the Pilgrims of Plymouth*, ed. Jordan D. Fiore (Plymouth, MA: Plymouth Rock Foundation, 1985), 67–69.

[24] Diana Karter Appelbaum, *Thanksgiving: An American Holiday, An American History* (New York: Facts on File Pub., 1984), 9.

[25] This editing was exposed in *Education Update*, Heritage Foundation, 10:3 (Summer 1987). Quoted in Robert P. Dugan, *Winning the New Civil War: Recapturing America's Values* (Portland, OR: Multnomah, 1991), 149–50.

Unit Ten

HOLLYWOOD HISTORY

The entertainment industry has entered the field of creative editing in an animated version of the story of Pocahontas, the Native American woman who pleaded with her father to spare the life of John Smith. Pocahontas later became a Christian and married another colonist, John Rolfe. But this episode will all be deleted from an animated retelling of the story. Kendall Hamilton of *Newsweek* offers the following report on the newly designed and politically correct Pocahontas:

> The film's P.C. prospects are… helped by the exclusion of Pocahontas's potentially, er, problematic later years, in which she was kidnapped by settlers and, after converting to Christianity, married one of her captors. Male domination fantasy! Subversion of morally superior indigenous culture! Well, maybe, but [Producer James] Pentecost says such considerations weren't a factor: "We didn't really sidestep any of it for any reason other than this was the most direct way to tell the story and the clearest." Pass the peace pipe.[26]

While this might be the *official* explanation from Disney, my guess is that the studio was pressured by Native Americans to hide Pocahontas's "mistake" of rejecting her native religion.

WILLIAM HOLMES McGUFFEY'S ECLECTIC READERS

A study of the historical record reveals that religion played a major role in the development of the public school curriculum. "Textbooks referred to God without embarrassment, and public schools considered one of their major tasks to be the development of character through the teaching of religion. For example, the *New England Primer* opened with religious admonitions followed by the Lord's Prayer, the Apostles' Creed, the Ten Commandments, and the names of the books of the Bible."[27]

The most widely used textbook series in public schools from 1836 to 1920 were William Holmes McGuffey's *Eclectic Readers*. More than 120 million *Readers* were sold during this period. The *Readers* stressed religion and its relationship to morality and the proper use of knowledge. In an introduction for a reissue of the *Fifth Reader*, historian Henry Steele Commager writes:

> What was the nature of the morality that permeated the *Readers*? It was deeply religious, and… religion then meant a Protestant Christianity… The world of the *McGuffeys* was a world where no one questioned the truths of the Bible or their relevance to everyday contact… The *Readers*, therefore, are filled with stories from the Bible, and tributes to its truth and beauty.[28]

Competing textbooks of the same era contained varying amounts of biblical material, but *McGuffeys* contained the greatest amount—"more than three times as much as any other text of the period."[29] Subsequent editions of the *Readers*—1857 and 1879—showed a reduction in the amount of material devoted to biblical themes. Even so, the 1879 edition contained the Sermon on the Mount, two selections from the Book of Psalms, the Lord's Prayer, the story of the death of Absalom (2 Samuel 18), and Paul's speech on the Areopagus (Acts 17). The Bible was still referred to as "'the Book of God,' 'a source of inspiration,' 'an important basis for life,' and was cited in support of particular moral issues."[30]

ANTISEPTIC TEXTS

Since the nineteenth century, secularists have been gradually chipping away at the historical record, denying the impact Christianity has had on the development of the moral character of the United States. In 1898 Bishop Charles Galloway delivered a series of messages in the Chapel at Emory College in Georgia. In his messages he noted that "books on the making of our nation have been written, and are the texts in our colleges, in which the Christian religion, as a social and civil factor, has only scant or apologetic mention.

[26] Kendall Hamilton, "No Red Faces, They Hope," *Newsweek* (November 21, 1994).
[27] Whitehead, *Rights of Religious Persons in Public Education*, 41–42.
[28] Quoted in Ibid., 42.
[29] John H. Westerhoff, "The Struggle for a Common Culture: Biblical Images in Nineteenth-Century Schoolbooks," *The Bible in American Education*, eds. David L. Barr and Nicholas Piediscalzi (Philadelphia, PA: Fortress Press, 1982), 32.
[30] Ibid., 28.

This is either a fatal oversight or a deliberate purpose, and both alike to be deplored and condemned. A nation ashamed of its ancestry will be despised by its posterity."[31]

The 1980s saw an even greater expurgation of the impact the Christian religion has had on our nation. So much so that even People for the American Way had to acknowledge that religion is often overlooked in history textbooks: "Religion is simply not treated as a significant element in American life—it is not portrayed as an integrated part of the American value system or as something that is important to individual Americans."[32] A 1994 study of history textbooks commissioned by the federal government and drafted by the National Center for History in the Schools at UCLA concluded that religion "was foolishly purged from many recent textbooks."[33] In 1990, Warren A. Nord of the University of North Carolina wrote:

> What cannot be doubted is that our ways of thinking about nature, morality, art, and society were once (and for many people still are) fundamentally religious, and still today in our highly secular world it is difficult even for the nonreligious to extricate themselves entirely from the webs of influence and meaning provided by our religious past… To understand history and (historical) literature one must understand a great deal about religion: on this all agree. Consequently, the relative absence of religion from history textbooks is deeply troubling.[34]

The removal of the topic of religion from textbooks is not always motivated by a desire to slam Christianity. Textbook publishers fear special interest groups that scrutinize the material for any infraction, whether it be religious, racial, sexual, or ethnic. For example, "the 1990 Houghton Mifflin elementary series first made special efforts to include material (and in state hearings received savage criticism from militant Jews, Muslims, and fundamentalist Christians)."[35] The easiest way to placate these diverse groups is to remove all discussion of the topic. This deletion of material is either outright censorship or else a reluctance to fight ideological wars, but whatever the case, failure to deal factually with the past distorts a student's historical perspective. This has happened to such an extent that even when religious themes are covered "their treatments are uniformly antiseptic and abstract."[36]

---

*This essay originally appeared as a chapter in the book *America's Christian History: The Untold Story*

Gary DeMar, *America's Christian History: The Untold Story* (Atlanta: American Vision, 1994), pp. 21–34.

**Reproduction rights granted by Gary DeMar and American Vision.

[31] Charles B. Galloway, *Christianity and the American Commonwealth* (Nashville: Methodist Episcopal Church, 1898), 15.

[32] Joan Delfattore, *What Johnny Shouldn't Read: Textbook Censorship in America* (New Haven, CT: Yale Univ. Press, 1992), 85.

[33] This is also the conclusion of the editorial writers of the *Marietta Daily Journal*: "History needing revision" (October 30, 1994). The National Standards for United States History has called for the restoration of the role religion played in the founding of America while pushing a "politically correct" agenda in nearly everything else. See Lynne V. Cheney, "The End of History," *Wall Street Journal* (October 20, 1994).

[34] Quoted in *History Textbooks: A Standard and Guide*, 1994–95 Edition (New York: American Textbook Council, 1994), 32.

[35] Ibid.

[36] Ibid., 33.

CENSORING THE PAST
ESSAY QUESTIONS

Answer the questions below on a separate sheet of paper and be prepared to review your answers in class.

1. How does censorship compare to protesting?

2. How does censorship compare to discernment?

3. What are some examples of historical revision in public schools?

4. What is an example of censorship through omission in public schools?

5. What were curriculum materials like in public schools before the middle of the twentieth century?

"THE RELIABILITY OF SCRIPTURE"
WITH TODD COTHRAN

PART ONE: THE OLD TESTAMENT

I. Three Categories of Evidence

    A. Transmission

    B. Archaeological record

    C. Fulfilled prophecy

II. Transmission

    A. Jewish scribes

        1. Reproduction process

        2. Error prevention

    B. God's will

    "Moses wrote all the words of the Lord." — Exodus 24:4

    Joshua also "wrote these words in the Book of the Law of God." — Joshua 24:26

    Samuel "told the people the ordinances of the kingdom, and wrote them in the book and placed it before the Lord." — 1 Samuel 10:25

    "Take for yourself a large tablet and write on it in ordinary letters." — Isaiah 8:1

    C. _Dead Sea Scrolls_ (1947)

    "Even though the two copies of Isaiah discovered in Qumran Cave 1 near the Dead Sea in 1947 were a thousand years earlier than the oldest dated manuscript previously known (A.D. 980), they proved to be word for word identical with our standard Hebrew Bible in more than 95 percent of the text. The 5 percent of variation consisted chiefly of obvious slips of the pen and variations in spelling." — Archer Gleason, *A Survey of Old Testament Introduction*

III. Archaeology

    A. Ebla Tablets (1974)

        1. Greatly weakens the Documentary Hypothesis — writing was around during Moses

        2. Written _1,000_ years before Moses

B. Archaeology suggests or proves…

    1. That Israel derives its ancestry from _____Mesopotamia_____ (Genesis 11:27–12:4)

    2. That language arose from a common origin

    3. That _____Jericho_____ and several others cities thought to be legend actually existed

    4. That the Hittite civilization…

        i. Existed at time of Abraham

        ii. Lasted over 1,200 years (doctorate from University of Chicago)

C. Latest discoveries

    1. **Tell Dan** in northern Galilee—found remains of a black basalt stele (stone slab)

        i. "The King of Israel"

        ii. "House of _____David_____"

    2. **Tell es-Safi** (the biblical city of "Gath of the Philistines")—found small ceramic shard that mentions two names remarkably similar to the name "_____Goliath_____"

"The science of modern archaeology and historical philology actually provides verification of the most ancient biblical texts. Whereas… throughout the nineteenth century and almost up to the Second World War, systematic criticism of the Old Testament texts tended to destroy their historicity, and to reduce the Pentateuch, in particular, to mere myth or tribal legend, the trend over the last half-century has been quite in the opposite direction." — Paul Johnson, *The Quest for God*

IV. Fulfilled Prophecy

A. Provides more than _____2,000_____ prophecies that validate its historical claims

B. All biblical prophecies concerning events up to the present time have come to pass.

C. Messianic Prophecies

    1. His _____birthplace_____

"But as for you, Bethlehem Ephrathah, too little to be among the clans of Judah, from you One will go forth for Me to be ruler in Israel." — Micah 5:2

"They said to him, 'In Bethlehem of Judea; for this is what has been written by the prophet: "And you Bethlehem, land of Judah are by no means least among the leaders of Judah; for out of you shall come forth a ruler who will shepherd my people Israel."'" — Matthew 2:5–6

2. His _attitude_ toward accusers

"He was oppressed and He was afflicted, Yet he did not open His mouth; like a lamb that is led to the slaughter, and like a sheep that is silent before its shearers." — Isaiah 53:7

"Then Pilate said to Him, 'Do you not hear how many things they testify against You?' And He did not answer him with regard to even a single charge, so that the governor was quite amazed." — Matthew 27:13–14

3. His _burial_ in a rich man's tomb (Joseph of Arimathea: Matthew 27:57–60)

"His grave was assigned with wicked men, yet He was with a rich man in His death, because He had done no violence, nor was there any deceit in His mouth." — Isaiah 53:9

4. His _resurrection_

"For Thou wilt not abandon my soul to Sheol; neither wilt Thou allow Thy Holy One to undergo decay." — Psalm 16:10

"Brethren, I may confidently say to you regarding the patriarch David that he both died and was buried, and his tomb is with us to this day. And so, because he was a prophet, and knew that God had sworn to him with an oath to seat one of his descendants upon his throne, he looked ahead and spoke of the resurrection of the Christ, that He was neither abandoned to Hades, nor did His flesh suffer decay." — Acts 2:29–31

D. 60 major prophecies and 270 ramifications

1. *Objection*: Many prophecies were manufactured after the fact

2. *Objection*: Many prophecies are obscure

TOPIC	OT PROPHECY	NT FULFILLMENT
Born of seed of woman	Genesis 3:15	Galatians 4:4
Line of Abraham	Genesis 12:2	Matthew 1:1
Line of Jacob	Numbers 24:17	Luke 3:23, 34
Line of Judah	Genesis 49:10	Matthew 1:2
Line of Jesse	Isaiah 11:1	Luke 3:23, 32
Line of David	2 Samuel 7:12–16	Matthew 1:1
Virgin Birth	Isaiah 7:14	Matthew 1:23
Birthplace	Micah 5:2	Matthew 2:6
Sold for 30 Shekels	Zechariah 11:12	Matthew 26:15

Forsaken by disciples	Zechariah 13:7	Mark 14:50
Silent before accusers	Isaiah 53:7	Matthew 27:12–19
Crucified with thieves	Isaiah 53:12	Matthew 27:38
No bones broken	Psalm 22:17	John 19:33–36
Scourging and death	Isaiah 53:5	John 19:1, 18
Rich man's tomb	Isaiah 53:9	Matthew 27:57–60
Resurrection	Psalm 16:10; 22:22	Matthew 28:6
Ascension	Psalm 68:18	Luke 24:50–53

PART TWO: THE NEW TESTAMENT

I. Objection One: Oral tradition is unreliable

A. Oral tradition was held in the highest regard.

B. Jewish children were taught to remember oral material accurately.

C. Oral tradition was handed down collectively to the entire community.

D. Exodus 24:4; Joshua 24:26; 1 Samuel 10:25; Isaiah 8:1; 1 Corinthians 14:37; Revelation 1:19

II. Objection Two: Written by men

A. Writers were inspired by God

"Biblical inspiration may be defined as God's superintending of the human authors so that, using their own individual personalities—and even their writing styles—they composed and recorded without error His revelation to humankind in the words of the original autographs."
— Ron Rhodes, *Answering the Objections of Atheists, Agnostics and Skeptics*

B. To what extent were the writers controlled by the Holy Spirit?

"Prophecy [or Scripture] never had its origin in the will of man, but men spoke from God as they were carried along by the Holy Spirit." — 2 Peter 1:21

Paul said he spoke "not in words taught us by human wisdom but in words taught by the Spirit, expressing spiritual truths in spiritual words." — 1 Corinthians 2:13

III. Objection Three: Writers were biased

A. Some of the most reliable reports of the Nazi Holocaust were from Jews.

"We did not follow cleverly invented stories when we told you about the power and coming of our Lord Jesus Christ, but we were eyewitnesses of his majesty." — 2 Peter 1:16

"That which was from the beginning, which we have heard, which we have seen with our eyes, which we have looked at and our hands have touched—this we proclaim concerning the Word of life." — 1 John 1:1

B. Other considerations

   1. Apostles had little to __gain__ and almost everything to __lose__

   2. New Testament writers gave up their lives in defense of what they saw.

   3. They kept in __embarrassing__ details about themselves

      i. Jewish people's unfaithfulness to God

      ii. Peter denying Christ three times

      iii. Peter being addressed as Satan

      iv. Disciples scattering when Christ was arrested

      v. Thomas's doubt about the resurrection

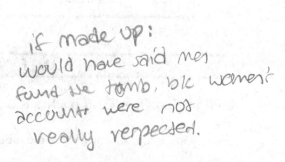
if made up: would have said men found the tomb, b/c women's accounts were not really respected.

IV. Objection Four: Too much time had passed

  A. The time between these two events (the writing of the original and the copying of the oldest extant manuscript) is extremely short

    1. Important because the shorter the time, the more reliable a text is considered

      i. Ancient classics have an average gap of over __1,000__ years

      ii. A 700-year gap is considered good among works of antiquity

    2. **John Ryland's manuscript** (oldest copy of New Testament)

      i. Contains fragments from John (John 18:31–33, 37–38)

      ii. Dates to approximately A.D. 117–138

    3. **Bodmer Papyri**

      i. Contains most of the Gospels of Luke and John

      ii. Dates to approximately A.D. 200

    4. **Chester Beatty Papyri**

      i. Contains almost all of the New Testament (including large portions of the Gospels)

      ii. Dates to approximately A.D. 250

5. **Codex Sinaiticus** (The British Museum)

   i. Contains the entire NT and parts of the OT

   ii. Dates to approximately A.D. 340

6. **Codex Vaticanus** (Vatican Library)

   i. Contains most of the Bible

   ii. Dates to approximately A.D. 325–350

7. **Codex Alexandrinus** (The British Museum)

   i. Contains most of the Bible

   ii. Dates to approximately A.D. 450

8. **Codex Bezae** (Cambridge University Library)

   i. Contains parts of the NT and most of the Gospels (written in Greek and Latin)

   ii. Dates to approximately A.D. 450–550

B. The New Testament compared to other documents of antiquity

AUTHOR	DATE WRITTEN	EARLIEST COPY	NUMBER OF COPIES	ACCURACY OF COPIES
Caesar	1st century B.C.	A.D. 900	10	———
Tacitus	A.D. 100	A.D. 1100	20	———
Thucydides	5th century B.C.	A.D. 900	8	———
Herodotus	5th century B.C.	A.D. 900	8	———
Homer	9th century B.C.	———	643	95%
New Testament	1st century A.D.	2nd century A.D.	5,000+	99+%

Unit Ten

C. Non-Christian accounts

1. **Tacitus** (ca. A.D. 55–120): Roman historian, *Annals*

2. **Suetonius** (ca. A.D. 120): Roman historian, *Life of Claudius*

3. **Josephus** (A.D. 37–97): Jewish Historian, *Antiquities*

4. **Pliny the Younger** (A.D. 112): Roman governor, *Epistles X*

5. **Jewish Talmud** (commentary on Jewish law, completed A.D. 500)

6. **Lucian** (second century A.D.): Greek satirist

D. General reports of Jesus and Christianity

1. Provocative teacher, a wise and virtuous man from the region of Judea

2. Reportedly performed miracles and made prophetic claims

3. Jewish leaders condemned him for acts of sorcery and apostasy

4. Crucified by the Roman procurator Pontius Pilate

5. Christians reported that he had risen from the dead

6. Roman Christians charged with crimes and met horrific persecution

7. First-century Christians worshiped Jesus Christ as God

8. Disciples were known for their courage and virtue

> "To be skeptical of the resultant text of the New Testament books is to allow all of classical antiquity to slip into obscurity, for no documents of the ancient period are as well attested biographically as the New Testament." — John Warwick Montgomery, *History and Christianity*

> "The excessive skepticism of many liberal theologians stems not from a careful evaluation of the available data, but from an enormous predisposition against the supernatural." — Millar Burrows, *What Mean These Stones?*

V. Truth: Myths and legends did not have sufficient time to develop and be recorded

A. Gospels (Matthew, Mark, Luke/Acts, and John)—probably written in early 50s and 60s

B. None mention noteworthy events between A.D. 60 and 70

1. Persecution of Christians instigated by the Roman emperor ___Nero___ (mid-60s)

2. The martyrdom of James (brother of Jesus), Peter, and Paul (62–66)

3. The fall of Jerusalem and destruction of the Temple under Roman general Titus (70)

C. Conclusion: Span of two full generations is insufficient

VI. Eyewitness Accounts of Historical Events

A. Luke 1:1–4; John 19:35; 1 Corinthians 15:3–8; Galatians 1:11–12; 2 Peter 1:16; 1 John 1:1–2

B. Actively attempted to squelch rumors before they could spread (John 21:22–25)

If the Gospel writers had departed from historical fact (either by exaggeration or outright invention), hostile witnesses familiar with the events of Jesus' life could have and would have exposed them.

VII. Other Known Mythical Writings

A. The Bible is neither bizarre nor frivolous, as in Greek mythology

B. Jesus' miracles were always done within the context of his ministry, specifically to give glory to God and to meet legitimate human need.

"THE RELIABILITY OF SCRIPTURE"
VIDEO QUESTIONS

Answer the questions below on a separate sheet of paper and be prepared to review your answers in class.

PART ONE

1. What was significant about the 1947 discovery of the Dead Sea Scrolls?

2. How does archaeology support the reliability of the Old Testament?

3. What are some of the latest discoveries that support the reliability of the Old Testament?

4. How should we respond to the claim that many prophecies were manufactured after the fact?

5. How should Christians respond to the claim that many prophecies are so obscure that a variety of events could be interpreted as fulfillment?

PART TWO

6. How should Christians respond to the claim that the oral tradition from which the New Testament was written was unreliable?

7. What is meant by the phrase "the Scriptures were inspired by God?"

8. What are some problems with the claim that the New Testament is unreliable because the gospel writers were biased?

9. How should Christians respond to the objection that the New Testament is unreliable because too much time passed between the original authorship and the date of the earliest copy?

10. How can Christians be sure that the Gospels do not contain myth and legend?

"THE HISTORICAL JESUS"
WITH KEVIN BYWATER

I. Critical Timeline

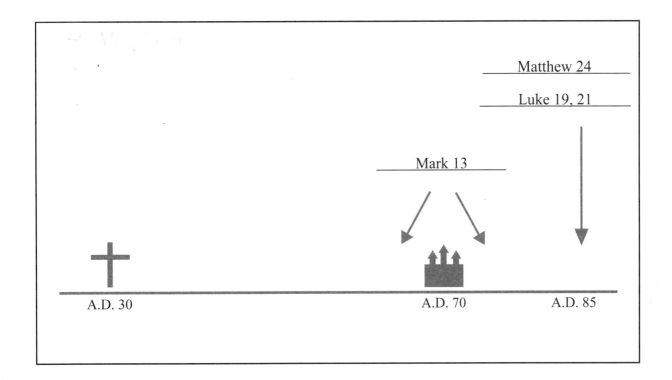

Matthew 24

Luke 19, 21

Mark 13

A.D. 30

A.D. 70

A.D. 85

II. Synoptic Gospels: Mark, Matthew, and Luke

A. Dated after 70 A.D. by some scholars

B. _The Olivet Discourse_: A speech in which Jesus predicts the destruction of the temple within one generation

C. Temple demolished in 70 A.D.

III. Methodological Naturalism: the process of interpreting history as purely natural events

A. Assumption: God does not intervene in history.

B. Miracles and prophecies do not occur.

C. Jesus' prophecy must have therefore been added by someone else after the event.

Unit Ten

IV. Jesus Seminar: a group of scholars and others who vote on the saying of Jesus

    A. _____Scientism_____: Truth can only be know through science

    B. Prophecy is actually historical fiction or retrojected legends.

V. Reconstructing History

    A. When was Acts written?

        1. Consider Luke's dual focus: Peter (1–12), then Paul (13–28)

        2. Consider Luke's tendencies: persecutions and deaths of leaders

            i. Jesus (2:23)

            ii. Stephen (7:60)

            iii. James (12:2)

        3. No mention of _____Paul's_____ death—A.D. 64

        4. Acts was likely written before A.D. 64

    B. When was Luke written?

        1. Luke/Acts was a two volume set

        2. Luke was therefore written before Acts (possibly A.D. 62)

    C. When was Mark written?

        1. Luke most likely used Mark as a source

        2. Mark was therefore written before Luke (possibly A.D. 60)

VI. Additional Warrants for Earlier Dates

    A. No mention of _____Nero's_____ persecution (A.D. 64–68)

    B. No mention of the fall of _____Jerusalem_____ (A.D. 70)

        1. No residue indicating it was past event

        2. No New Testament book mentions it as past

VII. Gospels' Tendencies Regarding Fulfilled Prophecy

A. Old Testament prophecies as fulfilled

    1. Throughout Matthew

    2. Luke 24:25–27

B. Consider the sufferings and resurrection of Jesus

    1. Prophesied: e.g., Matthew 16:21

    2. Noted as fulfilled:

        i. His sufferings:

            1) Peter disowning Jesus three times (Mark 14:74)

            2) On the road to Emmaus (Luke 24:6–8)

        ii. His resurrection:

            1) Matthew 28:6

            2) Mark 16:6

            3) Luke 24:6–8

            4) John 20:9

C. Yet not even a hint indicating that the Olivet Discourse had been fulfilled

VIII. Why Do Critics Date Matthew and Luke So Late?

A. Anti-Semitism—e.g. Matthew 23

    1. Christians kicked out of synagogues in A.D. 85

    2. After A.D. 85 Christians added anti-Semitic language to the words of Christ

    3. _____Jews_____ condemning Jews was normal and prophetic

        i. Isaiah 1:21

        ii. Jeremiah 3:6

        iii. Jeremiah 9:26

        iv. Isaiah 1:4

B. What we find in the Gospels is thus not anti-Semitism

Unit Ten

IX. Presence of What Became Irrelevant

A. Temple service

B. Sabbath

X. Lack of What Later Was Relevant

A. Circumcision of Gentiles

B. Marriage to unbelievers

C. Spiritual gifts

D. Church structure

E. Roles of women

F. Food restrictions

XI. Additional Indicators of Historicity

A. Diversity among the Gospel accounts

B. Retention of embarrassing elements

1. Was Jesus unable to heal? (Mark 6:5–6)

2. Is Jesus good? (Mark 10:18)

3. His family opposed him (Mark 3:21)

4. He was baptized by John

C. The quality and purpose of the miracles

D. Distinction between Christian prophets and the words of Jesus

1. John (Revelation 2–3)

2. Agabus (Acts 11:28; 21:10–11)

3. Paul (1 Corinthians 7:10,12)

XII. Final Observations

A. The Gospel accounts are ___summaries___ and ___paraphrases___

B. What language did Jesus speak? ___Aramaic___

C. In what language were the gospels written? ___Greek___

D. What does this imply?

    1. The gospels are translations

    2. Some of their differences may thus be explained

"THE HISTORICAL JESUS"
VIDEO QUESTIONS

Answer the questions below on a separate sheet of paper and be prepared to review your answers in class.

1. Why do critical scholars date the Synoptic Gospels after A.D. 70?

2. What is the Jesus Seminar? How do they interpret Scripture?

3. What case can be made for dating Acts and the Synoptic Gospels before A.D. 70?

4. What are some additional considerations for dating Acts (and consequently the Synoptic Gospels) before A.D. 70?

5. What are the Synoptic Gospels' tendencies toward the recording of prophecies?

6. Why do critics date Matthew and Luke around A.D. 85?

7. Are the Gospels anti-Semitic?

8. If the Gospels were written later, what might we expect to find that we do not?

9. What are some additional indicators for the historicity of the Gospels?

10. How might Christians explain some of the differences among the accounts of the Gospels?

DEAR DOUG
WRITING ASSIGNMENT

Hey there!

Spring—it's so close I can almost taste it! I'm about ready to crawl out of my skin from being cooped up all winter doing nothing but studying. I'll be so glad when finals are over—I won't have to read a textbook for months!

Speaking of which, I've got a history exam I'm supposed to be cramming for right now. The gang met at the library last night to discuss some questions the professor gave us to research and write about. I guess I've always thought history was dull, but that everything written down actually happened… well, was based on fact at least. But Paige said that history isn't objective at all, since it's always told from the perspective of the winner. Do you think that is true?

Sarah said that there's no point to history, since everything that happens in life is based on chance. I would've put that attitude down to the blues (she got dumped last week), but Mark agreed with her. He said that the only way history means anything is if mankind helps to guide it in a positive direction. Do you agree that history doesn't have a point?

While we're on the subject, Nathan asked me the other day if I thought the stories in the Bible were actually true or if they were just myths people wrote to communicate truth. When I said that I've always believed the events in the Bible actually took place, he asked me what proof I had. I couldn't give him anything satisfying. I've never questioned what my Sunday school teachers told me. How do you know that the Bible is accurate and reliable?

I suppose history is important, but I'm more interested in the present. I mean, history's already happened and can't be changed, but that doesn't necessarily mean it's not important. Does Christianity have anything to say about history?

By the way, you probably want to know the latest on Amber and me. We've been hanging out together a lot, but she seems different somehow. She's quicker to get mad at me when the slightest hint of religion crosses my lips. I'm not sure what to do exactly. Your letters have gotten me more interested in worldviews and the Bible, and I don't want to slip back into being a wimpy Christian. But I've gotten really close to Amber and don't want to lose her either. I'm just not sure what to do. Anyway, I've got to go… procrastination is getting me nowhere!

Keep in touch,
Doug

Unit Ten

UNDERSTANDING THE TIMES

Conclusion

Topics:
Evangelism
Leadership

A Summit Ministries Curriculum

SECTION OUTLINE

180-DAY SYLLABUS

DAY	IN CLASS	HOMEWORK	
1	WATCH "Worldview Witnessing" video	READ <u>UTT</u> Textbook 'Conclusion 11.1-11.2'	
2	REVIEW "Worldview Witnessing" video questions	READ <u>UTT</u> Textbook 'Conclusion 11.3'	
3	READ <u>UTT</u> Textbook 'Conclusion 11.3'		
4	REVIEW <u>UTT</u> Textbook 'Conclusion 11.3' questions	READ <u>UTT</u> Textbook 'Conclusion 11.4'	
5	READ <u>UTT</u> Textbook 'Conclusion 11.5-11.6'	READ <u>UTT</u> Textbook 'History 10.5'	
6	REVIEW <u>UTT</u> Textbook 'Conclusion 11.4-11.5' questions		
7	WATCH "Secrets of the World Changers" video P1–2		
8	WATCH "Secrets of the World Changers" video P3–4		
9	WATCH "Secrets of the World Changers" video P5–6		
10	REVIEW "Secrets of the World Changers" video questions		
11	TAKE Final Test		
12			
13			
14			
15			

90-DAY SYLLABUS

DAY	IN CLASS	HOMEWORK	
1	WATCH "Worldview Witnessing" video	READ <u>UTT</u> Textbook 'Conclusion 11.3'	
2	REVIEW "Worldview Witnessing" video questions	READ <u>UTT</u> Textbook 'Conclusion 11.4-11.5'	
3	TAKE Final Test		
4			
5			

"WORLDVIEW WITNESSING"
WITH KEVIN BYWATER

I. _____: The defense of the Christian faith; to present reasons for why you believe what you believe

    A. Engaging the war of worldviews

        1. Jude 3

        2. 1 Peter 3:15–16

        3. Acts 17:2–4

    B. You can either ___dodge___ the bullets or ___pursuade___ your opponent
                                                   (disarm)

    C. Difficulties in apologetics

        1. Too many ___issues___

        2. Too little time

        3. Too much ___fear___

II. What happens when worldviews clash?

    A. ___Convert___

    B. Cower

    C. ___Compromise___

    D. Confirm

III. Developing probing and persuasive apologetics:

    A. Attitude: Refutation vs. ___pursuading people___

    B. Strategy: ___Questions___ vs. Statements

C. Probing the Worldview Iceberg:

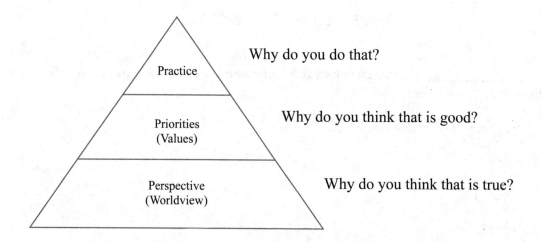

Practice	Why do you do that?
Priorities (Values)	Why do you think that is good?
Perspective (Worldview)	Why do you think that is true?

D. Some discerning and "disarming" questions:

1. What do you mean by ___that___?

2. How did you come to that ___conclusion___?

   i. Where did you get that information?

   ii. How do you know that to be true?

3. Have you ever considered (fill in the blank)?

   "Remember the 'golden rule' of asking questions: Ask of others only what you're willing for them to ask of you."

IV. Testing worldviews

A. Look for logical inconsistencies

B. Look for ___self-refuting___ ideas

C. Is the worldview actually livable?

D. It must be able to explain ___reality___

"WORLDVIEW WITNESSING"
VIDEO QUESTIONS

Answer the questions below on a separate sheet of paper and be prepared to review your answers in class.

1. What is apologetics? What are three key verses used in the discussion of apologetics? How are these verses applied?

2. What four things can occur when worldviews clash?

3. How does one persuade using apologetics?

4. What are some questions that can help us understand another's worldview? What are some discerning and disarming questions that can help others think through their worldview?

5. What are some good tests for worldview viability?

UNDERSTANDING THE TIMES
CONCLUSION QUESTIONS

Answer the questions below on a separate sheet of paper and be prepared to review your answers in class.

CONCLUSION 11.3

1. Why does it take faith to be an atheist?

2. According to naturalism, which came first: mind or matter? Why?

3. What are evolution's two biggest hurdles? Why?

4. Is there ample evidence for humanity's sinful nature?

5. What problems stem from the promotion of non-traditional families?

6. What are some inconsistencies inherent in the Marxist utopian worldview in general and socialism in particular?

7. What does Christianity postulate as the root of humanity's problems? How does Christianity propose to transform society?

8. What legal problems arise from the Secular Humanist and Marxist worldviews? How do Christians view the discipline of law?

9. What is scientism? What problems arise from this belief when applied to ethics?

10. What problems arise from scientism when applied to psychology?

CONCLUSION 11.4

11. What two things should Christians keep in mind when defending the biblical worldview?

12. Why is religious pluralism logically impossible?

13. What is wrong with the parable of the elephant?

14. Why can ethical relativists not live consistently?

15. What are a couple of areas of commonality Christians can use when speaking with someone who has been captured by the New Age worldview?

16. **Why is the Postmodern view of reality self-defeating?**

17. **What is wrong with the Postmodern view of language?**

18. **Why is the Postmodern rejection of truth and metanarratives incompatible with Christianity?**

19. **How are Postmodernists inconsistent when it comes to the subject of "social justice?"**

20. **How is the Postmodernist approach to history inconsistent?**

"SECRETS OF THE WORLD CHANGERS"
WITH JEFF MYERS

I. Living Like Royalty

"God uses ordinary people, with ordinary talents, to put forward into leadership situations so [they] can make an impact on the world for Jesus Christ."

  A. The person in the Bible who typifies leadership as it relates to young people is _____, who was…

    1. Probably a _____.

    2. Put in a position of great responsibility

    3. Responded with creativity and courage

      "For if you remain silent at this time, relief and deliverance for the Jews will arise from another place, but you and your father's family will perish. And who knows but that you have come to royal position for such a time as this?" — Esther 4:14

      "But you are a chosen people, a royal priesthood, a holy nation, a people belonging to God that you may declare the praises of Him who called you out of darkness into His wonderful light." — 1 Peter 2:9

  B. You were born to be _____.

II. The Foundation of Leadership From a Biblical Standpoint

  A. Jesus on leadership: "If anyone wants to be first he must be the very last, and the _____ of all." — Mark 9:35

  B. *Doulos*: One who _____ becomes a slave

    "Leadership is a willingness to rise to the bottom." — Dr. Glen Schulz

  C. You lead in direct proportion to your willingness to support the weight of your followers.

    "The more responsibility you are willing take for the lives of others, the more of a leader you will be."

  D. _____: A person who views the world from God's perspective, who exercises his or her gifts and talents with excellence and perseverance, and who strategically plans to serve others.

Conclusion

III. Four Aspects of a Breakthrough

A. _____: Seeing the world as God sees it

B. _____: Knowing where you fit in God's plan

C. _____: Getting the energy to live out God's plan

D. _____: Organizing your life around God's plan

PART TWO

IV. The Big Picture: Developing a Strategic Vision

"The first thing that distinguishes world-changing leaders from everyone else is their vision of the world. They have a stronger sense of how to influence the world through determination and creativity."

"The secret to discovering a sense of vision is learning to see the world as God sees it."

V. Strategic _____: Seeing the World As God Sees It

A. The lack of vision _____.

"Where there is no vision, the people perish." — Proverbs 29:18

B. Vision-driven people see the world…

1. The way it _____ is

…and…

2. The way they want it _____

C. Four characteristics that cause us to lose our vision

1. __Relativism__: People can't distinguish right from wrong

2. __Apathy__: People stop caring about others

3. __Cowardice__: People become too fearful to act on what is right

4. __Tyranny__: Those in power force their self-serving preferences on others

"In the absence of a biblical morality, a new elite will always come forward to dictate arbitrary absolutes to society." — Francis Schaeffer

5. This vision leads to: __Oppression__

"When the righteous thrive, the people rejoice; when the wicked rule, the people groan." — Proverbs 28:12

Conclusion

D. Four characteristics of an alternative vision:

1. ___Discernment___ : The ability to distinguish right from wrong and to prefer the right

2. ___Conviction___ : A personal concern about right and wrong for yourself and others

"See to it that no one takes you captive through hollow and deceptive philosophy." — Colossians 2:8

3. ___Courage___ : Overcoming fear to stand for right and oppose evil

4. ___Peace___ : Those in power rule by objective timeless standards of maintaining freedom with restraint

5. This vision leads to: ___Prosperity___

"Misfortune pursues the sinner, but prosperity is the reward of the righteous." — Proverbs 13:21

E. How to get a vision:

1. ___Notice___ the problem (Nehemiah)

2. ___Sense___ the urgency (Esther)

3. ___Anticipate___ involvement (Isaiah)

4. ___Commit___ to action (Deborah)

"In many ways, getting a vision is a skill, and like any skill, it improves with practice. As you improve your ability to get a vision of the world around you, you will improve in your influence in the lives of other people; and as a result, you will move toward becoming a world-changing leader."

PART THREE

VI. Living Like A Winner: Developing a Strategic Mission

"The second thing that distinguishes world-changing leaders from everyone else is their ability to tap into their reservoir of talents and gifts, in order to get more out of every situation and make the most of every opportunity."

VII. Strategic ___Mission___ : Knowing Where You Fit in God's Plan

A. Three crucial facts of Scripture that give us a sense of mission

1. God ___made___ you

"For you created my inmost being; you knit me together in my mother's womb. I praise you because I am fearfully and wonderfully made." — Psalm 139:13–14

2. God has ___gifted___ you to achieve

   "There are different kinds of gifts but the same Spirit… Now to each one the manifestation of the Spirit is given for the common good." — 1 Corinthians 12:4–7

3. God ___directs___ you through your actions

   "In his heart a man plans his course, but the Lord determines his steps." — Proverbs 16:9

B. How to develop a mission

   1. **R**___eview___: Look for clues in your life experiences

   2. **A**___nticipate___: Look ahead to determine a course of action

   3. **C**___onsult___: Get help from the "Solomons" in your life

   4. **E**___nact___: Do your best, recognizing that God will steer you

   "Your sense of mission does not emerge from other people. It comes from living out the design that God has given to you—that unique ability to do what he specifically has called you to do. And as you live out that sense of mission, you will become a world-changing leader who will make a difference in the world for Jesus Christ."

PART FOUR

VIII. Leadership Fitness: Developing Strategic Motivation

"The third thing that distinguishes world-changing leaders from everyone else is the way they use their energy to accomplish the things that they can accomplish."

IX. Strategic ___Motivation___: Getting the Energy to Live Out God's Plan

"Perseverance means moving on in spite of great difficulties, taking on the challenges, climbing the mountains of life, and continuing on even in the face of great obstacles."

"We develop a strategy… and then eventually our strategy begins to turn into stress."

A. How to deal with the stresses of life

   1. ___Stress___: A condition existing because of strain or deformation

   2. ___tension___: Either of two balancing forces tending to cause strain or deformation

   3. Stress is bad, but tension can be good

   4. ___Equilibrium___: A state of balance or equality between opposing forces

Conclusion

B. Developing equilibrium

    1. Recognize _destructive_ responses [to stress]

    2. Write down what is _bothering_ you

    3. Define a _sunset_ for each activity

    4. Don't _sacrifice_ your basic needs (sleep, food, exercise)

C. Staying motivated

    1. Understand true motivation

    Motivation: "A temporary condition in which individuals direct high levels of concentration and attention toward the competent completion of a task."— Professors Beatty and Payne

    2. A strategy for successful advancement

        i. Plan

        ii. Attack

        iii. Establish

        iv. Regroup (rest)

    3. Other ideas for staying motivated

        i. Challenge yourself regularly

        ii. Study heroes

        iii. Redeem the pockets of time

        iv. Maintain spiritual disciplines   _5 mins a day_

    "The way to stay motivated is to understand the sequence of plan, attack, establish, regroup; and to maintain the basic disciplines of using your time wisely. As you do those kinds of things, you will discover that motivation for most people is not a persistent state of high energy and a positive attitude; but the ability to press on in spite of great difficulties."

PART FIVE

X. Developing a Strategic Plan: Organizing Your Life around God's Plan

"The fourth thing that distinguishes world-changing leaders from everyone else is the way they plan carefully to achieve well-defined goals."

XI. Strategic Plan : Organizing Your Life around God's Plan

A. Learning to redeem the time .

"Be very careful how you live, making the most of every opportunity, because the days are evil." — Ephesians 5:15–16

1. Get a _planner_ and use it

2. Plan at the _beginning_ of the week

3. Plan based on your _mission_ and goals

4. _Focus_ on one or two areas each day

B. Learning to set _goals_

1. R_ecord_: Write it down

2. E_nvision_: Imagine the benefits

3. A_sk_: Seek help from experts

4. C_ollect_: Gain skills and knowledge

5. H_one_: Develop a plan of action

PART SIX

XII. As Soon As You Commit to This Process, _Satan_ Will Attack You!

> *Dear Christian Wimp:*
>
> *Who do you think you are? You'll never pull this off! See enclosed list.*
> *Your adversary, Satan*
>
> *Reasons why you'll never make it as a leader:*
> * *You don't have enough clout*
> * *No one will pay attention*
> * *You'll be too afraid*
> * *You're no match for me*

A. **Satan's attack:** "You don't have enough ___clout___"

Response: Your weakness is God's ___strength___

"Brothers, think of what you were when you were called. Not many of you were wise by human standards; not many were influential… But God chose the foolish things of the world to shame the wise; God chose the weak things of the world to shame the strong… so that no one may boast before him." — 1 Corinthians 1:26–29

B. **Satan's attack:** "No one will pay attention to you. You are too ___young___"

Response: Don't be intimidated… set the ___standard___

"Don't let anyone look down on you because you are young, but set an example for the believers in speech, conduct, faith, love, and purity." — 1 Timothy 4:12

C. **Satan's attack:** "You'll be ___too afraid___"

Response: God has given you ___boldness___

"For God did not give us a spirit of fear, but a spirit of power, of love, and of self-discipline." — 2 Timothy 1:7

D. **Satan's attack:** "You're no ___match___ for me"

Response: ___Victory___ is inevitable

"What, then, shall we say in response to this? If God is for us, who can be against us?… In all these things we are more than conquerors through him who loved us." — Romans 8:31, 37

XIII. What Is Worth Living (and Dying) For?

"The sin of our time is the sin that believes in nothing, cares for nothing, seeks to know nothing, interferes with nothing, enjoys nothing, hates nothing, finds purpose in nothing, lives for nothing, and remains alive because there is nothing for which it will die." — Dorothy Sayers

"SECRETS OF THE WORLD CHANGERS"
VIDEO QUESTIONS

Answer the questions below on a separate sheet of paper and be prepared to review your answers in class.

1. What did Jesus say about leadership? What are the characteristics of a Christian leader?

2. What is a strategic vision? What are four characteristics that cause us to lose our vision? What are four characteristics for an alternative vision? How do we get a vision?

3. What is a strategic mission? What are three crucial facts of Scripture that give us a sense of mission? How do we develop a mission?

4. What is a strategic motivation? How does one stay motivated?

5. What is a strategic plan? How do you redeem time? How do you set goals?

WORLDVIEW TRAINING

STUDENT MANUAL

UNDERSTANDING THE TIMES

Fact Sheets

A Summit Ministries Curriculum

Apologetics
Fact Sheet

KEY TERMS:

Argument from Design: an argument that states that if something exists that is designed, then it must have a designer

Apologetic [from the Greek word *apologia*]: An answer or a reasoned defense*

Apologetics: The field of theology that seeks to provide a reasoned defense of the Christian faith

Kalam Cosmological Argument: A rational reflection of three exhaustive dilemmas regarding the origin of the cosmos: 1) Did the universe have a beginning or has it always existed? 2) Was the beginning caused or uncaused? 3) Was the agent of cause personal or impersonal?

Negative Apologetics: Answers to objections to the Christian faith (defensive)

Positive Apologetics: Supplying reasons for believing the Christian faith (offensive)

Transcendental Argument: A rational comparison of atheism and theism that focuses on the practical outcomes of both worldviews

---

KEY VERSES:

Matthew 22:34–40   2 Corinthians 10:4–5   1 Peter 3:13–16
Acts 17:16ff   Colossians 2   Jude 3
Romans 12:1–4

KEY ORGANIZATIONS:

American Vision | www.americanvision.com | 770.222.7266 |

Biblical Worldview | www.christianworldview.net |

Christian Answers | www.christiananswers.net |

Christian Apologetics & Research Ministry | www.carm.org |

Christian Research Institute | www.equip.org | 888.700.0274 |

Probe Ministries | www.probe.org | 972.480.0240 |

Tekton Apologetics Ministries | www.tektonics.org |

Stand to Reason | www.str.org | 800.273.2766 |

Summit Ministries | www.summit.org | 719.685.9103 |

---

* Our familiarity with the term apology usually derives from the context of saying we are "sorry" for something we did that was wrong. This is not the original sense of the term. As can be seen from the Greek, an "apologetic" is a reasoned defense of action(s) or belief(s).

Fact Sheets

KEY PUBLICATIONS:

Areopagus Journal | **Apologetics Resource Center** | www.arcapologetics.org | 205.408.0136 |

Biblical Worldview | **American Vision** | www.americanvision.org |

Christian Research Journal | **Christian Research Institute** | www.equip.org |

First Things | **Institute of Religion and Public Life** | www.firstthings.com |

Southern Baptist Journal of Theology | **Southern Baptist Theological Seminary** | www.sbts.edu |

Summit Journal | **Summit Ministries** | www.summit.org |

KEY SOURCES:
(recommended titles appear in brown)

GENERAL APOLOGETICS

Bahnsen, Greg L. *Always Ready: Directions for Defending the Faith*. Atlanta: American Vision, 1996.

Beckwith, Francis, William Lane Craig, and James Porter Moreland, eds. *To Everyone an Answer: A Case for the Christian Worldview*. Downers Grove, IL: InterVarsity, 2004.

Beisner, E. Calvin. *Answers for Atheists, Agnostics, and Other Thoughtful Skeptics: Dialogs About Christian Faith and Life*. Wheaton, IL: Crossway, 1993.

Carroll, Vincent, and Dave Shiflett. *Christianity on Trial: Arguments against Anti-religious Bigotry*. San Francisco: Encounter Books, 2002.

Copan, Paul. *That's Just Your Interpretation: Responding to Skeptics Who Challenge Your Faith*. Grand Rapids, MI: Baker, 2001.

Corduan, Winfried. *No Doubt About It: The Case for Christianity*. Nashville: Broadman & Holman, 1997.

Evans, C. Stephen. *Pocket Dictionary of Apologetics and Philosophy of Religion*. Downers Grove, IL: InterVarsity, 2002.

Follis, Bryan A. *Truth with Love: The Apologetics of Francis Schaeffer*. Wheaton, IL: Crossway, 2006.

Geisler, Norman L. *Baker Encyclopedia of Christian Apologetics, Baker Reference Library*. Grand Rapids, MI: Baker, 1999.

———. *Christian Apologetics*. Grand Rapids, MI: Baker, 1976.

Geisler, Norman L., and Peter Bocchino. *Unshakable Foundations*. Minneapolis: Bethany, 2001.

Geisler, Norman L., and Ronald M. Brooks. *When Skeptics Ask*. Wheaton, IL: Victor, 1990.

Geisler, Norman L., and Paul K. Hoffman. *Why I Am a Christian: Leading Thinkers Explain Why They Believe*. Grand Rapids, MI: Baker, 2001.

Kreeft, Peter. *Fundamentals of the Faith: Essays in Christian Apologetics*. San Francisco: Ignatius, 1988.

Kreeft, Peter, and Ronald K. Tacelli. *Handbook of Christian Apologetics: Hundreds of Answers to Crucial Questions*. Downers Grove, IL: InterVarsity, 1994.

Lewis, C. S. *Mere Christianity*. San Francisco: HarperSanFrancisco, 2001.

———. *The Pilgrim's Regress: An Allegorical Apology for Christianity, Reason, and Romanticism*. Grand Rapids, MI: Eerdmans, 1992.

McDowell, Josh. *Josh McDowell Answers Five Tough Questions*. Wheaton, IL: Tyndale, 1991.

———. *The New Evidence That Demands a Verdict*. Nashville: Thomas Nelson, 1999.

McDowell, Josh, and Bob Hostetler. *Beyond Belief to Convictions*. Wheaton, IL: Tyndale, 2002.

McGrath, Alister E. *Explaining Your Faith*. Grand Rapids, MI: Baker, 1996.

———. *Intellectuals Don't Need God and Other Modern Myths: Building Bridges to Faith through Apologetics*. Grand Rapids, MI: Zondervan, 1993.

Moreland, James Porter. *Scaling the Secular City: A Defense of Christianity*. Grand Rapids, MI: Baker, 1987.

Fact Sheets

Nash, Ronald H. *Faith and Reason: Searching for a Rational Faith.* Grand Rapids, MI: Baker, 1988.

Noebel, David A. *Understanding the Times: The Collision of Today's Competing Worldviews.* Manitou Springs, CO: Summit Press, 2006.

Plantinga, Alvin. *Warranted Christian Belief.* New York: Oxford University Press, 2000.

Pratt, Richard L. *Every Thought Captive: A Study Manual for the Defense of Christian Truth.* Phillipsburg, NJ: Presbyterian & Reformed, 1979.

Rhodes, Ron. *Answering the Objections of Atheists, Agnostics, and Skeptics.* Eugene, OR: Harvest, 2006.

Samples, Kenneth R. *Without a Doubt: Answering the 20 Toughest Faith Questions.* Grand Rapids, MI: Baker, 2004.

Schaeffer, Francis A. *Death in the City.* Wheaton, IL: Crossway, 2002.

———. *The God Who Is There.* Downers Grove, IL: InterVarsity, 1998.

Strobel, Lee. *The Case for Christ: A Journalist's Personal Investigation of the Evidence for Jesus.* Grand Rapids, MI: Zondervan, 1998.

Wright, N. T. *Simply Christian: Why Christianity Makes Sense.* San Francisco: HarperSanFrancisco, 2006.

Van Til, Cornelius. *The Defense of the Faith.* Philadelphia: Presbyterian & Reformed, 1955.

PROOF OF GOD

Boa, Kenneth, and Robert M. Bowman. *20 Compelling Evidences That God Exists: Discover Why Believing in God Makes So Much Sense.* Tulsa, OK: RiverOak Publishing, 2002.

Geisler, Norman L., and Frank Turek. *I Don't Have Enough Faith to Be an Atheist.* Wheaton, IL: Crossway, 2004.

McGrath, Alister E. *Intellectuals Don't Need God and Other Modern Myths: Building Bridges to Faith through Apologetics.* Grand Rapids, MI: Zondervan, 1993.

Moreland, James Porter. *Scaling the Secular City: A Defense of Christianity.* Grand Rapids, MI: Baker, 1987.

Moreland, James Porter, and Kai Nielsen. *Does God Exist? The Great Debate.* New York: Prometheus, 1993.

Nicholi, Armand M. *The Question of God: C. S. Lewis and Sigmund Freud Debate God, Love, Sex, and the Meaning of Life.* New York: Free Press, 2002.

Plantinga, Alvin. *God and Other Minds: A Study of the Rational Justification of Belief in God.* Ithaca, NY: Cornell University Press, 1990.

———. *God, Freedom, and Evil.* Grand Rapids, MI: Eerdmans, 1977.

PROBLEM OF EVIL/PAIN

Lewis, C. S. *The Problem of Pain.* San Francisco: HarperSanFrancisco, 2001.

Plantinga, Alvin. *God, Freedom, and Evil.* Grand Rapids, MI: Eerdmans, 1977.

Wright, N. T. *Evil and the Justice of God.* Downers Grove, IL: InterVarsity, 2006.

Zacharias, Ravi K. *Deliver Us from Evil: Restoring the Soul in a Disintegrating Culture.* Dallas: Word, 1996.

Art & Culture
Fact Sheet

Key Verses:
Exodus 35:30–35   Ephesians 5:19
Colossians 3:16   Philippians 4:8

Key Organizations:

Art and Christianity Enquiry | www.acetrust.org | 020.7374.0600 |

Center for the Study of Popular Culture | www.rightwingwatch.org |

Christians in the Arts Networking | 617.783.5667 |

Christians in the Visual Arts | www.civa.org | 978.867.4124 |

Image | www.imagejournal.org | 206.281.2988 |

Key Publications:
Books and Culture | **Christianity Today** | www.christianitytoday.com/bc/ |

Key Quotes:

"Art worthy of a Christian is defined by skilled human creativity that reflects God's truth or God's beauty."[1]

"Ironically, the ability to say that a work of art can be aesthetically good, but false in the worldview it assumes provides an opportunity for the cultivation of moral capacities that popular culture cannot offer."[2]

"The best way to overcome banality is to demand something better—to seek out, as Paul wrote in Philippians, whatever is noble, right, pure, admirable, and to 'think on these things. Paul is commanding us to discipline ourselves to reflect on excellence. And he doesn't limit that to spiritual things, either. The command applies to everything—the music we listen to, the books and magazines we read, the films we watch."[3]

"Issues of quality and standards have been foolishly abandoned by liberals, who now interpret aesthetics as nothing but a mask for ideology. As a result the far right has gained enormously. What madness is abroad in the land when only neoconservatives will defend the grandeur of art? This does not mean that Christianity can be successfully expressed in every style. Some styles are wholly interwoven with aberrant philosophies (indeed, such styles are often nothing more than philosophical statements, which is why they are so bad aesthetically). Sometimes, Christians follow a particular style uncritically without recognizing the implicit contradictions between their faith and the style they are using to express it. Such incompatibility between form and content results in bad Christian art. (Late Victorian sentimentality, heavy metal nihilism, and pop culture consumerism would not seem to accord with a Biblical sensibility, but such misbegotten hybrids fill the Christian bookstores.)"[4]

[1] J.F. Baldwin, Jr., Summit Ministries Open Forum, July 12, 1994.
[2] Kenneth A. Myers, *All God's Children and Blue Suede Shoes* (Wheaton, IL: Crossway, 1990), 98.
[3] Chuck Colson, "Elvis Mania," *Breakpoint with Chuck Colson*, June 1993, 17.
[4] Gene Edward Veith, Jr., *State of the Arts: From Bezalel to Mapplethorpe* (Wheaton, IL: Crossway, 1991), 165.

KEY SOURCES:

(recommended titles appear in brown)

ART

Brand, Hilary and Adrienne Chaplin. *Art and Soul: Signposts for Christians in the Arts*. Carlisle, CA: Piquant, 2001.

Rookmaker, H. R. *Modern Art and the Death of a Culture*. Westester, IL: Crossway, 1994.

Ryken, Leland. "The Creative Arts," *The Making of a Christian Mind: A Christian World View and the Academic Enterprise*, Arthur Frank Holmes, ed. Downers Grove, IL: InterVarsity, 1985, 105–131.

———. *The Liberated Imagination: Thinking Christianly About the Arts*. Wheaton, IL: H. Shaw, 1989.

———. "The Paradisal Imagination." *Christianity and the Arts 4* (1997): 6–10.

Ryken, Philip Graham. *Art for God's Sake: A Call to Recover the Arts*. Phillipsburg, NJ: P&R Publishers, 2006.

Schaeffer, Francis A. *Art and the Bible*. Downers Grove, IL: InterVarsity, 1973.

Turner, Steve. "Being There: A Vision for Christianity and the Arts." *Trinity Seminary Review 21* (1999): 25–33.

Veith, Gene Edward. "Christianity and Culture: God's Double Sovereignty." *Modern Reformation 6*, no. 1 (1997).

———. "Must Art Be 'Christian' To Be Good." *Christianity Today*, February 1984, 69.

———. "A New Creative Force." *Christianity and the Arts 4* (1997): 37, 39–40.

———. *State of the Arts: From Bezalel to Mapplethorpe*. Wheaton, IL: Crossway, 1991.

CULTURE

Barzun, Jacques. *From Dawn to Decadence: 500 Years of Western Cultural Life*. New York: HarperCollins, 2000.

DeMoss, Robert G. *Learn to Discern*. Grand Rapids, MI: Zondervan, 1997.

Ferguson, Everett. *The Church of Christ: A Biblical Ecclesiology for Today*. Grand Rapids, MI: Eerdmans, 1996.

Hayes, Edward L. and Charles R. Swindoll. *The Church: The Body of Christ in the World of Today*. Nashville: Word, 1999.

Lewis, C. S. *The Abolition of Man*. San Francisco: HarperSanFrancisco, 2001.

Medved, Michael. *Hollywood vs. America: Popular Culture and the War on Traditional Values*. Grand Rapids, MI: Zondervan, 1992.

Myers, Ken. "Is Popular Culture Either?" *Modern Reformation 6*, no. 1 (1997).

Minnery, Tom. *Why You Can't Stay Silent: A Biblical Mandate to Shape Our Culture*. Wheaton, IL: Tyndale, 2001.

Myers, Ken. *All God's Children and Blue Suede Shoes*. Westchester, IL: Crossway, 1989.

Newbigin, Lesslie. *Foolishness to the Greeks: The Gospel and Western Culture*. Grand Rapids, MI: Eerdmans, 1986.

Postman, Neil. *Technopoly: The Surrender of Culture to Technology*. New York: Vintage, 1993.

Rookmaker, H. R. *Modern Art and the Death of a Culture*. Westester, IL: Crossway, 1994.

Schaeffer, Francis A. *A Christian View of Philosophy and Culture*. Westchester, IL: Crossway, 1982.

EDUCATION

Black, Jim Nelson. *Freefall of the American University: How Our Colleges Are Corrupting the Minds and Morals of the Next Generation*. Nashville: WND Books, 2004.

D'Souza, Dinesh. *Illiberal Education: The Politics of Race and Sex on Campus*. New York: Free Press, 1991.

Shortt, Bruce N. *The Harsh Truth About Public Schools*. Vallecito, CA: Chalcedon Foundation, 2004.

Sowell, Thomas. *Inside American Education: The Decline, the Deception, the Dogmas*. New York: Free Press, 1992.

Shapiro, Ben. *Brainwashed: How Universities Indoctrinate America's Youth*. Nashville: WND Books, 2004.

Stormer, John A. *None Dare Call It Education*. Florissant, MO: Liberty Bell Press, 1998.

ENTERTAINMENT

Gabler, Neal. *Live the Movie: How Entertainment Conquered Reality*. New York: Knopf, 1998.

Godawa, Brian. *Hollywood Worldviews: Watching Films with Wisdom and Discernment*. Downers Grove, IL: InterVarsity, 2002.

Postman, Neil. *Amusing Ourselves to Death: Public Discourse in the Age of Show Business*. New York: Viking, 1985.

Bioethics & Ethics
Fact Sheet

Key Terms:

ETHICS	**Cultural Relativism:** The belief that truth and morals are relative to one's culture **Karma:** The total effect of one's actions and conduct during each phase of existence, determining his/her destiny **Moral Absolutes:** The belief that an absolute ethical standard exists for all individuals regardless of era or culture **Moral Relativism:** The ethical belief that morals are relative to the individual **Proletariat Morality:** The ethical belief that whatever advances the proletariat and the cause of communism is morally good and whatever hinders the proletariat or communism is morally evil **Utilitarianism:** An ethical framework that posits that all action should be directed toward achieving the greatest utility for the greatest number of people (that the end justifies the means)
ABORTION	**Law of Biogenesis:** Living things reproduce after their own kind **Embryo:** An unborn baby from conception to the eighth week of gestation **Fetus:** An unborn baby from the eighth week of gestation until birth
BIOETHICS	**Bio:** Natural and living **Bioethics:** Right conduct in the area of biotechnology **Imago Dei:** Possessing the image of God **Personhood:** The debate in philosophy over what constitutes "being a person" **Viability:** The ability to survive on one's own and grow to adulthood
BIOTECHNOLOGY*	**Biotechnology:** Industrial use of living organisms or the application of technique to living organisms **Artificial Intelligence:** An artificial mechanism that can mimic human thinking and independence **Cybernetics:** Integration of man and machine **Nanotechnology:** Engineering and manufacturing at the molecular level **Stem Cell:** Cells in your body that have not been diversified into heart cells, brain cells, etc. **Transgenics:** Insertion of DNA of one species into the genetic code of another species **Xenotransplantation:** The use of animal tissues, organs, or cells transplanted to or used for contact with human subjects

*For additional terms, see www.biotechterms.org

Summit Ministries © 2009

EUTHANASIA	**Active Euthanasia (also known as mercy *killing*):** Occurs when a medical professional deliberately acts to cause the death of a patient

Passive Euthanasia (also known as mercy *dying*): Occurs when a medical professional withdraws extraordinary medical treatment consequently allowing a patient's demise

Voluntary Euthanasia: Occurs when an uncoerced patient chooses to end his or her life

Involuntary Euthanasia: Occurs when a second party makes the decision about whether active or passive measures should be taken to end a patient's life |

KEY FACTS:

ABORTION*	**Statistics:**
- Approximately 126,000 abortions are performed worldwide each day
- Approximately 46 million abortions are performed worldwide each year
- The lifetime average worldwide is about 1 abortion per woman

The Unborn:
- Day 30—heart begins to beat
- Day 40—displays measurable brainwaves
- Day 45—identifiable arms and legs
- Day 70—fingers and genitals appear and the child's face is recognizably human
- The majority of abortions are preformed between the seventh and tenth weeks |
| EUTHANASIA | **Jurisdictions with laws that specifically permit euthanasia:**
- Oregon
- The Netherlands
- Belgium |
| STEM CELL | **Embryonic Stem Cell Research:**
- **K**ills the embryo when extracted
- Provides no scientific achievement

Non-embryonic (Adult) Stem Cell Research:
- Does not kill a human being
- Continues to provide great scientific advancement |

KEY VERSES:

Genesis 1:26–31; 9:6	Proverbs 14:12; 16:25; 24:11–12	1 Corinthians 6:12–20
Exodus 20:13; 21:22–23	Isaiah 5:20–23	Matthew 7:13
Deuteronomy 32:39	Amos 5:15	Romans 1:18–32; 12:9
Psalm 12:8; 139:13–16	Jeremiah 1:5	Hebrews 5:14
Job 42:1–6	Mark 1:41	James 1:27; 2:14–17

*For additional statistics, see The Alan Guttmacher Institute, www.agi-usa.org

KEY ORGANIZATIONS:

BIOETHICS	**Center for Bioethics and Human Dignity** | www.cbhd.org | 847.317.8180 | **Council for Biotechnology Policy** | www.waragainsttheweak.com | 888.257.7730 | **Do No Harm** | www.stemcellresearch.org | 202.347.6840 |
ABORTION	**Concerned Women for America** | www.cwfa.org | **Crisis Pregnancy Centers** | www.crisispregnancy.com | 480.446.0500 | **Eagle Forum** | www.eagleforum.org | 618.462.5415 | **Justice for All** | http://jfaweb.org | 316.683.6426 | **Life Training Institute** | http://prolifetraining.com | 719.264.7861 | **National Right to Life** | www.nrlc.org | 202.626.8800 |

KEY QUOTES:

ETHICS

"The fundamental question of ethics is, who makes the rules? God or men? The theistic answer is that God makes them. The humanist answer is that men make them. This distinction between theism and humanism is the fundamental division in moral theory."[1]

"No inherent moral or ethical laws exist, nor are there absolute guiding principles for human society. The universe cares nothing for us and we have no ultimate meaning in life."[2]

"We can rationally discuss and argue with each other about right and wrong without resorting to the claim that ethical judgments are merely subjective or relative and that all such judgments have equal validity. For to claim the latter logically leads one to the bizarre judgment that Mother Teresa is no more and no less virtuous than Adolf Hitler."[3]

"If there is no absolute beyond man's ideas, then there is no final appeal to judge between individuals and groups whose moral judgments conflict. We are merely left with conflicting opinions."[4]

ABORTION

"Many people are very, very concerned with children in India, with the children of Africa where quite a few die of hunger, and so on. Many people are also concerned about all the violence in this great country of the United States. These concerns are very good. But often these same people are not concerned with the millions who are being killed by the deliberate decision of their own mothers. And this is what is the greatest destroyer of peace today—abortion, which brings people to such blindness."[5]

---

[1] Max Hocutt, "Toward an Ethic of Mutual Accommodation," *Humanist Ethics*, Morris B. Storer, ed. (Buffalo: Prometheus Books, 1980), 137.
[2] William Provine, "Scientists, Face It! Science and Religion are Incompatible," *The Scientist* (September 5, 1988).
[3] Frank Beckwith, "Philosophical Problems with Moral Relativism," *Christian Research Journal* (Fall 1993).
[4] Francis A. Schaeffer, *How Should We Then Live?* (Old Tappan, NJ: Fleming H. Revell, 1976), 145.
[5] Mother Teresa, quoted in Cal Thomas, "Meek Mother Teresa delivers a verbal knockout punch," *Colorado Springs Gazette Telegraph* (February 9, 1994).

Fact Sheets

"'The nurses have to look at the ultrasound picture to gauge how far along the baby is for an abortion, because the larger the pregnancy, the more you get paid. It was very important for us to do that. But the turnover definitely got greater when we started using ultrasound. We lost two nurses—they couldn't take looking at it. Some of the other staff left also.' What about the women having the abortions? Do they see the ultrasound? 'They are never allowed to look at the ultrasound because we knew that if they so much as heard the heartbeat, they wouldn't want to have the abortion.'"[6]

"The fact that restricting access to abortion has tragic side effects does not, in itself, show that the restrictions are unjustified, since murder is wrong regardless of the consequences of prohibiting it; and the appeal to the right to control one's body, which is generally construed as a property right, is at best a rather feeble argument for the permissibility of abortion. Mere ownership does not give me the right to kill innocent people whom I find on my property, and indeed I am apt to be held responsible if such people injure themselves while on my property. It is equally unclear that I have any moral right to expel an innocent person from my property when I know that doing so will result in his death."[7]

"A nurse who had worked in an abortion clinic for less than a year said her most troubling moments came not in the procedure room but afterwards. Many times, she said, women who had just had abortions would lie in the recovery room and cry, 'I've just killed my baby. I've just killed my baby.' 'I don't know what to say to these women,' the nurse told the group. 'Part of me thinks "Maybe they're right."'"[8]

BIOETHICS

"Cloning and the biotech agenda are even worse news for human dignity than abortion. Not only are we taking upon ourselves the godlike prerogative of ending human life as we choose, but we also are attempting to appropriate the prerogative of making human life as we choose."[9]

EUTHANASIA

"It's sad to say, but euthanasia will someday be legalized. There's already a thrust for it legislatively. We shouldn't allow for exceptions because hard cases make bad law. But some doctors are already deciding when the quality of life is over. A lot of it goes on without being prosecuted."[10]

KEY SOURCES/CRITIQUES:
(recommended titles appear in brown)

ETHICS

Bennett, William J. *The Book of Virtues: A Treasury of Great Moral Stories*. New York: Simon & Schuster, 1993.
———. *The Moral Compass: Stories for a Life's Journey*. New York: Simon & Schuster, 1995.
Burke, Thomas J., ed. *The Christian Vision: Man and Morality*. Hillsdale, MI: Hillsdale College Press, 1986.
Chamberlain, Paul. *Can We Be Good without God?* Downers Grove, IL: InterVarsity, 1996.
Davis, John Jefferson. *Evangelical Ethics: Issues Facing the Church Today*. Phillipsburg, NJ: P&R Pub., 2004.
Douma, Jochem. *Responsible Conduct: Principles of Christian Ethics*. Phillipsburg, NJ: P&R Publishers, 2003.
Geisler, Norman L. *Christian Ethics* (Grand Rapids, MI: Baker, 1989.
———. *Ethics: Alternatives and Issues*. Grand Rapids, MI: Zondervan, 1971.
Grenz, Stanley J., and Jay T. Smith. *Pocket Dictionary of Ethics*. Downers Grove, IL: InterVarsity, 2003.
Lewis, C. S. *God in the Dock: Essays on Theology and Ethics*. Grand Rapids, MI: Eerdmans, 1970.

---

[6] Dr. Joseph Randall, who performed over 32,000 abortions, quoted in David Kupelian and Mark Masters, "Pro-Choice 1991: skeletons in the closet," *New Dimensions* (September/October 1991).
[7] Pro-choice philosopher Mary Anne Warren, quoted in Randy Alcorn, *Pro Life Answers to Pro Choice Arguments* (Portland: Multnomah, 1992), 86.
[8] Diane M. Gianelli, "Abortion providers share inner conflicts," *American Medical News* (July 12, 1993).
[9] Charles Colson, *Breakpoint Radio Broadcast* (January 2, 2003).
[10] "A matter of life and death," Assemblies of God, USA, at http://pentecostalevangel.ag.org/

Fact Sheets

Rae, Scott B. *Moral Choices: An Introduction to Ethics*. Grand Rapids, MI: Zondervan, 2000.

Torrance, Alan and Michael Banner, eds. *The Doctrine of God and Theological Ethics*. Edinburgh: T&T Clark, 2005.

Wenham, Gordon J. *Story as Torah: Reading Old Testament Narrative Ethically*. Grand Rapids, MI: Baker, 2004.

Wilkens, Steve. *Beyond Bumper Sticker Ethics: An Introduction to Theories of Right & Wrong*. Downers Grove, IL: InterVarsity, 1995.

ABORTION (CRITIQUE)

Alcorn, Randy C. *Prolife Answers to Prochoice Arguments*. Portland: Multnomah, 1992.

———. *Why Prolife?* Sisters, OR: Multnomah, 2004.

Beckwith, Francis. *Abortion and the Sanctity of Human Life*. Joplin, MO: College Press, 2000.

———. "Abortion, Bioethics, and Personhood: A Philosophical Reflection." *Review of Ethics in a New Millennium. Southern Baptist Journal of Theology 4*, no. 1 (2000): 16–25.

———. *Politically Correct Death: Answering the Arguments for Abortion Rights*. Grand Rapids, MI: Baker, 1993.

———. "Roe V. Wade: Its Logic and Its Legacy." *Southern Baptist Journal of Theology 7*, no. 2 (2003): 4-28.

Beckwith, Francis and Norman L. Geisler. *Matters of Life and Death: Calm Answers to Tough Questions About Abortion and Euthanasia*. Grand Rapids, MI: Baker, 1991.

Brown, Harold O. J. *Death before Birth*. Nashville: Thomas Nelson, 1977.

Farish, Stephen E. "Biblical Principles Touching on the Question of Abortion and the Sanctity of Human Life." *Southern Baptist Journal of Theology 4*, no. 1 (2000): 76–85.

Fournier, Keith A. and William D. Watkins. *In Defense of Life: Taking a Stand against the Culture of Death*. Colorado Springs, CO: NavPress, 1996.

Garton, Jean Staker. *Who Broke the Baby?* Minneapolis: Bethany, 1998.

Gorman, Michael J. *Abortion and the Early Church*. Downers Grove, IL: InterVarsity, 1982.

Grant, George. *Grand Illusions: The Legacy of Planned Parenthood*. Nashville: Cumberland House, 2000.

Hoffmeier, James Karl, ed. *Abortion: A Christian Understanding and Response*. Grand Rapids, MI: Baker, 1987.

Kasun, Jacqueline R. *The War against Population: The Economics and Ideology of World Population Control*. San Francisco: Ignatius, 1999.

Koop, C. Everett and Francis A. Schaeffer. *Whatever Happened to the Human Race?* Westchester, IL: Crossway, 1983.

Koukl, Greg. "Only One Question: Compelling Answers to the Abortion Rights Challenge." *Areopagus Journal 1*, no. 4 (2001): 11–17.

Mitchell, C. Ben. "Persons Beyond Roe V. Wade: The Post-Human Age?" *Southern Baptist Journal of Theology 7*, no. 2 (2003): 68–77.

———. "The Legacy of Roe V. Wade for Bioethics." *Southern Baptist Journal of Theology 7*, no. 2 (2003): 30–39.

Montgomery, John Warwick. *Slaughter of the Innocents: Abortion, Birth Control, and Divorce in Light of Science, Law, and Theology*. Westchester, IL: Cornerstone, 1981.

Moreland, James Porter and Norman L. Geisler. *The Life and Death Debate: Moral Issues of Our Time*. New York: Praeger, 1990.

Weldon, John Ankerberg. "What Does the Bible Teach About Abortion?" *Areopagus Journal 1*, no. 4 (2001): 7–10.

BIOETHICS

Beckwith, Francis and Norman L. Geisler. *Matters of Life and Death: Calm Answers to Tough Questions About Abortion and Euthanasia*. Grand Rapids, MI: Baker, 1991.

Cameron, Nigel M., Scott E. Daniels, and Barbara White, eds. *Bioengagement: Making a Christian Difference through Bioethics Today*. Grand Rapids, MI: Eerdmans, 2000.

Fournier, Keith A. and William D. Watkins. *In Defense of Life: Taking a Stand against the Culture of Death*. Colorado Springs, CO: NavPress, 1996.

Kilner, John Frederic, C. Christopher Hook, and Diane B. Uustal, eds. *Cutting-Edge Bioethics: A Christian Exploration of Technologies and Trends*. Grand Rapids, MI: Eerdmans, 2002.

Koop, C. Everett and Francis A. Schaeffer. *Whatever Happened to the Human Race?* Westchester, IL: Crossway, 1983.

Moreland, James Porter, and Norman L. Geisler. The Life and Death Debate: Moral Issues of Our Time. New York, NY: Praeger, 1990.

Fact Sheets

CLONING

Annas, G. J. "Why We Should Ban Human Cloning." *New England Journal of Medicine 339*, no. 2 (1998): 122–25.

Kilner, John Frederic and C. Ben Mitchell. *Does God Need Our Help? Cloning, Assisted Suicide, and Other Challenges in Bioethics*. Wheaton, IL: Tyndale, 2003.

Lester, Lane P. and James C. Hefley. *Human Cloning: Playing God or Scientific Progress?* Grand Rapids, MI: Fleming H. Revell, 1998.

Robertson, J. A. "Human Cloning and the Challenge of Regulation." *New England Journal of Medicine 339*, no. 2 (1998): 119–22.

EUTHANASIA (CRITIQUE)

Kilner, John Frederic. *Life on the Line: Ethics, Aging, Ending Patients' Lives, and Allocating Vital Resources*. Grand Rapids, MI: Eerdmans, 1992.

———. *Who Lives? Who Dies? Ethical Criteria in Patient Selection*. New Haven, CT: Yale University Press, 1990.

Kilner, John Frederic, Arlene B. Miller, and Edmund D. Pellegrino, eds. *The Center for Bioethics and Human Dignity Presents Dignity and Dying: A Christian Appraisal*. Grand Rapids, MI: Eerdmans, 1996.

Kilner, John Frederic and C. Ben Mitchell. *Does God Need Our Help? Cloning, Assisted Suicide, and Other Challenges in Bioethics*. Wheaton, IL: Tyndale, 2003.

Kilner, John Frederic, Robert D. Orr, and Judy Allen Shelly, eds. *The Changing Face of Health Care: A Christian Appraisal of Managed Care, Resource Allocation, and Patient-Caregiver Relationships*. Grand Rapids, MI: Eerdmans, 1998.

Orr, Robert D. "The Physician-Assisted Suicide: Is It Ever Justified." *Areopagus Journal 1*, no. 4 (2001): 20–26.

Pankratz, H. Robert C. and Richard M. Welsh. "A Christian Response to Euthanasia, Part 1." *U-TURN 3*, no. 2 (1995).

———. "A Christian Response to Euthanasia, Part 2." *U-TURN 3*, no. 3 (1995).

Stewart, Gary. *Basic Questions on End of Life Decisions*. Grand Rapids, MI: Kregel, 1998.

MORAL ABSOLUTES

Copan, Paul. "'Who Are You to Judge Others?' in Defense of Making Moral Judgments." *Areopagus Journal,* vol. 1, no. 3 (July 2001).

Henry, Carl F. *Christian Personal Ethics*. Grand Rapids, MI: Eerdmans, 1957.

McDowell, Josh and Norman L. Geisler. *Love Is Always Right: A Defense of the One Moral Absolute* (Dallas: Word, 1996).

MORAL RELATIVISM

Beckwith, Francis and Gregory Koukl. *Relativism: Feet Firmly Planted in Mid-Air* (Grand Rapids, MI: Baker, 1998).

Feinberg, John S. and Paul D. Feinberg. *Ethics for a Brave New World*. (Wheaton, IL: Crossway, 1993).

George, Robert P. and John J. Diluilo. *The Clash of Orthodoxies: Law, Religion, and Morality in Crisis*. Wilmington, DE: Intercollegiate Studies Institute, 2001.

Kilpatrick, William. *Why Johnny Can't Tell Right from Wrong*. New York: Simon & Schuster, 1992.

Wiker, Benjamin. *Moral Darwinism: How We Became Hedonists*. Downers Grove, IL: InterVarsity, 2002.

PERSONHOOD

Beckwith, Francis J. "Abortion, Bioethics, and Personhood: A Philosophical Reflection." *Southern Baptist Journal of Theology 4*, no. 1 (2000): 16–25.

Mitchell, C. Ben. "Persons Beyond Roe V. Wade: The Post-Human Age?" *Southern Baptist Journal of Theology 7*, no. 2 (2003): 68–77.

Moreland, J. P. and Scott B. Rae. *Body and Soul: Human Nature and the Crisis in Ethics*. Downers Grove, IL: InterVarsity, 2000.

Fact Sheets

REPRODUCTION

Kilner, John Frederic, Paige C. Cunningham, and W. David Hager, eds. *The Reproduction Revolution: A Christian Appraisal of Sexuality, Reproductive Technologies, and the Family*. Grand Rapids, MI: Eerdmans, 2000.

Kilner, John Frederic, Rebecca Davis Pentz, and Frank E. Young, eds. *The Center for Bioethics and Human Dignity Presents Genetic Ethics: Do the Ends Justify the Genes?* Grand Rapids, MI: Eerdmans, 1997.

Stewart, Gary. *Basic Questions on Sexuality and Reproductive Technology* Grand Rapids, MI: Kregel 1998.

ROBOTICS AND ARTIFICIAL INTELLIGENCE

Craelius, W. "The Bionic Man: Restoring Mobility." *Science 295*, no. 5557 (2002): 1018–21.

Gomes, L. "No Need to Worry, Your Computer Isn't after Your Job." *Wall Street Journal* (2002).

Vogel, G. "Part Man, Part Computer: Researcher Tests the Limits." *Science 295*, no. 5557 (2002): 1020.

SOCIAL INVOLVEMENT

Grant, George. *Bringing in the Sheaves: Transforming Poverty into Productivity*. (Brentwood, TN: Wolgemuth & Hyatt, 1988.

———. *The Micah Mandate*. Chicago, IL: Moody, 1995.

Henry, Carl F. *Aspects of Christian Social Ethics: The Payton Lectures, 1963*. Grand Rapids, MI: Eerdmans, 1964.

STEM CELL RESEARCH

Barinaga, M. "Fetal Neuron Grafts Pave the Way for Stem Cell Therapies." *Science 287*, no. 5457 (2000): 1421–22.

Perry, D. "Patients' Voices: The Powerful Sound in the Stem Cell Debate." *Science 287*, no. 5457 (2000): 1423.

Regalado, A. ""Supercell" Controversy Sets Off a Scientists' Civil War." *Wall Street Journal* (2002).

Weissman, I. L. "Stem Cells: Scientific, Medical, and Political Issues." *New England Journal of Medicine 346*, no. 20 (2002): 1576–79.

———. "Translating Stem and Progenitor Cell Biology to the Clinic: Barriers and Opportunities." *Science 287*, no. 5457 (2000): 1442–46.

BIOLOGY & SCIENCE
FACT SHEET

KEY TERMS:

Big Bang: A theory of the cosmos' origin; a giant explosion around 14 billion years ago which expanded rapidly, cooled, and coalesced into the universe of today

Cambrian Explosion: The sudden geological appearance of most major groups of animals

Cosmic Evolution: The progression of collective humanity toward an age of higher consciousness

Creationism: the scientific theory that God was directly involved in creating the universe and all living kinds of plants and animals, including mankind

Darwinism: The scientific theory that proposes that gradual changes accumulated over vast periods of time resulting in the evolution of the species

DNA: The storehouse containing all the genetic information necessary for life

Homology: The study of the similarity in structure between different organisms

Icons of Evolution: Distortions of pro-evolution evidence commonly found in textbooks

Intelligent Design: The study of information and design in life and the cosmos

Irreducible Complexity: The philosophical concept that considers the complexity of living organisms—if any part is removed, the system loses function

Macro-evolution: The origin of fundamentally new organisms and plants from other forms of life

Micro-evolution: Small changes within the species of a gene pool

Mutation: Changes in genetic makeup

Natural Selection: The natural process of choosing favorable characteristics and eliminating unfavorable ones through such things as competition, predators, geography, and time

Neo-Darwinism: The theory that new species arise from natural selection acting over vast periods of time on chance genetic mutations in reproductively isolated populations

Second Law of Thermodynamics: A natural law that states that although the total energy in the cosmos remains constant, the amount of energy available to do useful work is always decreasing

Spontaneous Generation: The theory that non-living matter gave rise to living organisms

Punctuated Equilibrium: The theory of evolution that proposes that evolutionary changes occur over a relatively quick period of time, followed by periods of little to no evolutionary change

Teleology: The study of design and purpose in nature

Theistic Evolution: The belief that God works through the natural process of evolution

KEY VERSES:

Genesis 1

Mark 10:6

Ephesians 5:19

Philippians 4:8

Hebrews 11:3

KEY ORGANIZATIONS:

Answers in Genesis | www.answersingenesis.org | 859.727.2222 |

Access Research Network | www.arn.org | 719.633.1772 |

Creation Research Society | www.creationresearch.org | 928.636.1153 |

Discovery Institute | www.discovery.org | 206.292.0401 |

Institute for Creation Research | www.icr.org | 800.337.0375 |

KEY QUOTES:

EVOLUTIONISTS

"Evolution is a fact amply demonstrated by the fossil record and by contemporary molecular biology. Natural selection is a successful theory devised to explain the fact of evolution."[1]

"Man is the result of a purposeless and natural process that did not have him in mind. He was not planned. He is a state of matter, a form of life, a sort of animal, and a species of the Order Primates, akin nearly or remotely to all of life and indeed to all that is material."[2]

"Biology teaches us that the species man was not specially created but is merely, in a long chain of evolutionary changes of forms of life, the last link, made in the likeness not of God but of nothing so much as an ape."[3]

"With me, the horrid doubt always arises whether the convictions of man's mind, which has been developed from the mind of lower animals, are of any value or at all trustworthy. Would any one trust in the convictions of a monkey's mind, if there are any convictions in such a mind?"[4]

CREATIONISTS/ID

"The essential point of creation has nothing to do with the timing or the mechanism the Creator chose to employ, but with the element of design or purpose. In the broadest sense, a 'creationist' is simply a person who believes that the world (and especially mankind) was designed, and exists for a purpose."[5]

"Science is possible only because we live in an ordered universe which complies with simple mathematical laws. The job of the scientist is to study, catalogue and relate the orderliness in nature, not to question its origin. But theologians have long argued that the order in the physical world is evidence for God. If this is true, then science and religion acquire a common purpose in revealing God's work."[6]

---

[1] Carl Sagan, *Dragons of Eden* (New York: Random, 1977), 6.

[2] George Gaylord Simpson, *The Meaning of Evolution* (New Haven, CT: Yale University Press, 1971), 345.

[3] Kurt E. M. Baier, "The Meaning of Life," *Critiques of God*, Peter Angeles, ed. (Buffalo, NY: Prometheus, 1976), 315.

[4] Charles Darwin quoted in Francis Darwin, ed., *The Life and Letters of Charles Darwin*, Vol. 1 (London: J. Murray, 1888), 316.

[5] Phillip E. Johnson, *Darwin on Trial* (Downers Grove, IL: InterVarsity, 1993), 113.

[6] Paul Davies, *God and the New Physics* (New York: Simon & Schuster, 1983), 144.

Fact Sheets

"A science which deals with origin events does not fall within the category of empirical science, which deals with observed regularities in the present. Rather, it is more like a forensic science, which concentrates on unobserved singularities in the past. That is, a science about origins is a singularity science about the past; it differs from a scientific understanding about singularities in the present. A science about the past does not observe the past singularity but must depend on the principle of uniformity (analogy), as historical geology and archaeology do…

Just as a forensic scientist tries to make a plausible reconstruction of an unobserved (and unrepeatable) murder, so the evolutionist and creationist attempt to construct a plausible scenario of the unobserved past singularities of origin. So neither view is operation science. Rather, both are in the domain of origin science…

Some events of origin may have nonnatural primary intelligent causes. But to insist on finding a natural cause where there is evidence for primary intelligent causes is like demanding that a geology class remain at Mount Rushmore until it discovers some natural process of erosion to explain the faces formed on the mountainside."[7]

KEY SOURCES—EVOLUTIONISTS:

ASTRONOMY
Sagan, Carl. *Cosmos*. New York: Random, 2002.

COSMOLOGY
Dawkins, Richard. *The Blind Watchmaker*. New York: Norton, 1996.
Smoot, George and Keay Davidson. *Wrinkles in Time*. New York: W. Morrow, 1993.

DARWINISM
Darwin, Charles. *The Descent of Man and Selection in Relation to Sex*. Princeton: Princeton Univ. Press, 1981.
———. *On the Origin of Species*. Mineola, NY: Dover, 2006.

NEO-DARWINISM
Dawkins, Richard. *The Selfish Gene*. New York: Oxford University Press, 1989.
Sagan, Carl. *The Dragons of Eden*. New York: Random, 1977.

PALEONTOLOGY
Raup, David M. *The Nemesis Affair: A Story of the Death of Dinosaurs and the Ways of Science*. New York: Norton, 1999.
Raup, David M. and Steven M. Stanley. *Principles of Paleontology*. San Francisco: W. H. Freeman, 1978.

PHYSICS
Asimov, Isaac. *Asimov on Physics*. Garden City, NY: Doubleday, 1976.
———. *Understanding Physics*. New York: Walker, 1966.

PUNCTUATED EVOLUTION
Eldredge, Niles. *Reinventing Darwin: The Great Debate at the High Table of Evolutionary Theory*. New York: Wiley, 1995.
———. *Time Frames: The Rethinking of Darwinian Evolution and the Theory of Punctuated Equilibria*. New York: Simon & Schuster, 1985.
———. *Why We Do It: Rethinking Sex and the Selfish Gene*. New York: Norton, 2004.
Gould, Stephen Jay. *The Structure of Evolutionary Theory*. Cambridge, MA: Belknap of Harvard Univ. Press, 2002.

[7] Norman L. Geisler and J. Kerby Anderson, *Origin Science: A Proposal for the Creation-Evolution Controversy* (Grand Rapids, MI: Baker, 1987), 14, 25, 30.

KEY SOURCES—CREATIONISTS/ID:
(recommended titles appear in brown)

SCIENCE

Davies, P. C. W. *God and the New Physics*. New York: Simon & Schuster, 1983.

Jastrow, Robert. *God and the Astronomers*. New York: Norton, 1992.

Moreland, James Porter. *Christianity and the Nature of Science*. Grand Rapids, MI: Baker, 1989.

Pearcey, Nancy and Charles B. Thaxton. *The Soul of Science: Christian Faith and Natural Philosophy*. Wheaton, IL: Crossway, 1994.

DARWINISM (CRITIQUE)

Bird, Wendell R. *The Origin of Species Revisited*. New York: Philosophical Library, 1989.

Copan, Paul and William Lane Craig. *Creation out of Nothing*. Grand Rapids, MI: Baker, 2004.

Denton, Michael. *Evolution: A Theory in Crisis*. Bethesda, MD: Adler & Adler, 1986.

Gish, Duane T. *Evolution, the Fossils Say No!* San Diego: Creation-Life, 1979.

Johnson, Phillip E. *Darwin on Trial*. Downers Grove, IL: InterVarsity, 1993.

———. *Defeating Darwinism by Opening Minds*. Downers Grove, IL: InterVarsity, 1997.

Lester, Lane P., Raymond G. Bohlin, and V. Elving Anderson. *The Natural Limits to Biological Change*. Dallas: Probe, 1989.

Lubenow, Marvin L. *Bones of Contention: A Creationist Assessment of Human Fossils*. Grand Rapids, MI: Baker, 2004.

Milton, Richard. *Shattering the Myths of Darwinism*. Rochester, VT: Park Street, 1997.

Morris, Henry. *The Long War against God*. Green Forest, AR: Master, 2000.

Simmons, Geoffrey S. *What Darwin Didn't Know*. Eugene, OR: Harvest, 2004.

Taylor, Ian T. *In the Minds of Men: Darwin and the New World Order*. Toronto: TFE, 1984.

Wells, Jonathan. *Icons of Evolution: Science or Myth?* Washington DC: Regnery, 2000.

Wise, Kurt P. *Faith, Form, and Time: What the Bible Teaches and Science Confirms About Creation and the Age of the Universe*. Nashville: Broadman & Holman, 2002.

INTELLIGENT DESIGN

Behe, Michael J. *Darwin's Black Box: The Biochemical Challenge to Evolution*. New York: Free Press, 1996.

Dembski, William A. *The Design Revolution: Answering the Toughest Questions About Intelligent Design*. Downers Grove, IL: InterVarsity, 2004.

———. *Intelligent Design: The Bridge between Science & Theology*. Downers Grove, IL: InterVarsity, 1999.

———. *Mere Creation: Science, Faith and Intelligent Design*. Downers Grove, IL: InterVarsity, 1998.

———. *No Free Lunch: Why Specified Complexity Cannot Be Purchased without Intelligence*. Lanham, MD: Rowman & Littlefield, 2002.

Dembski, William A. and Michael Ruse. *Debating Design: From Darwin to DNA*. New York: Cambridge Univ. Press, 2004.

Johnson, Phillip E. *Defeating Darwinism by Opening Minds*. Downers Grove, IL: InterVarsity, 1997.

McGrath, Alister E. *Dawkins' God: Genes, Memes, and the Meaning of Life*. Malden, MA: Blackwell, 2005.

Moreland, James Porter. *The Creation Hypothesis: Scientific Evidence for an Intelligent Designer*. Downers Grove, IL: InterVarsity, 1994.

Thaxton, Charles B., Walter L. Bradley, and Roger L. Olsen. *The Mystery of Life's Origin*. New York: Philosophical Library, 1984.

NATURALISM (CRITIQUE)

Johnson, Phillip E. *Reason in the Balance: The Case against Naturalism in Science, Law and Education*. Downers Grove, IL: InterVarsity, 1995.

———. *The Wedge of Truth: Splitting the Foundations of Naturalism*. Downers Grove, IL: InterVarsity, 2000.

Fact Sheets

CULTS
FACT SHEET

KEY TERMS:

Cult: A system of religious veneration and devotion directed toward a particular figure or object; a religion

Modalism: The belief that there is only one person in the godhead who appears as three persons: the Father in the Old Testament, the Son in the New Testament, and the Holy Spirit today

Pseudo-Christian Religion: A group of people gathered around an individual (a group of individuals or an organization), who, while claiming to be the true Christian Church and teach true Christianity, actually distort and deny the foundational and distinctive doctrines of the Christian faith

Tri-theism: A belief in three separate gods: Father, Son, and Spirit

Trinity [Trinitarianism]: The belief in one God in three persons: Father, Son, and Spirit

Unitarianism: The belief that the Father is God, the Son is merely a creature, and the Holy Spirit is an impersonal force

KEY VERSES:

Psalm 119:105
Proverbs 30:5–6
John 17:17
Romans 5:12ff
2 Corinthians 11:1–15

Galatians 1:6–9; 2:21
Ephesians 2:1ff
Colossians 2:13
1 Timothy 2:5

2 Timothy 3:15–17
Titus 2:11–14; 3:4–8
2 Peter 1:3; 3:15–16
1 John 4:1–6

KEY ORGANIZATIONS:

Christian Research Institute | www.equip.org | 888.700.0274 |

Cult Information Centre | www.cultinformation.org.uk |

Cult FAQ | www.cultfaq.org |

Rick A. Ross Institute | www.rickross.com | 201.434.9234 |

Watchman Fellowship, Inc. | www.watchman.org | 205.833.2858 |

Wellspring | www.wellspringretreat.org | 740.698.6277 |

KEY PUBLICATIONS:

Spiritual Counterfeits Project | **Spiritual Counterfeits Project** | www.scp-inc.org |

KEY QUOTES:

MORMONS

"The Bible is the word of God, written by men. It is basic in Mormon teaching. But the Latter-day Saints recognize that errors have crept into this sacred work because of the manner in which the book has come to us. Moreover, they regard it as not being complete as a guide… Supplementing the Bible, the Latter-day Saints have three other books: the Book of Mormon, the Doctrine and Covenants, and the Pearl of Great Price. These with the Bible constitute the standard works of the church."[1]

"Many men say there is one God; the Father, the Son and the Holy Ghost are only one God. I say that is a strange God anyhow—three in one, and one in three! It is a curious organization… All are to be crammed into one God, according to sectarianism. It would make the biggest God in all the world. He would be a wonderfully big God—he would be a giant or a monster."[2]

"I have always declared God to be a distinct personage, Jesus Christ a separate and distinct personage from God the Father, and that the Holy Ghost was a distinct personage and a Spirit; and these three constitute three distinct personages and three Gods."[3]

"I am going to tell you how God came to be God. We have imagined and supposed that God was God from all eternity. I will refute that idea, and take away the veil, so you may see… he was once a man like us; yea, that God himself, the Father of us all, dwelt on an earth, the same as Jesus Christ himself did; and I will show it from the Bible… Here, then, is eternal life—to know the only wise and true God, and you have got to learn to be Gods yourselves, and to be kings and priest to God, the same as all Gods have done before you."[4]

"The Church of Jesus Christ of Latter-day Saints discounts the notion of Original Sin and its ascribed negative impact on humanity… [W]e believe that we are not born sinners… In other words, we're born good; we learn to sin as we grow older."[5]

"Indeed, we honor and respect Adam and Eve for their wisdom and foresight. Their lives in the Garden of Eden were blissful and pleasant; choosing to leave that behind so they and the entire human family could experience both the triumphs and travails of mortality must not have been easy. But we believe they did choose mortality, and in so doing made it possible for all of us to participate in the Heavenly Father's great, eternal plan."[6]

JEHOVAH'S WITNESSES

"Is [the Bible] too puzzling and complex to be understood? Can the average person understand it? What help is needed for one to grasp the meaning of the Scriptures?… It is obvious that we need help if we are to understand the Bible… [T]he fact is that we cannot understand the Bible on our own. We need help… Jehovah, through his organization, however, has allowed his loyal servants to understand its meaning today… You too can gain this understanding with the assistance of those who are experienced in 'handling the word of the truth aright'… All who want to understand the Bible should appreciate that the 'greatly diversified wisdom of God' can become known only through Jehovah's channel of communication, the faithful and discreet slave [i.e. The Watchtower Bible and Tract Society]."[7]

"Jesus Christ further deserves honor because He is Jehovah's chief angel, or archangel." Footnote 9: "Why do we conclude that Jesus is the archangel Michael… ?"[8]

"In [the] beginning the Word was, and the Word was with God, and the Word was a god."[9]

---

[1] Gordon Bitner Hincklye, *What of the Mormons? A Brief Study of the Church of Jesus Christ of Latter-Day Saints* (Salt Lake City: Church of Jesus Christ of Latter-Day Saints), 9, 11.

[2] Joseph Fielding Smith, *Teachings of the Prophet Joseph Smith* (Salt Lake City: Deseret Book, 1976), 372.

[3] Ibid., 370.

[4] Ibid., 345–46.

[5] Russell M. Ballard, *Our Search for Happiness: An Invitation to Understand the Church of Jesus Christ of the Latter-Day Saints* (Salt Lake City: Deseret Book, 1993), 87.

[6] Ibid.

[7] *The Watchtower* (October 1, 1994), 4 ,6 ,8.

[8] *The Watchtower* (February 1, 1991), 17.

[9] John 1:1 from *The New World Translation of the Holy Scriptures*.

Fact Sheets

KEY CRITIQUES:

CULTS

Breese, Dave. *The Marks of a Cult: Warning Signs of False Teachings*. Eugene, OR: Harvest, 1998.

Geisler, Norman L. and Ron Rhodes. *When Cultists Ask: A Popular Handbook on Cultic Misinterpretations*. Grand Rapids, MI: Baker, 1997.

Gomes, Alan W. *Unmasking the Cults: Zondervan Guide to Cults & Religious Movements*. Grand Rapids, MI: Zondervan, 1995.

Hexham, Irving. *Pocket Dictionary of New Religious Movements*. Downers Grove, IL: InterVarsity, 2002.

House, H. Wayne. *Charts of Cults, Sects, and Religious Movements*. Grand Rapids, MI: Zondervan, 2000.

Martin, Walter Ralston and Ravi K. Zacharias. *The Kingdom of the Cults*. Minneapolis: Bethany, 2003.

Passantino, Robert, Gretchen Passantino, and Raymond Schafer. *Answers to the Cultist at Your Door*. Eugene, OR: Harvest, 1981.

Rhodes, Ron. *The Challenge of the Cults and New Religions: The Essential Guide to Their History, Their Doctrine, and Our Response*. Grand Rapids, MI: Zondervan, 2001.

Sire, James W. *Scripture Twisting: 20 Ways the Cults Misread the Bible*. Downers Grove, IL: InterVarsity, 1980.

MORMONISM (CRITIQUE)

Abanes, Richard. *Becoming Gods: A Closer Look at 21st Century Mormonism*. Eugene, OR: Harvest, 2004.

Beckwith, Francis, Norman L. Geisler, Ron Rhodes, Phil Roberts, and Jerald and Sandra Tanner. *The Counterfeit Gospel of Mormonism*. Eugene, OR: Harvest, 1998.

Beckwith, Francis, Carl Mosser, and Paul Owen, eds. *The New Mormon Challenge: Responding to the Latest Defenses of a Fast-Growing Movement*. Grand Rapids, MI: Zondervan, 2002.

Blomberg, Craig, and Stephen Edward Robinson. *How Wide the Divide? A Mormon and an Evangelical in Conversation*. Downers Grove, IL: InterVarsity, 1997.

Cowan, Marvin W. *What Every Mormon Should Ask*. Eugene, OR: Harvest, 2000.

Carrigan, Cky John. "The Mormon Mirage." *Southwestern Journal of Theology* 46, no. 2 (2004).

Hinckley, Gordon Bitner. *What of the Mormons? A Brief Study of the Church of Jesus Christ of Latter-Day Saints*. Salt Lake City: Church of Jesus Christ of Latter-Day Saints, 1947.

Holding, James Patrick. *The Mormon Defenders: How Latter-Day Saint Apologists Misinterpret the Bible*. Miami: Tektonics Press, 2001.

McKeever, Bill and Eric Johnson. *Mormonism 101: Examining the Religion of the Latter-Day Saints*. Grand Rapids, MI: Baker, 2000.

Reed, David A. and John R. Farkas. *Mormons: Answered Verse by Verse*. Grand Rapids, MI: Baker, 1992.

Rhodes, Ron. *The 10 Most Important Things You Can Say to a Mormon*. Eugene, OR: Harvest, 2001.

Rhodes, Ron and Marian Bodine. *Reasoning from the Scriptures with the Mormons*. Eugene, OR: Harvest, 1995.

Smith, Joseph Fielding. *Teachings of the Prophet Joseph Smith*. Salt Lake City: Deseret Book, 1976.

JEHOVAH'S WITNESSES (CRITIQUE)

Bowman, Robert M. *Jehovah's Witnesses, Jesus Christ, and the Gospel of John*. Grand Rapids, MI: Baker, 1989.

———. *Understanding Jehovah's Witnesses: Why They Read the Bible the Way They Do*. Grand Rapids, MI: Baker, 1991.

———. *Why You Should Believe in the Trinity: An Answer to Jehovah's Witnesses*. Grand Rapids, MI: Baker, 1989.

Reed, David A. *Answering Jehovah's Witnesses: Subject by Subject*. Grand Rapids, MI: Baker, 1996.

———. *Jehovah's Witnesses: Answered Verse by Verse*. Grand Rapids, MI: Baker, 1986.

Rhodes, Ron. *Reasoning from the Scriptures with the Jehovah's Witnesses*. Eugene, OR: Harvest, 1993.

ECONOMICS
FACT SHEET

KEY TERMS:

Capitalism: an economic system based on the peaceful and free exchange of goods and services where all or most of the means of production and distribution (land, factories, railroads, etc) are privately owned and operated for profit

Economic Determinism: The belief that economics (the modes of production and exchange) determines the entire course of history; the social, political, and moral processes of life

Interventionism: Political activity undertaken by a state to influence aspects of economy usually in order to uphold certain moral values

Socialism: An economic system in which the ownership and operation of the means of production and distribution (land, factories, railroads, etc) are controlled by the government. According to Marxism, socialism (i.e. abolition of private property) is the transitional phase between capitalism and communism

Stewardship: The science, art, and skill of responsible and accountable management of resources. Christians believe that God is the ultimate owner of everything and that human beings have been given the responsibility to manage and care for his creation

Universal Enlightened Production: The belief that positive thought creates wealth

KEY FACTS:

- Christians must act on God's commands to help those who cannot help themselves
- Capitalism is the best strategy for defeating poverty
- Capitalism takes human nature into account

KEY VERSES:

Exodus 20:15, 17
Proverbs 11:24–26; 16:8;
  17:5; 19:17; 21:13; 22:9,
  28:27; 29:7; 31:8–9
Ecclesiastes 5:19

Acts 4:32-37; 20:35
1 Corinthians 16:2
2 Corinthians 8–9
Philippians 4:12–13

2 Thessalonians 3:7–13
1 Timothy 5-6; 6:6-10, 17–19
James 1:27; 2:14–17
1 John 3:16–18

KEY QUOTES:

"Christians need to care about the poor: that is one side of Christian social concern. But they also need to become informed about the relevant philosophical, political, and economic issues that ground wise and efficient policies to help the poor. Unfortunately, many Christians act as though the only thing that counts is intention. But when good intentions are not wedded to sound economic theory, good intentions can often result in actions that produce consequences directly opposite to those we planned."[1]

"Just before the collapse of socialism in the Soviet bloc, Lutheran sociologist Peter Berger wrote a marvelous book about the newly industrializing countries of East Asia. These 'little tigers,' or 'little dragons' as they're sometimes called, are part of a capitalist revolution and, as Berger documents, they are defeating poverty at an amazing rate.

---

[1] Ronald H. Nash, *Poverty and Wealth: The Christian Debate Over Capitalism* (Westchester, IL: Crossway, 1986), 9.

He compares them to the Third World nations that have tried socialism for the last three decades and finds that none of the latter have grown, and indeed, that most have moved backward."[2]

"[A]ll men have different gifts, talents, interests, and abilities. Left free, they will exercise those in different ways and will produce different fruits. The only way to arrive at equal fruits is to equalize behavior; and that requires robbing men of liberty, making them slaves."[3]

"If poverty (the lack of money) really were what ails the poor, supplying vast amounts of money surely would alleviate it. But after thirty years of Great Society-style, 'War on Poverty' welfare programs—programs that have transferred (in 1990 dollars) more than $3.6 trillion to the poor—poverty is still winning. We ought to think about that for a minute: In the last thirty years, we gave a million dollars to America's poor nearly four million times over, yet all the while poverty got worse. If the money earmarked for poverty relief in this year's federal budget alone were given to the poor directly, we would have enough funds to raise every man, woman, and child in America above the poverty line and have a cool $60 billion left over to celebrate our victory." Nearly 40 percent of those the U.S. government defines as 'poor' own their own homes—homes that have more living space than that enjoyed by most middle class Europeans. 'Poor' ought to retain its earlier definition: the lack of food, shelter, or clothing. And while we are engaged in the task of redefining, we ought to remind ourselves that the definition of compassion is not increased control of private income by government."[4]

"The century-old question—Does any given 'scheme of help... make demands on men to give themselves to their brethren?'—is still the right one to ask. Each of us needs to ask that question not in the abstract, but personally. We need to ask ourselves: Are we offering not coerced silver, but our lives? If we talk of crisis pregnancies, are we actually willing to provide a home to a pregnant young woman? If we talk of abandoned children, are we actually willing to adopt a child? Most of our twentieth-century schemes, based on having someone else take action, are proven failures. It's time to learn from the warm hearts and hard heads of earlier times, and to bring that understanding into our own lives."[5]

KEY ORGANIZATIONS:

Acton Institute | www.acton.org | 616.454.3080 |

American Enterprise Institute for Public Policy Research | www.aei.org | 202.862.5800 |

Cato Institute | www.cato.org | 202.842.0200 |

Foundation for Economic Education | www.fee.org | 914.591.7230 |

Heritage Foundation | www.heritage.org | 202.546.4400 |

Hoover Institute | www.hoover.org | 650.723.1754 |

Independent Institute | www.independent.org | 510.632.1366 |

Library of Economics and Liberty | www.econlib.org |

Ludwig von Mises Institute | www.mises.org | 334.321.2100 |

Property and Environment Research Center | www.perc.org | 406.587.9591 |

[2] K. E. Grubbs Jr., "A New 'Liberation Theology' for the World: Faith and the Free Market," *Imprimis*, March 1991.
[3] E. Calvin Beisner, *Prosperity and Poverty: The Compassionate Use of Resources in a World of Scarcity* (Westchester, IL: Crossway, 1988), 54.
[4] Michael Bauman, "The Dangerous Samaritans: How We Unintentionally Injure the Poor," *Imprimis 23*, no.1 (1994).
[5] Marvin Olasky, *The Tragedy of American Compassion* (Washington DC: Regnery, 1992), 232–33.

Fact Sheets

KEY PUBLICATIONS:

Freeman Journal | **Foundation for Economic Education** | www.fee.org | 800.960.4333 |

KEY SOURCES/CRITIQUES:
(recommended titles appear in brown)

ECONOMICS

Carson, Clarence Buford. *Basic Economics*. Wadley, AL: American Textbook Committee, 1988.

Gregg, Samuel. *Economic Thinking for the Theologically Minded*. Lanham, MD: Univ. Press of America, 2001.

Gwartney, James D., Richard Stroup, Dwight R. Lee, and James D. Gwartney. *Common Sense Economics: What Everyone Should Know About Wealth and Prosperity*. New York: St. Martin's, 2005.

Hazlitt, Henry. *Economics in One Lesson*. New Rochelle, NY: Arlington House, 1979.

Heilbroner, Robert L. *The Worldly Philosophers: The Lives, Times, and Ideas of the Great Economic Thinkers*. New York: Simon & Schuster, 1999.

Sowell, Thomas. *Applied Economics: Thinking Beyond Stage One*. New York: Basic, 2004.

———. *Basic Economics: A Common Sense Guide to the Economy*. New York: Basic, 2007.

———. *Marxism: Philosophy and Economics*. New York: Quill, 1985.

CAPITALISM VS. SOCIALISM

Gilder, George F. *Wealth and Poverty*. San Francisco: ICS, 1993.

Griffiths, Brian. *The Creation of Wealth: A Christian's Case for Capitalism*. Downers Grove, IL: InterVarsity, 1984.

Nash, Ronald H. *Poverty and Wealth: The Christian Debate over Capitalism*. Westchester, IL: Crossway, 1986.

Novak, Michael. *The Spirit of Democratic Capitalism*. Lanham, MD: National Book Network, 1991.

Schaeffer, Frankie, ed. *Is Capitalism Christian? Toward a Christian Perspective on Economics*. Westchester, IL: Crossway, 1985.

Soto, Hernando de. *The Mystery of Capital: Why Capitalism Triumphs in the West and Fails Everywhere Else*. New York: Basic, 2000.

PRIVATE PROPERTY

Bethell, Tom. *The Noblest Triumph: Property and Prosperity through the Ages*. New York: St. Martin's, 1998.

INTERVENTIONISM/SOCIALISM (CRITIQUE)

Dalrymple, Theodore. *Life at the Bottom: The Worldview that Makes the Underclass*. Chicago: Ivan R. Dee, 2001.

Gilder, George F. *Wealth and Poverty*. San Francisco: ICS, 1993.

Griffiths, Brian. *The Creation of Wealth: A Christian's Case for Capitalism*. Downers Grove, IL: InterVarsity, 1984.

Hazlitt, Henry. *The Critics of Keynesian Economics*. Lanham, MD: University Press of America, 1983.

———. *The Failure of the New Economics*. Lanham, MD: University Press of America, 1983.

Nash, Ronald H. *Poverty and Wealth: The Christian Debate over Capitalism*. Westchester, IL: Crossway, 1986.

Novak, Michael. *The Spirit of Democratic Capitalism*. Lanham, MD: National Book Network, 1991.

Schaeffer, Franky, ed. *Is Capitalism Christian? Toward a Christian Perspective on Economics*. Westchester, IL: Crossway, 1985.

Soto, Hernando de. *The Mystery of Capital: Why Capitalism Triumphs in the West and Fails Everywhere Else*. New York: Basic, 2000.

STEWARDSHIP

Beisner, E. Calvin and Fieldstead Institute. *Prosperity and Poverty: The Compassionate Use of Resources in a World of Scarcity*. Westchester, IL: Crossway, 1988.

Blomberg, Craig. *Neither Poverty nor Riches: A Biblical Theology of Material Possessions*. Grand Rapids, MI: Eerdmans, 1999.

Fact Sheets

WELFARE (CRITIQUE)

Dalrymple, Theodore. *Life at the Bottom: The Worldview that Makes the Underclass*. Chicago: Ivan R. Dee, 2001.

Grant, George. *Bringing in the Sheaves: Transforming Poverty into Productivity*. Brentwood, TN: Wolgemuth & Hyatt, 1988.

———. *The Dispossessed: Homelessness in America*. Ft. Worth: Dominion Press, 1986.

———. *In the Shadow of Plenty: Biblical Principles of Welfare and Poverty*. Ft. Worth: Dominion Press, 1986.

Nash, Ronald H. *Social Justice and the Christian Church*. Lanham, MD: University Press of America, 1990.

Neuhaus, Richard John. *Doing Well and Doing Good: The Challenge to the Christian Capitalist*. New York: Doubleday, 1992.

———. *Welfare Reformed: A Compassionate Approach*. Phillipsburg, NJ: P&R Publishers, 1994.

Olasky, Marvin N. *The Tragedy of American Compassion*. Wheaton, IL: Crossway, 1992.

HISTORY
FACT SHEET

KEY TERMS:

Creation, Fall, Redemption: The progression of events in God's creation—that all was created good, but mankind rebelled against God and requires divine redemption. Thus, all of creation is sacred and stands under the blessing, judgment, and redeeming purposes of God

Economic Determinism: The belief that economics is the only driving force in history

Evolutionary Godhood: The New Age belief that the divine is the source of evolutionary force and that we are growing toward godhood

Historical Determinism: The Muslim belief that history is not made up of a series of chance happenings; rather, Allah superintends history throughout time, guiding it toward an expression of his will

Historical Evolution: The belief that history is to be understood in terms of unguided evolution but which can now be guided by the ingenuity of mankind

Historical Materialism: The methodological approach to the study of society, economics, and history that looks for the causes of developments and changes in human societies through economic analysis (e.g. social classes, political structures, ideologies, etc.)

Historical Revisionism: The rewriting/editing of the past to serve an ideological purpose
Historicism: The view that past beliefs, morals, and truths should only be understood in relation to the cultural/historical periods in which they arose, not according to any eternal standard of morality and truth

Jihad: An Arabic word that means "striving in the way of God." This striving can take a number of forms, including the daily inner struggle to be a better person or armed struggle fought in defense of Islam

Nihilism: The view that the world, and especially human existence, is without meaning, purpose, comprehensible truth, or essential value

KEY VERSES:

Genesis 3:15	John 1:14	1 Timothy 3:16
Judges 2:10; 21:25	Galatians 4:4	

KEY PUBLICATIONS:

Archaeology Odyssey | **Biblical Archaeology Society** | www.bib-arch.org | 800.221.4644 |

Biblical Archaeology Review | **Biblical Archaeology Society** | www.bib-arch.org | 800.221.4644 |

Bible Review | **Biblical Archaeology Society** | www.bib-arch.org | 800.221.4644 |

Christian History | **Christianity Today** | www.christianhistory.net |

Fact Sheets

KEY SOURCES:

(recommended titles appear in brown)

CHURCH HISTORY

Harrison, R. K. *Old Testament Times: A Social, Political, and Cultural Context.* Grand Rapids, MI: Eerdmans, 2005.

Kennedy, D. James and Jerry Newcombe. *What If Jesus Had Never Been Born?* Nashville: Thomas Nelson, 1994.

Noll, Mark A. *Turning Points: Decisive Moments in the History of Christianity.* Grand Rapids, MI: Baker, 2000.

Shelley, Bruce L. *Church History in Plain Language.* Dallas: Word, 1995.

Stark, Rodney. *The Rise of Christianity: How the Obscure, Marginal Jesus Movement Became the Dominant Religious Force in the Western World in a Few Centuries.* San Francisco: HarperSanFrancisco, 1996.

Tenney, Merrill Chapin. *New Testament Times: Understanding the World of the First Century.* Grand Rapids: Eerdmans, 2004.

HISTORICITY OF BIBLE AND CHURCH

Blomberg, Craig. *The Historical Reliability of John's Gospel.* Downers Grove, IL: InterVarsity, 2002.

————. *The Historical Reliability of the Gospels.* Downers Grove, IL: InterVarsity, 1987.

Copan, Paul, ed. *Will the Real Jesus Please Stand Up? A Debate between William Lane Craig and John Dominic Crossan.* Grand Rapids, MI: Baker, 1998.

Craig, William Lane. *Knowing the Truth About the Resurrection: Our Response to the Empty Tomb.* Ann Arbor, MI: Servant, 1988.

Free, Joseph P. and Howard Frederic. *Archaeology and Bible History.* Grand Rapids, MI: Zondervan, 1992.

Geisler, Norman L. *Systematic Theology.* Minneapolis: Bethany, 2002 (Vol. 1, Chapters 25 and 26).

Habermas, Gary R. and Michael R. Licona. *The Case for the Resurrection of Jesus.* Grand Rapids, MI: Kregel, 2004.

Kitchen, K. A. *The Bible in Its World: The Bible and Archaeology Today.* Exeter, RI: Paternoster, 1977.

————. *On the Reliability of the Old Testament.* Grand Rapids, MI: Eerdmans, 2003.

Nash, Ronald H. *The Gospel and the Greeks: Did the New Testament Borrow from Pagan Thought?* Richardson, TX: Probe, 1992.

Thompson, J. A. *The Bible and Archaeology.* Grand Rapids, MI: Eerdmans, 1982.

Wilkins, Michael J. and James Porter Moreland. *Jesus under Fire.* Grand Rapids, MI: Zondervan, 1995.

[1] Ronald H. Nash, *Christian Faith and Historical Understanding* (Dallas, TX: Probe, 1984), 112.

Homosexuality
Fact Sheet

Key Verses:

Genesis 19:1–29   Romans 1:25-32   1 Timothy 1:10
Leviticus 18:22; 20:13   1 Corinthians 6:9–11

Key Organizations:

Genesis Counseling | www.genesiscounseling.org | 714.508.6953 |

Desert Stream Ministries | www.desertstream.org | 816.767.1730 |

Exodus International | www.exodusinternational.org | 407.599.6872 |

Love Won Out | www.lovewonout.com | 800.232.6459 |

Family Research Council | www.frc.org | 800.225.4008 |

Focus on the Family | www.fotf.org | 800.232.6459 |

Key Quotes:

"It never dawned on these people that my pain was a very real cry to be whole, to be well. A 15-year old crying out for love, and getting instead an empty excuse for healing, empty words that said, 'there are no absolutes,' 'lose your inhibition,' 'experiment with your sexuality.' Think about it… at fifteen, confused and alone, what effect would those words have?… You see, I was one of those children. I was a homosexual. And I am one of the lucky ones… I got out alive."[1]

"But this strategy [of viewing the homosexual struggle as a civil rights issue] is based on two assumptions: that sexuality is equivalent to race in terms of discrimination, and that the full equality of homosexuals can be accomplished by designating gay people as victims. Both are extremely dubious. Unlike blacks three decades ago, gay men and lesbians suffer no discernible communal economic deprivation and already operate at the highest levels of society: in boardrooms, governments, the media, the military, the law and industry."[2] [A pro-homosexual publication]

"As more and more homosexuals come out of hiding, the reality of gay economic and political and education achievement becomes more evident. And as that happens, gay people who insist they are oppressed will increasingly, and not always unfairly, come off as yuppie whiners, 'victims' with $50,000 incomes and vacations in Europe. They may feel they are oppressed, but they will have a harder and harder time convincing the public."[3] [A pro-homosexual publication]

---

[1] Jeff, "Open Letter from a Survivor," *CFV Report*, Volume 9 (October 1993).
[2] Andrew Sullivan, "The Politics of Homosexuality," *The New Republic* (May 10, 1993).
[3] Jonathan Rauch, "Beyond Oppression," *The New Republic* (May 10, 1993).

Fact Sheets

KEY SOURCES/CRITIQUES:

(recommended titles appear in brown)

HOMOSEXUALITY

Balch, David L., ed. *Homosexuality, Science, and the 'Plain Sense' of Scripture*. Grand Rapids, MI: Eerdmans, 2000.

Haley, Mike. *101 Frequently Asked Questions About Homosexuality*. Eugene, OR: Harvest, 2004.

BIBLE AND CHURCH

Bahnsen, Greg L. *Homosexuality, a Biblical View*. Grand Rapids, MI: Baker, 1978.

Cowan, Steve B. "Abandoning Nature: An Argument against Homosexuality." *Areopagus Journal 1*, no. 4 (2001): 33–36.

Dallas, Joe. *A Strong Delusion: Confronting The "Gay Christian" Movement*. Eugene, OR: Harvest, 1996.

DeYoung, James B. *Homosexuality: Contemporary Claims Examined in Light of the Bible and Other Ancient Literature and Law*. Grand Rapids, MI: Kregel, 2000.

Gagnon, Robert A. J. *The Bible and Homosexual Practice: Texts and Hermeneutics*. Nashville: Abingdon Press, 2001.

Grant, George and Mark Horne. *Unnatural Affections: The Impuritan Ethic of Homosexuality and the Modern Church*. Franklin, TN: Legacy Communications, 1991.

Jones, Stanton L. and Mark A. Yarhouse. *Homosexuality: The Use of Scientific Research in the Church's Moral Debate*. Downers Grove, IL: InterVarsity, 2000.

Mazzalongo, Michael. *Gay Rights or Wrongs: A Christian's Guide to Homosexual Issues and Ministry*. Joplin, MO: College Press, 1995.

White, James R. and Jeffrey D. Niell. *The Same Sex Controversy: Defending and Clarifying the Bible's Message About Homosexuality*. Minneapolis: Bethany, 2002.

Wilder, Terry L. "What the New Testament Does and Does Not Teach About Homosexuality." *Areopagus Journal 1*, no. 4 (2001): 28–32.

Wold, Donald J. *Out of Order: Homosexuality in the Bible and the Ancient Near East*. Grand Rapids, MI: Baker, 1998.

CAUSES AND COUNSELING

Dallas, Joe. *Desires in Conflict*. Eugene, OR: Harvest, 2003.

Konrad, J. A. *You Don't Have to Be Gay: Hope and Freedom for Males Struggling with Homosexuality or for Those Who Know of Someone Who Is*. Hilo, HI: Pacific, 1992.

Riley, Mona and Brad Sargent. *Unwanted Harvest?* Nashville: Broadman & Holman, 1995.

Wolfe, Christopher, ed. *Same-Sex Matters: The Challenge of Homosexuality*. Dallas: Spence, 2000.

Worthen, Anita and Bob Davies. *Someone I Love Is Gay: How Family and Friends Can Respond*. Downers Grove, IL: InterVarsity, 1996.

POLITICAL ACTION

Burtoft, Larry. *Setting the Record Straight: What Research Really Says About the Social Consequences of Homosexuality*. Colorado Springs, CO: Focus on the Family, 1994.

Grant, George and Mark A. Horne. *Legislating Immorality: The Homosexual Movement Comes out of the Closet*. Chicago: Moody, 1993.

Kennedy, D. James and Jerry Newcombe. *What's Wrong with Same-Sex Marriage?* Wheaton, IL: Crossway, 2004.

Magnuson, Roger J. *Are 'Gay Rights' Right? A Report on Homosexuality and the Law*. St. Paul, MN: The Fund, 1985.

Satinover, Jeffrey. *Homosexuality and the Politics of Truth*. Grand Rapids, MI: Baker, 1996.

Stanton, Glenn T. and Bill Maier. *Marriage on Trial: The Case against Same-Sex Marriage and Parenting*. Downers Grove, IL: InterVarsity, 2004.

Law & Politics
Fact Sheet

Key Terms:

Law

Critical Legal Studies: The deconstruction of law used to discover its subjective meaning and biased intent

Divine Law: Any law that comes directly from the character of God via special revelation

Natural Law: Physical and moral laws revealed in general revelation and built into the structure of the universe (as opposed to the laws imposed by human beings)

Positive Law [or Legal Positivism]: The Humanistic legal school of thought that claims laws are rules made by human beings and that there is no inherent or necessary connection between law and morality

Proletariat Law: A legal system established by state authority that favors the interest of the working people

Shari'ah Law: Islamic law derived from the Qur'an and the Hadith and applied to the public and private lives of Muslims within Islamic states. Shari'ah law governs many aspects of day-to-day life—politics, economics, banking, business, contracts, social issues, etc

Self-law: The New Age legal perspective that maintains that actions are lawful only if honorable to the god within and unlawful if imposed by an outside authority

Politics

Anarchy: The complete absence of government and law

Communism: A dream of future utopia brought about by a proletariat revolution and ultimately leading to a classless society in which all property is publicly shared and each person works and is paid according to his or her abilities and needs

Global Islamic States: The vision of many Muslims to bring all nations under Shari'ah law, whether accomplished through peaceful means or jihad

Identity Politics: A political ideology which seeks to advance the interests of particular groups in society which have been perceived to be the victims of social injustice

Justice, Freedom, Order: Principals of human governments instituted by God to protect the innocent, punish the guilty, and preserve the rights of all people against the sinful tendencies of mankind

Leftism: An ideological approach to politics emphasizing the state's role in bringing about social justice, with a special focus on helping the poor or oppressed (due to race, gender, or sexual orientation)

Liberalism: A political tradition emphasizing personal liberties and equality over traditional moral concerns; specific policies include a woman's right to an abortion, promotion of same-sex marriage, equal rights for women, and redistribution of wealth to help the poor

New World Order: The New Age belief that (given each person's evolution toward collective consciousness) humanity will eventually develop the capacity for worldwide self-government

Secular World Government: A non-religious political body that would make, interpret, and enforce a set of laws internationally

Self-government: The New Age political perspective that maintains that each divine individual is evolving the ability to govern him or herself

Social Justice: An ambiguous term used to denote a wide range of meaning—anything from basic social equality (e.g. right to life and liberty) to the equalization of wealth and special rights for minority groups

Statism: A political system in which the concentration of economic controls and planning are placed completely in the hands of a highly centralized government

Theocracy: Any government ruled by a power claiming divine sanction, e.g. ancient Israel and a number of Islamic nations

---

KEY VERSES:

Deuteronomy 2:37–38;
  4:5–6; 5; 6
Psalms 1–2; 11:11; 14:43;
  19:7–9; 119; 29:2

Zechariah 8:16
Jeremiah 27:5–9, 12
Daniel 2:20-21

Romans 13:1-10
1 Timothy 1:8–11; 2:1
1 Peter 2:13–14

KEY ORGANIZATIONS:

American Center for Law and Justice | www.aclj.org | 800.296.4529 |

American Family Association | www.afa.net |

American Vision | www.americanvision.org | 770.222.7266 |

Eagle Forum | www.eagleforum.org | 618.462.5415 |

Family Research Council | www.frc.org | 800.225.4008 |

Heritage Foundation | www.heritage.org | 202.546.4400 |

The Leadership Institute | www.leadershipinstitute.org | 703.247.2000 |

The Rutherford Institute | www.rutherford.org | 434.978.3888|

Justice Fellowship | www.pfm.org | 877.478.0100 |

KEY PUBLICATIONS:

Citizen Magazine | **Focus on the Family** | www.family.org | 800.232.6459 |

World Magazine | www.worldmag.com | 800.951.6397 |

Human Events | www.humanevents.org | 800.787.7557 |

"We are a religious people whose institutions presuppose a supreme being."[1]

"To cut off Law from its ethical sources is to strike a terrible blow at the rule of law."[2]

"Government policies of accommodation, acknowledgment, and support for religion are an accepted part of our political and cultural heritage...Any approach less sensitive to our heritage would border on latent hostility toward religion."[3]

"[The] Establishment Clause permits government some latitude in recognizing and accommodating the central role religion plays in our society."[4]

"Why have law and order deteriorated so rapidly in the United States? Simply because for many years it has been commonly taught that life is a random, accidental phenomenon with no meaning except the purely materialistic one. Laws are merely a matter of human expediency. Since humans are allegedly accidents, so are their laws."[5]

"If man cannot know, according to a higher law, what is just or right in a given situation, he cannot protest and criticize legitimately any particular course of action as unjust."[6]

"God has called the Church to serve. And through service He grants us favor with the people. This is a fundamental principle of dominion in the Bible: dominion through service."[7]

"[C]hristians have an important role to play in the organization that most people think of as 'government'—the state. Indeed, believers have a Biblical obligation to be involved in civic affairs, since that sphere, no less than the private realm, is subject to God's rule and requires a generous dose of Christian 'salt.'"[8]

"If while evangelizing we abandon the sociopolitical realm to its own devices, we shall fortify the misimpression that the public order falls wholly outside the command and will of God, that Christianity deals with private concerns only; and we shall conceal the fact that government exists by God's will as His servant for the sake of justice and order."[9]

"Christians realize that man's fallen nature has severe implications for every aspect of his life, including the political realm. The American system of checks and balances, therefore, is embraced by Christians in their political theory because it is a genuine attempt to curtail man's sinful tendencies not only among the private citizens but also among their governors. A Christian worldview is also indispensable for guaranteeing basic human rights for individuals. Because the Christian believes man is created in the image of God, he believes that each individual has value."[10]

"One of the most startling commentaries on this century is the fact that millions more have died at the hands of their own governments than in wars with other nations—all to preserve someone's power."[11]

---

[1] Justice William O. Douglas, Zorach v. Clausen, 343 U.S., 313 (1952).
[2] Russell Kirk, "The Christian Postulates of English & American Law," *Journal of Christian Jurisprudence* (Tulsa: Oral Roberts Univ., 1980), 66.
[3] Justice Anthony M. Kennedy, County of Allegheny v. ACLU, 492 U.S., 657 (1989).
[4] Ibid.
[5] A. E. Wilder Smith, *The Creation of Life* (Costa Mesa, CA: TWFT Publishers, 1970), ix.
[6] John W. Whitehead, *The Second American Revolution* (Westchester, IL: Crossway, 1982), 88.
[7] George Grant, *The Changing of the Guard: Biblical Principles for Political Action* (Ft. Worth: Dominion Press, 1987), 126.
[8] Doug Bandow, *Beyond Good Intentions: A Biblical View of Politics* (Westchester, IL: Crossway, 1988), 148.
[9] Carl F. H. Henry, *Twilight of a Great Civilization* (Westchester, IL: Crossway, 1988), 20.
[10] David A. Noebel, *Understanding the Times: The Religious Worldviews of Our Day and the Search for Truth* (Manitou Springs, CO: Summit Press, 1991), 624–625.
[11] Chuck Colson, *Kingdoms in Conflict* (Grand Rapids, MI: Zondervan, 1987), 270.

Fact Sheets

KEY CHRISTIAN SOURCES/CRITIQUES:

(recommended titles appear in brown)

LAW

Bastiat, Frédéric, *The Law*. Irvington-on-Hudson, NY: Foundation for Economic Education, 1998.

Bork, Robert H. *The Tempting of America: The Political Seduction of the Law*. New York: Free Press, 1990.

McConnell, Michael W. "The Origins and Historical Understanding of Free Exercise of Religion," *Harvard Law Review*, Vol. 103, no. 1410 (1990).

Titus, Herbert W. *God, Man, and Law: The Biblical Principles*. Oak Brook, IL: Institute in Basic Life Principles, 1994.

VanGemeren, Willem. *The Law, the Gospel, and the Modern Christian*. Grand Rapids, MI: Zondervan, 1993.

Wright, Christopher J. H. *An Eye for an Eye: The Place of Old Testament Ethics Today*. Downers Grove, IL: InterVarsity, 1983.

POLITICS

Amos, Gary T. *Defending the Declaration: How the Bible and Christianity Influenced the Writing of the Declaration of Independence*. Brentwood, TN: Wolgemuth & Hyatt, 1989.

Bandow, Doug and Fieldstead Institute. *Beyond Good Intentions: A Biblical View of Politics*. Westchester, IL: Crossway, 1988.

Bauman, Michael and David W. Hall, eds. *God and Caesar*. Camp Hill, PA: Christian Publications, 1994.

Burke, Thomas J. and Lissa Roche. *Man and State: Religion, Society, and the Constitution*. Hillsdale, MI: Hillsdale College Press, 1988.

Colson, Charles W. and Ellen Santilli Vaughn. *Kingdoms in Conflict*. New York: W. Morrow, 1987.

Doner, Colonel V. *The Samaritan Strategy: A New Agenda for Christian Activism*. Brentwood, TN: Wolgemuth & Hyatt, 1988.

Eidsmoe, John. *God and Caesar: Biblical Faith and Political Action*. Westchester, IL: Crossway, 1984.

Evans, M. Stanton. *The Theme Is Freedom: Religion, Politics, and the American Tradition*. Washington DC: Regnery, 1994.

Grant, George. *The Changing of the Guard: The Vital Role Christians Must Play in America's Unfolding Political and Cultural Drama*. Nashville: Broadman & Holman, 1995.

Hall, David W. *Savior or Servant: Putting Government in Its Place*. Oak Ridge, TN: Kuyper Institute, 1996.

Hart, Benjamin. *Faith and Freedom: The Christian Roots of American Liberty*. Dallas: Lewis & Stanley, 1988.

Neuhaus, Richard John. *The Naked Public Square: Religion and Democracy in America*. Grand Rapids, MI: Eerdmans, 1984.

Rushdoony, Rousas John. *Politics of Guilt and Pity*. Vallecito, CA: Ross House, 1995.

Schlossberg, Herbert. *Idols for Destruction: Christian Faith and Its Confrontation with American Society*. Washington DC: Regnery, 1990.

Smith, Gary Scott, ed. *God and Politics: Four Views on the Reformation of Civil Government*. Phillipsburg, NJ: Presbyterian & Reformed, 1989.

ABORTION

Beckwith, Francis. *Politically Correct Death: Answering the Arguments for Abortion Rights*. Grand Rapids, MI: Baker, 1993.

Beckwith, Francis J. "Roe V. Wade: Its Logic and Its Legacy." *Southern Baptist Theological Journal* 7, no. 2 (Summer 2003): 4–28.

Fournier, Keith A. and William D. Watkins. *In Defense of Life: Taking a Stand against the Culture of Death*. Colorado Springs, CO: NavPress, 1996.

Grant, George. *Grand Illusions: The Legacy of Planned Parenthood*. Nashville: Cumberland House, 2000.

Kasun, Jacqueline R. *The War against Population: The Economics and Ideology of World Population Control*. San Francisco: Ignatius, 1999.

CHURCH AND STATE

Cord, Robert L. *Separation of Church and State: Historical Fact and Current Fiction*. Grand Rapids, MI: Baker, 1988.

Eidsmoe, John. *Christianity and the Constitution: The Faith of Our Founding Fathers*. Grand Rapids, MI: Baker, 1987.

Whitehead, John W. *The Second American Revolution*. Elgin, IL: D. C. Cook, 1982.

HOMOSEXUALITY

Burtoft, Larry. *Setting the Record Straight: What Research Really Says About the Social Consequences of Homosexuality*. Colorado Springs, CO: Focus on the Family, 1994.

Grant, George and Mark A. Horne. *Legislating Immorality: The Homosexual Movement Comes out of the Closet*. Chicago: Moody, 1993.

Kennedy, D. James and Jerry Newcombe. *What's Wrong with Same-Sex Marriage?* Wheaton, IL: Crossway, 2004.

Magnuson, Roger J. *Are 'Gay Rights' Right? A Report on Homosexuality and the Law*. St. Paul: The Fund, 1985.

Satinover, Jeffrey. *Homosexuality and the Politics of Truth*. Grand Rapids, MI: Baker, 1996.

Stanton, Glenn T. and Bill Maier. *Marriage on Trial: The Case against Same-Sex Marriage and Parenting*. Downers Grove, IL: InterVarsity, 2004.

Fact Sheets

LEADERSHIP
FACT SHEET

KEY VERSES:

Proverbs 29:18   Ephesians 5:15–16

Esther 4:14   Romans 12:1–5

KEY ORGANIZATIONS:

Growing Leaders | www.growingleaders.com | 678.367.4187 |

Injoy | www.injoy.com | 800.333.6506 |

Myers Institute | www.myersinstitute.org | 423.570.1000 |

The Leadership Institute | www.leadershipinstitute.org | 800.827.5323 |

Passing the Baton International | www.passingthebaton.org | 423.570.1000 |

Summit Ministries | www.summit.org | 719.685.9103 |

KEY PUBLICATIONS:

Discipleship Journal | **NavPress** | www.navpress.com/dj | 800.366.7788 |

Student Leader | **American Student Government Association** | www.asgaonline.com | 352.373.6907 |

KEY QUOTES:

"Now Faithful play the Man, speak for thy God: Fear not the wicked's malice, nor their rod: Speak boldly man, the Truth is on thy side; Die for it, and to Life in triumph ride."[1]

"A ship in the harbor is safe, but that is not what ships are for."[2]

"You never conquer a mountain. Mountains can't be conquered; you conquer yourself—your hopes, your fears."[3]

"Champions know that success is inevitable; that there is no such thing as failure, only feedback."[4]

"The quality of a man's life is in direct proportion to his commitment to excellence."[5]

"Our plans miscarry because they have no aim. When a man does not know what harbor he is making for, no wind is the right wind."[6]

---

[1] John Bunyan
[2] John A. Shedd
[3] Jim Whitaker (first American to reach the summit of Mount Everest)
[4] Michael J. Gelb
[5] Vince Lombardi
[6] Seneca

"I studied the lives of great men and famous women, and I found that the men and women who got to the top were those who did the jobs they had in hand, with everything they had of energy and enthusiasm."[7]

"Life, like war, is a series of mistakes, and he is not the best Christian nor the best general who makes the fewest false steps. Poor mediocrity may secure that; but he is the best who wins the most splendid victories by the retrieval of mistakes. Forget mistakes: organize victory out of mistakes."[8]

"But when I said that nothing had been done I erred in one important matter. We had definitely committed ourselves and were halfway out of our ruts. We had put down our passage money—booked a sailing to Bombay. This may sound too simple, but is great in consequence. Until one is committed, there is hesitancy, the chance to draw back, always ineffectiveness. Concerning all acts of initiative (and creation), there is one elementary truth the ignorance of which kills countless ideas and splendid plans: that the moment one definitely commits oneself, then Providence moves too. A whole stream of events issues from the decision, raising in one's favor all manner of unforeseen incidents, meetings and material assistance, which no man could have dreamt would have come his way." Leadership is not so much the exercise of power itself as the empowerment of others."[9]

KEY SOURCES:
(recommended titles appear in brown)

Boice, James Montgomery. *Ordinary Men Called by God: A Study of Abraham, Moses, and David*. Grand Rapids, MI: Kregel, 1998.

Borthwick, Paul. *Leading the Way: Leadership Is Not Just for Super Christians*. Colorado Springs, CO: Navpress, 1989.

Castle, Tony. *Lives of Famous Christians: A Biographical Dictionary*. Ann Arbor, MI: Servant Books, 1988.

Cole, Edwin Louis. *Courage: Winning Life's Toughest Battles*. Southlake, TX: Watercolor, 2002.

Cowart, John W. *People Whose Faith Got Them into Trouble: Stories of Costly Discipleship*. Downers Grove, IL: InterVarsity, 1990.

De Pree, Max. *Leadership Is an Art*. New York: Currency, 2004.

Engstrom, Theodore Wilhelm. *The Making of a Christian Leader*. Grand Rapids, MI: Zondervan, 1976.

Fisher, Roger, Alan Sharp, and John Richardson. *Getting It Done: How to Lead When You're Not in Charge*. New York: Harper, 1998.

Foxe, John. *Foxe's Book of Martyrs*. Nashville: Thomas Nelson, 2000.

Hyde, Douglas Arnold. *Dedication and Leadership: Learning from the Communists*. Notre Dame, IN: University of Notre Dame Press, 1966.

Johnston, Ray. *Developing Student Leaders: How to Motivate, Select, Train, Empower Your Kids to Make a Difference*. Grand Rapids, MI: Zondervan, 1992.

Kouzes, James M. and Barry Z. Posner. *The Leadership Challenge: How to Keep Getting Extraordinary Things Done in Organizations*. San Francisco: Jossey-Bass, 1995.

Mattson, Ralph. *Visions of Grandeur: Leadership That Creates Positive Change*. Chicago: Moody, 1994.

Sanders, J. Oswald. *Spiritual Leadership*. Chicago: Moody, 1994.

Stanley, Andy. *The Next Generation Leader: 5 Essentials for Those Who Will Shape the Future*. Sisters, OR: Multnomah, 2003.

Stanley, Paul D. and J. Robert Clinton. *Connecting: The Mentoring Relationships You Need to Succeed in Life*. Colorado Springs, CO: NavPress, 1992.

Wilkins, Michael J. *Following the Master: Discipleship in the Steps of Jesus*. Grand Rapids, MI: Zondervan, 1992.

[7] President Harry Truman
[8] W. H. Murray
[9] Warren Bennis

Fact Sheets

Philosophy & Logic
Fact Sheet

Key Terms:

LOGIC

Deductive Reasoning: The process of reasoning that starts with an accepted rule and generalizes it to a specific situation in order to reach a conclusion; the conclusion is absolutely certain (e.g. if 5+4 = 9 and 6+3 = 9, then 5+4 = 6+3)

Fallacy: An error in either inductive or deductive reasoning

Inductive Reasoning: The process of reasoning that starts with a general principle and moves toward a rule in order to draw a conclusion; the conclusion is not "absolutely certain" (e.g. a court trial)

Logic [from the Greek *logos*]: The study of reasoning

The Principle of Excluded Middle: A is not non-A (e.g. white is not non-white)

The Principle of Identity: A is A (e.g. white is white)

The Principle of Non-contradiction: A thing cannot be both A and non-A at the same time and in the same sense (e.g. a color cannot be both white and blue)

PHILOSOPHY

Anti-realism: The belief that reality is subjectively constructed by human thought

Correspondence Theory of Truth: The belief that a statement is true if it corresponds to the facts of reality

Cosmology: The study of the structure, origin, and design of the universe

Deconstruction: A theory of literary criticism that seeks to expose the hidden assumptions and prejudices of the author of any written text, emphasizing the underlying racist, sexist, homophobic, or bourgeois bias of authors from the Western philosophic tradition

Dialectical Materialism: The belief that in everything there is a thesis (the way things are) and an antithesis (an opposition to the way things are), which must inevitably clash. The result of the struggle and merging that comes from the clash is the synthesis, which becomes the new thesis. This new thesis will eventually attract another antithesis, and produce a new synthesis

Epistemology: The study of knowledge

Metaphysics: The study of ultimate reality

Mind/Body Problem: The study of the relationship of the mind (e.g. mental events, mental functions, mental properties, and consciousness) to the physical body

Naturalism [or Materialism]: The philosophical belief that reality is composed solely of matter and that all phenomena can be explained in terms of natural causes e.g., law of gravity

Non-naturalism: The belief that everything is a part of God. The things that we can see and feel are only a manifestation of spirit, and all matter will melt away when universal consciousness is achieved

Ontology: The study of existence and being

Realism: The belief that what one encounters in the world exists independently of human thought

Supernaturalism: The belief that reality is more than nature; that a transcendent agent intervenes in the course of natural law

KEY VERSES:

Genesis 1:1
Deuteronomy 6:5
Matthew 22:37
John 1:1

Romans 12:2–3
1 Corinthians 1:18–2:16
2 Corinthians 10:5
Colossians 1:17

Colossians 2:3–8
2 Timothy 3:16
Revelation 19:13

KEY ORGANIZATIONS:

Fallacy Files | www.fallacyfiles.org |

Internet Encyclopedia of Philosophy | www.iep.utm.edu |

Logical Fallacies | www.logicalfallacies.info |

Stanford Encyclopedia of Philosophy | http://plato.stanford.edu |

KEY PUBLICATIONS:

Philosophia Christi | **Evangelical Philosophical Society** | www.epsociety.org |

KEY QUOTES:

"A little philosophy inclineth man's mind to atheism, but depth in philosophy bringeth men's minds about to religion."[1]

"5% think, 10% think they think, 85% would rather die than think."[2]

"Arguments, like men, are often pretenders."[3]

"For we let our young men and women go out unarmed in a day when armor was never so necessary. By teaching them to read, we have left them at the mercy of the printed word. By the invention of the film and the radio, we have made certain that no aversion to reading shall secure them from the incessant battery of words, words, words. They do not know what the words mean; they do not know how to ward them off or blunt their edge or fling them back; they are a prey to words in their emotions instead of being the masters of them in their intellects... We have lost the tools of learning, and in their absence can only make a botched and piecemeal job of it."[4]

---

[1] Hugh G.Dick, ed., *Select Writings of Francis Bacon* (New York: Random, 1955), 44.
[2] Anonymous
[3] Plato
[4] Dorothy Sayers, speech at Oxford, 1947, quoted in Roy Maynard, "Trivium Pursuit," *World* (October 8, 1994).

KEY SOURCES:
(recommended titles appear in brown)

LOGIC

Bluedorn, Nathaniel. *The Fallacy Detective: Thirty-Six Lessons on How to Recognize Bad Reasoning.* Muscatine, IA: Christian Logic, 2003.

Bluedorn, Nathaniel and Hans Bluedorn. *The Thinking Toolbox: Thirty-Five Lessons That Will Build Your Reasoning Skills.* Muscatine, IA: Christian Logic, 2005.

Capaldi, Nicholas. *How to Win Every Argument.* New York: MJF, 1999.

Copi, Irving M. and Carl Cohen. *Introduction to Logic.* Upper Saddle River, NJ: Prentice Hall, 2005.

Engel, S. Morris. *With Good Reason: An Introduction to Informal Fallacies.* Boston: St. Martin's, 2000.

Geisler, Norman L. and Ron Brooks. *Come, Let Us Reason: An Introduction to Logical Thinking.* Grand Rapids, MI: Baker, 1990.

Schick, Theodore and Lewis Vaughn. *How to Think About Weird Things.* Boston: McGraw-Hill, 2005.

Walton, Douglas N. *Informal Logic: A Handbook for Critical Argumentation.* New York: Cambridge Univ. Press, 1989.

PHILOSOPHY

DeWeese, Garrett J. and J. P. Moreland. *Philosophy Made Slightly Less Difficult.* Downers Grove, IL: InterVarsity, 2005.

Gaarder, Jostein. *Sophie's World.* New York: Farrar, Straus & Giroux, 1994.

Geisler, Norman L. and Paul D. Feinberg. *Introduction to Philosophy: A Christian Perspective.* Grand Rapids, MI: Baker, 1980.

Moreland, J. P. *Love Your God with all Your Mind.* Colorado Springs, CO: NavPress, 1997.

———. *Scaling the Secular City: A Defense of Christianity.* Grand Rapids, MI: Baker, 1987.

Moreland, J. P. and William Lane Craig. *Philosophical Foundations for a Christian Worldview.* Downers Grove, IL: InterVarsity, 2003.

Nash, Ronald H. *Life's Ultimate Questions: An Introduction to Philosophy.* Grand Rapids, MI: Zondervan, 1999.

———. *Worldviews in Conflict: Choosing Christianity in a World of Ideas.* Grand Rapids, MI: Zondervan, 1992.

Pearcey, Nancy. *Total Truth: Liberating Christianity from Its Cultural Captivity.* Wheaton, IL: Crossway, 2004.

Plantinga, Alvin. *Warranted Christian Belief.* New York: Oxford University Press, 2000.

Schaeffer, Francis A. *A Christian View of Philosophy and Culture.* Westchester, IL: Crossway, 1982.

CHRISTIAN MIND

Blamires, Harry. *The Christian Mind: How Should a Christian Think?* Ann Arbor, MI: Vine, 2004.

———. *The Post-Christian Mind: Exposing Its Destructive Agenda.* Ann Arbor, MI: Vine, 1999.

———. *Recovering the Christian Mind: Meeting the Challenge of Secularism.* Downers Grove, IL: InterVarsity, 1988.

Boice, James Montgomery. *Mind Renewal in a Mindless Age: Preparing to Think and Act Biblically.* Grand Rapids, MI: Baker, 1993.

Lewis, C. S. *Mere Christianity.* San Francisco: HarperSanFrancisco, 2001.

Moreland, J. P. *Kingdom Triangle: Recover the Christian Mind, Renovate the Soul, Restore the Spirit's Power.* Grand Rapids, MI: Zondervan, 2006.

———. *Love Your God with All Your Mind.* Colorado Springs, CO: NavPress, 1997.

Moreland, J. P. and William Lane Craig. *Philosophical Foundations for a Christian Worldview.* Downers Grove, IL: InterVarsity, 2003.

Noebel, David A. *Understanding the Times: The Collision of Today's Competing Worldviews.* Manitou Springs, CO: Summit Press, 2006.

Pearcey, Nancy. *Total Truth: Liberating Christianity from Its Cultural Captivity.* Wheaton, IL: Crossway, 2004.

Plantinga, Alvin. *Warranted Christian Belief.* New York: Oxford University Press, 2000.

Sire, James W. *Discipleship of the Mind: Learning to Love God in the Ways We Think.* Downers Grove, IL: InterVarsity, 1990.

———. *Habits of the Mind: Intellectual Life as a Christian Calling.* Downers Grove, IL: InterVarsity, 2000.

Fact Sheets

Psychology
Fact Sheet

Key Terms:

Higher Consciousness: The ever-increasing awareness of one's spiritual essence and the underlying spiritual nature in all things

Psychological Dualism (Mind/Body): The belief that the mind and the body exist as separate entities, i.e. the mind is not mere matter

Psychological Monism: The belief that the mind and the body exist as part of the same entity, i.e. the mind is a part of the material body

Self-actualization: The highest level of a person's potential and the ultimate goal of Maslow's "hierarchy of needs" (a theory contending that as humans meet their basic needs, they seek to satisfy successively higher needs)

Socially-constructed Selves: The belief that one's identity is constantly changing as a result of ever-changing social factors

Traditional Behaviorism: A branch of psychology which asserts that human behavior can be reduced into terms of principles that do not require consideration of unobservable mental events, such as ideas, emotions, and a mind, i.e. a form of materialism which claims that all human behavior is the result of materialistic processes and not the free will of the mind

Key Verses:
Luke 1:46–47
Titus 2:13

Key organizations:
Focus on the Family | www.fotf.org | 800.232.6459 |

Key Quotes:
"He breathed into his nostrils the breath of life and man became a living soul." — Genesis 2:7

Key Christian Sources:
(recommended titles appear in brown)

Dualism
Moreland, J. P. and Scott B. Rae. *Body & Soul: Human Nature & the Crisis in Ethics.* Downers Grove, IL: InterVarsity, 2000.

Homosexuality (Causes and Counseling)
Dallas, Joe. *Desires in Conflict.* Eugene, OR: Harvest, 2003.
Konrad, J. A. *You Don't Have to Be Gay: Hope and Freedom for Males Struggling with Homosexuality or for Those Who Know of Someone Who Is.* Hilo, HI: Pacific, 1992.

Riley, Mona and Brad Sargent. *Unwanted Harvest?* Nashville: Broadman & Holman, 1995.

Wolfe, Christopher, ed. *Same-Sex Matters: The Challenge of Homosexuality*. Dallas: Spence, 2000.

Worthen, Anita and Bob Davies. *Someone I Love Is Gay: How Family and Friends Can Respond*. Downers Grove, IL: InterVarsity, 1996.

SECULAR PSYCHOLOGY (CRITIQUE)

Justman, Stewart. *Fool's Paradise: The Unreal World of Pop Psychology*. Chicago: Ivan R. Dee, 2005.

Kilpatrick, William. *The Emperor's New Clothes*. Westchester, IL: Crossway, 1985.

———. *Psychological Seduction: The Failure of Modern Psychology*. Ridgefield, CT: Roger A. McCaffrey, 1983.

Milton, Joyce. *The Road to Malpsychia: Humanistic Psychology and Our Discontents*. San Francisco: Encounter Books, 2002.

Vitz, Paul C. *Faith of the Fatherless: The Psychology of Atheism*. Dallas: Spence, 1999.

———. *Psychology as Religion: The Cult of Self-Worship*. Grand Rapids, MI: Eerdmans, 1994.

Radical Environmentalism
Fact Sheet

Key Terms:

Animal Rights: A form of Radical Environmentalism which places non-human species on par with human beings both intrinsically and morally

Deep Ecology: A form of Radical Environmentalism that places an intrinsic value on all nature. This position leads to an ecocentric system of environmental ethics instead of an anthrocentric (people centered) or theocentric (God centered) system

Eco-terrorism: Acts of violence, sabotage, vandalism, property damage, or intimidation committed against individuals and companies in the name of environmentalism

Environmentalism: A broad term that connotes concern and stresses the need for the protection and preservation of the environment. Environmentalists usually operate through peaceful methods of social action (e.g. political lobbying, public awareness campaigns, etc.)

Green Party: A political party with radical environmentalist leanings. Founded in Hobart, Australia in 1972; since that time it has gained, to varying degrees, popularity throughout the world

Radical Environmentalism: An extreme form of environmentalism that views humanity as a mere animal and a plague upon nature and the environment. Radical environmentalists often resort to non-traditional forms of activism (e.g. eco-terrorism)

Key Verses:

Genesis 1; 3:17–19; 9:2–3   Romans 8:18–23   Hebrews 1:3
Psalms 8:4–8; 115:16   Colossians 1:17   2 Peter 2:12

Key Organizations:

Capital Research Center | www.greenwatch.org | 202.483.6900 |

CO$_2$ Science | www.co2science.org | 480.966.3719 |

Competitive Enterprise Institute | http://cei.org | 202.331.1010 |

Enviro Truth | www.envirotruth.org | 202.543.4110 |

Friends of Science Society | www.friendsofscience.org |

Global Warming | www.globalwarming.org |

Heritage Foundation | www.heritage.org | 202.546.4400 |

Cornwall Alliance for the Stewardship of Creation | www.stewards.net | 703.569.4653 |

Junk Science | www.junkscience.com |

Property and Environment Research Center | www.perc.org | 406.587.9591 |

Fact Sheets

KEY QUOTES:

"Human beings inhabit no more than 3 percent of the land surface of the earth. What's more, the amount of habitable land is not limited. Singapore was once marshland. Much of Holland was once under water… To put the matter in perspective, if the world's 5.4 billion people were put in Jacksonville, Florida, each person would have four square feet to stand in. In Texas each person would have at least fourteen hundred square feet, the area of a good-sized two-bedroom apartment."[1]

"The advocates of government family planning have their own set of justification, thinly disguised to avoid arousing resistance to population control. Sex education, for instance, will overcome 'ignorance' and 'fears and anxieties', and the adolescent pregnancy programs will in turn 'reduce teenage pregnancy and prevent abortion.' Not reported in the headlines, but frankly admitted in the programs, is the truth: the limitation of population. Equally absent from the news are the results of the government programs—no improvement in the psychological or physical health of the young and no reduction in pregnancy or abortion. Nor, ironically, is there any proof that they have reduced fertility. What the programs have achieved, and to a frightening degree, is the power and influence of the clique advocating government family planning, which it well understands is an essential intermediate step toward comprehensive population control."[2]

[Regarding old growth forests, atmospheric CO_2, and the "Greenhouse Effect":]
"Mature trees, like all living things, metabolize more slowly as they grow old. A forest of young, vigorously growing trees will remove five to seven tons more CO_2 per acre than old growth. There are plenty of good reasons to preserve old growth forests, but redressing the CO_2 balance is not one of them. If we were really interested (as we should be) in reducing atmospheric CO_2, we should be vigorously pursuing reforestation and the planting of trees and shrubs, including in urban areas, where local impacts on the atmosphere are greatest.

"Reforestation has been going on through enlightened forestry practices on private lands by timber companies and as a result of changes in agricultural and land use. In the United States, the average annual wood growth is now more than three times what it was in 1920, and the growing stock has increased 18 percent from 1952 to 1977. Forests in America continue to increase in size, even while supplying a substantial fraction of the world's timber needs."[3]

KEY PROPONENTS:

- Lester Brown (President of *The World Watch Institute*)
- Paul Ehrlich
- David Foreman (founder of *Earth First!*)
- Al Gore (former U.S. Vice President)
- Les Knight (founder of *Voluntary Human Extinction Movement*)
- Arne Naess (Norwegian philosopher of ecology)
- Peter Singer (Princeton University)

KEY PROPONENT SOURCES:

ANIMAL RIGHTS

Singer, Peter. *Animal Liberation: A New Ethics for Our Treatment of Animals*. New York: Random, 1975.
———. *In Defense of Animals: The Second Wave*. Malden, MA: Blackwell, 2006.

---

[1] Sheldon L. Richman, "Much Ado About Nothing: Population Growth as Promise, Not Problem," *The World & I*, vol. 8, no. 6 (1993): 374–75.
[2] Jacqueline Kasun, *The War Against Population: The Economics and Ideology of Population Control* (San Francisco: Ignatius, 1988), 206.
[3] Dixy Lee Ray with Lou Guzzo, *Trashing the Planet* (New York: HarperCollins, 1990), 36.

Fact Sheets

ECOLOGY

Brown, Lester Russell. *Plan B 2.0: Rescuing a Planet under Stress and a Civilization in Trouble*. New York: W.W. Norton, 2006.

Brown, Lester Russell and Earth Policy Institute. *Eco-Economy: Building an Economy for the Earth*. New York: W.W. Norton, 2001. Brown, Lester Russell and Worldwatch Institute. *State of the World 2001: A Worldwatch Institute Report on Progress toward a Sustainable Society*. London: Earthscan, 2001.

Brown, Lester Russell, Janet Larsen, Bernie Fischlowitz-Roberts, and Earth Policy Institute. *The Earth Policy Reader*. New York: W.W. Norton, 2002.

Gore, Albert. *Earth in the Balance: Ecology and the Human Spirit*. Boston: Houghton Mifflin, 2000.

Næss, Arne and David Rothenberg. *Ecology, Community, and Lifestyle: Outline of an Ecosophy*. New York: Cambridge University Press, 1989.

POPULATION CONTROL

Ehrlich, Paul R. and Anne H. Ehrlich. *The Population Explosion*. New York: Simon & Schuster, 1990.

KEY SOURCES/CRITIQUES:

(recommended titles appear in brown)

Avery, Dennis T. *Saving the Planet with Pesticides and Plastic: The Environmental Triumph of High-Yield Farming*. Indianapolis: Hudson Institute, 2000.

Bailey, Ronald. *Earth Report 2000: Revisiting the True State of the Planet*. New York: McGraw Hill, 2000.

Bast, Joseph L., Peter Jensen Hill, and Richard Rue. *Eco-Sanity: A Common-Sense Guide to Environmentalism*. Lanham, MD: Madison Books, 1994.

Beisner, E. Calvin. *Prospects for Growth: A Biblical View of Population, Resources, and the Future*. Westchester, IL: Crossway, 1990.

———. *Where Garden Meets Wilderness: Evangelical Entry into the Environmental Debate*. Grand Rapids, MI: Eerdmans, 1997.

Kasun, Jacqueline R. *The War against Population: The Economics and Ideology of World Population Control*. San Francisco: Ignatius, 1999.

Kaufman, Wallace. *No Turning Back: Dismantling the Fantasies of Environmental Thinking*. New York: Basic, 1994.

Lomborg, Bjørn. *The Skeptical Environmentalist: Measuring the Real State of the World*. New York: Cambridge University Press, 2001.

Ray, Dixy Lee and Louis R. Guzzo. *Environmental Overkill: Whatever Happened to Common Sense?* Washington DC: Regnery, 1993.

———. *Trashing the Planet: How Science Can Help Us Deal with Acid Rain, Depletion of the Ozone, and Nuclear Waste (among Other Things)*. Washington DC: Regnery, 1990.

Rubin, Charles T. *The Green Crusade: Rethinking the Roots of Environmentalism*. New York: Free Press, 1994.

Sanera, Michael and Jane S. Shaw. *Facts, Not Fear: Teaching Children About the Environment*. Washington DC: Regnery, 1999.

Simon, Julian Lincoln, ed. *The State of Humanity*. Cambridge, MA: Cato Institute, 1995.

Young, Richard A. *Healing the Earth: A Theocentric Perspective on Environmental Problems and Their Solutions*. Nashville: Broadman & Holman, 1994.

Fact Sheets

SCRIPTURAL RELIABILITY
FACT SHEET

KEY TERMS:

Critical Methodology: Various methods of examining the Bible with the aim of discovering its "genuineness"

Documentary Hypothesis: A hypothesis derived from criticism which asserts that the Pentateuch is a compilation of various sources usually identified as J.E.P.D.—Yahwist author, Elohist author, Deuteronomist author, and Priestly author

Form Criticism: The means of study and investigation of a biblical writing's structural form. The goal is to discover the "pre-historical" oral and written traditions that gave rise to the text

Redaction Criticism: The study and investigation of a biblical writing to discern how a text has been "edited." The goal is to discover what the ancient writer actually wrote as opposed to what has been handed down to us

Source Criticism: The study and investigation of biblical writings according to their sources of origin

Textual Criticism: The means of study and investigation of biblical writings used to discover the "original wording." The goal is to discover what the ancient writer actually wrote as opposed to what has been handed down to us

The Quest for the Historical Jesus: A movement within secular Christian scholarship that is seeking to discover the "true historical Jesus." Those that are part of this quest assume that Jesus was neither the Son the God nor a performer of miracles.

KEY VERSES:

Psalm 14:1; 199:89   Luke 1:1–4; 16:17; 21:33   Hebrews 11:6
Isaiah 40:8   Acts 1:1-3; 2:32   1 John 1:1-3
Matthew 5:18; 24:35   1 Corinthians 15:1–9   Revelation 22:18–19
Mark 13:31   2 Timothy 3:16

KEY ORGANIZATIONS:

Biblical Archaeology Society | www.bib-arch.org | 800.221.4644 |

KEY PUBLICATIONS:

Archaeology Odyssey | **Biblical Archaeology Society** | www.bib-arch.org | 800.221.4644 |

Biblical Archaeology Review | **Biblical Archaeology Society** | www.bib-arch.org | 800.221.4644 |

Bible Review | **Biblical Archaeology Society** | www.bib-arch.org | 800.221.4644 |

KEY QUOTES:

"The earliest preachers of the gospel knew the value of...first-hand testimony, and appealed to it time and again. 'We are witnesses of these things,' was their constant and confident assertion. And it can have been by no means so easy as some writers think to invent words and deeds of Jesus in those early years, when so many of His disciples were about, who could remember what had and had not happened…

"And it was not only friendly eyewitnesses that the early preachers had to reckon with; there were others less well disposed who were also conversant with the main facts of the ministry and death of Jesus. The disciples could not afford to risk inaccuracies (not to speak of willful manipulation of the facts), which would at once be exposed by those who would be only too glad to do so. On the contrary, one of the strong points in the original apostolic preaching is the confident appeal to the knowledge of the hearers; they not only said, 'We are witnesses of these things,' but also, 'As you yourselves also know' [Acts 2:22]. Had there been any tendency to depart from the facts in any material respect, the possible presence of hostile witnesses in the audience would have served as a further corrective."[1]

"There is no body of ancient literature in the world which enjoys such a wealth of good textual attestation as the New Testament."[2]

"There is, I imagine, no body of literature in the world that has been exposed to the stringent analytical study that the four gospels have sustained for the past 200 years. This is not something to be regretted: it is something to be accepted with satisfaction. Scholars today who treat the gospels as credible historical documents do so in the full light of this analytical study, not by closing their minds to it."[3]

"Skepticism toward the reliability of Scripture seems to survive in many academic circles despite the repeated collapse of critical theories. One still finds a disposition to trust secular writers whose credentials in providing historical testimony are often less adequate than those of the biblical writers. Not long ago many scholars rejected the historicity of the patriarchal accounts, denied that writing existed in Moses' day, and ascribed the Gospels and Epistles to second-century writers. But higher criticism has sustained some spectacular and even stunning reverses, mainly through the findings of archaeology. No longer is it held that the glories of King Solomon's era are literary fabrication, that 'Yahweh,' the redemptive God of the Hebrews, was unknown before the eighth-century prophets, or that Ezra's representations about the Babylonian captivity are fictional. Archaeologists have located the long-lost copper mines of Solomon's time. Tablets discovered at Ebla near Aleppo confirm that names similar to those of the patriarchs were common among people who lived in Ebla shortly before the events recorded in the later chapters of Genesis took place."[4]

KEY SOURCES:
(recommended titles appear in brown)

CANONIZATION, INSPIRATION, AND INERRANCY
Bruce, F. F. *The Books and the Parchments*. Westwood, NJ: Revell, 1963.
———. *The Canon of Scripture*. Downers Grove, IL: InterVarsity, 1988.
———. *The New Testament Documents: Are They Reliable?* Grand Rapids, MI: Eerdmans, 1981.
Carson, D. A. and John D. Woodbridge, eds. *Hermeneutics, Authority, and Canon*. Grand Rapids, MI: Academie, 1986.
Comfort, Philip Wesley, ed. *The Origin of the Bible*. Wheaton, IL: Tyndale, 2003.
Geisler, Norman L., ed. *Inerrancy*. Grand Rapids, MI: Zondervan, 1980.
Warfield, Benjamin and Samuel G. Craig. *The Inspiration and Authority of the Bible*. Philadelphia: Presbyterian & Reformed, 1948.

HISTORICITY OF CHRISTIAN WORLDVIEW
Blomberg, Craig. *The Historical Reliability of John's Gospel*. Downers Grove, IL: InterVarsity, 2002.
———. *The Historical Reliability of the Gospels*. Downers Grove, IL: InterVarsity, 1987.

---

[1] F. F. Bruce, *Are the New Testament Documents Reliable?* (Grand Rapids, MI: Eerdmans, 1960), 45–46.
[2] F. F. Bruce, *The Books and the Parchments* (Westwood, NJ: Revell, 1963), 178.
[3] Craig Blomberg, *The Historical Reliability of the Gospels* (Downers Grove, IL: InterVarsity, 1987), ix.
[4] Carl F. H. Henry, "The Authority of the Bible," *The Origin of the Bible*, Philip Wesley Comfort, ed. (Wheaton, IL: Tyndale, 1992), 17.

Fact Sheets

Copan, Paul, ed. *Will the Real Jesus Please Stand Up? A Debate between William Lane Craig and John Dominic Crossan*. Grand Rapids, MI: Baker, 1998.

Craig, William Lane. *Knowing the Truth About the Resurrection: Our Response to the Empty Tomb*. Ann Arbor, MI: Servant, 1988.

Free, Joseph P. and Howard Frederic. *Archaeology and Bible History*. Grand Rapids, MI: Zondervan, 1992.

Geisler, Norman L. *Systematic Theology*. Minneapolis: Bethany, 2002 (Vol. 1, Chapters 25 and 26).

Habermas, Gary R. and Michael R. Licona. *The Case for the Resurrection of Jesus*. Grand Rapids, MI: Kregel, 2004.

Kitchen, K. A. *The Bible in Its World: The Bible and Archaeology Today*. Exeter, RI: Paternoster, 1977.

———. *On the Reliability of the Old Testament*. Grand Rapids, MI: Eerdmans, 2003.

Nash, Ronald H. *The Gospel and the Greeks: Did the New Testament Borrow from Pagan Thought?* Richardson, TX: Probe, 1992.

Thompson, J. A. *The Bible and Archaeology*. Grand Rapids, MI: Eerdmans, 1982.

Wilkins, Michael J. and J. P. Moreland. *Jesus under Fire*. Grand Rapids, MI: Zondervan, 1995.

TEXTUAL CONSISTENCY

Archer, Gleason Leonard. *Encyclopedia of Bible Difficulties*. Grand Rapids, MI: Zondervan, 1982.

Kaiser, Walter C. *Hard Sayings of the Bible*. Downers Grove, IL: InterVarsity, 1996.

Geisler, Norman L. and Thomas A. Howe. *When Critics Ask: A Popular Handbook on Bible Difficulties*. Wheaton, IL: Victor, 1992.

Hayley, John W. *Alleged Discrepancies of the Bible*. New Kensington, PA: Whitaker House, 2004.

SOCIOLOGY
FACT SHEET

<u>KEY TERMS:</u>

Classless Society: The Marxists vision of a future society free from class antagonism, which will purportedly be brought about by the establishment of communism and the demise of oppressive capitalism

Family, Church, State: The Christian belief that society is divided into three God-ordained institutions

Feminism: A broad term that connotes concern and stresses equality between the sexes

Non-traditional Family: A number of alternatives to traditional marriage including modified open marriage, triads, cooperatives, collectives, urban communes, extended intimates, swinging, group marriage, same-sex marriage, part-time marriage, etc.

Polygamy, Mosque, Islamic State: The Islamic belief that society is composed of three institutions: family (which can be polygamous), Mosque, and State

Polymorphous Sexualities: The belief that individuals can exist in more than one gender form—based upon one's sexual identity and preference—(including gay, bi-sexual, lesbian, transgendered, transsexual, etc.)

Radical Feminism: An extreme form of feminism that rejects any inherent differences between the sexes. Radical feminism seeks to challenge all traditional gender standards. Radical feminists often belittle other women who have chosen the occupation of wife and/or mother. They also generally promote promiscuity, lesbianism, abortion, and state-run child care

Sexual Egalitarianism: The belief that all sexual practices—which are based on preference and sexual identity (or polymorphous sexualities) and not physical characteristics—are equal

<u>KEY VERSES:</u>	FAMILY	MEN
CHILDREN Exodus 20:12 Proverbs 1:8; 6:20; 17:17 Ephesians 6:1–3 Colossians 3:20	Psalm 33:10–11;103:9 Proverbs 11:11; 14:43; 29 Daniel 2:20-21 Romans 13:1–7 1 Timothy 2:1 1 Peter 2:13–14	Psalm 112 Luke 12:39 Ephesians 5:25–33; 6:4 Colossians 3:19 1 Timothy 3:1–8; 5:8 Titus 1:7-9; 2:6–8
CHURCH Matthew 18:15–20 Acts 20:28 1 Corinthians 5:9-13; 11:17–26; 12:4–31 Ephesians: 3:6–10; 5:21–24 Colossians 1:13–20	**MARRIAGE** Genesis 1:26–27; 2:18–25 Malachi 2:14–16 1 Corinthians 11:11 Hebrews 13:4	**WOMEN** Proverbs 13:4–5; 31:10–31 Ephesians 5:22–24 Colossians 3:18 1 Timothy 5:10–14 Titus 1:3–5 1 Peter 3:4

Fact Sheets

KEY ORGANIZATIONS:

American Family Association | www.afa.net |

Concerned Women for America | www.cwfa.org | 202.488.7000 |

Eagle Forum | www.eagleforum.org | 618.462.5415 |

Family Research Council | www.frc.org | 800.225.4008 |

Focus on the Family | www.fotf.org | 800.232.6459 |

Promise Keepers | www.promisekeepers.org | 866.776.6473 |

KEY QUOTES:

"For this reason a man will leave his father and mother and be united to his wife, and the two will become one flesh."— Ephesians 5:31

"The Christian worldview is intimately familiar with the experience of emptiness, with the despair and impotence that radical feminists—like all of us—seek to escape. We call this experience the human condition. Christians know the dark night of the soul, but we also know that self-glorifying rage will only plunge us deeper into the abyss."[1]

"Feminists are becoming difficult to identify, not because they do not exist, but because their philosophy has been integrated into mainstream society so thoroughly. The philosophy is almost unidentifiable as feminist, for it is virtually indistinguishable from mainstream."[2]

"Feminism freed men, not women...feminism gave men all the financial and personal advantages over women. The truth is, a woman can't live the true feminist life unless she denies her child-bearing biology. The reality of feminism is a lot of frenzied and overworked women dropping kids off at day-care centers. Women should get educations so they can be brainy in the way they raise their children. Women and men are not equal, they are different. The economy might even improve if women came home, opening up jobs for unemployed men, who could then support a wife and children, the way it was, pre-feminism."[3]

KEY SOURCES:
(recommended titles appear in brown)

CHURCH

Bonhoeffer, Dietrich and John W. Doberstein. *Life Together*. San Francisco: HarperSanFrancisco, 1993.

Clapp, Rodney. *A Peculiar People: The Church as Culture in a Post-Christian Society*. Downers Grove, IL: InterVarsity, 1996.

Ferguson, Everett. *The Church of Christ: A Biblical Ecclesiology for Today*. Grand Rapids, MI: Eerdmans, 1996.

Hayes, Edward L., Charles R. Swindoll, and Roy B. Zuck. *The Church: The Body of Christ in the World of Today*. Nashville: Word, 1999.

Minnery, Tom. *Why You Can't Stay Silent: A Biblical Mandate to Shape Our Culture*. Wheaton, IL: Tyndale, 2001.

Nouwen, Henri J. M. *My Sister, My Brother: Life Together in Christ*. Iamsville, MD: Word Among Us Press, 2005.

---

[1] Katherine Kersten, "How the Feminist Establishment Hurts Women," *Christianity Today* (June 20, 1994).
[2] Mary A. Kassian, *The Feminist Gospel* (Westchester, IL: Crossway, 1922), 251.
[3] Kay Ebeling, "The Failure of Feminism," *Newsweek* (November 19, 1990).

Roberts, Wes and Glenn Marshall. *Reclaiming God's Original Intent for the Church*. Colorado Springs, CO: NavPress, 2004.

Stark, Rodney. *The Rise of Christianity: How the Obscure, Marginal Jesus Movement Became the Dominant Religious Force in the Western World in a Few Centuries*. San Francisco: HarperSanFrancisco, 1997.

FAMILY

Allender, Dan B. and Tremper Longman. *Intimate Allies*. Wheaton, IL: Tyndale, 1995.

Andrews, Robert. *The Family: God's Weapon for Victory*. Mukilteo, WA: Winepress, 2002.

Crabb, Lawrence J. *The Marriage Builder: A Blueprint for Couples and Counselors*. Grand Rapids, MI: Zondervan, 1992.

Dobson, James C. and Gary Lee Bauer. *Children at Risk: The Battle for the Hearts and Minds of Our Kids*. Dallas: Word, 1990.

Elliot, Elisabeth. *Passion and Purity: Learning to Bring Your Love Life under Christ's Control*. Grand Rapids, MI: Fleming H. Revell, 2002.

Gairdner, William D. *The War against the Family*. Toronto: Stoddart, 1992.

Gilder, George F. *Men and Marriage*. Gretna, LA: Pelican, 1986.

Pride, Mary. *All the Way Home: Power for Your Family to Be Its Best*. Westchester, IL: Crossway, 1989.

Schlafly, Phyllis, ed. *Who Will Rock the Cradle? The Battle for Control of Child Care in America*. Dallas: Word, 1989.

Thoburn, Robert. *The Children Trap: Biblical Principles for Education*. Nashville: Thomas Nelson, 1986.

Thomas, Gary. *Sacred Marriage: What If God Designed Marriage to Make Us Holy More Than to Make Us Happy?* Grand Rapids, MI: Zondervan, 2000.

STATE

Bauman, Michael and David W. Hall. *God and Caesar*. Camp Hill, PA: Christian Publications, 1994.

Burke, Thomas J. and Lissa Roche. *Man and State: Religion, Society, and the Constitution*. Hillsdale, MI: Hillsdale College Press, 1988.

Eidsmoe, John. *God and Caesar: Biblical Faith and Political Action*. Westchester, IL: Crossway, 1984.

Hall, David W. *Savior or Servant? Putting Government in Its Place*. Oak Ridge, TN: Kuyper Institute, 1996.

Smith, Gary Scott. *God and Politics: Four Views on the Reformation of Civil Government*. Phillipsburg, NJ: Presbyterian & Reformed, 1989.

RADICAL FEMINISM

Blotnick, Sully. *Otherwise Engaged: The Private Lives of Successful Career Women*. New York: Facts on File, 1985.

Browne, Kingsley. *Biology at Work: Rethinking Sexual Equality*. New Brunswick, NJ: Rutgers Univ. Press, 2002.

Farrell, Warren. *The Myth of Male Power: Why Men Are the Disposable Sex*. New York: Berkley, 2001.

Graglia, F. Carolyn. *Domestic Tranquility: A Brief against Feminism*. Dallas: Spence, 1998.

Levin, Michael E. *Feminism and Freedom*. New Brunswick, NJ: Transaction, 1987.

Mitchell, Brian. *Weak Link: The Feminization of the American Military*. Washington DC: Regnery, 1989.

Rhoads, Steven E. *Taking Sex Differences Seriously*. San Francisco: Encounter Books, 2004.

Sayers, Dorothy L. *Are Women Human?* Grand Rapids, MI: Eerdmans, 2005.

Schlafly, Phyllis. *Feminist Fantasies*. Dallas: Spence, 2003.

Sommers, Christina Hoff. *The War against Boys: How Misguided Feminism Is Harming Our Young Men*. New York: Simon & Schuster, 2000.

———. *Who Stole Feminism? How Women Have Betrayed Women*. New York: Simon & Schuster, 1994.

Tooley, James. *The Miseducation of Women*. Chicago: Ivan R. Dee, 2003.

THEOLOGY
FACT SHEET

KEY TERMS:

THEOLOGY

Atheism: The denial of the existence of a supernatural God

Death of God Theology: A movement which flourished in the 1960s and 1970s, essentially promoting the idea that religion did not need to invoke "God" in the area of theology

General Revelation: God's communication—through nature and conscience—regarding his existence

Neo-orthodoxy: reacting to liberalization in theology, this movement stressed 1) the primacy of revelation while downplaying natural theology and human reason and 2) the near total transcendence and incomprehensibility of God.

Panentheism: the view that God is immanent, yet still transcendent, within the universe

Pantheism: The belief that god is everything and everything is god

Post-conservative Christianity [or Emergent Church]: a relatively new movement of Christians who are incorporating elements of postmodernism into their theology

Religious Pluralism: The belief that one should be tolerant of all religious beliefs since no one religion can be true

Special Revelation: God's specific communication—through the Bible and Jesus Christ—about salvation and himself

Theism: The belief in the existence of a supernatural God

Trinitarian Theism: The belief in one god who exists as three separate persons—Father, Son, and Spirit

HERMENEUTICS

Biblical Criticism: The study and investigation of biblical writings in order to understand the circumstances, background, history, language, authorship, and audience of the text

Exegesis: Extracting the author's original meaning from a text

Hermeneutics: The science of biblical interpretation used to discover the accurate meaning of a given text

Isogesis: Reading a personal bias into the text

RELIGIOUS PLURALISM

Inclusivism: The general sense that Jesus Christ is somehow superior to other religious figures and that salvation is somehow based upon his person and work

Particularism [also, negatively, Exclusivism]: The historical Christian view that the Bible is God's Word and that the person and work of Jesus Christ is the only means of salvation

Pluralism: The view that Christianity and Christ are not unique or superior to other religions or religions figures. Salvation can be found through means other than Jesus Christ.

Restrictivism: The view that only those who hear and respond to the Gospel of Jesus Christ will be saved [all restrictivists are particularists, but not necessarily vice-versa]

Universalism: The belief that everyone (or virtually everyone) will find salvation after death

KEY VERSES:

Genesis 1:1
Proverbs 10:28; 29:1
Ecclesiastes 7:29
Matthew 4:1–11; 9:6;
  23:14; 24:46

Mark 1:12–13; 12:40
Luke 4:1–13; 20:47
John 3:36; 5:29; 6:33; 14:6
Acts 4:12
Colossians 2:9

1 Timothy 1:17; 6:16
2 Timothy 3:16–17
Hebrews 4:12
1 John 5:12
Revelation 13:3; 14:11

KEY ORGANIZATIONS:

Evangelical Theological Society | www.etsjets.org | 502.897.4387 |

National Association of Evangelicals | http://nae.net | 202.489.1011 |

KEY PUBLICATIONS:

JETS | **Evangelical Theological Society** | www.etsjets.org | 502.897.4387 |

KEY PLURALISM FACTS:

- Sixty-four percent of Americans believe, "Christians, Jews, Buddhists, Muslims and all others pray to the same God, even though they use different names for that God."[1]
- Sixty-four percent of Americans agree with the statement, "All religions are equally good."[2]
- Sixty-two percent of those surveyed agreed that, "It does not matter what religious faith you follow because all faiths reach similar lessons about life."[3]
- Fifty percent of all teenagers and 30 percent of born-again teens agree, "It does not matter what religious faith you follow because all faiths teach similar lessons."[4]
- Fifty-five percent of all teenagers and 36 percent of born-again teenagers believe, "Muslims, Buddhists, Christians, Jews, and all other people pray to the same God, even though they use different names for their God."[5]

KEY QUOTES:

"Even the most tolerant pluralist has difficulties with the aspect of Hinduism which justifies the inequalities of Indian society by its insistence upon a fixed social order, or forcibly burning alive a widow on her late husband's funeral pyre."[6]

"The apostles asserted that Christ alone is the truth in the midst of a world that is more religiously diverse than any we have known in the West until recently."[7]

"'Why should I go to church,' someone once said to me, 'when I have no religious needs?' I had the audacity to reply, 'Because Christianity's true... The needs religion fills are relevant to an assessment of its truth... but were it merely a matter of finding religion to be helpful, then a religious commitment would not be essentially different from a personal preference. We would rightly say that just as some people prefer chocolate to other flavors of ice cream, some people prefer to be Christian than something else or nothing at all merely as a matter of taste. But when

---

[1] George Barna, *What Americans Believe* (Ventura, CA: Regal Books, 1991), 210–12.
[2] *Religion in America, 1996* (Princeton: Princeton Religion Research Center, 1996), 74.
[3] George Barna, *Absolute Confusion* (Ventura, CA: Regal Books, 1994), 207.
[4] George Barna, *Generation Next: What You Should Know About Today's Youth* (Ventura, CA: Regal Books, 1995), 79, 103.
[5] Ibid., 76, 103.
[6] Alister McGrath, *A Passion for Truth: The Intellectual Coherence of Evangelism*. (Downers Grove, IL: InterVarsity, 1996), 190.
[7] David Wells, *No Place for Truth Or Whatever Happened to Evangelical Theology?* (Grand Rapids, MI: Eerdmans, 1993), 104.

Fact Sheets

something is said to be true, we have a very different situation, especially when it is said of religion. Christianity, as well as other religious claims, are so serious and so demanding personally that adherence to them cannot be properly described as merely a matter of personal taste.'"[8]

"If you had gone to Buddha and asked him, 'Are you the son of Brahma?' he would have said, 'My son, you are still in the vale of illusion.' If you had gone to Socrates and asked, 'Are you the son of Zeus?' he would have laughed at you. If you had gone to Mohammed and asked, 'Are you the son of Allah?' he would first have rent his clothes and then cut your head off. If you had asked Confucius, 'Are you Heaven?' I think he would have probably replied, 'Remarks which are not in accordance with nature are in bad taste.' The idea of a great moral teacher saying what Christ said is out of the question. In my opinion, the only person who can say that sort of thing is either God or a complete lunatic suffering from that form of delusion which undermines the whole mind of man.'"[9]

Key Proponents:
- John Hick (professor of theology at University of Birmingham, vice-president of the British Society for the Philosophy of Religion, and vice-president of The World Congress of Faiths)
- Wilfred Cantwell Smith (Dalhousie University at Halifax, deceased)
- S. Wesley Ariarajah (Drew University School of Theology)

Key Proponent Sources:

Ariarajah, S. Wesley. *The Bible and People of Other Faiths*. Geneva: World Council of Churches, 1985.

———. *Not without My Neighbour: Issues in Interfaith Relations*. Geneva: World Council of Churches, 1999.

Hick, John. *A Christian Theology of Religions: The Rainbow of Faiths*. Louisville, KY: Westminster/John Knox Press, 1995.

———. *God Has Many Names*. Philadelphia: Westminster Press, 1982.

———. *The Metaphor of God Incarnate: Christology in a Pluralistic Age*. Louisville, KY: Westminster/John Knox Press, 2006.

Hick, John and Paul F. Knitter. *The Myth of Christian Uniqueness: Toward a Pluralistic Theology of Religions*. Maryknoll, NY: Orbis, 1987.

Smith, Wilfred Cantwell. *The Meaning and End of Religion*. Minneapolis: Fortress Press, 1991.

———. *Towards a World Theology: Faith and the Comparative History of Religion*. Maryknoll, NY: Orbis, 1989.

Whaling, Frank and Wilfred Cantwell Smith. *The World's Religious Traditions: Current Perspectives in Religious Studies*. New York: Crossroad, 1984.

Key Christian Sources/Critiques:
(recommended titles appear in brown)

Atheism (critique)

Geisler, Norman L. and Frank Turek. *I Don't Have Enough Faith to Be an Atheist*. Wheaton, IL: Crossway, 2004.

McGrath, Alister. *The Twilight of Atheism: The Rise & Fall of Disbelief in the Modern World*. New York: Doubleday, 2004.

Moreland, J. P. and Kai Nielsen. *Does God Exist? The Great Debate*. New York: Prometheus Books, 1993.

Nicholi, Armand M. *The Question of God: C. S. Lewis and Sigmund Freud Debate God, Love, Sex, and the Meaning of Life*. New York: Free Press, 2002.

Plantinga, Alvin. *God and Other Minds: A Study of the Rational Justification of Belief in God*. Ithaca, NY: Cornell University Press, 1990.

Zacharias, Ravi. *A Shattered Visage: The Real Face of Atheism*. Brentwood, TN: Wolgemuth & Hyatt, 1990.

---

[8] Diogenes Allen, *Christian Belief in a Postmodern World* (Louisville, KY: Westminster/John Knox Press, 1989), 1.
[9] C. S. Lewis, *God in the Dock: Essays on Theology and Ethics* (Grand Rapids, MI: Eerdmans, 1970), 157–58.

Fact Sheets

BIBLE DOCTRINE

Erickson, Millard J. *Christian Theology*. Grand Rapids, MI: Baker, 1998.

Geisler, Norman L. *Systematic Theology*. Minneapolis: Bethany, 2002.

Grudem, Wayne A. *Bible Doctrine: Essential Teachings of the Christian Faith*. Grand Rapids, MI: Zondervan, 1999.

————. *Christian Beliefs: Twenty Basics Every Christian Should Know*. Grand Rapids, MI: Zondervan, 2005.

————. *Systematic Theology: An Introduction to Biblical Doctrine*. Grand Rapids, MI: Zondervan, 1994.

Henry, Carl F. H. *God, Revelation, and Authority*. 6 vols. Wheaton, IL: Crossway, 1999.

Plantinga, Cornelius. *Engaging God's World: A Christian Vision of Faith, Learning, and Living*. Grand Rapids, MI: Eerdmans, 2002.

HERMENEUTICS

Carson, D. A. *Exegetical Fallacies*. Grand Rapids, MI: Baker, 1996.

Cowan, Steven B. "Scripture Interprets Scripture: The Role of Theology in Biblical Interpretation." *Areopagus Journal 6*, no. 1 (2006): 22–28.

Fee, Gordon D. and Douglas K. Stuart. *How to Read the Bible Book by Book: A Guided Tour*. Grand Rapids, MI: Zondervan, 2002.

————. *How to Read the Bible for All Its Worth*. Grand Rapids, MI: Zondervan, 2003.

Grenz, Stanley J., David Guretzki, and Cherith Fee Nordling. *Pocket Dictionary of Theological Terms*. Downers Grove, IL: InterVarsity, 1999.

LaHaye, Tim. *How to Study the Bible for Yourself*. Eugene, OR: Harvest, 1998.

Lemke, Steven W. "Good Hermeneutics: Rightly Dividing the Word of God." *Areopagus Journal 6*, no. 1 (2006): 7–13.

Patzia, Arthur G. and Anthony J. Petrotta. *Pocket Dictionary of Biblical Studies*. Downers Grove, IL: InterVarsity, 2002.

Peterson, Eugene H. *Eat This Book: A Conversation in the Art of Spiritual Reading*. Grand Rapids, MI: Eerdmans, 2006.

Russell, Walt. *Playing with Fire: How the Bible Ignites Change in Your Soul*. Colorado Springs, CO: NavPress, 2000.

Sire, James W. *Scripture Twisting: 20 Ways the Cults Misread the Bible*. Downers Grove, IL: InterVarsity, 1980.

Snyder, Jason. "Getting the Whole Story: The Importance of Context in Biblical Interpretation." *Areopagus Journal 6*, no. 1 (2006): 14–18.

Sproul, R. C. *Knowing Scripture*. Downers Grove, IL: InterVarsity, 1977.

PANTHEISM (CRITIQUE)

Clark, David K. and Norman L. Geisler. *Apologetics in the New Age: A Christian Critique of Pantheism*. Grand Rapids, MI: Baker, 1990.

Groothuis, Douglas. *Unmasking the New Age*. Downers Grove, IL: InterVarsity, 1986.

RELIGIOUS PLURALISM (GENERAL)

Adler, Mortimer Jerome. *Truth in Religion: The Plurality of Religions and the Unity of Truth*. New York: Macmillan, 1990.

Carson, D. A. "The Challenges of Contemporary Pluralism." *Southern Baptist Journal of Theology 1*, no. 2 (1997): 4–37.

————. *The Gagging of God: Christianity Confronts Pluralism*. Grand Rapids, MI: Zondervan, 1996.

Cowan, Steven B. "Do All Religions Lead to God?" *Areopagus Journal 1*, no. 3 (2001): 7–12.

Detzler, Wayne A. "Evangelism and the Peril of Pluralism." *Christian Apologetics Journal 4*, no. 2 (2005): 45–62.

Geisler, Norman L. "Religious Pluralism: A Christian Response." *Christian Apologetics Journal 4*, no. 2 (2005): 1–28.

Groothuis, Douglas. *Are All Religions One?* Downers Grove, IL: InterVarsity, 1999.

Leffel, Jim and Dennis McCallum. "Postmodern Impact: Religion." *The Death of Truth*, Dennis McCallum, ed. Minneapolis: Bethany, 1996, 200-214.

Hexham, Irving. *Pocket Dictionary of New Religious Movements*. Downers Grove, IL: InterVarsity, 2002.

Hux, Clete. "What About Those Who Have Never Heard?" *Areopagus Journal 1*, no. 3 (2001): 22–25.

Nash, Ronald. "Can Someone Be Saved by Jesus without Faith in Jesus?" *Areopagus Journal 1*, no. 3 (2001): 13–20.

————. *Is Jesus the Only Savior?* Grand Rapids, MI: Zondervan, 1994.

Fact Sheets

Netland, Harold. *Dissonant Voices: Religious Pluralism and the Quest for Truth*. Grand Rapids, MI: Eerdmans, 1991.

———. *Encountering Religious Pluralism: The Challenge to Christian Faith and Mission*. Downers Grove, IL: InterVarsity, 2001.

Newbigin, Lesslie. "Confessing Christ in a Multicultural Society." *Evangelical Review of Theology 22*, no. 3 (1998): 264–73.

Phillips, Gary. "Religious Pluralism in a Postmodern World." *The Challenge of Postmodernism: An Evangelical Engagement*, David S. Dockery, ed. Grand Rapids, MI: Baker, 2001, 131-143.

Ryken, Philip Graham. *Is Jesus the Only Way?* Wheaton, IL: Crossway, 1999.

Veith, Gene Edward. "Spirituality without Truth." *Postmodern Times: A Christian Guide to Contemporary Thought and Culture*. Wheaton, IL: Crossway, 1994, 192–207.

Stackhouse, John Gordon. *No Other Gods before Me: Evangelicals and the Challenge of World Religions*. Grand Rapids, MI: Baker, 2001.

COMPARATIVE RELIGIONS

Anderson, J. N. D. *Christianity and World Religions: The Challenge of Pluralism*. Downers Grove, IL: InterVarsity, 1984.

Clarke, Andrew D. and Bruce W. Winter. *One God, one Lord: Christianity in a World of Religious Pluralism*. Grand Rapids, MI: Baker, 1992.

Corduan, Winfried. *Neighboring Faiths: A Christian Introduction to World Religions*. Downers Grove, IL: InterVarsity, 1998.

———. *A Tapestry of Faiths: The Common Threads between Christianity and World Religions*. Downers Grove, IL: InterVarsity, 2002.

Fernando, Ajith. *Sharing the Truth in Love: How to Relate to People of Other Faiths*. Grand Rapids, MI: Discovery House, 2001.

Partridge, Christopher H. and Douglas R. Groothuis. *Dictionary of Contemporary Religion in the Western World*. Downers Grove, IL: InterVarsity, 2002.

Van Voorst, Robert E. *Anthology of World Scriptures*. Belmont, CA: Wadsworth, 2005.

HELL AND SALVATION

Crockett, William V. and Stanley N. Gundry, eds. *Four Views on Hell*. Grand Rapids, MI: Zondervan, 1992.

Crockett, William V. and James G. Sigountos. *Through No Fault of Their Own: The Fate of Those Who Have Never Heard*. Grand Rapids, MI: Baker, 1991.

Erickson, Millard J. *How Shall They Be Saved: The Destiny of Those Who Do Not Hear of Jesus*. Grand Rapids, MI: Baker, 1996.

Nash, Ronald H. *Is Jesus the Only Savior?* Grand Rapids, MI: Zondervan, 1994.

Okholm, Dennis L., Timothy R. Phillips, and Stanley N. Gundry, eds. *Four Views on Salvation in a Pluralistic World*. Grand Rapids, MI: Zondervan, 1996.

Stott, John R. W. *The Cross of Christ*. Downers Grove, IL: InterVarsity, 2006.

Tiessen, Terrance L. *Who Can Be Saved: Reassessing Salvation in Christ and World Religions*. Downers Grove, IL: InterVarsity, 2004.

WORLDVIEW
FACT SHEET

KEY VERSES:

Proverbs 3:5–6   Romans 12:1–2   Colossians 1:15ff; 2:1–8

Acts 17:16 ff   2 Corinthians 10:4–5

KEY ORGANIZATIONS:

American Vision | www.americanvision.com | 770.222.7266 |

Christian Research Institute | www.equip.org | 888.700.0274 |

Probe Ministries | www.probe.org | 972.480.0240 |

Stand to Reason | www.str.org | 800.273.2766 |

Summit Ministries | www.summit.org | 719.685.9103 |

KEY PUBLICATIONS:

Areopagus Journal | **Apologetics Resource Center** | www.arcapologetics.org | 205.408.0136 |

Biblical Worldview | **American Vision** | www.americanvision.org | 770.222.7266 |

Christian Research Journal | **Christian Research Institute** | www.equip.org | 888.700.0274 |

First Things | **Institute of Religion and Public Life** | www.firstthings.com | 212.627.1985 |

Imprimis | **Hillsdale College** | www.hillsdale.edu/news/imprimis.asp | 517.437.7341 |

Southern Baptist Journal of Theology | **Southern Baptist Theological Seminary** | www.sbts.edu |

Summit Journal | **Summit Ministries** | www.summit.org | 719.685.9103 |

KEY QUOTES:

"A worldview is, first of all, an explanation and interpretation of the world and second, an application of this view to life. In simpler terms, our worldview is a view of the world and a view for the world."[1]

"The term worldview refers to any ideology, philosophy, theology, movement, or religion that provides an overarching approach to understanding God and the world. Specifically, a worldview should contain a particular perspective regarding each of the following ten disciplines: theology, philosophy, ethics, biology, psychology, sociology, law, politics, economics, and history."[2]

---

[1] William E. Brown and W. Gary Phillips, *Making Sense of Your World: A Biblical Worldview* (Salem, WI: Sheffield Publishers, 1996), 29.

[2] David A. Noebel, *Understanding the Times* (Eugene, OR: Harvest, 1991), 8.

"A world view is a way one views the whole world. And since people have vastly different views of the world, depending on the perspective from which they view the world, it is clear that one's world view makes a world of difference. A world view is a way of viewing or interpreting all of reality. It is an interpretive framework through which or by which one makes sense out of the data of life and the world."[3]

"So what is a world view? Essentially this: A world view is a set of presuppositions (assumptions which may be true, partially true or entirely false) which we hold (consciously or subconsciously, consistently or inconsistently) about the basic make-up of our world."[4]

"A worldview is not the same thing as a formal philosophy; otherwise, it would be only for professional philosophers. Even ordinary people have a set of convictions about how reality functions and how they should live. Because we are made in God's image, we all seek to make sense of life. Some convictions are conscious, while others are unconscious, but together they form a more or less consistent picture of reality."[5]

KEY SOURCES:
(recommended titles appear in brown)

Baldwin, J. F. *The Deadliest Monster: A Christian Introduction to Worldviews*. New Braunfels, TX: Fisherman, 2001.

Breese, Dave. *Seven Men Who Rule the World from the Grave*. Chicago, IL: Moody, 1990.

Burnett, David. *Clash of Worlds*. Nashville: Oliver Nelson, 1992.

Carson, D. A. *The Gagging of God: Christianity Confronts Pluralism*. Grand Rapids, MI: Zondervan, 1996.

Colson, Charles W. and Nancy Pearcey. *How Now Shall We Live?* Wheaton, IL: Tyndale, 1999.

Eckman, James P. *The Truth about Worldviews: A Biblical Understanding of Worldview Alternatives*. Wheaton, IL: Crossway, 2004.

Geisler, Norman L. *False Gods of Our Time*. Eugene, OR: Harvest, 1985.

Geisler, Norman L. and William D. Watkins. *Worlds Apart: A Handbook on World Views*. Grand Rapids, MI: Baker, 1989.

Guinness, Os and John Seel. *No God but God*. Chicago, IL: Moody, 1992.

Hoffecker, W. Andrew and Gary Scott Smith. *Building a Christian World View*. Phillipsburg, NJ: Presbyterian & Reformed, 1986.

Lewis, C. S. *The Pilgrim's Regress: An Allegorical Apology for Christianity, Reason, and Romanticism*. Grand Rapids, MI: Eerdmans, 1992.

Moreland, J. P. and William Lane Craig. *Philosophical Foundations for a Christian Worldview*. Downers Grove, IL: InterVarsity, 2003.

Nash, Ronald. *Worldviews in Conflict: Choosing Christianity in a World of Ideas*. Grand Rapids, MI: Zondervan, 1992.

Naugle, David K. *Worldview: The History of a Concept*. Grand Rapids, MI: Eerdmans, 2002.

Noebel, David A. *Understanding the Times: The Collision of Today's Competing Worldviews*. Manitou Springs, CO: Summit Press, 2006.

Olasky, Marvin N. and Joel Belz. *Whirled Views: Tracking Today's Culture Storms*. Wheaton, IL: Crossway, 1997.

Pearcey, Nancy. *Total Truth: Liberating Christianity from Its Cultural Captivity*. Wheaton, IL: Crossway, 2004.

Raeper, William and Linda Edwards. *A Brief Guide to Ideas*. Grand Rapids, MI: Zondervan, 2000.

Schaeffer, Francis A. *How Should We Then Live? The Rise and Decline of Western Thought and Culture*. Wheaton, IL: Crossway, 1983.

————. *Naming the Elephant: Worldview as a Concept*. Downers Grove, IL: InterVarsity, 2004.

Sire, James W. *The Universe Next Door: A Basic Worldview Catalog*. Downers Grove, IL: InterVarsity, 2004.

Sproul, R. C. *The Consequences of Ideas: Understanding the Concepts That Shaped Our World*. Wheaton, IL: Crossway, 2000.

[3] Norman L. Geisler and William D. Watkins, *Worlds Apart: A Handbook on Worldviews* (Grand Rapids, MI: Baker, 1989), 11.
[4] James W. Sire, *The Universe Next Door: A Basic Worldview Catalog* (Downers Grove, IL: InterVarsity, 1988), 17.
[5] Nancy Pearcey, *Total Truth* (Wheaton, IL: Crossway, 2004), 23.

Fact Sheets

WORLDVIEW: CHRISTIANITY
FACT SHEET

KEY VERSES:

1 Chronicles 12:32   1 Corinthians 2:16; 9:19–23   Colossians 2
Matthew 22:34–40   2 Corinthians 10:4–5   Philippians 2:5
Acts 17:16ff   Ephesians 4:22–24   1 Peter 1:13–16
Romans 12:1–2

KEY ORGANIZATIONS:

American Vision | www.americanvision.com | 770.222.7266 |

Barna Research Group | www.barna.org | 805.639.0000 |

Biblical Worldview | www.christianworldview.net |

Centurions Program | www.breakpoint.org/resources/centurions | 877.478.0100 |

Christian Research Institute | www.equip.org | 888.700.0274 |

Nehemiah Institute | www.nehemiahinstitute.com | 800.948.3101 |

Probe Ministries | www.probe.org | 972.480.0240 |

Stand to Reason | www.str.org | 800.273.2766 |

Summit Ministries | www.summit.org | 719.685.9103 |

Veritas Forum | www.veritas.org | 617.491.2055 |

KEY QUOTES:

"I now believe that the balance of reasoned considerations tells heavily in favour of the religious, even of the Christian view of the world."[1]

"The Christian belief system, which the Christian knows to be grounded in divine revelation, is relevant to all of life."[2]

"The basic problem of the Christians in this country in the last eighty years or so, in regard to society and in regard to government, is that they have seen things in bits and pieces instead of totals."[3]

---

[1] C. E. M. Joad, *Recovery of Belief* (London: Faber & Faber, 1955), 22.
[2] Carl F. H. Henry, *Toward a Recovery of Christian Belief* (Westchester, IL: Crossway, 1990), 113.
[3] Francis A. Schaeffer, *A Christian Manifesto* (Westchester, IL: Crossway, 1981), 17.

Fact Sheets

KEY SOURCES:
(recommended titles appear in brown)

CHRISTIAN WORLDVIEW (DEVELOPMENT)

Colson, Charles W. and Ellen Santilli Vaughn. *Against the Night: Living in the New Dark Ages*. Ann Arbor, MI: Vine, 1989.

DeMar, Gary. *Thinking Straight in a Crooked World*. Asheville, NC: American Vision, 2001.

Henry, Carl F. H. *The Christian Mindset in a Secular Society: Promoting Evangelical Renewal and National Righteousness*. Portland, OR: Multnomah, 1984.

Kennedy, D. James and Jerry Newcombe. *Lord of All: Developing a Christian World-and-Life View*. Wheaton, IL: Crossway, 2005.

Lewis, C. S. *Mere Christianity*. San Francisco: HarperSanFrancisco, 2001.

MacArthur, John, Richard Mayhue, and John A. Hughes, eds. *Think Biblically! Recovering a Christian Worldview*. Wheaton, IL: Crossway, 2003.

Noebel, David A. *Understanding the Times: The Collision of Today's Competing Worldviews*. Manitou Springs, CO: Summit Press, 2006.

Orr, James. *The Christian View of God and the World*. Grand Rapids, MI: Kregel, 1989.

Pearcey, Nancy. *Total Truth: Liberating Christianity from Its Cultural Captivity*. Wheaton, IL: Crossway, 2004.

Phillips, W. Gary and William E. Brown. *Making Sense of Your World: From a Biblical Viewpoint*. Chicago, IL: Moody, 1991.

Schaeffer, Francis A. *A Christian Manifesto*. Westchester, IL: Crossway, 1981.

————. *The Complete Works of Francis A. Schaeffer*. 5 vols. Westchester, IL: Crossway, 1982.

Walsh, Brian J. and J. Richard Middleton. *The Transforming Vision: Shaping a Christian World View*. Downers Grove, IL: InterVarsity, 1984.

Wright, N. T. *Simply Christian: Why Christianity Makes Sense*. San Francisco: HarperSanFrancisco, 2006.

BIBLE SURVEY

Arnold, Bill T. and Bryan Beyer. *Encountering the Old Testament: A Christian Survey*. Grand Rapids, MI: Baker, 1999.

Carson, D. A. and Douglas J. Moo. *An Introduction to the New Testament*. Grand Rapids, MI: Zondervan, 2005.

Dillard, Raymond B. and Tremper Longman. *An Introduction to the Old Testament*. Grand Rapids, MI: Zondervan, 1994.

Elwell, Walter A. and Robert W. Yarbrough. *Encountering the New Testament: A Historical and Theological Survey*. Grand Rapids, MI: Baker, 2005.

Wright, N. T. *The Resurrection of the Son of God*. Minneapolis: Fortress Press, 2003.

WORLDVIEW: COSMIC HUMANISM
FACT SHEET

KEY VERSES:

Genesis 1:1, 27
Psalm 115
John 1:1–3; 14:6

Acts 4:10–12
Romans 2:23
2 Corinthians 11:3–4, 13–15

Colossians 1:15–20; 2
Hebrews 9:27
1 John 1:7–10

KEY ORGANIZATIONS:

Christian Research Institute | www.equip.org | 888.700.0274 |

Spiritual Counterfeits Project | www.scp-inc.org | 510.540.0300 |

Summit Ministries | www.summit.org | 719.685.9103 |

Watchman Fellowship, Inc. | www.watchman.org | 205.833.2858 |

KEY QUOTES:

"The New Age movement… is an extremely large, loosely structured network of organizations and individuals bound together by common values (based in mysticism and monism—the world view that 'all is one') and a common vision (a coming 'new age' of peace and mass enlightenment, the 'Age of Aquarius')." [A]ll New Agers believe that 'all is one'—everything that exists consists of one and the same essence or reality. A second assumption is that this Ultimate Reality is neither dead matter nor unconscious energy. It is Being, Awareness, and Bliss (which is to say, a Hindu conception of God as an impersonal, infinite consciousness and force). The first two assumptions imply two more: all that is, is God (which is pantheism); and man, a part of 'all that is,' is likewise divine."[1]

All that is can form itself into individual droplets of consciousness. Because you are part of all that is, you have literally always been, yet there was the instant when that individual energy current that is you was formed. Consider that the ocean is God. It has always been. Now reach in and grab a cup full of water. In that instant, the cup becomes individual, but it has always been, has it not? This is the case with your soul. There was an instant when you became a cup of energy, but it was of an immortal original Being. You have always been because what it is that you are is God, or Divine Intelligence, but God takes individual forms… As that little form grows in power, in selfhood, in its own consciousness of self, it becomes larger and more Godlike. Then it becomes God."[2]

"There are two fundamental problems with the doctrine of theological monism. First, it is not really theology. We have always known that the universe exists; to simply change its name from 'universe' to 'God' is a meaningless tautology and does not answer the real questions of the origin and purpose of the world or the nature of God. Second, the 'God' of monism is fatally flawed. Since he (or 'it,' which is more accurate) is of one essence with creation and consciousness, God is thus the origin of the imperfection and evil in our world; the foulest deeds and thoughts of humanity literally become attributes of God."[3]

---

[1] Elliot Miller, *A Crash Course on the New Age Movement* (Grand Rapids, MI: Baker, 1989), 15–16.
[2] Gary Zukav (a New Ager), *The Seat of the Soul* (New York: Fireside, 1989), 185–86.
[3] Mark C. Albrecht, *Reincarnation: A Christian Critique of a New Age Doctrine* (Downers Grove, IL: InterVarsity, 1982), 106.

Fact sheets

KEY PROPONENT SOURCES:

Blavatsky, H. P. *The Secret Doctrine: The Synthesis of Science, Religion, and Philosophy*. Pasadena, CA: Theosophical University Press, 1977.

Campbell, Joseph and Bill D. Moyers. *The Power of Myth*. New York: Doubleday, 1988.

Capra, Fritjof. *The Tao of Physics: An Exploration of the Parallels between Modern Physics and Eastern Mysticism*. Boston, MA: Shambhala, 2000.

Castaneda, Carlos. *The Teachings of Don Juan: A Yaqui Way of Knowledge*. Berkeley, CA: Univ. of California Press, 1998.

Chopra, Deepak. *Ageless Body, Timeless Mind: The Quantum Alternative to Growing Old*. New York: Harmony, 1993.

Ferguson, Marilyn. *The Aquarian Conspiracy: Personal and Social Transformation in the 1980s*. New York: St. Martin's Press, 1980.

Fox, Matthew. *The Coming of the Cosmic Christ: The Healing of Mother Earth and the Birth of a Global Renaissance*. San Francisco: Harper & Row, 1988.

Gawain, Shakti. *Creative Visualization: Use the Power of Your Imagination to Create What You Want in Your Life*. Navato, CA: New World Library, 2002.

MacLaine, Shirley. *Out on a Limb*. New York: Bantam, 1983.

Muller, Robert. *New Genesis: Shaping a Global Spirituality*. Garden City, NY: Doubleday, 1982.

Peck, M. Scott. *The Road Less Traveled: A New Psychology of Love, Traditional Values, and Spiritual Growth*. New York: Simon & Schuster, 2002.

Pirsig, Robert M. *Zen and the Art of Motorcycle Maintenance*. New York: W. Morrow, 1999.

Prophet, Mark and Elizabeth Clare Prophet. *The Lost Teachings of Jesus*. Livingston, MT: Summit Univ. Press, 1986.

Spangler, David. *Emergence: The Rebirth of the Sacred*. New York: Dell, 1984.

KEY CHRISTIAN SOURCES/CRITIQUES:

(recommended titles appear in brown)

Albrecht, Mark. *Reincarnation, a Christian Appraisal*. Downers Grove, IL: InterVarsity, 1982.

Alnor, William M. *Ufos in the New Age: Extraterrestrial Messages and the Truth of Scripture*. Grand Rapids, MI: Baker, 1992.

Ankerberg, John, John Weldon, and Craig Branch. *Thieves of Innocence*. Eugene, OR: Harvest, 1993.

Clark, David K. and Norman L. Geisler. *Apologetics in the New Age: A Christian Critique of Pantheism*. Grand Rapids, MI: Baker, 1990.

Groothuis, Douglas. *Confronting the New Age: How to Resist a Growing Religious Movement*. Downers Grove, IL: InterVarsity, 1988.

———. *Deceived by the Light*. Eugene, OR: Harvest, 1995.

———. *Unmasking the New Age*. Downers Grove, IL: InterVarsity, 1986.

Halverson, Dean C. *Crystal Clear: Understanding and Reaching New Agers*. Colorado Springs, CO: NavPress, 1990.

Mangalwadi, Vishal. *When the New Age Gets Old: Looking for a Greater Spirituality*. Downers Grove, IL: InterVarsity, 1992.

Melton, J. Gordon, Jerome Clark, and A. Kelly Aidan. *New Age Encyclopedia*. Detroit, MI: Gale Research, 1990.

Miller, Elliot. *A Crash Course on the New Age Movement: Describing and Evaluating a Growing Social Force*. Grand Rapids, MI: Baker, 1989.

Noebel, David A. *Understanding the Times: The Collision of Today's Competing Worldviews*. Manitou Springs, CO: Summit Press, 2006.

Sire, James W. *Shirley MacLaine and the New Age Movement*. Downers Grove, IL: InterVarsity, 1988.

Rhodes, Ron. *The Counterfeit Christ of the New Age Movement*. Grand Rapids, MI: Baker, 1990.

Tucker, Ruth. *Another Gospel: Alternative Religions and the New Age Movement*. Grand Rapids, MI: Zondervan, 1989.

Worldview: Islam
Fact Sheet

KEY TERMS:

God: Allah

Islam: Submission to Allah

Muslim: One submitted to Allah

Muhammad: Ultimate and final prophet of Allah

Qur'an: Word of Allah

KEY FACTS:

STATS	• About 1/5th of the world's population is Muslim • Approximately three-quarters of Muslims are non-Arabs • About 5 million live in North America
DATES	• 570 AD — Muhammad is born • 610 AD — Muhammad receives his first visions • 622 AD — Muhammad flees to Medina (this event, known as the Hijira, initiates the Muslim calendar) • 630 AD — Muslims conquer Mecca • 632 AD — Muhammad dies • 636–640 AD — The early conquests of Damascus, Jerusalem, Egypt, and Persia • 650 AD — The canon of the Qur'an established
PILLARS	• The confession of faith: "There is no God but Allah, and Muhammad is his prophet" • Prayers five times a day, facing Mecca • Almsgiving (about 1/40th of income and holdings), primarily for the poor • Fasting during the month of Ramadan • Pilgrimage to Mecca
BELIEFS	• Monotheism • Prophets • Holy books • Angels and jinn • Judgment day • Muslims reject the Trinity • Muslims deny the deity and sonship of Jesus Christ • Muslims deny that Jesus died upon the cross, thus also denying his resurrection • Muslims assert that the Bible is untrustworthy, though the Qur'an is flawless • Muslims face a day of judgment based on good and bad works

---

KEY PROPONENT SOURCES:

Ahmad, Khurshic, ed. *Islam: Its Meaning and Message*. Leichester, UK: The Islamic Foundation, 1999.
Rahman, Fazlur. *Islam*. Chicago: University of Chicago Press, 1979.
Tabbarah, Afif and Rohi Baalbaki. *The Spirit of Islam: Doctrine and Teachings*. Beirut: Dar El-Ilm Lilmalayin, 1988.

Fact Sheets

KEY CHRISTIAN SOURCES/CRITIQUES:

(recommended titles appear in brown)

ISLAM (GENERAL)	Anderson, Norman. *Islam in the Modern World: A Christian Perspective.* Leicester, UK: APOLLOS/InterVarsity, 1990. Geisler, Norman L. and Abdul Saleeb. *Answering Islam: The Crescent in the Light of the Cross.* Grand Rapids, MI: Baker, 1993. Noebel, David A. *Understanding the Times: The Collision of Today's Competing Worldviews.* Manitou Springs, CO: Summit Press, 2006. Robinson, Stuart. *Mosques and Miracles.* Upper Mt. Gravalt, AU: City Harvest, 2004. Saal, William J. *Reaching Muslims for Christ.* Chicago, IL: Moody, 1991. Schmidt, Alvin J. *Failure of Islam, Triumph of the West.* Boston: Regina Orthodox Press, 2004. Shorrosh, Anis A. *Islam Revealed: A Christian Arab's View of Islam.* Nashville: Thomas Nelson, 1988. St. Clair-Tisdall, W. *Christian Reply to Muslim Objections.* Villach, Austria: Light of Life, 1980. Woodberry, J. Dudley, ed. *Muslims and Christians on the Emmaus Road.* Monrovia, CA: MARC, 1989.
HISTORY	Lewis, Bernard. *What Went Wrong? Western Impact and Middle Eastern Response.* New York: Oxford University Press, 2002. Trifkovic, Serge. *The Sword of the Prophet, Islam: History, Theology, Impact on the World.* Boston, MA: Regina Orthodox Press, 2002. Ye'or, Bat. *Islam and Dhimmitude: Where Civilizations Collide.* Teaneck, NJ: Fairleigh Dickinson Univ. Press, 2002.
BELIEFS	Halverson, Dean C. "Islam." *The Compact Guide to World Religions,* Dean C. Halverson, ed. Minneapolis: Bethany, 1996. 103–120. Markham, Ian S., ed. *A World Religions Reader.* Malden, MA: Blackwell, 2000. 301-331. Cragg, Kenneth. *The Call of the Minaret.* New York: Oxford University Press, 1956. Dashti, 'Ali. *23 Years: A Study of the Prophetic Career of Mohammad.* Translated by F. R. C. Bagley. London: George Allen & Unwin, 1985. Hamada, Louis. *Understanding the Arab World.* Nashville: Thomas Nelson, 1990.
RADICAL ISLAM	Bodansky, Yossef. *Bin Laden: The Man Who Declared War on America.* New York: Random, 2001. El Schafi, Abd. *Behind the Veil.* Caney, KS: Pioneer Book Company, 2001. Horowitz, David. *Unholy Alliance: Radical Islam and the American Left.* Washington DC: Regnery, 2004. Jabbour, Nabeel. *The Rumbling Volcano: Islamic Fundamentalism in Egypt.* Pasadena, CA: Mandate Press, 1993. Rashid, Ahmed. *Jihad: The Rise of Militant Islam in Central Asia.* New Haven, CT: Yale Univ. Press, 2002.

Fact sheets

WORLDVIEW: MARXISM
FACT SHEET

KEY TERMS:

Bourgeois: The social/economic class that owns private property and the means of production

Communism: The Marxist dream of a future utopia in which all resources for production are owned in common by a classless society

Communist Manifesto: The 1848 political tract issued by Karl Marx and Friedrich Engels which outlined the goal and means of achieving of a classless society (i.e. Communism) through a proletarian revolution

Marxism: The ideology of Karl Marx based upon atheism, dialectical materialism, evolution, and socialism

Proletariat: The working or labor class of society

KEY FACTS:

- Current Communist Countries:

World Ranking	Country	Population	Source
#1 (19.62%)	**China**	1,334,620,000	Chinese govt. population counter (Dec. 2009)
#13 (1.26%)	**Vietnam**	85,789,573	2009 census (Apr. 2009)
#47 (0.35%)	**North Korea**[1]	24,051,706	UN estimate (Oct. 2008)
#75 (0.16%)	**Cuba**	11,204,000	UN estimate (Jul. 2009)
#104 (0.093%)	**Laos**	6,320,000	UN estimate (Jul. 2009)

- Current Number of Citizens in Communist Countries (2009): 1.5 billion
- People Killed by Communism: 110,000,000[2]

KEY VERSES:

Exodus 20:15–17   Acts 5:1–4
Psalm 14   Ephesians 4:28

KEY ORGANIZATIONS:

Christian Anti-Communism Crusade | www.schwarzreport.org | 719.685.9103 |

KEY QUOTES:

[Pro-Marxist speaker] "I think I have to give an even broader historical characterization of the moment in which American Marxists find themselves and in which our pedagogical work takes its significance. Lenin said that the two necessary [but not sufficient] preconditions for social revolution arc a class-conscious proletariat and a revolutionary intelligentsia. If, as intellectuals, we can necessarily play only a marginal role in the development of the former, the

---

[1] Although North Korea has removed all communist terms from its constitution and officially declared itself to be a *socialist* state, in practice very little has changed. Some sources may not classify it as a communist state, however.
[2] http://www.hawaii.edu/powerkills/NOTE5.HTM

task of creating the latter is clearly our fundamental one. To create a Marxist culture in this country, to make Marxism an unavoidable presence and a distinct, original, and unmistakable voice in American social, cultural, and intellectual life, in short to form a Marxist intelligentsia for the struggles of the future—this seems to me the supreme mission of a Marxist pedagogy and a radical intellectual life today."[3]

"Marx… taught that God was a projection of man's radical alienation: from himself, from his labor, and from a human community cruelly divided by class barriers. Man's salvation, in Marx's view, thus lay within history, in the creation of a mundane utopia… Lenin, in turn, believed that the advent of this radically secular version of the coming kingdom could be dramatically accelerated by revolutionary action… Whereas Marx simply treated religion contemptuously as a source of man's alienation, Lenin hated the church and saw in it a powerful rival for hearts and minds… The communist animus against religion—and especially Christianity—was no accident: It was an essential part of the Marxist-Leninist package. A communism that had a benign view of Christianity was no more possible than a communism that had a benign view of democracy, or of market economies. Something had to give. As things worked out, of course, it was communism that 'gave.' And the delicious irony was that it 'gave' because what generations of communists took to be mere fantasy—the Christian faith of the people of central and eastern Europe—proved more attractive, more resilient, more revolutionary, and more accurate to human experience than the secular doctrine that proclaimed itself the ultimate expression of revolutionary consciousness."[4]

KEY PROPONENTS:

- Frederick Engels (Deceased)
- Frederic R. Jameson (Duke University)
- Frank Lentrichia (Duke University)
- V. I. Lenin (Deceased)
- Karl Marx; (Deceased)
- Herbert Marcuse (Deceased)
- Joseph Stalin (Deceased)

KEY PROPONENT SOURCES:

Marx, Karl. *Das Kapital*. Washington DC: Regnery, 2000.
Marx, Karl and Friedrich Engels. *On Religion*. New York: Schocken, 1964.
Marx, Karl, Friedrich Engels, et. al. *The Communist Manifesto*. New York: Oxford Univ. Press, 1998.
McFadden, Charles Joseph. *The Philosophy of Communism*. New York: Benziger Brothers, 1939.

KEY CHRISTIAN SOURCES/CRITIQUES:

Bauman, Michael and Lissa Roche, eds. *Man and Marxism: Religion and the Communist Retreat*. Hillsdale, MI: Hillsdale College Press, 1991.
Conway, David. *A Farewell to Marx: An Outline and Appraisal of His Theories*. New York: Penguin, 1987.
Courtois, Stéphane. *The Black Book of Communism*. Translated by Jonathan Murphy and Mark Kramer. Cambridge: Harvard Univ. Press, 1999.
McFadden, Charles Joseph. *Christianity Confronts Communism*. Chicago, IL: Franciscan Herald, 1982.
Noebel, David A. *Understanding the Times*. Manitou Springs, CO: Summit Press, 2006.
Schwarz, Frederick Charles. *Beating the Unbeatable Foe*. Washington DC: Regnery, 1996.
———. *You Can Trust the Communists to Be Communists*. Englewood Cliffs, NJ: Prentice-Hall, 1960.
Solzhenitsyn, Aleksandr. *The Mortal Danger: How Misconceptions About Russia Imperil America*. Translated by Michael Nicholson and Alexis Klimoff. New York: Harper & Row, 1980.
Sowell, Thomas. *Marxism: Philosophy and Economics*. New York: Quill, 1985.

---

[3] Frederic Jameson, in Stephen H. Balch and Herbert I. London, "The Tenured Left," *Commentary* 82:4 (October 1986).
[4] George Weigel, "The Collapse of Communism," *The World & I*, vol. 8 (May 1993), 372–73.

Worldview: Postmodernism
Fact Sheet

Key Terms:

Modernism: A broad and somewhat ambiguous term used to embrace a diverse range of arts, attitudes, philosophies, and cultural moods which emerged following the 18th century Enlightenment. Epistemologically it is characterized by a strong belief in rationalism and science as a well as a strong skepticism in both the supernatural and the authority of religion

Postmodernism: A broad and somewhat ambiguous term used to describe a philosophical and cultural reaction to the convictions of Modernism (which is sometimes equated with Humanism). Postmodernism is the philosophical proposal that reality is ultimately inaccessible by human investigation, that knowledge is a social construction, that truth-claims are political power plays, and that the meaning of words is to be determined by readers not authors. In brief, reality is what individuals or social groups make it to be

Metanarrative: a single overarching objective interpretation or narrative of reality

---

Key Facts:

- Seventy-two percent of Americans agree, "There is no such thing as absolute truth; two people could define truth in totally conflicting ways, but both could still be correct."[1]
- Seventy-one percent of Americans agree, "There are no absolute standards that apply to everybody in all situations."[2]
- Fifty-three percent of those who claim there is no such thing as absolute truth identify themselves as born-again Christians.[3]
- Forty-two percent of those who identify themselves as evangelical Christians agree, "There is no such thing as absolute truth; two people could define truth in totally conflicting ways but both could still be correct."[4]

Key Verses:

Joshua 24:14–15　　Proverbs 9:10　　John 1:17; 3–4; 14:6; 16:13; 18:38
Judges 17:6; 18:21　Isaiah 59:15　　Romans 1:18-32; 2:8–9
1 Kings 18:21　　　Jeremiah 7:28　　2 Timothy 2:15; 3:14–17
Psalm 31:5; 146:5–6　Malachi 2:6　　　2 John 4–6

Key Quotes:

POSTMODERNISTS	"For the pragmatist [postmodernist], true sentences are not true because they correspond to reality, and so there is no need to worry what sort of reality, if any, a given sentence corresponds to – no need to worry about what 'makes' it true."[5] "Truth isn't outside of power, or lacking in power: contrary to a myth whose history and functions would repay further study, truth isn't the reward of free spirits, the child of protracted solitude, nor the privilege of those who have succeeded in liberating themselves. Truth is a thing of this world: it is produced only by virtue of multiple forms of constraint. And it induces regular effects of power. Each society has its regime of truth, its 'general

---

[1] George Barna, *Virtual America* (Ventura, CA: Regal, 1994), 83, 283.
[2] Ibid., 85, 230.
[3] Ibid., 83.
[4] Ibid.
[5] Richard Rorty, *Consequences of Pragmatism* (Minneapolis: University of Minnesota Press, 1982), xvi.

politics' of truth: that is, the types of discourse which it accepts and makes function as true; the mechanisms and instances which enable one to distinguish true from false statements, the means by which each is sanctioned; the techniques and procedures accorded value in the acquisition of truth; the status of those who are charged with saying what counts as true."[6]

CRITIQUE

"There is one thing a professor can be absolutely certain of: almost every student entering the university believes, or says he believes, that truth is relative. If this belief is put to the test, one can count on the students' reaction: They will be uncomprehending. That anyone would regard the proposition as not self-evident astonishes them, as though he were calling into question 2+2=4… Openness—and the relativism that makes it the only plausible stance in the face of various claims to truth and various ways of life and kinds of human beings—is the great insight of our times… The study of history and of culture [according to this view] teaches that all the world was mad in the past; men always thought they were right, and that led to wars, persecutions, slavery, xenophobia, racism, and chauvinism. The point is not to correct the mistakes and really be right; rather it is not to think you are right at all. The students, of course, cannot defend their opinion. It is something with which they have been indoctrinated."[7]

"Ours is an age in which 'conclusions' are arrived at by distributing questionnaires to a cross-section of the population or by holding a microphone before the lips of casually selected passers-by in the street… In the sphere of religious and moral thinking we are rapidly heading for a state of intellectual anarchy in which the difference between truth and falsehood will no longer be recognized. Indeed, it would seem possible that the words true and false will eventually (and logically) be replaced by the words likable and dislikable."[8]

KEY PROPONENTS:

- Walter Truett Anderson
- Walter Brueggemann
- Jacques Derrida
- Stanley Fish
- Michel Foucault
- Jean Francois Lyotard
- J. Richard Middleton
- Richard Rorty
- Brian J. Walsh

KEY PROPONENT SOURCES:

Anderson, Walter Truett, ed. *The Truth About the Truth: De-Confusing and Re-Constructing the Postmodern World.* New York: Putnam, 1995.

———. *Reality Isn't What It Used to Be.* San Francisco: Harper & Row, 1990.

Derrida, Jacques. *Of Grammatology.* Translated by Gayatri Chakravorty Spivak. Baltimore: Johns Hopkins Univ. Press, 1998.

Fish, Stanley Eugene. *Is There a Text in This Class? The Authority of Interpretive Communities.* Cambridge: Harvard Univ. Press, 1980.

Foucault, Michel. *The Archaeology of Knowledge and the Discourse on Language.* New York: Knopf, 1972.

———. *Madness and Civilization: A History of Insanity in the Age of Reason.* Translated by Richard Howard. New York: Vintage, 1973.

———. *The Order of Things: An Archaeology of the Human Sciences.* New York: Vintage, 1994.

[6] Michel Foucault, "Truth and Power," *The Foucault Reader*, Paul Rabinow, ed. (New York: Pantheon, 1984), 72–73.
[7] Allan Bloom, *The Closing of the American Mind* (New York: Simon & Schuster, 1987), 25-26.
[8] Harry Blamires, *The Christian Mind: How Should a Christian Think?* (Ann Arbor, MI: Servant Books, 1963), 107.

Lyotard, Jean François. *The Differend: Phrases in Dispute.* Translated by Georges Van Den Abbeele. Minneapolis: Univ. of Minnesota Press, 1988.

———. *The Postmodern Condition: A Report on Knowledge.* Translated by Brian Massumi and Geoff Bennington. Minneapolis: Univ. of Minnesota Press, 1984.

Nietzsche, Friedrich. *Beyond Good and Evil.* Translated by Helen Zimmern. Mineola, NY: Dover, 1997.

———. *On the Genealogy of Morals.* Translated by Walter Arnold Kaufmann. New York: Vintage, 1989.

Rorty, Richard. *Achieving Our Country: Leftist Thought in Twentieth-Century America.* Cambridge: Harvard Univ. Press, 1998.

———. *Philosophy and Social Hope.* New York: Penguin, 1999.

———. *Philosophy and the Mirror of Nature.* Princeton: Princeton Univ. Press, 1979.

KEY CHRISTIAN SOURCES/CRITIQUES:

(recommended titles appear in brown)

Allen, David L. "Preaching and Postmodernism: An Evangelical Comes to the Dance." *Southern Baptist Journal of Theology 5*, no. 2 (2001): 62–78.

Beckwith, Francis and Gregory Koukl. *Relativism: Feet Firmly Planted in Mid-Air.* Grand Rapids, MI: Baker, 1998.

Cabal, Ted. "An Introduction of Postmodernity: Where Are We, How Did We Get Here, and Can We Get Home?" *Southern Baptist Journal of Theology 5*, no. 2 (2001).

Carson, D. A. *The Gagging of God: Christianity Confronts Pluralism.* Grand Rapids, MI: Zondervan, 1996.

Copan, Paul. *True for You, but Not for Me: Deflating the Slogans That Leave Christians Speechless.* Minneapolis: Bethany, 1998.

Dockery, David S., ed. *The Challenge of Postmodernism: An Evangelical Engagement.* Grand Rapids, MI: Baker, 2001.

Erickson, Millard J. "Foundationalism: Dead or Alive?" *Southern Baptist Journal of Theology 5*, no. 2 (2001): 20–32.

———. *Truth or Consequences: The Promise and Perils of Postmodernism.* Downers Grove, IL: InterVarsity, 2001.

Groothuis, Douglas R. *Truth Decay: Defending Christianity against the Challenges of Postmodernism.* Downers Grove, IL: InterVarsity, 2000.

Lundin, Roger. *The Culture of Interpretation: Christian Faith and the Postmodern World.* Grand Rapids, MI: Eerdmans, 1993.

McCallum, Dennis, ed. *The Death of Truth.* Minneapolis: Bethany, 1996.

Noebel, David A. *Understanding the Times: The Collision of Today's Competing Worldviews.* Manitou Springs, CO: Summit Press, 2006.

Norris, Christopher. *The Truth About Postmodernism.* Cambridge: Blackwell, 1993.

Parker, James. "A Requiem for Postmodernism, Wither Now?" *Southern Baptist Journal of Theology 5*, no. 2 (2001).

Schreiner, Thomas R. "The Perils of Ignoring Postmodernism." *Southern Baptist Journal of Theology 5*, no. 2 (2001): 2–3.

Veith, Gene Edward. *Postmodern Times: A Christian Guide to Contemporary Thought and Culture.* Wheaton, IL: Crossway, 1994.

WORLDVIEW: SECULAR HUMANISM
FACT SHEET

KEY TERMS:

Humanism: The belief that humanity is the highest of all beings and that truth and knowledge thus rest in science and human reason

Humanist Manifesto: The title of three manifestos laying out a secular humanist worldview. They are *Humanist Manifesto I* (1933), *Humanist Manifesto II* (1973), and *Humanist Manifesto III* (2000), although the latter is actually titled *Planetary Humanism*. The central theme of all three is the elaboration of a philosophy and value system that does not include belief in God

---

KEY VERSES:

Psalm 14:1   Romans 1:21–23   Colossians 2:1–8
Acts 17:16ff   2 Corinthians 10:5

KEY QUOTES:

HUMANISTS	"There is no place in the Humanist worldview for either immortality or God in the valid meanings of those terms. Humanism contends that instead of the gods creating the cosmos, the cosmos, in the individualized form of human beings giving rein to their imagination, created the gods."[1] "The classroom must and will become an area of conflict between the old and the new—the rotting corpse of Christianity, together with its adjacent evils and misery and the new faith of Humanism, resplendent in its promise of a world in which the never-realized Christian idea of 'Love thy Neighbor' will finally be achieved."[2]
CRITIQUES	"The ultimate failure of Secular Humanism is in the fact that of its very nature it promises what it cannot fulfill. By encouraging people to put their trust in earthly happiness it programs them for disillusionment. This is in large measure the reason why the history of the modern world has been characterized, intellectually, by philosophies of pessimism like Existentialism and by often-rancorous bitterness over various plans for worldly improvement. In the twentieth century, mass slaughter has been perpetrated not by religious believers in opposition to heresy but by secularists convinced that their plan for a worldly utopia is the only possible one."[3] "Bertrand Russell, a clear-headed liberal humanist, wrote as follows about what he called 'the night of nothingness': 'There is darkness without and when I die there will be darkness within. There is no splendor, no vastness, anywhere; only triviality for a moment, and then nothing.' That says it all. Whereas for the Christian nothing is finally trivial, for the humanist everything becomes finally trivial, death, as Russell says, producing precisely that effect."[4]

---

[1] Corliss Lamont, *The Philosophy of Humanism* (New York: Frederick Ungar Publishing, 1982), 145.
[2] John J. Dunphy, "A Religion for a New Age," T*he Humanist*, January/February 1983, 26.
[3] James Hitchcock, *What is Secular Humanism? Why Humanism Became Secular and How It Is Changing Our World* (Ann Arbor, MI: Servant Books, 1982), 141.
[4] J. I. Packer and Thomas Howard, *Christianity: The True Humanism* (Waco, TX: Word, 1985), 231–32.

KEY PROPONENT SOURCES:

SECULAR HUMANISM (GENERAL)

Huxley, Aldous. *Brave New World*. New York: Harper & Row, 1989.

Huxley, Julian. *The Humanist Frame*. London: Allen & Unwin, 1961.

Huxley, Julian, Gilbert Murray, and Joseph Houldsworth Oldham. *Humanism*. London: Watts & Co., 1944.

Kurtz, Paul, ed. *The Humanist Alternative: Some Definitions of Humanism*. Buffalo, NY: Prometheus, 1973.

———. *Humanist Manifesto 2000: A Call for a New Planetary Humanism*. Amherst, NY: Prometheus, 2000.

———. *Humanist Manifesto I and II*. Buffalo, NY: Prometheus, 1980.

———. *A Secular Humanist Declaration*. Amherst, NY: Prometheus, 1980.

———. *Skepticism and Humanism: The New Paradigm*. New Brunswick, NJ: Transaction, 2001.

Lamont, Corliss. *Humanism as a Philosophy*. New York: Philosophical Library, 1949.

———. *The Philosophy of Humanism*. Amherst, NY: Humanist, 1996.

Morain, Lloyd and Mary S. Morain. *Humanism as the Next Step*. Amherst, NY: Humanist, 1998.

Skinner, B. F. *Walden Two*. New York: Macmillan, 1976.

SECULAR HUMANISM AS A RELIGION

Dewey, John. *A Common Faith*. New Haven, CT: Yale University Press, 1991.

Huxley, Julian. *Religion without Revelation*. Westport, CT: Greenwood, 1979.

Kurtz, Paul. *Eupraxophy: Living without Religion*. Buffalo, NY: Prometheus, 1989.

Potter, Charles Francis. *Humanism: A New Religion*. New York: Simon & Schuster, 1930.

———. *Humanizing Religion*. New York: Harper, 1933.

Sellars, Roy Wood. *Religion Coming of Age*. New York: Macmillan, 1928.

KEY CHRISTIAN SOURCES/CRITIQUES:

(recommended titles appear in brown)

Geisler, Norman L. *Is Man the Measure? An Evaluation of Contemporary Humanism*. Grand Rapids, MI: Baker, 1983.

Hitchcock, James. *What Is Secular Humanism? Why Humanism Became Secular and How It Is Changing Our World*. Ann Arbor, MI: Servant, 1982.

LaHaye, Tim. *The Battle for the Mind*. Old Tappan, NJ: Revell, 1980.

LaHaye, Tim and David A. Noebel. *Mind Siege: The Battle for Truth in the New Millennium*. Nashville: Word, 2000.

McDowell, Josh and Don Douglas Stewart. *Understanding Secular Religions*. San Bernardino, CA: Campus Crusade, 1982.

Noebel, David A. *Understanding the Times: The Collision of Today's Competing Worldviews*. Manitou Springs, CO: Summit Press, 2006.

Packer, J. I. and Thomas Howard. *Christianity: The True Humanism*. Waco, TX: Word, 1985.